ELLIS ISLAND SCRAPBOOK

by Kevin Sherlock
Author of <u>Ellis Island -- When America Did Immigration Right</u>

BRENNYMAN BOOKS
AKRON, OHIO
UNITED STATES OF AMERICA

ELLIS ISLAND SCRAPBOOK by Kevin Sherlock

Copyright © 2010 by Kevin Sherlock

Published by Brennyman Books
PO Box 3988
Akron, Ohio 44314

Send direct inquiries or orders to the above address.

Printed in the United States of America.

All rights reserved. No part of this book may be reproduced or transmitted in any form or by any means, electronic or mechanical, including photocopying, recording, or by any information storage and retrieval system, without prior written permission of the author, except for the inclusion of quotes from the book in a review.

Cataloging in Publication Data

Sherlock, Kevin
    ELLIS ISLAND SCRAPBOOK
    Includes footnotes, bibliography, and index.

ISBN 978-0-9654036-2-7

1.   United States -- History.
2.   United States – Culture
3.   Genealogy -- United States
4.   Heritage – United States
5.   Immigration – History – United States.
6.   Ellis Island
7.   Current Events -- Non-Fiction -- United States

NOTE: Illustrations credited as known. The author searched within the limits of his ability to determine copyright or lack of same for each illustration. Those illustrations shown and not credited are thought to be in the public domain, due to the age of the illustration, copyright laws, and by representations made. If this is not the case for a particular illustration, the publisher agrees to pay the usual and customary usage fee to the legitimate copyright holder for the image, upon receiving legitimate proof of such holding.

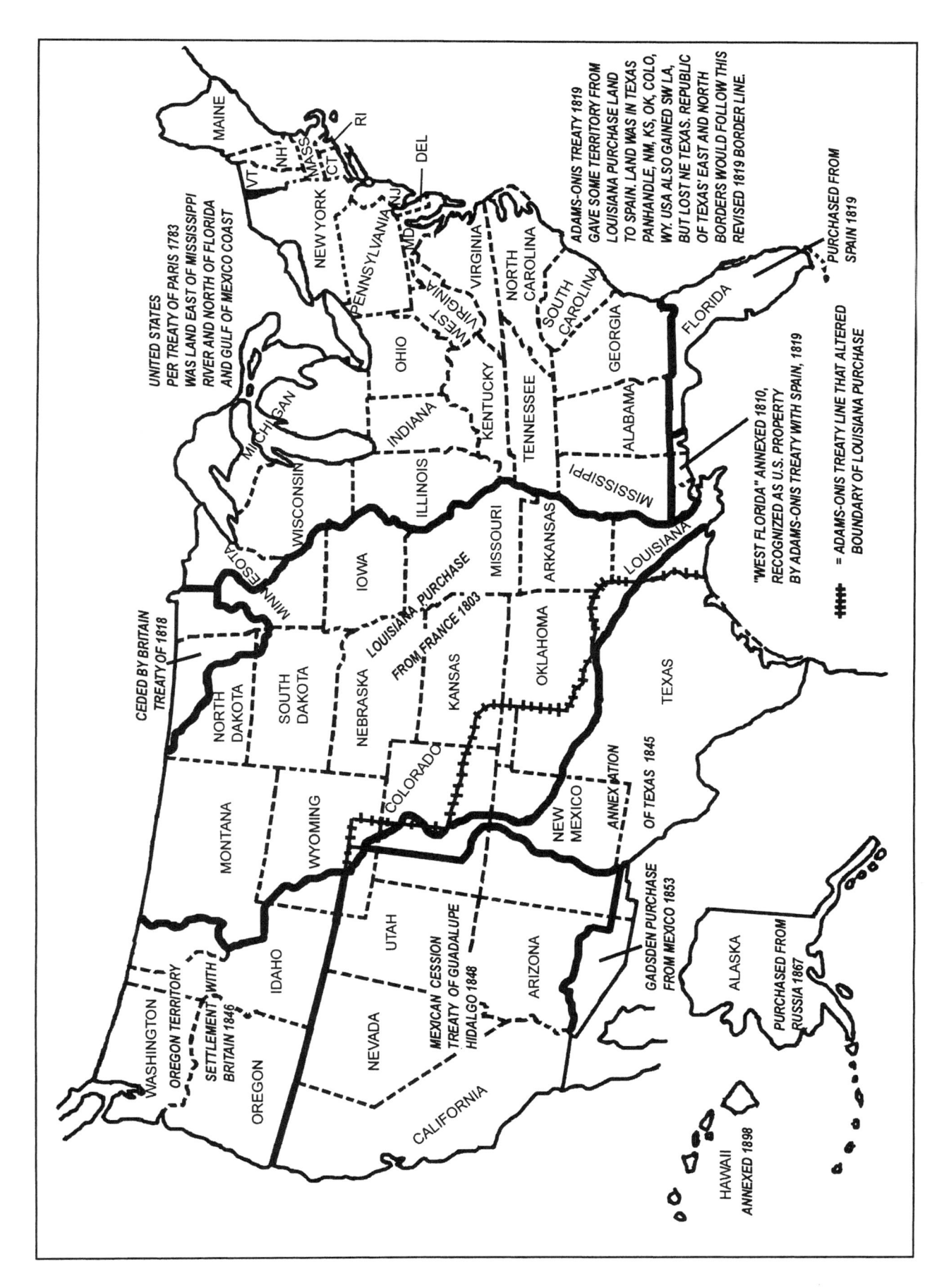

Map 1. Manifest Destiny – The Growth of the United States

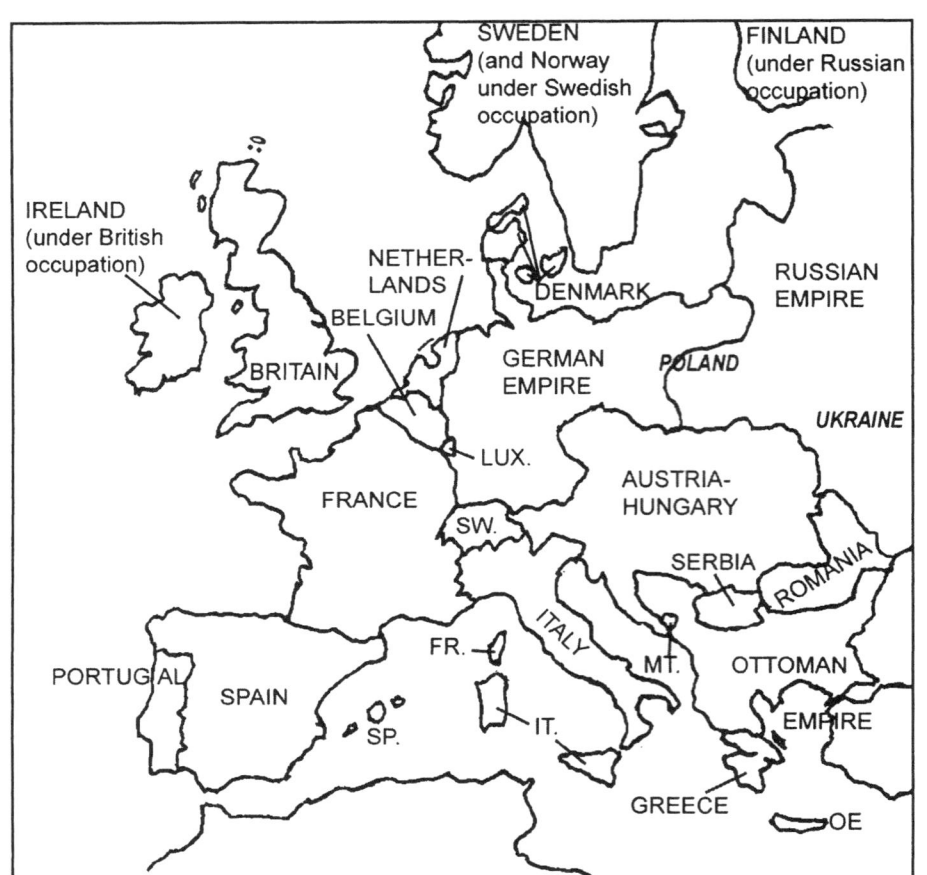

Map 2 (left). Europe in 1871, after the Franco-Prussian War and Italian Unification

Map 3 (below). Europe in 1914, just before the start of World War One

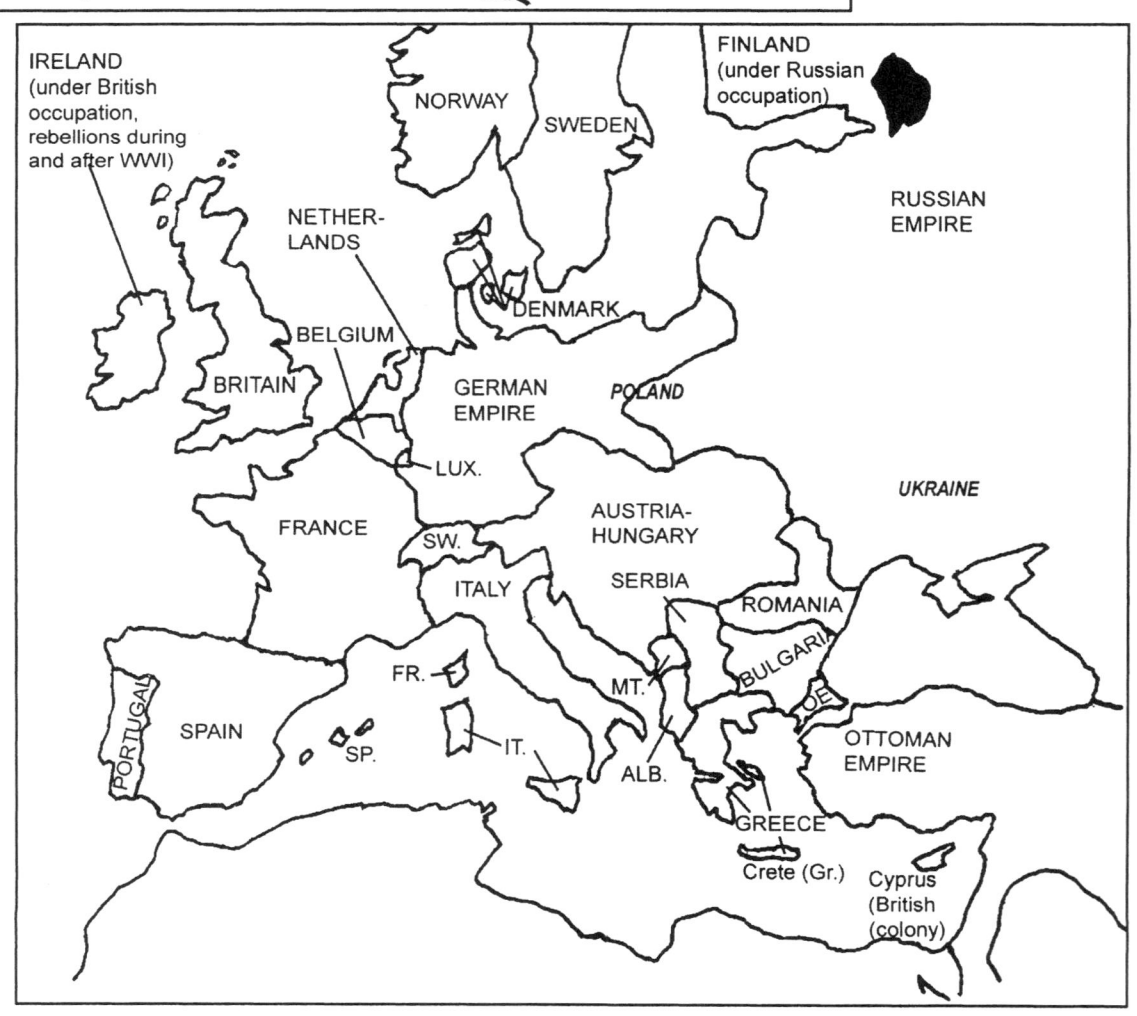

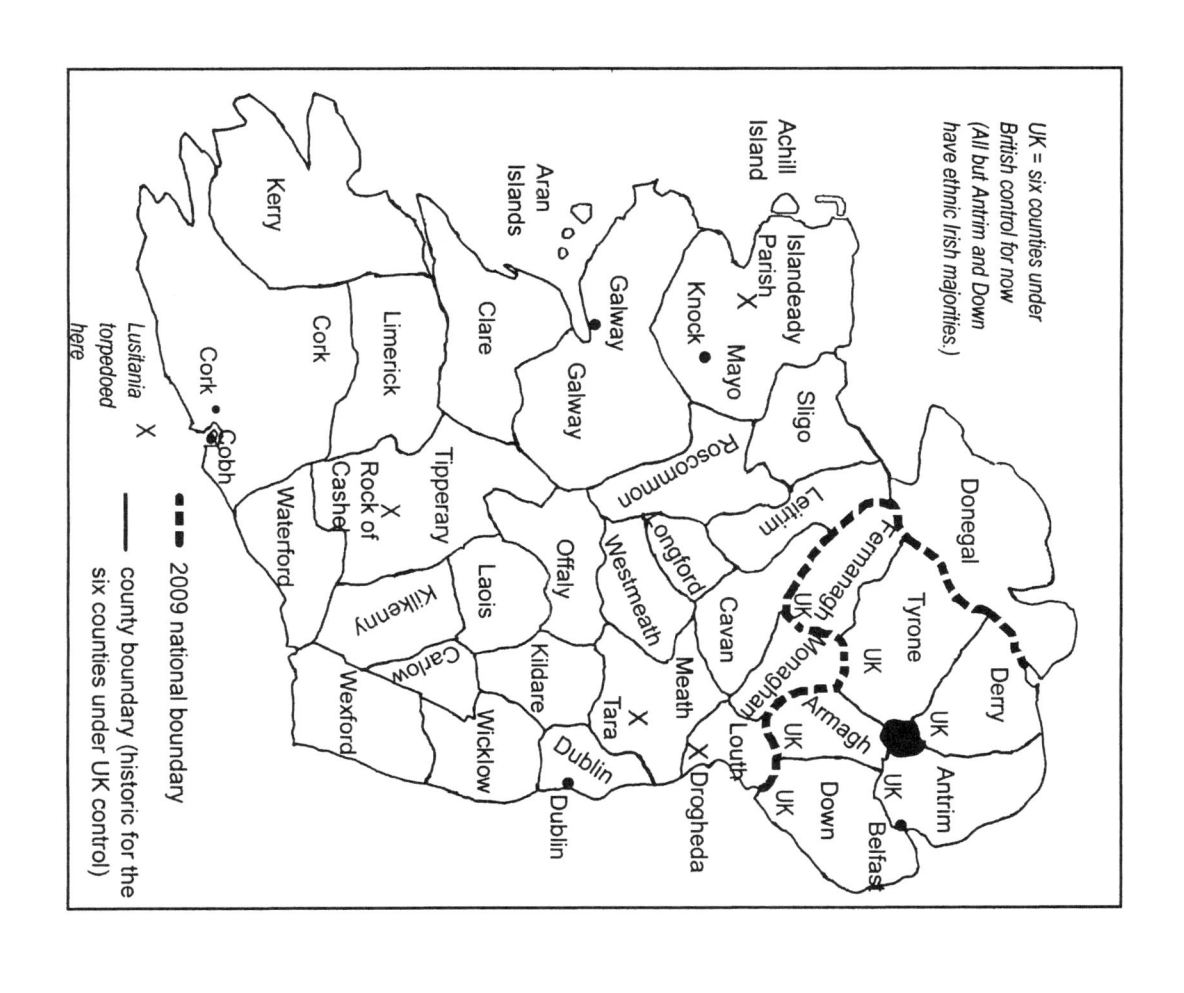

Map 4. Ireland's 32 Counties

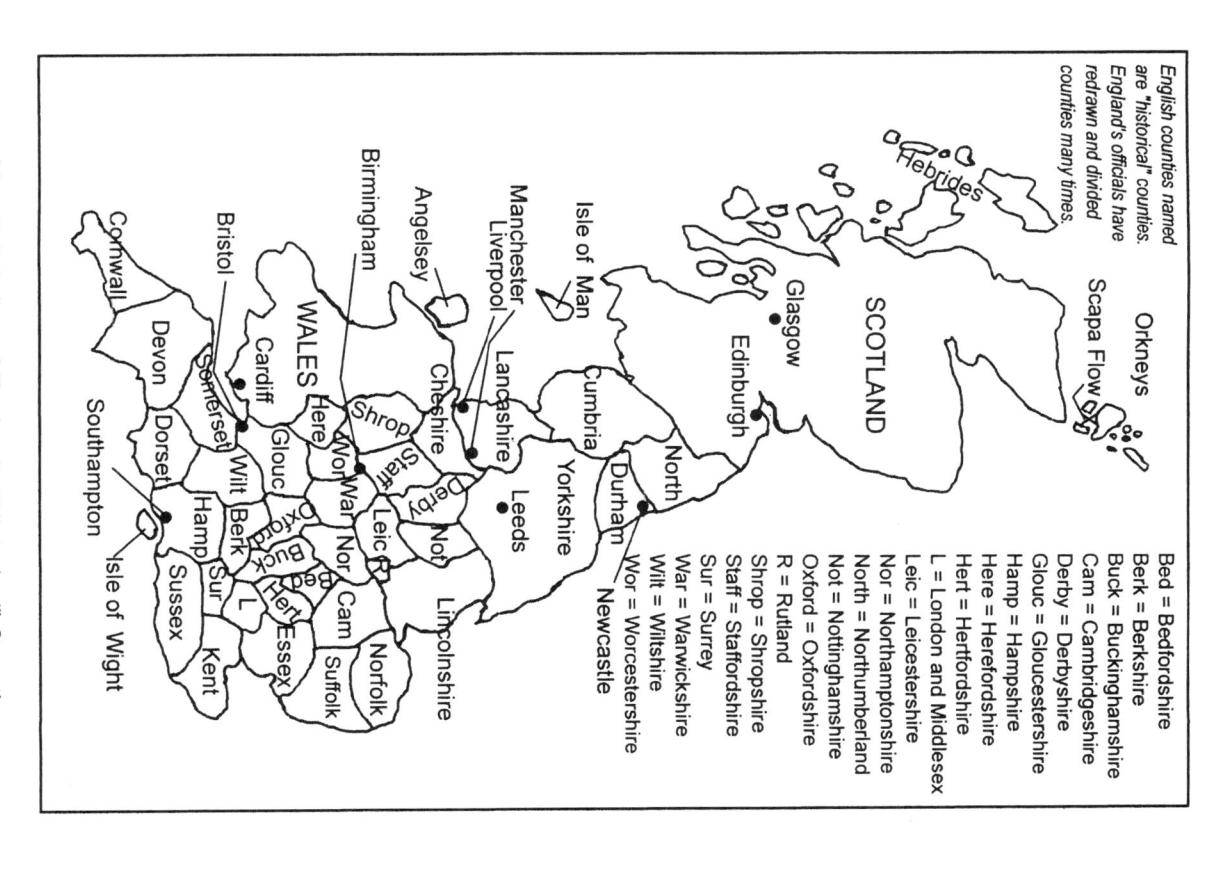

Map 5. Britain and England's "Historical" Counties

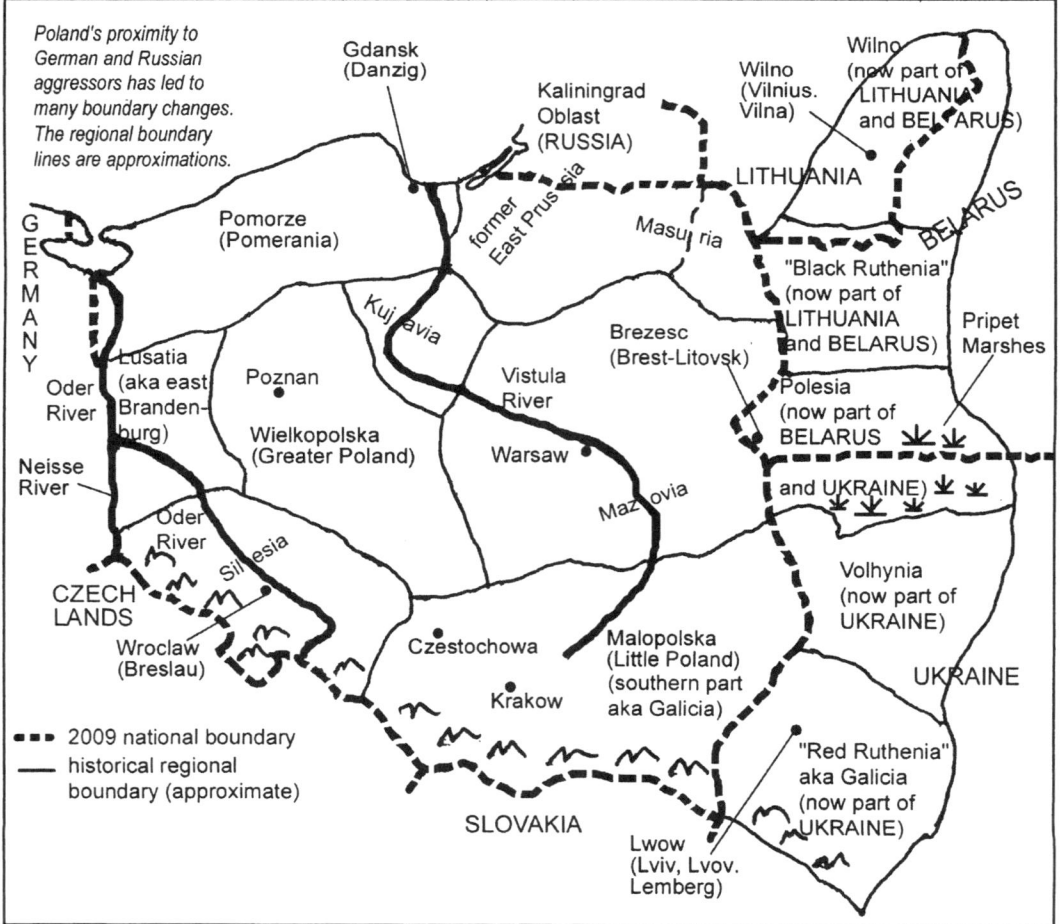

Map 6 (top). Spain's Historical Regions and Portugal

Map 7 (left). Poland's Boundaries and Historical Regions

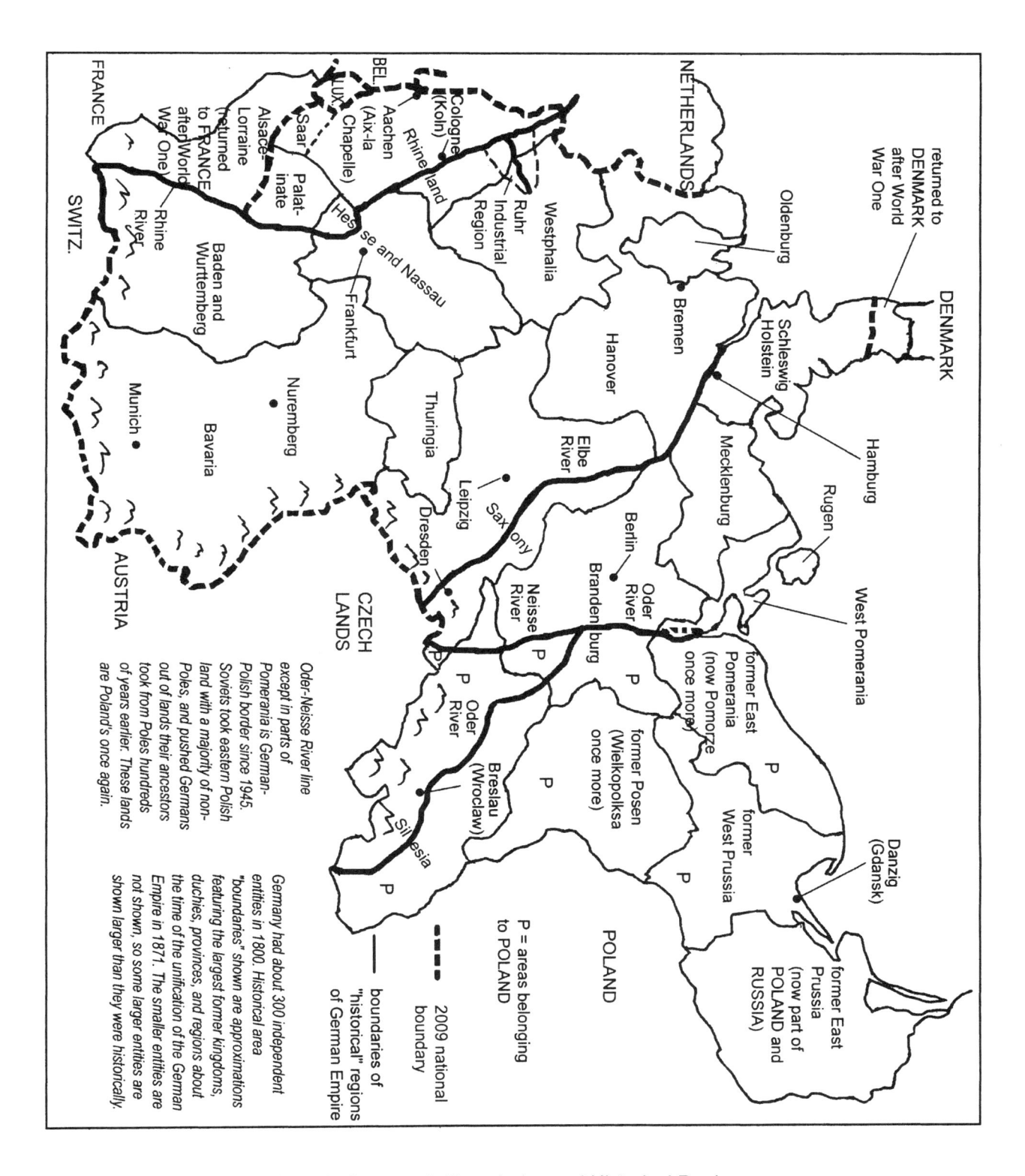

Map 8. Germany's Boundaries and Historical Regions

Map 9. France and its Regions

Map 10. Italy and its Regions

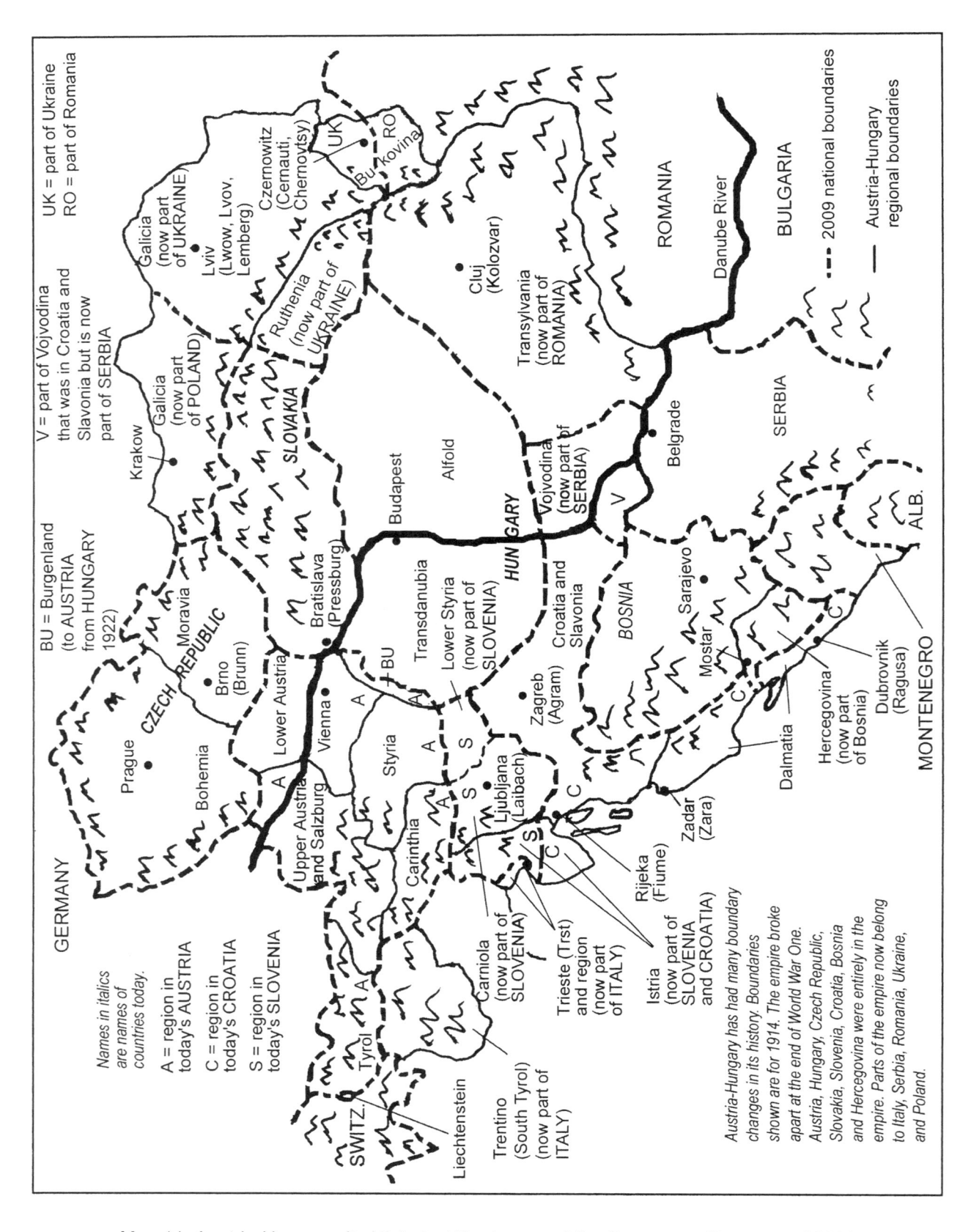

Map 11. Austria-Hungary, its Historical Regions, and the Successor States as of 2009

Map 12. The Balkans as of 2009

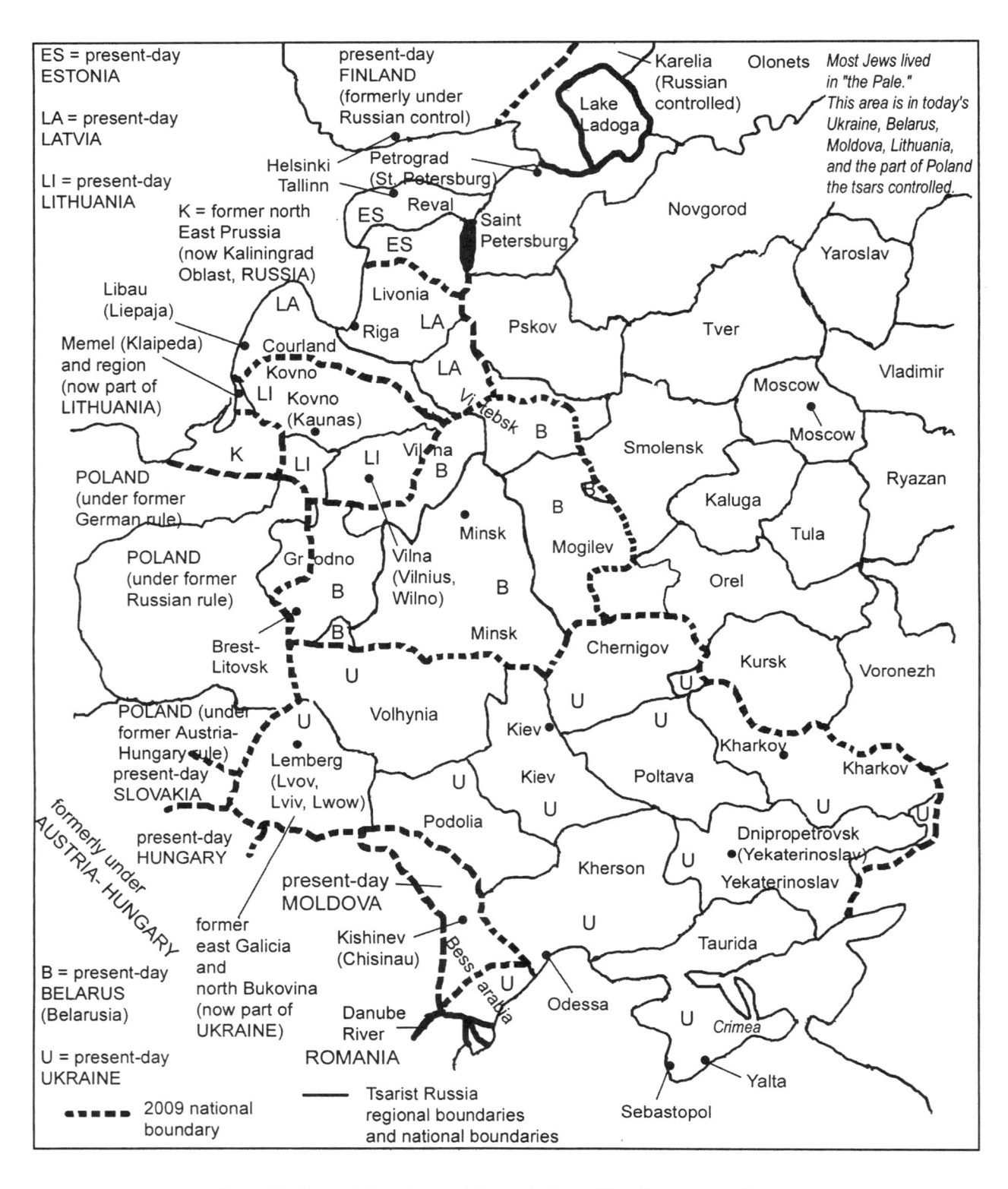

Map 13. Tsarist Russia, and Boundaries of the Successor States to the Former Soviet Union as of 2009

Map 14. Europe as of 2009

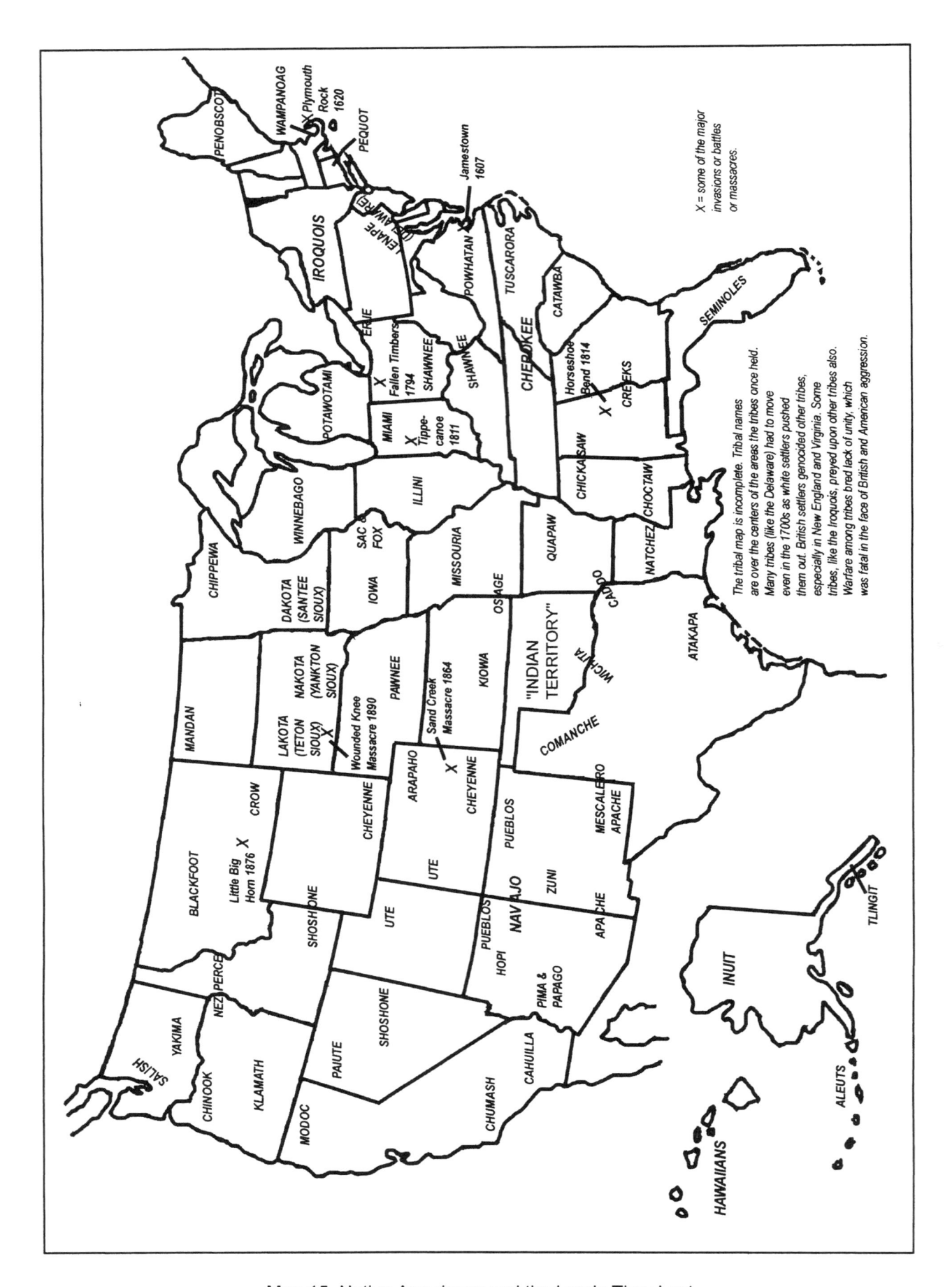

Map 15. Native Americans and the Lands They Lost

TABLE OF CONTENTS

Chapter	**Page**
Introduction	1
What Was Life In Europe Like?	3
Manifest Destiny, Magnificent Destination	43
Regulating Immigration from the American Revolution to the Early 1900s	83
The Lowdown on Steerage	111
What Was Immigrant Processing Like?	121
The Demise of Ellis Island	147
Memories are Made of These	159
The Truth About Ellis Island	229
The Closing of the Scrapbook	239
Index	247
Acknowledgments and Dedications	255
About the Author	256

DISCLAIMER

The purpose of this book is to inform and entertain. The author and publisher sell this book with the understanding they do not render legal advice. Neither the author nor the publisher assumes any responsibility for the misuse of information contained in this book. Neither the author nor the publisher assumes responsibility or liability for any damage or loss caused or alleged to be caused directly or indirectly by the information contained in this book.

Although the author and publisher have researched all sources to ensure the accuracy and completeness of information presented in this book, there is the possibility that typographical errors and content errors have gotten into the book. No human is perfect

Since books and documents available to the public within the life span of the author form the backbone of this book, the author and publisher have cited them in the text so you the reader will know where the information came from. The author and publisher assume no liability or responsibility for any possible inaccuracies in the sources quoted ... in any case, each strove within the limits of his abilities to be as accurate as the sources used

If you see an error, let the author know about it and he will correct it. The author and the publisher each can make errors despite diligence to keep the text accurate. Only Our Lord is perfect – and look how He has been resented for that through the centuries!

The author and the publisher assume no liability or responsibility for any possible damage caused or claimed to have been caused to those whose questionable behavior is mentioned in this book.

Writing the truth about the living whose shortcomings made this book, no matter how much it offends them, is absolutely a defense against libel. Freedom of speech and libel laws guarantee the right to satire and fair comment on the character and job performance of those individuals in the public eye. No one put a gun to their heads to make them act the way they do!

MAP NOTES

In America, the citizens of the 13 states made the Union, and American settlers organized the land of the other 37 states (often over the protests of the Mexican, Spanish, American Indian, and Hawaiian first settlers) and later applied for admission to the Union. In Europe, they didn't do it this way.

Because of the threat posed by Moslem, Asian, and Viking invaders, local strongmen set up local governments and made agreements with stronger regional lords. These lords made agreements with national leaders known as kings or emperors. The stronger helped the weaker, and drew labor and food and raw materials from the weaker. This series of agreements was known as feudalism. It was the only way at the time the people of Europe could defend themselves against the bloodthirsty vermin arrayed against them.

Regional governments often started as the holdings of a powerful lord who swore allegiance to a less-than-all-powerful king. In many cases, the people and leaders of these regions had rights as well as responsibilities, and they guarded their rights zealously.

The people of Europe tried to keep as much authority local as possible, but the rulers of Europe wanted all the power in their slimy hands. Wars, revolutions, and government dictates, almost always driven by someone's greed, continually changed the regional and national boundaries of Europe.

The maps of European nations in this book are an attempt by the author to show the historical regions of most of the countries of Europe. The maps of Europe, unless otherwise specified, tend to show regional boundaries from the 1870s, after the unification of Germany and Italy, and the reorganization of Austria-Hungary, to the eve of World War One in 1914. These maps also show 2009's boundaries.

The author is a better historian than he is a cartographer. However, these maps he drew are reasonable representations of the organization of Europe in the time of the Ellis Island Era.

His map of the growth of the United States does not show all the details of the Webster-Ashburton treaty that fixed the Maine boundary and other disputed parts of the American boundary with British-owned Canada in the 1840s. However, it accurately shows the growth of the nation. And the American Indians' map shows, by and large, the areas of the larger tribes the British and the Americans fought, defeated, and stripped of their land.

INTRODUCTION

One of the best reasons for the study of history is to learn how people have faced problems over time. The main purpose for this book is to give the American public a perspective of why people came to America, and how the officials in the late 1800s and early 1900s dealt with the issues immigration posed.

The vast majority of the immigrants who came to America in the Ellis Island Era wanted to become Americans and did so. They became real Americans in thought and in action. They assimilated. Many of them served in our nation's armed forces in World War One and their sons answered the nation's call in World War Two.

In the Ellis Island Era, America didn't import Europe's welfare recipients or Latin America's underpaid or Asia's slave laborers or the Middle East's jihadists. The people who came here in the Ellis Island Era had to support themselves, not come in on labor-undermining contracts, not have communicable diseases that threatened the American public, not come in illegally, and not have an attitude that was at odds with the American way of life. Those who couldn't or wouldn't meet these reasonable standards couldn't get in and were shipped back to where they came from.

The heyday of Ellis Island – from the 1890s through the 1920s – was a time when American officials did care about the good of Americans in regards to immigration. This is an approach our public officials ought to try now.

The second purpose of this book is to put faces on the people of history. This book gives you a people's history of the life of most people in Europe during the late 1800s and early 1900s. It also gives you a large number of human interest stories about the immigrants at Ellis Island and the American immigration agents who processed them.

The book lays out like this:

This first chapter of this book explains what life was like for most Europeans in the 1800s.

The second chapter explains how America got to be so big, and why America could accommodate immigrants.

The third chapter covers how Americans tried to regulate immigration from the time of George Washington to the presidencies of Theodore Roosevelt and William Taft. It mixes in sketches of American history during those times to give a frame of reference for the regulations.

The fourth chapter covers steerage.

The fifth chapter explains how Ellis Island operated from the 1890s to the Great Depression.

The sixth chapter covers immigration laws in the 1920s and the slowdown in immigration that led to the closing of Ellis Island as an immigration station.

The seventh chapter is a very large collection of short stories about the immigrants and immigration officials at Ellis Island.

The eighth chapter analyzes the Ellis Island Era. It displays statistics and debunks false legends. It explains why the "Ellis Island Approach" worked.

The final chapter is a wrap-up of the book.

Without question, much of this nation's foundation is from British dissenters who wanted freedom from the Crown. But much of the work on the foundation of America was also done by Spaniards and Mexicans and Frenchmen and Creoles who built cities in America before the American Revolution. St. Augustine, Florida, and Santa Fe, New Mexico are older than Boston and New York City. San Diego, San Francisco, and Los Angeles are older than Cincinnati, Cleveland, and Chicago. French-founded Detroit, New Orleans, and St. Louis also date back to the early and mid 1700s.

There were other builders of America. Despite American bigotry against Catholics, roughly 30 percent of the Continental Army was Irish. And roughly 5% to 10% of the soldiers and sailors in the ranks of the Patriots were black men whose ancestors were kidnaped and exiled from Africa to be sold and worked as slaves. The sad truth is many of our Patriots were slaves also.

The peoples of Europe who didn't want to bow to an inbred king or nobility or to a crooked parliament came to this nation and built it up. Many slaves were forced to come here, and they and their descendants added their own labor and intellect and talents to the national culture. It was this amalgamation of European, Native American, American Hispanic, and African cultures under a common belief in God and a sense of the rights and responsibilities of the people that made America into the greatest nation on earth.

History is not about forces, but about people. Plus, history is a story. It's fun to read about the foibles of the famous, and it's interesting to get a glimpse of how people lived in earlier times.

ELLIS ISLAND SCRAPBOOK

I try to put a human face on the millions of farming people and city people and others who lived and died unknown to all but their friends, their loved ones, their neighbors, their pastors or rabbis, and the people they worked for. When you put yourself in the shoes of these people, your ancestors, you begin to understand why they did what they did.

The maps provided show the jumbled state of affairs in Europe in the 1800s and early 1900s. They also show the regions of the countries so you can find them readily. If your ancestors came from Galicia (in Spain) or Galicia (in Poland or Ukraine), from Lorraine or Lombardy, Bavaria or Bohemia, or Mayo or Montenegro, you will be able to find these regions. The maps aren't fancy but they get the job done.

By the way, don't skip the footnotes. Many of the best anecdotes in this book are in the footnotes.

Since this book is an Ellis Island Era scrapbook, there ought to be plenty of pictures to show what our ancestors and our historical figures looked like. And so there are. This is our nation's historical family photo album. A picture collection of America during the Ellis Island Era would in many ways look like the art of Norman Rockwell and the photo album of your grandparents or great-grandparents. And besides, weren't our ancestors some fine-looking people?

This book is the sister book to Ellis Island -- When America Did Immigration Right. Both books cover the growth of America, the history of immigration regulation to the Ellis Island era, and immigration processing. This book has a short chapter on steerage, a large chapter on the lives of the peoples of Europe, and a huge chapter of true stories of Ellis Island people that the other book does not have. This book focuses on the people's history of Europe and those who left the continent, and on the stories of the people who came through Ellis Island and the people who worked at Ellis Island.

The other book also has larger chapters on American history from World War One up to World War Two, a chapter on the fight against "white slavery", and a chapter on two immigrant tragedies that happened a year apart – the Triangle Fire and the *Titanic* disaster. The other book focuses more on American history and also focuses more on the problems of immigration today.

We need to know where we came from and why our customs and traditions are what they are. Your generation didn't get to its position without standing on the accumulated experience of the people of the 160 or so generations from the time of the patriarch Abraham to the present.

Read, reflect, and enjoy. And thank God people in your family tree decided to try their luck here, in the greatest nation on earth.

Kevin Sherlock
Lincoln's Birthday, 2010

NOTES ON TERMS IN THIS BOOK

The "Ellis Island Era" is basically the four decades from the start of the 1890s through to the end of the 1920s. In this span came most immigrants before the 1960s.

The term "Native American Indian" or "American Indian" refers to the people who settled and populated the Americas before Columbus, the Vikings, or even Brendan the Navigator. This distinguishes them from the people from India in South Asia. I extend similar respect to the Inuit ("Eskimos") who first settled Alaska and the Polynesians who first settled Hawaii.

The term "Orthodox Jew" refers to Jews who practice Orthodox Judaism. The terms "Jew" and "Jewish" refer to people who practice one of the various forms of Judaism, and those who by blood (if not always observance) consider themselves Jewish.

The term "Christian" refers to Catholics, Orthodox Christians, and Protestants. Too many people incorrectly use the term "Christian" to refer to Protestants only. Catholics and Orthodox Christians believe in the divinity of Christ and His mission as Redeemer of mankind. Protestants got these beliefs (and the Bible) from Catholics and Orthodox Christians.

The term "Orthodox Christian" or "Orthodox" refers to the Christian churches which serve the majority of believers in Russia, Ukraine, and the Balkans, and some other lands. There are Orthodox Christians in America, also. Most of them have roots in the above-mentioned countries.

Some statistics I present in this book were reported by 12-month calendar years and others were reported by 12-month fiscal years. Unless there was an important reason to do so, I tended not to say which was a calendar year statistic and which was a fiscal year statistic.

I realize the term "corrupt politician" is redundant, but I use the term in this book anyway. I apologize for the extra ink used in printing this term.

WHAT WAS LIFE IN EUROPE LIKE?

Why would more than 30 million people leave Europe to come to America in the 1800s and 1900s? Why would they pull up roots and leave loved ones and come to a far away and unknown land? In order to understand the immigrants' mindsets, you have to understand what the conditions were in the lands they left behind. This chapter is a sketch of Europe in those times.

SNAPSHOTS OF EUROPE IN THE 1800s

The wars of Napoleon – the heir of the French Revolution – took up the first 15 years of the continent's calendar in the 1800s. After the British locked the Little Corporal on St. Helena, Europe quieted down some, but it was never truly at peace from the end if the Napoleonic Wars to the start of another general war in Europe – World War One – a century later.

At the end of the Napoleonic Wars, the French were free but resentful, a nation held in check only by the combined efforts of peoples with nowhere near the liberties they had. France had been the strongest power in Europe for almost 200 years. Losing this position (and losing the hundreds of thousands of strong young men who kept them in this position) galled and grieved the French greatly.

Here's how the rest of the continent looked at the end of the Napoleonic Wars in 1815:

The British government ruled England, Wales and Scotland. They occupied Ireland and treated the justifiably hostile Irish little better than slaves. Britain's navy was strong enough to fight and beat any other two nations' navies, and Britain's sailors proved it during the Napoleonic Wars. However, Andrew Jackson, William Henry Harrison, Winfield Scott, Jean Lafitte, Isaac Hull, Stephen Decatur, Oliver Perry, and other American heroes beat them on land and on water in the War of 1812.

Germany was a 39-entity puzzle; Prussia was its biggest piece. Kinglets and princelings ruled postage stamp sized storybook realms elsewhere in the Fatherland. Prussians also wrongfully held much Polish land.

Russian soldiers occupied Finland (which they took from the Swedes during the Napoleonic Wars), Ukraine, Belarusia (Belarus), Moldova (then called Bessarabia), the Baltic lands (Estonia, Latvia, Lithuania), the Caucasus land of Georgia and some of Armenia, and most of Poland. Many Russian soldiers and civilians lay dead; the people of their homeland had suffered greatly during the wars against Napoleon.

Austria's emperor ruled Austria, Hungary, the Czech and Slovak and Ruthenian lands, southern Poland, Galicia (southeastern Poland and northwestern Ukraine), Transylvania and Bukovina (northwestern and northern Romania), Vojvodina (northern Serbia), Croatia, Slovenia, and much of northern Italy (including Venezia, Lombardy and Tuscany).

The Turks occupied the rest of Serbia, Bosnia and Hercegovina, Albania, Greece, Macedonia, Bulgaria, and most of Romania. The Turks also occupied Armenian land, Cyprus, much of the Arabian peninsula, and present-day Iraq, Kuwait, Syria, Lebanon, Israel, and Jordan. Egyptian leaders would break their land free from the Turks in the 1800s, only to lose it to the grasping British later in the century. The local rulers of present-day Algeria, Tunisia, Morocco, and Libya were basically Moslem bandits, pirates and slavers. The Turks had loose control over or affiliations with all these areas except Morocco. American sailors and Marines fought some of these human vermin in the early 1800s. The French would occupy and rule Algeria and Tunisia later in the 1800s. The French (with Spanish help) would take over Morocco in the early 1900s. Likewise, the Italians would take Libya from the Turks a few years before the start of World War One.

Denmark and Sweden were free. So was poor and isolated little Montenegro. Switzerland was free once again, after a few years of French occupation.

Spain and Portugal were two proud but poor and battered nations after the Napoleonic Wars. Their royals and nobility had fled or had connived with Napoleon, and many of their "enlightened" had collaborated with him. In short, the countries' elites had sold out. The priests and people had waged guerrilla warfare against the French oppressors. The Iberian Peninsula was full of ruined towns and families mourning their dead. Meanwhile, Spain and Portugal's own colonists in Latin America were rebelling or soon would rebel and would throw out the Iberian noblemen who had ruled them.

Italy was a jumble of territories ruled by Austria, the Pope, and a number of comic opera local rulers. Many wanted to run Italy, therefore no one could.

The European powers took Belgium from France after the Napoleonic Wars and united it with the

Netherlands, which they also pried out of Napoleon's grip. The Dutch held Belgium until the Belgians forced their way out of the unhappy union in 1830.

The European powers took Norway from Denmark (a French ally) after the Napoleonic Wars and assigned Norway to Sweden (an enemy of France). The Swedes held Norway until the Norwegians got a divorce similar to Belgium's in 1905. The Danes still held Iceland and would do so until World War Two.

Throughout the 1800s, British soldiers forcibly held Ireland in the British Empire. Poland's people lost their freedom in the partitions of the 1770s and the 1790s. Poland lay dissected and divided between three greedy empires – Prussia, Russia, and Austria – throughout the 1800s. The Irish and the Poles would not take these oppressions passively.

The major countries during the 1800s and early 1900s fought each other, and so did the minor countries. Major countries fought minor countries, and once several minor countries took on a major country that was a threat to all of them.

Italy and Germany would each become united countries in the 1860s and 1870s, with considerable bloodshed.

The Serbs, Greeks, Romanians, Bulgarians, Macedonians, and Albanians would gain their freedom from the Turks by revolt and by warfare in the 1800s and the years of the early 1900s before World War One. The Turks slaughtered most of the Armenians under their control during World War One.

The Hungarians could not throw off the rule of the Austrian emperor, but they made so much trouble for him he left them as masters in their own house until they eventually separated from Austria at the end of World War One. The Poles would not regain their freedom until after World War One. World War One made it possible for the Czechs and Slovaks and Ruthenians and many Poles and Romanians to gain their freedom from the Austrians and Hungarians at war's end. World War One also made it possible for the Slovenes and Croats to leave the crumbling Hapsburg empire and join with the Serbs and the people of Montenegro and Bosnia and Hercegovina and most of the people of Macedonia to form Yugoslavia at war's end.

Most of the Irish won their freedom from Britain in a successful guerrilla war after World War One. The newly-free Poles would have to fight the Russians – now under Communist rule – for similar stakes and win in the same time period. Likewise, the people of Lithuania, Latvia, Estonia, and Finland were able to secure their freedom from the Soviet Union in the wake of Russia's slide into Communism toward the end of World War One.

The Communists would continue the oppression of the many in Russia and Ukraine and Belarusia after they overthrew the democrats who overthrew the Tsar. Many Poles and the people of the Baltic states would escape the Reds' grasp until World War Two. Then the Poles would suffer German and Russian invasion and partition, while the Baltic peoples would suffer Soviet occupation and later Nazi occupation. Eventually the Poles and the Balts would suffer re-occupation by the troops of the Soviet Union.

Most countries convulsed at least once during the 1800s and early 1900s due to a rebellion, a dynastic struggle for power, a revolution, the struggle of patriots for independence, or some or all of the above. No matter who won, the people almost always lost.

This was the civilized and progressive Europe many of our ancestors would flee from in the 1800s and early 1900s. Thank the Good Lord they came here to America.

WHY DID SO MANY PEOPLE LEAVE EUROPE?

Why did so many people leave Europe?

Leaving your homeland, traveling in a leaky overcrowded wooden ship teeming with vermin and eating wormy food and drinking bad water for weeks – or upgrading a few decades later to an overloaded stinking steamship packed like a city bus – only to come to a strange land and deal with people who more often than not don't speak your language and all too often treat you like dirt on the surface doesn't sound like a rational choice to make.

However, almost 38 million people made that choice from 1820 (when American officials started keeping detailed immigration statistics) through 1930, when American immigration laws and the Great Depression slowed the flood of immigrants to a trickle. **(1)**

Were the immigrants crazy? Were they overly optimistic? Or did they know what they were dealing with at home and decide to take a chance on a life in a foreign land that might turn out better? If Europe was so special, why did so many people leave it?

You won't get a long scholarly dissertation on the many reasons so many people made that choice in this chapter. Instead, you'll get a look at how life was for the vast majority of people who lived in Europe.

Try to put yourselves into the shoes, boots, clogs, and sandals of these people. Then it will be clear why a lot of them decided to come to America and help make this country the greatest nation on earth.

THE LIVES OF THOSE WHO FARMED

Farmers and other agricultural workers were the majority of the people of Europe in the late 1800s. Roughly 60 percent of the people of Europe worked the land in 1870. This percentage dropped by the early 1900s, but more people in Europe worked raising crops or tending herds than doing anything else. **(2)**

Most Europeans were peasants, and many were not long out of serfdom. Some peasants owned a few acres. Others rented land from a landlord. Still others were unable even to rent land, so they were laborers on the farms or estates of those who would hire them.

The countries of Europe still had nobility in the late 1800s and the early 1900s. In most countries, the feudal obligations of the peasants had ended only in the generations since the French Revolution.

What made a peasant different from a serf? A peasant, by law, could own or rent land. Most peasants were poor, but some were relatively prosperous, and a few made themselves into landlords and estate owners. A serf, by law, was bound to the land he worked and was virtually owned by his lord. Serfdom ended in Western Europe before it ended in Eastern Europe. Russia and most of the lands the Russian emperor controlled had serfdom until the 1860s, and there were serfs in the Balkans until the people of the Balkans ran the Turks out of their lands.

Imagine yourself living in a small wooden house, or a house made of sun-dried adobe or clay, or maybe a house with stone and mortar walls. If your house was made of kiln-fired brick or cut stones, you were lucky. If you lived where wood was plentiful, you would live in a log house. If you were very poor, your house might be little more than a hut made out of peat that you cut from the bog yourself ... or a furnished cave in the side of a hill.

Your house is a one-room or two-room dwelling, with a fireplace in the middle. Or if your house is bigger, there is a fireplace on each side of the house. The roof is thatched with straw or reeds, or is made of shingles, or maybe tile or slate. You have never seen electricity or indoor plumbing. Nor has anyone else in your village, or the surrounding villages.

Many of the implements in your house you have made yourself. Most of your pots and plates and jugs and other kitchenware the local blacksmith or tinsmith or potter or cooper has made for you. You and your wife have bought some items from a wandering peddler or a tinker.

You and your family members have two changes of clothing, and maybe one set of clothes for church and other special occasions. You may have shoes or boots, or wooden shoes, or leather sandals, or you might wrap your feet with rags. You might go barefoot for much of the year.

If you are a woman, you have given birth in your bed, or on the floor, or on the kitchen table. Or maybe you were in the fields working, when you felt you were about to give birth. And you cried out, and the women working with you helped you deliver your child.

If you have animals, their shed is next to your house, or their keep is underneath your house. If you are very very poor, the birds or pigs or sheep or goats might have shelter under the roof of your small house in a

ELLIS ISLAND SCRAPBOOK

dirt-floored room next to your family's living quarters.

You and your wife and children plant and harvest your potatoes and vegetables with simple hand tools. Your wife gardens by hand, and feeds the chickens or ducks or geese with grain she tosses out from her apron.

You plow with a wooden plow or a metal plow or a wooden plow with a metal plow edge and a horse or an ox or a donkey. (Metal plows will not be in widespread use in Europe until the second half of the 1800s.) If you don't own or can't rent a draft animal, you and your family break up the land with hoes and you drag a harrow to break up the clods of soil further. You sow the grain seeds by casting them on the newly-plowed or hoed soil.

You harvest grain with a sickle (or a scythe if you are strong enough and don't mind wasting some heads of grain). You thresh grain with a horse or a donkey or an ox. If you want it clean, you thresh the grain with a flail, a tool that looks like a martial artist's nanchukus. *(In fact, Oriental farmers use nanchukus to thresh rice. Their ancestors used them for threshing rice long before they used them as weapons.)* A hand threshing machine is available to you if you have the money for one or if your village has one. Horse-powered threshing machines become common in Europe in the mid 1800s, and steam-powered threshing machines finally reach many villages in the late 1800s or early 1900s. You put some grain aside for your family, and you sell the rest or use it to pay your rent. **(3)**

You don't throw away the straw after threshing the grain. You use straw to thatch your roof if you can't find the proper reeds for the job. Straw also makes good mulch for your fields and good bedding for people and animals alike.

During the harvest, you dig up and store potatoes and hope they will last you until you can get more next year. The ones that grow too many eyes in the winter you can cut up and plant to grow new potatoes the next year. Potatoes provide you with more food per unit of land than any other crop can provide.

You raise other root crops as well -- vegetables like turnips, beets, and parsnips. You put potatoes, turnips, beets, and parsnips in a cellar or in a shed or in the ground to preserve them over the winter and spring.

You grow, harvest, shell, and dry peas and beans. You grow, harvest and dry other fruits and vegetables.

You grow and harvest cabbage. You store cabbage in a cellar or in a shed or in the ground for use during the winter. You shred some of it, salt it, and drop it into large crocks. The cabbage ferments in its own juice, which preserves it, and your family eats sauerkraut for many a day.

Your village has an olive press or a seed press for making cooking oil out of olives or oil seeds. You go to the village miller to have your grain ground, or you grind some of it yourself in your own house if you can afford a grain mill.

If you have animals, you keep some for milk and breeding, and slaughter others for meat. You dry or salt or smoke the meat. You make sausage and other meat products out of the scraps and intestines.

Your wife churns butter from sheep's milk, goat's milk, or cow's milk, and she makes cheese from milk.

You and the other villagers cut hay in late spring and early summer, dry it, and store it in your barns for your animals over the winter. You and the other villagers harvest hay from your own land and from the hillsides and meadows for which the villagers have common use privileges.

You might grow corn, usually for your animals. Field corn can stay in the field until well into the fall, and the ears will dry on the stalks. (If you try to harvest the corn when it is too moist, it will rot in storage.) You pick the ears of corn by hand and set most of them aside for your animals. The rest you turn into corn meal. You feed the cornstalks to the cattle or burn them as fuel.

You might also grow mangels, a root crop, for your animals to eat during the winter. If food is scarce, then you will be eating mangels too.

In mountainous areas, there is less good land for farming. However, your animals can still graze the mountains and hillsides if you or your village has grazing rights. Someone in your family will take the animals to the nearby mountains in the summer and tend them and milk the female animals and make cheese. If you live in a mountainous country with a reasonably safe countryside, like Switzerland or Norway or Sweden, your older children can take the flocks and herds up to summer pastures in the mountains, and you are reasonably sure they will be safe. They live in huts, milk the female animals, and make cheese. You check on them from time to time to make sure they are safe, they are working, and they are not paying undue attention to teenagers of the opposite sex.

If you grow or can get grapes, you make your own wine. Your village often has a wine press. If grapes don't grow well in your area, you make your own hard cider from apples or you brew your own beer from grain.

In the wintertime, you might work with other men to cut down trees for lumber. The snow on the ground makes it a little easier for the horses or donkeys or oxen to drag the logs, and you have the time to do the logging, because your crops are harvested. You work at home making furniture for your family and other small items for sale in the local marketplace. Your wife sits by the fire and makes the family's clothes. Or she does some knitting or weaving or piecework to make the family some extra money in the wintertime.

During good years, you have enough to eat, and a little to sell for goods. During bad years, you go hungry at best and you starve to death at worst. Or you go into long-term debt, sometimes permanent debt. Or you are driven from the land and have to go to work in the cities.

If you own land at all, odds are overwhelming you are a smallholder. If you own 20 acres of farmland in most of Europe (or 40 acres of farmland land in colder, less productive Russia or Scandinavia), you are lucky. Such a holding will provide you and your family enough land for you to feed yourselves and have a reasonable amount to sell. Typically you own less land, and it is broken up into a couple of parcels somewhere near your village. You might need to rent land to raise enough crops to make ends meet. Or you might add to your income by working part-time on the estate of a nobleman or someone else with money. Or all too often you are a landless peasant who has to work full-time on an estate, or rent the land you work from a landowner in exchange for a share of the crops you raise.

Feudal obligations that peasants and serfs owed noblemen have ended in your country in your lifetime, or your father's lifetime, or your grandfather's lifetime, or your great-grandfather's lifetime... so the nobleman cannot legally tie you to the land, and you don't need his permission to marry. (Odds are, for many of you, your parents or grandparents or great-grandparents needed some nobleman's permission to marry!) However, a nobleman's word is still more important than yours, especially if he hauls you into court for some reason. "Equality before the law" is something you are not expecting to experience in this life.

At one time, the nobleman's warlord ancestors protected your serf ancestors in exchange for the right to work them like dogs, but that arrangement has changed. The nobleman might still work you like a dog. He can not punish you as viciously as his ancestors could punish your ancestors, but he is not powerful enough to protect you from the soldiers of an invading country (or soldiers of your own country's army) who march through your area. The noblemen of the 1800s all too often drink, wench, and gamble away the wealth you and the other peasants and your ancestors have made for their noble families. (That aspect of nobility hasn't changed over the centuries.)

You work a number of days each week for your noble or military landlord, or you pay him a certain amount of your cash or your produce and livestock. Your landlord makes you labor draining swamps, or felling timber, or planting, tending and harvesting his crops. Your landlord may have the duty to ensure the roads in his domain (such as they are) are in good repair ... and if he does, rest assured you will spend some of the year fixing roads for him. If your local nobleman doesn't have the power to make your do roadwork, your local government officials certainly do.

Maybe you have a small plot of land for yourself, maybe you don't. Maybe you get the right to gather firewood and draw water on your landlord's estate. If you hunt game on his land, he can punish you or even have you killed for poaching. He doesn't trust you ... armed wardens and guards, and mantraps around his manor house will kill you or hurt you severely if you decide to poach on his land or break into his manor.

You and the other peasant men bow, and your wife and the other peasant women curtsy to these well-heeled men and their wives. James Gerard, the American ambassador to Germany during World War One, said he went hunting with a count in Hungary. While he was waiting to shoot at game birds the count's men were driving his way, he said, "two peasant girls walked past me. One of them, to my surprise, caught hold of my hand, which she kissed with true feudal devotion. As a guest of the Count I was presumably of the noble class and therefore entitled by custom and right to this mark of subjugation." **(4)**

If your landlord and his guests are hunting, they all too often run their horses and dogs through your garden or your patch of grain. (All too often they do it to the fields of small independent peasant farmers also.) Gerard noted, "It is customary to hunt roebuck on these flat plains (of north Germany) from a carriage. In this way, a bullet, traveling at a downward angle, if the buck is missed, strikes the ground within a short distance. If one were to shoot lying down, kneeling, or standing, the danger to peasants in the fields would be very great." **(5)**

The local nobleman does not have the right to sample your daughter. However, if he decided to do so, he would probably not be in much hot water, unless you decide to kill him yourself. Rape is illegal, but the wealthy and the powerful tend to escape justice for such hateful offenses. Many noblemen corrupted the girls of their estates simply by using their power in service of their predatory lechery.

Having as a landlord someone from a wealthy merchant or banking or industrialist family often could leave you in as bad or worse straits.

Let's say a wealthy businessman owns the estate you farm on. He probably got to where he was through deceit and trickery, or out-and-out thievery or piracy.

He's worse in many cases than a nobleman or a noblewoman from an old titled family, because some nobles are actually decent men and women who tend to think of you as their wards or their adopted children instead of as merely their tenants. Such noblemen and noblewomen have trained their heirs to show some humanity to their tenants.

The businessman doesn't have the attachment of family to the place, or the noble family's tradition of looking after people. He has money but often no appreciation for the obligations of his station in life.

Your ancestors used to be able to graze their animals on the commons or on the church's lands. But then greedy nobles and the untitled rich got laws passed enclosing the commons to keep out the poor. The stolen commons lands then went to the highest bidders or bribers ... often for much less than they were worth. Or the government officials of your country confiscated the Church lands – bought by donations of your ancestors' labor and the nobleman's ancestors' money – and sold the stolen properties at low prices to friends of the regime. Who were these friends of the regime? Anticlerical businessmen, lawyers, speculators, and noblemen.

In times of crop failure, you have it very hard. If you rent land, your rent is still due, crop or no crop. If you own your own land, you are still short of food to sell, and maybe you are short of food to keep your family decently fed. And the government still wants their taxes. You may have to live off of grasses, or next year's seed, or you may starve to death or die of a disease that attacks your body because it is weakened by the effects of severe undernourishment.

In times of crop failures, the rulers don't want food riots in the cities, so it is easier for them to raid the countryside for food. They take your grain and your animals. Maybe they pay you, maybe they don't. Causing a couple of hundred peasant families to starve by stealing their crops is a lot easier for the government to handle than to having to shoot down thousands of angry slum dwellers for putting cities to the torch.

All of the above is what made the Famine in Ireland in the late 1840s so horrible. The potato crop, which fed most of the Irish, failed in consecutive years. Millions were reduced to eating grass and wild plants; many starved, and many many more died from diseases which killed them due to their weakened condition.

The Irish weren't the only people to suffer from the blight that cause their famine. The potato blight came to Europe, apparently in a shipload of seed potatoes from the United States to a port in Belgium in 1844. The crop disease spread through Europe in 1845 and 1846, causing large drops in the potato harvests in several countries.

The Irish suffered the worst because they were almost all tenant farmers who grew grain for sale and lived on potatoes and milk almost exclusively themselves. The rural poor could not afford the loss of income in keeping much grain for their own use. They grew potatoes for their own use because potatoes yielded more food per acre than any other crop in Ireland's soils and under Ireland's cool and rainy skies.

British authorities who ruled Ireland turned the natural disaster into a genocidal event against the Irish. They sent out British soldiers across the land to ensure grain and livestock would be shipped to Britain. Besides confiscating the grain and livestock the Irish tenants raised, the British authorities committed many other acts of callous indifference to the suffering of the Irish people. Ireland's population dropped almost by half in the decade following the start of the famine. More than one million people died of starvation or diseases which spread because the people were weak on starvation diets. At least two million more Irish had to emigrate. Most came to the United States. Others went to Canada, Britain, or Australia.

The potato blight also caused hunger and unrest in Germany and France in the same years, and was a factor in the revolutions that racked both lands in 1848. Unlike the Irish, a larger percentage of the rural poor in these countries owned their own land. In both lands, the peasants and tenants could often rely on other crops when the potatoes rotted in the field. Their own authorities, while harsh and crooked, at least were not foreign occupiers like those who ruled the Irish. This meant French and German authorities felt the need to address the effects of the potato crop failure much more urgently than the British officials did.

As a peasant or serf or landless tenant farmer, what are your means for redress of your grievances? The state and the courts are against you. You and the other peasants (or serfs) can sometimes strike back ... you can destroy the property of the rich, cripple or slaughter their livestock, withhold labor, hold back meat and other food, refuse to pay taxes, hide your daughters from them and their lecherous sons, hide your sons from military service, ostracize the government officials the state sends to enforce the state's demands, or maybe kill a few of the rich and the government officials. The richer people call you "backward." You may not have any schooling, but you know where your interests lie.

What keeps your life from being constant despair?

Your attitude and your ignorance help, to a certain extent. You accept your lot in life. You probably don't know how to read, and you often don't know what you have been missing.

But there is more than that. You realize life isn't totally without hope, or bright moments of joy, or consolation.

On Sundays you attend church and visit with the others after services. On market days you visit with others of your age and sex long after you're done buying and selling. The older girls and boys, and the younger men and women look forward to these days, so they can meet, and flirt, and court. Especially on Sundays after services they do so, because they have had their baths and they are wearing the clothes that make them the prettiest or the handsomest they can be during the week.

The church bells of your village ring the hours during the days as you work. The church bells ring in homage to Our Lord when Mass or Divine Liturgy or worship service starts. The church bells ring for joy for the young men and women for their weddings, and for their parental pride for children's baptisms, First Communions, and confirmations. For funerals, the church bells toll in sorrow and in somber anticipation of the destiny of the deceased and the majesty of God's judgment.

Those of you old enough to remember the plaintive little song "The Three Bells" of the late 1950s get the concept of the bells of the little Protestant church that rang for the birth, marriage, and death of Jimmy Brown. You also understand the idea of the prayers that the people of his congregation said for him for these events of his life and death. His preacher and the people of his little village gave thanks in times of joy and prayed in times of sorrow.

The church bells ring joyfully for holidays and times of national triumph. The church bells ring out alarms in case of fire or disaster or foreign invasion. In these times, the bells are a call for people to gather in the church for refuge or sanctuary. Many Catholic and Orthodox Christian churches in Eastern Europe and the Balkans are walled so the peasants can protect their families and offer more resistance to Moslem Turkish invaders. The church bells are a sign you can hear that your priest or minister is vigilant and is looking out for you.

If you live in a Catholic country or an Orthodox country, the holy days that the Church keeps give you some rest from the demands of your landlord. The priests don't have the power to make the nobles or the businessmen give the poor their due, but they do have the power to compel the nobles and the businessmen to rest their workers once or oftener a week.

In all of the countries, regardless of religion, there are some holidays or traditions which allow you to rest from work and enjoy yourself. Carnival before Lent, Eastertide, the oncoming of spring, the start of summer, the celebration when the harvest is done, Christmastime, New Year ... these are times where many of your happy memories lie.

The holidays and traditions link you to your past, and help you teach your children their faith and their heritage. You enjoy seeing the joy of your children.

You shed tears of gratitude and remembrance for your parents and the other adult relatives and friends who gave you love and joy when you were younger ... and you miss them most at holidays.

During these times, even the rulers of your area are a little less harsh. Perhaps they are feeling happier themselves at this time. Perhaps a few of them heed the advice one Spanish wise man gave to his king that a lord at festival time should show his subjects he is as happy for them in their celebrating as a benevolent father is for his children when they are playing happily. Why shouldn't people eat and drink and sing and dance with their friends and sweethearts? Why shouldn't the young men serenade the young women?

A wedding becomes a village event, as a young man and young woman join the ranks of the responsible married adults. The villagers take part in this joining of two young people together as a couple and a family. The eating and drinking, the singing and dancing, the rituals and customs of bringing the new wife and husband together in their new home ... they bring some fun to your life, and bring back memories when you and your spouse married.

People married young, because they could earn livings even as teenagers. In many European lands, a boy could marry if he was 14 or older, and a girl could marry if she was 12 or older, as long as his or her parents gave permission. These ages of consent for marriage were in effect in Britain until 1929! However, the laws and customs of the countries kept many other youths and maidens from marrying until they were older.

Bear in mind life was much shorter and children shouldered adult burdens much earlier in the olden days than they have done for the last three generations, starting with the baby boomers. A 14-year-old boy in the Europe or America of the late 1800s or early 1900s wasn't hanging out at the mall or playing soccer; he was working on a farm almost as effectively as a grown man and he had a man's work responsibilities. Likewise, a 12-year-old girl in the Europe or America of the late 1800s or early 1900s wasn't on the phone with her friends or hanging out at the mall; she was tending to the duties of hearth, home. garden, and farmyard – she could work almost as well at them as a mature woman. In short, boys and girls of that age and older had the responsibilities of young adults and could earn livings as adults in the economies of their homelands. **(6)**

However, in many countries, sons and daughters were still under the rule of their parents until well into their 20s. On the parish marriage record of one of my Czech ancestors in the mid-1800s is the notation he married his first wife "with her parents' permission," although she was 24! A key reason many young people emigrated to America was the tyranny of their parents.

Even death in your village – a sad event – still brings you and the other villagers together. The priest's solemn and majestic Requiem Mass for the dead person, and his reminder that God holds in the palms of His almighty hands the soul of a poor person who lives a decent life brings reassurance to people with few possessions other than faith, hope, and love. (For the deceased who were Protestants or Jews, the good minister's or rabbi's religious service would be less formal than the majestic liturgies of the Catholic and Orthodox faiths, but surely heartfelt.) The king and the dictator and the lord and the wealthy merchant discriminate against you, but God Almighty does not. The outpourings of love and sympathy to the bereaved from their families and neighbors, the wake, and the other rituals surrounding the burial of the deceased sustain those who lost their loved one. You feel good and blessed in doing your part to help, and you have some reassurance you and yours will receive help in your darkest hours.

* * * * * * *

Here's the overall picture of the farmer, peasant, tenant farmer, and landless farmhand in mid to late 1800s Europe.

If your country is England, or Scotland, or Wales, Henry VIII or his evil daughter Queen Elizabeth or some other royal pirate took the Church's lands and deeded them to their lackeys for free or at low prices. This hurt many peasants (and the poor in the towns) because the parishes and monasteries helped support the poor with charity and with paying jobs. **(7)**

But the royal pirates (and the nonroyal pirates like Cromwell) didn't stop there.

Your peasant ancestors had the right to graze their animals in the noblemen's fields over the winter after the harvest. They also had the right to collect wood, cut hay, and graze animals in the village commons (crop land and pasture land the village's residents owned in common) or "wastelands" (unfarmed lands, usually poorer pasture land or swamp or scrub forest). The commonly-owned meadows provided hay for the peasants' animals in winter; under normal situations animals were not allowed in commonly-owned meadows. A "village green" was a field inside a farming village for protecting livestock and for holding farm markets and other village events.

Henry VIII and Elizabeth and their successors on the throne allowed the nobles to "enclose" the commonly-owned lands with hedges or stone fences. This kept in the nobles' herds, and kept your ancestors out. Your ancestors lost the right to graze animals and cut hay and collect firewood on these lands. They lost the right to rent many of these lands. The loss of firewood, grazing lands, haying fields, and rentable croplands pushed many peasants into abject poverty and forced them to leave the villages.

By about 1830, the rich had enclosed virtually all of the once-open farmland in England. Their cattle and sheep grazed where once your ancestors had grazed their own animals and raised their own crops.

Formal feudalism has long been dead in Britain, but that doesn't mean your life is that much better. Parliament has cut the power of the throne, but has increased the power of the moneyed, in whose interests they rule.

Odds are you are landless tenants or you own too little land to be a successful small farmer. Your village and many others are emptying of people because the tenant farmers and many of the small landowning peasants can no longer make livings as farmers. If you haven't already done so, you are considering giving up farming and moving to a city and finding work there in one of the many factories that have sprung up during the 1800s. **(8)**

If you live in Sweden or Denmark or Prussia or Saxony or Hanover or elsewhere in northern Germany, the situation is similar. When kings and princes in these lands turned Protestant in the 1500s, they needed their nobles to become Protestants with them so the nobles wouldn't be tempted to overthrow them. If a nobleman was a member of a different religion than his king or queen or prince, he had a ready excuse to revolt ... he could claim his ruler forfeited his right to the nobleman's obedience because he had joined a "false religion" and was "in revolt against God." Noblemen and noblewomen were not known for their piety, but like the elites in all ages, they were very good about making excuses for their actions.

The rulers wanted more money to expand their governmental power. So they took the Church's land as plundering armies take spoil from a war, and doled it out to reward the nobles who turncoated with them. What lands the rulers didn't give out they kept and had these lands run like estates, with the profits going to their coffers.

Later on, especially when the Industrial Revolution started, rich merchants and industrialists acquired estates cheaply and claimed it was God's will that they engaged in predatory landlord practices which wound up depriving the people of honest livings. Sadly, too, many ministers who depended upon the wealthy classes for support were not going to preach sermons against the piracy and lechery of their benefactors.

If you lived in northern Germany, your family didn't become free from serfdom until the early 1800s in many cases. The king of Prussia, by far the largest north German state, abolished serfdom during the Napoleonic Wars. Napoleon did it in much of the rest of Germany after his armies seized German territories.

Germany was not unified in the early and mid 1800s. It was a collection of small states, and conditions for the peasants and other farm workers went from bad to worse the farther north and east you went in the Fatherland.

If you lived in Sweden, your ancestors had much better odds of being free landowning peasants. But chances are still more than 50-50 you are a laborer on a nobleman's estate in the mid 1800s. **(9)**

If you live in Norway, your land went from being united with Denmark for roughly 400 years to being ruled by Sweden after the Napoleonic Wars. You might be a free landowning peasant, or you might be a laborer on a nobleman's estate. Odds are good you work as a fisherman and/or a logger, and your wife and children work your little farm while you are fishing or logging.

If you live in Finland, your homeland went from roughly 650 years of Swedish rule to Russian rule during the Napoleonic Wars. However, the Tsars allow you and most of your people to be free peasants instead of serfs because that's what most of the country folk of Finland were when Tsar Alexander I's army took your land from the Swedes in 1809. Many of you are loggers a good part of the year.

In Denmark, there is not enough land to go around. So many of those who want to farm have to leave the land. In Norway, Sweden, and Finland, there is not enough _good_ land to go around. The growing season is short; it is too cold for much farming. The number and percentage of landless peasants rises dramatically in the 1800s. So many of those who want to farm have to leave.

If you live in Italy or Spain or Portugal or Austria or Hungary or Bavaria or elsewhere in southern Germany – all places which are mostly Catholic – seizure of many of the Catholic Church's lands took place under the rules of "enlightened despots" like Hapsburg emperor Joseph II in Austria and Hungary in the 1780s, or during the Napoleonic Wars in portions of Italy and Germany, or later in the 1800s (Spain in the 1830s, some parts of Italy, as late as the 1860s). In most of these lands, the politicians grabbed the land but they did not give it to the people. They sold it to their wealthy friends for pennies on the dollar, and received bribes or cuts of the sale proceeds. **(10)**

Of course, having a Catholic ruler was no guarantee you as a peasant or a landless farmworker or a serf weren't going to suffer oppression. Sadly, most rulers of all religions (and the atheists and agnostics too) believed (and will always believe) in one thing -- take advantage of those below them. And since you as a peasant or a landless farmworker or a serf are at the bottom of the social ladder in Europe, you would suffer under misrule, just like millennia of your ancestors did.

If you live in southern Germany or Austria or Hungary, your family didn't become free from feudalism and/or serfdom until the late 1700s or early or mid 1800s in many cases. **(11)**

Hapsburg emperor Joseph II announced the end of formal serfdom in Austria and Hungary and in other parts of his empire in the 1780s. However, he didn't follow up to verify the nobles were obeying his decree. Many feudal practices which allowed noblemen to oppress the peasants remained in place in the Hapsburg dynasty's domains. During the revolutions of 1848-1849, the Austrian government ended the remaining feudal practices to keep the peasants from joining the rebellions. They allowed the landless peasants to acquire land from noblemen's estates by paying taxes over time to compensate noblemen for the land they lost, and they ended the forced labor of peasants on landlords' estates. The rebel Hungarian government did likewise to gain the support of the peasants, at the urging of Lajos (Louis) Kossuth, one of the leaders of the 1848-1849 Hungarian uprising against Austria's Hapsburg dynasty.

Italy, like Germany, was not unified in the early and mid 1800s. It was a collection of small states, and conditions for the peasants went from bad to worse the farther south you went on the Italian boot. Napoleon ended many practices of feudalism and/or serfdom in much of Italy when his armies overthrew local kings and drove Austrian armies from Austrian-occupied portions of Italy. In northern Italy, there were many peasants who owned their own farms. However, most farmland south or Rome was in the hands of a few large estate owners and most of the people were tenants or field hands.

Spain and Portugal didn't have feudalism and serfdom in the way other European countries had it because the rural poor of these lands took an active part in pushing the Moslems out of the Iberian peninsula. Also, their colonies in the New World offered opportunities to the poor, so many Spaniards and Portuguese who might have otherwise had to live in servitude sought their fortunes in Latin America in the 1500s, 1600s, and 1700s. However, noblemen still held lots of land, and they still took advantage of the tenant farmers and farm hands who depended on them for employment.

There was another problem with farming in the sunny peninsulas. If you live in Spain, Portugal, or Italy, in most cases, the land doesn't get nearly the rain it could use. Irrigation would not become widespread in these countries until the 1900s.

Of course, life was no garden party for farmers in northern Europe either. Odds are the farmers usually got reasonable amounts of rainfall (and sometimes way too much rain), but not a lot of warmth. Europe was in the grip of the "Little Ice Age" from the early 1600s to the late 1800s. **(12)**

If you are a small farmer in France, at least the politicians allowed some of your ancestors to buy some land after they confiscated it from the nobility and the Church during the Revolution. But they didn't distribute too much to the many. The revolutionary leaders, Napoleon, and their successors sold off much of this land to their friends ... and to the descendants of nobles who were smart enough to leave France during the Revolution with their money and their heads. **(13)**

In France, odds are you own enough land to make a living as a small farmer. Your land is some of the best land in Europe, with a decent supply of water, winters that are not too cold, and summers that are not too hot. Anyone who has been to France realizes why many people would want to stay there if they could.

Things are not as good in Switzerland and the Low Countries. In Switzerland the land is too poor, in Belgium you worry about invading armies, and in the Netherlands you worry about the sea constantly threatening to overwhelm the dikes and flood your land. In all of these countries, there is not enough good farmland to go around.

If you live in Ireland, you are under occupation by a foreign power – Britain. Your ancestors weren't allowed to own land if they were Irish and Catholic. Usually the land laws kept land in the hands of the absentee British landlords. Or the Famine of the late 1840s caused your parents so much agony they had to give up the acre or so they owned to the British government so your family could get watery soup and exposure to government-backed attempts by religious charlatans to make you and your family become Protestants.

As impoverished tenant farmers or smallholders, your people used potato spades that were all wood except for the cutting surface, which was a strip of iron fastened to the large wooden wedge that formed the spade. Why? Because most country people couldn't afford shoes year-round and had to go barefoot much of the year. A metal potato spade would cut their feet. **(14)**

If you live in Russia, Ukraine, Belarusia, Moldova, Lithuania, Latvia, or Estonia, your people were still serfs until the 1860s, when Tsar Alexander II liberated the serfs. And after that they and you were very poor peasants owning hardly any land ... and you had to pay the government for the land so the government could reimburse the nobles for the land the government made them turn over to you. On top of that, you had to answer to the village council for how you used your land and when you could travel. **(15)**

If you are not Russian, you are under occupation by the Tsar's army and bureaucrats. Foreign businessmen exploit you and others in your homeland.

If you are Jewish in the Russian Empire, you are usually a tradesman, a peddler or a small businessman. Starting during the reign of Tsar Alexander III – who blames the Jews as a people for the bomb blast that caused his father Alexander II to die horribly – the government presses Jews to leave Russia. The government forbids Jews to own farmland except for some small parcels around Jewish towns in the far west of the Russian Empire (Lithuania, Poland, Belarusia, Ukraine). The nobles and government officials from time to time provoke some of your gentile peasant neighbors to rob, beat, and murder some of you (and rape your women) as a way of helping these peasants forget that they – the nobles and the government – are the culprits who are systematically taking advantage of the peasants. **(16)**

If you live in Poland, you are under occupation by a foreign power -- Russia or Prussia or Austria-Hungary. Their rulers partitioned your country in the late 1700s. Joseph II formally ended serfdom in Austrian-controlled Poland starting in the 1780s, but some practices of feudalism persisted until the revolutions of 1848-1849. The king of Prussia ended serfdom in Prussian-occupied Poland during the Napoleonic Wars. And the serfs in Russian-occupied Poland received their freedom in the 1860s, about the time the Russian serfs received their freedoms.

If you live in Slovenia, Bohemia, Moravia, Galicia, or Bukovina, you are under occupation by a foreign power ... you are in the part of Austria-Hungary ruled by Austrians. If you live in Slovakia, Ruthenia, Croatia, Dalmatia, Vojvodina, or Transylvania, you are under occupation by a foreign power ... you are in the part of Austria-Hungary ruled by Hungarians. As we mentioned earlier, Joseph II formally ended serfdom in Austrian and Hungarian-controlled lands, in the 1780s. However, many feudal practices which allowed noblemen to oppress the peasants remained in place in the Hapsburg dynasty's domains. The rival governments of Austria and rebel Hungary, during the revolutions of 1848-1849, ended the other feudal practices to keep the peasants from fighting against them. In the late 1860s, Hungary's leaders agitated for and received status equal to Austria in being able to rule their people locally and misrule the Slavs and Romanians they had power over.

Many of the nobles and moneymen in these lands own the land. Your local nobles often seek approval from the throne of the invaders (the Austrians and the Hungarians) who made these people's ancestors their lackeys. They don't seek legitimacy from you their people.

If you live in Bosnia, Hercegovina, Macedonia, Albania, parts of Greece or Serbia or much of Bulgaria, things are even worse. You are a landless serf or an almost landless peasant under Turkish occupation. (Bosnia and Hercegovina came under Austrian occupation in 1878, and most of the other lands didn't shed the Turkish yoke until the Balkan War of 1912-1913). Rainfall is often a problem as you try to raise enough produce to pay the Turks the taxes they impose on you. The Sultan's troops and officials rob, beat, and behead people regularly. The girls and young women in your family and other families can be raped early and often. They persecute you because you are an Orthodox Christian, worshiping Our Lord in a liturgy virtually unchanged since the time of St. John Chrysostom (who wrote the liturgy) in the late 300s AD.

If you live in the free parts of Greece, Serbia, Montenegro, Romania, or Bulgaria, things are somewhat better. You and most of your countrymen at least are free from the Turks, but not from the landlords. Many of your brothers and sisters are still in the hands of the Turks or the Russians or the Hungarians or the Austrians. Wars and raids are constant worries to you. Except for Romania, lack of rainfall is a constant threat to ruin your crops. However, you are free to worship God according to your faith – usually the Orthodox faith.

Throughout Europe, there are pressures on you and other farming people forcing you and them to leave the land.

Your life isn't easy. You are probably a landless tenant or you own too little land to be a successful farmer. If you haven't already done so, you are considering giving up farming and moving to a city and finding work there.

Laws of inheritance in your country decree you would have to leave what little land you have to only one of your children, and the rest would have to find work elsewhere.

Or the laws in your land would allow you to divide the small amount of your land among your offspring as you see fit. This results in ridiculously small strips of land scattered about the countryside surrounding your village. A peasant would spend much of his day going to and from his various small pieces of land, which were scattered and not big enough to farm efficiently.

In the late 1800s, technology is attacking your way of life.

Shipyard workers now build many steel ships and few wooden ships. The steel ships with their engines can hold more cargo, travel much faster, and travel more safely and dependably than the sail-driven and steam-driven wooden ships. This has taken away from the lumber barons of Scandinavia and Russia some very good clients, and has idled some of the lumbermen of Scandinavia and Russia. Coal is replacing wood as fuel in many of the homes of Europe. Electricity and gas are also becoming available in the cities of Europe. Although there is an increasing need for wood for building, for furniture, and for paper products, the downturn in demand of wood for shipbuilding and fuel hurts many people who make some or all of their livings by logging.

But the steel ships pose a worse threat to you than just the loss of a wintertime logging job. These ships can carry huge amounts of grain and salted meat from the United States, Canada, and South America. With the invention of refrigeration, the ships can even bring large amounts of meat, fruit and vegetables to Europe. And with the rise of railroads in Europe, middlemen can distribute all this food throughout the continent cheaply and quickly.

If you rent land, American corn and wheat -- raised and harvested by free men owning more and better land and better equipment -- are undercutting the price of the grain that you and the other renters of the large landowners' estates can raise by hand. So the large landowners are turning from raising crops to raising livestock. Or they are using machinery to help with the raising and harvesting of grain. Either way, they have figured out they don't need as many farmhands and tenants as they used to. They run you and others like you off the land you rent.

Refrigeration, fast ships, and American productivity are also attacking the citrus industry of Spain and Italy in particular, and the meat industry in Europe in general, causing many to lose their work. Meat coming from Argentina and elsewhere in South America is also driving down the price of meat for the people in the cities, and driving down the amount you can get for the animals you sell to the slaughterhouses.

If you are a small farmer who owns his own land, the lower cost of grain, meat, and produce from America and from larger farms in Europe worked with machinery is undercutting the price you can get for your crops ... money you need to stay afloat. Taxes rise, but your income doesn't. Odds are you can't afford machinery or your farm is too small for new machinery to help you much. Thanks to the factories, you and your wife are unable to earn as much making items in your home during the colder months when you can't raise crops. You are tempted to sell your farm and find work in the city.

In Germany, Count von Caprivi, who became chancellor after Kaiser Wilhelm II fired Bismarck, lowers tariffs to help German industries export more goods. Caprivi says, "Germany must either export people or goods." This hurts the Junkers – the Prussian land barons -- in the pocketbook because farm products from their estates cost more than meat and wheat coming in from America, Russia, or Austria-Hungary. The American competition hurts the smaller farmers even more because, unlike owners of large estates, they can not buy the machinery that would lower production costs, and their fields are too small for efficient use of this machinery. The Kaiser sacks Caprivi, and Germany's leaders restore the food tariffs to pacify the Prussian Junkers. But this does not stop the trend away from agriculture in Germany. In 1870, about two-thirds of the people work in agriculture; by 1914, only about one-third of the people work in agriculture. Since Germany's population almost doubles in that time, about 6% fewer people are working in agriculture in 1914 than in 1870. **(17)**

Britain's leaders have made their landowning aristocracy a little less wealthy, but they have broken their small farmers with a series of measures in the 1840s through the 1860s. They remove tariffs on food items, and by the 1870s British farmers can not compete with America's farmers pricewise. Most small farmers and landless farm workers have to leave the farms. The landowning aristocrats and the businessmen with lots of money buy up the land. The amount of money they can extort from their tenant farmers in Britain and Ireland (most of Ireland will not win independence until the 1920s) drops by at least a third from 1888 to 1901. They make up for it with other investments, and by renting their lands as hunting preserves and resorts, and remain very rich.

By 1901, only about a fifth of the British population is rural, and by 1914, British farms produce only a fifth of the food the people of Britain eat. This makes the British very dependent on trade with America and colonial exploitation of Canada and Australia and Ireland. This even makes Britain dependent on France, Denmark, and the Low Countries for vegetables and dairy products. This definitely makes Britain very vulnerable to submarine warfare. British greed for colonies and trade, and British dependence on a strong navy and merchant fleet will be key reasons World War One takes place and lasts as long as it will. **(18)**

In 19th Century Europe, like in too many "civilized" countries today, too many leaders don't think of farming as an industry a country should have for national security reasons. Politicians seeking power count heads and when they count more heads in the cities, they tend to favor lower food prices for the city dwellers. So they are for free trade in agriculture, which means they allow a large amount of food imports. If they decide to subsidize farmers to stay in business as a national defense measure, the public can still get cheaper food, and the farmers can still make a living. Of course the subsidy money would have to come from taxes or duties paid elsewhere (there is no free lunch), but such a subsidy program would benefit the poor in the cities and the poor in the countryside alike. Unfortunately, this kind of thinking is too advanced for the politicians.

In short, if you are a small farmer, a peasant, a tenant farmer, or a landless farm hand, there are very few places in Europe where you get what is rightfully yours.

There is less land to go around, and less work to go around, and less money coming your way as the 1800s become the 1900s. What you are getting paid for your labor is not going to increase relative to the cost of living. You are considering leaving the land to move to the city, or you are considering leaving your homeland altogether to try your luck in the New World.

THE LIVES OF THOSE WHO MINED

Not everyone who lived in the countryside farmed. The villages and small towns were home to blacksmiths and tinsmiths, carpenters and masons, weavers and tailors, millers and bakers, butchers and tanners, cartwrights and wagonmakers, vintners and brewers, coopers, fullers, chandlers, fletchers, and many other tradesmen ... tradesmen and their families who needed the business of the farmers.

Peddlers traveled from town to town with their wares in wagons. Tinkers also traveled from town to town and made repairs for people.

In areas where forests abounded, loggers lived. Along the seacoasts were ports large and small from which fishermen sailed to ply their trade.

In areas which had coal or metal ore, or stone for building, there were miners or quarrymen.

Spain, France, Germany, Britain, Sweden, Russia, and the Czech and Polish lands which Austria's emperor controlled had many mines. Wales and Bohemia in particular had many miners per capita, and many of the men from these lands would come to America to work in the coal and ore mines of this land.

If you are a miner, your day begins before sunrise. And from the mid-fall to the mid-spring, your day ends after sunset. Sunday, aptly enough, is the only day you can see the sun, because that's the only day of the week you're not working in the mine.

You use ropes and ladders to get into the mine and out of it. In some mines, you use two rods, moving a distance in one direction, and then reciprocating and moving the same distance in the opposite direction, to travel down into the mine, and then up out of it. You would have to step on the platforms fastened to the rod moving in the direction you wanted to go to move the way you wanted to. Your would step from the platform on one rod, drop 20 feet or so until a platform on a rod coming up 20 feet or so pulled even with the platform you were on, then you would step onto that platform, drop another 20 feet or so when it reciprocated and dropped, and so on, until you got to where you needed to go. In a 1000-foot-deep mine, it would take you about 20 minutes to get to the bottom of the mine, and another 20 minutes to travel from the bottom of the mine to the entrance of the mine at the end of the work shift. Owners installed these apparatuses so their workers wouldn't use too much strength getting to the parts of the mine they were working in.

You and your fellow workers use picks and shovels to dig the shafts into the ground so you could get at the veins of ore or the seams of coal that were worth mining. Later on, the mine owners introduce steam-powered drills and augers to bite into the veins of ore or the seams of coal. The horizontal passageways are often not tall enough for you to stand up in. Usually the size of the veins of ore or the seams of coal limited the size of the horizontal passageways; the mine owners didn't want to pay for drilling, blasting, and removing unusable rock.

You and your fellow workers dig or blast into the coal or the ore, load it onto carts, and move the carts to the mine shaft so others could raise them to the surface. As you dig and blast into the seam, you will have to reinforce the passages with heavy timbers to keep them from caving in on you. A lamp is your only light in these man-made tunnels. A helmet is your only protection.

If your mine owner values your services enough, he provides donkeys or large dogs to haul the carts to the mine shaft so they can be lifted to the surface. Otherwise you do it ... or boys do it. (As the 1800s progress, governments pass laws against girls and women working in the mines. Before, they had worked dragging or pushing mineral carts through the passages. As you could imagine, females could be preyed upon in the darkness of the passages of the mines.)

In coal mines, methane gas is a real hazard if it builds up to a certain percentage – about 5 to 15 percent. The spark from a lamp or your tools hitting rock or any explosive could ignite this gas and kill you all. So you keep a caged canary with you at all times. If the methane gas level goes high enough, the canary dies. And then you and the other miners had better clear out of the mine as fast as you can.

Another hazard is lack of oxygen. Mine engineers devised horse-driven fans to drive enough fresh air through the mine passages to keep you and the other miners (and the beasts of burden) from asphyxiating and dying from lack of oxygen. Later on, the engineers will use steam engines, and then electricity to get miners the air they need. As a bonus, they will discover ventilating a mine drives out some methane and other gases that are poisonous or explosive or hazardous in some other way to the lives and health of the miners.

A third problem is water. When you dig into the ground, you're bound to hit it. To prevent flooding of the mine, mine bosses had horses lowered into the mine and harnessed to drive pumps to remove the water. Steam engines have seen use since the 1700s in draining water from mines, but well into the 1800s, horses still did much of this work.

Well into the 1800s, the miners' own muscles and the muscles of draft animals supplied most of the raw power that ran the mines. Later in the 1800s, mine bosses used steam power, and later electrical power to drain water from the mines, ventilate the mines, lower men and equipment into the mines, and raise men, equipment, and minerals out of the mines. Likewise, they will bring machinery into mines to cut coal, drill rock, and extract ore, making your mine more productive and safer.

But you still work hard for what little you make. You might get to (or have to) live in a company-owned cottage. Odds are you don't belong to a union that could protect your rights. There is always the threat of sudden death in your work – you could fall to your death, be burned or shattered in a fire or an explosion, be crushed in a cave-in, die of asphyxiation or drowning, or be electrocuted. Then there is the very good possibility that mining would shorten your life without a tragic accident. You could overwork yourself and break your health, or you could get black-lung disease or silicosis from breathing in coal dust or rock dust daily. Since there are no worker compensation benefits, or labor standards to speak of until the late 1800s, you are gambling you will not die or become a cripple and leave your family destitute.

If you work in a quarry or an open pit mine, you don't face as many hazards as the underground miners. But falling rock, ore, or coal could still crush your head or bury you. Likewise, quarry owners and surface mine owners are every bit as tightfisted as the underground mine owners.

God help you if you are a serf or a prisoner condemned to work in a mine. Then the mine owner or the state doesn't care if you live or die. (Unlike you, even a low-paid free miner has job skills. This gives him some worth to his employer.) Your conditions are indescribably bad. In short, you are expendable. If you die, there will be others convicted by just or unjust judges to take your place.

Despite the dangers, you and many other people consciously decide to work as miners in the 1800s. The area you live in might have many mines, and many job opportunities. Many miners are skilled workers in comparison with farmers and most factory and workshop workers. Some mining jobs pay reasonably well compared with other jobs. Mining is a dirty and dangerous job, but a respected job for a worker.

Like the farmers, miners find some joy and consolation in life.

You and your fellow miners often form unions or guilds or other fraternal organizations. These organizations would offer you and your family some benefits when you needed them, and maybe help with the cost of a funeral when you or a loved one dies. You and your wife and your children socialize with other miners and their families. You have festivals, dances, and projects together, much like you have at your church. Besides being fellow townspeople, these other mining families are people who share your lifestyle.

Some mining companies provide decent housing to their miners. Perhaps you have a sturdy cottage. Living in a town sometimes gives your children the opportunity to get some schooling. Living in town also gives you and your wife more opportunities to do things in your spare time than you would have on a farm.

On Sundays you attend church and visit with the others after services. Sundays after services bring the older girls and boys and the younger men and women the same chances to socialize, because they have had their baths and they are wearing the clothes that make them the prettiest or the handsomest they can be during the week.

If you live in a Catholic country, your mine might close on a holy day and give you another well-deserved day of rest. Your miners' association might celebrate the feast day of the patron saint of the association. In all of the countries, regardless of religion, there are some holidays or traditions which allow you to rest from work and enjoy yourself.

Weddings and funerals in your mining town would have much the same impact on your life as they would on the lives of the peasants. The townspeople (especially from the miners' families) would take part in the wedding or the funeral. There would still be plenty of people to cheer the newlyweds and pray for the deceased and help their survivors.

The church bells ring in your town like the church bells ring for the people in the country. However, you fear one type of ringing the farmers don't have to worry about ... the insistent sad clanging of the bells when there has been an emergency or a disaster inside the mine. Those men who are off duty have to come and try to rescue the living and recover the bodies of the dead. The wives and children of those inside the mine wait outside and agonize over whether their husbands and fathers are coming home alive. All too often, their worst fears come true.

What would make you think about leaving the mines of Europe?

At best, the conditions for miners were not good. In many countries, miners' unions were illegal or were unpowerful. Remember, in the late 1800s, most countries in Europe were monarchies or empires. Even in Britain and France, two countries where people had the right to vote and organize unions, the authorities were on the side of the mine owners.

Some of the mines of Europe were becoming exhausted. For many other mines, the cost of mining the mineral was becoming more than the price selling the mineral would bring on the open market. Either of these problems would mean the miners would lose their jobs.

Another reason was there were more opportunities in other parts of the world. There were gold rushes or other stampedes for minerals in Australia, South Africa, Latin America, and North America. Of all of these countries, conditions seemed the best in the United States.

And some of you who worked as miners wanted to get out of the mines altogether. Maybe you could farm, or live in a city and make a living at a safer job. America seems to have more opportunities for this than your own homeland. **(19)**

THE LIVES OF THOSE WHO LIVED IN CITIES AND TOWNS

After the countryside, the cities where the people of Europe were most likely to live. In 1870, roughly 20% of population lived in cities or towns with populations above 5,000 people. **(20)**

After the end of feudalism, many of the newly-free peasants sold the small strips of land they held title to and moved to the cities looking for work. Or the great lords and merchants ran them off of their land. Rather than become beggars, they moved to the cities.

Here they joined those who couldn't inherit or buy land, ... the proletariat, or the rabble. The "proletariat" were unskilled and semiskilled laborers who, unlike skilled tradesmen or artisans, could not set their wages, but had to accept what miserly business owners and wealthy lords were willing to pay them for their work.

The first industry to mechanize was the fabric industry. The steel industry followed, and then so did the manufacturing of other goods.

If you live in a city, odds are you live in a slum. If your wife or daughter runs to and from the public fountain when drawing the family's water, you have "running water." Your wife buys wood or charcoal or coal and cooks on an iron stove. You have no refrigeration, and you can't afford ice. Your wife or oldest daughter shops almost daily for food.

If you live in a large city, you probably live in a stone or brick building. The city fathers learned from the fires sweeping through the city in earlier days to try to limit the number of wooden buildings.

However, you and your family share this building with dozens of other people. The stench from all that cooking, sweating, washing, and voiding is everywhere. Windows are your ventilation, and the building is drafty in the winter. You have no air conditioning in the summer. (Air conditioning is not even available to the *rich* in this era.) Your tenement is cold in the winter, hot in the summer, and dirty all year round.

To heat your room in the colder months, you buy coal or wood from a man who brings it to your building in a cart. You burn the fuel in a stove or a fireplace. In a way, it is good if the building is a bit drafty. It poses less of a risk of carbon monoxide poisoning, because the hazardous gas can't build up to a percentage strong enough so it can asphyxiate you and your loved ones. Oil lamps and candles are your nighttime light source. You and your family (and all the other people in your building) have to be careful with these, so no fire starts.

Bad water and open sewage do nothing to improve public health. You and other people use pots to answer the call of nature, or use outhouses. People pile their trash and excrement in huge piles in the alleys until the garbagemen can haul the mess away. Most cities and towns have a primitive sewer system at best. (London, for example, is plagued by the backup of the sewers when high tide backs up the Thames River. Also, the drinking water is questionable because it comes from the same river the sewers dump untreated waste into.) Some sewers are nothing more than trenches in the street to carry wastes into the nearest body of water. Germs from cesspools, from overused outdoor toilets, and from people relieving themselves on the filthy streets are constant igniters of local epidemics. **(21)**

The horses and donkeys that carry the loads leave loads of their own in the streets. Then there are those who are slovenly enough to empty their chamber pots into the streets from the windows up above. (Napoleon's father sued a family in Corsica for emptying their chamber pot – or maybe dishwater or kitchen waste -- out their windows onto his wife, Napoleon's mother. They had ruined her dress, and he won damages from them. Even in cities with sewers, filth builds up in the streets until the garbagemen get around to collecting it. Especially in the summer, the stench is overwhelming. But you get used to it. You have to. **(22)**

What is harder to get used to are the epidemics that rage through the cities. All those people living in close quarters with poor sanitation are bound to pass germs. And they do. People routinely drop like flies. (The people in the country can bury their own wastes, manure their gardens and fields with the animals' wastes, and burn their trash, so they can avoid many of the germs you can't. They also enjoy better food, and often homemade wine or beer (alcohol kills germs), so they are getting a healthier diet than you are.)

Another problem comes from the factories which provide you with your daily bread (what little you can buy on the starvation wage they pay you). The factories burn coal, and exhaust it unfiltered. This adds to the problem that you and many thousands of other workers living so closely packed together cause when you burn fuel to heat your home or cook your food.

Choking coal and chemical fogs roll over your city, dimming the sunlight and slowly poisoning you and the other residents. White clothes hung out to dry turn gray. The buildings you crowd into to live in turn gray. Even the trees outside your cities darken from the smoke. So do the insides of your lungs.

You breathe soot daily, and many other poisons besides. You suffer exposure to toxic chemicals, coal dust, or cotton dust. Mercury used for making felt for hats damages hatmakers' brains, causing them to twitch a lot more than the average person, and giving rise to the sad expression, "He's as mad as a hatter." The local hatter who suffers brain damage from breathing mercury while he works has it worse than you, but you're not breathing clean air like the peasants are, either. Sicknesses from breathing in the poisons the factories belch into the air bedevil you and other people.

You work in a factory, standing for hours at a machine and doing repetitive tasks. Your boss can fine you for talking, singing, or taking a break to answer the call of nature. In summer, the factory drips with humidity; in winter, the cold winds breeze through the factory. When there is work, you work 12 hours a day, six days a week. When there is no work, you starve or get by on the "charity" of a poorhouse with watered-down soup and separate living quarters for men, women, and children ... even for the married poor. Until the late 1800s, no country's politicians think of unemployment coverage.

Like miners, your day begins before sunrise, and from the mid-fall to the mid-spring, your day ends after sunset. Sunday, aptly enough, is the only day you can see the sun, because that's the only day of the week you're not working. Sometimes you can't, because many of the "better people" who own factories are openly contemptuous of religion, so they don't mind making you come to work on Sunday. Or the piously hypocritical factory owners attend services and take away your Sabbath and make you report for work while they are at church asking Jesus for more money.

Some of the bosses pay their workers on Saturday night in taverns they own, coming in very late with the payroll, trying to get their workers to drink away some of their weekly earnings while they wait for their pay.

Factory owners and managers devise other ways to skin you. Factory owners employ women to cause a labor surplus and shrink men's wages. Women are more docile than men, and will work for less. This depresses the wage of male workers. Factory owners also employ children to shrink women's wages. Children work in the countryside, say the bosses, so they can work in the factories ... where they are expected to do a man's work at a child's pay. The wages of male workers drops further.

Any child would tell the boss, if he or she dared speak up, that tending sheep and goats or picking fruit and vegetables in the sunshine is no comparison with being trapped in a building and working around noisy dangerous machinery.

Twelve, 14- and 16-hour days, often with no time off for Sunday, exhausts the men and women and children who toil in factories, not only in the countries under authoritarian rule, but in "liberal" Britain's factories as well. Cruel bosses beat and fine workers over trifles and threaten them with firing. These indignities rob the workers of their pride and their will to stand up for themselves.

In these factories, machines do not have safety guards. Workers routinely lose fingers, hands, arms, and eyes to the machines. Children suffer the most. Boys and girls who should be in school or in the fields are laboring in factories. They tire easier, and daydream, and are not as strong, or as tall ... so many of these little ones lose fingers or limbs or eyes, or occasionally even scalps to the machines.

Many children are taken out of orphanages, and are worked 10 to 16 hours a day by many factory bosses. The bosses are not above chaining children to their machines during their shifts, or locking them up at night to prevent them from running away. Children are easy prey to sex offenders among the bosses and the adult workers.

The family structure breaks down as most men can't earn enough to support their families, so their wives and children have to work for money also. This means the children receive very little parental supervision or love from their exhausted parents. Children who have parents caught in this situation often receive no schooling, and grow up illiterate and despairing. These unfortunates don't think they can ever improve their lots in life.

The housing shortage causes many men and women to cohabit without getting married. Predictably, the numbers of foundlings soar.

Crime is epidemic. Thievery flourishes; and many women feel compelled to sell themselves as prostitutes. For example, London, a city of about 2.5 million people in the mid 1800s, had 9000 registered prostitutes and perhaps another 70,000 who sold themselves without a license. If this estimate is accurate, then about one woman in ten (actually of younger women, maybe one in four or one in three) felt she had to take cash for sex in the British capital. **(23)**

What can you do about your conditions?

The guilds of craftsmen – the men who have recognized trades – look down on you. After all, they are often self-employed. The factory owners know it is in their own interests to keep you from organizing like the craftsmen do.

In many countries, labor unions are illegal. In countries where they are legal, they have little power. Officials send police and soldiers to beat and saber the workers. In countries like Britain and France, where unions are legal, judges swayed by position or bribes rule against unions and order the leaders jailed. Or factory owners can decide not to hire union members.

Resentment sets in, and sometimes you or workers you know riot. Government officials have the police beat you down ... and if the police can't or won't do it, then the soldiers certainly will. Then, of course, the politicians and those richer than you say the rioting (which was brought on by the injustice of the owners) is proof you are unworthy of justice.

As the Industrial Revolution advances, the industrialists squeeze the guild members also. In many places, the guilds – organizations of skilled tradesmen – used to determine quality standards for products to make sure some unscrupulous tradesman wouldn't undercut them. They also set standards for training people who wanted to enter the trades, and set obligations for master tradesmen to their apprentices.

The industrialists want none of this. They use money to influence government officials to take the power of setting quality and training standards away from the guilds. Why? They are greedy and cheap. The cloth, shoes, and other products their machines spit out won't for many years have the quality of goods a weaver or a shoemaker or another skilled tradesman could make, so their products obviously couldn't meet guild standards. Factory owners don't need skilled workers to run their machines. So they hire and fire without worrying about the quality of a worker's training.

Eventually, engineers and mechanics improve the machines for mass production to the point where many manufactured goods are as good or better than handmade goods. The manufacture of clothing, footwear, hardware, and household goods are hurting the businesses of the tailors, the weavers, the cobblers, the blacksmiths, the tinsmiths, the glass blowers, the potters, the cabinetmakers, and many other tradesmen in the villages and the towns.

If you have come in from the countryside, you are cut off from your roots in the city. If you were born in the city, you don't have much time for building new ties. Maybe your parish or congregation might offer you some solace. Or, if you don't want religion, there are other ways to spend your time.

Drink is one way you try to forget your troubles. Sex is another. In many cities, as many as one child in three is born to females who aren't married.

There are not enough priests or ministers to remind you of your duty to behave like children of God. Nor is there the social disapproval of the village or the small town toward the drunks, lechers, thieves, and loafers. Most city dwellers, like yourself, are too busy trying to survive to have the energy to build a strong community in the city like the people have in the country.

The churches don't seem to make much difference in the cities. Priests and ministers do not have much influence on the industrialists. Many of the upper classes are atheists, skeptics, or agnostics. They don't care much for someone telling them it is the will of God that they pay their workers fairly instead of treating them like slaves, and that they sell their customers quality products instead of shoddy junk.

Many of the rich have cast off religion and its demands for charity and morality. Even many among the wealthy who donate great sums to charity usually make this money by cheating their workers, paying them subsistence wages, or by cheating customers by making shoddy goods, or both. Their "charity" is a sham, the product of their thievery for public relations.

Many of the leading alleged thinkers of the day are lapdogs of the wealthy. The "thinkers" say the poor will always be poor anyway, so why help them? Malthus and his ilk say treating the poor fairly, or giving them charity when they are destitute is not useful, because they will only breed more poor. Opinion makers blame the plight of the poor on the poor themselves instead of on the greed of the landed aristocrats and the industrial and merchant magnates who squeeze every penny of profit out of the poor that they can squeeze.

Darwin's concepts of natural selection find enthusiastic listeners among many capitalists, who justify their piracy as the result of their being fitter to survive than the poor. (Many earlier capitalists liked John Calvin's teachings favoring usury, wealth accumulation, and industriousness; they felt they had his religious approval to gouge others and work their employees long hours for little pay.) They feel God smiles on the prosperous, even though too many of the prosperous obviously ignore the commandments against coveting property, lying, theft, and murder. Anti-religious "liberals" are against the poor for different reasons ... they say the poor are too stupid to deserve better, that natural selection made the more able people rich. They try to keep the laborers in the cities from having the right to vote, because they rightly fear the proletariat will vote for more radical politicians than themselves.

All too often, the ministers of churches treat the rich with kid gloves, because their own personal interpretation of the Bible tells them God is blessing the rich with material goods because they are chosen people. It doesn't seem to occur to these ministers that these people are rich because they abuse their free will to violate the commandments against covetousness and theft, and they ignore the words of St. Paul and of Our Lord Himself that no one should deprive the worker of his just wages.

The result of generations of this sort of thinking is predictable. For example, vocations for the Protestant clergy would drop in Britain. Also many of the "educated" "no longer regarded religion as the central theme of life." **(24)**

James Gerard, the American ambassador to Germany during World War One (and nominally a Protestant), would say something similar about religion in predominantly Lutheran Germany during World War One:

"I saw no signs of any great religious revival, no greater attendance at the churches. Perhaps this was because I was in the Protestant part of Germany where the church is under the direct control of the government and where the people feel that in attending church they are only attending an extra drill, a drill where they will be told of the glories of the autocracy and the necessity of obedience. In fact, religion may be said to have failed in Germany and many state-paid preachers launched sermons of hate from their state-owned pulpits." (25)

In Protestant countries, there is an official religion that the king, queen, kaiser, kaiserin (empress), nobility, and Parliament give lip service to while they pursue their own vices. Since the established church is subservient to the state, little pressure for reform comes from the pulpits. Many of those who consider themselves intellectuals are atheists or agnostics. In the cities, you can avoid religion and pursue vice without too many problems. There are plenty of women who have little to sell but themselves, and too few husbands and fathers and brothers to protect them.

In Catholic countries, the monarchs and government leaders are usually anticlerical. And so are the upper classes, those who consider themselves intellectuals, and the industrialists. To them, you are a bumpkin if you show any faith. To them, Pope Leo XIII is a troublemaker who presumes to tell your leaders to stop making wars of unjust conquest, start allowing the poor to attend school and receive religious education, and start enacting laws to protect the rights of the workers. How dare the Pope blame socialism and communism on the greed of the capitalists and imperialists? Just like in the Protestant countries, you can avoid religion and pursue vice in the cities without too many problems. In fact, the theaters and opera houses in France and Italy are bound to contain performances more salacious than those in many Protestant countries.

In Orthodox countries, only Russia has cities of any size. Yet the pattern in Russia is largely the same as in the Protestant countries. The Tsar and Tsaritsa (empress) and the nobles have too much authority, and the church hierarchy are nearer the throne than they are to the people. Priests and monks who defend the people often meet bad ends. Moscow and St. Petersburg and the larger provincial cities have the same kinds of vice that flourish elsewhere in Europe. You can avoid religion and pursue vice in the cities without too many problems.

Many otherwise decent people, scandalized by the bad example in morals and lack of charity shown by church leaders, quit organized religion altogether.

Often enough, the tide of misery rising in the cities has simply overwhelmed the work of the good-hearted priests, nuns, brothers, ministers, deaconesses, rabbis, and the charitable lay people who donate to their causes. They care deeply and they do their best, but poverty in the city is a harder thing to deal with than poverty in the country. In the country, even the poorest can grow food and trade labor for rent and clothes. In the city, everything must be paid for in money, from the roof over a person's head to the food and clothes he or she needs. If someone can't get a job, he or she can't get the cash needed to live.

If the cities are so horrible, why are people coming to the cities in droves?

In many cases, they have to. There is no more land to farm for them to claim and cultivate. Or they have lost their land. Or the jobs that used to be available to them in the countryside are gone. On the other hand, there is work (and some handouts) for people in the cities.

The cities offer some advantages to people, besides someplace to go if they can't farm.

The Industrial Revolution, which brutalized the first couple of generations of industrial workers in each country, eventually improves the lots of millions of city dwellers.

More efficient grain and livestock farming in the Americas drops the price of grain and meat. Steam-powered railroad trains rush the food to Latin American and North American ports, coal-powered (and later oil-powered) steel ships speed the food to Europe, and European trains bring this food to the cities. Some European leaders subsidize their own farmers to produce food, but allow lower-cost imported food into their countries to keep the masses in the cities from rioting. Workers start having more of their paychecks free to spend on items other than food.

Better machinery starts to produce better products at more reasonable costs. Workers in the city are able to afford more products. Better scientists and engineers and doctors and better public health practices cut down the size and severity of epidemics and industry-related illnesses.

As more people learn how to read, the newspapers gain importance in passing on ideas and information. The rise of the telegraph, steamship, railroad, and telephone brings news from distant countries to people in Europe more quickly. In the cities, it is easier to organize masses of discontented people to protest injustices. Urban mobs force the leaders to change some of the most unfair laws. The more astute leaders – often out of shrewd selfishness instead of goodness – change other unfair laws on their own to win the approval of more people and retain political power.

Odds are in late 1800s urban Europe, you and your wife have little or no education. However, with luck and determination, you might find a job other than unskilled factory work. You might be able to better yourself.

Your children might or might not be able to go to school now. But they would have even less of a chance to go to school in the countryside. If your boys can get through school somehow, they might be able to become businessmen or white-collar professional men. The less able boys can still become government employees. Even your girls could consider becoming teachers or nurses.

You as a city dweller are not as restricted by customs and your neighbors as you would be in a farming village. You have more freedom of association in the city; there are more people to meet and get to know. Since fewer people know you really well, gossip and busybodying doesn't affect you as much in a city as it would in a village. If you are a member of a minority group, you might find a large community of your ethnic group or religion in the city. This surely would be better than isolation among people hostile to your origin or creed.

If you are religious, you can belong to a parish or congregation in the city, and have some ties to your fellow worshipers like the people in the rural villages have. However, religion does not have quite the visceral impact on your life that it would in your rural village.

The church bells are not the only loud sound in the city. The noises of the factory horns, the dull noises of the crowds, the clanging of the fire bells, and the clattering of the constant horse and wagon traffic and rail traffic compete with the church bells for your attention.

As more and more countries' leaders fund public schools and insist children attend them, the priests and nuns lose much of their hold on the education of children. Many nations' leaders even seize Church schools and ban orders of nuns and brothers and priests who had taught children for centuries. Many self-satisfied snobs and government bureaucrats look down on religion and on the faithful.

The parish in the city has more competition for social life than the parish in the country. In the country, only the village tavern and market day compete with the church's Sundays and holidays and pageants and weddings. In the cities, there are hundreds of taverns and cafés and fancier places as well. There are many fraternal organizations that are not connected to any church.

There is more entertainment in the city. If you can afford it, you can take it in. The city has better musicians and singers, because there are more people concentrated in the city to be paying customers. Likewise, there are more plays to choose from than the religious pageants of the village churches. In fact, if you would prefer to avoid religion altogether, the city is really your place.

Things are far from fine in the cities, but your family has come to the city seeking work and you have stayed because you have adapted to city life. There is more squalor, but there are more opportunities. Politicians sooner or later will have to better your lot in life, with better wages, safer workplaces, and some protection in times of unemployment, injury, and old age if they don't want constant rioting. You might not see these changes in your lifetime, but maybe your children will in theirs.

Then maybe you are thinking of coming to America. The word you hear is that workers in America get better pay, and live in better conditions. There is no hereditary nobility in America. And even though there are plenty of robber barons who run America's industry and commerce, they don't have the power that European lords of commerce and industry have. And Americans can throw out the thieves who rule them at election time.

A FEW NOTES ON RELIGIOUS PERSECUTION

Those of you who are Catholics have already heard from Protestants and Jews and atheists how oppressive the popes and the Inquisition supposedly were, so you're used to the flak. Believe it or not, your religion doesn't hold the record for persecution.

Since America is mostly a Protestant country, you who are Protestants have probably never heard the ugly truth that your spiritual ancestors were the most violently intolerant of the Christians.

British and Lutheran and Calvinist "witch burners" in Britain, Germany, and elsewhere in Europe murdered 35,000 to 100,000 people (the vast majority were women), many more people than the Spanish Inquisition's officers ever executed for all reasons. **(26)**

Oliver Cromwell and other like-minded Protestant Englishmen murdered close to a million Catholic Irish in a religious and ethnic pogrom in the 1640s and 1650s. By comparison, those who ran the Spanish Inquisition – widely considered the bloodiest Catholic enterprise – executed about 5500 to 32,000 heretics, child molesters and rapists in positions of authority, and suspected Jewish and Moslem fifth-columnists (those who posed falsely as converts and usually supported

ELLIS ISLAND SCRAPBOOK

Spain's Moslem enemies) in three and a half *centuries* from 1480 to 1830. **(27)**

Our collective ignorance of these facts stems from our national origin as colonies of Britain, whose leaders and opinion makers have been incredibly anti-Catholic and anti-Spanish for centuries. British rulers made money from their pirates who plundered Spanish gold fleets and Spanish colonies in the New World. Even in our time, when Prince Charles of England was romantically linked with pretty Catholic Princess Marie-Astrid of Luxembourg in 1979 and 1980, Protestant bigots in Britain and then-prime minister Margaret Thatcher opposed him breaking the nation's three-centuries old law against a potential ruler of Britain marrying a Catholic. So the big-eared heir married Diana and kept Camilla on the side. Princess Marie-Astrid married another nobleman and lived happily ever after.

The British weren't the only bigots. In 1545, John Calvin's lackeys in Geneva, Switzerland burned 20 people to death on witchcraft charges for allegedly conspiring to use the black arts to spread an epidemic. By the way, Calvin the coward would not minister to the victims of the epidemic because he was afraid of getting sick. Suspected witches were not Calvin's only victims. From 1542 through 1546, Calvin's first five full years in power in Geneva during his comeback, his town councilmen had the executioners burn 35 people at the stake (including the 20 alleged witches burned in 1545), hang 13 other people, and behead 10 other people. One of those was a girl whose pretty head was cut off because she reportedly struck her parents.

By comparison, officials in Spain recorded executing six people for witchcraft over a period of several centuries. The officials of the Inquisition had a hand in almost none of these executions. Spain, Portugal, and Ireland together have 17 recorded executions (and no more than 67 recorded and estimated executions of alleged witches) ***throughout their national histories***, compared to Calvin's Geneva's 20 in 1545.

On witch-burning, the Spanish Inquisition also compares well to the behavior of the English Puritan wingnuts of Salem, Massachusetts, who in 1692 hanged 19 people, crushed a man to death under rocks trying to get him to talk, and let four others die in jail after some delinquent teenage girls falsely accused them of witchcraft. The French Inquisition also cleared Joan of Arc of false sorcery and heresy charges, but English leaders ignored them and burned her at the stake anyway on the trumped-up charges for political and military reasons.

The last person to be executed on witchcraft charges in Europe was Anna Goeldi, a tall good-looking brunette who was the maid and mistress of a judge named Johannes Tschudi in the Swiss canton of Glarus. Evidently she stopped giving him sex, so he fired her. Anna threatened to reveal his adultery publicly. This would probably cost Tschudi his judge job and his spot as an elder at the local Protestant church, so he accused her of witchcraft. Given his standing relative to hers, it was a foregone conclusion Anna would get the shaft again. A swordsman beheaded Anna in the town square in 1782, the year after we beat the British at Yorktown. **(28)**

The non-established Protestant churches did not share in this trail of blood in Europe. Why? They never had enough power to do so. Otherwise they probably would have, as witnessed by the butchery of American Indians by the Pilgrims, the Puritans, the Huguenots, the Presbyterians, the Methodists, and their descendants.

The lack of American Indians in British-settled North America contrasts greatly with the huge numbers of American Indians in the Spanish-settled Americas. The British and their American descendants saw the American Indians as savages to be killed. The Spanish and their American descendants saw the American Indians as people to be worked, for sure, but also as people to be evangelized and assimilated. Queen Isabella of Spain was furious when Columbus brought her American Indians in chains, and she ordered them freed. She outlawed slavery in the New World, but after her death, corrupt rulers would allow it. And there was a lot of sexual mixing between the Spanish and the Indians as well. This accounts for the Mexicans and for many other mestizo peoples of Latin America.

Queen Isabella and King Fernando *did* expel the Jews from Spain. Why? Most of the leading Jews in Spain were on the losing side of Queen Isabella's war to drive the Moslem invaders out of Spain. The Jews as a group thus had to pay a heavy price for their leaders' alliances with the Moslems over the nearly eight centuries they oppressed the Spanish.

The Spanish rulers' treatment of the Jews was about average for Western Europe. English officials drove out the Jews from their lands in the late 1200s, and French officials did likewise in the early 1300s, and the Jews of those realms weren't supporting Moslem invaders who had oppressed the people for several centuries. In Germany, local officials conducted pogroms against Jews in the mid 1300s.

During the wars of the Protestant Reformation, Luther preached a pogrom against the Jews and got them driven from many parts of Germany. His opponent Charles V, the Catholic Holy Roman Emperor, was much more friendly to the Jews of Germany. (Charles V also ruled Spain. He was one of the many grandchildren of Fernando and Isabella.)

Charles II of England, Cromwell's enemy, allowed Jews to return to his realm in the 1660s. The Hapsburg Empire was up and down for Jews. Their status depended on the mood of the emperor or empress. The same held true among the states of Italy. Pope Alexander VI, the corrupt Borgia pope with several bastards (including Lucrezia Borgia) to his tally, took in many Jews who King Fernando and Queen Isabella exiled. Many popes followed his example in aiding Jews. (Even the falsely-maligned Pius XII did so. He paid ransoms to free Jews in Italy. He hid 3000 Italian Jews in his own summer palace near Rome from the Germans who essentially were occupying Italy after the overthrow of Mussolini. He also had hundreds of other Jews hidden from the Nazis in the Vatican itself. His diplomats, most notably the future Pope John XXIII, rescued thousands of Jews from Eastern Europe.)

Catholic Poland was considered the safest place for Jews in Europe during the Protestant and Catholic reformations, so many European Jews moved there. The Moslem Turks allowed Jews to live in the Balkans and in some other areas of their empire as second-class citizens. For awhile, Turkish-run Salonika (in Greece, city of the Apostle Paul's Epistles to the Thessalonians) became a predominantly Jewish city. However, the Moslems of Morocco weren't so hospitable. They robbed and murdered or left to die many Jews who fled from Spain. They also raped Jewish girls and women.

At the direction of Russia's leaders, Orthodox Christians persecuted Jews in the 1800s and early 1900s. When the Russians and Prussians and Hapsburgs cut up Poland in the late 1700s, Russia's leaders took the parts of the Polish state (Warsaw, eastern Poland, Lithuania, Belarusia, and western Ukraine) that had the most Jews. The Jews thus went from being reasonably secure in Poland to being targets of harsh persecution.

Jews suffered much more and oppressed much less in Europe because there were fewer of them. In areas where Jews had power, they behaved no better than the Gentiles toward people who believed differently than them. For example, Jews persecuted Orthodox Christians in Salonika. Discrimination and persecution are two of the baser instincts of fallen human nature in action.

Of course, the Moslem Turks and other Moslems who ran the Ottoman Empire treated Christians like slaves and Jews only a little better. The slave markets of Constantinople were always full of Orthodox Christian girls and Catholic girls from Ukraine, Armenia, Georgia, and the Balkans.

Moslems killed and enslaved millions during their wars of aggression against the people of Europe. The Crusades were attempts to stop these bloodthirsty vermin, and to guarantee Christians the right to make pilgrimages to the Holy Land. Moslems made slaves of European people on up to the 1900s. Moslems continue to make slaves of African people today.

In all too many Moslem countries, the penalty for leaving Islam is death. And in those Moslem countries where such a law is not on the books, there are sizeable minorities of people who would take it upon themselves to kill converts anyway. To the chagrin of non-Moslems and even to the dismay of many decent peace-seeking Moslems, this trend is as old as Mohammed himself.

Many Hindus are also not above murdering people of other faiths. They slaughtered hundreds of thousands of Moslems at or around the time of the partition of the Indian subcontinent into Hindu India and Moslem Pakistan after World War Two. Government-sanctioned murder of Catholics and Protestants by Hindu fanatics is an all-too-common occurrence in the India of today. So is human sacrifice of children for money and sexual gain. So is the murder of brides if their dowries are too small. **(29)**

In tallying the dead from sectarian violence, I am not counting those oppressors who died while persecuting others. Self-defense of the right to practice religion is justifiable. Moslem oppressors made the lives of the Christian peoples of much of Europe a living hell for centuries. The only way the Catholic and Orthodox peoples of these lands could practice their religions in peace was to drive the jihadists out. Likewise the Irish had every right to rebel against the British who destroyed their churches and murdered them and their priests and nuns. The Jews of the Warsaw ghetto were totally justified in killing the Nazis who would murder them and roughly six million other Jews in 12 short years.

By presenting these facts, I am not downgrading any religion. Religions thrive despite the bad example of their most powerful alleged adherents. You have no reason to apologize for what your fellow believers did or may have done centuries ago. (Just like America is great despite the many criminals who hold high office in this land.) But bigots against certain religions have exaggerated the numbers of crimes people of that faith committed, and have ignored the wrongs done by people who share their own creed (or lack of faith).

One of the worst bloodbaths in Europe before 1900 was ordered by the atheist and agnostic leaders of the French Revolution. The "enlightened" lawyers and fellow "liberals" of the Revolution who "freed France from the tyranny of the crown and the Church" sent roughly 30,000 men, women, and children from all walks of life to their deaths in the 18 months from the execution of incompetent King Louis XVI in January 1793 through the execution of the cunning self-righteous psychopath Robespierre in July 1794. About half of these unfortunates were guillotined; many of the headless were women. Most of those condemned went to their deaths with little or nothing in the way of a trial.

This does not count an estimated 100,000 to 300,000 men, women, and children the revolutionary army killed in Vendée and Brittany in western France during this time. Almost all of these victims were fervently Catholic peasants who rebelled against the lunatics who had taken control in Paris. The Girondists (moderate leftist lunatics) and Jacobins (radical leftist lunatics) alike in the French government ordered their soldiers to show the peasants no mercy. The peasant rebels – nicknamed the Chouans (screech owls) – resisted for awhile but then finally crumbled under the repeated assaults of government troops. The survivors carried on guerrilla warfare against the government for a couple of years, but could not save their people from the government troops' atrocities. The troops shot, hanged, drowned, beat to death, burned, and beheaded their female and male victims. They raped women and children, cut open pregnant women, and burned towns.

Napoleon Bonaparte, when ordered to take command of troops to crush the peasants and priests of the Vendée and Brittany, refused to do so. He said it was beneath him to shed French blood, especially when France had plenty of external enemies like the Prussians and Austrians and British to fight. After Napoleon overthrew the government and became dictator, he was conciliatory to the surviving rebels of these regions. **(30)**

The French Revolution was one of many godless pogroms against humanity. Atheistic Nazis and Communists would use similar "justification" to their mass murders of millions of innocent people in Europe in the 1900s.

MORALITY IN THE VICTORIAN AGE

It's hilarious but disturbing to hear those who call themselves professors and activists and artists talk about how sexually repressed people were in the Bad Old Days ... presumably to justify the open swine-in-rut behavior of too many men and the bitch-in-heat behavior of too many women today. Since the knowledge of history most of these people have apparently could be written on a piece of confetti, I'll say a few words about the "repressive morality" of the Bad Old Days here.

Throughout history there have been swings back and forth concerning what constitutes appropriate sexual conduct. The Middle East of Biblical times was a moral cesspool, like the Hollywood of today. The Rome of old started out reasonably pure for a pagan society, but degenerated into public lasciviousness. Ancient Greece was less bad only because there were fewer Greeks than Romans. The Greek city-state of Thebes even had an army unit called "The Sacred Band" – these were homosexuals who chained themselves to their favorite sex partners when they went into combat.

When Christianity spread throughout Europe, the Greeks, the Romans, and the barbarians who became Christians started to behave themselves a lot more than their ancestors did. Women had fewer rights than men in Christian society, but they had a much better standing in Christian society than they did in pagan societies. Jesus Christ Himself taught men that women had the equal dignity with men of being creatures created in the image and likeness of God. Jesus Christ also preached against divorce (which almost always favors men over women).

The Middle Ages had plenty of sexual misconduct by the royalty and nobility. There were popes who had bastard children. During the Renaissance and the Elizabethan Era, the degeneracy of the elites was an open bad example. In the 1700s and early 1800s, the mood of the Enlightenment and the Revolution was to attack the teachings of the Church, so it was again okay for the gentry and the merchants and the government officials to behave irresponsibly publicly.

By the mid-1800s, the pendulum had swung back a little. In this era, it was not considered proper decorum to carry on (at least to the knowledge of the public). This convention carried through the Victorian Age (named after Britain's Queen Victoria, who was on the throne from 1837 until 1901) and then into World War One ... the time frame of much immigration from Europe to America.

Victorian England's veneer of morality was a sham for many of the men and women of the aristocratic classes. Exclusive as nobility and interrelated as Arkansas, these British bluebloods carried on affairs with each other with the arrogance of royalty and the sleaziness of Hollywood. Serial infidelity, homosexuality, lesbianism, and bisexuality were okay as long as one didn't get publicly exposed. Sadly, the cheated-on spouse would lose his or her standing among the elite if he or she was indiscreet enough to make a stink of it so the British presses would have something to titillate the masses with ... at least those in the masses who could read. **(31)**

Many of France's political leaders and people of wealth, not to mention her writers, artists, actors, and musicians, were too straightforwardly lecherous to subscribe to the hypocrisy of upper-crust Victorian England. In other words, public figures in France openly had affairs instead of hiding their sins from the public, as British public figures did. French leaders, unlike their English counterparts or our own Bill Clinton, wouldn't dream of hypocritically appearing with a five-pound Bible in public the day after they got caught wenching in the brothels or romping at a country estate or a townhouse. (Being a public debaucher of course is evil in another way, because those who do so set bad examples for the young and encourage others to imitate them and wallow in their filth.)

The noblemen and the merchants and the bankers and the leaders of industry in Europe in the 1800s had the money to dally in style and the bad examples to follow on the thrones and in the blueblood stud books, errr, nobility registers of their countries.

Historically, most rulers fell laughably short when it came to behaving themselves sexually. In fact, many were publicly unfaithful enough so their mistresses were public figures. Louis XIV of France secretly married one of his mistresses after his wife died and he finally settled down. Peter the Great of Russia, one of the most enthusiastic lechers of all time, finally married one of his mistresses – big-boned buxom Katrina Skavronsky, who started life as an orphaned peasant girl in Lithuania – and she ruled as empress after his death. His enemy Charles XII of Sweden had three passions – wars of aggression, lechery, and decapitating sheep to strengthen his sword arm.

But hardly anyone matched the level of the royal rutting of Augustus the Strong, a king of Saxony in the 1700s. He fathered almost 400 bastards. He was such a scumbag he used at least one of his bastard daughters as his mistress.

Then there were those like Frederick the Great of Prussia, and William of Orange (the William in William and Mary of England) who had wives of convenience but found other males more to their liking sexually. Not surprisingly, neither produced offspring.

King James I of England (the King James who commissioned the bible that bears his name) was reportedly a switch-hitter because of his numerous handsome young favorites. James at least produced an heir ... Charles I, the king who would lose the head he needed to wear a crown.

Queens were not blameless either. Elizabeth I of England, who never married, lived up to her nickname "The Virgin Queen" almost as poorly as the entertainer Madonna has lived up to the standards of behavior of her given name. French queen Marie Antoinette allegedly let the Marquis de Lafayette (the very one who served gallantly in the American Revolution) service her. She allegedly offered him her honor, and he reportedly honored her offer. American Revolution naval hero John Paul Jones reportedly gave Catherine the Great of Russia waves of pleasure. Jones was one of the many studs in Catherine's bullpen. Queen Isabella II of Spain (the mid-1800s queen, not the great queen who defeated the Moors and sent Columbus to the New World) was like Catherine the Great in the boudoir, if not in the throne room.

Queen Isabella of Spain (Columbus' patroness and the scourge of the Moslems who had butchered her people for centuries) was a faithful and loving wife to King Fernando. She was also taller than him. But when his beady eyes focused too long on a lady at court, she would graciously have the damsel married off properly (with many gifts from her own largesse) and then would have her and her new husband transferred to perform duties of state far away from court.

Likewise, Maria Theresa, the Empress of Austria, loved her far less accomplished husband in spite of his occasional infidelities. She was faithful to him, even though *she* had the power as empress and he was only her consort. She kept him close enough to bear 16 (that's right, ten plus six) children by him. One of her daughters was the ill-fated royal slut Marie Antoinette.

Napoleon and his brothers and sisters had enough extramarital affairs to keep the tabloids in copy for a generation.

Old King Ludwig I of Bavaria had a mistress whose antics eventually helped cost him his throne in the mid 1800s. He had taken up with the dancer Lola Montez, the daughter of a British officer and a woman who was the illegitimate daughter of a British member of parliament. In Bavaria, whatever Lola wanted, Lola got. She meddled in politics so haughtily that she prompted rioting against herself in early 1848. Ludwig I had to banish her and grant the people more freedoms than he wanted to grant. He set aside his crown later that year.

Lola still had crowns of her own to seek. She wound up emigrating to America, and she spider-danced her way across the eastern United States in the early 1850s. She went out to California and entertained the miners, the sharpies, and the robber barons in the Golden State. She would die young in New York City just before the start of the Civil War. By then she had turned over a new leaf; at the time of her death she was helping prostitutes leave their degrading trade.

Instead of going much further with the antics of rulers, I'll note that the list of kings who kept their marriage vows was a short one, and the list of queens who did likewise wasn't that much longer.

Like the Clintons, the rulers of Europe had marriages of convenience, and inconvenient lovers sometimes wound up dead. Henry VIII was a prime example; he had Anne Boleyn (Wife No. 2) beheaded so he could marry Jane Seymour. Henry had Anne charged with incest, adultery, and witchcraft. Anne, by the way, had six fingers on one of her hands, and Henry claimed this was proof she was a witch. *Henry probably hadn't complained about the extra digit when she was caressing him!*

Henry VIII also had Katherine Howard (Wife No. 5) and her lady-in-waiting beheaded. Young Katherine had committed adultery in part to bear Henry a son, because she figured out he was impotent, and her older and much more experienced lady – like an escort service madam – aided her in entertaining her favorite young noble stud. Henry also had the young nobleman's head chopped off for his offense of looking for love in exactly the wrong place.

Catherine the Great allowed her husband to be murdered so she could rule Russia. Mary Queen of Scots married a divorced nobleman scandalously soon after the murder of her worthless husband (a precocious young lecher in his own right) because she was already pregnant with the nobleman's child. Henry VIII's own daughter Elizabeth had a number of gentlemen callers ... and one of them (Essex) wound up losing his head over her (figuratively and literally). Elizabeth also had Mary Queen of Scots, her own cousin, imprisoned and beheaded after the Scottish nobles Mary hadn't bedded and wedded overthrew her. Mary Queen of Scots, by the way, had earlier laughingly turned down cousin Elizabeth's suggestion she marry one of the falsely-advertised "Virgin Queen's" cast-off lovers.

One of the worst serial murderers of all time was the niece of a king. Hungarian countess Erzsebet (Elizabeth) Bathory, the "Blood Countess," was from a Protestant Hungarian noble family, and was the niece of Stefan Bathory, the king of Poland in the late 1500s. After her usually absent army officer husband died in the early 1600s, she (with the help of her lesbian lover and her female servants) sadistically slaughtered 300 to 650 peasant girls and young women to satisfy her twisted sexual preferences. When her "steady Betty" died, the countess recruited another sadistic lesbian to take her place. This woman had a penchant for the daughters of the nobility. The countess and her new lady were eventually caught, because grieving noblewomen whose daughters they butchered had more pull with the regime than grieving peasant mothers. Unfortunately, due to her late husband's service to the crown, and the regime's debt to her family, the authorities did not force Countess Erzsebet to kneel before the headsman but had her walled in a room inside her castle in Hungarian-ruled Slovakia and they suppressed the details of her many crimes and perversions. They slid food to her in her confinement daily until she died. Her companions in crime (those who procured victims for her), however, were either burned at the stake or beheaded. **(32)**

By the late 1800s, rulers tended to conduct themselves with more decorum. In other words, they were more discreet in their indiscretions. Of course King Edward VII, son of Queen Victoria, during his long tenure as Prince of Wales, was a notorious lecher during the era nicknamed for his mother. Queen Isabella II of Spain, his mother's contemporary, was overthrown, in part, because of her publicly scandalous behavior.

Emperor Franz Josef of Austria-Hungary, who had a very long reign of his own in the most of the same decades as Queen Victoria, turned to a succession of mistresses when his own wife Empress Elisabeth (Sissi) went on sexual flings and gambling binges across Europe. But Franz Josef was no Henry VIII; he loved his wayward wife and made sure she had plenty of money for her many road trips. He turned to the mistresses because Sissi essentially cut him off.

Their son, Crown Prince Rudolf, gave his wife Princess Stephanie venereal disease from one of his many romps in Vienna and elsewhere, rendering her sterile. Prince Rudolf then wanted to divorce poor Princess Stephanie (who was a 17-year-old virgin when he married her) so he could father children! He reportedly wound up killing his teenage mistress Maria Vetsera – a girl whose mother he had also known in the Biblical sense – in a hunting lodge before taking his own life.

The truth about the death of Crown Prince Rudolf and Maria Vetsera was never disclosed by Emperor Franz Josef. Soviet troops dug up Maria Vetsera's grave looking for jewels as they overran Austria in early 1945. A doctor examined Maria's skull and noted it bore no sign of a gunshot wound. This led the doctor and some historians to the conclusion Rudolf arranged for a doctor to perform an abortion on Maria, the doctor botched the abortion, she died in agony in Rudolf's arms at the hunting lodge, and he shot himself in a welter of guilt and remorse and despair. **(33)**

The royalty and upper nobility of Europe were plagued with the results of centuries of inbreeding and venereal disease. Crown Prince Rudolf's imperial Hapsburg family in particular had their share of morons, lunatics, and suicides because of all the copulating cousins. But no dynasty was safe. The Hanoverian and the Hohenzollern families who ruled Hanover and Britain, and Prussia, respectively, were interrelated and suffered from madness. And how else do you explain the "'54 Ford with both doors open" look of Britain's Prince Charles?

Rudolf's remote Hapsburg relative Don Juan of Austria, like many royal bastards, turned out to be an above-average leader. (He led Spanish and Italian and Croatian sailors to decisive victory against the Turkish fleet at Lepanto in 1571. This was the last major sea battle between galley fleets.) Don Juan's mother, a woman who his very capable father Charles V impregnated during a romp while he was a widower, was outside the family circle.

The closeness of kin in royal weddings in the 1800s caused another problem that had a negative effect upon history – hemophilia. Queen Victoria herself was a carrier of the hemophilia gene, as were many royal women related to her. (Queen Victoria's husband Prince Albert, by the way, was also her first cousin.) Queen Victoria's granddaughter Tsaritsa Alexandra of Russia was also a carrier. Because her son Alexei had hemophilia, and only the charlatan Rasputin seemed to be able to help him, she fell under the world-class reprobate's spell. Her infatuation with Rasputin helped him put a large number of unworthy men into place in Russia's government. Their incompetence and greed helped bring on the revolutions that would result in Russia falling into the clutches of Communist dictatorship.

Rasputin was a monk who became a free-lance wandering preacher with supposed gifts of healing, much like some of the charlatans in this country you see on TV. Although the Russian Orthodox Church leaders allow clerics to marry, they expect them to be examples of good behavior. Rasputin was enthusiastically not. Despite having a wife, he had sex with all classes of women in Russia, from peasant girls on up to noblewomen.

And Rasputin evidently didn't understand "no." Bishop Hermogen of Saratov, Rasputin's superior, found out Rasputin had raped an Orthodox Christian nun. Bishop Hermogen summoned Rasputin, interrogated him, and got him to admit to the rape. The furious bishop, a large powerful man, beat Rasputin with a heavy wooden cross and then started pummeling Rasputin's head with his fists. For penance, Bishop Hermogen ordered Rasputin to swear to renounce sex for life.

The only way the bishop was going to enforce that sentence was to castrate the Clintonian cleric. Rasputin ran away from the bishop's control and complained to Tsaritsa Alexandra. She ensured Bishop Hermogen lost his position by imperial decree. **(34)**

Rasputin enjoyed Tsaritsa Alexandra's protection. She had his apartment protected by police, and they often had to disarm angry husbands and lovers whose women had gotten too close and personal with the mad monk. His influence was so great over Alexandra that many people assumed she was one of his many conquests.

Even Queen Victoria herself supposedly had flings with John Brown, her Scottish equerry and hunting guide, after her husband Prince Albert died. But Victoria, ever the lady, did not broadcast any alleged indiscretion of hers.

So much for the scandals of the select. What about the commoners, your ancestors and ancestresses and mine?

People in England called condoms "French letters." In France, people returned the compliment by called condoms "English cloaks." Sigi Ernst, Vienna's condom king in the late 1800s, did not have to advertise what he sold in his ads, but in one such ad he told his clientele he was adding a more discreet entrance to his emporium of fornication aids. In Europe, homosexuality was often called the "Prussian malady," or a man suspected of homosexuality was said to have "Turkish tendencies." Adults were not ignorant of sexual misconduct, but were more prone to avoid public crudeness than they are now. **(35)**

Operas, operettas, novels, novellas, and plays in the late 1800s all too often celebrated, or at least excused infidelity and other forms of sleazy behavior. Many German playwrights went a step further; a century before their opposites in the American TV and movie trade, they drew in audiences by mixing sadistic and morbid violence with the illicit sex already in their scripts.

Houses of prostitution were common in Europe. And so were prostitutes without the overhead of a bordello. Prostitution was legal in many countries of Europe, and was tolerated almost everywhere else. In the mid-1800s, there were possibly as many as 80,000 prostitutes working in London. Also available were ladies of the nobility, the upper classes, and the "demimonde" (performers, gold-diggers, professional beauties, and other attractive females of easy virtue). Daniel Mannix, an American naval officer from the late 1890s through the late 1920s, in the book The Old Navy documented his bachelor runs through the countesses and chorus girls of Europe whenever sea duty took him there.

Ireland (despite being under British captivity) stood almost alone as a national society in opposition to this trend. Of course, the peasant women and girls of Europe, especially Eastern Europe, had reputations for modesty in dress and behavior. And peasant fathers and brothers, even in the Latin countries, protected their daughters and sisters with fists and weapons. But the cities of Europe and the café societies of Europe were loaded with lechers and their mistresses.

Uplifting plays like Edmond Rostand's patriotic and idealistic "Cyrano de Bergerac," penetrating yet sympathetic literature like Charles Dickens' portrayals of the poor in his novels, historical epics like Henryk Sienkiewicz's books about Poland and Quo Vadis, his epic book about the Christians in the days of Nero, and the introspective works of the great Russian authors stood out in Europe in the 1800s, in part because they were about more important themes than casual sex. These authors tried to reach the nobler emotions of their audiences and alert them to their countries' problems. In fact, a number of authors attacked Sienkiewicz in the early 1900s because he said truthfully that too many novelists, playwrights, lyricists, and librettists (opera and musical show lyricists) were peddling smut.

Up until the people understood medical care better, and medical care became better, women tended to have their babies at home. It wasn't until well into the 20th Century that married women would give birth at hospitals in large numbers. (Even in mid 20th Century

America, my wife was born at home.) Couples who could afford it had a doctor come to their homes and deliver the children; those with less money had the town midwife deliver the children. But many couples couldn't even afford the help of a midwife, so the wife gave birth alone, or with the help of her sisters. All classes tended to avoid the hospitals for childbirth.

All, that is, except for single women. The shame of being an unwed mother led many of these unfortunate women to hospitals to give birth, and then to quietly and tearfully slink away, leaving their children to be adopted or placed in orphanages.

Bastardy was not uncommon in Europe. In the 1860s, 6.5 percent of the mothers of England and Wales gave birth while unmarried. In Scotland, 10 percent of mothers were involved in bastardy, as were 10 percent of the Orange (Scottish and English) mothers of Ulster. About 10 percent of the mothers of Sweden and Norway gave birth out of wedlock; Danish mothers had a bastardy rate of 11 percent. Among most of the Lutheran states of Germany, 15 percent of the children were born to unmarried women. The more disciplined Protestants of Prussia had a 10 percent rate of bastardy; Catholic mothers in Prussia (which included many Poles) had a bastardy rate of 6.5 percent. Dutch and Swiss women had illegitimacy rates of about 5 percent; both countries had a ratio of three Protestants for every two Catholics.

In mostly Catholic Austria-Hungary, 11 percent of mothers gave birth out of wedlock. Italian and Spanish mothers had an illegitimacy rate of about 5 percent; French women and Belgian women had a bastardy rate of 7 percent. Irish women had the lowest rate of mothers out of wedlock in Europe among countries reporting – 3 percent. **(36)**

Abortion was also more common than people would suspect. Some shady midwives would perform abortions. So would some unscrupulous doctors. And so would certain others. One of the suspects in the unsolved case of Jack the Ripper (the demented savage who murdered women in London) was an abortionist. In this country, Frank Sinatra's mother was a midwife and abortionist in New Jersey in the early 1900s. And like the vast majority of doctors who perform abortions today, Mrs. Sinatra would wind up in court several times because she committed multiple acts of malpractice. **(37)**

In various countries, hired baby-killers, especially the midwives, were called "angel makers." Abortionist doctors were available to the rich throughout much of Europe. In France, whose historians were matter-of-fact about such things, it is estimated at least 100,000 and possibly as many as 400,000 French women underwent abortions each year in the early 1900s, before World War One.

Most customers were single women and prostitutes. Many were dragged in by boyfriends or pimps so the boyfriends wouldn't have to marry them or the pimps could put them back to work quicker. Some were married women who didn't want more children; often it was their husbands who sent them. Among the more prosperous classes, large families had become unfashionable, and in many cases, well-to-do parents who wanted their children to have substantial inheritances figured having fewer children would make this possible.

Occasionally an abortionist would be caught and punished – usually after he or she had bungled an abortion. Some – including the female abortionists – as a matter of justice would be imprisoned, or sometimes executed by hanging or beheading. However, just as laws against robbery and murder didn't deter robbers and other contract killers from their "trades," laws against performing abortions on demand didn't deter those who performed them. Despite the occupational hazards of prison and the scaffold, abortionists kept at their business because of the money involved.

Those who claim there were hundreds of thousands of women's deaths in Europe yearly because abortions were illegal are lying or are uninformed. Since abortions were illegal across Europe, a woman's death from abortion would lead to an investigation. An abortionist who wanted to keep his or her freedom or head would try to do the grisly job carefully to avoid detection. German doctors who performed forced abortions on Slavic women during World War Two understood this; they wanted cover because they believed they would face execution if Germany lost the war. American authorities sentenced only two Nazi officials to prison for imposing Hitler's forced abortion program on Slavs; they prosecuted no Germans for the forced abortion program Hitler ordered for German women. **(38)**

Of course the insidious double standard was in vogue in Europe in the 1800s and early 1900s, just like it was in America. If a bride was not a virgin when she got married, often she would have to wear black or some other color instead of a white dress at her wedding. In some cases, a widow – who of course had the right to "know man" – who remarried would wear black or some other dark color on her wedding day to indicate appropriate sorrow for her previous husband as well as the appropriate sexual experience of a mature previously-married woman.

Sometimes women wore colors other than white on their wedding days for different reasons. Some ethnic groups favored the multicolored approach for their females. And for others, times of mourning or liturgical seasons dictated their wedding dress. A picture of one of my German ancestresses shows her in purple on her wedding day. She got married during Lent, a time of fasting, not feasting.

One of the Czech ancestors of mine who came here about the time of the Civil War lost his first wife. She died after miscarrying a girl, who would have been their fifth child. Wife No.1, the records show, he married "with her parents' permission" 11 years earlier, although she was 24! Evidently, he liked women from her family, because he got her kid sister (who was 32 at the time and never married) pregnant three years after she (Wife No. 1) died, owned up to being the boy's father, had the boy baptized, and then married the sister. (There was no parental permission notation on that marriage!) One child later, the couple and the six children all came to "bohunk town" in Chicago. Their "love child" was one of my great-great-grandfathers.

Most people back then did behave themselves for a number of reasons ranging from religious belief to the desire to set a good example for their children to fear of public ostracism.

Meanwhile, the noblemen and noblewomen of the 1800s, and the mercantile and industrial elites of that day and the females who ran with them, were probably no less lecherous than the typical public figures of today. But in most cases they didn't expect to be given public acclaim for their degeneracy.

Bottom line? The common people, in other words, the ancestors of most of us, tended to pay more attention to religion than we do. Church attendance as a percentage of the population was higher in the 1800s and early 1900s than it is now. Our ancestors in the 1800s and early 1900s were more familiar with early death than we are and were more prone to worry about the states of their souls than we are. Also, they were more involved in religion than we are because religion was not considered as unfashionable back then as it is today. Fear of being branded an outsider has all too often molded the behavior of the many.

However, they were not as prudish as the degenerates of today who set themselves up as arbiters of fashion and the "scholars" of history like to claim. Men and women from Adam and Eve to all of us today have always been subject to temptation. And we all have fallen, because we as men and women have fallen natures. At the very least, most people of the Victorian Age had the common sense to try to keep their failings private, instead of sharing their dirt or trumpeting their failings as the new world order.

WARS AND RUMORS OF WAR

There was an overall threat of war that hung over Europe from the 1870s to the start of World War One in 1914. The people called the build-up of tensions around Europe the "Dry War" – in much the same way people called the decades of tension between the Soviet Union and the United States the "Cold War." Unlike Ronald Reagan, Pope John Paul II, Lech Walesa and Solidarity, and Lane Kirkland and the AFL-CIO, the leaders of Europe were unable to win the "Dry War" without a cataclysmic bloodbath.

The scramble for colonies in Africa and Asia pitted Britain against other nations. Since the British grabbed for by far the most colonies, they had more squabbles with the natives and with other European rivals. Britain nearly went to war with France, Germany, Russia, and the United States during this period ... all because of British greed for land.

By the end of the 1800s, the British had grabbed one-fifth of earth's surface. The British systematically plundered Africa, India, and China. British settlers overran Australia, New Zealand and Canada; British businessmen also took over South Africa with the help of the British army.

In 1900, the British held Egypt, Sudan, a strip of present-day Somalia, Uganda, Kenya, the land that would become Zambia, Zimbabwe, and Nyasaland (Malawi), Bechaunaland (Botswana), Nigeria, Gold Coast (Ghana), Sierra Leone, and Gambia in Africa.

They were also in the process of taking all of South Africa, and after World War One, they would take over most of Germany's colonies in Africa (Tanganyika, Southwest Africa, and Togo). In Asia in 1900, the British held "India" (which then included, besides India, today's Pakistan, Bangla Desh, and Burma), Ceylon (Sri Lanka), part of New Guinea, and Malaya and Sarawak (Singapore and today's Malaysia). In the Western Hemisphere, the British held British Guiana, British Honduras (Belize), Jamaica, and some other islands in the Caribbean Sea. The British also held a number of islands and enclaves at key points along the shipping routes of the world; the most well-known of these were Hong Kong, Gibraltar, Malta, Cyprus, Aden, and Zanzibar. Canada, Australia, and New Zealand were more or less voluntary parts of the British Empire; the people of Ireland were very involuntary subjects.

The total land mass of the world is not quite 58 million square miles. This includes Antarctica and all the islands, as well as the other continental masses. The British, whose home island is about the size of Minnesota (less than 90,000 square miles), ruled an empire of more than 11 million square miles in size. By comparison, the United States (including Alaska and Hawaii) are less than 3.7 million square miles in size.

The British had disputes with the French over territory in Africa. The British had disputes with the Russians over territory in Central Asia, and desired to keep Russia from ever gaining solid naval access to the

Mediterranean Sea, because Britain's leaders thought the Russian navy might interfere with their plunder of India. To that extent, the British would rather allow the Turks to commit repeated atrocities against the peoples of the Balkans instead of letting Russian troops punish the fez-wearing murderers for their crimes against humanity. The British clashed with the Germans in a number of areas, mostly colonial, naval, and trade issues.

The British tried to bully nations in Latin America, but at least here the United States invoked the Monroe Doctrine and made the British back off. Theodore Roosevelt also made the British back off when they tried to claim the Alaska Panhandle for their colony Canada in the wake of the 1898 Yukon gold rush. The posturing militaristic Germans might have posed the greatest threat to peace in Europe, but the greedy grasping British clearly posed the greatest threat to world peace.

Saying the British posed a greater threat to world peace than the Germans is like saying Hitler was more evil than Stalin. Understand Germany's leaders were not contestants for the Nobel Peace Prize themselves. Germany, a recently re-assembled nation, started competing with Britain and France for colonies and with Britain for naval superiority under the aggressive Kaiser Wilhelm II. German leaders built up the army into the continent's best, and intimidated all their neighbors by threatening to unleash their soldiers against them. German leaders also built up a navy powerful enough to provoke quarrels with other European powers, and with American naval officers too.

German propaganda stressed German military might in an attempt to cow the other European leaders. Kaiser Wilhelm II on occasion personally pointed out to foreign dignitaries who visited him the top German officers designated to lead the planned assault on France. Because the Germans were so dominant and domineering, the French and Russians had to keep large standing armies to be ready for them.

Kaiser Wilhelm, judging by some his public utterances, was an unbalanced meglomaniac. The Kaiser routinely said things that made other European heads of state worry about his intentions and sometimes his sanity. But compared to the Junkers and the chief military officers, he was mild.

Kaiser Wilhelm was more like the Wizard of Oz than the spiritual father of Adolf Hitler. He had considerable power as a ruler, but he kept it by being a royal demagogue. The Kaiser had to appear tough and crazy and arrogant to overcome his physical handicaps and to keep the army and the Junkers from undermining him or overthrowing him.

The Germans, by comparison with the British, got into the colonial business very late. They managed to grab Tanganyika, Southwest Africa, Cameroon, and Togo in Africa. They grabbed part of New Guinea and some islands in the Pacific Ocean, and they thought about grabbing the Philippines after the Spanish-American War. American leaders sent a large enough number of soldiers, sailors, marines, and ships to the Philippines to keep the Germans (and the equally militaristic and greedy Japanese) at bay. Teddy Roosevelt's rise to the Presidency did much to make the Germans behave.

Germany's colonies weren't exactly garden spots. More Germans "colonized" New York City, Chicago, St. Louis, Milwaukee, and "Zinzinnati" than any of the lands in Africa or Asia the Kaiser's men grabbed.

The French hated the Germans for taking Alsace and much of Lorraine from them. But the French also had a long hatred of the British, going back as far as Norman baron William the Conqueror, and extending through the ages of the Hundred Years War, Joan of Arc, Louis XIV, the French Revolution, and Napoleon ... roughly 800 years. Even Joan, the girl saint, personally called the English "Godons" – French for "God-damned."

The behavior of the British and German leaders was evil, but sadly not too much worse than those of other European powers.

The French, though less powerful than the British or the Germans, were world-class in their greed for colonies. The French colonial empire was larger than that of any other European nation except for the British Empire. The French, whose country is about the size of the states north and east of the Potomac River – Maryland, Delaware, Pennsylvania, New Jersey, New York, and New England (about 200,000 square miles before they regained Alsace and all of Lorraine), ruled an empire of about 5 million square miles in size.

The French colonized Algeria in the 1830s. By 1900, the French also gained control of Tunisia and most of Morocco in North Africa, the areas of west and central Africa that form today's countries of Mauritania, Mali, Niger, Chad, Senegal, Guinea, Ivory Coast, Upper Volta aka Burkino Faso, Dahomey aka Benin, Central African Republic, Gabon, and Congo (Brazzaville), an enclave on the Red Sea next to Ethiopia they called French Somaliland, and the large island of Madagascar. After World War One, they would take over Germany's African colony of Cameroon (Kamerun). The French also took Indochina (today's Laos, Cambodia, and Vietnam) in Asia, and some other islands in the Indian Ocean and the Pacific Ocean. They held French Guiana (which had the truly evil penal colony on Devil's Island) and some islands in the Caribbean Sea.

The leaders of Austria-Hungary and Russia had rival designs on the Balkans. Russia's leaders wanted Constantinople, and with it access to the Mediterranean

Sea. Some of the leaders of Austria-Hungary wanted Serbia and Macedonia down to the port of Salonika for better access to the Mediterranean Sea; Franz Ferdinand opposed this lust because he felt the empire had too many rebellious Serbs as it was.

The leaders of France and Britain and Italy also had designs on the Turks' Middle East possessions. Germany pushed for control of the Turks' economy. Russia and Britain had rival spheres of influence in Persia (present-day Iran). The major European colonial powers and Japan lusted for control of China.

Even lesser states like Italy, Spain, Portugal, Denmark, Belgium, and the Netherlands had colonies. The Italians held most of present-day Somalia and Eritrea. In the 1890s, the Italians tried to subjugate Ethiopia, but the African Christian people of that land slapped down the Italians in humiliating fashion. In a war with Turkey in 1911 and 1912, the Italians did manage to take Libya away from the Turks.

The Portuguese held Angola and Mozambique in southern Africa, and also held some other small strips of land and islands in and around Africa, India, the East Indies, and China. The Spanish held Cuba, Puerto Rico, the Philippines, and some Pacific islands until the United States took away the first three possessions after the Spanish-American War and Spain's leaders sold the Pacific islands to the Germans. The Spanish held onto a strip of Morocco, some desert land called Spanish Sahara south of Morocco, Equatorial Guinea in central Africa, and some islands off the African coast.

The Belgians held a huge piece of Africa consisting of the land of the Congo River basin; at the time it was called the Belgian Congo. On independence, this land would be called Congo, then Zaire, and once again Congo. They also held what is now Rwanda and Burundi. The Dutch held Surinam in South America, some islands in the Caribbean Sea, and the so-called "Dutch East Indies" (today's Indonesia). The Danes held Iceland, Greenland, and those Virgin Islands that the British hadn't grabbed. American officials would buy Denmark's Virgin Islands during World War One.

At the start of World War One, the Turks still held the lands that make up present-day Iraq, Syria, Lebanon, Israel, Jordan, and much of Saudi Arabia and the other states of the Arabian peninsula.

The greedy Europeans treated the Africans as little more than slaves. German chancellor Otto von Bismarck convened the Berlin Conference in late 1884 and early 1885 as a way of playing off the various colonial nations against each other. (At the time, 80% of black Africa was under black African rule.)

The European delegates divided Africa like a pie, drawing borderlines across areas that divided tribal groups from each other and lumping rival tribal groups into proposed colonies to serve the desires of European politicians and colonial corporations, not the people of Africa. Shortly, in all of Africa, the Christian king of Ethiopia and the freed resettled American slaves who ran Liberia would be the only blacks running independent African countries.

So much of the ethnic strife that has plagued Africa throughout the 20th Century and into this century is due to that three-month conference of greedy Europeans.

By the way, when I say "tribal groups" and "ethnic strife," I could be talking about Europe as well. Their hatreds and greeds weren't any more civilized than those of the Africans; only their means of murdering other people were more up-to-date.

A rival series of alliances pitted Germany and Austria-Hungary against England, France, and Russia. Italy played the prostitute, seeking to couple with the countries which would pay the most. Italy's leaders had an open treaty with Germany and Austria-Hungary, and a secret treaty with France.

Militarism and blind nationalism also helped rise the specter of war. After the Prussians won three quick wars in the 1860s and 1870s, other nations raised their military spending and increased their drafts, hoping to get results like Bismarck. Politicians wrapped themselves in their nations' flags in part to gain popularity and in part to deflect public view from their many failures. The rival nations' presses were only too happy to demean other nations as a way of building up their own nations. Politicians and media figures preached quasi-pagan worship of the state instead of worship of God Who demands the politicians and the people of all states to live by the Ten Commandments.

How did this affect the people of Europe?

In the countryside, a common scene was the hated local sheriff notifying young peasant men they were drafted. These young men knew they would be little more than cannon fodder for unjustifiable wars.

In Austria-Hungary, the Austrians and Hungarians ruled Slavs and Romanians, so naturally the subject peoples were not enthused about fighting for their despised masters. Likewise, Poles, Balts, Jews, and Ukrainians under Russian rule had no desire to die for the Tsar. Nor did Poles under German control want to die for the Kaiser. Nor did Irish peasants want to further the cause of their British oppressors.

Wars hit the peasants hardest. Most peasants were poor. All they had of value were their sons and daughters. The state wanted their sons as cannon fodder. The state wanted their daughters as uniform makers or munitions makers ... and all too often the state wanted them as the spoils of war.

The wars took the sons immediately. Many of them died on distant battlefields, or they limped home crippled or blind or otherwise too weak to do serious farmwork anymore.

But the rest of the peasants suffered too. The young women lost men who should have been their husbands.

Governments raised taxes, which cost the peasants more and more of their crops and livestock. Large landlords either evaded the taxes or transferred them to the backs of their tenants.

Think of the poor peasants who lived in the paths of the armies. Soldiers confiscated the peasants' livestock and grain, bivouacked in their fields and barns, raided the houses, and fornicated with the peasant girls – either with the girls' consents, or against the girls' wills. Farms, livestock, crops, daughters, all ruined.

On their way home, the soldiers repeated the process. And these were the soldiers of the same country, of the government supposedly protecting their peasants!

Soldiers of an invading army naturally behaved much worse. What they couldn't loot, they destroyed. The girls who wouldn't give in they raped and often killed.

They grabbed teenagers off the streets of the villages and made slave laborers of them. Their leaders had officers who took inventory of the wealth of a conquered area, and they ordered the local people to hand it over. They vandalized homes and barns, they burned churches, and they desecrated graveyards. Even the bones of the dead were not safe.

On their way home, these soldiers repeated the process.

The constant upheavals throughout Europe, and the wars and rumors of war hit the average people the hardest. If the loss of farms or the danger and drudgery of mine or factory work couldn't make them leave, certainly the oppression and warfare could.

Tensions increased as Europe went deeper into the 1900s. Nearly every year would see some sort of "crisis" that would bring Europe to the brink of general war. Finally general war – the war they called the Great War and the war we know as World War One came in 1914. This four-year war would kill millions of soldiers, sailors, airmen, and civilians. This war would feature the use of poison gas, submarine warfare, starvation blockades, air combat and aerial city bombing, machine guns, modern artillery, and tanks. This war would topple the emperors of Germany, Austria-Hungary, Russia, and the Ottoman Empire. This war would spawn the Communist takeover of Russia, and the Nazi takeover of Germany.

Does it surprise you at all that the heaviest period of European immigration to America came during the years 1900 to the summer of 1914?

WHAT MADE YOUR ANCESTORS LEAVE?

Every adult and every unaccompanied teenager who got on a boat for America had his or her own special reason for leaving the homeland.

The inability to earn a living in the home country was as big a reason as any. If there was not enough land to farm, or if there were not enough jobs in the cities and towns to go around, then immigration sure beat starving or living like a beggar. Many husbands and wives made the difficult decision to leave behind their loved ones and start anew because they had to.

Many young adults left because their parents were good-hearted and wanted to help their children as they reached adulthood, but were desperately poor. They couldn't afford a dowry, or an inheritance for all of their children, and the unlucky daughters and sons would have to make their own starts in life. With few chances in their home villages and towns, they often left their homelands altogether.

The spreading of the news about the opportunities in America gave many Europeans the dream of becoming better off in America. Many hoped to become rich in America. Many others dreamed of earning enough money in America to come home and buy a nice sized farm or start a business in the home country. Still others with talent wanted to try their luck in America because they foresaw themselves being unable to rise in the homeland, where rank and privilege all too often crowded out energy and talent.

Certainly many people came because of oppression against them for religious or ethnic or political reasons. Huge numbers of Irish, Poles, and Jews left Europe for these reasons. So did many Czechs, Slovaks, Ruthenians, Romanians, Slovenians, Croatians, Serbs, Greeks, Balts, Armenians, and Ukrainians. Many of the German immigrants in the mid 1800s left for these reasons also. In the 1800s and early 1900s, many people who were part of an ethnic or religious minority in their homelands felt the pressure to leave because the authorities and the people in the majority felt free to abuse them.

Many young people fled from their abusive parents and relatives. In the old country, many parents treated their sons and daughters like indentured servants once they

FARMING: FOUNDATION OF EUROPEAN SOCIETY

Top: Horses were the power of choice on farms throughout Europe until the second half of the 1900s. These horses were still in harness in Slovakia in 2001. Photo by author.

Center: Peasants' farm houses were simple structures. The design featured a large central room around the fireplace. Sometimes the married couple had a private room, sometimes they didn't. The loft of the house often served as sleeping areas for the children. If the family had taken an elderly relative in, she usually got to sleep by the fire. This Slovak cabin was made of logs, but many other peasant homes were made of brick, stone, or clay. Martin Skansen (outdoor museum), Martin, Slovakia. Photo by author.

Bottom left: The center room of this clay farm house was where the wife and daughters cooked and made clothes. The whole family took their occasional baths in this room. The father and his sons would make furniture or other items for sale in this room in the wintertime. The family ate in this room, and entertained in this room. Several of the family members slept in this room at night. Martin Skansen, Martin, Slovakia. Photo by author.

Bottom right: "The Spinner" by Ignat Bednarik. Farm people built their own homes, made their own clothes, and did many other things to help themselves that they traditionally get no credit for. This Romanian female pictured was typical of farm women across Europe in her work ethic and her skill. Permission obtained.

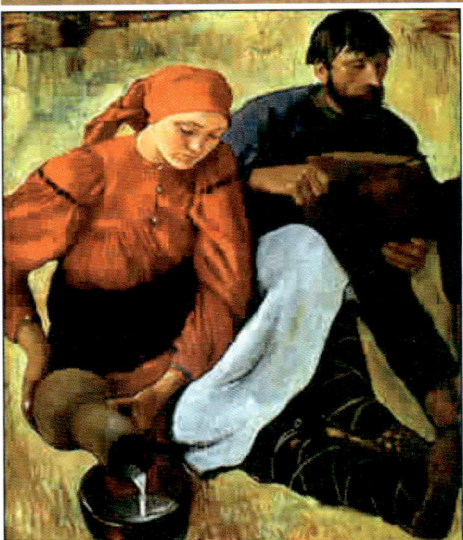

CROP HARVESTING IN EUROPE

"There is a season, turn, turn, turn .... a time to sow, a time to reap." Springtime was the plowing season for grain and vegetable crops. Early summer brought the wheat harvest. Other grains' harvesting came later. Late summer and early fall brought the potato harvest and the fruit harvest. Typically, cherries are harvested in early summer, then apricots, plums, grapes, and then apples. Berries ripen all through the summer.

Farming people were constantly busy. And due to drought or downpour or frost or blight or hailstorm or windstorm, or government seizure or pillaging armies, they might have little or nothing to show for their efforts. Without the many millions of those who farmed – as small farmers or laborers or serfs, there would be no food surplus to feed those who lived in the cities.

"The (Grain) Harvesters", **top left**, by French painter Henry Moret, and "Peasants", **center**, by Russian artist Z. Serebryankova, are in the public domain. "The Grape Harvest", **top right**, and "The Potato Harvest", **bottom left**, are by Mary Petros. The picture of the Polish hay raker, **below**, is courtesy of Alamy.

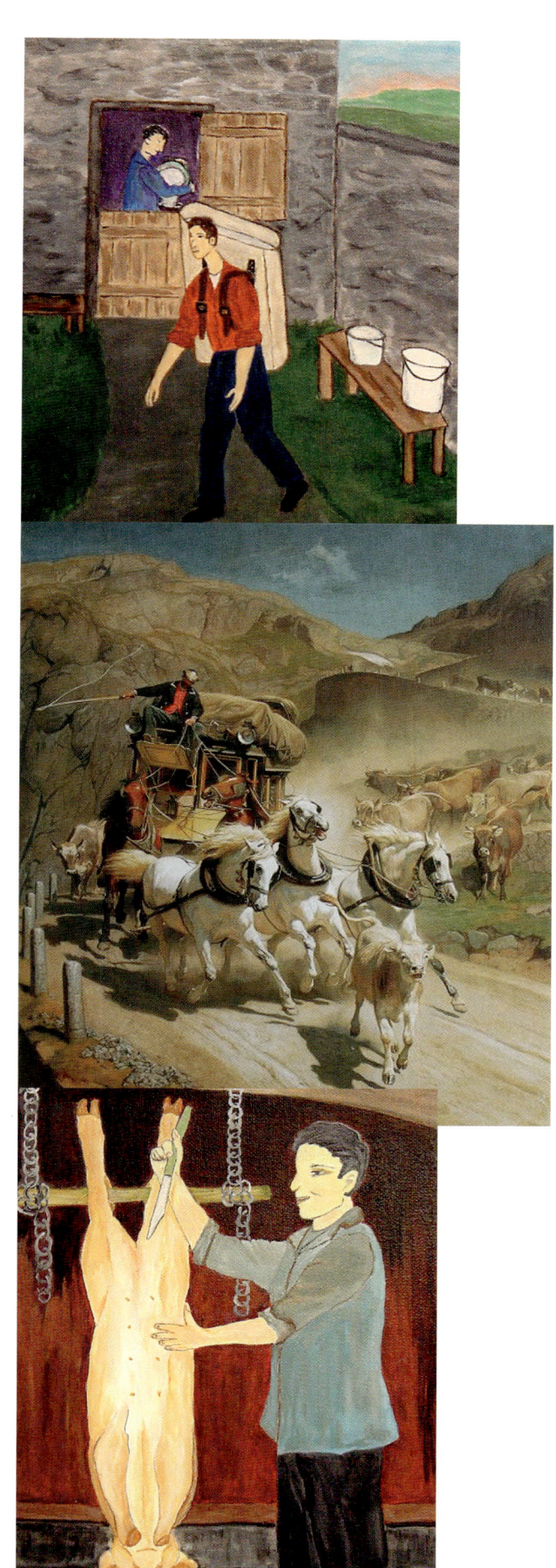

LIVESTOCK IN EUROPE

Europe's people lived close to the soil. Farm people milked animals to make dairy products, they sheared them for wool, and they slaughtered them for meat and hides. Farm people also used them as beasts of burden. Even poultry provided eggs, meat, and feathers. Stock work was hard, and sometimes dangerous. Rudolf Koller's painting, **center**, shows a mail coachman having trouble stopping his team from running through a cattle drive in the Alps. Public domain.

In today's societies, most people would lack the guts to do the chores their ancestors had to do daily to feed themselves. Yet they look down on those whose labors feed them. "The Dairymen," "The Shepherds," and "The Hog Slaughterer", **top left, top right, bottom left,** are all by Mary Petros. English goose girl picture, **below,** is by William Hankey; public domain.

OTHER EUROPEAN CROPS

Top left: Iberian, Italian, Balkan, and south of France farmers have grown olives for millennia. This grove is in Spain. Public domain.

Top right: Swedes, shown here in a 1918 photo, Finns, and other Scandinavian and Slav workers logged commercially. Public domain.

Center left: Turkish girl picks cotton, 1930s. Cotton will grow in the warmer areas of Europe and the Middle East if there is enough water. Government of Turkey. Ataturk no doubt authorized this photo to show he had overthrown the militant Islamists who had run his land for centuries, and that in the new Turkey, women were not abject slaves anymore.

Center right: Orange grove, Ventura County, California. The Spanish brought citrus crops to America. Italians also raise lots of citrus fruit. Photo by author.

Bottom: Basque herder moves sheep wagon in Montana, 1940s. To help the wool and sheep meat industry in the American West, American lawmakers allowed Basques who were professional shepherds an immigration exemption. The Basque homeland is in the far north of Spain and in southwest France. Credit: Library of Congress.

FISHERMEN FED MANY IN EUROPE

Top left: "Norwegian Fishing Village" by Mary Petros. Note the gutted fish drying on the racks. The subfreezing winter temperatures make the area a giant freezer, preventing the fish from spoiling while allowing them to dry.

Top right: "Mending Nets" by Mary Petros. The Greeks, shown here, and the Italians, Spanish, Portuguese, French, and Croatians all fished the Mediterranean Sea and its tributary seas.

Bottom left: "Blessing the Fleet" by Mary Petros. Fishing was and is a hazardous trade. The village Catholic priest or Orthodox priest blessed the fishermen's boats and the fishermen regularly, because they could use all the prayers and blessings for safety they could get. The Portuguese, shown here, were great sailors and explorers.

Bottom right: Detail from "Dutch Pinkie Coming to Anchor" by Henry Chase. The North Sea, where these Dutch fishermen plied their trade, is a stormy body of water. It appears calm to one side of the vessels, but the darkening skies on the other side bode the fishermen no good. Credit: National Park Service.

MINING WAS A TOUGH LIFE

Top left: This was the pithead of one of the shafts of the Příbram mining complex in Bohemia. The Příbram mine in the 1800s was the richest silver mine in the Hapsburg Empire. The mine complex also contained ores of lead, zinc, and other metals. The Nazis and Communists later forced political prisoners to mine uranium ore here. Overwork and radiation poisoning killed these unfortunates. Today it is a vast museum. Photo by the author.

Top right: Open pit iron mine in Urals, 1910. Russian photographer Sergei Prokudin Gorskii caught these workers carting iron ore from an open pit mine. The work was safer than in an underground mine, but still no picnic. Public domain.

Center: British coal miners, 1890s. The man on his side is undercutting the coal seam so the other man can cut the coal out more readily. Low pay and miserable conditions drove many miners to migrate to America. Public domain.

Bottom: Irish farmer cuts peat for his hearth, 1920s. Peat, a high-carbon turf in bogs, burns well enough that it has warmed homes in the Emerald Isle from prehistoric times to the present. Firms "harvest" peat, but many people cut their own supplies. Irish Tourist Association.

Above: Grand Duchess Elisabeth was Russian Tsaritsa Alexandra's sister. After the assassination of her husband, she became an Orthodox nun. Communists murdered her during the Russian Civil War. She has been declared a saint and martyr.

Left: Montenegrins, without fezzes, battle the Turks in 1876. They, the Serbs, the Bulgarians, and the Greeks continually rose against the Turks for religious and national freedom. Painting by Petar Lubarda.

ORTHODOX CHRISTIANS
live mostly in the Balkans and in Russia and Ukraine. They absorbed the blows of Mongolic and Moslem invaders for centuries.

Top left: Hagia Sophia (Holy Wisdom) Church, Constantinople. Eastern Roman (Byzantine) emperor Justinian had this magnificent church built in the 500s AD. It was almost like the "St. Peter's" of the Orthodox Christians. Following in the footsteps of Constantine, Justinian built an empire in the Balkans, the Near East, and Italy. He and his successors bought Europe roughly nine centuries of protection from Turkic and Middle Eastern invaders. When the Turks finally took Constantinople in 1453, they desecrated the great church and then turned it into a mosque. Painting by Eileen Sherlock.

Top right and bottom right: Young couple from Georgia in clothes their ancestors wore; painting of 1800s Armenian woman by Frederick Bridgman. The Georgians and the Armenians live in the Caucasus region between the Black Sea and the Caspian Sea. They have suffered greatly for their faith at the hands of the Turks and the Iranians. Both pictures public domain.

THE ROLE OF THE FAITH

The Church played a huge role in the lives of the people. The clergy tended to the spiritual needs of the people and the corporal needs of the desperately poor. On the orders of Christ, the Church elevated women from slaves to partners of men with the sacrament of matrimony. The Church's priests prepared the faithful to face death with courage and a soul forgiven of sin.

Many clergymen and women practiced and taught trades, like this Orthodox nun making pottery. The Church also taught the young, sometimes with the okay of the state, but often in defiance of the state, especially in countries like Ireland and Poland. The Polish priest shown here is violating Prussian or Russian law. The Jews faced discrimination in Europe. They faced persecution in the Russian Empire, yet they persevered.

Top left: "The Baptism" is by Hungarian artist Istvan Csok. **Bottom left:** "Children of Desze," by Austrian artist Marianne Stokes, shows girls at an Orthodox Christian worship service in Romania. **Top right:** "Countryside School" is by Polish artist Artur Grottger. **Bottom right:** Sergei Prokudin Gorskii photo shows Jewish children receiving instruction in Russia in the early 1900s. All public domain. **Center:** "Orthodox Nun Makes Pottery" is by Mary Petros.

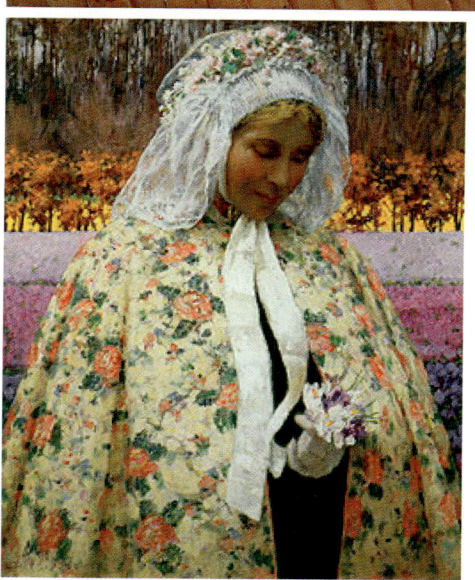

FAMILY AND COMMUNITY

The family could be a very large influence for good. The blessings of parents for marriage, and the constant prayer of the faithful for the dead were natural actions that showed love and charity. And who does not enjoy a wedding or a holy day celebration?

Top left and bottom left: "The Parents' Blessings" and "The Mourner," by Mary Petros, show life in the Czech lands and old Slovakia. **Top right:** "Balkan Wedding Party," by Mary Petros, shows a celebration in Bulgaria.

Center: "Easter in Brabant" by George Hitchcock shows a young Flemish woman celebrating the Resurrection of Our Lord. The Flemish live in Belgium and the Netherlands. They are related to the Dutch; most of them who profess a faith are Catholics. Public domain.

Bottom right: Portuguese girls prepare for a procession after Mass on the festival of the Holy Spirit (Pentecost). After the procession, the parishioners would feed the poor. Portuguese took the custom with them to California; these girls were pictured on Pentecost 1942 at a Catholic church in Santa Clara. Credit: Library of Congress.

FESTIVALS AND HOLIDAYS

The peoples' lives were not ones of total drudgery unrelieved by happiness. Even the poorest of peasants could enjoy a festival, a religious holiday, or a celebration like a wedding.

Top left: "Irish Dancers" by Mary Petros.

Top right: "Christmas 1914." Christmas had a secular "winter festival" tint as well as a religious meaning in Europe. Easter had more of an emotional pull on the people, because the long winter was ending at Easter, and so was the fasting. Also, Easter is the greatest day on the Christian calendar, while Christmas is not a holy day of obligation for many Protestants. In fact, killjoys Calvin and Cromwell forbade celebrating Christmas! So did Puritans, who treated Christmas as a work day! People in Catholic countries and Orthodox countries celebrated Christmas as a holy day and as a festival. St. Nicholas Day (December 6) in many Catholic, Protestant, and Orthodox Christian lands was a gift-giving day. Germans brought the Christmas tree to the Christmas season. (Even Luther liked Christmas trees with candles.) This German woman trimming a tree outdoors is somber; her people and those across Europe were at war in 1914. Public domain.

Bottom left: "Shoeing the Bride." Summer festivals and harvest festivals often featured farcical rituals for young adults. Check out the women cheering the "blacksmith" on at this Ruthenian festival in Svidnik, Slovakia. Credit: "35 Rokov Muzeum Ukrajinskej Kultury vo Svidniku" by Miroslav Sopoliga, a Slovak govt. museum book.

Bottom right: "Temptation of Good by Evil." Many festivals featured a pageant, like this one in Belarus, and often the theme was good vs. evil. Unwarped people wanted the former to prevail. Credit, Oleg Babinets, Belarus; www.babinets.com.

PEOPLE CAME TO CITIES AND TOWNS seeking jobs and better times. The people found company as well as work in the cities and larger towns. They did their best to relieve the drudgery of their everyday lives. **Top left:** "Vendors in Balkan Town" by Mary Petros. In the marketplace, people could find food, merchandise, gossip, and companionship. The town shown is in Serbia. **Top right:** "Washday" by Mary Petros. Many cities and small towns had wash houses for the women to do laundry. Women visited while they worked. **Below left:** "City Street in Italy" by Mary Petros. The cities of Europe buzzed with life. The lines above the streets were aflutter with drying laundry. **Below right:** Hungarian women prepare for a folk dance during a town festival. They and their ancestresses loved to look their best on Sundays and holidays. Even today the womenfolk of Hungary and other lands in Eastern Europe are as pleasing to the eye as any on Earth. **Center:** Even Gypsies and semi-nomadic shepherd people of the Balkans needed some goods from towns, and came in to trade. This early 1900s shepherdess was wearing a silver "crown" and "belt" jewelry, flashable precious metal assets. (Even today, females in these groups openly wear coins on their clothing.) Was she a Moslem, or a Christian girl trying to hide her looks from the Moslems for her own safety?

THE INDUSTRIAL REVOLUTION made Europe a continent full of city dwellers. **Top left:** The Coalbrookdale coking coal and cast iron complex in England was a major employer in the 1700s and early 1800s. **Top right:** The British-developed steam engine liberated factories from dependence on water power. British and American inventors built machines which could make thread and cloth and remove trash from cotton cheaply; the fabric and clothing industries mechanized soon afterward. This Swedish woman is making wool thread with the aid of the machines, early 1900s. Both public domain; painting is by Philippe de Loutherbourg.

Center left: Improved techniques in mass-producing good steel and the invention of machine tools made mighty factories like the Skoda Works in the Czech lands practical. Britishers, Americans, and Germans led the way in heavy industry. Credit: Czechoslovak Legation.

Bottom: Better process control and packing practices made mass food canning and whisky production (Jameson distillery, Ireland) practical. Photo by author.

Center right: Factory owners would hire women. Some got jobs because of their dexterity and attention to detail. Others got jobs to break the pay scale for men. This young lady worked in a factory in one of the Baltic countries in the 1920s.

PROS AND CONS OF LIFE IN CITIES AND TOWNS

Top: Drab, dirty, and unsanitary conditions prevailed in many factory towns, like this British city Gustave Doré pictured. Public domain. **Center right:** Officials made sure cities became cleaner, and cities were places where people could socialize as well as merely work. Bratislava, Slovakia street scene photo by author. **Center left:** "Maslenitsa" by Boris Kustodiev This was "Pancake Week" – the last week before the start of Lent, which was a festival time in Old Russia. There was social action even in smaller cities and larger towns during the dead of winter, as this Russian town scene shows. Public domain.

Bottom left: A moment of weakness and the double standard made many pregnant unmarried girls leave home for the anonymity of the city. Many stories had the theme "farm girl is loved and left, and has to leave her village." Many Nordic teen girls herded in the summer, giving them time alone for young bucks. Scandinavia, Scotland, and Germany had high rates of bastardy. Painting by Anders Zorn. Public domain.

Bottom right: Prostitution was illegal, but was often tolerated and regulated for VD. Many governments and "entrepreneurs" parasitically made money off of the degradation of the prostitutes. "Albertine (and prostitutes) at the Police Doctor's Waiting Room" by Christian Krohg, public domain.

WOMEN IN TROUBLE

Top left: Protestant "reformers" locked women accused of sexual immorality in this cage in Levoca, Slovakia when they ran the town. Problem? Men knew who to solicit next time. **Center left:** Englishmen ducked nags and scolds. Was this wet-bodiced victim an ancestress of Hillary or Laura Schlessinger? **Top right:** Calvinists, Lutherans, and Puritans believed in witches. This was bad news for many women, like Anna Goeldi, pictured, a housemaid who had sex with a Swiss politician. He falsely accused her of witchcraft in 1782 to get rid of her; his friends in the Protestant council judging her case had her tortured and condemned her. A swordsman cut off her head in the town square.

Royal women ran into trouble too. **Top center:** Mary Queen of Scots sought sanctuary in England when Scot nobles overthrew her. Her own cousin Elizabeth I (the pirate queen) had her beheaded in 1587. **Bottom left:** Marie Antoinette goes to the guillotine in 1793. Leftist lawyers and politicians who overthrew her husband had hundreds of thousands of innocents murdered. **Center right:** Empress Elisabeth "Sissi" of Austria-Hungary was stabbed to death by an Italian anarchist while on vacation in Switzerland in 1898. Levoca photo by author; Mary Queen of Scots by Rowan Lazar, others public domain.

Princesses ran into trouble also. **Bottom center:** Princess Tatiana, pictured, and her sisters Olga, Maria, and Anastasia were victims of Communists. Reds shot the three older sisters with their parents in 1918. Anastasia reportedly escaped, but was captured and murdered later. Her remains were not found with those of her sisters and parents. **Bottom right:** Nazis kidnaped Princess Mafalda in 1943 when her father the king of Italy switched sides in World War Two. They raped her, flung her in a concentration camp, and let her bleed to death in 1944. Both public domain.

IMMIGRANTS CAME HERE FOR MANY REASONS

Top left: Many young men in Europe came to America to avoid being used as cannon fodder in a war. The great-uncle of the author's wife wasn't so lucky. He had to serve in the army of Austria-Hungary. Later, he and the author's wife's great-aunt lived in their village in Slovakia. **Top right:** Some cowardly European guys left pregnant girlfriends behind. Some single moms left Europe to avoid the merciless people in their villages. Women who weren't virgins often had to marry in a color other than white. One pair of the author's great-grandparents were Germans. She wore a purple dress to her wedding because they married during Lent. One of the author's Czech ancestresses was already a single mom (by her eventual husband) who presumably had to wear black at her wedding. **Bottom:** Croatian artist Maxo Vanka painted this mural of peasants praying the Angelus (the noon prayer) in St. Nicholas Croatian Catholic Church in the Pittsburgh area. Eastern Europeans made good Americans, but understandably they longed for their loved ones in the old country. Credit: St. Nicholas Croatian Catholic Church, Diocese of Pittsburgh. **Center:** Emperor Karl and Empress Zita, the last rulers of Austria-Hungary. They were exiled after World War One, and he died in 1922. Zita would flee to America during World War Two when Hitler sought to execute her. Her sons served in the U.S. armed forces and U.S. government during the war.

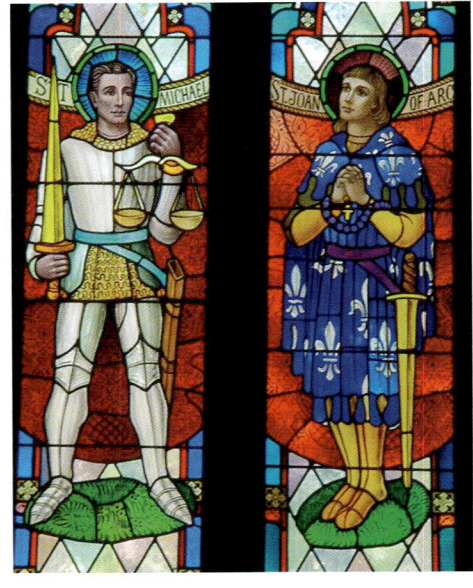

EUROPE'S IMMIGRANT CULTURE IN AMERICA

Top left: After Mass in honor of the Virgin Mary's assumption into Heaven, these Italian-American girls parade through the streets of Cleveland's "Little Italy" in costumes of the regions of their ancestral land. Italian mariners like Columbus, Cabot, and Verrazano charted the New World. The Italian presence in America cannot be ignored. Photo by author. **Center:** Jews brought their own brand of performance art to America. They have done well in music and film. "Fiddler on the Roof," about the Jews of Old Russia, is one of America's best-loved musicals. Credit: Alamy. **Bottom left:** A Russian-American girl carries bread and salt in a welcome ceremony traditional to Russians and Ukrainians and Belarusians. She is performing at a charity event as a member of a dance troupe affiliated with an Orthodox Christian church in Ohio. Photo by author. **Bottom right:** Irish-American re-enactor wears the uniform and carries the colors of one of the regiments of the Irish Brigade of the Union Army during the Civil War before a veterans' parade in Cincinnati on Pearl Harbor Day. Note the Irish harp brass on his cap. Photo by author. **Top right:** Stained glass window in the Catholic chapel at the U.S. Military Academy, West Point, New York. Catholic donors paid to build the church in the early 1900s when Congress would not. Fittingly, St. Michael the Archangel and Joan of Arc are two military saints who represent the Church Militant. Photo by author, a former parishioner.

were old enough to earn their keep, and then earn their parents extra money as workers. Many parents farmed out their teenage children to greedy relatives who took advantage of them. Many of these young men and women mistreated in these ways escaped to America.

Other young people ran to escape arranged marriages to people they didn't want for spouses. Too many parents in the old country tried to live off the generosity a rich son-in-law might show them. For money too many parents were willing to condemn their daughters to unhappy marriages.

Many young men fled for a related, but less noble reason. They got their girlfriends pregnant, and they ran away like cowards to escape their obligations, while their girlfriends were stuck with the shame, the abuse of their neighbors, and the cost of raising a child without a man to help her. Many pregnant girls and young women had to leave because their parents banished them or they were unwilling to face the unfriendly scrutiny of other villagers.

Many young men fled to escape another kind of embrace – that of the state. Draft-age young men often left their villages a step ahead of the officers whose job it was to get them into uniform to fight the peasants and proletarians of other countries, or to oppress other farm workers and city laborers in their own countries.

Many people fled because they were common criminals, as opposed to those who had to flee because they committed illegal but not immoral political offenses. Many Americans of British ancestry who brag their ancestors were here before the American Revolution would not be pleased to know their illustrious forebears were pickpockets or prostitutes. Likewise, there were those from all countries of Europe who came to America in the 1800s and 1900s whose criminal behavior would not make their descendants proud. Once Ellis Island and other federal immigration stations were in operation, the number of criminals escaping to America dwindled as the inspectors started screening them out.

All the desires to leave would be wasted emotions if there weren't places that were easy and cheap for people to move to. The mid to late 1800s had a number of factors that allowed many millions of people to leave Europe.

The advance of technology enabled people to make good livings as farmers and ranchers in the vast lands of the United States, Canada, Brazil, Argentina, and Australia. Farming machinery improved crop yields per farmer, railroads made it easier for farmers to get their crops and animals to market, and refrigeration and steamships even allowed growers and ranchers in these countries to export meat and produce to Europe. The Spanish had introduced ranching and farming practices to the New World that would help build Texas and California into agricultural powerhouses.

Officials in the United States gave huge amounts of land to the railroad companies when they built railroads into the Great Plains states and the western states. The railroad companies wanted passengers and freight to haul, so they were willing to sell the land to American "pilgrims" (think Jimmy Stewart in the movie "The Man Who Shot Liberty Valance") and immigrants at reasonable rates. The railroads made it relatively easy for people to settle in the American West.

In many of these countries there were precious metal and precious stone strikes that fired the imagination of the world. There was a gold rush in California in the late 1840s and 1850s, a silver strike in Nevada in the early 1860s, gold rushes in Alaska and in the nearby Canadian Yukon region in the 1890s, and several other smaller "rushes" in the other western states in the late 1800s and early 1900s. There were also major mining booms in places like South Africa, Australia, and Brazil in the late 1800s and early 1900s.

The Industrial Revolution began in Britain, whose practical scientists and businessmen were able to turn scientific discoveries into cash. But fueled by the railroad industry, the steel industry, the oil and coal industries, and the Civil War, the Industrial Revolution went farther in the United States. The United States was a young big country that was not held in check by tradition like Britain was. Its cities needed building, not renovating. American entrepreneurs soon found ways to turn inventions into money, and they needed people to work in the mills and factories to make the goods that made them big money.

The development of mass steelmaking techniques made it possible to build ships of steel and propel them with steam engines. Steel steamships started replacing wooden sailing ships in the late 1800s. The new steamships were faster and more reliable than the sailing ships, and they could haul more cargo – and more huddled masses of people.

Shipping companies made a great deal of money hauling bulky cargoes like grain, sugar, hides, cotton, timber, and metal from North America and Latin America to Europe. However, they sailed with virtually empty holds from Europe to the Western Hemisphere. Then the shippers hit on the idea of hauling people in the holds of their ships on the voyages from Europe to America. Other steel ships, while built exclusively to handle passengers, were still designed to move large numbers of people in cramped quarters for very little cost.

Steamship companies could now offer people passage to the New World at a price they could afford, and still make the steamship companies good money.

What helped the steamship companies further (besides the desperation of many to leave Europe and the desire of some government leaders and industrial leaders in the New World to get cheap labor to build their countries) was the development of two other fields – education and communications.

In the United States, Catholic priests, nuns, brothers, and laypeople established schools for their children. Some Protestant ministers and laypeople did likewise. Others without major ties to religion pushed the idea of compulsory school attendance, and taxpayer funding for schools. The spread of religious schools and government-run schools improved the literacy of the American public. **(39)**

Advances in communications shrunk the time it took for news to travel between continents. Samuel Morse invented the telegraph in the late 1830s. Cyrus Field in 1866 put telegraph wires under the Atlantic Ocean to provide speedy communication with Europe. Alexander Graham Bell invented the telephone in 1876, which sped communications further. Marconi would make the first trans-Atlantic wireless telegraph transmission in 1901. This would lead to radio. A free press in the United States, bolstered by energetic reporters, almost instantaneous communication, and the support of many people who could now read, spread the word about what it was like to live in the United States.

Reliable mail service between the New World and Europe, supported by steam-powered trains and ships, also spread the word about the opportunities on the west side of the Atlantic Ocean. Europeans learned that America was free, safe, and unhindered by nobility. They learned a person born poor could rise to be president, like Andrew Jackson, or Honest Abe Lincoln.

People in Europe learned land was there for the taking if they wanted to homestead. People in Europe learned American factories paid better wages than the factories of Europe, because there was more work to do than skilled hands to do it, and because many American workers – who had never been as servile as European workers – quit jobs, moved, or started their own companies if they didn't like their bosses. Many millions of people started thinking about saving some money and coming to the United States. They knew the building of railroads in Europe made it easier to get to port cities, and steamships made it cheaper to sail across the Atlantic Ocean.

Not all the immigrants came to the United States. Most of the immigrants from Spain and Portugal emigrated to Latin America, where they knew the language. Many of those who emigrated from Italy likewise landed up in Latin America, especially in Argentina.

Some English and Scottish and Welsh emigrants moved to Canada, which was still a British possession almost until World War II. So did settlers from colder portions of Europe, like Scandinavia, Ukraine, and Russia. Still, more of the people from these countries chose to come to the United States, because it was a more free and less harsh place to live than Canada.

The word also got to the villages of Europe that America was safe from war. Except for the Civil War, and except on the frontier, white people were safe from war and the corresponding pillage, arson, and rape. In the Civil War, the women and girls in the paths of the armies were essentially safe from rape. This was due in large part to the discipline exerted by the military leaders on both sides, but it was also due in huge part to the innate decency of the Union and Confederate soldiers alike.

In fact, during the Civil War, Union authorities court-martialed and dismissed from service General John Turchin, for reportedly urging his soldiers to burn and loot an Alabama town and rape some of the women. Turchin, a Russian native, was disciplined for playing by European rules. Abraham Lincoln eventually restored Turchin to rank, after Turchin's wife traveled to Washington and pleaded his case personally. General Turchin did get told not to play war that way again.

Lincoln's people scoured Europe for talented military officers early in the Civil War, because most of the best American officers had defected to the Confederacy. Many veterans of the wars and rebellions in Europe, especially German and Irish refugees, did serve in the Union Army. Lincoln offered the great Garibaldi himself command in the Union Army during the Civil War, but the Italian patriot turned him down. Lincoln's army did include a regiment called the Garibaldi Guard (the 39th New York), which was as diverse as Europe in miniature. Their colonel was a Hungarian. The soldiers were natives of Italy, Hungary, Croatia, Ukraine, Switzerland, Germany, Portugal, Spain, France, and England. **(40)**

In America, some bigotry against Catholics and Jews was standard practice and sometimes was government policy, but pogroms against Europeans were not. Of course, the leaders of the U.S. government ordered many acts of genocide committed against the native American Indians during this time. Also, lynchings of blacks in the South were common, race murders of Mexicans in the West and Southwest happened all too frequently, and the killings of Chinamen out West all too often got little police attention. Likewise, "Jim Crow" laws codified discrimination against blacks, and members of the Ku Klux Klan and other organized bigots abused the blacks in a manner similar to the pogroms against the Jews in the Russian Empire.

A desire to leave, a good place to go to, and a reasonable way to get there all contributed to the decisions of millions of Europeans to start anew in the United States. Now you see why your ancestors left. They wanted to leave, and they were able to do so.

America was light-years ahead of Europe politically and socially when it came to having a level society where people of talent and drive could rise. In 1829, most people in Russia, Ukraine, the Baltic lands, and Poland were serfs. Many in Central Europe, though formally not serfs, lived in conditions not much better. Most people in France, Germany, and Italy were only one or two generations out of serfdom. The Balkans were under Turkish enslavement. Most Irish were landless tenants exploited by British landlords. Most Spaniards and Portuguese lived in grinding poverty. Life wasn't a bowl of cherries for the people of Scandinavia, Switzerland, Britain, or the Low Countries either.

By comparison, in 1829 America, Andrew Jackson, the son of an impoverished hillbilly widow, became president of the United States. He made his fortune in Tennessee, the first state where poverty did not keep a man from voting. And about 100,000 mountaineers, rednecks, and other proud Americans of less than genteel upbringing descended upon Washington and cheerfully trashed the White House while drunkenly celebrating Jackson's inauguration day. Why? Because one of theirs had become president, he was taking up residence in their house, and the whisky was free.

In the Europe of the 1800s, those called "liberals" paid lip service to the workers and peasants and servants but usually wanted to limit the right of workers and peasants and servants to vote because they looked down on them. They were willing to let the less educated (rebelling peasants and other farm workers, tradesmen, and laborers) get shot for them in rebelling while they reaped the benefits of redistribution of power. They also wanted to limit the power of the nobility because most of them were not nobles. Most liberals were atheists, agnostics, or tepid Christians who believed the state should rule the church. Many liberals wanted to deny women the right to vote because women tended to practice religion more than men. Liberals from that era tended to come from the classes of lawyers, bureaucrats, and professors. Many capitalists, hoping for free trade legislation and laws to break the economic power of skilled tradesmen so they (the capitalists) could increase their profits, also were liberals. Liberals of course supported reforms, as long as these wouldn't cost them money or power. Liberals opposed kings and dictators because they wanted power for themselves, not because they intended to share power with the downtrodden. In short, there was no great philosophical difference between these people and those who call themselves liberals who hold power in Europe (and America) today.

In the Europe of the 1800s, those called "conservatives" were usually those who held power and didn't want to give it up. They wanted to limit the right of workers and peasants and servants to vote because they looked down on them. They were willing to let the less educated (the soldiers and policemen) get shot for them resisting rebellions while they reaped the benefits of power and money. They wanted to limit the rights of people like lawyers and professors because most of them were not lawyers or professors. Most conservatives were agnostics or tepid Christians who believed the state should rule the church. Conservatives from that era were estate holders or large businessmen or nobility or career military people. Some clergymen were conservatives because they thought the rulers would support their churches, or at least wouldn't confiscate what they had. Conservatives of course opposed reforms that would cost them money or power. Conservatives supported kings and dictators as long as these men protected their rights and their property, but could switch sides on a dime if kings or dictators wanted to take their rights or property. In short, there was no great philosophical difference between these people and those who call themselves conservatives who hold power in Europe (and America) today.

The main difference between "liberals" and "conservatives" in Europe was that "conservatives" were usually more honest about their selfishness than "liberals" were.

By comparison, America was a nation without nobility, or without a white serfdom, or without an upper crust of lawyers or businessmen scheming to stir the masses to rebel so they could misrule in the place of the nobility. The American Revolution, the Constitution, and later reforms had put power into the hands of a much greater percentage of Americans than any revolution and aftermath had done for people in any European country. Blacks in Southern States before the Civil War were mostly slaves, and after the Civil War they were definitely treated like dirt, but the average landless peasants in Europe were not much better off, and some were worse off. America had more than its share of shysters and snake-oil salesmen and thieves and petty tyrants, but most of the men who governed the country were essentially patriotic and committed to democracy, regardless of party.

How else can we compare America to Europe? In the early 1900s, Americans had the freedom and the cussedness to elect a man like Teddy Roosevelt – a man so gung-ho he lost an eye in a White House boxing match with one of his Secret Service men – to lead them, in no small part because this cowboy, police commissioner, war hero, outdoorsman, and hard-driving reformer was the type of man Americans were proud of and wished they could be. By comparison, most of Europe still called some morbidly inbred king or emperor or kaiser or tsar or sultan their boss. And in the "democracies" of France and Britain, a clutch of greasy debauched inbred bribetakers ran things.

For many of you, thanks to those who passed through Ellis Island, you, your parents, your grandparents, and maybe your great-grandparents missed out on living in the way of World War One, World War Two, Nazi occupation, and/or Soviet occupation. The descendants of these immigrants, you included, have lived in the greatest nation on earth because of them.

Thank God for their willingness to give America a try, and the resulting better life you have now.

END NOTES

1. Statistics come from the Annual Report of the Commissioner General of Immigration, 1931, listed on Page 195 of the Historic Research Study, Statue of Liberty – Ellis Island National Monument, by Harlan D. Unrau, National Park Service, 1984.

2. Figures for estimate of the rural population of Europe come from European Historical Statistics 1750-1970 by B.R. Mitchell. My estimates come from the following reported statistics for the occupations of employed adult males in "agriculture, fishing, and forestry" in these countries:

Britain (1871)	20% of 8.23 million
Ireland (1871)	54% of 1.74 million
France (1866)	47% of 11.07 million (not counting Alsace-Lorraine, lost in 1870)
Belgium (1866)	45% of 1.58 million
Netherlands (1859)	41% of 0.94 million
Switzerland (1890)	46% of 0.89 million
Sweden (1870)	62% of 1.13 million
Norway (1875)	39% of 0.53 million
Finland (1880)	72% of 0.36 million
Denmark (1870)	48% of 0.85 million
Germany (1882)	43% of 13.37 million (and occupied Poland and Alsace-Lorraine)
Poland (1897)	48% of 2.24 million (Russian occupied Poland only)
Russia (1897)	63% of 23.96 million (includes Ukraine, Baltics, Belarusia, Moldova, Georgia, Armenia, Turkestan, Siberia also)
Austria-Hungary (1880)	59% of 11.61 million (includes rest of Poland, Slovenia, Croatia, Czech., Slovakia, Ruthenia, Galicia, Vojvodina, Bukovina, and Transylvania)
Italy (1871)	61% of 9.26 million
Spain (1877)	72% of 5.73 million
Portugal (1890)	68% of 1.58 million

The vast majority of these men worked on farms. (Statistics for women were more spotty, so I used stats for males ... and if a man was in agriculture, his wife was almost always in agriculture also.) Since nations reported as late as 1897, my estimate of at least 60% for 1870 Europe comes from the higher rural percentages from before 1870, and from the absence of statistics from the Balkans, where the people were overwhelmingly rural.

3. Sources of information about farm tools include Ways of Old: Traditional Life in Ireland, by Olive Sharkey, and Slovakia: European Contexts of the Folk Culture, edited by Ratislava Stoličná.

4. The source is Face to Face With Kaiserism, by James Gerard, Chapter X.

5. The source is Face to Face With Kaiserism, Chapter XI.

6. Britain's Age of Marriage Act, which raised the age of marriage to 16 for boys and girls, became law in 1929. Girls in America (like Loretta Lynn, for example) and many other states married very young even into the 1960s.

An 1899 Catholic catechism – The Catechism Explained, by Rev. Francis Spirago (page 654) – also listed 12 and 14 as marriageable age for girls and boys with their parents' permission.

In the late 1800s, teenagers could earn a living. People lived much shorter lives so they tended to marry young. Since girls in Europe and America on average started menstruating at an older age in the 1800s than girls do now, most girls were well into their teens before they could bear children, and by then they were in prime physical shape to bear and raise children. They would presumably have more energy and more patience with little ones than women in their 30s would have.

Immigrants from Moslem and Hindu countries have some disgusting and un-American ideas regarding arranged marriage, dowry murders, and "honor killings" of girls, so lawmakers may have to tighten American immigration and marriage laws to combat such abuses. British authorities in 2007 had to do so because of the problem of predatory Moslems and Hindus abusing marriage visas, according to Britain's Sunday Times (3/25/2007).

The age of sexual consent laws are under attack by opponents of religion, like homosexuals and abortion providers. Organized homosexual predators have pushed to lower the age of consent in this country for the past generation, so they could prey on young boys. Planned Parenthood and other abortion providers almost always refuse to report pregnant girls barely old enough not to believe in Santa Claus, even though these girls are usually the victims of incest, rape, or statutory rape.

Colorado lawmakers in 2006 had to amend their laws because appellate court judges made an idiotic ruling that common law statute allowed common-law hookups for girls as young as 12 and boys as young as 14, according to a 7/5/2006 Associated Press story. The reporter noted a 38-year old predator tried to use the common law statute to escape a jail term for impregnating a 15-year-old girl. He had to go to jail because state authorities wouldn't grant him a marriage license to marry the girl he sexually abused, even though her knucklehead mother okayed it.

7. A source of information about this piracy is A History of England, by David Willson (pages 242-245, and 281-285). Another is Hilaire Belloc's book How the Reformation Happened (pages 68-75, 92-94, 97, and 115).

8. Sources of information about the rural people leaving the land in Britain include A History of England (pages 262-265, 491-492, and 544), and The Western Experience by multiple authors (page 461).

9. A source of information about rural conditions in Sweden is Swedish History in Outline by Jörgen Weibull (page 63).

10. Sources of information about the grabbing of Catholic Church lands in predominantly Catholic countries include The Western Experience (pages 691, 692, and 886), A Survey of European Civilization by Wallace Ferguson and Geoffrey Bruun (page 634), The History of Spain: From the Musulmans to Franco by Louis Bertrand and Charles Petrie (page 323), The Spanish Civil War by Hugh Thomas (pages 13 and 34), and Napoleon Bonaparte by Vincent Cronin (page 261).

11. Sources of information about the end of serfdom in southern Germany, Italy, and the Hapsburg Empire are The Course of Civilization by Joseph Strayer, Hans Gatzke, and E. Harrison Harbison (Volume 2, page 98), and Napoleon Bonaparte (pages 261 and 339).

12. A source of information about the "Little Ice Age" is Environmental Geoscience by Arthur and Alan Strahler (page 458).

13. A source of information about the grabbing of Catholic Church lands in France is The Course of Civilization, (Volume 2, page 117). Another is Napoleon Bonaparte (56-57, 215).

14. Sources of information about rural conditions in Ireland and Irish farm tools include The Great Hunger: Ireland 1845-1849, by Ms. Cecil Woodham-Smith, The Story of the Irish Race by Seumas MacManus, and Outlines in Irish History: Eight Hundred Years of Struggle by Seumas Metress. The kind people of the Knock Folk Museum in Knock, County Mayo, Ireland, and of the Famine Museum in Strokestown, County Roscommon, Ireland also provided us with great information about rural conditions in Ireland and Irish farm tools when we visited these museums.

15. Sources of information about the end of serfdom in the Russian Empire include The Course of Russian History by Melvin Wren (pages 407-412) and An Introduction to Russian History and Culture by Ivar Spector (pages 132-140).

16. Sources of information about the condition of Jews in the Russian Empire is The Course of Russian History (pages 446-448) and A History of the Jews (358-363) by Paul Johnson.

17. The Caprivi quote and German agricultural facts came from The Second Reich by Harold Kurtz (pages 66-68). Another source for the German agricultural facts is Modern and Contemporary European History (1815 - 1940) by J. Salwyn Schapiro (pages 400 and 408).

18. Sources for facts about British agriculture and farm land rents are Modern and Contemporary European History (1815 - 1940) (pages 137-138 and 283-284), and A History of England (pages 617-619, 635-637, and 672-674).

19. I covered the coal industry as a reporter and wrote technical manuals for mining machinery for some years, so I have a working knowledge of some mine conditions and improvements. However, the good people of the Mining Museum of Příbram, Czech Republic provided us with a great deal of information about European mining techniques in the 1800s and the lives of the miners in the 1800s when we visited this museum.

20. Figures for the urban population of Europe come from the report "Urbanisation 1700-1870" by Paolo Malanima and Oliver Volckart. Their work was funded by the London-based European think tank Centre for Economic Policy Research.

21. A source of information about city sanitation in general and London in particular is The Western Experience (pages 834-835 and 852). Another is "The History of Sanitary Sewers" by Jon Schladweiler of the Arizona Water Pollution Control Association.

22. The source for the fouled dress story is Napoleon Bonaparte (page 24).

23. A source of information about the estimated number of prostitutes in London is The Western Experience (page 835).

24. The source of the clergy vocation drop in Britain is A History of England (page 604).

25. The source of this quote was Face to Face With Kaiserism, Chapter IX.

26. Sources of information on executions for witchcraft suspects include Jenny Gibbons' article "Recent Developments in the Study of the Great European Witch Hunt," first published in the publication The Pomagranate: A New Journal of Neopagan Thought in 1998, and Ronald Hutton's unpublished article "Counting the Witch Hunt," which he purportedly made available to Wiccan and modern pagan groups.

Jenny Gibbons noted, "The Inquisition almost invariably pardoned any witch who confessed and repented." Ms. Gibbons at the time of publication was a self-described pagan, a resident of Oregon, and holder of a graduate degree in medieval history; presumably she hadn't changed her husband into a toad. Several pagan and Wiccan webmasters reprinted Ms. Gibbons' article, implying they gave it credibility. Some pagan and Wiccan websites also referenced Hutton's estimates on numbers of people killed for witchcraft-related convictions. Hutton, a Briton and the author of The Pagan Religions of the Ancient British Isles, was considered friendly and unfriendly to the pagan and Wiccan movements, depending on which of these people was speaking.

Ms. Gibbons and Hutton estimated between 35,000 and 65,000 people were executed for witchcraft and related offenses, a much lower bracket than many in the Wiccan cause and in the anti-Christian movements claim. Another reputed analytical expert, Brian Levack, in his book The Witch-Hunt in Early Modern Europe estimated about 60,000 people were executed for witchcraft and related offenses. Anne Barstow, in Witchcraze, estimated about 100,000 executions. These researchers' work tended to blame Protestant "reformers" and civil authorities in areas where Protestants were dominant for the most executions. The Lutheran areas of Germany, and Calvinist areas in nearby countries had the highest number of witch executions, while England and Scotland also had active witch hunts. Ireland, Spain, and Portugal had the fewest, and Italy seemed a relatively safe place for broom riders before the 20th Century.

Some modern pagans and Wiccans, like Ms. Gibbons, have accepted historical work showing their role models to be much less persecuted in Medieval, Renaissance, and Reformation Europe than some of the propagandists in these movements would have people believe.

Another source of information on the execution of suspected witches is Richard Green's treatise "How Many Witches," made available through The Holocaust History Project, a tax-exempt Jewish group whose members make available information about the Nazi genocide of the Jews. Possibly this group was peeved by some wild feminists' and witch conspiracy believers' claims that roughly 10 million women were executed on false witchcraft charges in Europe in a 400-year period. If true, this would have eclipsed the number of victims of Hitler's holocaust by four million. (Only the slaughters of the Slavs by Nazis and Communists in the 1900s exceeded the Jewish Holocaust as the Number One genocide in Europe in terms of total number of murders.) Green said while it was sad that anyone was executed on a false charge of witchcraft, it was patently untrue based on population numbers that so many as 10 million women died as condemned witches.

27. Sources for statistics on the Irish dead as the result of the English war upon them from 1641 through 1652 include The Story of the Irish Race (page 432) and Outlines in Irish History: Eight Hundred Years of Struggle (page 27). A source of information on Cromwell's part in the murder of so many Irish is A History of England (pages 391-392).

Figures on the number of victims of the Spanish Inquisition vary somewhat. William Walsh, in his book Isabella of Spain, The Last Crusader (pages 167-181, 210-218, 260-281), claimed the officers of the Spanish Inquisition had about 2000 people executed while Tomás de Torquemada ran it from its start in 1480 to his death in 1498. Adrian Shubert, in his book The Land and People of Spain (pages 80-82), proposed officers of the Inquisition had about 5000 people executed from 1480 to 1530. He also reported Inquisition officers handed down 500 death sentences from 1540 through 1700. Paul Johnson, in his book A History of the Jews (pages 226-229), asserted officers of the Inquisition had 20,000 people executed from 1480 through 1540. He asserted Inquisition officers had another 12,000 or so people executed from 1540 through 1790.

28. In 1558 and 1559, Geneva had about 20,000 residents. In these two years, Calvin had his henchmen punish 414 of them – one out of every fifty residents. But that was a sign he had the people of Geneva sufficiently cowed. Calvin's spies and police could have women punished for serving too much food or sweets at a meal, or for wearing a dress or a hairstyle not deemed proper. Men were put in the town pillory for playing cards or dice. Calvin's agents could invade homes to quiz people on their religious knowledge, snoop on their personal lives, and inventory women's shoes, dresses, and jewelry. Adults and children received punishment for verbally disagreeing with Calvin, for inattention or inappropriate laughter during his sermons, and for a host of other pissant infractions that made the Spanish Inquisition look like the ACLU.

Sources of information on Calvin's personal life and his rule of Geneva (including information and statistics on those he had punished) include Philip Schaff's work The History of the Reformation (Volume VIII, The Swiss Reformation, Section 107), Schaff's work Encyclopedia of Religious Knowledge (Volume II), and Stefan Zweig's book The Right to Heresy (Chapter 2). Schaff was a Swiss-born Protestant theologian who emigrated to America in the 1800s.

Info on the Salem Witch Trials comes from "The Witchcraft Trials in Salem: A Commentary" by Douglas Linder for University of Missouri Kansas City's law school.

Info on Anna Goeldi comes from the British Sunday Telegram (2/7/2007). Swiss authorities were still balking at exonerating the woman more than two centuries after a leering jeering mob watched a swordsman cut off her comely head. What do you expect from a government whose members can deny wrongdoing in hiding Nazi-stolen loot?

29. A source on dowry murders in India is Michael and Hyman Kublin's book India (page 205). They said greedy people committed perhaps several thousand such murders a year. They also noted (page 167) at least 500,000 Moslems, Hindus, and Sikhs died (and at least another 12 million or so people had to flee from their homes to an area on the subcontinent where their religion was the majority) because of sectarian violence among them during the 1947 partition of India and Pakistan. Do a search on the Internet for news articles of Hindu violence against Catholics and Protestants, and you will find many on such attacks, rapes, arsons, and murders in the 2000s. Greedy Hindu landlords are angry at the conversion of many "Untouchables" to Catholicism. These poor people, who do the most menial labor in India, are gaining assertiveness, in part due to the help of the priests and nuns. Hindu extremists, who owe their political power to their ability to inflame the masses, are also directing this evil talent at Protestant preachers who proclaim the Gospel in an in-your-face style. They claim it is insulting to the Hindu deities.

30. A source for the number of victims of the Reign of Terror is Stanley Loomis' book Paris in the Terror (page 328). Another is The Western Experience (page 751). Some encyclopedias use a figure of about 20,000 guillotinings, other executions, and mob murders of prisoners in Paris, and a roughly equal number of guillotinings, firing squad executions, artillery fire executions, and other government sanctioned killings of political prisoners in the rest of France. Sources of information on the crushing of the people of Vendée and Brittany include Vincent Cronin's book Napoleon Bonaparte and Sophie Masson's 1996 article "Remembering the Vendée" in the Australian magazine Quadrant. The editors of Godspy magazine reprinted the article with Sophie's permission in 2004.

A disturbing filmclip of the guillotining of a character played by actress Charlotte Turckheim that is easy to find on the Internet came from the French movie "Chouans!" about the peasant uprising in Vendée and Brittany.

Aleksandr Solzhenitsyn spoke at the dedication of the Vendée Memorial in 1993, the 200th anniversary of the uprising in the Vendée and in Brittany. He considered Robespierre and his kind to be cut from the same cloth as the Communists.

Religious-tinted violence pales in comparison with atheist-ordered mass murder in the 1900s and in the 2000s. The activities of those who turned their backs on religion – and especially rejected the demands for ethical conduct that only revealed religions can logically make – have done much more harm to humanity in the past century than the religious persecutions in Europe did, or maybe even the jihadists of Islam have done.

For victim body count, the gold medal goes to the atheistic Communists in China, and the silver medal goes to the atheistic Communists of the Soviet Union. The satanic Hitler and his atheistic Nazis, and Japan's crazed militarists are also in this conversation, in terms of murders per armed thug. Each of these regimes murdered in the tens of millions of people.

The atheistic sociopaths Hitler and Stalin and their minions, the atheistic buffoon Mussolini, the pagan psychopaths who ran Japan, and the atheistic and agnostic grasping cowards who ran France and Britain were all responsible for World War Two. But even they finally found enlightenment. These self-deifying leaders who were to blame for that cataclysm all discovered after they died there is a God, He was displeased with their actions, and it's damned uncomfortable in Hell!

31. A source of information about the debauched lifestyles of Britain's upper classes is The Proud Tower by Barbara Tuchman (Chapter 1).

32. Information on Blood Countess Erzsebet Bathory comes from The Rough Guide to the Czech and Slovak Republics by Rob Humphreys (pages 402-403), and from Court TV's Crime Library website.

Here's a lesser-known account of another blueblood bimbo's private reign of terror. One of the noblewomen of Russia during the time of Catherine the Great bought serfs for 10 rubles apiece and in 10 years tortured 140 of them to death. Most of the victims were serf women and serf girls. A source for the story of this evil bitch is A Picture History of Russia (page 99), edited by John Martin.

33. Zita von Hapsburg, the last empress of Austria-Hungary, told Austrian officials after World War Two that when she and her husband became the rulers of the empire, they came across a file in Franz Josef's records that purported to have the inside information on the deaths of Rudolf and Maria. The file had blank papers, she said.

Zita blamed the French government. She claimed they wanted to detach Austria-Hungary from the alliance with Germany. In her opinion, the plot was to assassinate Franz Josef so Rudolph, a France-lover and an opponent of his father's policies, could come to the throne. When Rudolph refused to participate, she claimed, assassins killed him and Maria too, to hush her up for good. I believe Zita to be wrong on this; if Rudolph and Franz Josef were French assassins' targets, the old emperor would have no reason to cover up the cause of his son's death. He simply would prevail upon Germany to help him punish the French. In 1889, France did not have an alliance with Britain or Russia; they would be isolated and helpless against German and Austro-Hungarian attack. Franz Josef okayed war on Serbia in 1914 after Serb militants murdered his successor and nephew Franz Ferdinand and his wife Sophie. He did this even though he and his nephew butted heads repeatedly, and he and his court blackballed Sophie during her entire marriage to his nephew for not having enough noble blood. Tragically, this escalated into World War One, the suicide of Europe.

Others have blamed Franz Josef, German agents, Maria's uncles, and others for the deaths of Rudolph and Maria. Each of these speculations has evidence to support and reject it. Evidently, forensic evidence indicated one shot was fired. So did Vatican archives; a papal official had done his own spadework at the site of the killings. The botched abortion theory is at least consistent with forensic evidence (only one shot fired, no gunshot wound to Maria's skull, but a massive one to Rudolph's head), Rudolph's sexually loose behavior and power, the remorse any man who was not a monster would feel watching a girlfriend die painfully and in fear, and the need Franz Josef had to cover up the circumstances of his son's death from the people he ruled and from Catholic authorities, who would be prone to deny a suicide a public funeral.

34. The source of information about Rasputin's rape of a nun, the beatdown Bishop Hermogen gave him, and the punishment the bishop received is Nicholas and Alexandra by Robert Massie (pages 211-212).

35. The anecdote about the Viennese condom king comes from A Nervous Splendor, by Frederic Morton (page 195).

36. These statistics came from Cardinal James Gibbons' 1879 book The Faith of Our Fathers (page 304). Statistics on illegitimacy in Europe in the first decade of the 1900s from the Statesman's Yearbook show similar rates of bastardy for the countries listed.

37. The sources of my remarks about Dolly Sinatra and the malpractice records of abortion providers with doctor's licenses come from His Way by Kitty Kelley and from the public records I laid out in my books Victims of Choice and The Scarlet Survey. There is nothing novel about abortion doctors botching abortions. America's civil courts and coroners' offices are full of such cases since Roe vs. Wade.

38. Figures on abortions in France come from pages 601-602 of A History of Private Life: From the Fires of Revolution to the Great War edited by Michelle Perrot. The chapter containing these statistics was written by Alain Corbin. Corbin noted virtually all women undergoing abortions at the start of the 1800s were young single women and widows. As the years flew by, Corbin noted, proportionally more and more married women (including those whose husbands were impotent or not sexually active) underwent abortions. This book also noted infanticide of bastard victims was all too common in France in the 1800s. In the second half of the 1800s, Mme. Perrot and Anne-Martin Fugier noted (page 200), as many as a thousand women in any given year would go on trial for infanticide.

French abortionists were not alone in committing large numbers of abortions. Ratislava Stoličná and Katarina Apáthyová-Rusnáková, in the book Slovakia: European Contexts of the Folk Culture, (pages 181-183) noted many Protestants in Slovakia and elsewhere in Europe -- especially Calvinists -- preferred one-child families. The mothers all too often aborted younger brothers and sisters for superficial reasons so one child could gain a better education and a full inheritance. Germany had many abortionists and tens of thousands of abortions per year, said Planned Parenthood's Margaret Sanger in her 1938 autobiography (page 285).

The last woman executed for performing abortions in France was Marie Louise Giraud. Besides cheating on her husband, this paragon of feminism rented rooms to prostitutes, and as an abortionist she evidently profited from one of the occupational hazards of their trade. She probably collaborated with the Nazis, which was common among those in the French sex trade during occupation in World War Two. Her boyfriend reportedly did. The Nazis encouraged abortion among captive peoples, but the Vichy French government did not encourage French women to kill their young. Vichy French officials guillotined Mme. Marie in 1943. A French movie loosely based on Marie's fate came out in the 1980s with well-known actress Isabelle Huppert playing the beheaded abortionist. Marcel Petiot, a French abortionist who posed as a Resistance fighter to swindle desperate Jews and murder them, died on the guillotine in 1946. *Live by the sword, die by the sword.*

After World War Two, American judges of the Nuremberg Military Tribunal convicted two Nazi officials of a group named "Race and Settlement Main Office (RuSHA)" for "encouraging" and "pressuring" (using tactics short of coercion) and coercing non-German women (mostly Slavs) into undergoing abortions. They and a dozen other Nazi vermin in this evil group also stood charged of forced Germanization of blond intelligent captives, forced evacuations and resettlements of non-German civilians, plunder of property, kidnapping Slavic children, taking away Slavic women's babies if they were forced laborers, hampering reproduction of non-German nationals, punishment of foreigners for having sex with Germans, and being SS members.

Lead prosecutor James McHaney considered the unborn children as humans entitled to protection of the law. The Nazis used abortion to hold down the Slavic population and keep females from captive countries available for slave labor. He argued even if non-German women "consented" to abortions, the taking of the unborn babies' lives were crimes in and of themselves. (McHaney's remarks were in his opening statements for the U.S. vs. Ulrich Greifelt et. al. case.)

Nazi SS defendant Richard Hildebrandt complained in reply, "Up to now nobody had the idea to see in this interruption of pregnancy a crime against humanity."

A 1943 Nazi memo McHaney introduced as evidence noted "chiefly reactionary Catholic physicians" refused to perform abortions on the captive Slav females. The memo writer said other doctors would perform them once they were "made to understand" abortions of Slavs would lead to fewer enemies of the Reich. The memo writer also noted some doctors wanted anonymity for performing abortions or cover by inducing abortions on captive women without their knowledge (presumably while they were anesthetized). Why? So the doctors could escape execution in case Germany was to lose the war. (These items come from the trial transcript, pages 1076-1099, courtesy of the Mazal Library.)

The judges convicted Hildebrandt and another SS officer named Otto Hofmann of the abortion specifications in addition to their other crimes. The other male defendants drew sentences ranging from time served to life imprisonment for the non-abortion offenses they committed. A Nazi female escaped conviction. U.S. general Telford Taylor, the chief military prosecutor, criticized these judges for excessive leniency in his "Final Report to the Secretary of the Army on the Nuernberg [sic] War Crimes Trials."

Other war crimes trial judges sentenced "Euthanasia Program" chief Doctor Karl Brandt and six other Nazi medicos to death for their crimes. McHaney also prosecuted these vermin. Brandt, probably the highest ranking doctor in the Third Reich and an intimate of Hitler, performed abortions and "euthanized" the aged, crippled, retarded, and infirm. He and these other mad scientists also planned, managed, and performed thousands of unspeakably vile and cruel (and usually fatal) experiments on many unfortunates. Brandt and other sadistic and/or cowardly German doctors also murdered at least 275,000 people under the "Euthanasia Program," murdered another 100,000 or so "mental defectives" (with the aid of Germany's shrinks), and forcibly sterilized 400,000 Germans and others. They also performed at least 50,000 "eugenically directed" abortions on German females. (In other words, the fraus and frauleins were pregnant with potential defective babies, were handicapped themselves, or the fathers were non-Germans.)

Brandt was not sentenced for committing the many abortions he committed on "defective" German females or on German females deemed likely to give birth to handicapped or retarded children or on German females who were pregnant by non-Aryans. Nor was any other German doctor. Nor did Brandt or any other German receive punishment for the forced "euthanizing" of German nationals. Why? Because Allied judges ruled abortion and euthanasia of said "inferior people" and "subhumans" was legal in Nazi Germany because the victims were Germans. It was okay for scum like Brandt, Mengele, and a host of other sadistic murderers with medical degrees to commit these crimes on their own people. You have to go to law school to think like that.

Since Hitler and the Nazis wanted soldiers, they wanted the Fatherland's females to produce as many healthy children as possible, even if it meant they had to resort to fornication or adultery. Hitler regarded Germans as little more than intelligent breeding stock, so he made it illegal for German females in most cases to undergo abortions for reasons of personal immorality or personal convenience. But enforcement of this policy was far from airtight. Besides, Hitler used abortion as a lethal weapon against non-Germans and against those Germans he deemed unfit. Hitler was no Puritan; he was a bisexual teetotaling drug addict and a vegetarian animal lover who had committed incest with his niece. (The source of info on Hitler and the Nazis comes from William Shirer's epic work The Rise and Fall of the Third Reich.)

Josef Mengele escaped prosecution for the thousands of sadistic experiments he performed and the many thousands of victims he ordered executed at Auschwitz by fleeing to Argentina. He worked there as an abortionist (which was illegal in Argentina) and a friend of his bribed a judge to release Mengele and drop a homicide case against the Auschwitz butcher after Mengele botched an abortion on a young woman and she died. (The source is the New York Times, 2/11/1992.)

Further sources on the Nazi doctors include an article titled "The Third Reich – German Physicians Between Resistance and Participation" in the International Journal of Epidemiology by E. Ernst (Feb. 2001; 30:37-42), and the U.S. Holocaust Memorial Museum.

Since abortion was also a criminal offense in most states in America before 1973, any woman or girl dying of an abortion would bring the attention of homicide detectives to the abortion provider who caused her death. Most abortionists before 1973 in states where abortion was outlawed were doctors who did them illegally. Vital statistics reports show the numbers of such deaths were nowhere near the thousands per year claimed by fanatical abortion supporters. Today's abortion providers don't have to worry about criminal prosecution, or in most cases, even medical board reprimand when their acts of malpractice lead to deaths or permanent disabilities of women and girls. Their customers do have to worry about their lack of skill because in most cases they have been unable to do well in legitimate medicine. No balanced doctor aspires to be an abortionist.

39. Horace Mann, considered the father of public school systems in America, talked Massachusetts officials into getting into the public school business by claiming they would counteract Catholic influences in the state. Mann unwittingly helped cause the founding of many Catholic schools, because many Catholic parents wanted to shield their children from the anti-Catholic bigotry of many public school faculty members. From Mann's time until the 1960s, America's public schools had a nondenominational Protestant bent. Now they are bent against Catholics and Protestants alike.

A source of information about Horace Mann is in The Persistent Prejudice by Michael Schwartz (pages 188-189). Mann was also a temperance freak and a believer in phrenology, which is like "palmistry of the skull" (a great quote by Schwartz) in that its quacks claim they can determine character based on head shape. These people, in other words, are pinheads.

40. The source for the Turchin incident is The Civil War: Strange & Fascinating Facts by Burke Davis (page 229). The source for the Garibaldi Guard is The Civil War: Strange & Fascinating Facts (page 93).

Map 16. Europe in the 1920s, after the Peace Treaties, Revolutions, and Boundary Wars

WHAT WAS LIFE IN EUROPE LIKE?

MANIFEST DESTINY, MAGNIFICENT DESTINATION

Very few people want to leave their homelands if they are content. Many Europeans were not content. They gave up lifestyles they knew and made a crapshoot on what life would be like in a strange continent. More than 30 million people came from Europe to America from the century or so between the end of the War of 1812 and the start of the Great Depression.

In order to take on that many people, America had to live up to its billing as a much better place to be than crowded, poverty-stricken, war-torn, and oppressive Europe. America also had to be able to accommodate all the new arrivals.

This chapter will cover how the Spanish, French, English, and others settled America, how the English and their descendants wiped out the American Indians, and how Americans increased the size of the United States to its present boundaries.

This chapter will also cover the story of America's Mormons, who effectively seceded from the Union and got away with it for decades. Their story is in this chapter to explain what our leaders finally had to do to a quasi-militarily organized group of people who violated American law behind the guise of religion. It is an object lesson and precedent for what we might have to do as a nation against militant Islamists.

This chapter will also give a roundup of where America's immigrants came from in the Ellis Island era. And this chapter will explain how America's economy expanded so rapidly that America was able to put all these immigrants to work.

THE FIRST SEVERAL MILLION PEOPLE JUST SHOWED UP

In the beginning there were no immigration laws. People just showed up.

The first Americans, the people we call American Indians and Eskimos, settled the American Hemisphere from north to south thousands of years before the white man. Meanwhile, Polynesians settled on the Hawaiian Islands.

The Vikings were the next to show up, sort of. They tried to colonize Greenland. They sailed south, along the Canadian and American coast. American Indians along the Atlantic seaboard drove them off.

People from Iberia were the next to show up. The Portuguese pretty much kept to Brazil. The Spanish settled elsewhere in South America, and in Mexico, in Central America, on the Caribbean Islands, and in the present-day United States, long before the English came. (Santa Fé, New Mexico is 50 years older than Boston. St. Augustine, Florida is 65 years older than Beantown.)

The English showed up next, but briefly at first. The first English settlers tried North Carolina in the 1580s, but disappeared. They were supposedly killed or enslaved by the native American Indians.

The French showed up next. They would settle first in Quebec in the early 1600s, and later in Acadia (now called Nova Scotia), some islands in the Caribbean, Louisiana, along the Great Lakes, and along the Mississippi River and the Ohio River.

The English showed up again, in Virginia in 1607, and in Massachusetts in 1620. In the area that became the 13 Colonies, religious fanatics populated New England and massacred the American Indians who had helped them. English adventurers and lowlifes settled Virginia, and treated the American Indians likewise. Even the gentle Quakers who first settled eastern Pennsylvania in the late 1600 had no trouble cheating the American Indians or hiring those who would resort to violence to expel the American Indians.

Lord Baltimore, one of the few Catholics who was a friend of the king of England, got the right to establish Maryland as a colony for Catholics. His brother did so in 1634. Lord Baltimore's relatives tried to ensure the settlers lived peaceably with the American Indians, and they allowed Protestants and Jews to come to Maryland. The Anglican governor of Virginia formed a war party, and invaded Maryland in 1644. He had priests arrested and sent to England in chains. Those he couldn't catch his minions drove out. Eventually the more numerous Protestant immigrants voted to strip Catholics in Maryland of many of their civil rights. Catholics could not inherit land, educate their children as Catholics, attend Mass in public, serve as lawyers, or serve as public officials. **(1)**

The Dutch showed up in the 1620s, and settled in New York. The Swedes showed up in the 1630s and settled in Delaware, then the Dutch took Delaware over in 1655. The English took New York over from the Dutch in the 1660s ... and Delaware, too, while they were at it.

ELLIS ISLAND SCRAPBOOK

New Jersey started out as wealthy businessmen's colonies. Puritans and their enemies also settled in New Jersey. Controversies involving who had authority and valid title to the land (and the associated massive fraud involved) set the pattern for official corruption in New Jersey for centuries to come.

The Carolinas also started out as wealthy businessmen's colonies. Soon malcontents from New England and Virginia came there. So did small farmers from Britain's holdings in the West Indies. Rich British landowners had forced them out, and they turned the islands they stole from the small farmers into sugar cane plantations, which they brought slaves to work on.

Georgia started as a debtor and penal colony for poor whites from England. Many other pickpockets and prostitutes were forced to come to the other colonies; their descendants would eventually lord it over non-English immigrants because their dissolute ancestors were "early Americans."

What happened to the American Indians in the Eastern United States?

They lost because they didn't unite to fight the European invaders. And the American Indians along the Eastern Seaboard had the bad luck to be in land the English coveted.

The English settlers brought over with them the entitlement mentality. If they wanted the land, they killed or ran off the people who were living on it, and used the natives' different religion as an excuse to rob them and kill them. The English first tried this approach against the Catholic Irish in the 1500s, under Henry VIII and his bastard daughter Elizabeth, the Pirate Queen. English leaders King James I and Oliver Cromwell and William of Orange in the 1600s, in their theft of Irish land and the killing of the Irish people, would give the colonists of America a pattern to follow.

Purists point out William of Orange was not totally English, but a half-breed Dutchman who got the English throne when Parliament overthrew James II – a Catholic convert – and put William's business-arrangement wife Mary (James II's still-Protestant daughter) and himself on the English throne. William, also a Protestant, was height challenged and posture challenged — a polite way of saying he was a short hunchback. William's mother was James II's sister Mary. William was James II's son-in-law and nephew. In other words, for a wife of convenience, William married his first cousin. Did inbreeding lead to their failure to produce heirs? Probably not. William of Orange and Mary had no children because William preferred buggery with males to sexual intercourse with females.

The English applied the smash-and-grab tactics that they perfected in Ireland to the American Indians. The English in Virginia kidnaped and raped Pocahontas to gain leverage against her tribe. Tobacco entrepreneur John Rolfe was sexually attracted enough to Pocahontas to force marriage on her and show her off in England, where she died at the age of 21. Rolfe's countrymen stole enough from Pocahontas' people that the natives finally had enough and killed several hundred English settlers. The English responded by killing men, women, and children of her tribe and other tribes in the area for years, and burning them in their villages after signing peace treaties with them. **(2)**

Likewise, the Pilgrims and their rival Puritans killed American Indians in New England and praised God for the land they could steal. These godly buckle-hatted men sold the surviving Indian captives into slavery ... they even sold American Indians they could capture as slaves to the Moslems in North Africa! By the 1700s, there would be only few more American Indians in New England than members of Teddy Kennedy's family in Mothers Against Drunk Driving. **(3)**

Coming from the land of tulips and windmills didn't make the Dutch any less bloodthirsty. The Dutch killed peaceable American Indians in today's New York and New Jersey. The Dutch, by the way, were the first Europeans to bring blacks from Africa to the present-day United States to be sold as slaves. The Dutch sold slaves to the English colonists as well as to their own people. **(4)**

All the colonial nations of Europe would allow enslavement and transportation of Africans to the New World as slaves. Queen Isabella of Spain (Columbus' sponsor) forbade slavery, but her successors didn't have her morality.

French colonists tended to treat American Indians with dignity, while Spanish colonists wrongly tended to treat American Indians like peons. But at least the Spanish tried to teach the American Indians European ways so they could make it in Spanish New World society. The different Latin approach in part came from the different religious mindset of the French and Spanish. Catholic religious leaders – reinforced at different times by people like Queen Isabella and the Jesuits – determined American Indians had immortal souls and were children of God also. This meant – on paper, at least – that the French and Spanish colonists were not supposed to slaughter the Indians but to try to convert them, and introduce them to European ways. The missions that dot the Spanish-settled parts of America are proof they spent plenty of time and money doing so.

The French and Spanish certainly did not look down on Indian women but married them (and fornicated with them) readily. The proof is in the pudding; in Mexico and many other countries in Latin America, most people are mestizos – people of mixed Spanish and American Indian blood. In Canada, there are métis – people of mixed French Canadian and American Indian blood.

Spanish rule in the Western Hemisphere proved to be much easier on the American Indians than rule by those of British blood. In the Spanish-settled American states, there tend to be a higher proportion of American Indians than there are in most of the rest of the Lower 48 United States, or in English-speaking Canada. (Oklahoma has a large number of American Indians because white Americans exiled many of their ancestors to the place – then known as "the Indian Territory" – after taking their land.) This doesn't even count the huge number of American Indians in Mexico or elsewhere in Latin America.

In 1763, after winning the French and Indian War, the British took Quebec, Acadia (which the British renamed "Nova Scotia"), and France's other holdings in Canada. They also took French-settled land between the Appalachians and the Mississippi River. The British forcibly exiled most of the French settlers of Acadia during the French and Indian War. Many Acadians made their way to Louisiana, which would remain under French control until the end of the war, when the French ceded the Louisiana Territory to Spain. The descendants of these unfortunates would bear the nickname of "Cajun" after the land they were exiled from. The British also took Florida and the eastern Gulf Coast from the Spanish.

In the century before the American Revolution, people from Germany, Switzerland, Ireland, Scotland, and Wales would also come to the 13 colonies. So would the Huguenots – French Protestants escaping a milder persecution in Catholic France than the harsh persecution by the Protestant English that the Irish were escaping. Enough of these people – and enough of the descendants of the jailbirds, holy rollers, shady ladies, con artists, and malcontents from England – would rebel against English authority and develop the best experiment in liberty the world would ever see.

Protestantism had an unintended but positive impact on the people of English, Scot, Welsh, Huguenot, Dutch, and German blood in America in the 1700s which led to the American Revolution, and to the American way of life. The Puritans, Anglicans, Baptists, Presbyterians, Methodists, and other Protestant colonists all thought theirs was the only true faith. But even within these churches, there was no unanimity among the people over what the tenets of their faiths should be. Many believers figured their own views on the precepts of their faith were as good as anyone else's. Since all these churches recognized individual interpretation of the Bible, people could and did dissent from the teachings of ministers and often started their own congregations. There developed among the people a lack of respect for formal religious authority if they believed this authority conflicted with their own consciences ... or often merely their own desires.

This mindset transferred over to politics. The American colonists would in time have no problem with disputing the regulations and commands that came from the royal governors or from Parliament if they didn't agree with them. In a society where everyone could be his own pope spiritually, it was only natural that people in time came to believe they could rule themselves without any help from an inbred king, a debauched nobility, or a grasping Parliament. This mass realization of the people led to the founding and the building of the finest nation the world has ever seen.

George Washington and other American officers and enlisted men, and with aid from French, Irish, German, and Polish officers, French, Spanish, and black Haitian troops, French and Spanish seamen, French priests, and French, Spanish, and Dutch foreign aid, fought a war against Britain from 1775 to 1781. The Americans, aided with the foreign help, most of it coming from Catholic people of Catholic lands, beat the British and won freedom from Britain.

Roughly one-third of the Continental Army was of Irish blood, although less than 10 percent of the people of the 13 colonies were of Irish blood. People from the Emerald Isle percentagewise were much more patriotic for America than WASP Americans because they understood better than anyone else how oppressive the British could be, and they didn't want any more of it in America. Many of the WASPs favored the continuation of British rule; these native traitors were called Tories. Many would flee to Canada or England after the war. Some say the spiritual descendants of the Tories would ensconce themselves in Ivy League schools and in the State Department.

Many Americans of Irish ancestry who were Protestants – some as the descendants of those forcibly converted in Ireland, and others who turned to the Protestant denominations because the British and American Anglicans and Puritans kept Catholic priests out of most of the 13 colonies -- had not lost their distrust of the British. A large proportion of these people – to include a 13-year-old Andrew Jackson – also were in the ranks of the Patriot forces.

Also, 5 to 10 percent of all soldiers and sailors who fought for America's liberty were blacks. Many who were slaves gained their freedom after the war. In some horrible cases, these black patriots were returned to slavery, gypped and betrayed by the men they helped liberate from the British.

HOW AMERICA GOT TO BE SO BIG

At the time of the American Revolution, there were about three million people living in the 13 colonies plus today's Vermont and Maine. By comparison, there were about nine million people living in Britain (England, Scotland, and Wales).

Ben Franklin and his fellow diplomats made a favorable agreement with the British after the American Revolution which enabled the Americans to take most of the land between the original 13 states and the Mississippi River. The states of Kentucky, Tennessee, Alabama, Mississippi, Ohio, Indiana, Illinois, Michigan, and Wisconsin – and some of Minnesota -- would arise on these lands. (In New England, Vermont became a state in 1791 and Maine would become a state a generation later.) The Spanish, as practical allies of the Americans, recovered Florida and the eastern Gulf Coast from the British.

If it hadn't been for the anti-Catholic bigotry of the people of New England, America might have gotten Canada as well. England's rulers, who were militant anti-Catholics themselves, had during the French and Indian War exiled the French living in Acadia. There were too many French settlers in Quebec to exile, so the British left them in place. The British were at least smart enough to grant some religious toleration to the Catholic French of Quebec in 1774, a year before the American Revolution. They knew the French settlers of Quebec distrusted the bigoted New Englanders nearby, so they hoped to enlist the French to fight the New Englanders. The French in Quebec would not help their British masters suppress the American Revolution. But they would not respond to American overtures to join them in throwing off England's yoke during the American Revolution either, because they thought the Americans would persecute them for their religion. **(5)**

American settlers and American troops ran the American Indians off of the land they got from the British. In the Great Lakes region, British agitators armed American Indians to try to slow the advance of the Americans. Mad Anthony Wayne's troops beat warriors of the Miami tribe at Fallen Timbers in Ohio in 1794. William Henry Harrison's troops beat Shawnee warriors under the Shawnee Prophet at Tippecanoe in Indiana in 1811. Harrison and his Americans invaded Ontario in 1813 during the War of 1812, beat the British at Thames, and killed the great chief Tecumseh in the battle. Tecumseh, the Shawnee Prophet's brother, was the Shawnee chief who tried to organize the tribes (and secure cynical British help) against the American settlers and soldiers. In the South, Andrew Jackson's militiamen would crush Creek warriors at Horseshoe Bend in Alabama in 1814, also during the War of 1812. Both Jackson and Harrison would later become presidents largely due to their military prowesses.

Americans weren't stopping at the Mississippi. In 1800, Napoleon invaded and occupied Spain. He forced the Spanish to give up the Louisiana Territory. When Thomas Jefferson was president in the first decade of the 1800s, he sent envoys to France to try to buy New Orleans and the surrounding area so the settlers in the Mississippi, Tennessee, and Ohio valleys could send their goods to Europe and to the eastern United States through the port of New Orleans. In those days, there were no railroads. River boats and ocean-going ships were the cheapest and most reliable forms of freight transportation. Napoleon, in need of cash for his wars in Europe, and grimly aware France had no effective access to American colonies as long as rival Britain ruled the seas, in 1803 offered to sell the American government New Orleans, and all the land France claimed west of the Mississippi River. In exchange for $15 million and the promise of religious tolerance and citizenship for Catholic French and Spanish residents of the land, Jefferson's envoys brought home serious bacon – the title to land for the United States that would include most of present-day Louisiana, all of present-day Arkansas, Missouri, Iowa, and Nebraska, virtually all of South Dakota, much of Minnesota, most of North Dakota, Montana, Wyoming, Oklahoma and Kansas, and a large chunk of Colorado.

About the time of the War of 1812, American settlers started squatting on the strip of Gulf Coast territory that Spain owned, which now is part of Alabama, Mississippi, and eastern Louisiana. Napoleon, still lord of Spain, chose to do nothing about it, because he was still at war all over Europe.

After the War of 1812 (which Andrew Jackson and his militiamen and Jean Lafitte's privateers ended successfully by soundly thrashing the British at New Orleans in early 1815), British agitators armed American Indians in Spanish-held Florida. The tribesmen attacked settlers in Alabama and Georgia. Andrew Jackson and his men invaded Florida in 1818, defeated the American Indians, took Pensacola, and hanged two Britishers who had been selling the natives firearms. This created a row with Britain and Spain; John Quincy Adams turned it to America's advantage. He proposed since the Spanish government couldn't control the British or the American Indians in Florida, Americans would be happy to pay $5 million to take Florida off their hands. The Spanish sold Florida to the United States in 1819. Americans also got formal title to the Spanish Gulf Coast land they had been squatting on. Adams and his Spanish counterpart made some border adjustments between the Louisiana Territory, the Oregon Territory, and Spanish holdings in Texas, the Rocky Mountains, and California. Spain would lose these holdings two years later when the Mexicans revolted successfully.

Deportation and massacre of the remaining American Indians in the Southeast accelerated during Jackson's presidency (1829-1837) and continued into the 1840s.

A gold rush on Cherokee land in Georgia sped up the theft of Cherokee land – which the literate and politically savvy Cherokees held by valid American title – and the exile of the Cherokees. American settlers, backed by president Andrew Jackson and his successor Martin Van Buren, forced the Creek, Choctaw, Chickasaw, and Cherokee people to take the "Trail of Tears" to the "Indian Territory" in present-day Oklahoma.

Some Seminoles also went under force to the Indian Territory. But many of the Seminoles refused to move from Florida. American troops butchered most of them where they lived. Some remained in Florida, retreating deep into the swamps; others belatedly joined the exile.

In the Old Northwest, American settlers and soldiers forced out the Shawnee, the Miami, the Delaware, and smaller tribes. American settlers and soldiers in the 1830s forced tribes in Illinois to move across the Mississippi River into Iowa. They also beat Chief Black Hawk's braves when they tried to defend their homes.

American politicians, by negotiating with the British who held Canada, won a treaty that settled the northern boundary of the country along the 49th Parallel from Minnesota to the Rocky Mountains in 1818. By threat of seizure of land in what is now British Columbia, American president James Polk in 1846 got the British to settle the northern boundary of the country from the Rocky Mountains to the Pacific Ocean along the 49th Parallel. Thus, by these two agreements, the land that forms today's states of Washington, Oregon, and Idaho, portions of Minnesota, North Dakota, Montana, and Wyoming, and a small piece of South Dakota became American property. American negotiators settled Maine's boundary with the British in 1842.

American politicians were ruder to Mexico. Mexicans overthrew Spanish rule in 1821 and took over Spanish-held land from California to Colorado to Texas. The new Mexican government invited Americans to settle in Texas as long as they obeyed Mexican laws. American settlers in Texas revolted in 1835 after the Mexican government outlawed slavery and outlawed further American immigration to Texas. The Americans lost at the Alamo but won at San Jacinto in Texas in 1836. They formed the temporarily independent country of Texas, which was populated largely by Americans from the Southern states.

Polk brought Texas into the United States in 1845, and tried to buy California, and all the land between California and Texas from the Mexicans. Mexican leaders would not sell. The Mexicans also had issues as to what constituted Texas. Americans said the Rio Grande was Texas' southern border, and that Texas also should include the eastern half of present-day New Mexico, a large chunk of Colorado, a piece of Wyoming, a corner of Kansas, and what is now the Oklahoma Panhandle. The Mexicans said the boundary should be the Nueces River, farther north into Texas, and they thought Texas should be much smaller in the west also.

Mexican troops crossed the Rio Grande in early 1846 and attacked American soldiers under the command of General Zachary "Rough and Ready" Taylor. The Mexican War was on. Brave and well-led American soldiers beat the brave but poorly-led Mexican troops. Americans took California. General Taylor led his army into northern Mexico. General Winfield "Fuss and Feathers" Scott led another army into central Mexico and they captured Mexico City in 1847.

Ironically, the best Mexican outfit was the San Patricio brigade – a unit composed of Irish and Irish-American deserters from American units. Some Americans had been looting Mexican churches – Catholic churches, of course – and some of these animals raped Mexican women and girls, and the chain of command did nothing about it. So some of the American soldiers of Irish blood who were disgusted with the anti-Catholic bigotry of many of their comrades deserted and fought for Mexico. The Americans hanged or whipped and face-branded the few "Patricios" ("Patricks") whom they captured.

American politicians harvested the fruits of victory against Mexico, bringing into the United States California, and land that would become Nevada, Utah, most of Arizona and New Mexico, much of Colorado, and some of Wyoming, Kansas, and Oklahoma. Texas' border would be the Rio Grande. Americans paid the Mexican government $15 million for all this land. American officials purchased some more land from Mexico in 1853 for $10 million, which would give the southern boundaries of Arizona and New Mexico their final shape. This piece, known as the Gadsden Purchase, offered the easiest route for a railroad from the South to California, because the Rocky Mountains are relatively low in this area and there is a good pass through the mountains.

Certain Southerners weren't satisfied with this haul. General Taylor became President Taylor in 1849. Despite owning a large plantation and many slaves, Taylor opposed the extension of slavery in the West. He encouraged American settlers in California and New Mexico to apply for statehood, knowing their state constitutions would ban slavery. California's gold miners and gold seekers loathed slavery, not because of any early call to brotherhood with blacks, but because allowing slavery in California meant wealthy slaveholders could put slaves to work in the creeks of California to compete with them in panning for gold. Mexicans and Spaniards in the Golden State also opposed slavery.

Leading Southerners opposed statehood for these areas because there would be more free states than slave states in the Union, which would cost the pro-slavery southerners their deadlock in the Senate. Some threatened rebellion and secession. Taylor said he would crush secessionists and hang captured rebels.

Congressmen tried to bypass Taylor with the so-called Compromise of 1850. Taylor opposed them, but he died in July 1850. His replacement, the nonentity Millard Fillmore, allowed the Compromise of 1850 to become law. It allowed California in as a free state, barred New Mexico, and pushed a meaner Fugitive Slave Act that allowed assorted peckerwoods and other white trash to become federal slave catchers.

Some Americans, fearing the eventual statehood of more free states, talked of gaining Latin American land for slave empires suited for tropical plantation agriculture. (Minnesota and Oregon would become free states in the late 1850s. Pro-slavery Democrats failed in their ploy to bring Kansas into the Union in the late 1850s as a slave state.) The Spanish refused to sell Cuba, so some of these men made attempts to take Cuba by force in the 1840s and 1850s, and they also tried to grab Central America from the natives in the 1850s and in 1860. Spanish and Central American soldiers shot some of the adventurers when they caught them. The South's loss of the Civil War and the outlawing of slavery in America ended further American attempts to grab territory for slavery in the Caribbean islands and Central America.

After the Civil War, Russian officials offered to sell Alaska to the United States. Russia was the only major country in Europe whose leaders favored the Union in the Civil War. They had used the friendship to hide some of their warships in American ports when British naval officers considered attacking them. Russian authorities knew they didn't have the sea power to hold Alaska, so that's why they made the offer.

William Seward, Secretary of State for Andrew Johnson, successor to martyred Abraham Lincoln, convinced Johnson and Congress to make the deal. In 1867, Americans bought Alaska from Russia for $7.2 million.

Critics called Alaska "Seward's Folly" or the "American Icebox." But it was a wise deal for America that paid off many times over, in oil, gold, timber, and fishing. The purchase of Alaska also has paid off in protecting America from Japan and the Soviet Union.

The acquisition of Hawaii was less honorable, but was a good idea. American evangelizers had been coming to Hawaii to do good; they gave the natives Bibles and took their land, so they did well. American businessmen didn't even give the natives Bibles, but in 1893 brought about the overthrow of Hawaiian leader Queen Liliuokulani, a Hawaiian patriot who resented the commercial domination of her island by American sugar and pineapple plantation owners. President William McKinley engineered the annexation of Hawaii in 1898, the year of the Spanish-American War.

Hawaii has served since then as a naval base for American military men to protect America's West Coast. Of course, the money the islands have generated in sugar, pineapples, coffee, and tourism haven't hurt America either.

In the late 1800s, American diplomats tried to buy some Caribbean islands, but failed. In the Spanish-American War, American servicemen did take Cuba, the Philippines, and Puerto Rico from Spain, but later freed Cuba and gave Puerto Ricans American citizenship in 1917. American officials granted the peoples of the Philippines independence after World War Two. (They had earlier paid Spain $20 million for taking the Philippines.)

In 1917, American officials purchased some of the Virgin Islands from Denmark for $25 million. We bought the islands to protect the Carribean Sea approaches to the newly-open Panama Canal. Teddy Roosevelt had obtained the Canal Zone during his first term, and the American-built canal was open for business in 1914. The inept Jimmy Carter signed away the Panama Canal in the late 1970s; the canal turnover actually took place during Bill Clinton's corrupt administration. **(6)**

HOW THE WEST WAS WON, OR LOST

Americans didn't expand their country in a vacuum. Sadly, they crushed people who were already there. As Americans won the West, other people lost it. This section discusses this achievement and human tragedy.

By the end of the Mexican War, the United States government held about three million square miles ... much larger than Europe if you don't count the part of Europe that the Russian czar ruled. Much of the western part of the United States was mountainous, or barren desert, or high plains which were unbearably cold and snow-drifted in the winter. American Indians ruled the Great Plains, making overland trips from the eastern side of the country dangerous.

However, the land was there for the taking, if you were brave enough, or hardy enough, or greedy enough, or crazy enough. Spanish-style ranching was possible. So was Spanish style orchard and vineyard farming, if you and other settlers near you had the endurance to build irrigation ditches. So were mining and logging. So was regular commerce, if you wanted to sell guns, gear, and grub to the miners and would-be cattle barons and would-be timber barons who came west to seek their fortunes. People could farm quietly in the West, as they had done in the East, South, and Midwest, and many would do so. Other people chose to sneak out of town ahead of their debts or the local lawmen back East and start life anew.

The Gold Rush drew thousands of fortune seekers to California in the late 1840s and early 1850s. A large silver strike drew others to Virginia City, near Lake Tahoe in Nevada in the late 1850s. Further discoveries of precious metals and not-so-precious but worthwhile metals like copper, lead, and zinc would draw thousands more westward to work in the mines throughout the West.

American settlers stole the land of many Spaniards and Mexicans living in California. Even though the Treaty of Guadalupe Hidalgo, which ended the Mexican War, guaranteed citizenship and property rights to the people living in the territories Americans took from Mexico, American judges and lawmen found ways to invalidate the land titles of the Spaniards and Mexicans, and then steal their land. They even stole land from Hispanics who helped the American cause in the Mexican War, much like some Americans re-enslaved blacks who fought as Patriots in the American Revolution.

Kansas drew settlers to farm its soil. Kansas also drew big-time trouble. Proslavery settlers (with the connivance of leading Southern Democrats and doughface Democrat presidents Franklin Pierce and James Buchanan, and with the armed help of proslavery white trash from Missouri) attacked antislavery settlers, hoping to overpower them and bring Kansas into the Union as a slave state. This would give slaveholders help in the Senate. Vicious partisan warfare, combining some of the worst elements of the coming Civil War with Wild West banditry, erupted between Southerners and Northerners in the state. Lincoln's Senate race opponent Stephen Douglas and some Northern Democrats joined Republicans in Congress to smash the proslavery Democrats' ploy to make Kansas a slave state.

Eventually the far more numerous freesoilers beat back the slavery boosters, and "Bleeding Kansas" joined the Union as a free state in 1861, the first year of the Civil War. The Civil War brought more bloodshed to Kansas, as units of Southern guerrillas and outlaws operating out of refuges in the counties of western Missouri bordering Kansas raided the new state and killed hundreds of its settlers.

Union general Thomas Ewing and his men eventually forcibly removed most people from four proslavery counties of Missouri after William Quantrill and his Rebel raiders burned Lawrence, Kansas and killed most of the men in town in 1863. A year later, Ewing's brother-in-law General William T. Sherman would do the same thing to the people of Atlanta. How did Kansans feel about the situation? Many Kansas counties now bear the name of Sherman and other Union generals and Northern political figures.

The Civil War caused a real need for gold from California and silver from Nevada. The precious metals helped pay for the Union's war effort. Silver-rich Nevada came in as a free state (and anti-Mormon state) in 1864. Back east, in 1863, mountaineers loyal to the Union seceded their counties from Virginia and entered their counties into the Union as West Virginia.

Abraham Lincoln, besides running the Civil War to a successful conclusion, had the energy to put into place the Homestead Act, the Morrill Act, and the Pacific Railroad act. The Homestead Act, which allowed people to claim title to certain types of government-owned land if they lived on it and farmed it for five straight years, made it possible for many poorer Americans to move west, especially after the Civil War. The Morrill Act started the land grant colleges, which greatly advanced American agriculture and industry. The Pacific Railroad Act helped railroad companies build the cross-country railroads to the Pacific Coast. All of these measures benefited the West in particular and the country in general. They definitely helped open the West to more settlement.

Americans missed a chance to increase the size of the country even more after the Civil War. The British helped the South during the Civil War by building many ships which Rebel navy men used to attack Union commercial and military ships. These ships caused so much damage that some American leaders, after the Civil War, decided to ask for Canada as compensation from the ever-devious British. And if the Brits refused, some Americans argued, maybe America should take Canada by force.

Meanwhile, Civil War veterans of Irish blood plotted to seize Ontario and Quebec to hold them for ransom to free Ireland from British tyranny. Irishmen from both North and South banded together, bought weapons and gear from the War Department for pennies on the dollar, and moved into Ontario. These Irish natives, and Americans of Irish blood, known as "Fenians," beat Canadian militiamen and British regulars in two small battles in 1866.

The Irishmen's "Fenian Raid" into Canada was now a complication to American diplomacy. So Andrew Johnson, who succeeded the martyred Abraham Lincoln as president, had Ulysses Grant and George Meade (the general who won over Lee at Gettysburg) lead troops to seal the Canadian border to keep more Irishmen from joining the Fenians already in Canada. The Fenians, cut off from their American bases, had to return to America.

Eventually the British paid $15.5 million to settle American claims in the early 1870s. The British also gave Canadian settlers more of a say in how Canada was being run ... to hold the loyalty of the locals to the Crown in case Americans decided they wanted Canada in the future.

Andrew Johnson helped the Mexicans instead of trying to seize the rest of Mexico. During the Civil War, France's Napoleon III overthrew Mexico's government and installed a puppet regime under Archduke Maximilian Hapsburg of Austria, the brother of Austrian emperor Franz Josef. This was a violation of the Monroe Doctrine, but Abraham Lincoln was in no position to do anything about it during the Civil War. After the Civil War, Johnson sent general Phil Sheridan and 50,000 troops to Texas to prepare to run the French out.

The move worked. The French left Mexico, and Benito Juárez regained power as Mexico's president. He had Maximilian captured and shot. Maximilian's widow Carlota made it back to Europe but died insane.

After the Civil War, railroad barons opened up the American West for further settlement. Laborers from Ireland and many veterans of the Civil War pushed a railroad west from Omaha through Nebraska and Wyoming and into northern Utah. Meanwhile, laborers including many Chinese blasted through the Sierra Nevada mountain range and built rails east from Sacramento through Nevada and to the linkup with the westbound railroad in Utah in 1869.

Other railroad men built lines which linked Minnesota with Seattle and Tacoma by way of North Dakota, Montana, and Idaho. Others built a line that connected southern California with New Orleans by way of Arizona, New Mexico, and Texas, and still another line that connected southern California with Kansas City by way of Arizona, New Mexico, Colorado, and Kansas. Others built track that linked the three states of the Pacific Coast.

The railroad men usually got title to thousands of square miles of land along their rights of way from the government; they usually also received payments for each mile of track they laid. Some land they sold to settlers, from very cheap to very high, depending on how close to a railroad town the land was. Other land the railroad men sold to speculators and government officials, who charged other settlers exorbitant prices for land they themselves had bought cheaply.

The West, especially California and Nevada, would have developed faster if railroad barons hadn't bled many of their customers dry. Collis Huntington, an owner of the Central Pacific Railroad, (which he and his partners later renamed the Southern Pacific) would make farmers and businessmen show railroad officials their books. Huntington would have his minions charge the farmers and businessmen so much for shipping they had barely enough profit left over to stay in business. Huntington bought politicians and judges to protect his company's piracy. The plundering of Huntington and partners Leland Stanford, Charles Crocker and Mark Hopkins retarded growth of industry and agriculture in the areas the Southern Pacific traveled as long as they controlled the railroad. **(7)**

However, in the long run, the railroads did more good than harm. Expansion of the railroads provided a fast and cheap way to bring settlers west, bring manufactured goods the settlers wanted west, and bring cattle, grain, minerals, and timber the settlers provided back east.

The railroads also made it possible for more farming people from Europe to settle in the Plains states and further west. Germans, Scandinavians, and Slavs could and did form farming communities in Kansas, Nebraska, the Dakotas, and Minnesota. Skilled miners and laborers who were willing to work in the mines found their way west from Europe to the Rocky Mountain states. Loggers from Europe came to anyplace out west where there was logging to do.

People coming west brought about the near-extermination of the American Indian communities. It didn't have to be that way, but that's how it turned out.

American policy toward the American Indians was the natural descendent of British policy toward the American Indians. American policy was to move red people off of land white people wanted to settle.

American soldiers forced the American Indians to move repeatedly. American soldiers and settlers massacred American Indian communities repeatedly. In the Great Plains, where American Indians were the strongest, the soldiers, settlers, commercial hunters, rich men on hunting excursions, and railroad company hunters killed millions of buffaloes. This deprived the American Indians of buffalo meat and hides, which weakened them severely.

Here are a few red-letter years in the genocide of red men and red women:

In the 1850s, settlers in California virtually wiped out the peaceable local American Indians. They sold thousands of surviving children into slavery, and gang-raped and forced into prostitution many of the best-looking young women and older girls. In 1850, when California entered the Union, there were about 100,000 American Indians in the Golden State. By the end of the decade, there were about 30,000. **(8)**

In 1855, government agents tried to force American Indians in Washington onto various reservations. The American Indians rose after settlers and prospectors started stealing their land. After a three-year campaign, U.S. troops beat the American Indians.

In 1862, Santee Sioux Indians, restricted to reservations in Minnesota, suffered a crop failure. The government owed money to the Sioux but the agents had not paid it, Army officers would not give the Sioux food, and white merchants would not give them credit. The Sioux rebelled, swarmed off the reservations, and killed hundreds of whites, including the merchants who intended to starve them. Union Army soldiers eventually beat the braves at Wood Lake. Many Santee fled to the Dakotas, but about 2000 surrendered. The soldiers hanged 40 of the Santee warriors before Abraham Lincoln could put a stop to the hangings.

In 1864, Colorado militiamen under a minister named Reverend J.M. Chivington sneak-attacked 450 Cheyenne and Arapaho men, women, and children who – at the invitation of the U.S. government – were camping at Sand Creek, Colorado. They killed about 300 American Indians, mostly women and children. Indian fighter Kit Carson called Chivington and his men cowards. Their despicable act did bring American Indian retribution on whites in Colorado for several years.

General Sherman had his soldiers blast Captain Jack and his Modoc tribe out of the lava beds of far northern California. The settlers had wanted his tribe's land, and Captain Jack was brazen enough to try two white man's tricks – he killed settlers and he sprung an ambush during a peace negotiation. He killed General Edward Canby in the process, and Sherman said the Modocs deserved "utter extermination." The Modocs surrendered to Sherman's subordinate General Jefferson Davis (ironically he was a Union general in the Civil War by the same name as the leader of the Confederacy) in 1873; he had Captain Jack hanged.

Roughly 2000 Sioux and Cheyenne led by Sitting Bull, Crazy Horse, and Gall killed General George Custer and his entire group of about 250 soldiers in battle at Little Big Horn River in Montana in 1876. This victory over Custer and his cavalry encouraged federal officials to step up their efforts to wipe out American Indians on the northern plains.

Crazy Horse and a band of Sioux surrendered in 1877. Four months later, a soldier bayoneted Crazy Horse to death. After years of guerrilla warfare and living on the lam as fugitives in Canada, Sitting Bull and the few braves under his command surrendered to U.S. Army officers in 1881. Sitting Bull toured with Buffalo Bill Cody's Wild West Show in 1885 (nine years after Little Big Horn), and was a huge draw. In his tribal regalia, the great chief inspired fear and admiration among the palefaces who came to see the shows. Sitting Bull also gave fellow Cody star Annie Oakley her nickname of "Little Sure Shot." She would grow fond of the old warrior. But Sitting Bull was disgusted by the neglect of the poor he saw in the cities back East. He said American Indians would never treat their own that way. Sitting Bull gave away most of his earnings to poor people and returned to his tribe. U.S. government officials would never allow him to tour with Buffalo Bill in America again.

Government agents in 1877 ordered the Nez Percé tribe out of their land in the area where Oregon, Washington, and Idaho meet. As the Nez Percé prepared to leave, white settlers stole hundreds of their horses. The enraged Nez Percé killed about 20 settlers, which gave the U.S. Army the excuse to attack them. Chief Joseph decided to take the Nez Percé into Canada to escape. The tribe fought several battles with the soldiers, and they almost made it into Canada, but soldiers finally cut off their escape route in northern Montana just miles from the Canadian border. Chief Joseph had to surrender.

The "last stand" of the Sioux tribe came in 1890. Wovoka, a Paiute tribesman, preached to American Indians that they should go back to their old ways and reject the white man's way of life. Wovoka said this would help bring the dead American Indians back to life and make the white men go away. Many American Indians believed Wovoka's message, which was a mixture of Christian and American Indian beliefs. Whites called Wovoka's religious ceremony the "Ghost Dance."

The revival made the soldiers and settlers in the Great Plains nervous. American authorities shot and killed Sitting Bull while arresting him in mid-December 1890. Two weeks later, at the end of December 1890, American cavalrymen surrounded and arrested a band of several hundred Sioux, and forced them to stop at

Wounded Knee Creek, South Dakota. The Sioux camped overnight, and then the soldiers disarmed them the next morning. The troops then started firing on the Sioux, who defended themselves with their bare hands and any weapons they could grab. When the smoke cleared, 29 soldiers and more than 200 Sioux men, women, and children lay dead, including their chief Big Foot.

In Arizona, settlers took thousands of Apaches as slaves .... and forced the prettiest women and older girls into prostitution. Army officers ambushed Apache leaders who came to meet with them. It was only natural that Cochise and other Apache chiefs would rise against this sort of treatment. In 1871, whites in Tucson showed their good will by massacring about 100 Apaches who had turned themselves in at a nearby Army fort; this made the Apaches even more determined to hold out. General George Crook, an Indian fighter who actually dealt honestly with American Indians, finally convinced Cochise and most of the Apaches to go to reservations. Cochise died of natural causes in 1874.

Crook worked to keep the settlers and government swindlers from taking advantage of the Apaches. Crook's superiors removed him from his post after Apache leader Geronimo failed to surrender to him, and replaced him with Indian fighter (and Indian hater) General Nelson Miles. In 1886, Apache scouts whom Crook recruited talked Geronimo into quitting the warfare and going to a reservation, but Miles had Geronimo and his men (and the Apache scouts too) imprisoned in Florida. General Crook died in 1890 while trying to get the Apaches released, or at least resettled as free men in the Indian Territory.

It might have depressed the Apaches to go even to the Indian Territory. For in 1889, American politicians showed how low they could go when they allowed American settlers to steal even the Indian Territory from the American Indians who had to live there because generations of American politicians had decided to make them go there. By 1907, the Indian Territory would become the state of Oklahoma. **(9)**

Those who romanticize the American Indians do not mention the American Indians were often inhumane to each other before the white man's coming. Ritual torture and cannibalism were part of many tribes' way of life. The tortures they practiced on each other would nauseate all but the most psychopathic among you. The Aztecs were bloodthirsty people who preyed upon weaker Indian tribes. They publicly butchered and ate many thousands of other Indians. Members of these victimized tribes were willing to help Cortes against the Aztec oppressors. But the admitted savagery of American Indian tribes toward each other does not excuse the behavior of the whites — usually British and later American settlers and officials -- who as Christians were presumably not supposed to cheat, steal from, murder, or rape the American Indians.

In 1600, there were roughly two million to perhaps five million American Indians in what is now the Lower 48 states of America. There were maybe 100,000 to 200,000 American Indians and Eskimos in what is now Canada and Alaska. Some claim there were many times this number of natives; if that was true the English settlers and their descendants the Americans would have had much more trouble beating them. Also, there would have been more tangible evidence of the presence of so many natives, like more settlements, burial grounds, or other places showing human habitation or use. There would also be many more Americans who could legitimately claim American Indian blood.

Even with three centuries to increase their numbers, the native peoples of what is now America did not do so. That's because the diseases and the weapons of the whites killed them much faster than they could reproduce. By 1900, there were only about 250,000 native American Indians and Eskimos. Most of these lived in the American Southwest, where the first white settlers were Spanish. Some American Indians died at the hands of rival tribesmen, but most died due to the attacks and the diseases of the European colonists and their descendants. Even counting the intermarriage of American Indian and white people through these centuries (which usually involved people of Spanish or French blood), the drop in the numbers of American Indians was spine-chilling.

By comparison, Mexico's population was perhaps 9 to 11 million American Indians before Cortes landed in the early 1500s. The American Indian population nosedived dramatically, then started to recover by 1900. Of the 13 million or so people in Mexico that year, about a million were of European ancestry, and of the other 12 million, half were pure-blood American Indians, and half were mestizos.

The trends of American Indian and Eskimo numbers in British-controlled Canada paralleled those in the United States. There was a drastic drop in the numbers of these peoples in the 1800s, and then a recovery in numbers of natives by the 1960s. The United States' American Indian and Eskimo (Inuit) population in 1960 was 600,000 to 700,000.

Figures for the rest of Latin America are sketchier. But most of the people of Bolivia are American Indians, and in Paraguay, Peru, Ecuador, and Colombia, American Indians and mestizos far outnumber people of European origin. In Chile and Venezuela, Indians and mestizos are large minorities. In Argentina and Uruguay, whites predominate to a larger extent than whites do in the United States, and in Brazil, whites barely outnumber blacks and mulattoes. The whites of these lands killed off or intermarried with the relatively few American Indians who they found when they colonized these lands. Most of the people of the countries of Central America are American Indians and mestizos. **(10)**

This book doesn't have room to list all the crimes American government officials, military leaders, settlers, and businessmen committed against the American Indians. Nor does it have enough space to identify each treaty violation the whites committed against the American Indians from the time of the Cavaliers and the Pilgrims until the massacre of the Sioux at Wounded Knee in 1890, the year after the Sooners and others stole the Indian Territory itself from the American Indians. We mention some of the more important events of the struggle between the red man and the white man to show what it cost in lives and suffering to make the country open for American-style settlement.

Americans would also find other types of native people to dispossess in the 1800s. In 1867, America bought Alaska from Russia for $7.2 million and inherited a few thousand Eskimos and American Indians.

The first generations of Russian explorers and Siberian pioneers (from the 1740s through the 1790s) killed most of the natives on the Aleutian Islands. In 1799, one Russian entrepreneur won the fur monopoly, and he and his key people obeyed the Russian government's command to treat the natives better. Orthodox missionary priests came from Russia to work among the Eskimos and the American Indians, and won many converts to their faith. The Russian priests and company authorities treated the Eskimos and American Indians firmly but paternally, somewhat like the way the Spanish treated the American Indians in the lands they occupied. Alaska is the only state where the Orthodox Christian faith is among the leading faiths of the residents. **(11)**

When the Russians left, the Eskimos and American Indians had little protection. Owners of a monopoly granted by the U.S. government for seal hunting let their hunters decimate the seal herds, leaving Eskimos little to hunt. They likewise nearly eliminated the walrus and caribou herds. Other Americans likewise cheated the Eskimos and weakened them with bad whisky, infected prostitutes, and other diseases such as tuberculosis. Some Eskimo men took to summer-long drunks instead of hunting to stock up for the winter; their families starved. Some Eskimo women took to prostitution. The Eskimo population dropped dramatically again.

Protestant minister Sheldon Jackson tried a novel approach for Americans – he tried to keep Christ in Christianity in his dealings with the Eskimos. He set up schools for the Eskimos in their settlements, sought medical and legal help for them, and even had them taught how to herd and raise reindeer so they could make a living to replace their old trade of hunting.

A gold rush in the 1890s in the Nome area on Alaska's west coast made "America's Icebox" very profitable all of a sudden. Other gold strikes along the Yukon River in Alaska and in the Klondike district, in Canada's nearby Yukon Territory, brought more gold rushers to the Far North and made the Alaska Panhandle boundary an issue between Britain and America. Teddy Roosevelt used a little gunboat diplomacy to back off the British (who still basically ran Canada) and retain the Panhandle for America.

Meanwhile, Manifest Destiny was hitting the Hawaiian Islands with tidal wave force. American whaling crews had been sailing to Hawaii for almost a century, looking for provisions and looking for female companionship. American missionaries followed, bringing Bibles, a professed disgust over the sexual morals of the locals and the sailors, and a yen for profitable government office with the Hawaiians' king. Behind them came the sharpies, who would complete the conquest of the Hawaiians. Everyone brought diseases, venereal or otherwise, and decimated the native Hawaiians. The population of the natives dropped from about 300,000 in the late 1700s to about 70,000 in the 1850s. **(12)**

The sharpies conned the Hawaiian king into allowing foreigners to own land. The sharpies became sugar and pineapple plantation owners, and they imported Chinese and Japanese laborers to work their estates. Soon the Hawaiians were minorities in their own islands. The sugar barons forced the king and his legislature to give up power. When he died in 1891, his sister Liliuokulani ruled as queen. She tried to regain the monarchy's power and reduce the influence of the sugar and pineapple barons.

In 1893, at the request of greedy American sugar barons, American official John Stevens ordered American Marines on an American warship in Hawaiian waters to take part in a coup to overthrow Queen Liliuokulani. Sanford Dole, the son of a missionary, and a relative to pineapple baron James Dole, managed the coup that booted Queen Liliuokulani off of her throne. The American businessmen petitioned for the United States to annex Hawaii. Being part of America would give the sugar barons tariff-free benefits in the American sugar market. President Grover Cleveland sent an emissary to Hawaii to investigate, and learned most Hawaiians wanted Queen Liliuokulani to continue ruling them. He refused to annex Hawaii, but did nothing to throw the piratical Americans out of power. President William McKinley engineered the annexation of Hawaii in 1898, the year of the Spanish-American War.

Not all white people in Hawaii coveted the Hawaiians' land. Belgian priest Joseph De Veuster, aka Father Damien, ran a leper colony on Molokai. Father Damien, like Rev. Sheldon Jackson in Alaska, tried to serve instead of lording it over those he came to serve.

When Father Damien died of leprosy himself in 1889, a self-satisfied Protestant minister in Honolulu named Hyde libeled him in a letter to another minister, claiming Father Damien got the disease from having sex with the lady lepers. The great author Robert Louis Stevenson lambasted Hyde in public because Father Damien had set an example of Christian charity that was all too rare. Stevenson also predicted Hyde would only be remembered for suffering a written scourging at his (Stevenson's) hands. He was right.

What was the result of the growth of America at the expense of the American Indians, the Spanish, the Mexicans, the Eskimos, and the Hawaiians?

In 1840, Europe (including Russia west of the Urals) had about 250 million people on roughly 3.8 million square miles of land. The United States (which included America east of the Mississippi River, Louisiana, Arkansas, and Missouri – the three states west of the Mississippi River in 1840, and the rest of the Louisiana Purchase) had 17 million blacks and whites on 1.8 million square miles of land.

In 1900, Europe (including Russia west of the Urals) had about 425 million people on the same 3.8 million square miles of land. The 45 American states (and the territories of Oklahoma, Arizona, and New Mexico, which would soon become states) had 76 million people (including American Indians) on about 3 million square miles of land. **(13)**

The bottom line? America had plenty of land for Europe's huddled masses to come to. And now you have a thumbnail sketch of how we got it.

THE RELICS OF BARBARISM

The emptiness of the American West had drawn other members of Protestant America – the Mormons – westward in the 1840s. The Mormons were industrious, thrifty, and well-organized, on paper the perfect WASPs. However, their acquisitiveness and their perceived oddball beliefs led many Americans to loathe them.

Joseph Smith started the Mormon religion in upstate New York in 1830. He claimed he dug golden tablets from the ground, deciphered them, and determined they said one of the lost tribes of Israel migrated to America. Some people believed him and followed him. Smith led his followers to Missouri, where they alienated the locals by discriminating against non-Mormons. They also befriended free blacks in this slave state, but held slaves themselves. The locals ran the Mormons out of Missouri; they eventually started a settlement in Nauvoo, Illinois.

Smith decided to exclude blacks from the Mormon hierarchy, possibly to curry favor with the locals. However, he openly started to preach in favor of polygamy. This truly angered other Christians against the Mormons. Non-Mormons considered polygamy, along with slavery, one of the "relics of barbarism."

Smith and other elders had been practicing polygamy secretly before he made his desires, errr, doctrine public. Dr. John Bennett allegedly helped cover up the sexual use of many of the publicly single females in Nauvoo who were privately in polygamous setups with Smith and other Mormon elders by performing abortions on them. Smith ran out Bennett after they quarreled over who would get possession of a 19-year-old cutie named Nancy Rigdon.

In 1844, Smith tried to destroy the printing press of an opponent who exposed the sect's polygamy. Lawmen arrested Smith and his brother and held them in a nearby jail. Vigilantes, angered at the grasping ways of the Mormons in mammon and mates, broke into the jail and killed them.

After the death of Joseph Smith, the leaders of this now-openly polygamous sect sought to build a state away from other Americans, who hated them. Most Mormons, under the lead of Brigham Young, decided to head west. Using U.S. Army maps, good scouting, and solid planning, they moved to present-day Utah in the late 1840s. Brigham Young started the settlement in the Salt Lake area in the summer of 1847. This took place during the Mexican War; Utah went from nominal Mexican control to nominal American control and definite Mormon control.

Other Mormons in a rival sect led by James Strang (which by now included reputed abortionist John Bennett) didn't go west but instead headed north. They first settled in Wisconsin, but then took over Beaver Island – an aptly named place for the practice of polygamy – in Lake Michigan in 1848. When they became a majority, the Mormons took control of local government and looted the county treasury for "tithes", tried to beat (literally) tithes out of the Irish-American fishermen and their families who were already living on the island, and eventually forbade non-Mormons from fishing in the waters around the island. They ran the non-Mormons off of the island in a couple of years, and tried to spread their tentacles to the mainland of Michigan.

Strang had himself crowned "king" of Beaver Island. The Mormons under his leadership committed the federal crimes of timber theft, mail interference, and counterfeiting to supplement their earlier state crimes of land theft, fishing rights theft, assault and battery, and tax money theft (not to mention polygamy), but federal prosecutors as inept as some of those today could not win any convictions on the federal charges they brought against the Strangites.

When the government fails to protect the people, the people have to protect themselves. And in the 1850s, they weren't afraid to do so. So the people who Strang and his followers had abused planned to evict them from Beaver Island in 1856. Their plans were aided by a fatal row over females among some of the Strangite menfolk just before the non-Mormons attacked.

One of the disgruntled Strangites was a man who couldn't get enough action even in a cult that allowed polygamy. So he committed old-fashioned adultery and Strang ordered him whipped for his sin. Another had married a girl who Strang evidently got the hots for. (There were also insinuations this girl had a crush on one of Strang's "plural wives.") The young husband feared losing his pretty young wife and being castrated at Strang's orders. (Mormon elders under Joseph Smith and Brigham Young who wanted pretty young wives from time to time resorted to ordering their followers to castrate young men who would not give up their cute sweethearts.) So the vengeful adulterer and the man afraid of losing his wife and his manhood shot and beat Strang and left him for dead.

Within days, anti-Catholic journalists of the day noted, "a mob" of "drunken vigilantes" from Mackinac Island (code words for the Irish-American fishermen, some of them distant relatives of the author) drove the Mormons off of Beaver Island. Strang died of his wounds in Wisconsin shortly after the Irish-Americans repossessed the island and the fisheries he and his followers had stolen from them. His five wives, four of whom were pregnant at the time of his demise, eventually hooked up with other men, some of whom were non-Mormons.

Meanwhile, Mormons in Utah were safe from federal justice and other Americans for awhile, because there were very few Americans settled around them for awhile. This didn't mean Americans respected them. Many Americans viewed the Mormons in Utah as freaks of nature. Mormon leader Brigham Young, virtually a dictator over the lives of his flock, had 27 or 28 "wives" but who's counting? Non-Mormons nicknamed him "Bring 'em in Young" for his lechery. The one "wife" who sued Young for divorce wrote an exposé about him titled "Wife No. 19." Young won the suit because the U.S. government didn't recognize the polygamous "marriage." Federal authorities essentially considered her and Young's other "wives" to be concubines and Young to be a whoremonger.

Many other members of the Mormon hierarchy also had "plural wives". Most Mormons had only one wife, but the wealthy Mormons took several. This meant there would be a very high proportion of unmarried young men in Utah unless the church leaders could get females from outside Utah. Church agents even actively "hunted" female game in Britain and Scandinavia to convince them to embrace the Latter Day lifestyle.

The Mormons did make the desert bloom by their hard work, and they made good money selling supplies at high prices to the settlers heading to California. No one has ever denied their energy or their discipline. However, they did harass the non-Mormons heading west through Utah, which made them criminals.

The most brutal incident took place in 1857, when Mormons in southern Utah – probably with the connivance of Brigham Young himself – butchered the men, women, and older children of a wagon train headed to California. They also looted the pilgrims of all their possessions and money. Young's adopted son John Lee – who had close to a score of "plural wives" himself – commanded the Mormon militiamen who committed the mass murders. Two teenage sisters begged for mercy as about 120 of their fellow wagon train members lay dead; the Mormons raped and murdered them. They escaped punishment for the mass murders (called the Mountain Meadows Massacre) for a number of years by blaming the atrocity on Ute Indians.

The Mormons kidnaped and raised the 17 surviving small children, who were all seven years old or younger, thinking they would be too young to remember the shootings and dismemberments of their parents and older siblings. In 1859, a government agent, two noted frontiersmen, and U.S. Army troops took the 17 surviving children from their Mormon kidnapers and returned them to relatives in Arkansas. One younger child would later testify he saw a Mormon woman wearing the dress of his mother, after another Mormon had stripped her hatcheted corpse of the garment. Other children would recount the horror of watching the Mormons butcher their parents and older brothers and sisters.

The Mormons confronted and threatened federal troops and law enforcement officials many times from the 1850s through the 1880s. The Mormons tried to colonize Southern California, Nevada, Idaho, Wyoming, Arizona, and Colorado. Brigham Young advocated slavery and at the same time said it wouldn't be profitable in Utah. The Mormons stayed neutral during the Civil War. Young used his militia to murder Mormon separatists during the Civil War.

The Mormons escaped justice during the Civil War because Abraham Lincoln had bigger problems to deal with than a group of deviants who most Americans of that era considered were hiding behind a religion with no more perceived credibility than what Scientology has today. But the Mormons in effect had seceded from the Union and were just as quick to interfere with or threaten federal officers as the Southerners were. Besides, they committed other crimes against the social order besides polygamy .... the worst were the murders of non-Mormons and their own dissidents and their own womenfolk who got too friendly with non-Mormons. Justice demanded a penalty for the Mormons similar to what the Union Army had inflicted on the people of the Confederacy.

After the Civil War, Generals Sherman and Sheridan wanted to crush the Mormons like they had done to the Southerners, because of the Mormons' defiance of laws, their cheating of non-Mormons passing through Utah, and the murders they committed. Mormons shot, stabbed, or beat to death some non-Mormon men who they had legal difficulties with, or who were consorting with Mormon women. Also, Mormons had beheaded some Mormon women, apparently for the "crime" of getting too friendly with American soldiers stationed in Utah. (Soldiers testified to finding two of these women's severed heads.) It made little sense to bring these crypto-jihadists and "honor killers" before a jury of their Mormon peers because Mormon jurymen essentially refused to convict their own when they victimized non-Mormons or Mormons who strayed.

General Sherman sent Young a telegram threatening to allow his soldiers to avenge non-Mormon victims, but received no orders to make good on that threat. General Sheridan set up a base near Provo, Utah, but received no orders to proceed against the Mormons. Neither Andrew Johnson, nor Ulysses Grant, who succeeded Johnson as president, would unleash Sherman and Sheridan on the Mormons. However, neither president would allow Utah to become a state because of polygamy and because of Brigham Young's cultlike control of his followers.

Federal authorities indicted Young and other Mormon leaders on polygamy charges in 1871, but the Supreme Court voided all verdicts against Mormons decided by juries with no Mormon members. Mormons vastly outnumbered non-Mormons in Utah, so the justices ruled a jury in Utah without Mormons would be a violation of the right to jury in front of peers. So the Feds dropped the case against Young and his underlings in 1872, because they knew no Mormon would vote to convict them.

The Supreme Court has always had its share of knucklehead political lawyers. The Dred Scott, Plessy v. Ferguson, and Roe v. Wade decisions are just some of their best-known idiotic rulings. Since the Mormons were essentially an organized group of outlaws who could justify committing violent crimes and crimes of dishonesty against those not of their own kind, and who also advocated a degenerate lifestyle (polygamy) that violated the law of the land, none of them should have been seated on a jury trying people for violating a law they agreed should be violated.

It would be like trying a planter after the Civil War for resuming the practice of slavery; his wealthy Southern peers would not vote to convict him either. It would be like trying a Mob boss before a jury of other organized criminals; they wouldn't convict one of their own. It would be like trying a Saudi national for "honor killing" his daughter in front of a jury of Arabs who believe in that damnable practice; they would acquit him in a heartbeat.

Despite the Supreme Court ruling, some federal officials kept up the pressure on Young and the Mormons. Young essentially gave up his boy John Lee to appease those who were calling for his death for leading the Mountain Meadows Massacre two decades earlier. Authorities shot Lee to death at the scene of his great crime in 1877 after he was convicted. Brigham Young died later in 1877.

Federal lawmakers in 1882 finally passed an anti-polygamy law – the Edmunds Act – that the Supreme Court couldn't overturn. Federal marshals descended upon Utah, located polygamous families, and had the "husbands" prosecuted and sent to prison. The Mormons tried to shield these families, but their willingness to protect their polygamous brethren – who were usually the richest Mormons – weakened as the Feds applied pressure to whole communities. Why should working stiff Mormons who got by honorably with one wife cover for richer elders who kept multiple Mormon mamas?

Eventually Mormon leaders had the "revelation" that polygamy was not essential to their religion. After making the Mormons wait a couple of years to ensure the leaders wouldn't backslide into polygamy again, American officials allowed Utah into the Union in 1896. Mormons – who certainly deserve credit for much hard work in settling Utah in the American style – have dominated this state ever since.**(14)**

History repeated itself in a macabre way in 2001. Mormon officials, led by Brigham Young's adopted son, perpetrated the Mountain Meadows Massacre on September 11, 1857. An exact gross of years to the day later, jihadists perpetrated the 9/11 murders. Unlike Brigham Young, the al-Qaeda vermin cheerfully claimed responsibility for the murders their scum committed. Young professed astonishment that his many sermons and directives and other verbal and written orders preaching "blood atonement" and violence against non-Mormons were acted upon by scum under his command like his adopted son. Mormon apologists for Young today admit he ordered his people not to sell food to non-Mormon travelers like the massacre victims that year, and they admit Mormons committed the murders, instead of blaming it on "Injuns."

The reason we are discussing the problems the Mormons posed to the rest of America in the 1800s in a book about immigration is not to make fun of the Mormons today. The reason is to inform the American people of their right to restrict or deport those who import anti-American practices into the country and define these evil acts as part of their religion in order to practice them.

The Mormons learned their lesson. Since the 1890s, when their leaders sued for peace with America and agreed to live under American laws, many Mormons have served this country in war and in peace with honor like those of the Catholic, Orthodox Christian, Jewish, and other Protestant faiths.

Our lawyers and judges seem to work on precedent more than they seem to work on common sense, so at least We The People have a great precedent to present (the treatment of the Mormons) in prosecuting the criminals among us who act according to the dictates of their twisted consciences.

No individual or group has the right to practice crimes like polygamy, honor killings, clitorectomies on little girls, slavery, or jihadist murders of non-Moslems and claim these execrable practices are Moslem practices protected by the freedom of religion clause of the U.S. Constitution. Nor do Hindus have the right to impose a caste system, sacrifice screaming children to false goddesses, or commit dowry murders just because they can get away with it in India. Our public officials understood this in the 1800s and acted accordingly. We need to make the current crop of lowlifes in high places act in similar fashion.

THE ROLL CALL OF IMMIGRANTS BY DECADE

When America's welcome mat was out in the 1800s and early 1900s, who wiped their feet on it?

There are not many people of French blood in the United States. But when the country was young, French people were many of the first immigrants in the early 1800s.

America's first alliance was with France. The French had helped the Patriots in the American Revolution. French thinkers, writers, and speakers admired America's form of government. America remained friendly toward France during the regimes of Louis XVI, the Revolutionary government, the Directorate, and Napoleon without getting involved in the human tragedies of the Reign of Terror and the Napoleonic Wars. America had an undeclared war with France over ship seizures in the late 1790s, but there was more good will by and large between America and France than between America and Britain.

In the 1810s, some French emigrants came after the fall of Napoleon. (Napoleon's own brother Joseph was in this number and settled down for awhile in New Jersey.) They followed many Frenchmen and Frenchwomen seeking to keep their necks from underneath the blade of the guillotine during the French Revolution in the 1790s. The Dupont family came to America around 1800, started making gunpowder in Delaware, and their descendants colonized the tiny state financially.

The French had been in America for a long time. French priests and trappers had explored the Great Lakes and the Mississippi and Ohio Valleys, and a few French settlers lived in the Midwest along these waterways. French colonists and French exiles from Acadia (which the British renamed Nova Scotia – New Scotland – after they deported the French) had settled in New Orleans and surrounding areas in the Deep South. Paul Revere and George Washington had French Huguenot (Protestant) ancestry.

The French, mostly a combination of Catholic and agnostic people, had sided with the Americans against the British in the American Revolution. The French and their black Haitian subjects had fought for America in the American Revolution. Other French people who lived in Louisiana had fought with Andrew Jackson against the British at New Orleans at the end of the War of 1812.

Roughly five million people came to America between 1820 and the start of the Civil War in this, the last era where sail-powered wooden ships hauled the vast majority of passengers and freight.

From 1820 through 1830, roughly 100,000 people came from Europe. Of these, 54,000 came from Ireland, 27,000 came from Britain (including Scotland and Wales), 9000 came from France, and 8000 came from the various German states.

From 1831 through 1840, roughly 500,000 Europeans came to America. Of these, 207,000 came from Ireland, 152,000 came from the various German states, 76,000 came from Britain (including Scotland and Wales), and 46,000 came from France. Another 14,000 came from Canada, 7,000 came from Mexico, and 12,000 came from the West Indies.

From 1841 through 1850, roughly 1,600,000 Europeans came to America. Of these, 781,000 came from Ireland, 435,000 came from the various German states, 267,000 came from Britain (including Scotland and Wales), and 77,000 came from France. Another 42,000 came from Canada, 3,000 came from Mexico, and 14,000 came from the West Indies. This was the decade of the Great Hunger aka the Potato Famine in Ireland, and the decade of the Revolution of 1848, and crop failures in France and in the German states. This was also the decade of the Mexican War and the Gold Rush in California. During this decade Texas joined the Union and Americans took what is today California, Nevada, Utah, most of Arizona and New Mexico, much of Colorado, and parts of Wyoming, Kansas, and Oklahoma from the Mexicans. This land they conquered, along with Texas, contained perhaps 100,000 Mexicans and Spaniards and even more American Indians, none of whom were counted as immigrants. Under the treaty American officials signed with the Mexican government, the Mexican citizens in these lands became American citizens.

From 1851 through 1860, roughly 2,500,000 Europeans came to America. Of these, 952,000 came from the various German states, 914,000 came from Ireland, 424,000 came from Britain (including Scotland and Wales), and 76,000 came from France. Also 25,000 came from Switzerland and 21,000 came from Norway (which was part of Sweden until 1905). Another 59,000 came from Canada, 3,000 came from Mexico (during the decade the U.S. bought land from Mexico – the Gadsden Purchase -- containing a few thousand Mexicans and American Indians not counted as immigrants), and 11,000 came from the West Indies. About 41,000 Chinese came to America, almost all in the wake of the Gold Rush and other developments on the West Coast. The Irish and Germans continued to come in the wake of famine and turmoil in their homelands.

Immigration by Decade, 1820-1930

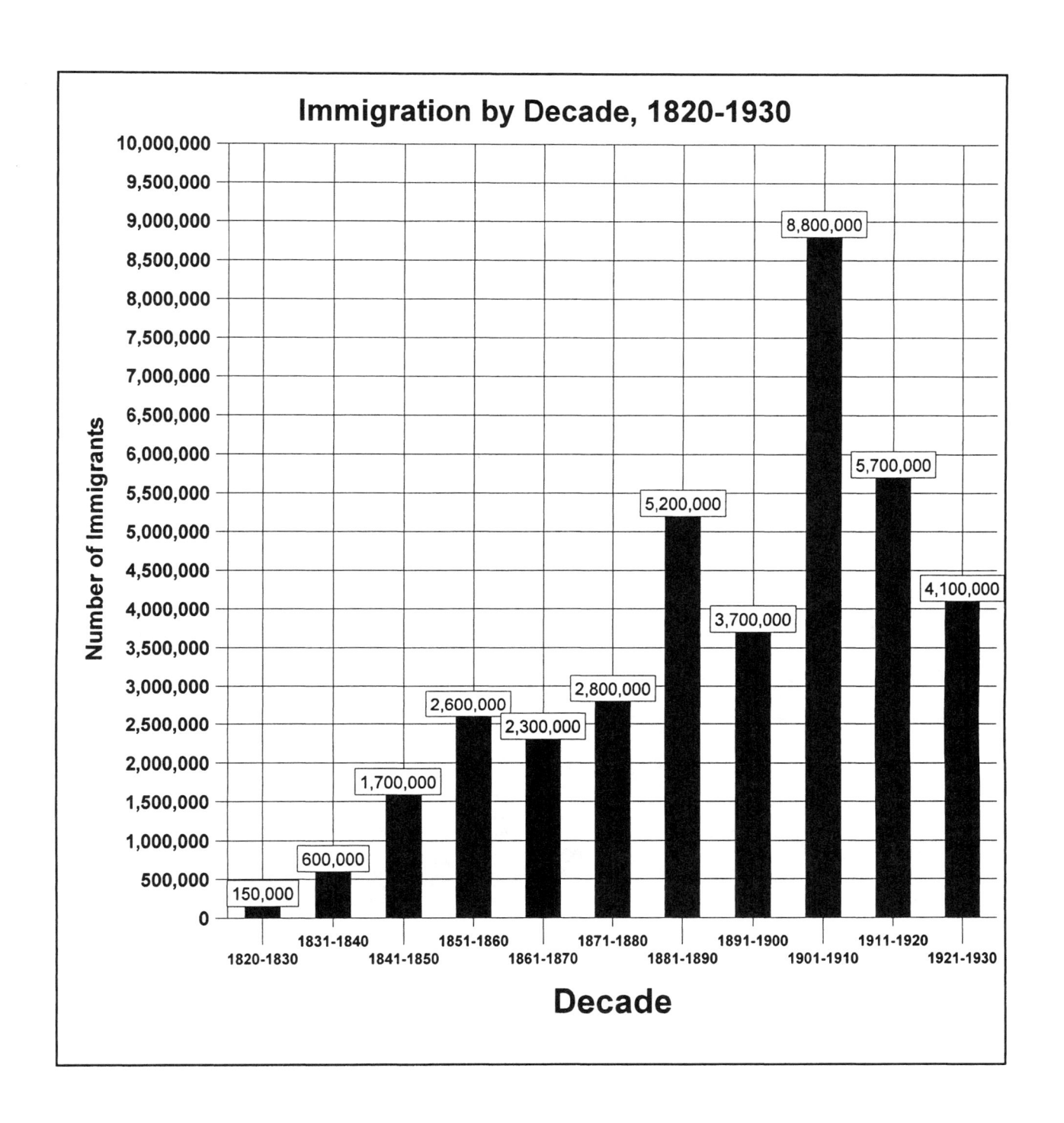

Decade	Number of Immigrants
1820-1830	150,000
1831-1840	600,000
1841-1850	1,700,000
1851-1860	2,600,000
1861-1870	2,300,000
1871-1880	2,800,000
1881-1890	5,200,000
1891-1900	3,700,000
1901-1910	8,800,000
1911-1920	5,700,000
1921-1930	4,100,000

Note: Totals include people counted coming from non-European countries as well as European immigrants.

ELLIS ISLAND SCRAPBOOK

Except for those few who were able to walk or ride from Mexico or Canada, these people sailed to America on sail-powered wooden ships under Spartan conditions. Many others didn't make it because their ships sank, or they died of hunger or disease at sea.

Steam-powered ocean-going vessels were in service before the Civil War, but their use increased dramatically during the 1860s and 1870s. The earliest steamers used paddlewheels to drive them. Then steam-driven propellers replaced the paddlewheels. Finally, steel hulled ships replaced the wooden steamships.

More than 10 million people came to America between 1861 and 1890 ... the last three decades of the pre-Ellis Island era. This was more than double the flow of immigrants of the previous 40 years.

From 1861 through 1870, the decade of the Civil War, roughly 2,100,000 Europeans came to America. Of these, 787,000 came from the various German states, 436,000 came from Ireland, and 607,000 came from Britain (including Scotland and Wales). Also 36,000 came from France, and 23,000 came from Switzerland.

During the 1860s, the first large numbers of people started coming from Scandinavia. From 1861 through 1870, about 72,000 came from Norway, 38,000 came from Sweden, and 17,000 came from Denmark. Another 154,000 came from and through Canada (largely French Canadians), 2,000 came from Mexico, and 9,000 came from the West Indies. About 64,000 Chinese came to America; many would help build the first transcontinental railroad.

From 1871 through 1880, roughly 2,300,000 Europeans came to America. Of these, 718,000 came from the now-unified Germany, 437,000 came from Ireland, and 548,000 came from Britain (including Scotland and Wales). Also 72,000 came from France, 17,000 came from the Netherlands, 7,000 came from Belgium, and 28,000 came from Switzerland. Also 95,000 came from Norway, 116,000 came from Sweden, and 31,000 came from Denmark.

During the 1870s, the first large numbers of people started coming from southern and eastern Europe. From 1871 through 1880, about 56,000 came from the newly-unified Italy, 14,000 came from Portugal, 39,000 came from the Russian Empire (many of these were Poles and Jews, and some were Ukrainians, Finns, Lithuanians, Latvians, and Estonians), 73,000 came from Austria-Hungary (which included Czechs, Slovaks, Ruthenians, Slovenes, Croatians, and some Poles, Ukrainians, Serbs, and Romanians). Also 13,000 others came from Poland who were not counted as subjects of Germany, Russia, or Austria-Hungary.

From 1871 through 1880, another 384,000 came from and through Canada (largely French Canadians), 5,000 came from Mexico, and 14,000 came from the West Indies. About 123,000 Chinese came to America, and another 10,000 came from Australia and New Zealand.

From 1881 through 1890, roughly 4,700,000 Europeans came to America, double the number who came the previous decade.

Why the increase? Many shipping companies put large numbers of steel-hulled vessels into commission during this decade. (Some had done so already in the 1870s.) These newer ships could hold more people and go faster. This rise in shipping capacity made it easier and cheaper to transport people to America. The immigrants didn't need as much food or water per voyage because the ships were faster, and because they could hold more people, the steel ships cut the cost per passenger of carrying people from Europe to America.

Of the Europeans came to America, 1,453,000 came from Germany, 655,000 came from Ireland, and 807,000 came from Britain (including Scotland and Wales). Also 50,000 came from France, 54,000 came from the Netherlands, 20,000 came from Belgium, and 82,000 came from Switzerland. Also 177,000 came from Norway, 392,000 came from Sweden, and 88,000 came from Denmark.

From 1881 through 1890, about 307,000 came from Italy, 17,000 came from Portugal, 213,000 came from the Russian Empire (many of these were Poles and Jews, and some were Ukrainians, Finns, Lithuanians, Latvians, and Estonians), and 354,000 came from Austria-Hungary (which included Czechs, Slovaks, Ruthenians, Slovenes, Croatians, and some Poles, Ukrainians, Serbs, and Romanians). Also 52,000 others came from Poland who were not counted as subjects of Germany, Russia, or Austria-Hungary.

From 1881 through 1890, another 393,000 came from and through Canada (many French Canadians, but also many Europeans who British steamship companies routed through Canada to avoid American taxes and immigration laws), 2,000 came from Mexico, and 29,000 came from the West Indies. About 62,000 Chinese came to America, as the immigration laws cutting down on Chinese immigration began to take effect. Another 7,000 came from Australia and New Zealand.

From 1891 through 1920 – the busiest years of the "Ellis Island era" – more than 18 million people came to America. This was close to double the flow of immigrants of the previous 30 years.

The 1890s saw the opening of Ellis Island and a number of immigration laws aimed at regulating the flow of people to America. The flood of people through Canada and by rail to the United States due to crooked

British shipping and immigrant screening practices slowed to a trickle due to these laws. Immigration fell to 70% of what it was during the previous decade. However, bigots in America grew angrier as the people from southern and eastern Europe kept coming in even larger numbers, while Anglo-Saxon, Teutonic, and Nordic immigration fell off dramatically.

From 1891 through 1900, roughly 3,600,000 Europeans came to America, more than a million fewer than the previous decade. Part of this was due to the hard times in America in the 1890s; the country's people suffered the worst depression the country had had in its history.

Another reason was the improving standard of living in Germany, Britain, Ireland, the Low Countries, Scandinavia, Switzerland, and France, which up to this point had been the European countries most likely to have immigrants coming to America. In Germany especially, the development of industry, and the German government's policy supporting industry led to many more jobs for Germans and less pressure on them to leave. Nearly a million fewer Germans came to America in the 1890s than had come in the 1880s. The other countries named above all sent many fewer immigrants to America in the 1890s than they had done in the 1880s. These drops more than canceled out a doubling of immigration from Russia and the countries of Southern and Eastern Europe.

Of the immigrants, 505,000 came from Germany, 388,000 came from Ireland, and 272,000 came from Britain (including Scotland and Wales). Also 31,000 came from France, 27,000 came from the Netherlands, 18,000 came from Belgium, and 31,000 came from Switzerland. Also 95,000 came from Norway, 226,000 came from Sweden, and 50,000 came from Denmark.

From 1891 through 1900, about 652,000 came from Italy, 28,000 came from Portugal, 505,000 came from the Russian Empire (many of these were Poles and Jews, and some were Ukrainians, Finns, Lithuanians, Latvians, and Estonians), and 593,000 came from Austria-Hungary (which included Czechs, Slovaks, Ruthenians, Slovenes, Croatians, and some Poles, Ukrainians, Serbs, and Romanians). Also 97,000 others came from Poland who were not counted as subjects of Germany, Russia, or Austria-Hungary. Also 13,000 came from independent Romania, 16,000 came from independent Greece, and 27,000 came from "Turkey in Asia" – almost of these people were Lebanese, Syrians, or Armenians fleeing Turkish oppression.

From 1891 through 1900, another 3,000 came from and through Canada, 1,000 came from Mexico, and 33,000 came from the West Indies. About 15,000 Chinese came to America, and 26,000 came from Japan. Another 3,000 trickled in from Australia and New Zealand.

The first decade of the 1900s was the heyday of Ellis Island. More than double the amount of Europeans came during this decade than had come in the previous decade.

Scandinavian and British immigration increased, and German and Irish immigration fell off. Immigration from Italy, Russia, and eastern Europe mushroomed. In Italy's case, conditions were poor – but Italy's immigration statistics were inflated. Many Italian men would come to America, work, and return to Italy. Then they would come back to America. Pogroms in Russia and constant tensions between Russia, Austria-Hungary, Germany, the Turks, and the Balkans encouraged many in Russia and Eastern Europe to get while the getting was good.

From 1901 through 1910, roughly 8,100,000 Europeans came to America. Of these, 341,000 came from Germany, 339,000 came from Ireland, and 526,000 came from Britain (including Scotland and Wales). Also 73,000 came from France, 48,000 came from the Netherlands, 42,000 came from Belgium, and 35,000 came from Switzerland. Also 191,000 came from newly-independent Norway, 250,000 came from Sweden, and 65,000 came from Denmark.

From 1901 through 1910, about 2,046,000 came from Italy, 69,000 came from Portugal, 1,597,000 came from the Russian Empire (many of these were Poles and Jews, and some were Ukrainians, Finns, Lithuanians, Latvians, and Estonians), 2,145,000 came from Austria-Hungary (which included Czechs, Slovaks, Ruthenians, Slovenes, Croatians, and some Poles, Ukrainians, Serbs, and Romanians). All of those who came from Poland who were counted as subjects of Germany, Russia, or Austria-Hungary. Also 53,000 came from independent Romania, 168,000 came from independent Greece, 39,000 came from Serbia, Bulgaria, and Montenegro combined, 80,000 came from "Turkey in Europe" – almost all of these people were Bulgarians, Greeks, Serbs, Macedonians, and Albanians fleeing Turkish oppression, and 77,000 came from "Turkey in Asia" – almost all of these people were Lebanese, Syrians, or Armenians fleeing Turkish oppression. Even 28,000 people came from Spain – a country whose immigrants almost always went to Latin America – in the decade after the Spanish-American War.

From 1901 through 1910, another 179,000 came from and through Canada, 50,000 came from Mexico, and 108,000 came from the West Indies. Canada was again becoming more of a way station country for European and now Asian immigrants instead of a source country for immigrants, although French Canadians continued to come to New England and the Middle Atlantic states. About 21,000 Chinese came to America, and 130,000 came from Japan. The large amount of Japanese coming to America led president Theodore Roosevelt to get Japan to agree to restrict immigration in the later part of the decade. Another 7000 came from Africa, and another 12,000 came from Australia and New Zealand.

The second decade of the 1900s was the decade of World War One. The Germans and the British, whose merchant fleets carried the most immigrants to America, were in a life-or-death struggle on the high seas. Since Britain's surface fleet was stronger, Germany's ships and Austria-Hungary's ships stayed bottled up in port. British ships, like the *Lusitania*, were targets for German submarines. The Germans and the Turks bottled up Russia's ships. French and Italian ships, like British ships, could sail, but they were also targets for German submarines. Immigrants were rightfully concerned about being aboard ships that could be targets of naval gunfire, submarine torpedoes, or anti-ship mines in the North Sea, so relatively few came to America during World War One, even before America declared war on Germany in 1917.

Other factors held down immigration as well. Just before World War One, troops of the Balkan countries retook Macedonia and surrounding areas from the Turks, and Albania became free. Instead of fleeing frm the Turks, many people in their newly-freed homelands decided to stay put. Because of World War One, millions of young men who were soldiers and sailors – the type of people most prone to come to America – would lay dead on the battlefields and under the waves. After World War One, Germans, Balts, Poles, and Russians fought over the land that became the Baltic countries. Soldiers in these fights died – without much notice, perhaps, like the soldiers in the Balkan warfare – but they were just as dead as the dead in World War One.

Millions of civilians in Germany, Austria-Hungary, Poland, Russia, Armenia, and the Balkans also died, from the British hunger blockade, from crop destructions and seizures by whatever army happened to hold an area, and from Turkish and Communist atrocities. Many of these unfortunates would have wanted to emigrate if only they could have done so.

The net result? **From 1911 through 1920**, only about half as many Europeans came to America as came during the previous decade. Roughly 4,400,000 Europeans came to America. Of these, 144,000 came from Germany, 146,000 came from Ireland, and 341,000 came from Britain (including Scotland and Wales). Also 62,000 came from France, 44,000 came from the Netherlands, 34,000 came from Belgium, and 23,000 came from Switzerland. Also 66,000 came from Norway, 95,000 came from Sweden, and 42,000 came from Denmark.

From 1911 through 1920, about 1,110,000 came from Italy, 69,000 came from Spain, 90,000 came from Portugal, 921,000 came from the Russian Empire (many of these were Poles and Jews, and some were Ukrainians, Finns, Lithuanians, Latvians, and Estonians), 896,000 came from enemy Austria-Hungary (most of whom were Czechs, Slovaks, Ruthenians, Slovenes, Croatians, and some Poles, Ukrainians, Serbs, and Romanians trying to escape their own emperor and his henchmen). All but 5000 of those who came from Poland who were counted as subjects of Germany, Russia, or Austria-Hungary. Also 13,000 came from independent Romania, 184,000 came from independent Greece, 23,000 came from independent Serbia, Bulgaria, and Montenegro combined, and 79,000 came from "Turkey in Asia" – almost all of these people were Lebanese, Syrians, or Armenians fleeing Turkish oppression. Also, 55,000 came from "Turkey in Europe" – almost all of these people were Bulgarians, Greeks, Serbs, Macedonians, and Albanians fleeing Turkish oppression before the victors of the Balkan Wars limited Turkey in Europe to the area around Constantinople. After the Balkan soldiers liberated their compatriots from the Turks, fewer people from the Balkans would want to flee the Turks because they were free.

From 1911 through 1920, another 742,000 came from and through Canada (mostly through instead of from), 219,000 came from Mexico, 123,000 came from the West Indies, and 59,000 came from Central and South America. About 21,000 Chinese came to America, and 2,000 came from Japan. Another 8000 came from Africa, and another 12,000 came from Australia and New Zealand.

Most of the people listed as coming from Canada were European immigrants and Asian immigrants who came to Canada and tarried a while before coming to America. People from the Indian subcontinent – then under British rule – used Canada as a way to sneak into California. British shipping companies profited from landing foreigners in Canada, where immigrants would not be unduly regulated if they intended to eventually enter the United States. Many Mexicans came to America during World War One to replace American laborers who had gone off to fight in the war.

The third decade of the 1900s was the decade when America's leaders greatly restricted immigration. During this decade, roughly four million people would come to America; a third of these came from and through Canada and from Mexico. Not quite double that amount came from Europe directly.

Even though World War One was over, there were still plenty of reasons for people to want to leave. But due to the immigration quota laws, only about half as many people came from Europe as had done so in the previous decade.

After World War One, the Poles, Czechs, Slovaks, Ruthenians, Croatians, Slovenes, Lithuanians, Latvians, Estonians, Finns, many Romanians and Serbs, and most of the Irish became free. Many people from these lands who might have emigrated if oppression at home had continued would instead try to stay at home and help build their nations.

The Russians dropped out of World War One, suffered some German and later some Allied occupation, endured a civil war, and lost a war to the Poles, all by 1921. Pro-democracy people overthrew the Czar in 1917, and later that year the Communists overthrew the democrats. The Baltic countries became free, as did Poland and Finland. Moldova joined Romania. The Communists retook Ukraine, which was briefly independent. After World War One, the Communists and their rivals fought a horrible internal war in which millions of civilians and soldiers died. The victorious Communists murdered their opponents and locked the country's borders, so immigration from Russia virtually ceased.

From 1921 through 1930, roughly 2,500,000 Europeans came to America. Of these, 412,000 came from defeated Germany, 221,000 came from mostly-independent Ireland, and 330,000 came from Britain (half of whom were Scots). Also 50,000 came from war-ravaged France, 27,000 came from the Netherlands, 16,000 came from war-ravaged Belgium, and 30,000 came from Switzerland. Also 69,000 came from Norway, 97,000 came from Sweden, 32,000 came from Denmark, and 17,000 came from newly-independent Finland.

From 1921 through 1930, about 455,000 came from Italy, 29,000 came from Spain, and 30,000 came from Portugal. From Russia and Ukraine, 61,000 came; 6000 came from newly-independent Lithuania, 3000 came from newly-independent Latvia, and 2000 came from newly-independent Estonia.

World War One killed Austria-Hungary, the "prison of nations." From the lands of the dead empire, 33,000 came from Austria, 31,000 came from Hungary, 102,000 came from newly-independent Czechoslovakia (which included Czechs, Slovaks, and Ruthenians), 49,000 came from the enlarged Yugoslavia (Serbia with Slovenes, Croatians, Montenegrins, Macedonians, and Bosniaks added). From reborn Poland came 228,000 people. Also 68,000 came from Romania (which was enlarged with Transylvania and Moldova), 51,000 came from Greece (whose own people had to give home to a million Greeks fleeing Turkey), and 3,000 came from violence-torn Bulgaria.

World War One also killed the Ottoman (Turkish) Empire. During World War One, the Turks murdered more than a million Armenians. After the war, the British and French grabbed Syria, Lebanon, Jordan, and Israel, and set up Iraq and Arabia and assorted shiekdoms on the Arabian Peninsula as independent and semi-independent states. Turkish officers patriotically overthrew the sultan when he agreed to allow the British, French, and Italians to partition Turkey itself. The Turks beat the Greeks, who were acting as Britain's stooges, and murdered many civilian Greeks living in Turkey. The Turks also went back to genociding the Armenians.

Roughly 15,000 came from "Turkey in Europe" – these people were mostly Bulgarians, Greeks and Armenians fleeing Turkish oppression, or refugees from Russia and Ukraine fleeing Communism by way of Constantinople. Another 19,000 came from "Turkey in Asia" – almost all of these people were Armenians and Greeks fleeing Turkish oppression.

From 1920 through 1930, another 925,000 came from and through Canada (mostly through instead of from), 459,000 came from Mexico, 75,000 came from the West Indies, and 58,000 came from Central and South America. About 30,000 Chinese came to America, and 33,000 came from Japan. Another 6000 came from Africa, and another 8000 came from Australia and New Zealand.

From 1820 through 1930, Europe sent more than 32 million immigrants to the United States. The rest of the world sent another 5 million. Not counted were the hundreds of thousands of blacks who were forcibly seized in Africa and shipped to America. The legal importing of slaves had ended in 1808, but some slave ships still called on American ports without punishment to the captains or the shipowners. After the external slave trade ended, truly depraved slaveowners encouraged black women to have many children, and sold them like livestock.

Most of the people listed as coming from Canada in the early 1900s were European immigrants or Asian immigrants who used Canada as a "prep school" or as a way station to America.

As for Mexico, that unhappy land was in tumult during the 1910s and 1920s. The long-time dictator Porfirio Diaz was overthrown in 1911, and rival groups clashed for almost a decade until Alvaro Obregón wound up winning the revolution in 1920. His hand-picked successor Plutarco Calles in the 1920s instituted one-party rule in Mexico and brutally persecuted the Catholic Church.

Mexico is overwhelmingly a Catholic country, but its government is by law and by practice anti-clerical to this day. This is because government leaders, bureaucrats, and other elites are anti-clerical. Depending on who enforces the law, it was and still can be illegal for priests to wear clerical garb in public, and for nuns to wear their habits (uniforms) in public. Catholic schools and hospitals face discriminatory regulations that secular schools and hospitals escape.

Many Mexicans came to America in the 1910s and 1920s to escape the tumults and persecution. Many others came to seek higher wages. **(15)**

ELLIS ISLAND SCRAPBOOK

THE ROLL CALL OF IMMIGRANTS BY BLOOD

ENGLISH, SCOTS, AND WELSH

Roughly 2,620,000 people came to America from England from 1830 to 1931. During this time, another 730,000 people came to America from Scotland, and another 90,000 came to America from Wales. Roughly 790,000 people came from Britain in this period whose records didn't specify which part of Britain they came from.

IRISH

Ireland's immigration was huge relative to her population. The impact Irish immigrants have had on America has been huge in proportion to Ireland's population. Between 1820 and 1931, roughly 4,590,000 Irish came to America. Among these were ancestors of mine.

There had to be a reason why so many people were willing to leave such a small country besides the usual desire for a better life that motivated most immigrants to come to America. Ireland ranks – along with Britain, Italy, and Germany – as one of the top four countries of Europe in sending immigrants to America. Ireland at the start of the Great Hunger in 1845 had about 8 million people. Since each of the other three countries had many times more people than Ireland, the British rulers had to be very selfish and hateful to cause so many Irish – including my own ancestors -- to leave their homeland.

GERMANS

From 1820 through 1931, roughly 5,900,000 people came from German ruled lands to America. The vast majority of these were Germans, although some were Poles (even though immigration officials tried to count the Poles separately), and some were other minorities (French and Danes) who were under German occupation. This figure does not count the Germanic peoples of Switzerland or Austria; they are counted elsewhere.

FRENCH

From 1820 through 1931, roughly 580,000 French came to America. This is a very small number compared with the number of people in France in that era. In France, there was inefficiency, yes, but the French took care of their own. The French people would not tolerate the cruelest unsafe and miserable conditions of the factories and mines that the workers of Britain and Germany had to work in. Most of the French were proud of their beautiful country and they thought they had a stake in its success. As a result, very few French left France.

ITALIANS

From 1820 through 1931, roughly 4,660,000 people came from Italy to America. Poverty drove most Italians to immigrate. For every immigrant who came from northern Italy, five came from southern Italy. The numbers may be skewed because many men came back and forth repeatedly before choosing either to stay in America or return home for good.

In 1910, the Italian government claimed Italy had lost up to 5.5 million people permanently to the Western Hemisphere. At first glance, the Italian government's numbers look a little high, but they were probably not too far off the mark. As benchmarks, Italian officials claimed Italy lost 350,000 emigrants in 1900 and 530,000 emigrants in 1910. If this is correct, Italian immigration to Argentina and Brazil and elsewhere in Latin America would have approached 250,000 in 1900 and exceeded 300,000 in 1910, for U.S. immigration officials reported 102,000 immigrants from Italy in 1900 and 223,000 immigrants from Italy in 1910.

From 1857 through 1910, at least one million Italians emigrated to Argentina. As of the 1960s, roughly 40 percent of Argentines reported having at least some Italian blood. In that era, a similar number of Italians emigrated to Brazil. But since Brazil was and is a much more populous country than Argentina, the immigration of the Italians didn't affect Brazil as greatly.

In the 1920s, American officials greatly restricted immigration to the United States. This affected Italians more than any other group of Europeans. Immediately before World War One, the largest numbers of immigrants to America came from the Russian Empire, Austria-Hungary, and Italy. After World War One, the Red slavemasters of the Soviet Union essentially forbade their subjects to leave the workers' paradise. The former Austria-Hungary after World War One broke down into several small countries with shattered economies and millions of dead. Italy still had many people willing and able to leave; most of them wound up emigrating to Argentina and Brazil.

At the end of this section is a discussion on why reported immigration figures from Italy and some other lands may be much higher than net immigration figures.

SPANISH AND PORTUGUESE

The problems of their homelands led many Spanish and Portuguese to emigrate. Most people with power (like those everywhere) believed in little more than rights and enrichment for themselves. The factions in these countries did not believe in compromise, so fighting resulted, and so did repression of those who lost — and harm to those unlucky enough to be in the way.

People from Spain had colonized much of the territory of the United States, but America would come under rule by Anglo-Saxon Americans who openly hated the Spanish. So the immigrants from Spain tended to go to Argentina and other countries in Latin America their countrymen had colonized in previous centuries instead of to the United States. Likewise, immigrants from Portugal tended to go to Brazil instead of to the United States.

Roughly 170,000 Spaniards came to the United States between 1820 and 1931. Roughly 250,000 Portuguese came to the United States in the same period.

By comparison, from 1851 through 1930, roughly four million Spaniards left Spain for the Latin American countries of the New World. And from 1851 through 1920, about 1,400,000 Portuguese came to the New World, almost exclusively to Brazil. From 1921 through 1930, perhaps another 300,000 to 400,000 Portuguese came to the New World, almost exclusively to Brazil.

These numbers may be skewed because many men came back and forth repeatedly before choosing either to stay in Latin America or return home for good.

Perhaps half of the Spaniards and Portuguese returned to their homelands when they could. Most Spanish immigrants to Latin America went to Argentina, the most European in climate and culture of Spain's former possessions. Many Spaniards emigrated to Uruguay and Portuguese-speaking Brazil also. The balance of Spaniards emigrated to Chile, Peru, Mexico, and other countries in Latin America. From 1851 through 1930, roughly one million Spaniards emigrated to Argentina and stayed. This implies at least another million Spaniards stayed in Argentina for awhile – as seasonal workers or as workers seeking to save some money by working overseas a few years – and came home. It is not unreasonable to think a similar proportion of Spaniards and Portuguese did likewise elsewhere. In fact, immigration statistics into Spain during and after World War One indicate almost as many people came into Spain as left Spain.

America's immigration figures did not tabulate Basques. Most of these people came from the Basque lands of northern Spain, and a few came from adjoining territory in southern France. Many Basque sheepherders and their families came to the Rocky Mountain states.

Another 760,000 people from Mexico, Spain's most populous former colony, came to the United States legally in that time span. From Central America and South America came another 160,000 people in this time period; virtually all of these countries had been Spanish or Portuguese possessions. And another 430,000 or so people came to the United States from the West Indies; most of these people came from islands like Cuba, Puerto Rico, and Hispaniola, all of which had been Spanish colonies. (Haiti on the western side of Hispaniola, had later been a French colony. Jamaica, a Spanish colony until the English seized it during the Cromwell dictatorship, was a British colony during the Ellis Island era.)

Of course, this does not count the few thousand Spaniards the United States gained in buying the Louisiana Purchase in 1803, or in buying Florida in 1819. Nor does it count the Spaniards and Mexicans the United States gained in admitting Texas to the Union in 1845, or the Spaniards and Mexicans the United States gained in the Mexican Cession and the Gadsden Purchase (California, Nevada, Utah, Arizona, New Mexico, much of Colorado, and some of Wyoming, Kansas, and Oklahoma). Perhaps 100,000 Spaniards and Mexicans became American citizens after the statehood of Texas and the Mexican War even though they didn't migrate to America. *America migrated to them!*

CANADIANS

British-run Canada was a source of illegal immigrants from Europe and Asia during the Ellis Island era. It was also a conduit for many Europeans who wanted to come to America who avoided the Ellis Island "experience." So of the 2,920,000 or so immigrants listed as coming from Canada from 1820 through 1931, many were not Canadians.

Some Anglo Canadians and French Canadians came to America before the Civil War. From the end of the Civil War to 1890, hundreds of thousands of French-Canadians came to America, primarily to New England and the Mid Atlantic states. The flow stalled in the 1890s, then resumed in the years before World War One and resumed again in the 1920s.

Various estimates say about 900,000 French Canadians emigrated to the United States from 1820 to 1931. Probably an equal number of Canadians with roots in Britain or Ireland emigrated to the United States during this time. This means at least 1.1 million people used Canada as a conduit or a stopover point from Europe or Asia to come to America. Most of these interlopers did so in the 1910s and the 1920s. **(16)**

ELLIS ISLAND SCRAPBOOK

DANES, NORWEGIANS, SWEDES, AND FINNS

From 1820 through 1931, roughly 330,000 people came from Denmark to America. Another 1,210,000 or so came from Sweden and a further 800,000 or so came from Norway during this period. (Immigration officials noted the difference between the Swedes and the Norwegians even though the Swedes ruled the Norwegians.) Proportionately, Norwegians were more prone to come to America than Swedes, because there were only about half as many Norwegians as Swedes. The Danes, proportionately, were the most prone to stay home of these three groups of Scandinavians.

The Russian tsars ruled the Finns from 1809 through 1917, so the numbers of Finnish immigrants are not documented as well as the numbers of other Scandinavian immigrants. From 1898 – when U.S. officials started counting them -- through 1914, about 190,000 Finns came to the United States. Before 1898, perhaps about another 20,000 Finns came to the United States. From 1915 through 1931, another 40,000 or so Finns came to the United States. This is a total of about 250,000 Finnish immigrants. Perhaps this total counts some people of Estonian blood. The language of the Estonians (and their Lutheran faith) is similar to the language of the Finns, so some immigration officials could have counted them with the Finns.

The best-known Scandinavian immigrant to the United States – a man who came to America as a child from Norway in the 1890s – gained fame in connection with his association with another ethnic group in America. His name? Knute Rockne, player and coach of the University of Notre Dame's Fighting Irish. Also during the Roaring Twenties, "Untouchable" Eliot Ness (whose parents were Norwegian immigrants), and aviator Charles Lindbergh (whose father was a Swedish immigrant and a congressman) would add color to one of America's most colorful decades.

SWISS

Between 1820 and 1931, roughly 290,000 Swiss came to America.

Among these immigrants was John Sutter of California Gold Rush fame. He fled a wife and a Swiss debtor's prison, and wound up in California in 1839. He got a land grant of 76 square miles in the Sacramento area from the Mexican government and started a ranching, wheat growing, and lumber operation.

Sutter and his men built a fort in what is present-day Sacramento, an 18-foot-high wall with cannon towers that enclosed a 150 foot by 500 foot area. "Sutter's Fort," besides giving good protection to his workers, served as their home, storehouse, blacksmith shop, and tannery. Sutter's men rescued what was left of the Donner Party, the people who resorted to cannibalism to stay alive when they got trapped in the snows of the Sierra Nevada range.

Fame doesn't always mean fortune. Sutter lost everything when gold was discovered on his land. His workers left to search for gold and thousands of prospectors and others ran him off of his land. He died in poverty.

I mention Sutter here because most Swiss didn't make the splash he made. Sutter greatly helped the development of America. Sutter bought out the Russians who had colonized land north of San Francisco and acquired their cannons in the transaction. He and his men ran British Hudson Bay Company trappers out of Northern California. They thus played a role in keeping the ever greedy British from stealing California as a colony. For this act Sutter and his men deserve America's eternal gratitude.

DUTCH AND BELGIANS

Between 1830 and 1931, roughly 250,000 Dutch came to America to farm and to work in the cities. Of course, there were those Dutch who came to New York in the 1600s when their flag flew over the New York City area and the Hudson Valley. The Dutch had a long history of making good in America. Three presidents (Van Buren and both Roosevelts, all native New Yorkers) had Dutch ancestry.

Only about 150,000 people from Belgium came to America. There was more land for farming in Belgium, and there were more manufacturing jobs available. However, among the immigrants Belgium sent to America was Father Pierre De Smet, who evangelized American Indians, built schools for them, and pushed (unsuccessfully) for decent treatment for them. Another was Father Joseph De Veuster aka Father Damien, the saint and martyr to leprosy who aided the lepers in the Hawaiian Islands. Like their country's exports of cut diamonds, these immigrants were few in number but very valuable to the people they served.

JEWS

From 1898 – when U.S. officials started counting them -- through 1931, roughly 1,910,000 people they called "Hebrews" came to the United States. Without question, the motivator for most of the Jewish immigrants was flight from oppression.

Of these immigrants, about 1,550,000 Jews came before the end of 1918. Roughly a million of these Jews came from the Russian Empire (mostly from central and eastern Poland, Galicia, elsewhere in Ukraine,

Belarusia, and Lithuania) from 1898 through 1914; another 400,000 came from Austria-Hungary (mostly from Galicia and southern Poland) from 1898 through 1914. The remainder came from Germany and western Poland (which the Germans held), Romania, or other countries before World War One, or came during World War One.

From 1919 through 1931, about 360,000 "Hebrews" came to the United States from Russia, Eastern Europe, Germany, and elsewhere in Europe.

From 1871 (when the first immigrants from Eastern Europe came in quantity) through 1898, about 600,000 people came from Russia, and about 840,000 people came from Austria-Hungary. Also about 160,000 others came from Poland during this time who were not counted as subjects of Germany, Russia, or Austria-Hungary; maybe 40,000 of these people were Jews. And about 10,000 people, mostly Jews, came from independent Romania. Maybe 650,000 of these 1.6 million people were Jews – roughly 500,000 of these were from Russia. Also, from 1871 through 1898, roughly 2.6 million people came from Germany (which owned part of Poland); maybe another 100,000 to 150,000 of these people were Jews. This is a total of about 2,510,000 to 2,560,000 Jews.

The estimates of the numbers of Jews points to problems in estimating the number of immigrants from Eastern Europe and Russia – political instability and divided homelands. There were three large empires in Eastern Europe in the 1800s – Austria-Hungary, Russia, and the Ottoman Empire. Poland was occupied by Russian, Austro-Hungarian, and German troops. The Ottomans held Bulgaria, Greece, Serbia, Montenegro, Albania, and most of Romania at the start of the 1800s. By the start of World War One, all of these peoples would be free of the Turks. But many Romanians were still subjects of Austria-Hungary or Russia. The Turks also held many Armenians and the Lebanese, the Syrians, the peoples of present-day Iraq, the Holy Land, and much of present-day Saudi Arabia. Besides more than half of Poland, the Russian tsars also held Ukraine, some of Armenia, Georgia, Finland, Estonia, Latvia, Lithuania, and present-day Belarusia and Moldova. Franz Josef, the emperor of Austria-Hungary from the end of our Mexican War (1848) until just before we entered World War One (1916) ruled the Austrians, the Hungarians, the Czechs, the Slovaks, the Ruthenians, many Poles, some Ukrainians, many Romanians, some Serbs, the Croatians, the Slovenes, and the people of Bosnia and Herzegovina. He also was the emperor over some Italians. So if the following estimates of peoples seem uneven, this is why.

American immigration officials kept statistics on immigrants by country of residence since 1820 but did not keep statistics by nationality until 1898. Also, immigrant groups tend to inflate the number of their people who came to America. Therefore, the statistics I report on the various peoples who came to America from the lands of Eastern Europe and Russia are estimates on my part, using immigration statistics and other sources.

POLES

From 1898 – when U.S. officials started counting them as ethnic Poles -- through 1914, about 1,400,000 Poles came to the United States. From 1915 through 1931, another 110,000 or so Poles came to the United States. (This includes 85,000 Poles who left the reborn state of Poland for the United States from the end of World War One through 1931. According to the records, 230,000 people came to America from the resurrected Polish state from 1919 through 1931; the other 145,000 or so who left for America were Lithuanians, Ukrainians, Russians and Belarusians, or Jews.)

Before 1898, maybe about 160,000 or so people from the Polish provinces of the German, Austrian, and Russian empires came to the United States. Possibly a quarter of these 160,000 people were Jews living in Poland, and the other 120,000 or more were Poles. Adding these people to the other Poles counted yields a total of about 1,630,000 Polish immigrants.

Of these Polish immigrants, perhaps two-thirds (a million or so people) who came before World War One were from the portion of Poland (Mazovia – the area of central and eastern Poland around Warsaw and Lodz, and Masuria – northeastern Poland) under the rule of the Russian Empire. Perhaps a quarter (400,000 or so people) were from the portion of Poland (western Galicia and Malopolska –the area of southern Poland around Krakow) under the rule of Austria-Hungary. The remainder were Poles from the portions of Poland (Silesia, Pomerania, Wielkopolska) under German rule.

How dissatisfied were the Poles? Despite there being about four Russians for every Pole in the Ellis Island era, Poles provided six times as many immigrants of Slavic blood to the United States as the Russians themselves did. The Poles had more mobility, and more dissatisfaction than the Russians had. (They had three foreign occupier regimes to hate – Prussia's and Austria's as well as Russia's.) They also had the connection with America ideals – their officers helped Americans gain independence, and Kosciuszko in 1794 had tried to bring America's ideals to the fight for liberation to Poland.

RUSSIAN EMPIRE AND SOVIET UNION

Roughly 3,340,000 immigrants came to America from the Russian Empire and the Soviet Union from 1820 through 1931. Besides Russians, this tally also includes Finns and Estonians, Lithuanians and Latvians, some Poles, some Ukrainians, and Belarusians, and a few Romanians, Moldovans, Armenians, and Georgians. It also includes a huge number of Jews.

The Jews and Poles were the people most likely to leave the Russian Empire. The Lithuanians and Finns, proportionately, were similarly dissatisfied. Then came the Ukrainians and Ruthenians. Of all the non-Russian groups who immigrated in large numbers, the Jews suffered most of all in Tsarist Russia, then the Poles and the Lithuanians. The Finns and Ukrainians and Ruthenians suffered less than the Poles and the Lithuanians, but their lives were still hard in their homelands. The pattern was the same in all cases – these people lived on Russia's western edges, they were non-Russian in blood, and they were tired of suffering at the hands of those who ran the Russian Empire.

Those who opted to come to America would escape World War One and/or the Russian Civil War and seven decades of brutal Communist repression. Those who hesitated lost.

Before 1871, fewer than 4000 people came to America from Russia. American officials brought America to about 400 Russians when they bought Alaska from the Russian government in 1867.

From 1871 (when the first immigrants from Eastern Europe came in quantity) through 1898, about 600,000 people came from the Russian Empire. The vast majority of these immigrants were Jews and Poles instead of ethnic Russians.

From 1820 to 1898, about 160,000 Poles came who were counted independent of the three empires which divided Poland; many of these people lived in what was the Russian Empire.

Leaders of the Soviet Union did not prevent 62,000 people from leaving the "workers' paradise" and coming to America from 1921 through 1931. Only about half of these "malcontents" were ethnic Russians. The balance were mostly Jews and Ukrainians.

From the end of World War One to 1931, another 18,000 or so people came from the new Finland, 2000 people came from the new Estonia, 4000 people came from the new Latvia, and 6000 people came from the new Lithuania. All of these people lived in land that had been part of the Russian Empire. Sadly for the people of Lithuania, Latvia, and Estonia, they would enjoy only two decades of freedom. Then they would suffer Soviet and Nazi occupation during World War Two, then they would endure almost five more decades of Soviet slavery until they won their freedom in 1991.

From 1898 through 1914, about 220,000 people who immigration officials called "Russians" came to the United States. Before 1898, hardly any ethnic Russians came to the United States. From 1915 through 1931, another 50,000 or so "Russians" came to the United States. This is a total of about 270,000 immigrants who were Russians and who the immigration officials counted as Russians.

There was no major distinction between the people of Belarusia and Old Russia before the Communist Revolution. (Some Belarusians were Catholics, but most were Orthodox Christians, like the Russians.) Belarusia has had the sad distinction of being the Belgium of Eastern Europe ... several European armies have come through the land to attack Moscow. Likewise, Russian and Soviet armies have used Belarusia as an invasion route to Poland and Germany. The Reds made Belarusia a "people's republic" within the Soviet Union after they seized power. Belarusia became free in the early 1990s and is now known as Belarus, but its retread Communist leaders have kept the new nation in virtual lockstep with Russia. Some people counted as ethnic Russians in the United States are of Belarusian heritage.

Before 1898, perhaps 20,000 people who immigration officials called "Lithuanians" came to America. From 1898 through 1914, about 250,000 people they called "Lithuanians" came to the United States. (Perhaps 20,000 of these people were Latvians; immigration people counted Latvians with the Lithuanians.) From 1915 through 1931, another 13,000 or so "Lithuanians" came to the United States, including 6000 people who came from the new Lithuanian state from 1921 through 1931. Another 4000 people came from the new Latvian state to the United States from 1921 through 1931. This is a total of about 290,000 immigrants from these two Baltic nations; the vast majority of these were Lithuanians.

Virtually all Lithuanians who emigrated left the Russian Empire. (The Germans held Klaipeda (Memel) and the surrounding area until the end of World War One; some Lithuanians came from this area. A few came from Vilnius (aka Wilno or Vilna) and the surrounding countryside after Polish troops took this land – which had large numbers of Poles also -- from Lithuania after World War One.) The Russian leaders had targeted Lithuanians as rebels and as allies of Poland – and as Catholics. (Most Latvians were less rebellious and were Lutherans; their ancestors had converted when Prussian Germans and the Swedes controlled them.)

A small number of Armenians (some of whom were under Russian or Soviet rule until the 1990s) and

Georgians (who were also under Russian or Soviet rule until the 1990s) came to America. Most Armenians who came to America were under Turkish rule; that's why they fled. Besides the Nazis, the Turks had the only government in Europe that made the Russian Empire and the Soviet Empire look somewhat benevolent to ethnic and religious minorities.

Finnish and Estonian immigration is covered with the other Scandinavians. Jewish and Polish immigration is covered previously as well.

UKRAINIANS AND RUTHENIANS

Before 1898, maybe about 5000 or so people who immigration officials called "Ruthenians" came to the United States. (By this name, they meant Ukrainians as well as the Ruthenians tucked up in Ruthenia in the Carpathian Mountains.) From 1898 through 1914, about 255,000 "Ruthenians" came to the United States. From 1915 through 1931, another 15,000 or so "Ruthenians" came to the United States. This is a total of about 275,000 Ruthenian and Ukrainian immigrants.

Of these Ruthenian and Ukrainian immigrants, perhaps 80,000 to 100,000 were Ukrainians from the portion of Ukraine under Russian rule. Perhaps another 30,000 to 50,000 were Ukrainians from the portion of Ukraine (eastern Galicia) under the rule of Austria-Hungary. Perhaps 130,000 to 150,000 people were Ruthenians from their impoverished Carpathian homeland.

Ukraine was briefly independent from early 1918 through the Russian Civil War. The Ukrainians suffered genocidal rule from Soviet commissars until World War Two. The Communists essentially murdered five million to seven million Ukrainians by confiscating their food and starving them during the winter of 1932-1933. The Communists were so hateful to the Ukrainians that many Ukrainian men fought in World War Two on the side of the Germans, and many others fought against the armies of both totalitarian regimes. During World War Two, the Nazis as well as the Communists oppressed the Ukrainian people in some of the most hideous ways imaginable. The Soviets resumed their monopoly of slavery over Ukraine after World War Two and remained as masters of Ukraine until the breakup of the Soviet Union in 1991.

THE FORMER HAPSBURG EMPIRE

Roughly four million immigrants came to America from the Hapsburg Empire (also known as Austria-Hungary) from 1820 to 1914. This includes Slovenians and Croatians, Czechs and Slovaks, some Poles, some Ukrainians, Ruthenians, Bukovinans, some Romanians, some Serbs, some Hercegovinans, and some Bosniaks. (A "Bosniak" is a Bosnian who is Moslem. Bosnians who are Christians usually count themselves as Croatians or Serbs.) This also includes a large number of Jews. Another 25,000 or so subjects of Austria-Hungary managed to gain entry to America during the four years of World War One.

From 1820 to 1898, about 160,000 people from Poland came who were counted independent of the three empires which divided Poland; some of these people lived in what was Austria-Hungary.

From the end of World War One to 1931, another 110,000 or so people came from the new Czechoslovakia, about 230,000 came from the reborn Poland, 50,000 or so came from the new Yugoslavia, and about 70,000 came from the enlarged Romania. All of the Czechs and Slovaks, some of the Poles, about half of the people in the new Yugoslavia, and some of the people coming from Romania lived in land that had been part of Austria-Hungary. Also, about 65,000 people came from the new ethnic but vastly smaller states of Austria and Hungary. This tallies to about 250,000 to 300,000 people.

HUNGARIANS

Before 1898, perhaps 150,000 to 200,000 Hungarians came to the United States. From 1898 through 1914, about 460,000 people who immigration officials called "Magyars" came to the United States. From 1915 through 1931, another 40,000 or so "Magyars" came to the United States. This is a total of about 650,000 to 700,000 Hungarian immigrants.

CZECHS AND SLOVAKS

Before 1898, perhaps 150,000 to 200,000 Czechs came to America. Among these were ancestors of mine. From 1898 through 1914, about 140,000 people who immigration officials called "Bohemians and Moravians" came to the United States. From 1915 through 1931, another 30,000 or so "Bohemians and Moravians" came to the United States. This is a total of about 320,000 to 370,000 Czech immigrants.

About as many of the earlier Czechs were Protestants and "free-thinkers" (agnostics) as were Catholics. The Czechs tended to come to America much earlier than most of the rest of the minorities of Austria-Hungary. Half of the Czechs took to farming in the Midwest and in Texas; most of the rest of the minorities of Austria-Hungary tended to work in mines in the countryside or work in factories in the cities.

Before 1898, perhaps about 50,000 Slovaks came to the United States. From 1898 through 1914, about 480,000 Slovaks came to the United States. Among these were my wife's ancestors. From 1915 through 1931, another

70,000 or so Slovaks came to the United States. This is a total of about 600,000 Slovak immigrants.

CROATIANS AND SLOVENES, BOSNIANS AND HERCEGOVINANS

Before 1898, perhaps 50,000 Croatians and Slovenians came to the United States. (Immigration officials didn't count people of the two groups separately.) From 1898 through 1914, about 460,000 Croatians and Slovenians came to the United States. From 1915 through 1931, another 30,000 or so Croatians and Slovenians came to the United States. One of these was the father of a former girlfriend of mine. This is a total of about 540,000 Croatian and Slovenian immigrants. Austria-Hungary's rulers ruled these lands until the end of World War One.

This doesn't count Croatians bundled with the roughly 50,000 "Dalmatian, Bosnian, and Herzegovinan" immigrants recorded from 1898 through 1914. Some of these people were Croatians. Austria-Hungary held Dalmatia – Croatia's seacoast – from after the Napoleonic Wars to the end of World War One. Austria-Hungary's leaders sent troops to occupy Bosnia and Hercegovina in 1878 (the Turks had run these areas), and annexed them in 1908. The Hapsburgs would hold these lands until the end of World War One. Virtually all the "Dalmatian, Bosnian, and Herzegovinan" immigrants came from 1898 through 1914. Hardly anyone from these lands came to America before 1898. From 1915 through 1931, another 3000 or so "Dalmatian, Bosnian, and Herzegovinan" immigrants came to the United States. These lands would become part of Yugoslavia -- along with the rest of Croatia, Slovenia, Vojvodina, Serbia, Montenegro, and most of Macedonia -- after World War One. Perhaps 25,000 to 30,000 of these immigrants were Catholic South Slavs, most of whom could count as Croatians, for an overall total of at least 560,000 Croatians and Slovenes.

SERBS, MONTENEGRINS, MACEDONIANS, AND BULGARIANS

From 1898 through 1914, about 145,000 "Bulgarians, Serbs and Montenegrins" came to the United States. Before 1898, hardly any "Bulgarians, Serbs and Montenegrins" came to the United States. From 1915 through 1931, another 25,000 or so "Bulgarians, Serbs and Montenegrins" came to the United States. This is a total of about 170,000 Serb, Montenegrin and Bulgarian immigrants. (This includes Macedonian immigrants, who spoke a language similar to Serbs and Bulgarians, and lived in territory that mostly went to Serbia and later Yugoslavia. Immigration officials did not count Macedonians as a separate ethnic group.)

Since there were about 16 immigrants from Yugoslavia for every immigrant from Bulgaria from 1921 through 1931 (most of these years were "quota years" in which immigrants were admitted to America based on a percentage already in the country), and since Serbs, Macedonians, and Montenegrins made up a little more than half the people of postwar Yugoslavia (and a little less than half the immigrants from the new Yugoslavia to America in this time), I estimate about 150,000 of these immigrants were of Serb, Montenegrin, or Macedonian blood, and about 20,000 were of Bulgarian blood.

Unfortunately, immigration officials lumped the immigration figures from the three kingdoms together. From 1898 through 1918, roughly 60,000 Serbs and Montenegrins and Bulgarians immigrated from territory their respective kingdoms controlled, and another 90,000 or so Serbs and Montenegrins and Bulgarians immigrated from Balkan territory controlled by the Turks before World War One, or from Balkan territory controlled by Austria-Hungary before World War One. Of these 90,000, I estimate more than half were Serbs from Vojvodina or Bosnia, areas which were under the rule of Austria-Hungary until the end of World War One, and fewer than half were Serbs or Bulgarians from areas which were under the rule of the Turks. The ruler of Serbia didn't gain control of Macedonia or Kosovo, or areas of southern Serbia from the Turks until after the First Balkan War in 1913. Likewise, the ruler of Montenegro gained some South Slav land in 1913 that up to that time had been under the rule of the Turks. The ruler of Bulgaria gained Eastern Rumelia from the Turks in 1885, and some of Macedonia and Thrace from the Turks after the First Balkan War in 1913. The Bulgarians lost coastal western Thrace to Greece after World War One.

This doesn't include Serbs and Montenegrins bundled with the 53,000 or so "Dalmatian, Bosnian, and Herzegovinan" immigrants recorded from 1898 through 1931. Perhaps 10,000 to 15,000 of these immigrants were Orthodox South Slavs, most of whom could count as Serbs or Montenegrins, for an overall total of at least 160,000 Serbs and Montenegrins.

GERMANS OF AUSTRIA-HUNGARY

What about the Austrians and the other Germans who were dominant in Austria-Hungary? So what about them, American immigration officials responded.

American immigration officials didn't consider Germans from Austria-Hungary (the Austrians, Sudeten Germans of Bohemia and Moravia, and other Germans in places like Slovakia and Hungary and Transylvania and Bukovina) to be a separate nationality from Germans from the "Fatherland" (the German Empire).

Subtracting the people who emigrated from Austria-Hungary who were not German from the total number of people American officials noted were from Austria-Hungary gives a rough estimate of Austrians and other Germans who emigrated from the Hapsburg Empire. From 1871 through 1890, about 100,000 to 150,000 Austrians and other Germans from the empire came to the United States. From 1891 through 1900, about 150,000 to 200,000 Austrians and other Germans from the empire came to the United States. From 1901 through 1910, about 300,000 to 350,000 Austrians and other Germans from the empire came to the United States. From 1911 through 1918, about 100,000 Austrians and other Germans from the empire came to the United States. From 1918 through 1931, about 30,000 people came from Austria to the United States. In all, maybe around 680,000 to 830,000 Austrians and other Germans from the Hapsburg Empire came to the United States.

THE FORMER OTTOMAN EMPIRE

Very few people from the Balkans were able to come to America. They were too poor, and free to move much too late in comparison with other people in Europe, thanks to the Turks.

From 1881 to 1931, roughly 360,000 people escaped the Ottoman Empire and Turkey and came to the United States. (Hardly anyone came to America from the Ottoman Empire before 1881.) Of these, 155,000 escaped "Turkey in Europe" (the Balkans) and 205,000 escaped "Turkey in Asia" (basically Turkey, Armenia, Syria, and Lebanon).

From the end of World War One to 1931, about 40,000 people came from the severely shrunken Turkey. After the war, Turkey would consist of the Anatolian Peninsula in Asia and Constantinople and the bit of land surrounding it in Europe. About 24,000 of these people came from "Turkey in Asia" – mostly Armenians and Greeks, and another 17,000 of these people came from "Turkey in Europe" – again, mostly Greeks and Armenians.

Lebanon and Syria were under French control after World War One. About 13,000 people left these lands to come to America.

From the end of World War One to 1931, another 55,000 or so people came from Greece, about 4000 came from Bulgaria, about 2000 came from the new Albania, and 50,000 or so came from the new Yugoslavia. In the years before World War One, the villages of many of these people had been under Turkish misrule.

Speaking of the Turks, only 23,000 of them came to America from 1898 to 1931.

GREEKS

Before 1898, about 12,000 Greeks, virtually all from the kingdom of Greece, came to the United States. From 1898 through 1914, about 370,000 Greeks came to the United States. Of these, about 280,000 came from the kingdom of Greece, and most of the rest came from Turkish-occupied land. From 1915 through 1931, another 145,000 or so Greeks came to the United States. Of these, about 115,000 came from the kingdom of Greece, and most of the rest came from Turkish-occupied land.

This is a total of about 530,000 Greek immigrants. Of these, about 410,000 came from the kingdom of Greece and most of the other 120,000 came from Turkish-occupied land. The Turks ruled Epirus (northwestern Greece), most of Thessaly (central and northern Greece), Salonika (Thessalonika) and the surrounding area of southern Macedonia, Thrace (from Salonika to Constantinople), and Crete (nominally), all areas (except Thrace and the city of Salonika itself) overwhelmingly Greek, until after the First Balkan War in 1913. Many Greeks also lived in Constantinople (Istanbul), and Smyrna (Izmir) and other port towns of western Turkey until the Greek government brought the remaining one million or so ethnic Greeks in Turkey to Greece in the 1920s to protect them from retaliatory slaughter by the Turks in the wake of the Greeks' suicidal invasion of Turkey after World War One.

ROMANIANS, BUKOVINANS, AND MOLDOVANS

Romanians were totally independent of the Turks (but not of the Hapsburgs or the Romanovs) when their period of immigration to America really began. In all, about 150,000 Romanian immigrants came to America from 1898 through 1931.

Before 1898, about 10,000 people, mostly Jews, came to America from the kingdom of Romania. Another 10,000 or so people, mostly Jews, came to America from Romania in 1899 and 1900. Hardly any Romanians came to America during that time.

From 1898 through 1914, about 130,000 Romanians — including some from Bukovina -- came to the United States. (Bukovina is tucked into the Carpathian Mountains just east of Ruthenia. Today Bukovina is divided between Romania and Ukraine.) Of these, about 65,000 came from the kingdom of Romania and most of the remaining 65,000 or so came from Transylvania and Bukovina, areas which were under the rule of Austria-Hungary. A small number of Romanians came from Bessarabia (present-day Moldova) which was under Russian rule until 1918, and then was part of Romania until the Russians reseized it in 1940. Since the early 1990s, Moldova has been independent.

From 1915 through 1931, another 20,000 or so Romanians came to the United States. Of these, fewer than 5000 – mostly from outside of the kingdom of Romania – fled during World War One. From 1919 through 1931, about 70,000 people came from the expanded kingdom of Romania, which now also had Transylvania, Bukovina, Bessarabia (present-day Moldova), and southern Dobrujda (a Bulgarian-populated area between the Danube River and the Black Sea that Romania would hold until 1940), besides Wallachia and Moldavia. However, only about 15,000 of these were Romanians. The other 55,000 or so were of Hungarian, Jewish, Ukrainian, or Russian blood.

ALBANIANS

American immigration officials did not count Albanians as a separate ethnic group before the end of World War One. They didn't have to. The mostly Moslem Albanians weren't breaking down doors and gates at Ellis Island. Only about 2000 Albanians came to America from the end of World War One to 1931. Many of these immigrants were Catholics and Orthodox Christians.

ARMENIANS

From 1898 through 1914, about 55,000 Armenians came to the United States. Before 1898, hardly any Armenians came to the United States. From 1915 through 1931, another 30,000 Armenians came to the United States. This is a total of about 85,000 Armenian immigrants. A large number of Armenians lived across the border in the part of Armenia in the Russian Empire, and later the Soviet Union, but hardly any of these Armenians fled their homeland to come to America. Many more Armenians could have come to America if the Turks hadn't murdered so many of them.

LEBANESE AND "SYRIANS"

From 1898 through 1914, about 90,000 people who immigration officials called "Syrians" came to the United States. These were mostly Christian Lebanese and Syrians and Assyrians. Before 1898, hardly any Lebanese or Syrians or Assyrians came to America. From 1915 through 1931, another 20,000 or so "Syrians"came to the United States. This is a total of about 110,000 Lebanese and Syrian and Assyrian immigrants. **(17)**

NET IMMIGRATION (IMMIGRANTS ALLOWED IN MINUS IMMIGRANTS WHO RETURNED HOME)

American immigration officials for many years did not keep track of the number of people who emigrated from America. But the number of people who came to America and then went back to Europe was large.

From 1892 through 1900 – the first nine years Ellis Island was open – roughly 1.9 million males and 1.2 million females emigrated to the United States. From 1901 through 1910, roughly 6.1 million males and 2.7 million females emigrated to the United States. From 1911 through 1920, roughly 3.6 million males and 2.1 million females emigrated to the United States. From 1921 through 1930, roughly 2.3 million males and 1.8 million females emigrated to the United States. These figures include boys and girls as well as men and women. From 1892 through 1930, 6.1 million more males emigrated to America than females; the great majority of the extra males were adults.

Many men and some women went back to their homelands, and many came back to America a second time or more. My wife's Slovak grandmother and my own Irish great-grandmother were two of these many people. Since they already had legal status in America, they were probably counted as travelers instead of departures. Most of those who came to America – except in the first decade or so of the 1900s – did it once and stayed.

Since American women tended to marry American men, the immigrant males had to marry immigrant females in America or in the home country. Of course, not all men and women married ... among the immigrants were groups of priests and nuns whose vows forbade this. Likewise, there were those who chose not to marry, and there were those who couldn't find someone who would have them. And there were many women from time immemorial to almost the present day who never married because they sacrificed their lives to care for parents or relatives. But the math says in the busiest Ellis Island era years there was a surplus of 6.1 million male immigrants. Not all that many wound up living without female companionship for life.

Even with all the deaths working immigrants suffered in industrial accidents and suffered as crime victims, they come nowhere near filling the disparity in numbers between males and females who came to America. <u>*Most of these "extra" men obviously came to America to work for a few years, and then returned to their home countries with their savings*</u>.

Italian males were particularly prone to do this. Many Italians sent money home to help their families. Several records of returns indicate there were far more Italian male immigrants than female immigrants, and more

Italian male returners than men of any other ethnic groups in the Ellis Island era. Some estimates say more than 50% of Italian men who came here returned to Italy, or made more than one immigration here before staying for good. Fewer Spaniards and Portuguese came to the United States, but their percentages were probably similar, based on how many of them went back and forth between Iberia and Latin America.

These sources also indicate 30% or so of Slav and other Eastern European men who came here returned home, or made more than one trip here before staying for good. Many men from places like Poland, Slovakia, Croatia, Hungary, and Greece also returned to their homelands in very high numbers after earning enough money for their plans.

Jews were the least likely to return to Europe, because most of them were fleeing oppression. They had nothing to return to. The Irish were almost as prone as the Jews to be "one and done" in terms of numbers of trips across the Atlantic Ocean as immigrants. Some estimates say about 2% of Jews and about 5% of Irish returned to Europe for good. Also the ratio of women to men was about 1 to 1 for these groups, which indicates family flight and also flight for single adults of both sexes. The Irish, like the Jews, were victims of oppression where they came from.

People from Western Europe (Britain, the Low Countries, Switzerland, Germany, France) and from Scandinavia (Denmark, Norway, Sweden, Finland) were in between these two extremes. Estimates say between 10% and 20% of these people returned to Europe for good or made multiple immigrations.

There are no thorough statistics from the Ellis Island era on immigrant departures because American officials didn't start keeping them until late in the first decade of the 1900s. Before the advent of reliable steamship travel and cheap steerage tickets, there was little returning. World War One and the later quotas and finally the Great Depression put an end to wholesale temporary immigration for work in the Ellis Island era. Estimates indicate about four million Europeans went home for good in the Ellis Island era. This does not count the roughly 160,000 people who American authorities deported for various violations of the law they committed. Nor does it count the 400,000 or so people American authorities barred from entering the country as immigrants. **(18)**

A likely alternative figure is perhaps nine million of the 37 million or so immigrants (32 million from Europe, and 5 million from elsewhere in the world) returned to their homelands. This comes from subtracting the 6 million extra males (most were suspected temporary immigrants) from the 37 million gross immigration figure to get 31 million people, then estimating perhaps 10 percent of all other immigrants returned to their homelands. This much higher estimate still means 28 million people came here for good from 1820 through 1930 – including my ancestors and my wife's ancestors, and many of your ancestors as well.

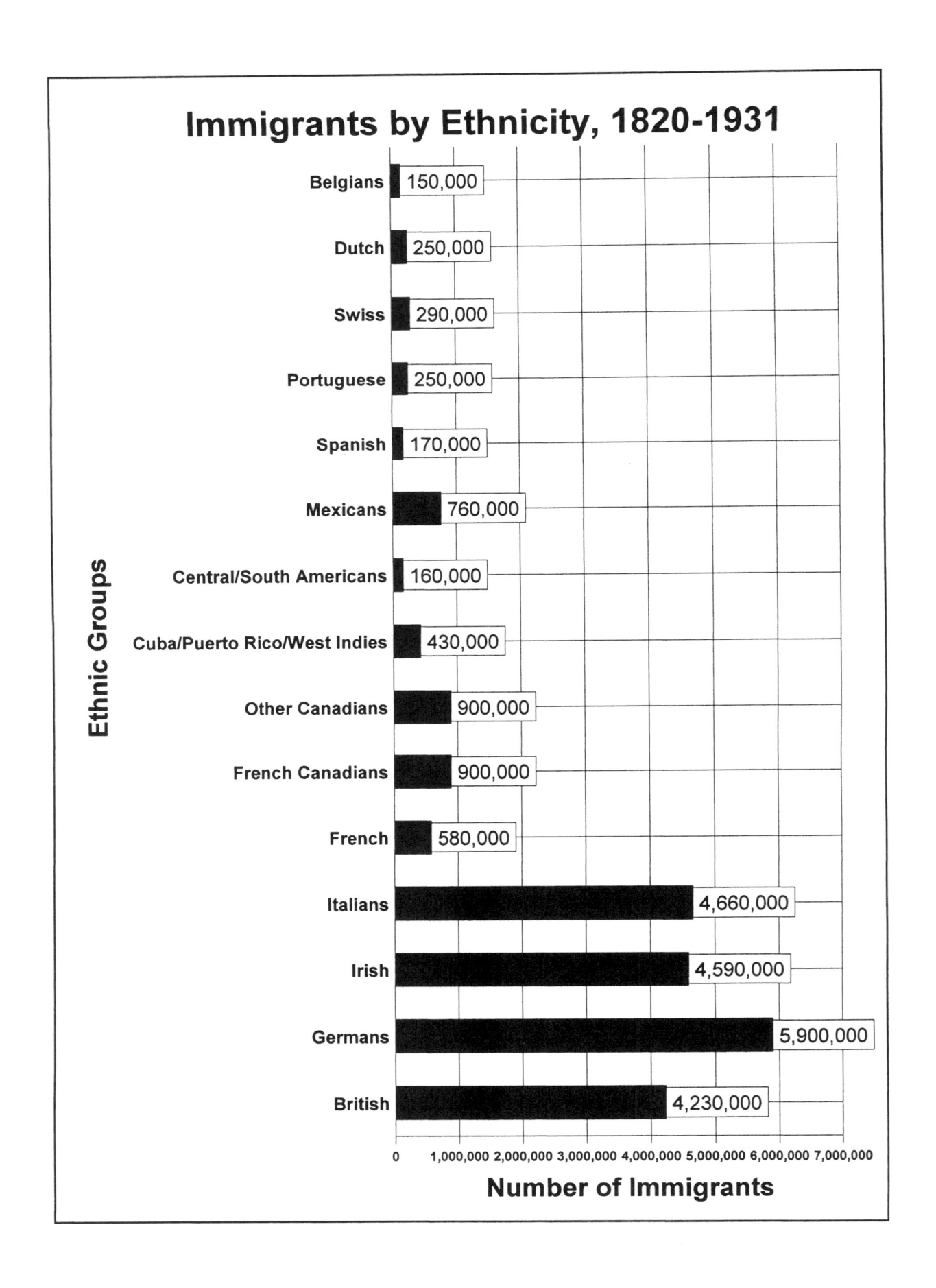

Immigrants by Ethnicity, 1820-1931

Ethnic Group	Number of Immigrants
Belgians	150,000
Dutch	250,000
Swiss	290,000
Portuguese	250,000
Spanish	170,000
Mexicans	760,000
Central/South Americans	160,000
Cuba/Puerto Rico/West Indies	430,000
Other Canadians	900,000
French Canadians	900,000
French	580,000
Italians	4,660,000
Irish	4,590,000
Germans	5,900,000
British	4,230,000

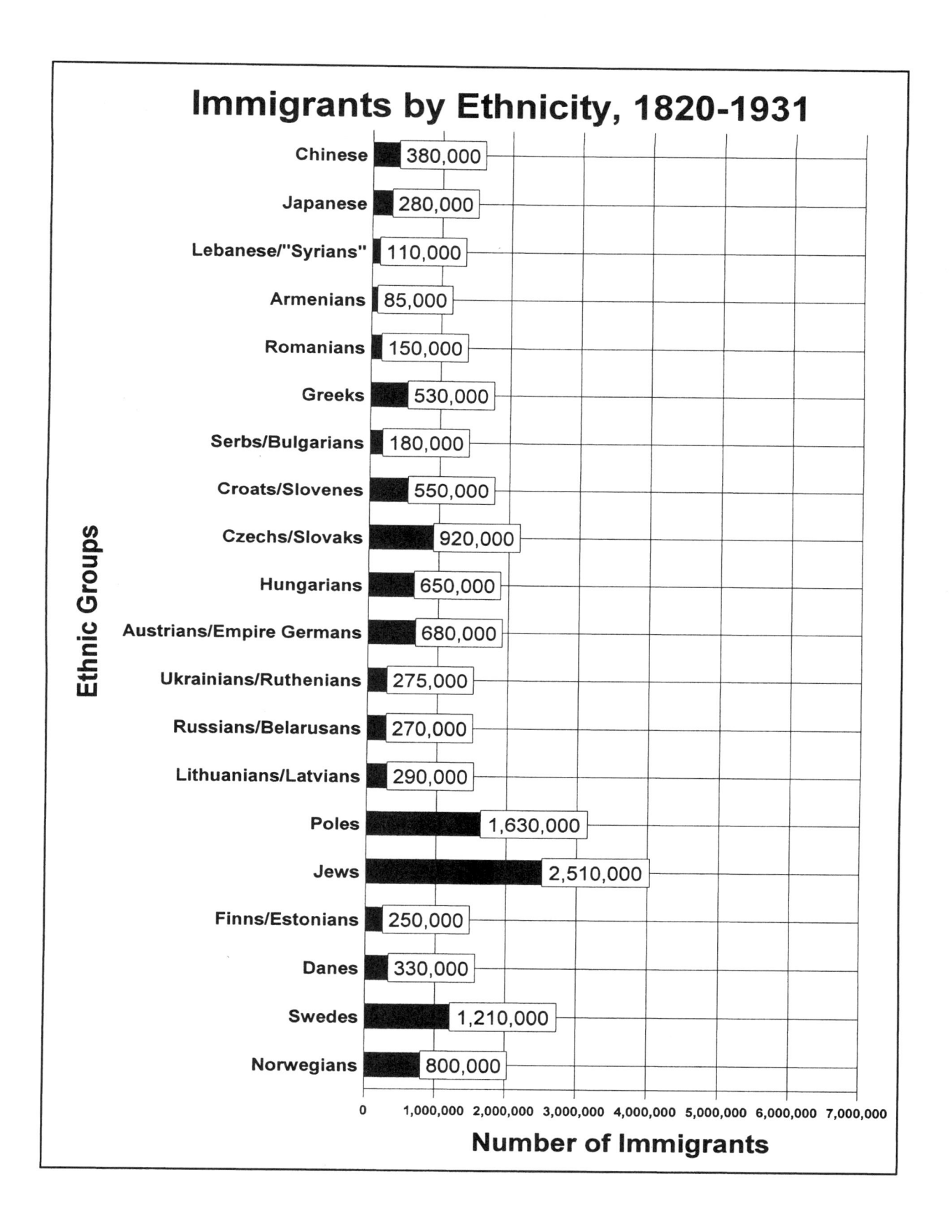

Immigrants by Ethnicity, 1820-1931

Ethnic Group	Number of Immigrants
Chinese	380,000
Japanese	280,000
Lebanese/"Syrians"	110,000
Armenians	85,000
Romanians	150,000
Greeks	530,000
Serbs/Bulgarians	180,000
Croats/Slovenes	550,000
Czechs/Slovaks	920,000
Hungarians	650,000
Austrians/Empire Germans	680,000
Ukrainians/Ruthenians	275,000
Russians/Belarusans	270,000
Lithuanians/Latvians	290,000
Poles	1,630,000
Jews	2,510,000
Finns/Estonians	250,000
Danes	330,000
Swedes	1,210,000
Norwegians	800,000

ELLIS ISLAND SCRAPBOOK

WHY AMERICA WAS ABLE TO TAKE IN THE IMMIGRANTS

America took in the immigrants because there was plenty of land, and there was plenty of work for the immigrants and everyone else to do.

The Spaniards introduced Spanish-style ranching (men on horses controlling large free-ranging herds of livestock to get the most dollar value out of rangeland that was of poor quality) to the areas that would become present-day California and Texas. They also introduced farming, irrigation, winemaking, mining, schooling, and skilled trades to these areas. The Spanish also taught these skills to American Indians who would learn them. This would "civilize" the areas the Spanish colonized and make the lands easier for Americans to use once they seized them during and after the Mexican War.

The Industrial Revolution had started in England, but people in the Northeastern and Midwestern states would push it much faster.

In the late 1700s, English immigrant Samuel Slater brought the know-how on how to build cotton thread spinning machines to America. At roughly the same time, Eli Whitney invented the cotton "gin," which made cotton a feasible cash crop in America for those who had enough land to plant the crop and enough slaves to pick it. Whitney also hit upon the idea of interchangeable parts to provide muskets on contract to the American government when John Adams was president. *(Despite his brainstorm, he was late in delivering the firearms. This was possibly the first American defense contract overrun.)* Whitney's first idea would make cotton an inexpensive cloth but retard the progress of the Industrial Revolution in the Southern states and lead indirectly to the Civil War. His second idea would make the success of the Industrial Revolution possible.

The power loom made commercial clothmaking feasible. Fabric mills sprung up in New England in the early 1800s using cheap waterpower and cheap farmgirl labor. Eventually steam engines would replace waterpower. Eventually many fabric making companies moved their mills south, where cheaper Southern labor would replace New England labor.

The first practical steam engine was the work of Scotsman James Watt in the late 1700s. In the early 1800s American Oliver Evans developed a steam engine that could power factory machinery. The rise of the steam engine, which engineers and mechanics improved upon all through the 1800s, meant factories didn't have to depend on water power. They could burn coal, wood, or oil and make steam power to weave cloth, mill grain, saw timber, or do other tasks wherever men decided to install them.

The steam engine also made faster travel possible. In the very early 1800s, American Robert Fulton built a feasible commercial steamboat, and soon American state governors and private companies were having canals built to move goods by water. The country needed laborers to dig these canals, and workers to build the boats to travel them.

Britishers invented the steam locomotive and railroads. But Americans laid down many more miles of track to connect their cities. They needed to, for America was a much bigger country ... the island of Britain is only about the size of Minnesota, or smaller than New York, New Jersey, and Pennsylvania put together. The country needed laborers to lay the rails, mine the coal that fed the locomotives, and make the steel that made the locomotives and rails possible.

Shipbuilders would combine steel and steam to build ships that could carry cargos and passengers quicker and safer than wooden ships.

Railroads and ships needed lots of steel. American William Kelly in the late 1840s and Briton Henry Bessemer in the 1850s developed pneumatic converters to make large batches of high-quality steel cheaply.

Iron works and steel mills sprung up in Pennsylvania to be near the supply of high-quality coal that steelmaking required. (It takes much more coal as fuel than iron ore as raw material to make steel.) Railroads and ships brought the coal and the iron ore to the steel mills, and factories rose to build locomotives, rails, rolling stock, bridges, ship hull steel, and steamship parts. Steam-driven pumps kept many coal mines dry and provided power to perform many tasks in these mines, making it easier and cheaper to mine coal.

In the 1840s, John Deere built a steel plow factory in Illinois; the steel plows helped farmers bust prairie sod better than they could with a wooden or cast iron plow. At about the same time, Cyrus McCormick built a factory for horse-pulled reapers in Chicago. This invention cut grain-harvesting time. Threshing machines and mowing machines would follow. These devices made it possible for farmers to raise more crops. Even humble barbed wire made it possible for farmers to retain livestock and protect their fields, especially in the Great Plains.

Steamboats and trains would carry the extra grain, which made it easier and cheaper to feed people who were coming to work in mills and factories in the expanding cities. Eventually steam-powered machinery would find use on many farms.

Steam-driven saw mills and grain mills would make it easier to make lumber and process grain for people.

Steamboats and trains would carry these products also.

Edwin Drake erected the first commercial oil drilling rig in Pennsylvania in 1859. Men built refineries to make crude oil into kerosene and other products. Kerosene would light America's homes and businesses. Refiners would eventually figure out how to make diesel oil and gasoline, which would make the diesel engine and the gasoline engine feasible.

Thomas Edison invented the light bulb in 1879 and introduced the direct-current electric power plant in the 1880s. George Westinghouse, Serb immigrant Nikula Tesla, and German Jewish immigrant Charles Steinmetz developed alternating current and alternating current power plants and transformers, which were more efficient at bringing electricity to businesses and homes. Tesla developed alternating current motors, which were more useful than steam-driven machinery.

Electric motors replaced steam power for driving machines in many factories. Electricity replaced kerosene and candles in homes and businesses. Electricity would make commercial refrigeration feasible, which in turn prolonged the freshness of meat, fish, dairy products, and produce, making it possible to feed more people more nutritiously and more cheaply.

Mining engineers developed techniques for making mines safer to work in and more profitable to operate. Metallurgical engineers discovered processes that made it easier to extract metal from ore. Chemical engineers discovered processes that made it easier to refine oil, and make products from coal. Mechanical engineers and industrial engineers made better machine tools and designed more effective processes to manufacture the goods people needed.

A number of inventors would make internal combustion engines (diesel engines and gasoline engines) practical. Such engines would power locomotives, cars, trucks, and tractors, starting in earnest in the first decade of the 1900s. The internal combustion engine would make it possible for Orville and Wilbur Wright to power their first airplane in 1903.

Charles Goodyear in 1839 discovered vulcanizing, a process to make rubber useable in industry. Rubber would gain use as a waterproof material that could be used to make a number of products. Likewise, chemists discovered how to use coal to make plastics.

American Samuel Morse in the late 1830s invented the telegraph, which helped not only the railroad industry, but other businessmen who needed information quickly. Soon journalists were also using the telegraph to report the news. Cyrus Field in 1866 first put telegraph wires under the ocean to provide speedy communication with Europe.

Better printing presses allowed newspapermen, magazine editors, and book publishers to sell printed matter to people cheaply. Because most people in America could read, and because there was freedom of expression, there was a market for their publications.

Teachers in Catholic schools, other religion-based schools, and public schools taught most Americans reading, writing, arithmetic, and a number of other useful subjects. Americans could understand more ideas, spread them, and make use of them, thanks to these teachers.

Scottish immigrant Alexander Graham Bell invented the telephone in 1876, which sped communications further. Marconi would make the first trans-Atlantic wireless telegraph transmission in 1901. This would lead to radio.

In the mid and late 1800s, Europeans like Frenchman Louis Pasteur, German Robert Koch, and Britisher Joseph Lister studied germs and provided ways to kill them. Pasteur and Koch developed vaccines and treatments to kill germs. Lister is considered the father of antiseptic surgery.

Europeans and Americans developed sewer systems, water processing plants, and other sanitation practices, which made it possible for larger amounts of people to live in cities without regularly dying of epidemics. Electricity made it possible to provide public transportation, lighting, and power to homes and industries in the cities more safely.

These inventions, discoveries, improvements, and applications made it possible to feed vast numbers of people, move raw materials and goods, and make modern industry and modern cities possible. In so many ways these inventions, discoveries, improvements, and applications were interdependent or contingent. In other words, someone had to discover or invent something that would in turn make something else possible, and that advance would in turn lead to other advances. All of these helped make America the leading industrial and agricultural nation on the globe.

The American system did not penalize initiative. This made it easier for people to produce the inventions, discoveries, improvements, and applications that led to the industrialization of America. There were no established cartels or government officials waiting to crush new ideas, or bleed them of profit, like in Europe. A very high proportion of investment capitalists in America were willing to gamble on promising ideas, and cash in on the results. American academia, much less formal than Europe's, was more receptive to ideas. Since America was a new country, there wasn't a strong enough financial establishment and landed aristocracy to hold people back (except for the South, which paid dearly for its wealthiest citizens' fixation on slave-raised cash crops) If someone thought his hometown was too stifling, he could move away and do better elsewhere.

What was the upshot of all of this?

America, from its very beginnings until well into the 20th Century, was going to need extra help. America had room and good land for farmers willing to work and raise food. America needed miners to mine coal, iron ore, and other metals. America needed workers to build the railroads, locomotives, canals, and steamboats to take the minerals to the factories. America needed loggers to provide the lumber to build ships, railroad cars, and houses. America needed laborers to work in the factories and build the cities the factories were in. America needed the trained technical people and the thinkers and entrepreneurs to make things happen.

America back in the day needed immigrants. America had room available for immigrants willing to come, earn their way, and assimilate into American society. And from the 1700s through the Ellis Island era, most immigrants were willing to become real Americans and contribute to the nation.

THE EMIGRANT EMPRESS

In the 1940s, Americans would open their doors to a European empress who came to America as a refugee. For a decade or so she would join the people she had once ruled.

Zita Bourbon-Parma von Hapsburg, the former empress of Austria-Hungary, came to the throne in 1916 with her husband Karl when his great-uncle Franz Josef died. The imperial couple lost their thrones late in 1918, when World War One collapsed their empire. They went into exile, Karl died in the early 1920, and Zita would live in very modest circumstances in European exile with her eight children. But she saw to it that they got schooling and training.

Zita's oldest son Otto, who would have been a ruler if she and her husband Karl hadn't been forced out of Austria and Hungary, was under a sentence of death from Hitler because he publicly opposed joining Austria to Nazi Germany. Otto worked against Hitler's seizure of Austria, and when Hitler succeeded, he moved the family to Belgium, in whose army his uncles Sixtus and Xavier (brothers of his mother Zita) had served in World War One. The family, with the help of Portuguese diplomat Aristides Sousa Mendes, fled to Portugal when Belgium fell to the Germans, and then to America. Otto also worked with Sousa to help get Jews out of Nazi-occupied Europe.

Zita lived in New York and Quebec throughout the 1940s. In one of her public appearances in the 1940s, she attended the installation of the Byzantine Catholic bishop of Pittsburgh. (The great Catholic preacher Bishop Fulton J. Sheen, then a monsignor, gave the sermon at this event.) The Slovaks and Ruthenians who brought this form of Catholicism to America came from lands that for hundreds of years were under the rule of the Hapsburg family she married into. Zita was of French, Italian, and Portuguese ancestry.

In the 1950s Zita returned to Europe. Otto and some of her other children would rise to prominence in the professions and they were able to make her last four decades of life very comfortable. Zita died in a convent in Switzerland in 1989 and she was given a public funeral in Vienna – the city that she once ruled an empire from – that was more than worthy of a former empress. The sober and solemn rite was a moving spectacle that inspired many people to reflect on the vanity of human life and the reality of eternal life. **(19)**

Unlike many of the immigrants today, Zita and her children and nephews did not show ingratitude to the people who gave them sanctuary. Once he came to America, Otto von Hapsburg worked as a civilian to help America's war effort; American officials would not allow him to serve in the military. His brothers and his cousins fought in the ranks of America's armed forces. Despite being a prominent journalist and a European politician, Otto von Hapsburg tried to be a friend of the United States in his writings and in his political acts.

Ironically, many of the "best and brightest" of Otto von Hapsburg's never-to-be-realized domain and the other lands of Europe left for America because of his ancestors and others in the ruling classes of Europe. So did many, many, many peasants and laborers, who added their own efforts to America.

All of these solid people could have contributed to making Europe stronger, if only the elites and their bureaucrats in their homelands had been willing to provide the people with security and fair treatment. When the leaders failed the people, some people rebelled, and many more simply left to find better lives in America. With their blood, sweat, and tears, and their desire to become real Americans, they would help build their adopted homeland, the United States, into the mightiest nation in the world.

END NOTES

1. The account of the governor of Virginia sending armed invaders into Maryland and jailing and driving out priests, and the account of English officials and Protestant settlers persecuting Catholics comes from Michael Schwartz's book The Persistent Prejudice (pages 25-28). Cardinal James Gibbons, the bishop of Baltimore in the late 1800s and early 1900s, also commented on the laws against Catholics in Maryland in his book The Faith of Our Fathers (pages 192-197).

2. Information on the kidnaping and rape of Pocahontas comes from The American Heritage Book of Indians by William Brandon (pages 165-167), and from The True Story of Pocahontas by Linwood "Little Bear" Custalow, a member of Pocahontas' tribe.

3. Information on the abuses of the Puritans and Pilgrims comes from George Willison's book Saints and Strangers. This book, based on the Puritans' and Pilgrims' own records, and published in 1945, long before leftist and atheist political correctness dominated the history field, noted the Puritans' and Pilgrims' robbery and enslavement and butchery of the Indians (and to a lesser extent their mistreatment of rival Quakers).

Willison noted the Pilgrims' original pastor would not go with them from the Netherlands to New England because of their disagreeableness. Willison also noted these Protestants' hatred for the Catholic-style celebration of the Christmas and Easter holidays; they outlawed the celebration of Christmas for many years. He also reported the treason of many of their descendants who supported the British against the Patriots.

Willison also noted the Puritans' and Pilgrims' many sexual problems. An elder named Studley had to be drummed out before the Pilgrims came to America for serial adultery, incest, and child molesting. Prominent minister John Cotton had to be shipped out for sexually abusing young girls; he was allowed to pastor in South Carolina. Willison reported many bonneted women and buckle-hatted men had problems obeying the commandment against adultery, including one spirited matron who was punished for preferring to go native and cheat with red men. He also noted most weddings were civil weddings in Massachusetts in colonial days because the godly Protestants hated "popery." In other words, most Puritan and Pilgrim men and women wed in front of a magistrate instead of in church under the ministrations of a minister because Catholics had church weddings which priests solemnized. So the Puritans' and Pilgrims' ceremonies were more like a "civil union" than like the Sacrament of Matrimony.

Willison was not trying to tear these people down. He admired their guts, their hardiness, and their zeal. But as a good historian, he researched the truth and reported it.

4. Information on the Dutch abuse of American Indians comes from The American Heritage Book of Indians (pages 167-170), and from the book The Gateway States (page 33).

5. Ben Franklin, Jesuit priest John Carroll, and Maryland Catholic Charles Carroll visited Quebec's French leaders and priests in early 1776 to try to get them to join the American cause. They failed, in large part, because of the Quebecois' distrust of the bigotry of the American Protestants. Americans had attacked the Quebec Act of 1774 because it afforded tolerance to Quebec's French Catholics. Information on this ill-fated parley and the anti-Catholic prejudice in New England that caused it to fail comes from Bruce Lancaster's book The American Heritage Book of The Revolution (pages 142-143), and from Thomas Fleming's book Liberty! The American Revolution (pages 166-167).

6. The French had previously tried to build a canal across the isthmus of Panama (which was then part of Colombia) in the late 1800s. But the effort ended in failure, the deaths of more than 20,000 workers and engineers, and a huge financial and bribery scandal that involved many of France's politicians.

During the Spanish-American War, the crew of the Oregon, an American battleship, had to take it around the bottom of South America to join the American fleet in the Caribbean Sea. The ship's journey was widely publicized, and navalists like Theodore Roosevelt thundered for an American canal. When he became president in 1901, one of his first orders of business was to overturn an American-British agreement to jointly control a canal. Roosevelt got the British to back out, and he determined America would build a canal in Central America and guard it with military force.

A French engineer named Bunau-Varilla, who wanted to retrieve something for the French company involved, and the company's American fixer William Cromwell convinced Congress in 1902 to vote to continue the canal project in Panama (the Americans were leaning toward putting the canal in Nicaragua) and pay the French company $40 million in exchange for getting American title to the canal route and the survey work, the engineering documents, machinery, and other Panama assets the French company had.

The Colombians heard about the $40 million offer, and demanded a share of the money earmarked for the French firm. Their diplomats reached a tentative deal with the American government to get $10 million for 100 years of use of a six-mile wide swath of the Panama isthmus that contained the canal route and another $250,000 a year as part of the profit for the tolls the canal authorities would charge. However, the dictator of Colombia vetoed the deal, and demanded all of the $40 million.

The French agreement with the Colombian government was due to end in late 1904. Then the Colombians could cut the failed French out entirely and make their own deal with the Americans. Roosevelt was at first agreeable to the Colombian offer, but then he got itchy to start work on the canal. He didn't want to wait until late 1904.

Bunau-Varilla convinced American officials they could engineer a "revolution" in Panama against the Colombian government. Locals in Panama rebelled roughly once a year; Roosevelt had been helping Colombian officials keep a lid on the rebels so the local railroad across the isthmus (which Americans built and had used for decades) could keep running.

Without committing formally to the scheme, Roosevelt in essence assisted the "revolt" to make the deal happen. An American warship showed up off of Panama, and Panamanian and American railroaders, some other locals, and some Colombian soldiers who were bought off carried out the revolt. The American warship's officers and crew, by forcibly protecting Americans in the area and by negotiation, persuaded the Colombian soldiers who wanted to quell the rebellion to back off and go home.

The locals set up a government. Bunau-Varilla, who funded the rebellion, got himself appointed as Panama's envoy. He said the new government would accept $10 million and $250,000 a year in exchange for American ownership, not lease, of a 10-mile swath through Panama for the canal. And by the way, the French company would still get the $40 million. Congress and Teddy Roosevelt accepted these more generous terms very quickly. The Panamanian leaders were outraged over the Frenchman's sellout in giving the land away, but agreed to abide by it.

Roosevelt got the canal started. U.S. Army doctors beat the yellow-fever that had killed so many men working for the French two decades earlier. U.S. Army engineers led the assault on the hills, swamps, and other terrain features that had blocked the French. By 1914, the Panama Canal was ready for ship traffic.

The Panama Canal was an impressive achievement, but like the winning of the West, there was something wrong about it. The sordid deal between Bunau-Varilla and Theodore Roosevelt basically cheated the Colombians out of a fair share of the money the canal has earned over the last century.

Roosevelt should have bought the canal zone in Panama from Colombia, left the eastern half of Panama in Colombian hands, and let the western half of Panama merge with Costa Rica or become a smaller independent state. Or he should have paid Colombia the $40 million and secured title to the Canal Zone. (In the 1920s, Americans did pay the Colombians $25 million for the takeover.)

Instead, we got a tainted land deal from the new Panamanian government that cut the little made-up country in half. In Teddy Roosevelt's time, this didn't matter. No tinpot dictator from Panama would get a hearing from our government if he tried to evict the Americans from the Canal Zone. Instead, he would find himself dead or in exile, and his subjects would find American soldiers and marines occupying the land.

But times had changed by our nation's bicentennial. (The author, a military veteran, was in Jungle School in the Canal Zone on July 4, 1976.) Prominent American leftists in the 1960s and 1970s bemoaned the "injustice" of "American occupiers" "splitting a sovereign state in two." They forgot to mention the locals could never have built the canal whose tolls propped up their country; America did it for them. They also forgot to mention Panamanians owed their independence to America. Lyndon Johnson, a president whose regime was riddled with corruption and incompetence, suggested giving up the canal.

In early 1977, the author took leave, visited his congressman in Washington, and urged him not to give away the Panama Canal. Any American who has seen the Canal like the author has can only stand in awe of the genius and courage of the men of this land who conquered the jungle, the terrain, and yellow fever to build it. However, the stupidity and/or corruption of globalists like Jimmy Carter and Henry Kissinger led American officials to give the Canal Zone to the *bandidos* who ran Panama.

In 1997, while Bill Clinton was president, the Red Chinese government firm Hutchison Whampoa Ltd. won contracts from the Panamanian government to operate the port facilities on both ends of the Panama Canal. In a national emergency, the Chinese could sabotage the canal, which still allows the quick transoceanic passage of a large amount of America's commerce. Clinton did nothing to stop the Chinese grab of these ports.

Clinton had personally assisted COSCO (China Ocean Shipping Company), a shipping firm owned by the Chinese military, in its attempt to lease a former U.S. Navy base at the port of Long Beach, California. Members of Congress in 1998 killed Clinton's bid to let the Chinese in by amending a defense spending bill to forbid port officials from granting the lease and not allowing the president the power to waive restrictions on the Chinese.

The Chinese Army used a COSCO ship in an attempt to smuggle 2000 AK-47 assault rifles into California for sale to street gangs in 1996 via two other Chinese government owned firms. U.S. Customs agents boarded the ship while it was in Los Angeles' harbor. They had to do so because a Clinton minion tipped off the Chinese about the agency's impending bust, according to U.S. Customs officials. Janet Reno or one of her people at the Justice Department had the perpetrators released, and they fled to China. The Red Chinese firms also tried to smuggle in shoulder-fired anti-aircraft missiles, rockets, and rocket launchers. Guess how these weapons would have been used if they had succeeded. A year later, Janet Reno was dodging questions from Congressmen on why the Clinton administration had allowed COSCO a lease at the port of Long Beach despite this act of murderous smuggling.

In the past few decades, Colombian drug lords have repaid America's removal of Panama from their ancestors many times over. How? They have flooded our country with drugs. They have made back the money we should have paid the Colombian people many times over by supplying the many dopers in government, media, entertainment, college campuses, law offices and elsewhere in American society with the marijuana and cocaine and other little helpers these losers seem to require to get through the day.

Info on the Panama Canal comes from Nathan Miller's book Theodore Roosevelt: A Life (pages 398-409), the book U.S. Overseas (pages 120-123 123), and David McCullough's epic book The Path Between the Seas (pages 329-402).

Info on the Panama Canal surrender and Chinese control of the port facilities comes from a 12/14/1999 BBC News article. Info on Clinton and COSCO comes from World Net Daily (9/21/1998). Info on the Red Chinese gunrunning operation that had inside help from Clinton operatives comes from Charles Smith's article for Newsmax (12/9/2002). Other sources for the dealings of Clinton with the Chinese, the Chinese control of Panama Canal ports, the Chinese export of weapons to criminals and other unsavory characters in America, and the dodging of Janet Reno include Congressman Duncan Hunter's article in the 4/21/1997 issue of Insight on the News, the 5/14/1998 Congressional Review (pages S4864-S4867), an article in Human Events (3/6/2006), and Charles Smith's 6/17/2000 article for World Net Daily.

7. Information on the railroad barons' gouging comes from Irving Stone's book Men To Match My Mountains (pages

AMERICAN REVOLUTION

Left: April 19, 1775 was the day armed Americans first stood up to British aggression, at Lexington, Massachusetts. The armed Patriots defended themselves when fired upon, then escaped a much larger British force. American militia stood up to the British at nearby Concord, shown here, and prevented them from seizing American weapons. Patriots harried the Redcoats on their retreat to Boston. Credit: U.S. National Guard.

Below: Washington and Von Steuben made the 8500 or so ragged Americans who survived the Valley Forge, Pennsylvania encampment the winter of 1777-1778 into real soldiers. These men would never again lose to the British in battle. Re-enaction photo by author.

Center left: Tadeusz Kosciuszko, a Polish officer, also aided Washington. So did Lafayette, a French officer. Casimir Pulaski, another Polish officer, died in combat in American service. Roughly 30% of the Continental Army was Irish, and 5% to 10% of America's Revolutionary War soldiers and sailors were blacks. Credit: Kosciuszko Society.

Bottom: American soldiers storm British defenses at Yorktown, Virginia. The Brits surrendered October 19, 1781, 6-1/2 years after Lexington and Concord. Credit: U.S. Army.

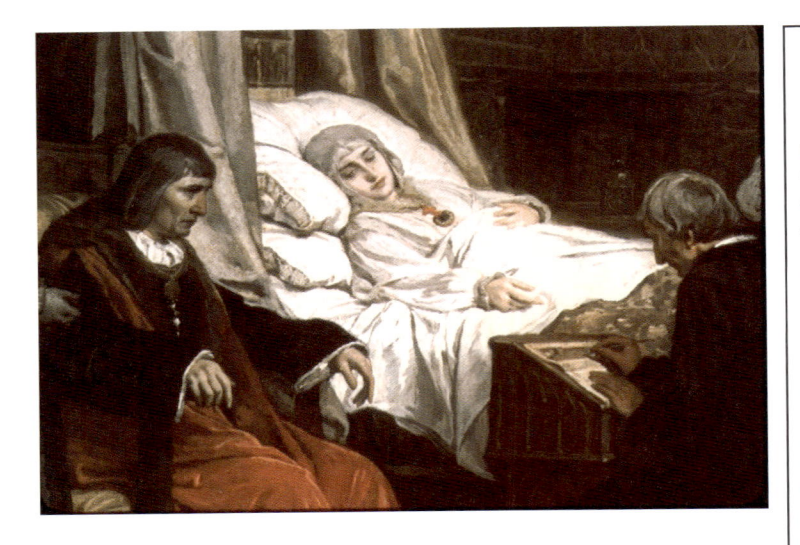

SPAIN'S CONTRIBUTIONS TO AMERICA

Left: Crusader Queen Isabella is the mother of the Spanish nation. She united Spain by seeking out and marrying husband King Fernando of Aragon, and letting him mesh his realm in eastern Spain with her realm of Castile in central and northern Spain. They ruled as equals. She and he led and paid for the fighting men who pushed the bloodthirsty Moslems out of Spain. She also bankrolled Columbus' voyage on the chance he might find something of value. She also forbade enslavement of the American Indians. (It happened after her death, shown here in the painting "Testament of Isabella the Catholic," by Eduardo Rosales. King Fernando is by her bedside and Cardinal Cisneros is writing down her orders.) Thanks to the warrior queen, the Spanish beat the British to the U.S. by about half a century.

Center: Queen Isabella ordered the evangelization of American Indians and the integration of American Indians into Spanish American society. Catholic priests built missions, ministered to the Indians, and taught them farming methods and skilled trades. Santa Ysabel Mission, in San Diego County, California, is one of many missions built in the Spanish style. There are far more American Indians in America and elsewhere in the Western Hemisphere where the Spanish ruled than where the British ruled. Photo by author.

Below left: The grounds of San Fernando Mission in Los Angeles County contain a Catholic church, a museum, a seminary, a cemetery, and a park. This Hispanic bride has just been married at the church over Christmastime. Photo by author. Disclosure: The author has visited and participated in many religious services at this great mission over the years. He also has a little Spanish blood, of which he is proud.

Below right: The Mission Bells of San Carlos Borromeo de Carmelo Mission. Better known as "Carmel Mission," this Monterey County mission is where Padre Junípero Serra, founder of the California mission system, is buried. He and his subordinates founded 21 missions along the California coast, each about a day's journey on foot apart. Photo by author.

Top left, top right, and center: The Spanish introduced winemaking, irrigated farming, and cattle and sheep ranching to America. Spanish vaqueros had driven cattle for many years to better pastures in their dry homeland. They applied this method of livestock raising to the dry regions of present-day Texas, New Mexico, Arizona, and California. The Spanish, besides introducing grapes and walnuts (the grove of trees at right), introduced olives, citrus fruit, and various vegetables to California, Texas, and other areas they settled. They also brought horses in large numbers, thus also inadvertently increasing the mobility of the American Indians. The Spanish also helped the Patriots against the British. Photos by author.

Bottom: It took a Spanish ship many many months to sail from Spain around Cape Horn at the bottom of South America to California. Even ships from Peru and western Mexico were rarities. So the appearance of a Spanish ship off the coast of California was a big event for the Spanish settlers of San Diego, Santa Barbara, Monterey, and San Francisco, Spanish towns in California with harbors. Credit: Eileen Sherlock.

FRANCE'S MARKS ON AMERICA

Joan of Arc (seen in the mural Lionel Royer painted for the basilica in her home town of Domremy in Lorraine) was the mother of the French nation. She led men into combat against the English invaders, and had the rightful king crowned. She as a patriot set a great example for America's Patriots.

Joan was backstabbed by her government, and when she was captured in battle, her king didn't try to ransom her. The English abused her in prison, but could not break her. They burned her at the stake on May 30, 1431. Joan was a devout and zealous Catholic, and she was cheerful and kind. She wanted to marry, and she had France's bravest and manliest men at her beck and call ... yet she behaved herself despite her power. That is a sign of heroic virtue!

French explorers and priests like Father Marquette, **left**, explored the Great Lakes and Mississippi Valley. The French founded New Orleans, St. Louis, and Detroit. The Cathedral of St. Louis in New Orleans, **below left**, is a shining example of French architecture. The French also settled Quebec and the Maritime area of Canada. During the French and Indian War, the British exiled the French of Acadia to Louisiana and elsewhere (**below right**, picture by Charles Jeffreys), and renamed the area Nova Scotia. They broke up many families in the process. Americans would call the French exiles from Acadia "Cajuns." George Washington had French ancestry, as did Paul Revere and John Sevier. Lafayette and the French aided the Patriots against the British.

THE AFRICANS -- IMMIGRANTS AGAINST THEIR WILL

Upper left: Dutch slavers brought the first African slaves to English buyers in Jamestown, Virginia in 1619. Slave-trading vermin often displayed pretty female slaves naked or almost naked. Credit: Granger.

Center: Slaves were demeaningly auctioned like livestock; slave traders ruthlessly split families. Credit: Library of Congress.

Upper right: The Union Army freed many slaves during the Civil War, like this family in South Carolina. Many slaves freed themselves by running away and crossing into Union lines. Credit: Library of Congress.

Bottom: The Underground Railroad was **not** the creation of politically correct liberals, but mostly of blacks themselves. They had to get away from their masters, travel by night, and get into free states like Pennsylvania, Ohio, Indiana, Illinois, and Iowa, which bordered the northernmost slave states Delaware, Maryland, Virginia (which before the Civil War included West Virginia), Kentucky, and Missouri. Others, like Frederick Douglass, used papers free blacks provided them to escape to the North. Some blacks helped fugitives get out of the South. Some whites like Levi Coffin did help the escaping slaves once they got into the North, as this painting by Charles Webber shows.

THE EVIL EMPIRE STRIKES BACK

Left: George Washington, shown awarding medals to his men, distrusted the British in particular and European politicians in general. So he worked to strengthen America's army and navy. Credit: U.S. Army

Center: Adams and Jefferson and Congress weren't as wary as Washington. So the British struck like pirates. They started kidnaping American sailors from port taverns and docks to force them into service in the British navy. They got more brazen and started taking men off of American merchant ships. This immoral enslavement policy of the British was called "impressment." Public domain.

Below left: Congress awoke belatedly to the British threat. They ordered the building of some magnificent warships, such as the USS Constitution (aka "Old Ironsides"), pictured here. American seamen proved more than a match in one-on-one fights against the British in the upcoming War of 1812. Photo by author.

Bottom right: The British burned the White House and Washington in August 1814. James Madison and most government officials and civil servants fled. Dolley Madison and some servants stayed to gather archives and other papers of national interest, silver, and the portrait of George Washington. They escaped with these items just before the redcoats hit town. Compare this with Hillary Clinton looting the White House of about $200,000 in items for herself when she left in 2001. People loved Dolley Madison because of her courage, her graciousness, and her bubbly fun-loving personality. Zachary Taylor visited her and called her "America's First Lady." All presidents' wives have had this title since. Credit: Emile Dodamead, James Madison Museum

AMERICA HOLDS, WINS, AND EXPANDS

Top left: The British decide to attack and loot Baltimore. In September 1814, British gunners shelled Fort McHenry from their ships. Fort McHenry's men held, saving the people of Baltimore. Francis Scott Key viewed the bombardment from a British ship (he was aboard trying to get captives released). The bomb bursts' lighting "gave proof through the night that our flag was still there." The re-enactment shows this nicely. Credit: National Park Service.

Top right: Andrew Jackson leads frontier militiamen, Creoles, free blacks, and "pirates" to victory in the Battle of New Orleans. Old Hickory's men, covered by field fortifications, killed the British commander and killed or wounded about half of his men; the Brits fled. Almost no Americans died. Herbert Morton Stoops portrayed the action of this January 1815 battle.

Center right: Andrew Jackson, by Thomas Sully. Jackson was a man of great resolve, who had common sense as well as anger. Jackson killed a man in a duel for falsely saying Jackson's wife was an immoral woman. **Center left:** Americans defeat Mexicans in the Mexican War. The efforts of these men confirmed the addition of Texas to the Union, added California and other parts of the Southwest to the Union, and secured the West from British poaching. Credit: Addresses and Papers of the Presidents, 1897, per Descendants of the Veterans of the Mexican War.

Bottom: Commodore Sloat lands Marines at Monterey, California, in July 1846, before declaration of war. This move weakened the Mexicans, and the British, who also had designs on California. W.A. Coulter illustration.

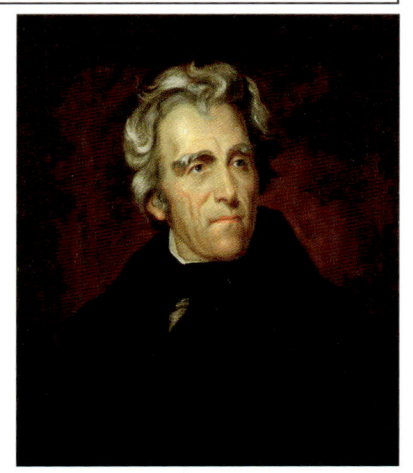

THE PIONEER SPIRIT

In several decades of the 1800s, Americans occupied land from the Mississippi River to the Pacific Ocean. They organized this vast land into American communities.

Top: "Lewis and Clark" by Eric von Schmidt. Napoleon sold the Louisiana Purchase to America when Jefferson was president. He sent the Lewis and Clark expedition to explore what we bought. Sacajawea is coming to embrace her brother Cameahwait, a Shoshone leader. He sells Lewis and Clark fresh horses. Sadly and ironically, the black man carrying the U.S. flag is York, Clark's slave.

Center: Hundreds of thousands of people headed west in covered wagons with some cooking and clothes-making gear, farming tools, seeds, weapons, and provisions. The woman at Fort Sutter is explaining the pioneer journey to tourists. Ignorant California officials want to close Sutter's Fort and other historical sites.

Bottom left: Swiss immigrant John Sutter left a wife and debts behind in Europe to come to America. He organized Americans, Mexicans and Indians to build Sutter's Fort for protection, and he ran a huge logging, ranching, and grain-producing settlement. His men saved many pioneers from death. They also helped prevent British agents from setting up a colony in California when the Russians withdrew. When gold was found at Sutter's sawmill, his people left him, and gold-hungry Americans took away his land. Sacramento now sits on top of his land.

Bottom right: Gold miners used water pressure to crumble streamside rock formations to extract gold. This water cannon is on the site of Sutter's sawmill, east of Sacramento.

Photos by author.

Settlers built towns, and men set up stage coach lines and teamster lines to connect the towns. Eventually men built railroads to link the American West to the rest of the nation. **Top:** Girl admires horses of a stage coach driver in Columbia, California, a gold mining town that is now a state park. **Bottom left:** Workers lay track; California State Railroad Museum. Clueless and alien California politicians want to close this park also. Photos by author.

Center: Pioneers homesteaded from the Great Plains to the Pacific Coast, like the four Chrisman sisters (center), who staked out a piece of western Nebraska and built this sod house. Credit: Library of Congress and Nebraska Historical Society.

Bottom right: The West wasn't truly settled until the ladies came West to civilize the menfolk. Western men gave women the right to vote before the men back East did. Photo by author.

THE CIVIL WAR

Wealthy slaveholders' militant defense of slavery — even at the expense of the Union — was the greatest single cause of the Civil War.

Left: Abraham Lincoln (speaking) and Stephen Douglas (in gray at Lincoln's right) debated slavery in the Illinois senate election of 1858. Thousands rode horses or walked to see these patriots. Douglas won the race; Lincoln beat him and two other rivals in the presidential election two years later. Public domain.

Bottom left: The South's brave men and women rallied gallantly for a bad cause. The vast majority of Southern soldiers owned no slaves. They felt they were defending their homes. Spy Belle Boyd gives Stonewall Jackson key intelligence that helped him win battles against Union troops. Painting by Mark Korolev; sold to raise money for preserving Belle Boyd's home in Martinsburg, West Virginia.

Below: There were free blacks in America, almost all in the North, but they didn't enjoy the same rights as white Americans did. These re-enactors showed this wrong at the Old State Capitol in Springfield, Illinois. Photo by author.

Above: Pickett's Charge at Gettysburg, July 3, 1863, was the climax of the Civil War – and a rare blunder of Robert E. Lee's. Union soldiers shot up his Rebels and broke the attack. Lee had to retreat from Pennsylvania with the men he still had. Credit: gettysburgreenactment.com.

Below: "Strike for God and Country," by Don Stivers. Irish soldiers in Union blue with Old Glory and green flag charge Rebels at Spotsylvania in May 1864. Grant took charge against Lee in Virginia, but there was still no quit in the Southerners. Meanwhile, General Sherman was leading a collateral ancestor of the author and 90,000 other Yankees thru Georgia. The war ended in Union victory (and American victory) in April 1865.

Above: More than 600,000 men in uniform died in the Civil War. Many were married men; there were hundreds of thousands of young widows across America mourning their husbands. Mary Lincoln would mourn her murdered husband too. Honest Abe died on Good Friday, like Our Lord. Photo of this beautiful charming re-enactor by author.

Below: "Home at Last" by Don Stivers. Almost 300,000 free and escaped slave blacks served in the Union Army. Thousands more escaped slaves helped the Union Army in other ways. Surely they deserved to share in the fruits of victory.

AMERICAN INDIANS
lost their lands and often their lives when the settlers came. **Top left**: "Abduction of Pocahontas" by Jean Louis Gerome, summed up British Indian policy: rape, enslavement, and murder. **Bottom:** "Trail of Tears" by Robert Lindneux (courtesy Woolaroc Museum, Oklahoma) shows the forced exile of the Cherokees, Choctaws, Creeks, Chickasaws, and Seminoles from the Southeast to Oklahoma. Sooners would eventually steal Oklahoma from the American Indians, too. **Left:** Geronimo, the Apache on the right, and his warriors fought long and hard against the whites who broke their treaties and abused their people. **Top right:** Catholic Church, San Antonio de Pala Mission, San Diego County, California. American Indians built and decorated this Spanish mission church. Spanish rule was far less brutal than British. Photo by author.

Top left: "Custer's Last Stand" by Elk Eber. Sioux warriors killed Custer and all of his men at Little Big Horn in Montana in June 1876. Eber's father was German; his mother was a Sioux named Little Elk who witnessed the battle.

American response was quick and savage. Army units attacked and broke the Sioux. **Center left:** Sitting Bull had to lead his band into Canada to escape Uncle Sam's wrath. But the British made him leave. USGS photo. **Center right:** When Sitting Bull was shot to death in December 1890, his friend Annie Oakley, who Sitting Bull nicknamed "Little Sure Shot," said someone should hang for the crime. Public domain. **Bottom left:** Hundreds of Sitting Bull's tribesmen and women were murdered at Wounded Knee, South Dakota just after Christmas 1890. Soldiers buried the dead in a mass grave. U.S. Army photo.

Bottom right: These American Indian girls in Arizona, like thousands of others across the West, were herded onto reservations and forced to abandon their way of life. Teachers and government agents tried to beat the American Indian spirit and customs out of them.

WORK OF THE IMMIGRANTS

Top: Irish immigrants did much of the digging of the canals of America in the first half of the 1800s. They did this work even in the South, because they were expendable, while a worked-out slave would cost his master money. Credit: National Park Service, Ohio and Erie Canal National Corridor.

Center: These Irish workers and other Civil War veterans built the Transcontinental Railroad west through Nebraska and Wyoming to Utah. General William Tecumseh Sherman, who led his men in the destruction of Southern railroads a few years earlier, was an engineer and one of the key leaders in the successful effort to build the rails that tied the West Coast to the rest of the country. Chinese and American workers built the stretch east from California through Nevada to Utah. The woodcut is by Alfred Waud.

Bottom: These Swedes left their snowbound homeland to try their hands at farming in Kansas. Credit: Library of Congress and Kansas Historical Society.

Top: Slavic men were many of the workers in the steel mills — like this one in Pennsylvania — and the coal mines of this nation. Credit: Lewis Hine, New York Public Library.

Center: These Finnish people and other Scandinavians came to places like Minnesota, Wisconsin, Michigan, Washington, and Oregon to work as loggers, like they did in their homeland. Credit: Finland National Immigration Institute.

Bottom right: Mexicans have worked the ranches and farms of California, Texas, Arizona, New Mexico, and Colorado, from the time of Spanish and Mexican settlement of the West to the present. Credit: Library of Congress.

Bottom left: Edward Sherlock, great-grandfather of the author, emigrated from Ireland to Chicago. He was a butcher in Drogheda, Ireland, then a slaughterer in Chicago. He died of TB that he contracted in his trade, like many other poor souls did back in the day. RIP, Great-grandpa Sherlock, RIP.

Bottom line: Immigrants kept some of their customs, but they tried to become real Americans and achievers instead of loafers, criminals, jihadists, spies, and separatists.

EUROPEANS BROUGHT CHRISTIANITY to America. Some, like Joseph De Veuster, aka Father Damien, a Belgian Catholic priest, heroically practiced what they preached. Living our faith unhypocritically is something we are all called to do.

Left: Father Damien with lepers at Molokai, Hawaii. He died of leprosy in 1889 after ministering to the lepers for many years. Photo courtesy Cathedral of Our Lady of Peace, Honolulu.

Right: "Mayflower Compact" by N.C. Wyeth. Dissident English Protestants who opposed the Protestantism of King James (he of the King James bible) make a citizens' agreement before landing in Massachusetts. Protestants' rejecting Catholic orthodoxy led to arguments with other Protestants, and then to questioning of kings. This questioning of authority and the compromise among equals of different opinions led to American style democracy. Credit: Granger

Below left: Holy Assumption Orthodox Church, Kenai, Alaska. Russian Orthodox priests and other priests from the Balkans brought this faith to America. Credit: National Park Service.

Below right: San Diego (St. James) Parish, Santa Fé, New Mexico. This is the oldest parish or congregation in the United States; priests have said Mass here since the early 1600s. Photo by author.

294-301, 328-329).

8. Information on the tragic drop in the American Indian population of California comes from The American Heritage Book of Indians (page 305).

9. Excellent sources of information on the wars against the American Indians are Dee Brown's book Bury My Heart at Wounded Knee, the book The Plains States, and The American Heritage Book of Indians.

10. Statistics on the of American Indians in North America and South America before 1900 are at best educated guesses. The American Heritage Book of Indians (pages 3-15, 82, and 403) lists some numbers that seem reasonable. Guenter Lewy, in a 11/22/2004 article in George Mason University's History News Network, reported various estimates, and concluded (wrongfully) the drastic drop in numbers of American Indians was not genocide, but mere tragedy.

11. Statistics and some historical information on Alaska natives and Russian settlers comes from the books The American Heritage Book of Indians (pages 283-284) and the book The Frontier States (pages 14-15, 35). Further info on Sheldon Jackson comes from an article Stephen Haycox wrote for The Pacific Historian (Spring 1984).

12. Statistics and some historical information on Hawaii comes from the book The Frontier States (pages 94-97), John Garraty and Robert McCaughey's book The American Nation (pages 630-632), the book The National Experience (pages 496-497), and George Knoles' book The New United States: A History Since 1896 (page 50).

13. Statistics for European and American populations come from Brian Mitchell's book European Historical Statistics 1750-1970, Terry Jordan's book The European Culture Area, and the U.S. Department of Commerce book set Historical Statistics of the United States (Bicentennial Edition).

14. Information on Joseph Smith, Brigham Young, and the "mainstream" Mormons comes from Men to Match My Mountains (pages 94-100, 178-185, 213-226, 266-274, 329-351, 411-423), from Lucius Beebe and from Charles Clegg's book The American West – The Pictorial Epic of a Continent (pages 351-363), and from Robert Hine's book The American West (pages 228-234). Other information on these Mormons comes from the Winter 2003 Utah Historical Quarterly (page 14), and the article "Mormon Blood Atonement: Fact or Fantasy?" by Jerald Tanner and ex-Mormon Sandra Tanner (who like many in Utah claims descent from Brigham Young through one of his more than two dozen "wives") in the April 1997 Salt Lake City Messenger.

Information on the Strangites comes from "The Man Who Shot Strang" in the 10/10/2002 Beaver Beacon, the Beaver Island Historical Society, a June 1970 American Heritage article by Robert Weeks, an excerpt of Vickie Speek's book God Has Made Us a Kingdom by Signature Books, and an article by Jenny Nolan in the 1/29/1996 Detroit News.

Information on the Mountain Meadows Massacre comes from Will Bagley's article "Rescue of the Mountain Meadows Massacre Orphans" in the February 2005 issue of Wild West Magazine, from Cecilia Rassmussen's 6/29/2003 article in the Los Angeles Times, and from Douglas Linder article

"The Mountain Meadows Massacre of 1857 and the Trial of John D. Lee" on the University of Missouri Kansas City law school website. (Linder has written a series of articles on famous trials.) Further "blood atonement" and massacre information comes from a paper Will Bagley wrote titled "Will You Love That Man or Woman Enough to Shed Their Blood?" Bagley presented it at a conference on new religion studies in Utah in June 2002. The Church of Jesus Christ of Latter Day Saints (Mormon) official website www.lds.org carried an article from the church's September 2007 Ensign magazine by Richard Turley which attempts to exonerate Young for the Mountain Meadows Massacre. I also spoke with Burr Fancher, a descendant of a victim of the Mountain Meadows Massacre. He is an officer in the Mountain Meadows Massacre Foundation, a group of descendants and collateral relatives of victims of the atrocity and students of history whose aim is not to let this atrocity remain hidden and its victims go unmemorialized.

The abortion allegation come from the American Heritage article and the testimony of Mormon woman Sarah Pratt, which was in a reprint of Wilhelm Ritter von Wymetal's muckraking book Joseph Smith: The Prophet, His Family, and His Friends (pages 60-63). The book was first published in 1886 in Salt Lake City(!)

A personal note: My Catholicism didn't prevent Brigham Young University officials from offering me a scholarship to attend their well-respected college in the early 1970s. I interviewed with Mormon officials about their offer, and they treated me cordially. However, I instead chose to attend Loyola University for that year (all you anti-Jesuit conspiracy theorists take note); I paid most of my tuition with my earnings from a job as a mechanic and laborer in a paper mill. I then received an appointment to attend the U.S. Military Academy; I graduated from USMA and served as an officer in the U.S. Army. I would later take biology classes at the University of Dayton (a Catholic school) and organic chemistry courses at Xavier University in Cincinnati in the 1990s (all you anti-Jesuit conspiracy theorists take note again) to prepare for further forensic science and toxicology studies.

15. Statistics on immigration come from the immigration tables of the Historic Research Study, Statue of Liberty – Ellis Island National Monument, by Harlan D. Unrau, National Park Service, 1984. I did some math to come up with totals.

16. Estimates on immigration from Canada comes from the Catholic Encyclopedia, Damien-Claude and Claude Belanger's 1999 article "French Canadian Emigration to the United States 1840-1930," thanks to Marionopolis College, and an article "The Eldorado to the South: French-Canadians in the U.S.," on the Duke University website. These sources note there were 1.2 million Canadians in America, according to the 1900 census, and there were 400,000 French Canadian natives in the U.S. and another 700,000 who claimed one or both parents were French Canadians (the net number of French Canadians would be 1.1 million minus the deceased ancestors). This implies about an even distribution of French Canadian and non-French Canadian immigrants. The Belangers gave a firm estimate of 900,000 French Canadian immigrants from 1840 through 1930. My estimate of an equal number of non-French Canadians comes from the rough ratio of 1:1 the 1900 census figures imply.

The website canadianconnection.com carried this quote from a 1920s Canadian politician: "Canada cannot afford to be a preparatory school for people from European countries whose ultimate destination will be with our neighbours [sic] to the south." In other words, the Canadians were aware Europeans used their land to prepare to come to America. An article by William Siener, titled "Through The Back Door: Evading the Chinese Exclusion Act Along The Niagara Frontier, 1900 to 1924," outlined Canadian complicity in the smuggling of Chinese illegals into America. Congressmen made similar note of British and Canadian perfidy in smuggling unfit immigrants in their comments in support of various immigration reform bills in the late 1800s and the early 1900s.

A 1910 article in the Review of Reviews titled "Canada's Plan of Averting the Yellow Peril" said it was the duty of Canadians as British subjects to help Britain maintain friendly relations with Asian nations. Therefore the article's author said Canadian officials used personal diplomacy with the Chinese, Japanese, and British colonial authorities in Asia to regulate immigration. The author said many Indians from India were fighting British battles as soldiers, so that was to their credit. The author mocked Theodore Roosevelt but noted Canadian authorities used similar methods in dealing with would-be Asian immigrants. The article shows the subservience of Canadians to the British lead in handling immigration (the Canadians and British routinely violated American immigration regulations to make extra money for the British Empire).

17. Statistics on ethnicities of the immigrants comes from the Unrau study. Sources of immigration statistics specific to the Spanish, Portuguese, and Italians include J. Halcro Ferguson's book The River Plate Republics (page 30), Latin America: Geographical Perspectives (pages 417-419), and Brian Mitchell's book European Historical Statistics 1750-1970 (pages 135-149). I did some math and estimation to come up with totals.

18. Sources for estimates of immigrants who returned to Europe include Mark Wyman's book Round-Trip to America: The Immigrants Return to Europe, 1880-1930, and commentary on same by Hans Storhaug in a lecture he presented in 2002, and Donna Przecha's article "Immigrants Who Returned Home." Hard figures came from the Unrau study.

19. We leave this chapter with an account of the event in Empress Zita's 1989 funeral which made many people reflect on the meaning of life and the states of their souls. (The quotes which follow are more or less what the speakers said, given translation issues and slightly conflicting reports from observers.)

Six black horses drew the century-old royal hearse carrying Empress Zita's casket in a procession through the streets of Vienna.

When the pall bearers tried to bring Zita's casket into the *Kapuchinerkirk*, a Catholic Church run by the Capuchin monks which has served as the church where many requiem Masses for Hapsburg family members have taken place, a member of the funeral procession knocked on the massive wooden doors to have them opened. A monk inside the church thundered, "Who goes there?"

The mourners replied, "Zita, her imperial, royal, and apostolic majesty, Empress of Austria and Queen of Hungary, and all her domains."

The monk shouted, "I know her not!" He would not open the doors to the church.

Someone knocked again. The monk inside the church thundered, "Who disturbs our peace?"

The mourners replied, "Zita, the Queen of Bohemia, Dalmatia, Slavonia, Galicia, Queen of Jerusalem, Grand Duchess of Tuscany and Krakow." (These were some of her many titles as empress.)

The monk shouted, "I do not know her!" He kept the doors closed.

Someone knocked a third time. Once again, the monk inside the church demanded in an unfriendly voice to know who was bothering him.

This time the mourners replied, "Zita von Hapsburg, a lowly sinner humbly begging forgiveness before the throne of God."

The monk announced in a friendlier voice, "Enter, and find rest." Then the massive doors of the church swung open wide.

What was the moral of this ritual? All people, no matter how mighty they were in their earthly lives, are still small and imperfect figures in the presence of God Almighty. He grades everyone on his or her merits against His very objective set of measurements: Did you do My will to the best of your abilities? Did you obey the Ten Commandments and the Golden Rule? Did you love Me, and did you love your neighbor as yourself? God expects people to live according to His commandments, and He gives no man or woman favorable treatment due to his or her status in earthly life come Judgment Day.

REGULATING IMMIGRATION FROM THE AMERICAN REVOLUTION TO THE EARLY 1900s

In the first century of America's free existence, virtually the only national laws concerning immigration were laws designed to aid immigrants in coming to the United States. There was virtually no federal regulation of immigration. There was no immigration station at Ellis Island. Immigrants came by ship to American seaports, debarked, and were free to go wherever they could.

In 1795, Congress enacted the first comprehensive American naturalization law. (An earlier 1790 law had one paragraph of text.) They required free white foreigners to reside in America for five years, renounce their allegiance to any foreign government, swear an oath of allegiance to America and the U.S. Constitution, and display "good moral character." They forbade anyone who fought for the British in the Revolutionary War to become citizens unless the legislature of his state was willing to vote in his favor. President George Washington signed the bill into law.

Immigrants to America came in through a handful of seaports and border stations throughout the 1800s. Some crossed in from Mexico and Canada, often illegally, like millions do today. Until the 1920s, most illegals were Europeans or Asians who sneaked in through Canada.

Until the Louisiana Purchase, all American seaports were on the Atlantic coast. America would not have a seaport on the Pacific coast until fur traders built Astoria, Oregon after the Lewis and Clark expedition of the early 1800s. Americans and Britons, wary of each other, jointly occupied the Pacific Northwest region, and Americans would start coming in large numbers to the region in the 1840s. In 1846, the British saw the light and relinquished their claim on "the Oregon Country" – the area that is now Washington, Oregon, Idaho, and parts of Montana and Wyoming. The 49th Parallel would officially be America's boundary with Canada from Minnesota to the Pacific Ocean.

America would not have any ports in California until the Mexican War, which also started in 1846, about the time President James Polk's men settled the Canadian border issue with the British. In the 1800s very few immigrants other than Mexicans or Chinese came to America via the Pacific coast seaports. Since most immigration until the 1960s was from Europe, most immigrants came in through the Atlantic coast ports.

The Erie Canal – built not long after the War of 1812 – linked the Great Lakes states by water to the Hudson River, which flows to the Atlantic Ocean by New York City. The canal gave New York City's port an advantage no other Atlantic port had – a direct water connection to the Midwest. New York City soon became the dominant American seaport because of this water link. From after the War of 1812 until the 1960s, more than half of all immigrants to the United States landed at New York City.

In 1819, Congress enacted the Steerage Act, their first attempt at making conditions reasonable for immigrants and their first attempt to figure out who was coming to America. They required sailing ships transporting passengers to America to carry adequate provisions for passengers for the journey across the ocean, they limited the number of people that could be on a sailing ship as passengers coming to or leaving any American port, and they required ships' officers to submit passenger lists to the local American customs official of the American port in which they docked. In 1847 and in 1855, Congress updated this law to make conditions better for passengers.

The first formal immigration station in New York City was at Castle Garden. In the early 1800s it was known as Castle Clinton, because it was a small fort with cannons on the southern end of Manhattan Island, in an area called "The Battery." It formed part of the harbor defense fortifications of New York City. (A "battery" is an artillery unit similar in size to an infantry company; that's why the area was called "The Battery.") After the War of 1812, New York City got the land from the U.S. Government; the demobilized fort got the name "Castle Garden." Castle Garden became a park; the great Swedish singer Jenny Lind performed there in 1850. In 1855, New York state officials put Castle Garden to use as a place to process immigrants.

During the 1820s and 1830s, more immigrants came from Ireland than any other country. Certain Protestant bigots claimed the presence of the Irish was a threat to the United States. They conveniently failed to mention that the greatest threat to American liberty was Protestant England – whose leaders waged war against America twice already – during the Revolution and the War of 1812. British law forbade the Irish to have most civil liberties the British people had; British law also denied certain civil liberties to Catholics in Britain. The American bigots also forgot a large percentage of Washington's Continental Army had been Irish.

Samuel Morse, who later invented the telegraph, made his fortune publishing anti-Catholic books. He claimed the Pope and the Austrian emperor were in league to take over America, and many yokels and bluenoses believed him. He argued for restricting immigration, banning Catholics from public office, and closing Catholic schools. Anti-Catholic mobs in Boston and

Philadelphia burned Catholic schools and churches. Catholics were galled that their tax money, along with everyone else's, supported Protestant private schools and anti-Catholic public schools. Catholics had to build their own schools with their own money so their children could go to school without hearing anti-Catholic bigotry from the teachers and principal.

During the 1840s, the first decade which saw more than a million immigrants, 781,000 of these came from Ireland. This was the decade of the Great Hunger (the Potato Famine) in Ireland. Likewise, in this decade, 435,000 came from the German states, and another 77,000 came from France. The peoples of Germany and France experienced crop failures and revolutions that failed. Almost all of the Irish immigrants were Catholics, and a large percentage of the German and French immigrants were also Catholics. **(1)**

In that decade, the United States defeated Mexico – an almost entirely Catholic country with anticlerical leaders – in the Mexican War. A quarter of the soldiers in America's small victorious army were Irish-born. Ironically, Mexico's best unit, the San Patricio (Saint Patrick) Brigade, was made up of deserters from the American army of Irish blood. Also, as a result of the successful war with Mexico, American officials granted citizenship to many Mexican and Spanish nationals who lived in California and elsewhere in the newly-won Southwest. The Gold Rush in California at the end of the Mexican War brought many thousands of people to California from other countries, as well as from the rest of America, in a search for wealth.

In the 1850s a party comprised entirely of anti-Catholic bigots – who called themselves the "American Party," while everyone else aptly called these wingnuts the "Know-Nothings" -- rose on a platform calling for restricting immigration, banning Catholics from public office, and closing Catholic schools. Know-Nothing rioters killed people in St. Louis, Cincinnati, and Louisville – all cities welcoming many German Catholic immigrants -- in the 1850s.

Naturally, the Know-Nothings seized power among the anti-Irish in Calvinist and Unitarian Massachusetts. Know-Nothings also gained elsewhere. In the 1854 congressional election, voters elected 43 Know-Nothings to Congress and five to the Senate. There were 27 others who won elections who were members of Know-Nothing lodges. Know-Nothing candidate Millard Fillmore, the nonentity who served out Zachary Taylor's term as president after some doctors committed malpractice and killed "Old Rough and Ready" while treating him for a digestive tract disorder, got almost a quarter of the popular vote in the presidential election of 1856. **(2)**

The Know-Nothings – like the Whigs – dissolved on the slavery issue, and soon disappeared as a formal party. The bigots – depending on their views on slavery – joined the Democrats or the new Republican party. (Know-nothings of a different sort dominate both parties now.)

In the Civil War, close to 150,000 natives of Ireland served in the Union Army and Union Navy. Roughly 175,000 German-born men served in the Union Army and Union Navy. Roughly 40,000 Irish natives also served in the forces of the Confederacy; but relatively few Germans did so. **(3)**

After the Civil War, prejudice and discrimination still existed against the Irish and to a lesser extent the Germans, but these groups were now organized enough to protect themselves. Open bigotry against the newly-freed black slaves and the free blacks of America was widespread in America, but at least American-born blacks were now American citizens who could vote.

American Indians suffered a century of government-sponsored genocide in the 1800s. But many of them *did* receive American citizenship, through individual treaties their tribes signed with the American government, through marriage with whites, through military service, or through the 14th Amendment in 1868 if they lived in states or territories under effective American government control. Many tribes not under effective U.S. government control did *not* receive citizenship under the 14th Amendment. It would take the Indian Citizenship Act of 1924 to grant all American Indians American citizenship. **(4)**

From the 1870s until the 1920s, America's leaders would enact several laws to regulate immigration for the perceived benefit of America's citizens. First they restricted Asian immigration, then they federalized immigration, then they tried to improve screening of immigrants so those who came to America would not be a burden on American society. They decided to restrict virtually all Asian immigration. After World War One, they decided to greatly restrict all immigration.

IMMIGRATION LAWS FROM THE CIVIL WAR TO 1890

In the late 1800s, Congresses, not presidents, would usually lead on the immigration question and other questions of great importance to the Republic. From the assassination of Lincoln in 1865 to the assassination of William McKinley in 1901, Congress was a more active branch of the federal government than the presidency. Congress impeached and almost removed Lincoln's successor Andrew Johnson. Ulysses S. Grant was a sturdy, basically decent man and a great general, but he was a poor president because he was a novice at civilian politics. Many in Grant's administration were crooked, and their lust for undeserved wealth undermined his work.

Rutherford Hayes owed his election to questionable Electoral College maneuvering. In exchange for the electoral votes of some Southern states, he ended Reconstruction and allowed Southerners to persecute blacks. His questionable win earned him the nickname "Rutherfraud." Of course, his Democrat opponent Samuel Tilden carried some Southern states because the Ku Klux Klan and other organized bands of white trash prevented large numbers of blacks from voting. Hayes was also known for having a priggish wife who banned alcohol from the White House and for that act of unhospitality she got the nickname "Lemonade Lucy." James Garfield was shot to death months into his term. Chester Arthur was about as charismatic and accomplished a man as Millard Fillmore.

Grover Cleveland, the one Democrat president in this era, had a term in the mid 1880s and another term in the mid 1890s. He was an honest, able, and tough man, but still not a Lincoln. Cleveland, because he was honest, admitted to fathering a bastard child (who he was paying support for) during his first campaign for president, while his opponent James Blaine was not enough of a man to silence the anti-Catholic bigots around him in his campaign. Cleveland overwhelmingly won the Irish vote and got into the White House. Later, bachelor Cleveland would marry a young beauty named Frances Folsom and become a father while President.

Benjamin Harrison, whose term sandwiched between Cleveland's two terms, was not a bad man but was not a dynamic man as president. Like Hayes in 1876 and George W. Bush in 2000, Harrison had won the electoral vote against Cleveland but lost the popular vote. (Tilden owed his popular margin in 1876 to the suppression of blacks in the South who would have voted Republican. Al Gore owed his popular margin in 2000 to the widespread illegal voting of felons, mental patients, and unnaturalized aliens, and to the suppression of the absentee votes of military people.) Harrison's administration was the first to spend a billion dollars in a year in peacetime.

In the rematch election of 1892, Cleveland handily won both the electoral vote and the popular vote.

William McKinley followed Cleveland to the White House in 1897 after he handed William Jennings Bryan the first of his three presidential defeats. McKinley as a congressman designed tariffs that protected American industries and workers from cheap imports and won the support of bosses and laborers alike. As a lawyer, McKinley had defended strikers for free, an act untypical for a Republican.

While nowhere near as firebreathing as his subordinate and eventual successor Theodore Roosevelt, McKinley also favored expansion of American power. He was president during the Spanish-American War and he was the president who annexed Hawaii. McKinley also took Puerto Rico into American control and ordered the occupation of Cuba and the Philippines after our men beat the Spanish.

The locals in the Philippines at first welcomed American help in their uprising against Spanish colonial authorities. But some of them turned against the Americans when it became evident the Americans were going to take the Philippines as a colony for themselves. It took several years for American soldiers and marines to defeat the Filipinos, and they lost roughly 5000 men in the campaign.

The Filipino insurrectionists had courage and numbers, but American control was inevitable. Why? American military people had developed, over years of conflict with American Indians, a mixture of toughness and ruthlessness against opponents who could fight in an irregular style. They also were much better armed. And unlike today, American politicians in that era didn't quit on their military people.

Besides, the Germans and Japanese also had designs on the Philippines. It would not have been possible for the Filipinos to resist the Germans or especially the nearby Japanese if either of these colonialist powers decided they wanted the islands badly enough. American colonialism was the least distasteful option they had. American leaders sent a large enough number of soldiers, sailors, marines, and ships to the Philippines to keep the Germans and the equally militaristic and greedy Japanese at bay. Teddy Roosevelt's rise to the Presidency in 1901 did much to make the Germans and the Japanese behave.

The Americans also did much to control the Moros, the Moslem savages active on Mindanao, other islands in the Philippines, and other islands in present-day Indonesia (then under Dutch colonial rule). Moros would purposely run amok with swords and knives, killing many of the Filipinos, who were Catholics and

ELLIS ISLAND SCRAPBOOK

thus infidels worthy of death in the eyes of the Moslems. Moslems also kidnapped Filipino girls for use as sex slaves. American forces shot down these Moslem fanatics, burned their villages, and shelled the palace of a sultan who supported them. The Americans thus greatly diminished the Moslems' depredations.

Now that we've given a backdrop to the era, let's examine what Congress did about immigration in that time.

The first immigration law after the Civil War reflected the long-overdue realization that America's native-born and immigrant blacks deserved American citizenship. In 1870, Congress enacted and President Ulysses Grant signed into law a naturalization act that allowed people of African blood who were not born in the United States the ability to become naturalized citizens. This covered slaves brought to America illegally after 1808, and blacks from Africa and elsewhere (like the West Indies) who wished to come to America.

The second immigration law after the Civil War was aimed at would-be immigrants from China. Many Chinese had come to America during the California gold rush of 1849. Many more had come to the Western U.S. later to mine, build railroads, and perform other labor that would enable them to earn enough money to establish themselves nicely when they returned to China.

Some unscrupulous businessmen also imported women from the Far East to serve as prostitutes in the American West. Because of the general rowdiness of the West compared to "back East" (the Midwest, the South, and the Northeast), and because of the shortage of women compared to men in the West, prostitution was legal in many communities in western states and territories. Prostitution was also widely tolerated in areas where it wasn't legal.

Prostitution had been a major problem even in the Civil War. Washington and Richmond teemed with whores, and many followed the camps of the armies. Venereal diseases disabled thousands of soldiers. Officers and men chased after the shady ladies, ignoring their duties. Union general Joseph Hooker, a devotee of trashy women, gave a certain class of them his own last name as a professional nickname. Rebel general Earl Van Dorn was shot to death during the Civil War by an irate husband of a woman whose breastworks he had carried with her consent.

The Victorian Age had a lot more sexual misbehavior than the history books and novels will tell you about. Many cities around the country had red-light districts. In fact, Seattle city government for awhile existed almost entirely on licenses and fines on prostitution, alcohol, and gambling. When a women's group threw the rascals out of City Hall in the 1880s, the politicians they elected closed so many of the whorehouses, saloons, and gambling dens that the town went broke. **(5)**

The native Hawaiians were even more openly promiscuous in the 1800s. The local girls used to swim out to the whaling ships in their harbors to consort with sailors until American missionaries convinced native Hawaiian rulers to control their females.

Many unscrupulous western businessmen brought Chinese laborers to America to undercut the local laborers in the mines, on railroad crews, and elsewhere. Chinese people would work for less than native Americans or European immigrants who knew American customs would. Sometimes the Chinese had to; many of them came as indentured servants, little more than slaves.

The Chinese were not the only people in bondage in the Land of the Free in the 1870s. Many Americans in the West essentially used American Indians as slave laborers, especially in California, Arizona, and New Mexico. And peonage and convict labor camps were essentially extensions of slave labor – predominantly for blacks but also for many whites – in the South well into the 1900s. This of course does not count the millions of people in city tenements or company towns or sharecropper shacks laboring for pittances.

Many American working people hated the Chinese because they would work for lower wages and the bosses could make native laborers work for less also if there were Chinese around. American laborers added this legitimate grievance – although they should have focused on the greedy bosses who used the Chinese to underpay everyone – to their instinctive prejudices against the Chinese. The "Chinks" were yellow-skinned and slant-eyed. The men wore pigtails, both sexes did laundry, they worshiped pagan gods, they spoke an inscrutable language, they kept to themselves, and they didn't tell the Americans what they were thinking. In an era when most Americans openly called blacks "niggers", openly called Mexicans "greasers", and openly called American Indians "red-skinned savages," the Chinese weren't alone in being the victims of racial hatred.

Congress in an 1875 law made it illegal to supply coolie (unskilled Asian) laborers to the United States on contract. The law (called the Act of March 3, 1875) also made it illegal for Americans to bring people from China or Japan to America against their wills. The congressmen aimed at protecting American laborers against Chinese and Japanese competition, and also aimed at protecting natives of China and Japan against unscrupulous lords in their own countries and against robber barons in America.

The 1875 law also made it illegal to transport females from China or Japan for immoral purposes. The law made it illegal for any convicts to immigrate to America, except for those convicted of political offenses.

Congress followed up the 1875 law with a second law in 1882. This law, known as the Chinese Exclusion Act, stopped Chinese laborers from coming to America for the next 10 years. (The law did not restrict immigration of businessmen or other non-laboring professionals from China.) The law also barred Chinese immigrants who were not already citizens from obtaining American citizenship. The law allowed Chinese already legally in the United States to leave the country and come back as long as they had the paperwork showing they were legal residents. (Chinese immigrants as a class were not formally able to become citizens until the passage of the McCarran-Walter Act in 1952. Earlier laws (such as the Magnuson Act of 1943 and war brides laws) during and after World War Two enabled some Chinese to become citizens.)

Congress amended the Chinese Exclusion Act in 1884 to extend the 10-year ban on Chinese immigration for another 10 years. Chinese immigration dropped sharply, but never stopped.

Federal officials next enacted laws against foreign undesirables, not just the Chinese. In the 1880s, immigration was roughly double what it had been in the 1870s. American laborers started feeling the competition for work. State government leaders were trying to enact immigration restriction laws to protect American workers – who were voters – but federal judges declared these state laws unconstitutional because they supposedly restricted interstate commerce illegally.

Federal officials decided to address immigration as a whole in the 1880s. Congress passed the first such general immigration law in 1882. This law, the Act of August 3, 1882, barred convicts (except those convicted of political offenses), lunatics, idiots, and people liable to become public charges. The law also required any shipping company whose ships brought such people to the United States to return them to the countries they came from at their own (the shipping company's) expense.

The law also required a tax of 50 cents per person for those who arrived by water to defray costs of inspection. The law put overall supervisory responsibility in the hands of the U.S. Treasury Department, but put responsibility and authority for doing the hands-on work of conducting immigration inspections in the hands of the governors of states.

This law had two serious loopholes. It allowed state governments to enforce immigration policy, and it didn't tax people coming into the United States by land. Many state government workers were incompetent or crooked or both. At best, state government workers enforced the law unevenly. British shipping lines continued to take advantage of the second loophole by dropping off people at Halifax, Nova Scotia, and arranging for them to come by rail into the United States, dodging inspections and taxes. From 1881 through 1890, 393,000 came to the United States from Canada, roughly the same as the 384,000 who came from Canada to the United States from 1871 through 1880.

Congress then took aim at unskilled laborers from Europe whose presence was hurting the local workers. Unscrupulous businessmen – using false advertising – had been conning Europeans for years to come over to America to seek their fortunes. The shipping companies were only too happy to ship the immigrants to America in steerage so they could cash in on the traffic of the human cargo. When the immigrants showed up, there were often no opportunities like what the advertising promised. Or the wages the businessmen promised were high for Europe, but below the prevailing wages for America. This created an excess of labor in many areas. Since the immigrants needed to work to feed, shelter, and clothe themselves, they were willing to work for less money than the prevailing wages were for the industries whose owners lured them to America. Wages fell, severely hurting American workers.

Congress in 1885 enacted the Alien Contract Labor Law as a start at dealing with this abuse. This law made it illegal to import or assist in importing immigrants to America with any labor contract made before immigration of the immigrant to America. The law exempted certain skilled workers in industries not already established in the United States, entertainers, and relatives and friends of those already in the United States.

This law had several flaws. First of all, many unscrupulous businessmen hadn't even bothered to sign immigrants to labor contracts in the first place. They had just made promises of a better life that were tempting enough to lure the foreigners to America. Forbidding contracts would not curb this abuse.

Second, the law left responsibility for enforcement in the hands of the states. And finally, the law had no provisions for inspection of immigrants, deportations of violators of the law, or penalties on shipping companies who assisted immigrants in violating the law. In short, the law was a paper tiger.

UNCLE SAM TAKES OVER IMMIGRATION

The Alien Contract Labor Law was violated so often that even congressmen finally figured out the law needed fixing. In 1888, the House of Representatives authorized investigation of immigration.

The Congressional committee members investigated, and reported what many suspected. They determined European leaders were conniving to dump their convicts and paupers in the United States. They determined state government inspectors were checking immigrants too rapidly to do a thorough job. They determined paupers and convicts from Europe were getting by the inspectors. They determined that there were many violations of the Alien Contract Labor Law, and yet there were very few prosecutions and even fewer convictions of violators. They determined the taxpayers of New York (where most of the immigrants were coming to by ship) were having to pay $20 million a year to take care of illegal immigrants.

Later in 1889, President Benjamin Harrison's Secretary of the Treasury William Windom had issued an independent report of his own department's findings. Windom's people said it was difficult to throughly examine immigrants on "vessels that arrive crowded with immigrants all eager to land."

As bad a problem as this was, they said, it paled in comparison to the wrongdoing of British shipping company officials who sneaked around American laws to dump undesirables in the United States. They noted, "But a more serious difficulty, in the satisfactory administration of the law, is found in the facility with which prohibited persons may enter the United States from the British provinces (Canada) and Mexico. From November, 1888, to April, 1889, inclusive, twenty-eight British steamships landed 1,304 immigrants at Portland, Me., but they previously touched at Halifax (in Nova Scotia), and landed more than three times that number, most of whom, it is reported, came by rail through Canada into the United States without examination or restriction, and the steamships thereby escaped the payment of the passenger tax. Such unrestricted influx of immigrants has, it is believed, resulted in a large addition to the number who require public aid, and this increased the financial burden of the States and municipalities where they chance to fall into distress."

They recommended adding lepers, sufferers of "destructive and contagious diseases," and "all persons inimical to our social and political institutions" to the list of those barred from entering the United States.

They recommended making immigrants getting "character and fitness" certificates from American consuls in their countries.

They noted the main purpose of the Alien Contract Labor Law of 1885 was to protect American workers from unfair competition from foreigners willing to work for much less money. They said foreigners were breaking the law by coming to Canada and then sneaking into the United States by rail.

They noted the U.S. Treasury Department was supposed to supervise immigration. However, the federal agency contracted the work to the states. This led to problems in enforcing immigration laws, such as they were. State immigration officials were not under federal control. To resolve local jurisdictional disputes, Windom and his subordinates recommended the U.S. Treasury Department (his department) should take over immigration supervision from state immigration commissions.

In 1890, congressional investigators again confirmed American businessmen, foreign steamship companies, and British authorities in Canada were conspiring to flood the U.S. with illegal immigrants. They said the businessmen sent agents to Europe to lure the poor to come to America by promising them unrealistically good conditions, that steamship company executives likewise sent agents through Europe stimulating interest in steerage tickets, and that British authorities in Canada allowed these immigrants into Canada so they could make their way into America without being inspected. They blamed a division of authority between the U.S. Treasury Department and the states for American failure to punish these abuses. **(6)**

In early 1890, Windom decided the U.S. government should take over inspection and admission of immigrants in New York City. Treasury Department agents had determined Castle Garden was unsuitable to handle the tide of immigrants coming into New York City each day. Windom ended the federal immigration contract with New York state officials. Since New York City was the port of entry for most immigrants, this move in effect "federalized" most of the immigration inspection workload.

Per a congressional resolution of April 11, 1890, members of the House and Senate decided to make Ellis Island in Upper New York Bay the site of the new federal immigration station. Ellis Island was handy – it is just across the Hudson River from Castle Garden. Ellis Island is also directly north of Liberty Island, where the Statue of Liberty had been built just four years earlier. Ironically, a large number of people objected to putting an immigration station on Liberty Island, whose giant copper goddess was symbolically beckoning the foreigners to come to the Land of the Free. They said all the greasy foreigners would degrade the attractiveness of the monument. So it was Ellis Island or bust.

There was a bit of housekeeping to do before the feds could have the new facility built. Ellis Island and Liberty Island – which was called Bedloe's Island before Lady Liberty called it home – had both contained harbor defense fortifications from the time of George Washington's presidency to the Civil War, just like the Battery. Starting in 1861, the first year of the Civil War, the U.S. Navy used Ellis Island as a powder magazine, a place for storing gunpowder and other explosives. Before workers could build the immigration station, Navy men had to relocate the pyrotechnics to Fort Wadsworth on nearby Staten Island.

Castle Garden's era as the main immigration station in America would be done. The tiny converted artillery post, which had been stage to Jenny Lind and spider-dancing Lola Montez, and the site of the processing of millions of immigrants, closed in 1890. New York authorities, ticked off because the feds were taking over immigration processing from them, refused to allow the T-men to use Castle Garden.

But Windom and his people shrugged off the New Yorkers' tantrum. While workers were building the inspection station on Ellis Island, Treasury agents in 1890 and 1891 processed immigrants at their Barge Office facility on the Battery, close to Castle Garden. **(7)**

Meanwhile, Treasury Department agents kept examining immigration processing in an effort to improve it. The annual report of the Treasury Department for FY 1891 noted when federal authorities took over immigration processing from New York state officials in 1890, they saved expenses and collected more money from immigrants and steamship companies.

The report also noted federal officials in New York were deporting more aliens who were violating the Alien Contract Labor Law than New York state workers had been deporting for this cause. The authors wrote, "The defense of our wage workers against unfair competition is so essential a part of the industrial protective system of the country, that nothing should be left undone in legislation or administration to make it effective."

While acknowledging, "Our country owes too much in greatness and prosperity to its naturalized citizens to wish to impede the natural movement of such valuable members of society to our shores," the authors wrote, "The noticeable feature of our immigration in recent years has been a change in the character of many of the immigrants, who do not readily assimilate with our people, and are not in sympathy with our institutions."

In 1891, Congress and President Harrison put a new immigration law into effect, which put the states out of the immigration processing business. The law, known as the Act of March 3, 1891, ordered the U.S. Treasury Department to take over this mission in all states, like they had already done in New York City, the port taking in by far the most immigrants. The U.S. Treasury Department's Bureau of Immigration would handle processing of immigrants.

The law made it a violation for companies to encourage immigration by promising jobs in ads in foreign countries. The law also forbade foreign steamship companies from soliciting foreigners to become immigrants to America. It allowed the companies to advertise their prices, services, and schedules. (U.S. state governments got an exemption for their immigrant inducement programs.)

The law called for medical inspections of immigrants. The law also closed an earlier loophole allowing unlimited immigration of relatives and friends of people who had already gone to the United States.

Today, the U.S. government allows relatively unlimited immigration of relatives of Third World people who have already come to the United States. The practice is called "daisy chaining."

Months after the passing of the 1891 immigration law, the Bureau of Immigration had 24 inspection stations ready in seaports and at spots along the Canadian and Mexican borders. The U.S. Marine Hospital Service's doctors conducted medical inspections at these stations.

The new immigration code still had its problems. The authors of Annual Report of the Secretary of the Treasury for FY1891 noted immigration officials needed to do more to verify the criminal backgrounds of would-be immigrants. They said in so many words the worst criminals would lie about their situations.

They also noted more aliens were landing in Canada and coming to America by rail to avoid inspection and the immigration tax. The 1891 law allowed for only a few inspectors along the Canadian and Mexican borders.

They urged the process of "sifting immigrants" should at least begin in the immigrants' homelands. That way, they argued, "aliens of the prohibited classes shall not be permitted to come across the ocean to our ports, only to be sent back penniless and stranded."

They also urged a uniform inspection of rail passengers from Canada to stop illegals coming in from the north. They urged an international agreement with Britain and Canada, but said the United States should set up its own inspection process for rail passengers whether the British and Canadians liked it or not.

In the 1890s, American officials did further work on the immigration laws to protect Americans from hazards associated with allowing certain types of immigrants to come to America. In the 1890s, immigration would drop by about a million and a half people from what it had been in the 1880s.

Two laws members of Congress enacted in early 1893 started the trend for inspecting immigrants for health and suitability.

One law prevented the introduction of contagious or infectious diseases into the United States. This law allowed a countrywide ban of immigrants from places where cholera and other serious contagious and infectious diseases were epidemic, if quarantining immigrants from the country couldn't guarantee the safety of Americans.

The second law required captains of vessels to provide lists of passengers. Inspectors were required to hold immigrants not clearly entitled to enter the United States for hearings before boards of special inquiry. The law required consuls at seaports where ships were loading passengers for America to verify the lists and verify the immigrants had undergone physical exams, and that none of the passengers was as far as they knew, excludible. Steamship companies were required to post American immigration laws where they sold tickets. Twice a year, the companies had to send certifications to the U.S. Attorney General that they were doing so.

Later in 1893, U.S. Treasury Department officials put into effect a series of regulations designed to protect the rights of the American public, set standards for screening immigrants, and protect immigrants from unscrupulous steamship company officials.

The regulations deputized customs inspectors along the Canadian border to act as immigration officials to inspect those coming into America.

The regulations required ship captains bringing immigrants from ports or parts of countries where certain diseases were prevalent to present a statement certified by an American consular officer that all steerage immigrants he transported had been held for medical observation at a barracks facility at the port for five days before the voyage, and that these immigrants had had their clothes, baggage, and personal effects disinfected. They required leather shoes and boots and leather luggage cases to be disinfected with carbolic acid in water, and they required many other items to be steamed, boiled, treated with carbolic acid, or dipped in a mercury chloride solution.

The regulations ordered the steamship company which brought any immigrant who could not be admitted to the United States to pay for the feeding and lodging of the immigrant while he or she was detained for hearings if the board of special inquiry ruled to have the immigrant deported. Likewise, the regulations ordered the steamship company which brought any immigrant who couldn't gain entry to the United States to take him or her back to Europe at company expense.

A supplement to the regulations established medical exams for immigrants. The supplement also made shipping companies pay for the treatment of people who had become ill aboard ship until they were well enough to leave U.S. hospital facilities to enter the country or return to the port they came from. In some cases, at the discretion of the immigration commissioner, the American immigrant fund would cover expenses of those who were detained due to "accident or unavoidable circumstances."

The regulations and the supplement also established the practice of questioning immigrants for literacy and poverty. If an immigrant came in with $30 or less, the agents were to know about it. If an immigrant was deemed a person likely to become a public charge, he or she had the right to show proof of support from a spouse or relative to the immigration agents.

If the immigrant came illegally and became a public charge within a year of immigrating, the person or corporation or steamship company or railroad bringing the person to America in the first place would have to pay to have him or her deported. If the immigrant came legally, passed inspection, and then became a public charge (through permanent injury or ailment) within a year, the American government's immigrant fund would pay for the deportation.

The laws were designed to protect the rights of the American public to have immigration regulated and prevent infected immigrants from carrying contagious diseases to the country, to protect immigrants from unscrupulous steamship company officials, and to set an understandable standard for steamship companies and immigration officials alike. The rules were generally fair, except for the rule that specified an immigrant getting injured and disabled in the United States through the fault of another still was sent back. This was about a generation before worker compensation laws, so American workers who were disabled on the job suffered comparably in their own homeland. **(8)**

THE EARLY DAYS OF ELLIS ISLAND

Ellis Island opened for business January 1, 1892. Annie Moore, a 15-year-old girl from County Cork in Ireland, was the first immigrant to land and be processed at Ellis Island. After Annie signed the register, Colonel John Baptiste Weber, the first commissioner of the Ellis Island immigration station, presented her with a 10-dollar gold piece, the largest sum of money she had ever had. Annie and her two younger brothers who traveled with her celebrated the New Year by being admitted to the United States as legal immigrants.

Roughly 16 million people had come to America from 1820 to 1891, before inspectors at Ellis Island and other new immigration stations had even processed a single immigrant. Inspectors would admit 20 million immigrants into the United States – more than 14 million of them through the port of New York, and 12 million or so of the port of New York arrivals through Ellis Island – from 1892 through 1924, when the quota laws slowed the tide of immigrants to a trickle.

In the era when American officials were serious about regulating immigration, 70% of all immigrants would come through New York City for processing. The remainder came through smaller immigration stations in the major ports of the East Coast, the Great Lakes, the Gulf Coast, and the Pacific Coast, and similar facilities along the Mexican and Canadian borders. **(9)**

Joseph H. Senner served as Commissioner of Immigration at Ellis Island from 1893 to 1897. He was a German Austrian Jewish immigrant, born in Moravia (in what is now the Czech Republic), who left his faith and changed his last name from Samuely when he came to America, and got involved in America's German community. Senner, a newspaper man, was nominally a Republican. But he worked for the election of honest Democrat Grover Cleveland, and received the appointment a couple of weeks after Cleveland took office for his second term.

Senner had a staff of roughly 100 employees to inspect, process, detain, feed, provide medical care to, admit, or deport a couple of hundred thousand immigrants a year. Ellis Island's slowest year in Senner's term was 1897, when more than 180,000 immigrants passed through, and its busiest was 1893, when almost 450,000 immigrants passed through.

As the 1890s ran their course, more and more people from Southern and Eastern Europe immigrated to America. Some of them did not meet standards for admission as immigrants, and they started disturbances at Ellis Island. Following is an account of one of these fracases, from the New York Times on May 8, 1895:

Four Men Escape from Ellis Island

Over 100 Italians made a determined effort yesterday to break out of the detention pen at Ellis Island.

They rushed against the gates in a body, yelling and waving their arms to scare the guards. The place was in an uproar in a moment, the scared women and children huddling into corners, and the attendants running about for extra guards.

Finally, the Italian representative at Ellis Island, Prof. Aldini, mounted a desk and spoke to his angry countrymen. This had a quieting effect, and in half an hour there was again quiet in the pen.

Four men had escaped over the railing earlier in the day, and made their way to the New Jersey shore.

This was not an isolated incident. A reporter wrote the following in an article in the New York Daily Tribune for April 16, 1896:

Small riots that threatened to develop into trouble of a more serious nature are occurring daily among the many immigrants on Ellis Island, and the officials have become so apprehensive, that Dr. Senner yesterday telegraphed to the Treasury Department at Washington, asking permission to swear in a number of special constables to be used in keeping in subjection the unruly aliens. The Tribune has already told of the arrival of thousands of peasants, penniless and dirty for the most part, from the Mediterranean ports, and they are continuing to pour in daily.

On Sunday the steamship Bolivia brought into this port 1,376 of these people, and Alesia followed with over one thousand. The Werra yesterday brought in 756 and the steamships Victoria and Belgravis are now on the way here with an aggregate of 2,820 more.

Federal authorities allowed Senner to hire more help in 1896.

Senner recommended placing Ellis Island employees under civil service regulations to weed out the unfit. However, an 1896 executive order president Grover Cleveland signed doing this exempted the incumbent jobholders. They were classified as "civil servants" without having to take exams. In other words, they were grandfathered into their jobs without having to prove they were competent to hold them. From 1896 until 1900, only four new hires at Ellis Island came from the civil service list. The rest came from people who the Civil Service Commission certified on the word of politicians. This would in time lead to a corruption scandal at Ellis Island.

Private contractors provided baggage transportation service, food service, and money changing service at Ellis Island. In the first few years, the contractors won business by submitting the highest bid. (The Immigration Bureau was self-supporting; it took in more money in contracts and fees than it spent.) However, this didn't always mean the winning contractors provided the best services to the immigrants. They had the temptation to make their money by doing as little as possible for the immigrants or charging the immigrants as much as possible.

This changed in 1896, when immigration officials awarded contacts to vendors who would charge the least percentage of interest in changing money, ship baggage for the lowest amount per piece, and provide food at the lowest costs. This change in awarding contracts made services better for the immigrants. Of course there would still be individuals who overcharged for and underdelivered on food, deliberately short-changed immigrants in money exchanges, and stole baggage. However, the bidding system improved the overall level of contract services.

In June 1897, a nighttime fire burned down the wooden immigration station building and several other wooden buildings on Ellis Island. Fortunately, no one died or suffered serious injury in the fire. Federal officials decided to build brick, concrete, and steel buildings to replace them. Meanwhile, they temporarily shifted the processing of immigrants back to the Barge Office, on the Battery, close to Castle Garden. **(10)**

Senner left his position at Ellis Island in 1897, and President McKinley appointed Thomas Fitchie, a Brooklyn politician of Scottish ancestry, to replace him. Edward McSweeney, who had been the Assistant Commissioner of Immigration at Ellis Island since 1893, continued in this office under Fitchie.

During most of Fitchie's tenure as Commissioner of Immigration at New York City, construction workers were building better structures on Ellis Island. So immigrant processing in New York City continued at the Barge Office until December of 1900.

The Barge Office didn't have the space or the isolation for control purposes that Ellis Island had. Immigration officials had to rent houses near the Barge Office so they could have room for their hospital service and their detention areas. They also tied a steamboat to the wharf and used it as quarters for detained immigrants and hospital staffers.

Large-scale corruption returned to the immigration process. Unscrupulous employees charged friends and relatives of immigrants money to see them, and stole from the immigrants. Unscrupulous contractors overcharged immigrants for food and short-changed immigrants when they changed their European money into American money. (Federal authorities allowed moneychangers to charge a small percentage for profit, like a check cashing service, but they were grossly overcharging the immigrants beyond this allowable percentage.) Baggage theft was widespread. Some employees and contractors steered pretty single immigrants to people who forced them to work as prostitutes. **(11)**

Terence Powderly, a railroad machinist who had been mayor of Scranton, Pennsylvania as well as the leader of the Knights of Labor (one of America's first labor unions) had been one of the few prominent labor figures to work for the election of William McKinley in 1896. (McKinley was pro-industry and often was pro-labor as well.) Powderly, who also had become a lawyer after his time as head of his union, applied to become the Commissioner-General of Immigration. Powderly, the son of Irish immigrants, was a good man but a controversial figure. McKinley intended to appoint him, but ran into trouble on this. Most Republican senators were not pro-labor. Some Democrat senators were; they and many labor people were upset Powderly had worked for McKinley, so they called the appointment a payoff. The Senate would not at first confirm Powderly. So McKinley appointed Powderly to the post in 1897 on a recess appointment. The next year the Senate did confirm him.

Powderly's office was in Washington, but he would have to spend quite a bit of time checking on his subordinates in New York City. Powderly launched an investigation of the Barge Office. In 1900, at the conclusion of the investigation, Powderly had 11 immigration agents fired for various offenses stemming from the investigation. Their offenses ranged from overcharging for food, misleading immigrants about distances and destinations (meaning they overpaid for train tickets), charging immigrants' friends and relatives admission fees to allow them on Ellis Island, gypping immigrants in exchanging their European money for American money, cruelty, and other forms of petty theft.

"My chief regret," Powderly said, "was that I could not send some of the culprits to the penitentiary." **(12)**

Immigration officials had In 1899 decided to post a Marine Hospital Service surgeon in Naples to observe immigrants for any physical problems they might have that would prevent them from gaining entry to America once American agents inspected them in New York City or other ports where their ships might land them. Naples at this time was one of the busiest ports of departure for immigrants and also among the dirtiest and most disease-ridden.

The surgeon only had the authority to prevent people from boarding immigrant ships if they were suffering from communicable diseases. He managed to keep many other physical defectives from boarding the ships by telling the steamship company officials that American officials would probably refuse them entry and deport them at the steamship company's costs. It would take awhile before this practice of checking would-be immigrants before they got on ships would be mandatory practice. **(13)**

The Spanish-American War came in 1898, and it would have an indirect effect on the checking of would-be immigrants at at least one other port also.

Crooked contractors sold diseased beef to the U.S. Army, and the toxic meat poisoned many soldiers. Among them was a military band leader who had emigrated from Foggia, in the Apulia region of southern Italy. He had married an immigrant girl from Trieste – a seaport of mostly Italian and Slovenian people under the control of Austria-Hungary -- and their children would be born in America. He had joined the U.S. Army as a musician, and his children grew up in the West as he and his wife and children moved from Army post to Army post in the 1880s and 1890s.

He became deathly ill after eating the poisoned meat, and the Army discharged him. He took his wife and children back to Trieste, so she and their children could live with her relatives after he died. He died in 1901, and his oldest son, now 18, was able to find work as a clerk for the American consul's office in Budapest. The son was a native of America who could speak Italian ... and he quickly learned German and Croatian. He became the consular agent in Rijeka (which in those days was also called Fiume) when he was 20. Rijeka, near Trieste, was also a port city, and many people from Austria-Hungary would get on ships bound for America in the Croatian city's harbor.

About the time the young consul reported for duty in Rijeka, Britain's Cunard Line started sending two ships a month to the port to take emigrants to America. The consul read the immigration regulations he was supposed to enforce, and noted there was nothing specifying he should have immigrants inspected at the port for certain diseases and ailments that would keep them from gaining entry to America. However, if inspectors at Ellis Island or other American ports found would-be immigrants with these problems, they would bar them from entry and make them go back to Europe. The regs said a consul had to "certify to the health of all passengers and crews and give the ship a certificate that it had cleared from a port free from contagious diseases or illnesses subject to quarantine regulations and that bedding and other household goods had been properly fumigated." The consul believed it was wrong to allow immigrants to spend money to get to America, only to be turned back, so he got permission from his superiors to hire local doctors to inspect immigrants at Rijeka.

When the first Cunard Line vessel docked at Rijeka to load immigrants for America, the consul arrived with a doctor to have the immigrants inspected. The British sea captain and steamship line officials were furious when the consul demanded to inspect the immigrants for health problems. They refused, so the consul refused to give the ship a bill of health to land in America. When they saw the young consul was serious, they allowed inspection of the immigrants under protest. The British refused to pay the doctor's fee, so the consul made the Cunard Line post a bond before he would allow any more immigrants for America to board their ships. The Cunard Line threw in the towel, at least at Rijeka.

The young consul would spend 1903 through 1906 at Rijeka, and he would ensure the passage of close to 100,000 immigrants before coming back to America and working as an interpreter at Ellis Island to pay his way through law school. This young consul, Fiorello La Guardia, would gain a reputation for decisive action as a Congressman, a military officer, and mayor of New York City. He explained his first decisive action this way: "Inspection was speedy and efficient, and we saved many hundreds of innocent people from the expense of taking a trip all the way to New York only to be found inadmissable on health grounds and sent back."

La Guardia's idea of American-supervised health inspections done at ports of embarkation did not become government policy for a number of years. Even in the 1920s, when U.S. Public Health Service doctors examined many steerage-traveling immigrants in European ports before allowing them on the ships, doctors still examined most immigrants traveling steerage when they reached Ellis Island and other American immigration stations because it wasn't universal practice to screen immigrants overseas until the era of the Great Depression.

American authorities would start fining steamship companies for each immigrant they transported to America who was too diseased or otherwise physically unadmissible. They would also force the steamship companies to take them back to the ports they brought them from on their money. This system of fines and charges would force steamship companies to have immigrants inspected for diseases in European ports, but would not be as impartial as La Guardia's method of American supervision of the physical exam screening process. **(14)**

The new brick immigration station at Ellis Island was ready for business in December 1900. Immigration workers resumed processing immigrants on Ellis Island eight days before Christmas 1900. Thomas Fitchie at this time was still Commissioner of Immigration at New York City. Edward McSweeney was still Assistant Commissioner of Immigration at New York City. And William McKinley was still President. But their days all would be numbered.

ELLIS ISLAND WHILE THEODORE ROOSEVELT WAS PRESIDENT

The first decade of the 1900s was the heyday of Ellis Island. More than double the amount of Europeans came during this decade than had come in the previous decade. Most immigrants in Roosevelt's time were people from southern Italy, people from all over Austria-Hungary, Jews from Russia, and Poles from their occupied and divided homeland. Many Irish, Germans, and Britons came also ... but many many more came from Italy, Russia, and Austria-Hungary.

It would also be a decade of change and reform for the immigration process. This happened because Theodore Roosevelt was the president through most of the decade, and he picked men who thought like him to run the nation's immigration offices.

Ironically, Teddy Roosevelt became president because of the act of a son of Polish immigrants. This man, Leo Czolgosz, was the anarchist who shot President William McKinley in the gut while he was shaking hands at a fair in Buffalo on September 6, 1901. Cabinet members came to Buffalo to be with their chief; Roosevelt – who was vice-president at the time -- rushed from a camping trip to visit McKinley.

When Roosevelt visited his wounded chief, McKinley was in good spirits and appeared on the road to recovery. Roosevelt returned to his vacation in upstate New York because he and the other Cabinet members thought McKinley would pull through. He figured this act of going back on vacation might calm the public.

However, McKinley took a turn for the worse late September 12 and early September 13. McKinley's people sent for Teddy Roosevelt. That afternoon, an outdoors guide located the vice-president coming down from hiking up a mountain to tell him his boss was dying. Roosevelt hiked back to the lodge several miles away, then he and a driver hitched horses to a wagon and rode more than 40 miles through the mountains in a thunderstorm in the darkness (and they drove so hard they had to change for fresh horses two times on the way) to get to the nearest train station. They got there, mud-covered, as dawn was breaking on September 14, 1901. A telegraph was waiting for Roosevelt, telling him McKinley had died in the wee hours of the morning and he was now the President. Roosevelt took the train to Buffalo, met with the other Cabinet members and aides there, and took the oath of office in a private home that afternoon. **(15)**

Teddy Roosevelt would serve as president from 1901 to 1909. During Roosevelt's administration, more immigrants came to America than in any other similar length of time until the 1990s, when Bill Clinton and Congress decided to ignore enforcement of immigration laws.

Roosevelt was the most politically active president since Abraham Lincoln. He was more enthusiastic about using the power of the presidency than Lincoln. Roosevelt's mindset was crucial to how the American government would run immigration during his terms of office.

Roosevelt became president because an anarchist murdered his predecessor, so he wanted anarchists kept out of the country. Roosevelt hated corruption, so he insisted on honest administration. Roosevelt believed government officials should help the people instead of sitting on their hands while the rich and powerful took advantage of the people, so he insisted on fairness. Roosevelt believed the white race was superior to other races, but he respected Japan as a nation. He also tried to allow the immigration of skilled Chinese. Roosevelt was not bigoted against non-WASP whites, and he believed certain immigrants could strengthen America.

On a personal level, Teddy Roosevelt had a number of friends and acquaintances of many races, religions, ethnicities, levels of wealth, and stations in life. Roosevelt had many more friends who were cowboys than bluebloods. He was the first president to have a black to the White House as a dinner guest – he invited black educator Booker T. Washington shortly after he became president. (Lincoln had conferred with Frederick Douglass in the White House about the recruiting of blacks for the Union Army in 1864, but it was an office appointment instead of a dinner invite.) Roosevelt could treat American Indians and Spaniards one-on-one with respect, even though he had faced off against some braves in North Dakota and had fought in battle against the Spanish.

Teddy Roosevelt had his shortcomings. Like too many men with authority, it was hard for him to admit he was wrong after he rushed to judgment. Probably his worst such act was his decision to uphold the dishonorable discharging of 167 black soldiers stationed near Brownsville, Texas because white residents of that town falsely complained they had rioted. He couldn't admit that he had rushed to judgment and endorsed the punishing of these men after his underlings had botched the investigation and falsely accused the soldiers of covering up for other soldiers of their battalion who allegedly killed a white bartender and wounded a policeman.

Daniel Mannix, a naval officer who thought the world of Teddy Roosevelt because he made the U.S. Navy so powerful, was one of the minority who disapproved of how the incident was handled. He noted:

"A number of these Negro [sic] regiments were outstanding for their skill and pluck. It was a Negro [sic]

regiment that had distinguished itself at San Juan Hill, bravely charging the Spanish position when the white troops refused to advance. When one of those black regiments was in Texas they were attacked by a white crowd for having broken a local taboo, such as entering a restaurant reserved for whites or some such thing. In my opinion, those troopers would have been perfectly justified in taking their rifles and firing a volley into that mob of crackers and tarheels." **(16)**

Teddy Roosevelt didn't overcome Jim Crow. Of course, neither did elitist leftist Democrats Woodrow Wilson or Franklin Delano Roosevelt. In fact, Wilson and FDR used segregation to their advantage, keeping Southern Democrats loyal to them.

Aside from his substandard dealings with the black soldiers, Teddy Roosevelt believed in treating people fairly and having government employees serve the public instead of lording it over the public. He also believed in doing what he felt was right to protect America's interests. The men he picked to run the immigration services were like-minded men.

A scandal at Ellis Island in the summer of 1901, during McKinley's last few months as president, showed that many employees working at Ellis Island were still either corrupt or incompetent, even after Terence Powderly had the work force investigated and eleven of them fired. Some immigration agents were found to be extorting money from immigrants, and some New York City aldermen who performed civil marriage ceremonies overcharged immigrants and kicked back money to higher-ups, allegedly including Fitchie himself. Another facet of the scandal involved the sale of as many as 10,000 fraudulent citizenship papers to immigrants. **(17)**

Shortly after Roosevelt became president in September 1901, he decided to can Thomas Fitchie, the Commissioner of Immigration at Ellis Island. He also made up his mind to get rid of Edward McSweeney, Fitchie's assistant commissioner.

A few months later, Roosevelt replaced Fitchie with William Williams, a wealthy lawyer who had a good military record in the Spanish-American War. Teddy replaced McSweeney with Joseph Murray, an old friend of his.

Williams wasn't the Commissioner-General of Immigration (Terence Powderly held that title until mid 1902, and then Frank Sargent, a former official in the Brotherhood of Locomotive Firemen, held that title until well into 1908), but he was the Commissioner of Immigration at Ellis Island, the top man at the post where immigration was heaviest. Since he oversaw the processing of roughly two-thirds of all immigrants coming to America each year, any policies he put into effect would be important. Besides having so much local responsibility, Williams was an outspoken man, and he made sure his views were heard.

Williams was honest, direct, and decisive, the kind of man you would expect Teddy Roosevelt to ask to serve. Williams was also opinionated and somewhat prejudiced. He stepped on a lot of toes and angered everyone from dishonest contractors and scam artists posing as missionaries whom he banned from the island to immigrant aid society people who believed he was prejudiced against their countrymen to women workers who thought he was a male chauvinist.

Williams did have some prejudices against certain types of immigrants. However, he didn't let it affect his performance of his job. His personality almost sticks an index finger in your face as you read his reports and letters. Like his boss Teddy Roosevelt, Williams would be too blunt and too politically incorrect for the nation today, because too many of us are immature and are not adult enough to hear the blunt truth coming from our leaders.

Roosevelt fired Powderly in June 1902 on a trumped-up charge he had "coerced" McSweeney. The real reason was Powderly had made so many waves that many of the careerists in the Bureau of Immigration didn't like him. Powderly asked Roosevelt to have someone he trusted review the record of the investigation he (Powderly) ordered, and of his actions concerning McSweeney, and Roosevelt did so. Roosevelt learned the charges against Powderly were untrue, and Powderly had acted justly. Roosevelt would try to make it up to Powderly by appointing him as a special official of Department of Commerce and Labor in 1906 and sending him to Europe to determine the causes of immigration to America from each of the countries of Europe. In 1907, Roosevelt appointed Powderly chief of the Bureau of Immigration's Division of Information, a job Powderly would hold until 1921. Powderly would serve as a Labor Department official until his death in 1924. **(18)**

In February 1903, Congress at the request of Theodore Roosevelt, merged several federal subordinate agencies to form the Department of Commerce and Labor. One of the agencies winding up on the new cabinet-level agency was the Bureau of Immigration.

In March 1903, Congress passed another immigration bill. The 1903 law was legislation you would expect from government when Teddy Roosevelt ran things – an overhaul of previous laws that kept the good features of the old laws and removed their bad features, and added new provisions that made sense, resulting in a code that was workable and fair.

The law aimed at providing better inspection of immigrants, and excluding undesirables. An obvious result of the assassination of President McKinley by anarchist Leon Czolgosz was a provision for the exclusion of any anarchist or other person holding beliefs supporting the violent overthrow of an elected government.

McKinley, by the way, was not the only leader of a nation killed by anarchists in the years before this law went into effect. Anarchism was a force in Europe from the 1880s through World War One. European anarchists also assassinated Tsar Alexander II of Russia in 1881, French president Sadi Carnot in 1894, prime minister Antonio Canovas of Spain in 1897, Empress Elisabeth (Sissi) of Austria-Hungary in 1898, and King Umberto of Italy in 1900.

The assassination of Canovas had had disastrous results for Spain and a direct impact on the United States. Canovas was the best of the politicians who ran Spain in the late 1800s. The mediocrities who ran the country after he died blundered into war against an all-too-eager United States the next year.

Likewise, the assassination of Tsar Alexander II of Russia had an effect on America. His successors aimed policies against Jews, Poles, and other non-Russians in Russia and the lands the Russians controlled. This would translate into the immigration of millions of Jews and Poles and other non-Russians from the Russian Empire to America.

The law aka the Act of March 3, 1903, also strengthened the ban on prostitutes and pimps emigrating to America. The lawmakers put a fine of $5000 and a 1 to 5-year prison term on the books as punishment for those who imported females for prostitution.

"White slavery" (sex trafficking) was a huge evil then, as now, and unlike now, leaders in the early 1900s were more prone to do something about it. Teddy Roosevelt was the moral opposite of Bill Clinton. Inspectors of the Ellis Island era were "tough" on unaccompanied single women because they wanted to make sure these women were not prostitutes, or were not victims being trafficked as sex slaves, or were not so destitute they would feel forced to become prostitutes. Paternalism done the right way is a wonderful thing.

The 1903 law also excluded all polygamists (this was aimed at Moslems, pagans, and Mormons). Back in the day, the Mormons, before – and sometimes after – they swore off polygamy, sent proselytizers to Britain and Scandinavia to bring in women as converts to be polygamous wives for the leaders who could afford more than one wife and could put up with multiple cases of PMS under their roofs each month.

The 1903 law also excluded "persons who have been convicted of a felony or other crime or misdemeanor involving moral turpitude." ("Moral turpitude" means crimes of dishonesty, such as perjury, burglary, fraud, theft, embezzlement, and fencing stolen goods, or sexual crimes such as rape, sodomy, sexual assault, and child molesting, or acts of malicious violence such as murder, felony assault, and robbery, and acts against public decency such as adultery, incest, bigamy, homosexuality, and child abandonment.)

However, Congress didn't have any trouble with people whose rap sheets contained only political offenses (as long as they weren't anarchists). The law said, "Nothing in the Act shall exclude persons convicted of an offense purely political, not involving moral turpitude." After all, Roosevelt and the Congressional leaders realized political malcontents had founded the United States and their malcontent successors had made it the greatest nation in the world in little more than a century.

The 1903 law banned "all idiots, insane persons, epileptics, and persons who have been insane within five years or previous; persons who have had two or more attacks of insanity at any time previously; paupers; persons likely to become a public charge; professional beggars; persons afflicted with a loathsome or with a dangerous contagious disease."

The 1903 law also denied each immigrant the right to appeal the decision of a Board of Special Inquiry if the board members had ruled the immigrant unfit to enter because of physical or mental disabilities, or because of a "loathsome" or "dangerous contagious disease."

The 1903 law excluded people coming to America on labor contracts except for certain skilled workers whose employment would not put Americans out of jobs. The legislators made it illegal to assist or encourage immigration for jobs, and to offer contracts to foreigners in most cases, and the law carried a $1000 fine for violators. It also allowed anyone harmed by importing a contract worker (including the contract worker himself!) to sue the cheap labor importer; the private citizen or illegal alien and his lawyer could collect the $1000 fine instead of the government if his attorney filed before the government attorney filed.

This law didn't apply to contracts with domestic servants (the "Fifi" or "Lizzie" or "Maria" or "Helga" exception). Nor did it apply to white-collar professionals, clergymen, nuns, or entertainers. These folks could come in legally.

Actors, circus people, musicians, and singers didn't make the money they make now, and in the days before movies and radio and TV and recorded music, people took in their entertainment live. The "entertainer" provision was designed to encourage top-flight talent to come to America. Some immigrants would try to sneak in by falsely claiming they were singers or musicians. One of Williams' successors at Ellis Island, Henry Curran, would make a woman from Hungary show her talent with a violin, and admitted her into the country when she showed she was a virtuosa.

The 1903 law continued to make it a crime to knowingly immigrate illegally. The immigrant would have to pay his own way home, or those who conspired to help him immigrate illegally would have to do so. If the rejected immigrant was without money, then the American government (or the shipping company whose ship brought him – if it was provable that company officials were derelict in failing to keep him off their ship) would pay to ship him back.

Officials had been deporting some alien (foreigners who were not citizens) felons on the common-sense grounds that they couldn't come to America with a criminal record for nonpolitical crimes, so why should they be allowed to stay in America after robbing, beating, raping, or chiseling someone here? The 1903 law made it more easy to expel aliens from America who broke American laws. An alien who was in prison technically was a public charge, and as such, could be forced to leave the country. The law ordered immigration officials to check prisons as well as charitable institutions for aliens with an eye to deporting them as public charges.

The law also increased the amount of time an immigrant could be deported for being a public charge from one year to two years. This applied to immigrants with pre-existing problems, not to immigrant workers who became injured on the job in America.

The legislators also targeted shipping company officials and others who stood to profit from trafficking in illegals. They made it a crime to smuggle illegals or excludibles into America, punishable by a fiine of $1000 per illegal, and a prison term of three months to two years. They also made it a crime to knowingly assist anarchists into America, punishable by a $5000 fine and a prison term of 1 to 5 years They made it a crime for an anarchist or other subversive of the established order, or for any other immigrant who was in America illegally to apply for citizenship, and they made it illegal for anyone else to assist such illegals. Violators of these citizenship laws could cost the offender up to $5000, and one to ten years of penitentiary time.

Ship captains who landed aliens anywhere in America except at an immigration station faced a $100 to $1000 fine and up to a year in prison.

The lawmakers closed the loophole the British and Canadians had been exploiting in railroading immigrants into America without inspection or head tax.

Aliens could still sneak in by walking or by riding horses or by riding in horse-drawn sleds or wheeled vehicles like wagons or carriages across the border. They could also sneak in on small boats or in trains or inside those newfangled automobiles. But the law stopped some illegal immigration from Canada and Mexico. (Most were coming in illegally through Canada.)

Presumably to assist themselves and the federal bureaucrats in their judgment and in their deliberations, the legislators inserted a section into the law forbidding the sale of liquor in the Capitol Building. They didn't make it illegal for anyone to give them a snort or several before they attended to the nation's business.

The representatives and senators also wrote into the law a provision for making ship captains note which immigrants had the equivalent of less than $50. Although they did not enact a law requiring would-be immigrants to have a minimum amount of money to avoid vagrancy or pauperism, they did want to monitor how many very poor were trying to come to America.

The lawmakers also ordered ship captains to have would-be immigrants answer essentially the same questions that American inspectors would eventually ask immigrants. They made it illegal for ship captains to fail to have valid information about any immigrant they intended to land in America, and made such a failure a $10 fine per immigrant on whom information was missing.

The law also penalized shipping companies $100 per diseased person found in inspection in America for bringing any diseased person to America if a competent doctor in Europe or elsewhere outside of America could have detected the disease. The law also allowed American officials to forbid a ship carrying the diseased permission to land at any American port until the shipping company paid the fine. **(19)**

William Williams used the $100 penalty regulation like his own "Big Stick." He had the steamship companies fined $7500 (for 75 immigrants) the steamship companies brought to the United States negligently in June 1903.

He noted, "Already very clear signs exist that the law will hereafter be obeyed, and the former alleged inability on the part of some foreign surgeons to discover cases of favus and trachoma prior to embarkation is very rapidly disappearing. The bringing of diseased aliens, with or without a law to the contrary, is a reckless thing, if only on account of the ready disseminating of disease among the healthy immigrants." **(20)**

In other words, Williams said, some chiselers running a steamship line were willing to risk sickening many immigrants aboard a ship just to shoehorn a couple of sick people into steerage so they could collect a few dollars more.

Williams cared about the other immigrants as well as the American public. Williams fined and/or fired employees when he caught them or found out about them mistreating immigrants. He had businessmen investigated whom he suspected were defrauding the immigrants. He even barred some immigrant aid groups and clergy from Ellis Island when he determined they were corrupt.

Williams had definite ideas on the kinds of immigrants he wanted Americans to welcome, and the kinds he wanted kept out. In his annual report of 1903, Williams noted, "The great bulk of the present immigration settles in four of the Eastern States (New York, New Jersey, Massachusetts, Pennsylvania), and most of it in the large cities of those States. Notwithstanding the well-known demand for agricultural labor in the Western States, thousands of foreigners (from Italy, Austria-Hungary, and Russia) keep pouring into our cities, declining to go where they might be wanted because they are neither physically nor mentally fitted to go to these undeveloped parts of our country and do as did the early settlers from northern Europe."

"No one would object to the better classes of Italians, Austrians, and Russians coming here in large numbers; but the point is that such better element does not come, and, furthermore, the immigration from such countries as Germany and the British Isles [sic] has fallen to a very low figure."

"Past immigration was good because most of it was of the right kind and went to the right place. Capital can not, and it would not if it could, employ much of the alien material that annually passes through Ellis Island, and thereafter chooses to settle in the crowded tenement districts of New York."

Williams said at least 200,000 of the 650,000 who came to the country legally in 1902 were undesirable. He said they were "unintelligent, of low vitality, of poor physique, able to perform only the cheapest kind of manual labor, desirous of locating almost exclusively in the cities, by their competition tending to reduce the standard of living of the American wageworker, and unfitted mentally or morally for good citizenship."

He said undesirables "will be of no benefit to the country, and will, on the contrary, be a detriment, because their presence will tend to lower our standards; and if these 200,000 persons could have been induced to stay at home, nobody, not even those clamoring for more labor, would have missed them. Their coming has been of benefit chiefly, if not only, to the transportation companies which brought them here."

"I state without hesitation that the vast majority of American citizens wish to see steps taken to prevent these undesirable elements from landing at our shores. Attempts to take such steps will be opposed by powerful and selfish interests, and they will insist, among other things, on the value of immigration in the past to the United States and the enormous demand for labor, neither of them relevant as applicable to the particular question whether the undesirable immigrants should be prevented from coming here."

"Europe, like every other part of the world, has millions of undesirable people whom she would be glad to part with, and that strong agencies are constantly at work to send some of them here."

"Aliens have no inherent right whatever to come here, and we may and should take means, however radical and drastic, to keep out all those below a certain physical and economic standard of fitness and all whose presence will tend to lower our standards of living and civilization." **(21)**

Williams' remarks, true in most respects but unfortunately prejudiced in other respects, reflected the viewpoint of many Americans.

Williams was constantly defending his work and his staff's work at Ellis Island. Teddy Roosevelt, in response to Williams' critics in the German community of New York City, appointed a commission to investigate Williams and his people. The commissioners found the German critics of Williams and his people were – like the *Hindenburg* as it burst into flame – full of hot gas. **(22)**

The feisty Williams quit his job in January 1905. Why? Because he believed his assistant Joseph Murray -- an old friend of Roosevelt's whom Teddy had personally appointed – was unfit for the job and Roosevelt would not remove him from the post.

Teddy Roosevelt replaced Williams as Commissioner of Immigration at Ellis Island with Robert Watchorn. Watchorn, a coal miner since he was a boy, emigrated to America from England as a young man in 1880. Watchorn went to work as a miner in Pennsylvania, and saved enough to bring his parents and siblings to America. Watchorn became the first secretary and treasurer of the United Mine Workers union, and then served the chief factory inspector for the state of Pennsylvania. He had also served in the Immigration Service as an inspector at Ellis Island, then as the chief immigration officer monitoring Canadian immigration. Watchorn had trains inspected in Canada, and he went undercover in Canada to find out where most aliens were sneaking into America. As a result, he posted officials elsewhere along the Canadian border and inside Canada to guard against illegal immigration.

Theodore Roosevelt, although a Republican, did not look down on miners. Roosevelt helped settle the Coal Strike of 1902. He was the first president to intervene in a strike on the side of the public, and to give the striking workers a fair hearing, instead of paying undue respect to the demands of the robber barons. Because of this, Roosevelt had many friends in the United Mine Workers, from leader John L. Lewis to the rank-and-file miners.

While not as combative as Williams, Watchorn was as dedicated to America's people and to the fair treatment of the immigrants. Watchorn received higher marks for kindness than did the feisty Williams. A glimpse of his motivation comes from a letter he wrote to Teddy Roosevelt after receiving his appointment to succeed Williams. He wrote, "I do not know of a more important post at your disposal, Mr. President, than that for which you have thus chosen me. To dry tears, and to assuage grief, are works worthy of the noblest of our race; but to remove the cause for tears and grief, is a more laudable endeavor. Ellis Island is the one place where this can be done, in very great measure, by the one in authority there." **(23)**

Watchorn continued Powderly's and Williams' war against corruption. He designed standards for food, money changing, and baggage handling contracts to ensure quality service for fair prices. He also checked on companies which did business with immigrants after they left Ellis Island. In one case, he filed a complaint with the Interstate Commerce Commission against several railroad companies for gouging and mistreating immigrants leaving Ellis Island. Watchorn filed his case after he had one of his assistants, Philip Cowen, an American of German Jewish heritage, pose as an immigrant and travel the rails with immigrants.

In 1905 Roosevelt appointed men to examine how to manage the cases of immigrants seeking to become "naturalized" – in other words, become American citizens. On their advice, Congress in 1906 reorganized the Bureau of Immigration into the Bureau of Immigration and Naturalization. The bureau's Division of Immigration would screen immigrants, while the bureau's Division of Naturalization would maintain citizenship records and oversee local federal courts in the citizenship process. The Division of Naturalization would ensure immigrants seeking citizenship would file a standard application, pay a standard cost, and get equal justice at any federal court. Federal attorneys with the U.S. Justice Department would do case work relating to immigrants applying for citizenship.

Ellis Island was very busy when Commissioner Williams ran it. But the most immigrants per year landed at Ellis Island during Commissioner Watchorn's watch. The vast majority of immigrants during Teddy Roosevelt's presidency were Italians, Jews coming from the Russian empire, Poles from the three empires which held Poland captive, and people of many ethnicities coming from Austria-Hungary. These people were different in religion, customs, and personal habits than the British, German, and Scandinavian immigrants of previous decades. They aroused resentment in many Americans. Out on the West Coast, many Californians were angry over the large numbers of Japanese coming to the Golden State.

However, it was overstatement to say these "unwashed" aroused the same level of mindless hatred the Irish immigrants aroused when they came by the hundreds of thousands during and after the Great Hunger more than 50 years earlier. Angry Americans didn't form a party to fight these immigrants like the Know-Nothings had done to fight the Irish. But many Americans thought the government should do more to keep out people they called "Dagos," "Kikes," "Polacks," "Hunkies," and others from Eastern and Southern Europe. Likewise, they wanted the flow of peoples they called "slant-eyed Japs and Chinks" dried up. The politicians listened.

In 1907 Watchorn's staffers processed more than a million immigrants through Ellis Island. Early in that same year Congress adjusted immigration laws a little more with another immigration bill.

The new immigration law, formally known as the Act of February 20, 1907, was an update of the 1903 immigration law. It enabled immigration inspectors to exclude more kinds of immigrants. Besides criminals, anarchists, those guilty of acts of moral turpitude, and other problem immigrants who couldn't become American residents, immigration inspectors were to exclude imbeciles, feeble-minded persons, people with physical or mental defects that would harm their abilities to earn livings, tuberculosis sufferers, unaccompanied children 15 or younger unless they were coming to be with a parent who was legally in the United States, and persons who admitted to committing non-political crimes even when they weren't convicted of these crimes.

The 1907 law also increased the amount of time an immigrant could be deported for being a public charge from two years to three years. The law retained the clauses about treating criminals like public charges to make it easier to deport them.

The law also denied each immigrant the right to appeal the decision of a Board of Special Inquiry if the board members had ruled the immigrant unfit to enter because he or she had tuberculosis. They added this disease to the existing other mental, physical, and serious disease problems they allowed no appeal from in the 1903 law.

Unfortunately, the lawmakers weakened some of the 1903 law's punishments. They removed the specific punishments for illegals wrongfully becoming citizens. They also removed the specific penalites for wrongfully assisting illegals to become citizens.

The representatives and senators also allowed aliens facing deportation hearings to be free on bond pending final ruling on their cases. This would allow some wealthier aliens to jump bond.

The members of Congress kept the 1903 law's provision making it illegal for ship captains to fail to have valid information about any immigrant they intended to land in America. However, they capped the fine for such wrongdoing at $100 per ship. The 1903 law made the fine $10 per immigrant on whom information was missing.

The senators and representatives made it legal to deport alien females for engaging in prostitution or other immoral acts (like pornography) within three years of gaining entry to the United States. Prostitutes and white slaves from abroad soon learned to say they had been in the country longer than three years when policemen took them into custody. Regrettably, the congressmen did not apply the same punishment for those who lived off the proceeds of the sex trade, like pimps, madams, sex traffickers, and pornographers.

The 1907 law excluded those having tickets paid for by any private organization or foreign government. On the surface it might seem unfair to bar an immigrant from entry if a private organization or foreign government paid for him to come to America. However, some European governments were ethnically cleansing – for example, the Russian government wanted Jews, Poles, and other minorities to leave the Russian Empire. Likewise, all European countries had residents that the authorities and the public in those countries considered undesirable. They were dumping their misfits in America, and America's lawmakers, looking out for the good of Americans, wanted this to stop.

The 1907 law required better sanitation and less crowding on ships carrying immigrants. They ordered shipping companies to alter their ships to meet American steerage standards by the first day of 1909. Some steamship company officials used this requirement as an excuse to raise ticket prices instead of curbing their large profit margins. This kept some of the very poorest of Europe from immigrating, but most immigrants still managed to save their money for the higher fares. Still, the departure of many people from Europe would make opportunities for those poorest who couldn't afford to leave the home country because there was less competition for work and land.

The lawmakers retained most of the rest of the 1903 law. (However, they did drop the ban on selling booze in the Capitol building.) They added authorization and funding for a commission to study immigration. They gave the president the authority to sign international immigration agreements subject to the advice and consent of the Senate. They also allowed immigration officials to work with state officials in steering immigrants to states whose leaders wanted immigrants for certain purposes. **(24)**

The 1907 law did have some effect on admissions but not on the numbers of those who came to America. The flow of immigrants stayed between 750,000 and 1.3 million each year from 1907 until 1914, when World War One started. Immigration from Italy, Austria-Hungary, and the Russian Empire continued to be very high.

Immigration agents at Ellis Island and all other immigration stations had been barring 3500 to 9000 would-be immigrants a year in the years 1901 through 1904. From 1905 through 1908, the immigration agents at Ellis Island and all other immigration stations would bar 10,000 to 13,000 would-be immigrants a year. Most of those denied entry to the United States the inspectors ruled as "paupers or likely to become public charges."

Williams would return as Commissioner of Immigration at Ellis Island in 1909. During 1909, the immigration agents at Ellis Island and all other immigration stations would bar 10,411 would-be immigrants, but in the next three full years of his term at Ellis Island (1910-1912), the immigration agents at Ellis Island and all other immigration stations would bar 16,000 to 24,000 would-be immigrants a year. Most of those denied entry to the United States the inspectors ruled as "paupers or likely to become public charges." Evidently, inspectors enforced the law more literally during these years, especially those at Ellis Island, who processed roughly three-quarters of all immigrants during Williams' second watch there. **(25)**

Meanwhile, Roosevelt himself handled the problems of immigration from China and Japan.

In 1900, rebels in China, who foreigners nicknamed the "Boxers," rose against the Europeans who had carved China up like rival gangsters carve up turf. They attacked foreign-owned businesses and missions. They killed thousands of Chinese who had become Christians and they killed Catholic priests and nuns who worked among them. The Boxers beheaded several Protestant missionaries and their wives. They besieged for two months about 1000 foreigners and another 3000 Chinese Christians who had holed up in a section of Peking (Beijing) where the legation district was. (A legation is like an embassy, but with less prestige. The Europeans, Japanese, and Americans considered the Chinese as subhuman, unworthy of embassies. That's why they were so exploitative to the Chinese in the first place.)

The Chinese army had not intervened in the struggle because the corrupt and decrepit Dowager Empress Tzu Hsi had encouraged the Boxers. Finally a multinational force broke into Beijing and routed the Boxers. The leaders of several European nations, Japan, and America forced the Dowager Empress' government to pay hundreds of millions of dollars in penalties and allow the hated foreigners to rule sections of some of China's biggest cities.

American officials spent their cut of the money covering losses to Americans. But since they received much more money than they needed to cover all legitimate American claims, they refunded the balance to the Chinese government. China's rulers used the money to send Chinese students to study in America.

Although American businessmen were about as greedy as their European and Japanese rivals, Teddy Roosevelt (like McKinley) and his officials were much more ethical than their opposites in the European capitals and Tokyo in other ways as well. They tried to talk the Europeans and Japanese into acting more like reasonable businessmen and less like colonial masters, but did not make much of an impact.

The American public looked down on the Chinese as being backward pagans and feared American robber barons would use them as yellow slaves to break their wage scales. The Chinese Exclusion Act, enacted in 1882 and amended in 1884, had kept most would-be Chinese immigrants out of the United States. The related Chinese Exclusion Treaty was due to expire at the end of 1904.

American labor union leaders wanted to keep the Chinese excluded because they knew business owners would use the Chinese to reduce wages even more. American businessmen who sold products to China wanted the ban on Chinese immigration lifted.

China was still a quasi-colony of Europe, Japan, and America, but many of its "best and brightest" were planning to change this. Many patriotic Chinese – like the Japanese decades earlier – welcomed Western practices that would improve their nation but not the greedy Westerners who came with the practices. China still had a few years left under the corrupt and decrepit Dowager Empress Tzu Hsi. She died in 1908 and Chinese revolutionaries overthrew her successor in 1911 and essentially ended the dynasty.

China's emerging industrialist, merchant, intellectual, and student classes wanted better treatment from America. Chinese businessmen, travelers, students, and government officials who legally came to America complained that American immigration officials abused them and detained them in unsanitary facilities in San Francisco harbor.

Congress, on Roosevelt's urging, extended the Chinese Exclusion Act in 1904. Roosevelt wanted to protect American workers, and he also wanted to pick up some votes. He was running for a second term in 1904, and anti-Chinese sentiment ran high in the Pacific states. The Chinese Exclusion Treaty expired, but no new treaty took its place right away. So the status quo continued. Chinese laborers remained excluded. Other Chinese who traveled to America continued to suffer abuses.

Finally, the Chinese struck back. People in China, aided and abetted by Chinese businessmen in America, started threatening a boycott of American products in 1905.

Roosevelt continued to oppose the immigration of unskilled coolie laborers. However, he figured treating other Chinese nationals coming to America fairly would ease the tension. Roosevelt ordered American officials in China to start checking Chinese people applying to come to the United States. If an American official in China issued a Chinese person an entry certificate, Roosevelt ordered, then immigration officials in the United States would have to honor it instead of refusing the Chinese entry or soliciting bribes to allow them in. Roosevelt also ordered some immigration agents guilty of corruption or abusive behavior toward Chinese immigrants fired or otherwise punished. (This was already policy toward immigration agents guilty of corruption or abusive behavior toward other immigrants.)

Many people in China were not satisfied. They began the boycott in the summer of 1905. American products went unsold. Chinese servants quit working for Americans. Cynical Europeans, who essentially wouldn't even allow Chinese into their own countries, profited by selling more of their goods to the Chinese instead. The Europeans encouraged the boycott.

Many American business leaders who profited from the China trade urged Roosevelt to loosen restrictions on Chinese immigration. Instead, Roosevelt put pressure on the Dowager Empress' government to stop the boycott. Also, powerful Chinese businessmen who profited from the American trade started to lose money, and they appealed to her officials.

When persuasion didn't work, Roosevelt threatened a military strike on China. Chinese officials put an end to the boycott in 1906. Roosevelt, Congress, and American immigration officials continued to exclude coolie laborers from China, but on paper they made it easier for other Chinese to immigrate to America. Actual Chinese immigration to America stayed at about 2100 a year in the 1900s, and at about 2100 a year in the 1910s. American immigration officials would continue to enforce American laws limiting immigration from China. **(26)**

Roosevelt took a different approach to the Japanese. He respected Japan as a military power and understood the nation's need for respect. However, he was opposed to immigration of unskilled Japanese workers to the United States. Corrupt politicians in San Francisco made him take care of business with the Land of the Rising Sun.

Large commercial farm owners in California, who wanted cheap fruit pickers and farm workers, naturally opposed any move that would deprive them of Japanese labor. However, many California union people supported limiting Japanese immigrants. They didn't want their wages sneak-attacked.

San Francisco mayor Eugene Schmitz and his political boss Abe Ruef were in trouble for their many crimes. In 1906, the year of the San Francisco earthquake, they were facing indictment on corruption charges, so they decided to appeal to anti-Japanese bigotry to divert attention from their legal problems. Their people on the San Francisco school board late in 1906 voted to force all Oriental children into one school to segregate them from white children.

Teddy Roosevelt was not amused. The school board's action was a probable violation of a treaty America had with Japan about the treatment of its nationals.

Roosevelt's attorney general filed lawsuits against the San Francisco school board in 1907. Southern leaders lent their support to San Francisco officials. Why? Segregation of blacks was the law in their states. They didn't want this to change. Roosevelt the Republican had invited Booker T. Washington to the White House, so in the beady little minds of the segregationists, a successful attack upon segregation in San Francisco could lead Roosevelt to attack segregation of blacks in their own states.

Roosevelt had to tread with caution and wisdom. Since the San Francisco school segregation edict was only a decade or so after the Supreme Court's idiotic 1896 Plessy v. Ferguson case ruling okaying segregation, Roosevelt might have lost in court. Meanwhile, people in Japan rioted against Americans and Japanese papers in California made threats of bloodshed against Americans. (They were lucky they did it in California. In many other states in that era, they would have been lynched or at the very least their newspaper buildings would have and should have been burned to the ground.) Japanese politicians called for more military spending.

Roosevelt "invited" the school board members to come to Washington. Mayor Schmitz came with them. Roosevelt convinced them to revoke the segregation law. Roosevelt issued an executive order banning Japanese immigration via Mexico, Canada, and American-owned Hawaii.

Roosevelt – who personally helped negotiate the end of the Russo-Japanese War -- then used a little more of his diplomatic muscle later in 1907 on the Japanese. He convinced Japanese officials that the Congress was going to virtually exclude Japanese immigration like they had virtually excluded Chinese immigration. Japanese officials got the hint; in the so-called "gentlemen's agreement" with Roosevelt, they decided to restrict the immigration of their laborers to America.

In 1907, more than 30,000 Japanese immigrated to the United States; the number dropped to about 16,000 in 1908, and then varied from about 3,000 to 10,000 Japanese immigrants a year until 1925, when quotas took effect.

Roosevelt said, "The obnoxious school legislation was abandoned, and I secured an arrangement with Japan under which the Japanese themselves prevented any emigration to our country of their laboring people, it being distinctly understood that if there was such emigration the United States at once would pass an exclusion law. It was of course infinitely better that the Japanese should stop their own people from coming rather than that we should have to stop them; but it was necessary for us to hold this power in reserve."

Juries eventually found Eugene Schmitz guilty of extortion and Abe Ruef guilty of bribery. (Ruef bribed 11 of the 18 local supervisors, and he also tried to bribe jurors.) Both men did several years in jail. After Schmitz's release from prison, a forgiving and/or stupid electorate in San Francisco would vote him back into office as a local supervisor two different times. **(27)**

In the wake of the incident with Japan, Teddy Roosevelt sent a fleet of battleships and other vessels around South America and into the Pacific to perform naval training and gunnery practice. (The Panama Canal was still under construction.) Roosevelt intended that his Great White Fleet would show the Japanese – who had recently annihilated the Russian fleet in the Russo-Japanese War – some American muscle. He saw the fleet off in December 1907.

After the American fleet had made calls at the major ports of the nations of South America and was steaming toward America's West Coast ports in 1908, the Japanese government invited the fleet to Japan. Roosevelt and his admirals, wary of a Jap sneak attack plot, accepted the invite but had the ships' men on alert. They limited shore leaves in Japan, deployed ships defensively, and had men at the ready to fight any potential attacks. The Japanese were favorably impressed with the professionalism and good will of America's navy men; their visit to Japan was a diplomatic success for America. On the way home, the American fleet passed through the Suez Canal and rendered assistance to the victims of a huge earthquake in Italy. Theodore Roosevelt greeted the Great White Fleet as it returned to America in February 1909, 10 days before he left office. (Before FDR, Inauguaration Day was March 4 instead of January 20.)

Those who complain today about how bigoted and mean-spirited the immigration officials were a century ago need to remember men like Williams and Theodore Roosevelt were looking out for the nation's interests as well as the immigrants' interests. Unlike most federal-level politicians and officials today, Theodore Roosevelt and Williams put the good of the country ahead of their own political careers.

Williams was stern and somewhat bigoted. But despite his prejudices, he was an honorable man who punished those who mistreated the immigrants. Under his second watch, immigration agents kept out more people, but almost everyone from the areas of Europe he targeted still managed to gain entry to the United States. This meant Williams' personal prejudices did not extend to discrimination against non-WASP immigrants in how he had immigrants screened and treated.

Roosevelt's other Ellis Island boss Robert Watchorn was less stern and more likeable. He radiated more charm than Williams, but was just as dedicated to giving the taxpayers good service for their money. He was also deeply motivated to protect immigrants from those who would abuse them.

Roosevelt himself was forceful, but generous. Because he was forceful he was respected. Because he tried to help people he was loved by many. Like Williams, Roosevelt was somewhat bigoted as well. However, Roosevelt usually was able to do the right thing despite his prejudices. Teddy Roosevelt allowed more non-WASP immigrants into America than any other president until Bill Clinton. Clinton, of course, in the informed opinion of many, did so because he was looking to pad voter rolls in his favor as well as deliver cheaper grunt and techie labor for his corporate sponsors.

The record of history provides a yardstick to measure those who have held power. Compare Theodore Roosevelt with both George Bushes and the Clintons and Obama, who have repeatedly ignored the nation's interests and look out only for their own interests and the interests of the corporate leaders (campaign donors and friends) who want cheap labor, bailouts, and no trade regulations to interfere with their profits on Asian-made goods. It's obvious who the servant of the people was, and who the servants of their own demented egos and the pathological greed of their donors have been.

ELLIS ISLAND WHILE TAFT WAS PRESIDENT

William Howard Taft became president in 1909. As Theodore Roosevelt's vice-president, Taft benefited from Teddy's popularity like George Bush would benefit from Ronald Reagan's popularity. Taft, a tall obese man, was nowhere near as energetic as Teddy Roosevelt -- but who was? He and Roosevelt would finally have a falling-out. Their tiff split the Republican Party so badly that Democrat Woodrow Wilson would win the 1912 election while garnering only slightly more than 40% of the popular vote. Roosevelt, angry because GOP wheelhorses cheated him out of the nomination, ran as an independent and got many more popular votes and electoral votes than Taft.

History repeats itself. Eighty years later, a short big-eared billionaire named Perot who said he worried about the disruption of his daughter's wedding would draw enough voters away from the very flawed George Bush to allow the very flawed Bill Clinton to win the 1992 election with less than 45% of the popular vote.

Taft did continue many of Roosevelt's policies and rehired many of those who worked for Roosevelt. Among these was William Williams. He brought Williams back as Commissioner of Immigration at Ellis Island when Robert Watchorn resigned in 1909.

Taft in essence helped Watchorn resign. Watchorn was a kindlier man than Williams, but not as aggressive at refuting the lies his critics spread about him. Watchorn riled the corporate thieves who wanted to profit from the immigrant carrying trade, he riled the employment agencies whose owners wanted to exploit the immigrants as quasi-slave labor, and he riled the local contractors and petty thieves who wanted to cheat immigrants. All of these swindlers had friends among the crooked politicians in New York, New Jersey, and Washington. They had been pressing for Roosevelt to fire Watchorn. Of course that wouldn't happen.

But the huge number of immigrants Roosevelt's administration let into America riled the people who were Watchorn's natural allies – labor union people. Watchorn was a former labor official himself. His former comrades in the labor unions complained that allowing so many people into America was going to depress wages. And Watchorn came in for criticism from some of his own employees on Ellis Island, because the torrent of immigrants led him to work them harder. Taft decided not to reappoint Watchorn when he took office in 1909. **(28)**

Watchorn went on to other projects. He became an oil industry operator, and made quite a bit of money as a result. But the former coal miner didn't become a robber baron.

Taft didn't exactly reward the greedy for raising the uproar against Watchorn. He brought back the brass-knuckled William Williams to run Ellis Island.

Williams in his second term as commissioner almost immediately stirred up controversy by enforcing the "pauper" and "public charge" portion of the immigration law. In a memo he wrote for his agents, he acknowledged there was no legal minimum in cash an immigrant needed to enter America. However, he said, "In most cases it will be unsafe for immigrants to arrive with less than twenty-five ($25) besides railroad tickets to destination, while in many cases they should have more." He wanted inspectors to take this into consideration when deciding whether to admit immigrants.

Williams said common sense dictated setting a minimum amount of cash needed and letting would-be immigrants and shipping companies know what America expected of them. He blamed shipping companies for bringing large numbers of practically penniless people to America, where they would require charity to survive until they could eke out meager livings. As an example, Williams noted 189 of the 251 passengers a steamship offloaded at Ellis Island on the 4th of July 1909 had $10 or less.

There would be no formal requirement for an immigrant to show he or she had at least a certain amount of cash to avoid being sent back as a pauper for a few more years. But Williams instructed his inspectors to use the $25 amount as a guideline to determine if an immigrant could be excluded as being likely to become a public charge. He noted, "This notice is not, as many have claimed it to be, a rule under which inspectors must exclude immigrants with less than $25, and thus an attempt to create a property test not found in the statutes. It is merely a humane notice to intending immigrants that upon landing they will require at least some small amount of money with which to meet their wants while looking about for employment."

Many immigrants who were in their 20s in this period would say later the inspectors let them in despite not having $25 because they looked like vigorous young men and women. Others remembered it as a hindrance. **(29)**

Bringing in destitute immigrants was a big business not only for the shipping companies, but for immigration business operators. Williams in a 1910 report to Congress, noted these men would have agents operating in Europe tell immigrants to list the immigration business street address in America as a final destination address to fool the inspectors. He said a couple of the shipping companies also brought in large numbers of boys younger than 16 even though their parents were staying at home in Europe. **(30)**

Williams in his second term as boss at Ellis Island resumed his crusade against corruption. In 1910, he revoked the food service contract of the businessmen who held it because they were not feeding immigrants properly. In 1911, he ended the baggage handling contract of the contractor who had it because he and his people were cheating immigrants.

In 1910, Williams started an investigation that led to the prosecution and imprisonment of 15 officials of the Hellenic Transatlantic Steam Navigation company for smuggling diseased aliens into America. When the trials of some of the defendants were over in 1912, the federal prosecutor in Brooklyn wrote him the following letter summarizing the convictions:

Sir:

I have the honor to inform you that on Tuesday afternoon, the 25th instant, at 4:30 P.M. the officers of the S.S. Patris of the National Steam Navigation Company of Greece, who were found guilty on June 21st of conspiracy in smuggling or landing surreptitiously into the United States ineligible and diseased aliens in violation of the United States Immigration Laws, were brought before Judge Chatfield in the District Court for the Eastern District of New York and sentenced as follows:

Demetrios Bogiazides, master of the S.S. Patris, one year and one day in Atlanta Penitentiary, and to pay a fine of $1000.

Nicholas Bogiazides, Chief Officer of S.S. Patris, (son of the Master) one year and one day in Atlanta Penitentiary and to pay a fine of $1000.

Augoustis Fountes, Chief Commissary of S.S. Patris, ten months in Atlanta Penitentiary and to pay a fine of $1000.

Andreas Dambassis, Chief Steward of S.S. Patris, ten months in Atlanta Penitentiary and to pay a fine of $1000.

Nicholas Bistis, Doctor of S.S. Patris, six months in the prison at Mineola, L.I. and to pay a fine of $1000.

The Judge in imposing sentence on the defendants expressed his sorrow that he cannot reach for punishment Embyrikoe, Charalambos and Dapontes, the owners and managers of the steamship company in Greece, as the evidence proved that they were the arch-conspirators and the defendants knowingly became their conspirators and tools in effecting the a overt acts of the conspiracy here.

After the imposition of sentence the attorneys for the defence [sic] proposed that inasmuch the company itself had directed the smuggling operations and the profits accrued to the company, the burden should fall on the company, and they could arrange to pay any fine, no matter how big if the Court were disposed to decrease the imprisonment period imposed an the defendants. The Court stated that they might make an application to him before the defendants were sent to Atlanta, and he would think it over, although he did not believe in the practice or principle of imposing big fines and reducing the prison sentences. **(31)**

Williams again took aim at some of the self-styled immigrant aid groups and clergy from Ellis Island when he determined they were corrupt. He banned representatives of the Swedish Immigrant Home, St. Joseph's Home for the Protection of Polish Immigrants, and the Austrian Society of New York from coming to Ellis Island to waylay immigrants. This is what he wrote to the Austrian Society of New York when he revoked their privileges on Ellis Island in 1909:

Sir:

You have asked me to state why I withdrew from your society the privilege of being represented at Ellis Island. I proceed to comply with your request.

(1) For some time past the quarters in which your society receives immigrants have been maintained in a condition of almost indescribable filth and ordinary sanitary requirements have been disregarded. This condition of filth appears to have extended to everything in the house, including room, floors, closets, bedding and the solitary bath tub on the top floor. Foul odors have pervaded most of the quarters. These facts have at various times in 1908 and 1909 been reported to a Congressional Committee by Government agents who went to the house in order to investigate it. Further details as to what they found are on file in my office and open to inspection. The same atrocious conditions were on August 9, 1909, again witnessed and reported to me by an Inspector of this office. That all of these Government agents have been conservative in their statements is now conclusively proved by an investigation conducted a few days ago by the Health Department of the City of New York which shows the Home's quarters to be grossly unsanitary and filthy, some of them being offensive with decomposing animal and vegetable matter. As a result appropriate orders will be issued by the Health Department.

In view of what precedes I am amazed that you should have cared to write me under date of August 11, 1909, that "now the house is in a <u>clean, good condition.</u>"

(2) Your home is open to men and women alike, the records showing that a large number of both, including unmarried women, have been turned over to you. Nevertheless, you employ no matron, though your manager, at a recent hearing in my office, undertook to explain that his wife, who is most of the time in the kitchen, served also as matron. I have not only been unable to learn that there are any moral safeguards thrown around girls who reach your Home, but, on the contrary, it appears that they have been frequently exposed to coarse treatment and sounds of vulgarity.

(3) One of your chief duties in connection with immigrants going to your Home is to see to it that they promptly reach their relatives or friends, or secure proper employment, and you have been reporting to this office the alleged addresses showing where such immigrants have gone. For some time past some of these addresses have been under investigation. An agent who acted for the Congressional Committee above referred to reports that in the Spring of 1908 he found a large proportion to be false or fictitious. Out of a few which I have recently caused to be investigated I find a number to be wrong or worthless for all purposes for which the immigration authorities might require them.

Any one of the foregoing reasons justifies my statement that the Home of the Austrian Society is not a fit place for immigrants to go to. I could if I wished furnish further reasons for my action, but I deem the present ones sufficient.

*Respectfully,
(Signed) Wm. Williams
Commissioner*

Williams reinstated the privileges of the Austrian Society of New York, and then got word they had backslid. His follow-up letter to them in 1910 indicates why they were in his doghouse once again.

Sirs:

I had occasion last summer to withdraw your privilege of representation at Ellis Island by reason of the very bad conditions found to prevail in your so-called Immigrants' Home. Later I restored these privileges upon assurances that this Home would be conducted in a proper manner. Such, however, does, not appear to have been the case. During the month of April an agent of the North American Civic League for Immigrants (an organization composed of disinterested persons bent on protecting the immigrant after landing in New York City) spent two nights there. The beds she slept in had vermin and the mattress and bed clothing were filthy in the extreme. A serious cause of complaint last summer was that you employed no matron; nevertheless the only woman connected with the management on the occasion of this agent's visit was the cook, and she took no care of the girls. On the contrary these were looked after by two foul-mouthed men, who not only did all chamber work, but waked the girls in the morning. Instead of knocking on the door they walked in yelling "Aufstehen" ("Get up") and something in Polish. The girls who did not get up were shaken by these men who again came into the dormitory while the girls were dressing and made vulgar remarks concerning them in German and Polish. Further details I omit. These two men were not the only ones about the house who were vulgarly familiar with the female inmates. Upon leaving the agent paid the usual charges for board and lodging.

Last week I sent agents during the day time to inspect your new quarters at 84 Broad Street. They reported similar conditions as to the mattresses and bed-clothing. Two of the objectionable male employees were still there, also the same manager, who did not appear to be at all disturbed when his attention was called to the filth of mattresses and blankets. There was nothing to indicate the presence of a matron and the chamber work was still being done by men. It is an abuse of language to call such a place a "Home" for girls.

An Immigrant Society which is not conducted on a high plane of efficiency and decency by managers whose own sense of duty will make them unwilling to see it conducted in any other way, is not fit to be represented at a Government Station. Repeated experiences with your management, both on the part of this office and of a Congressional Committee, tend to show that it fails (whether purposely or otherwise I do not know or care) to grasp these facts. This office has lost confidence in it, and whether this confidence can be restored or whether, if there is to be a society for Austrian immigrants here, it must be a different one from yours, is a matter not necessary to discuss now. The immediate purpose of this letter is to give you notice that no further immigrants will be turned over to you at Ellis Island.

*Respectfully,
(Signed) Wm. Williams
Commissioner*

Williams conceded there were many legitimate charity organizations and missionary societies whose people helped the immigrants. But he wanted help from them in rooting out the crooks who posed as immigrant aid societies. He reported, "These could add still further to their usefulness if they would band together for the purpose of assisting the Government in detecting black sheep and the missionary for revenue, whose presence should be as unpleasant to them as it is to the commissioner." **(32)**

There is nothing new under the sun. People who say legitimate Moslem organizations should be outing people who recruit murderers and suicide bombers in Moslem circles are merely using the same approach Williams used in trying to get the legitimate operators to let him know about the crooks and vermin.

There was enough dislike of Williams among some of the organized immigrant groups that Congressman William Sulzer from New York, a Democrat, called for a Congressional investigation of Ellis Island in 1911. As a result, members of the U.S. House of Representatives investigated Williams, a Republican, and his staffers for "cruelty to helpless and unprotected immigrants." Certain immigrant protection group officials, foreign-language newspaper publishers, and those who resented Williams for his bulldog attitude in upholding immigration laws as he interpreted them witnessed against Williams.

Williams, in writing, and in his verbal testimony before the congressmen, said Sulzer and the witnesses were lying about their key charges, and offered proof to back his counterattack. He noted he was not going to argue every detail with his detractors because they were caught lying on the gist of their most important accusations.

Sulzer in essence took back his complaints, and instead asked for more money for Ellis Island's administration. Williams had proven to the congressmen's satisfaction the charges Sulzer and others had lodged against him were false. **(33)**

Two years later, Sulzer – who had become governor of New York – would himself would be on trial for misconduct in office. Sulzer committed the all-too-common crime of diverting campaign money to his own wallet. New York officials tried Sulzer, found him guilty, and removed him from office.

Besides the work of trust-busting officials, and the work of conservationist officials, Taft inherited another body of reform work from Teddy Roosevelt. It was the work if the Dillingham Commission on immigration reform. This commission, authorized by the Immigration Act of 1907 and chaired by Senator William Dillingham from Vermont, worked from 1907 to 1911 on the issues of immigration. The members of the commission keyed on the need to bar undesirable immigrants, the need to assimilate immigrants, and the need to prevent a flood of foreign workers who would allow corporate officials to lower the standard of living of American workers. They and the experts they contracted compiled more than 40 volumes of statistics, investigative testimony, and analysis on the facets of immigration, and in 1911, they released their findings.

The members of the commission made the following recommendations to make immigration laws better for the people of the United States and in some cases more fair for the immigrants:

> American officials should deport aliens who, within five years of admission to America, receive a felony conviction. (This was a no-brainer.)
>
> American officials in Europe should make arrangements with European officials to have would-be immigrants possess official certificates showing they had not committed any crimes that would exclude them from America. (In some cases this would work, but in many cases, immigrants were refugees from oppressive regimes. The European authorities would lie about these people, or refuse them permission to leave in the first place. Likewise, many European officials refused young men permission to leave because they wanted to draft them into their armies.)
>
> Immigrants becoming public charges within three years of admission to America should be deportable on a case-by-case basis. (This was aimed at saving American taxpayers money so they wouldn't have to support the shiftless. Someone hurt in an industrial accident would obviously have much more standing in such a hearing than someone who refused to work and became a professional beggar.)
>
> Male and female American immigration officers should travel in steerage undercover to ensure shipping companies comply with American laws. (Immigration agents who traveled incognito for the commissioners verified many instances of inexcusable conditions aboard such ships.)

Members of the Boards of Special Inquiry must meet certain standards of experience and training, their hearings must be public, and there must be an assistant secretary of Commerce and Labor (this department was later separated into the Department of Commerce and the Department of Labor) appointed to review decisions of Boards of Special Inquiry. (This was a no-brainer.)

States must regulate so-called "immigrant banks." (These were not banks, but businesses run by craftier people of the same ethnicity as immigrants from Southern and Eastern Europe. These people would hold immigrants' money "for safe keeping" or arrange to invest it in the home countries for the immigrants. The commissioners wanted to keep immigrants from being swindled, and they wanted the immigrants to keep more of their money in America as long as they were working in America. The commissioners did not attack immigrant community banks that operated as real banks.)

American officials should deport aliens who persuade immigrants not to assimilate and not become American citizens. (This was a no-brainer.)

American officials should encourage immigrants to move to rural areas where their labor would do the most good. They should also encourage immigrants to buy farms. (At this time, many rural workers were leaving farms and coming to the cities for higher paying jobs. There was beginning to be a labor shortage in the countryside. Part of it was man-made; rural employers were no more generous than urban employers. The commissioners were trying to get immigrants to sink roots in America as farmers instead of depressing urban wages as unskilled laborers.)

The Secretary of Commerce and Labor should rule on the importation of skilled laborers to establish certain industries only after investigating claims of businessmen and finding them to be valid as to the absence of such technical know-how among Americans. (This was a no-brainer aimed at protecting American workers.)

The commissioners made several recommendations to reduce the oversupply of unskilled workers in cities, and in places like mining communities and mill towns, where their presence was undercutting American laborers' wages. These included:

American officials should bar entry to unskilled men who come without wives or families. (This was aimed mostly at temporary laborers who intended to work only to save enough money to better themselves in the home countries. Their willingness to live in poverty to save money undercut Americans' wages.)

Would-be immigrants who couldn't read or write in any language should be denied entry.

Immigrants should show a higher minimum amount of money to immigration officials to gain entry.

The commissioners then made some recommendations to ensure future immigrants would reinforce instead of alter, overwhelm, or undermine American institutions. These included:

American officials should continue to exclude unskilled Chinese laborers, not formally restrict such workers from Japan (or Japanese-occupied Korea) unless the Japanese started abusing the "gentlemen's agreement" reached with Teddy Roosevelt, and make an agreement with the British to effectively prevent people from the Indian subcontinent (the British controlled it) from immigrating to America. (This was aimed at keeping America a Judeo-Christian nation. Not only did unskilled Asian workers break the wage scale; they did not tend to assimilate because their belief systems were greatly different than those of most Americans. Arabs and other Moslems were not specifically mentioned, but American officials did not admit many of them. Then, too, very few Moslems tried to emigrate to America. Even most of the immigrants from the Ottoman Empire – in which the Moslem Turks ruled Arab Moslems from much of the Arabian peninsula, present-day Iraq, Syria, Jordan, Lebanon, and Israel – tended to be Greek, Armenian, Lebanese, and Assyrian Orthodox and Catholic Christians.)

There should be a quota based on the percentage of ethnic groups already in America. (Most of the people on the commission were prejudiced in favor of a Wonder Bread-bland white Anglo-Saxon Protestant America. So they wanted to restrict immigration from Italy, Eastern Europe, and Russia.)

There should be a cap on the number of immigrants. (Some would argue this was racism on the part of the commissioners. Others would argue there were too many people coming as it was, and they were hurting the wage scale of American workers.) **(34)**

Williams agreed with most of what the commissioners recommended. He was also working for improving immigration laws for the benefit of Americans. He referred to Teddy Roosevelt's worry about incoming unskilled foreigners undercutting the American laborer and giving capitalists the excuse to reduce the standard of living because the foreigner would work for less and live in squalor because that's all he knew. He urged Congress to enact legislation to deport aliens who committed crimes in America.

Williams also urged Congress to close loopholes the steamship company officials used to evade the law. He noted steamship company operators were bringing insane people to America and escaping fines. The law forbade "idiots, imbeciles, and epileptics." Unscrupulous shipping line officials and their corrupt lawyers evidently argued insane people were not "idiots, imbeciles, or epileptics." Williams wanted insanity added to the list of reasons immigration officials could exclude would-be immigrants. Williams also wanted fines against steamship companies for committing certain violations doubled.

He also noted the law only fined shipping companies and captains for providing no information about aliens on their manifests. He wanted Congress to punish steamship lines for providing false or inaccurate information as well as providing no information.

Williams noted ship captains allowed unfit aliens to escape their ships and illegally enter the country. He also noted, "The contract labor law is constantly being violated on a large scale, and, while the immigration authorities detect many of the violations in individual instances, yet the wholesale violations they are usually unable to detect, with the result that thousands of aliens continue to come here every year as a result of encouragement and solicitation." He urged lawmakers to act against these abuses. **(35)**

Much of Williams' advice and the Dillingham Commission's recommendations would become law. But not right away. Many opposed the Dillingham Commission's and Williams' views on literacy and paupers. Taft vetoed an immigration bill containing a literacy test for adult immigrants and a minimum cash amount for entry. (Wilson would veto a ban on illiterate immigrants, but Congress would override his veto.)

During Taft's term in office, American lawmakers addressed three major scandals that affected immigration. One was the tragedy and shame of the trade in immigrant girls and young women for sex. The second was the tragedy of deaths at sea due to greedy and negligent shipping companies. The third was the exploitation of immigrants and Americans alike in sweatshops, factories, and other workplaces. The muckrakers and the Mann Act dealt with the first outrage. The sinking of the *Titanic* brought the second to light. And the horrible Triangle Fire forced the authorities to do something about the third.

It was a shame immigrants had to suffer and die for Americans to fight these abuses. But their suffering did not go in vain. The American public prodded American politicians to address the abuses that led to their deaths and suffering, and to the deaths and suffering of many more Americans as well. Theodore Roosevelt had shown it was possible for a government, only if properly led and staffed and motivated, to actually help people instead of harming them.

The hope Theodore Roosevelt gave Americans about the ability of the government to do right led generations of us to depend on his successors, and many thousands of federal, state, and local officials from then until now to do right also. American officials have gained much more power in the century or so since Theodore Roosevelt left office, but very few of them have governed in his spirit. Not every politician can be a Theodore Roosevelt, but sadly, all too many of them have been (or still are) Pee Wee Herman or Benedict Arnold.

END NOTES

1. Immigration statistics throughout this chapter come from the immigration tables of the Historic Research Study, Statue of Liberty – Ellis Island National Monument, by Harlan D. Unrau, National Park Service, 1984.

2. Information on the Know-Nothings and the anti-Catholic pogroms comes from Michael Schwartz's book The Persistent Prejudice (pages 38-60) and from James McPherson's book Battle Cry of Freedom (pages 130-144).

3. Sources for the number of Irish and German soldiers in the Civil War include William Burton's book Melting Pot Soldiers, and The Civil War Times (December 2003).

4. The 14th Amendment was aimed at giving freed slaves citizenship, not babies born to illegals. In that era, a baby born to foreign parents on American soil had the status of his or her parents – foreign nationals. This is as it should be.

Even many American Indians did not get citizenship under the 14th Amendment because their tribes were not under U.S. government control. In other words, the feds considered the Sioux, the Apaches, the Nez Percé, the Comanches, and many other tribes of the Great Plains and the West to be non-citizens and hostiles. Some American Indians gained citizenship under the Dawes Act of 1887 if they left the tribal life; of course this allowed the palefaces to grab more tribal land. Other American Indians who lived in frontier territories and states gained citizenship by marrying whites or blacks, or by serving in America's armed forces. To their shame, American leaders did not grant full citizenship to all American Indians until 1924, under the Indian Citizenship Act of 1924.

Thanks to the incompetence and chicanery of Lyndon Johnson, Teddy Kennedy and others in foisting the 1965 Immigration and Nationality Act on the American people, illegals since the mid 1960s often give birth to babies on American soil to get into the country legally as the parents of "American citizens." Teddy's brother Bobby was murdered by an Arab immigrant in 1968; his brother John was murdered by a Communist in 1963.

Irresponsible bureaucrats, members of Congress, judges, and presidents have undermined the 14th Amendment by allowing illegal foreign females to drop "anchor babies" on American soil and gain legal status as a result. They have been burdening the taxpayers with these illegals and their offspring, most of whom take in more taxpayer-covered services than they return in the form of labor.

5. The source for the Seattle tax crisis is William Speidel's book Sons of the Profits (pages 286-287).

6. The source for information on Treasury Department officials and Congressional findings from 1889 through 1891 is the Unrau study (pages 20-25).

7. Information on the federal takeover of immigration in New York City and the problems involving Ellis Island, Liberty Island, Castle Garden and the Barge Office come from the Unrau study, Edward Corsi's book In the Shadow of Liberty, Thomas Pitkin's book Keepers of the Gate: A History of Ellis Island, and Barry Moreno's book Encyclopedia of Ellis Island. Corsi was a commissioner of immigration at Ellis Island. Pitkin was a federal government historian at the Statue of Liberty. Unrau and Moreno are both well-respected National Park Service historians. Moreno is a historian at Ellis Island.

8. Info about immigration laws and policies in the early 1890s comes from the Unrau study (pages 25-39), and from the text of the Act of March 3, 1891 (26 Statutes at Large 1084-1086).

9. Other immigration stations the feds opened in the 1890s were in Boston, Philadelphia, and Baltimore. The feds also had an inspection station in Montreal, Quebec. They established other smaller immigration stations along the Canadian and Mexican borders in the 1890s.

There would later be smaller immigration stations in Buffalo, Detroit, Chicago, New Orleans, El Paso, Seattle, the San Francisco area, Los Angeles, and Honolulu. There would be even smaller immigration stations in the port cities of America, in some interior cities, and along the Canadian and Mexican borders.

By the 1920s, the second largest immigration station in terms of staffers and immigrants processed was Angel Island in San Francisco Bay. From 1910 to 1940 (when a fire at the administration building, and then World War Two intervened), the inspectors on Angel Island admitted about 200,000 immigrants, mostly Asians. This compares with the roughly 15.5 million immigrants the inspectors at Ellis Island and other New York City port inspectors processed from 1892 through 1940.

Information on these stations comes from Barry Moreno's book Encyclopedia of Ellis Island (pages 110-112).

Some people claim immigration agents processed a million people, mostly Chinese, at Angel Island. These claims don't jibe with the public record.

Per the Unrau study, American officials admitted about 900,000 people from Asia from 1820 through 1931. (The 1999 Statistical Yearbook of the Immigration and Naturalization Service claims 1.07 million people came from Asia from 1820 through 1940, but only 16,000 or so of these came from 1931 through 1940. They erroneously counted about 150,000 European immigrants from lands in the Balkans the Ottoman Empire controlled before World War One as part of the Asian count.)

Of Asians who came from 1820 through 1940, 382,000 came from China, 275,000 came from Japan, 206,000 came from the Ottoman Empire (and later Turkey after World War One), 10,000 or so came from the Indian subcontinent, and 43,000 others came from elsewhere in Asia. During this time, American officials also admitted almost 55,000 from Australia and New Zealand, and about 10,000 from the Pacific Islands not part of Asia. Most of the people from the Ottoman Empire sailed to the Atlantic ports of America.

The vast majority of Chinese (about 270,000) admitted came through Pacific Coast ports before 1882, the year the Chinese Exclusion Act became law. Most Japanese (about 150,000) admitted came before 1910. From 1910 through 1940 (the year fire shut down Angel Island as an immigration station), American officials admitted 58,000 Chinese, 122,000 Japanese, and 7000 from the Indian subcontinent total for all immigration stations across America.

The 1882 Chinese Exclusion Act, the 1907 "Gentlemen's Agreement" limiting Japanese immigration, the 1917 immigration law with the "Asian Barred Zone" provision, and the 1924 immigration law with national origin quotas were all in effect during some or all of the operating life of Angel Island as an immigration station. These all held down immigration from Asia.

Another ugly event held down immigration from China and Japan in the 1930s. The Japanese were carrying on a war of conquest and subjugation against the Chinese. The Japs controlled the coast of China and its approaches with their navy. (This was also the decade in which they captured and evidently raped Amelia Earhart repeatedly – before executing her – for scouting out their Pacific Island installations.) This cut down on immigration from both lands.

Bottom line? American officials admitted roughly 190,000 people from China, Japan, and the Indian subcontinent from 1910 through 1940 total for all immigration stations across America. American officials admitted 26,000 other Asians (not counting the mostly Christian refugees from the Ottoman Empire and the countries that succeeded its collapse in 1918) and 25,000 people from Australia, New Zealand, and the Pacific Islands from 1911 through 1940. In other words, there were about 240,000 immigrants total admitted from East Asia and South Asia and the Philippines and Oceania in these years. And not all of them were processed at Angel Island!

A more accurate estimate is that Angel Island immigration officials admitted about 200,000 immigrants. (They admitted some Latin American and a few European immigrants along with the Asians.)

Figures come from the 1999 Statistical Yearbook of the Immigration and Naturalization Service, and the Unrau study.

Some sources note American officials detained 175,000 Chinese and several thousand Japanese on Angel Island during its time in service. This is plausible, because many Chinese tried fraudulent means to come into America. A common scam for them was to claim being born in San Francisco before the devastating 1906 earthquake. They falsely claimed the earthquake destroyed their records. Many other Chinese claimed they were the sons or daughters of naturalized Chinese immigrants ... this racket was called the "paper son" and "paper daughter" racket. Former Ellis Island boss Edward Corsi, in his book In the Shadow of Liberty (pages 159-176) talked about these and other rackets he and his people had to combat. Many Japanese women came to America as "picture brides." In some cases, this was a scam to import Japanese females (often against their wills) for use as prostitutes. American officials were right to detain them and verify their alleged husbands' situations before admitting them. This saved many a Japanese woman and girl from sexual slavery.

ELLIS ISLAND SCRAPBOOK

10. Good sources on Senner and his term include the Unrau study (pages 208-215), Keepers of the Gate (Chapter II), and 3/29/1893 and 6/13/1893 New York Times articles.

11. Information on Fitchie and McSweeney and their stays in office comes from the Unrau study (pages 215-217), Keepers of the Gate (Chapter II), and the Publishing Society of New York reference Republicans of New York (page 285).

12. Information on Terence Powderly comes from his autobiography The Path I Trod (pages 298-300).

13. Information on the Naples surgeon posting comes from the Unrau study (page 40).

14. The information on Fiorello La Guardia and his family comes from his autobiography The Making of an Insurgent. La Guardia's comments on health inspections and the eventual adoption of overseas inspection of immigrants comes from his book (pages 53-57). Terence Powderly, in a 12/8/1906 letter to Theodore Roosevelt, (The Path I Trod, pages 303-304) made basically the same recommendation.

Barry Moreno, in his book Encyclopedia of Ellis Island (page 197) noted line inspections of immigrants for health problems at Ellis Island dropped drastically in the mid 1920s. Part of the reason undoubtedly was the Immigration Act of 1924, which drastically reduced the number of immigrants coming in at Ellis Island. Part of the reason was the adoption of La Guardia's practice of medically inspecting immigrants at the port of debarkation.

In 1926, the Surgeon General noted doctors in the previous 12 months intensively examined 73,000 third class (steerage) immigrants at Ellis Island, and briefly examined the other 51,000 third class (steerage) immigrants aboard ships because American doctors examined them overseas before they shipped to America (or because they had return permits). This information comes from the Unrau study (page 919).

All immigration stations had the same basic medical inspection process for immigrants. However, Ellis Island doctors saw so many more immigrants than doctors at other immigration stations that they developed more experience. Ellis Island's doctors also had a hospital, specialists, and a medical lab at their disposal.

15. Information on the assassination of McKinley and Roosevelt's race to Buffalo include Theodore Roosevelt: An Autobiography, Walter Lord's book The Good Years, and Edmund Morris' book The Rise of Theodore Roosevelt.

16. Mannix's remarks come from his book The Old Navy (page 152). Other information on the wrongful discharge of the black soldiers comes from Nathan Miller's book Theodore Roosevelt: A Life (pages 465-469), the Handbook of Texas Online's article "Brownsville Raid of 1906," and an article by Laura Tillman in the 6/18/2008 Brownsville (Texas) Herald. Richard Nixon reversed the dishonorable discharge, and ordered some separation pay to go to the surviving soldier of the 167 and to surviving widows.

17. Info on the further investigation of corruption at Ellis Island under Fitchie comes from Hans Vought's book The Bully Pulpit and the Melting Pot, an article by Henry Guzda in Monthly Labor Review, July 1986, and a 10/1/1902 New York Times article.

18. Information on the wrongful firing of Terence Powderly and his reinstatement elsewhere in the Roosevelt administration comes from The Path I Trod (pages 301-302, and 306).

19. Information on the Act of March 3, 1903 comes from the law itself (32 Statutes at Large, pages 1213-1222).

20. Information on Williams' fining of the steamship lines comes the Unrau study (page 43).

21. Comments from Williams' Annual Report for 1903 come from the Unrau study (pages 45-47).

22. Information on the clearing of William Williams comes from the Unrau study (pages 229-231).

23. Watchorn's letter is in the Unrau study (pages 235-236).

24. Information on the Act of February 20, 1907 comes from the law itself (34 Statutes at Large, pages 898-911).

25. Immigration statistics come from the Unrau study.

26. Information on the Boxer Rebellion and Theodore Roosevelt's handling of the Chinese boycott and Chinese immigration issues comes from George Knoles' book The New United States (pages 51-52), The Good Years (pages 9-40), and Howard Beale's book Theodore Roosevelt and te Rise of America to World Power (212-252).

27. Information on the run-in with Japan over the segregation law in San Francisco comes from Carey McWilliam's article in the Oscar Handlin-edited book Immigration as a Factor in American History (pages 171-177), Theodore Roosevelt: An Autobiography (pages 392-395), and The San Francisco Earthquake by Gordon Thomas and Max Morgan Witts (pages 276-281).

28. Information on the leaving of Watchorn comes from Henry Guzda's article in the July 1986 issue of Monthly Labor Review.

29. The sources for William Williams' quotes are his Annual Report dated 8/16/1909 in his papers (New York City Public Library) and the Unrau study (pages 251-252).

30. Information on Williams' charges against shipping companies and immigration business operators comes from the Unrau study (page 254).

31. Information on the jailed Greek shipping line smugglers comes from a 6/27/1912 letter to Williams in his papers (New York City Public Library).

32. Information on Williams' war against corrupt immigrant aid societies and homes comes from his 8/16/1909 and 5/24/1910 letters to the Austrian Society in his papers (New York City Public Library) and the Unrau study (pages 251-256).

33. Information on Williams' fight against Sulzer comes from his Annual Report dated 10/10/1911 in his papers (New York City Public Library) and the Unrau study (pages 262-264).

34. These recommendations come from the conclusions and recommendations portion of the Dillingham Commission report (pages 45-48).

35. Information on Williams' comments come from the Unrau study (pages 54-59).

THE LOWDOWN ON STEERAGE

Our ancestors who came to the Western Hemisphere before World War Two came by boat or ship. Even the American Indians and Inuit (Eskimos) too impatient to wait for sheet ice to form used boats to cross the Bering Strait from Siberia to Alaska. The Polynesians sailed across the Pacific Ocean to Hawaii in open boats.

The Spanish, French and British came on wooden ships like the Santa Maria or the Mayflower. So did the others who came here from Europe before the late 1800s.

Although we're ashamed as a nation to admit it, the slave ships brought a lot of unwilling immigrants to America. The Dutch started bringing enslaved Africans to America in 1619. The other seafaring European nations followed suit.

From 1619 to 1808, when American leaders made importing slaves from Africa illegal, roughly 500,000 blacks from Africa made it alive to America aboard slave ships. A couple hundred thousand other Africans died or were murdered aboard the slave ships, and the crew members tossed their bodies into the ocean. **(1)**

In the 1800s, sailing ships reached their peak in size and speed. Up until late in the century, the people from Ireland, Germany, and elsewhere in Europe sailed in large sailing ships or in less seaworthy vessels that were floating hells. The vast majority of the immigrants had almost no money, so they came as cheaply as they could in good and bad ships alike, in the steerage of these ships.

Why did they call it steerage?

A ship requires mechanical linkage from its wheel to its rudder for steering. The cables and hardware that transferred the helmsman's steering to the rudder had the collective nickname of "steerage." The lowest part of an oceangoing vessel, which held the steering gear, picked up the nickname as well.

The lowest part of the ship was the least desirable place to be on a voyage, but it was the cheapest. So the large majority of immigrants traveled in the steerage part of the ship.

Let's talk a little about the state of navies and merchant shipping during America's history as a background for why the steerage trade happened.

Britain had the best navy and the best commercial fleet in the world in most of the 1800s and early 1900s. Britain's fishing fleet helped feed the British. Britain's merchant fleet brought the food its people couldn't grow on the island, and brought the raw materials its people needed to make its products and even to make its ships. Britain's navy had kept Napoleon's army and many other armies from invading Britain. If British recruiters couldn't drum up enough men to serve as tars in the fleet that protected their home island and enabled them to be imperialists around the globe, British officials would send press gangs into the countryside and the slums to kidnap men into the navy. They likewise grabbed sailors off of merchant ships of Britain and of other countries, including America's.

In the years leading up to the War of 1812, British press gangs kidnaped as many as 10,000 Americans to serve in their navy. The Royal Navy's practice of pressing American sailors into British naval service was a supporting cause of the Revolutionary War and the key cause of the War of 1812. Britain's leaders didn't end this reprehensible way of getting sailors until well into the 1800s. **(2)**

Herman Melville's novel Billy Budd *and Walt Disney's excellent film "The Scarecrow of Romney Marsh" portrayed the evil practice of impressment. This film came out in the early 1960s (starring "Secret Agent Man" Patrick McGoohan) while Walt Disney was alive.*

During the 1700s, the 13 Colonies sold Britain lumber, naval stores (pitch used to caulk seams of ships, tar used to waterproof ship surfaces, and turpentine used in wood varnish), pig iron, whale oil, furs, tobacco, and potash. The 13 Colonies also sold lumber, meat, fish, grain, and rum to Spain. All of these were food or raw materials, and were bulky cargoes that took up a lot of room in a wooden sailing ship's hold.

After the American Revolution, the people of the United States greatly increased their navy, fishing fleet, and merchant fleet. The invention of the cotton gin made cotton America's most profitable export product. The Erie Canal, the Great Lakes, and the railroads linked the Midwest to New York City and the other ports on the Eastern Seaboard. The improvements in transportation and the development of better farm tools for the many small farmers of the Midwest made grain another key American export. New England whalers sent whale oil to Europe and American clippers even hauled Chinese tea to Europe. Shippers continued to haul American and Canadian lumber and fur across the Atlantic Ocean to buyers in Europe.

Shipbuilders in the mid 1800s were building sailing ships much larger than they had done so in the early 1800s. This dropped the price of hauling American goods to Europe, and increased trade to the extent there were about 4000 ships carrying American and Canadian goods to Europe in the 1840s. At this time, wooden paddlewheel steamships also started to make their mark in passenger service and high-value cargo shipping across the Atlantic Ocean. (Since they had to haul coal to make steam, they could carry less cargo than the largest sailing ships. But they didn't depend on the winds, so they could make the trips across the Atlantic Ocean faster.)

Britain's merchant fleet was still the world's largest fleet, but just before the Civil War, America's merchant fleet was the second largest. America's exports were still mostly food or raw materials. Likewise, many British ships hauled timber and fish to Britain from Canadian and American ports and fishing areas. These were bulky cargoes that took up a lot of room in a wooden sailing ship's hold. **(3)**

Shipowners didn't want their ships sailing from Europe to America empty. Besides making a trip that garnered no hauling fares, an empty ship on the open water of the ocean was more unstable than one loaded with cargo or ballast. So shipowners made more efforts to recruit people who wanted to leave Europe and come to America. They advertised, and they offered very low fares for people who were willing to travel in the holds of the ships.

People who took the shipowners up on their offer were tough or desperate or both. In the days before the Civil War, travel by sea was hazardous. Shipwrecks were common, because the ships were frailer than they are today, they had no radios or weather tracking capability, and their charts weren't as accurate. And once a ship sunk out at sea, everyone usually died. There were no search planes or helicopters or fast ships to help the victims.

For a sailing ship, changing weather could leave the ship becalmed ... stuck out on the ocean because there weren't favorable winds. Also it was much easier for food to spoil and for water to go bad then than it is now. And the close quarters and unsanitary conditions of traveling meant many of those in steerage could become sick and die. Then the crew would toss their bodies overboard.

Rude strangers in close quarters, crew members looking to molest women and girls, rats, storms, ship fires, bad food, and other problems made the crossing a prolonged ordeal. From England to America, a sailing ship voyage lasted about four to six weeks; often they lasted two to three months. About 10 percent of all immigrant travelers – mostly Irish and Germans – died of sickness during the voyage in any given year ... the famine years in Ireland naturally produced a larger percentage of deaths. **(4)**

During the Civil War, the Union Navy and the Confederate Navy combined had more ships than the British navy. Meanwhile, large steel propeller-driven steamships started to replace wooden sailing ships because they could run reliably even if the winds weren't favorable, and could be bigger to haul more coal and cargo and ride out tougher weather.

Britain won back the undisputed title of Queen of the Seas after the Civil War. Britain's leaders built up their navy and merchant fleet to exploit their colonies around the globe.

The Germans, under the impetus of Kaiser Wilhelm II, would build up their navy and commercial fleet in the late 1800s and early 1900s. The British took Kaiser Wilhelm's naval buildup as a threat, because they depended upon their navy for protection and upon their merchant fleet for food and raw materials. The naval race was a source of tension between these two predator nations that helped lead to World War One.

America's leaders let the U.S. Navy plunge into mediocrity after the Civil War. They scrapped old ships but built very few new ones to replace them. Eventually, America would have in Theodore Roosevelt a president who was serious about the country's navy and commercial shipping. He was the force behind the building of the Panama Canal and the buildup of the U. S. Navy. However, the U. S. Navy would not clearly surpass the British navy on the high seas until after World War One.

America's merchant shipping trade also dropped for awhile after the Civil War, then made a comeback. Just before World War One, Britain's merchant fleet was more than twice the size of America's, and America's was almost twice as big as Germany's. As far as navies went, Britain's was about twice as big as Germany's, and Germany's was a little larger than the U.S. Navy. **(5)**

American manufacturing output in the early 1900s equaled the combined outputs of Germany, Britain, and France, even though there were more people in the three European nations. American manufacturers started exporting machinery and other finished goods instead of letting European nations get all the trade in these items. However, American companies sold these goods to Japan, China, and Latin America, not to Europe. European people made machinery and finished goods of comparable value to American goods. So America continued to export mostly raw materials to Europe.

Just before World War One, the chief exports of America to Europe were cotton, grain, meat and dairy products, oil, coal, copper, lumber, and leather. All of these products were bulky. And in the era before World War One, American leaders had enough common sense to arrange a balance of trade that was so favorable to America that the value of products America exported was close to double the value of products America imported. **(6)**

This huge flow of bulky American foodstuffs and raw materials through the era between the Civil War and World War One, and the larger ships carrying the increasing amounts of cargoes meant there was even more room in the holds of ships sailing from Europe to America. These hold spaces of large steel steamships would be empty or have to hold some ballast coming westward across the Atlantic Ocean unless the steamship companies could convince enough low-income Europeans to go to America in the holds of their ships. (Since Americans were buying from their own manufacturers, European shipping companies had relatively light cargoes coming here instead of bulky loads of manufactured goods to dump here.)

So the European shipping companies really started advertising for Europeans who wanted to try their luck in America. They made the ticket prices cheap to get as many people to sail in steerage as possible.

In short, economics of the shipping trade and advances in shipping made large-scale immigration to America possible.

Here was the business thinking of the officials of the steamship companies:

If a steamship carrying immigrants from a British, French, Dutch, Scandinavian, or German port could make it to America in 8 to 12 days, and the steamship company spent roughly 50 cents to a dollar per steerage passenger per day in food and sanitation and supervision costs on these steerage passengers, they could make good money charging $15 to $30 per steerage passenger and taking several hundred of them to America. A steamship carrying immigrants from an Italian, Balkan, or Russian port would typically take 15 to 25 days to get to America, which meant the steamship company would have to spend more money on food and sanitation and supervision to transport these people. But the steamship company could still made money if its officials spent less on food and sanitation and supervision per person per day and really packed the immigrants into steerage. Ships from these ports commonly carried 1000 or more immigrants in steerage, and many of these people would need delousing or medical attention at Ellis Island.

A passenger steamship would carry passengers in first-class quarters or second-class cabins both ways across the Atlantic, and would make very good money transporting these higher fare paying customers. But even luxury liners like the doomed *Titanic* and the doomed *Lusitania* carried hundreds of poor immigrants in steerage. (The *Lusitania* also carried bulky war matériel as well as nonsteerage passengers from America to Britain during World War One on her return voyages to Britain; that was why a German submarine captain had her torpedoed in 1915.)

AN INVESTIGATION OF STEERAGE

To get a glimpse at people and conditions of earlier times, it is a good practice to read what was written about them while they were happening.

An American record on steerage I found was so good I am going to quote from it at length so you can see for yourself what steerage was like in the late 1800s and the early 1900s.

The Dillingham Commission, a U.S. Senate commission whose members studied immigration issues in the early 1900s, commissioned officials and undercover people to study steerage conditions. The 1909 report was extensive, but the gist of what the investigators and inspectors found they summed up quite nicely in a document they called Abstract of the Report on Steerage Conditions. Here it is.

The Immigration Commission's report on steerage conditions, which was presented to Congress December 13 1909, was based on information obtained by special agents of the Commission traveling as steerage passengers on 12 different transatlantic steamers, as well as on ships of every coastwise line carrying immigrants from one United States port to another. There had never before been a thorough investigation of steerage conditions by national authority, but such superficial investigations as had been made, and the many nonofficial inquiries as well, had disclosed such evil and revolting conditions on some ships that the Commission determined upon an investigation sufficiently thorough to show impartially just what conditions prevailed in the steerage. It is, of course, true that the old-time steerage with its inherent evils largely disappeared with the passing of the slow sailing vessel from the immigrant-carrying trade, but the Commission's investigation proved clearly that the "steerage" is still a fact on some ships, although on others it has been abolished. Indeed, the investigation showed that both good and bad conditions may and do exist in immigrant quarters on the same ship; but, what is of more importance, it showed that there is no reason why the disgusting and demoralizing conditions which have generally prevailed on immigrant ships should continue.

The complete report of the Commission upon this subject includes a detailed account of the experiences of an Immigration Commission agent it the steerage of three transatlantic ships, but for the purpose of this summary a more general description of conditions under which immigrants are carried at sea will suffice.

Because the investigation was carried on during the year 1908, when, owing to the industrial depression, immigration was very light, the steerage was seen practically at its best. Overcrowding, with all its concomitant evils, was absent. What the steerage is when travel is heavy and all the compartments filled to their entire capacity can readily be understood from what was actually found. In reading this report, then, let it be remembered that not extreme, but comparatively favorable, conditions are here depicted.

Transatlantic steamers may be classed in three general subdivisions on the basis of their provision for other than cabin passengers. These are vessels having the ordinary old-type steerage, those having the new-type steerage, and those having both. In order to make clear the distinction among these subdivisions, a description of the two types of steerage, old arid new, will be given.

The old-type steerage is the one whose horrors have been so often described. It is, unfortunately, still found in a majority of the vessels bringing immigrants to the United States. It is still the common steerage in which hundreds of thousands of immigrants form their first conceptions of our country and are prepared to receive their first impressions of it. The universal human needs of space, air, food, sleep, and privacy are recognized to the degree now made compulsory by law. Beyond that, the persons carried are looked upon as so much freight, with mere transportation as their only due. The sleeping quarters are large compartments, accommodating as many as 300, or more, persons each. For assignment to these, passengers are divided into three classes, namely, women without male escorts, men traveling alone, and families. Each class is housed in a separate compartment and the compartments are often in different parts of the vessel. It is generally possible to shut off all communication between them, though this is not always done.

The berths are in two tiers, with an interval of 2 feet and 6 inches of space above each. They consist of an iron framework containing a mattress, a pillow, or more often a life-preserver as a substitute, and a blanket. The mattress, and the pillow if there is one, is filled with straw or seaweed. On some lines this is renewed every trip. Either colored gingham or coarse white canvas slips cover the mattress and pillow. A piece of iron piping placed at a height where it will separate the mattresses is the "partition" between berths. The blankets differ in weight, size, and material on the different lines. On the line of steamers, where the blanket becomes the property of the passenger on leaving, it is far from adequate in size and weight, even in the summer. Generally the passenger must retire almost fully dressed to keep warm. Through the entire voyage, from seven to seventeen days, the berths receive no attention from the stewards.

The berth, 6 feet long and 2 feet wide and with 2 ½ feet of space above it, is all the space to which the steerage passenger can assert a definite right. To this 30 cubic feet of space he must, in a large measure, confine himself. No space is designated for hand baggage. As practically every traveler has some bag or bundle, this must be kept in the berth. It may not even remain on the floor beneath. There are no hooks on which to hang clothing. Almost everyone has some better clothes saved for disembarkation, and some wraps that are not worn all the time, and these must either be hung about the framework of the berth or stowed somewhere in it. At least two large transportation lines furnish the steerage passengers eating utensils and require each one to retain these throughout the voyage. As no repository for them is provided, a corner of the berth must serve that purpose. Towels and other toilet necessities, which each passenger must furnish for himself, claim more space in the already crowded berths. The floors of these large compartments are generally of wood, but floors consisting of large sheets of iron, were also found. Sweeping is the only form of cleaning done. Sometimes the process is repeated several times a day. This is particularly true when the litter is the leavings of food sold to the passengers by the steward for his own profit. No sick cans are furnished, and not even large receptacles for waste. The vomitings of the seasick are often permitted to remain a long time before being removed. The floors, when iron, are continually damp, and when of wood they reek with foul odor because they are not washed.

The open deck available to the steerage is very limited, and regular separable dining rooms are not included in the construction. The sleeping compartments must therefore be the constant abode of a majority of the passengers. During days of continued storm, when the unprotected open deck can not be used at all, the berths and the passageways between them are the only places where the steerage passenger can spend his time.

When to this very limited space and much filth and stench is added inadequate means of ventilation, the result is almost unendurable. Its harmful effects on health and morals scarcely need be indicated. Two 12-inch ventilator shafts are required for every 50 persons in every room; but the conditions here are abnormal and these provisions do not suffice. The air was found to be invariably bad, even in the higher inclosed decks where hatchways afford further means of ventilation. In many instances persons, after recovering from seasickness, continue to lie in their berths in sort of stupor, due to breathing vitiated air. Those passengers who make a practice of staying much on the open deck feel the contrast between the air out of doors and that in the compartments, and consequently find it impossible to remain below long at a time. In two steamers the open deck was always filled long before daylight by those who could no longer endure the foul air between decks.

Wash rooms and lavatories, separate for men and for women, are required by law, and this law also states that they shall be kept in a "clean and serviceable condition throughout the voyage." The indifferent obedience to this provision is responsible for further uncomfortable and unhygienic conditions. The cheapest possible materials and construction of both washbasins and lavatories secure the smallest possible degree of convenience and make the maintenance of cleanliness extremely difficult where it is attempted at all. The washbasins are invariably too few in number, and the rooms in which they are placed are so small as to admit only by crowding as many persons as there are basins. The only provision for counteracting all the dirt of this kind of travel is cold salt water, with sometimes a single faucet of warm water to an entire wash room. And in some cases this faucet of warm water is at the same time the only provision for washing dishes. Soap and towels are not furnished. Floors of both wash rooms and water-closets are damp and often filthy until the last day of the voyage, when they are cleaned in preparation for the inspection at the port of entry.

Regular dining rooms are not a part of the old type of steerage. Such tables and seats as the law says "shall be provided for the use of passengers at regular meals" are never sufficient to seat all the passengers, and no effort is made to do this by systematic repeated sittings. In some instances the tables are mere shelves along the wall of a sleeping compartment. Sometimes plain boards set on wooden trestles and rough wooden benches placed in the passageways of sleeping compartments are considered a compliance with the law. Again, when a compartment is only partly full, the unoccupied space is called a dining room and is used by all the passengers in common, regardless of what sex uses the rest of the compartment as sleeping quarters. When traffic is so light that some compartment is entirely unused, its berths are removed and stacked in one end and replaced by rough tables and benches. This is the most ample provision of dining accommodations ever made in the old-type steerage, and occurs only when the space is not needed for other more profitable use.

There are two systems of serving food. In one instance the passengers, each carrying the crude eating utensils given him to use throughout the journey, pass in single file before the three or four stewards who are serving and each receives his rations. Then he finds a place wherever he can to eat them, and later washes his dishes and finds a hiding place for them where they may be safe until the next meal. Naturally there is a rush to secure a place in line and afterwards a scramble for the single warm-water faucet, which has to serve the needs of hundreds. Between the two, tables and seats are forgotten or they are deliberately deserted for the fresh air of the open deck.

Under the new system of serving, women and children are given the preference at such tables as there are, and the most essential eating utensils are placed by the stewards and are washed by them. When the bell announces a meal, the stewards form in a line extending to the galley, and large tin pans, each containing the food for one table, are passed along until every table is supplied. This constitutes the table service. The men passengers are even less favored. They are divided into groups of six. Each group receives two large tin pans and tin plates, cups, and cutlery enough for the six; also one ticket for the group. Each man takes his turn in going with the ticket and the two large pans for the food for the group, and in washing and caring for the dishes afterwards. They eat where they can, most frequently on the open deck. Stormy weather leaves no choice but the sleeping compartment.

The food may be generally described as fair in quality and sufficient in quantity, and yet it is neither; fairly good materials are usually spoiled by being wretchedly prepared. Bread, potatoes, and meat, when not old leavings from the first and second galleys, form a fair substantial diet. Coffee is invariably bad and tea does not count as food with most immigrants. Vegetables, fruits, and pickles form an insignificant part of the diet and are generally of a very inferior quality. The preparation, the manner of serving the food, and disregard of the proportions of the several food elements required by the human body, make the food unsatisfying and therefore insufficient. This defect and the monotony are relieved by purchases at the canteen by those whose capital will permit. Milk is supplied for small children.

Hospitals have long been recognized as indispensable, and so are specially provided in the construction of most passenger-carrying vessels. The equipment varies, but there are always berths and facilities for washing and a latrine closet at hand. A general aversion to using the hospitals freely is very apparent on some lines. Seasickness does not qualify for admittance. Since this is the most prevalent ailment among the passengers, and not one thing is done for either the comfort or convenience of those suffering from it and confined to their berths, and since the hospitals are included in the space allotted to the use of steerage passengers, this denial of the hospital to the seasick seems an injustice. On some lines the hospitals are freely used. A passenger ill in his berth receives only such attention as the mercy and sympathy of his fellow-travelers supply.

After what has already been said, it is scarcely necessary to consider separately the observance of the provision for the maintenance of order and cleanliness in the steerage quarters and among the *steerage passengers. Of what practical use could rules and regulations by the captain or master be when their enforcement would be either impossible or without appreciable result with the existing accommodations? The open deck has always been decidedly inadequate in size. The amendment to Section 1 of the Passenger Act of 1882, which went into effect January 1, 1909, provides that henceforth this space shall be 5 <u>superficial</u> feet for every steerage passenger carried. On one steamer showers of cinders were a deterrent to the use of the open deck during several days. On another a storm made the use of the open deck impossible during half the journey.*

The only seats available were the machinery that filled much of the deck.

Section 7 of the law of 1882, which excluded the crew from the compartments occupied by the passengers except when ordered there in the performance of their duties, was found posted in more or less conspicuous places. There was generally one copy in English and one in the language of the crew. It was never found in all the several languages of the passengers carried, although if passengers of one nationality should understand this regulation it is equally important that all should.

Considering this old-type steerage as a whole, it is a congestion so intense, so injurious to health and morals, that there is nothing on land to equal it. That people live in it only temporarily is no justification of its existence. The experience of a single crossing is enough to change bad standards of living to worse. It is abundant opportunity to weaken the body and implant there germs of disease to develop later. It is more than a physical and moral test; it is a strain. And surely it is not the introduction to American institutions that will tend to make them respected.

The common plea that better accommodations can not be maintained because they would be beyond the appreciation of the emigrant and because they would leave too small a margin of profit, carries no weight in view of the fact that the desired kind of steerage already exists on some of the lines and is not conducted as a philanthropy or a charity.

THE NEW-TYPE STEERAGE

There is nothing striking in what this new-type steerage furnishes. On general lines it follows the plans of the accommodations for second-cabin passengers. The one difference is that everything is simpler proportionately to the difference in the cost of passage. Unfortunately the new type of steerage is to be found only on those lines that carry emigrants from the north of Europe. The number of these has become but a small per cent of the total influx.

Competition was the most forceful influence that led to the development of this improved type of steerage and established it on the lines where it now exists. An existing practical division of the territory from which the several transportation lines or groups of such lines draw their steerage passengers lessens the possibility of competition as a force for the extension of the new type of steerage to all emigrant-carrying lines. Legislation, however, may complete what competition began.

The new-type steerage may again be subdivided into two classes. The better of these follows very closely the plan of the second-cabin arrangements; the other adheres in some respects to the old-type steerage. These resemblances are chiefly in the construction of berths and the locations and equipment of dining rooms. The two classes will not be considered separately, but the differences in them will be noted. The segregation of the sexes in the sleeping quarters is observed in accordance with the law much more carefully in the new type of steerage than in the other. Women traveling without male escorts descend one hatchway to their part of the deck; men descend another, and families still another. Further privacy is secured by inclosed berths or staterooms. The berths are sometimes exactly like those in the old-type steerage in construction and bedding, but the better class are built like cabin berths. The bedding is in some cases not clean, but the blankets are always ample. Staterooms contain from two to eight berths. The floor space between is utilized for hand baggage. On some steamers special provision is made beyond the end of the berths for baggage. There are hooks for clothes, a seat, a mirror, and sometimes even a stationary washstand and individual towels are furnished. Openings below and above the partition walls permit circulation of air. Lights near the ceiling in the passageways give light in the staterooms. In some instances there is an electric bell within easy reach of both upper and lower berths which summons s steward or stewardess in case of need.

On some steamers stewards are responsible for complete order in the staterooms. They make the berths and sweep or scrub floors as the occasion requires. The most important thing is that the small rooms secure a greater degree of privacy and give seclusion to families. On most steamers some large compartments still remain. These are occupied by men passengers when traffic is heavy.

In spite of the less crowded conditions the air is still bad. Steamers that are models in other respects are found to have air as foul as the worst. The lower the deck the worse the air. Though bearing no odors of filth, it is heavy and oppressive. It gives the general impression of not being changed as often as it should be. Passengers who are able to go up on the open deck, and thus experience the difference between fresh air and that below, find it impossible to remain between decks long, even to sleep. The use of the open deck generally begins very early in the morning. Where there are not stationary washstands in the staterooms, and their presence is still the exception and not the rule, lavatories separate for the two sexes are provided. These are generally of a size sufficient to accommodate comfortably even more persons than there are basins. Roller towels are provided, and sometimes soap. The basins are of the size and shape most commonly used. They may be porcelain and cleaned by a steward, or they may be of a coarse metal and receive little care. The waterclosets are of the usual construction – convenient for use and not difficult to maintain in a serviceable condition. Floors are at all times clean and dry. Objectionable odors are destroyed by disinfectants. Bath tubs and showers are occasionally provided, though their presence is seldom advertised among the passengers, and a fee is a prerequisite to their use.

Regular dining rooms appropriately equipped are included in the ship's construction. Between meals these are used as general recreation rooms. A piano, a clock regulated daily, and a chart showing the ship's location at sea may be other evidences of consideration for the comfort of the passengers.

On older vessels the dining room occupies the center space of a deck, inclosed or entirely open, and with the passage between the staterooms opening directly into it; the tables and benches are of rough boards and movable. The tables are covered for meals, and the heavy white porcelain dishes and good cutlery are placed, cleared away, and washed by stewards. The food is also served by the stewards.

On the newer vessels the dining rooms are even better. In equipment they resemble those of the second cabin. The tables and chairs are substantially built and attached to the floor. The entire width of a deck is occupied. This is sometimes divided into two rooms, one for men, the other for women and families. Between meals men may use their side as a smoking room. The floors are washed daily. The desirability of eating meals properly served at tables and away from the sight and odor of berths scarcely needs discussion. The dining rooms, moreover, increase the comfort of the passengers by providing some sheltered place, besides the sleeping quarters, in which to pass the waking hours when exposure to the weather on the open deck becomes undesirable. The food on the whole is abundant and when properly prepared wholesome. It seldom requires augmentation from private stores or by purchase from the canteen. The general complaints against the food are that good material is often spoiled by poor preparation; that there is no variety and that the food lacks taste. But there were steamers found where not one of these charges applied. Little children receive all necessary milk. Beef tea and gruel are sometimes served to those who for the time being can not partake of the usual food.

Hospitals were found in accordance with the legal requirements. On the steamers examined there was little occasion for their use. The steerage accommodations were conducive to health, and those who were seasick received all necessary attention in their berths.

With the striking difference in living standards between old and new types of steerage goes a vast difference in discipline, service, and general attitude toward the passengers.

One line is now perhaps in a state of transition from the old to the new type of steerage. It has both on some of its steamers. The emigrants carried in its two steerages, however, do not radically differ in any way.

The replacement of sails by steam, with the consequent shortening of the ocean voyage, has practically eliminated the former abnormally high death rate at sea. Many of the evils of ocean travel still exist, but they are not long enough continued to produce death. At present a death on a steamer is the exception and not the rule. Contagious disease may and does sometimes break out and bring death to some passengers. There are also other instances of death from natural cause, but these are rare and call for no special study or alarm.

The inspection of the steerage quarters by a customs official at our ports of entry to ascertain if all the legal requirements have been observed is, and in the very nature of things must be, merely perfunctory. The inspector sees the steerage as it is after being prepared for his approval, and not as it was when in actual use. He does not know enough about the plan of the vessel to make his own inspection and so he sees only what the steerage steward shows him. The time devoted to the inspection suffices only for a passing glance at the steerage and the method employed does not tend to give any real information, much less to disclose any violations.

These, then, are the forms of steerage that exist at the present time. The evils and advantages of such are not far to seek. The remedies for such evils as now exist are known and proven, but it still remains to make them compulsory where they have not been voluntarily adopted.

THE COASTWISE TRAFFIC

A certain percentage of the immigrants who are distributed from New York City and other points travel toward their ultimate destination on smaller steamship lines in the coastwise trade. There seems to be no attention whatever paid to the accommodations for, or care of, immigrants on these ships. On one steamer investigated it was found that steerage passengers were carried in a freight compartment, separated from the rest of the vessel only by canvas strips, and that in this compartment the immigrants were not provided with mattresses or bedding. There was practically no separation between the women and the men. On this boat other passengers who pay the same price as do the immigrants have regular berths with mattresses and pillows, and a dining room is provided for their use. There is also separation of the sexes. The negroes [sic] who patronize this line are quartered in this compartment and receive for the same price much better treatment than do the immigrants. This line has carried as many as 200 immigrants on one trip in these freight compartments.

<u>Note</u>: This report came 13 years after the Plessy vs. Ferguson segregation case. Segregation was law in the South and common practice elsewhere. By comparing the treatment of immigrants with that of American blacks, who everyone knew was getting cheated on a regular basis, the author was saying the immigrant was <u>really</u> getting shafted.

On another line, which has accommodations in its ordinary boats for about 50 immigrants, the immigrants can obtain food such as is served to the crew, but the berths are in three tiers, instead of two as on the transatlantic boats. The immigrants are also allowed the freedom of the lower forward deck.

An investigator's description of the hardships of the immigrants on one Hudson River boat is as follows:

Forward of the freight, in the extreme bow of the boat, is an open space. I saw immigrants lying on the floor, also on benches, and some were sleeping on coils of rope, in some cases using their own baggage for head rests.

Conditions on the other line from New York to Albany were found to be similar, though in neither case was there any excuse for the crowding, as there was plenty of room on the boats.

Of a vessel in the coastwise trade an investigator's notes read as follows:

There was no attempt to separate the men from the women, and upon going into the sleeping quarters I found the women and men in all states of dress and undress (mostly the latter). Hot nights they slept on deck.

Sunday, at midnight, some man crept into the Polish woman's bunk and attempted an assault, but her cries drove him off.

Monday night about the same time, presumably the same man, now acknowledged to be a member of the crew – that information I obtained by talking to members of the crew – attempted, and perhaps succeeded, in assaulting the same woman.

The captain started an investigation, but what came of it I was unable to learn, as the matter was hushed up.

It is fair to state that this charge was taken up by the proper authorities, but that no further evidence could be obtained. The quarters of that particular boat were clean and well kept and the food fair.

It is satisfactory to learn that upon the steamers of the Panama Railroad and Steamship Line, practically owned and operated by the United States Government, the conditions and discipline were found to be good, the only complaint being as to the food, which was said to be of very poor quality and of very scanty allowance on one of the boats.

The general comment to make in relation to this class of transportation seems to be that the welfare of the immigrant is left entirely to the companies. If the line is humane and progressive, the immigrants are well treated. If it is not, the immigrants suffer accordingly. In all probability the condition of the immigrants on these ships could be made much better by the enforcement of existing statutes.

CONCLUSION

The report you just read was related to efforts of America's representatives, senators, and president Theodore Roosevelt, who in 1908 enacted a law mandating shipping companies to provide reasonable steerage accommodations for immigrants or face fines, delays in leaving American ports, and imprisonment of ship officers. Because of this law (formally known as 35 Statutes at Large 583-584), steerage after 1908 would be markedly better than what existed up to that time. Those who did the inspecting and the investigating did so to see where problems existed and how they could be solved.

Our leaders finally had to resort to fines, forced delays, and jail time to get some of the shipping company operators' attention. The efforts of American leaders in this regard were consistent with their efforts in the early 1900s to assist the American people from being exploited by unscrupulous bosses and businessmen.

Even the problems with American coastal ships, the report authors noted, could be solved by simply enforcing existing American laws. By comparison, British and other European shipping companies often legally hauled Jews seeking to escape Russia from Russian ports to British or German or Dutch or Scandinavian North Sea ports aboard smaller ships used to haul cattle, timber, or ore. The cattle boats in particular were offensive, as the holds for people were below the holds for cattle. Ship crews would flush out the excrement and urine from the cattle pens, but the flush water "often percolated on the passengers in the cramped holds below."

The "old steerage" ships' operators packed people in tightly, allowing for little or no privacy. At least one ship's crew, either out of a desire to maintain some order or out of a desire to mess with the steerage passengers, posted signs reading, "All couples making love too warmly would be married compulsorily at New York if the authorities deemed fit, or should be fined, or imprisoned." **(7)**

Compared with America's leaders, most other countries' lawmakers did much less for immigrants at sea. For example, British corporate officials did not properly test the *Titanic* before it made its maiden (and only) voyage. Crew members were unfamiliar with the massive ship and with each other. The captain was running the ship too fast for conditions among icebergs at night; officers wouldn't even give lookouts in the crow's nest binoculars to see icebergs sooner. Crew officers and crew members evidently kept the vast majority of steerage passengers away from the underfilled lifeboats, and they drowned or died of exposure. But the shipping company's officials got British maritime authorities to allow the *Titanic* and many other British vessels to sail without enough lifeboats for all the crew members and passengers. It wasn't illegal for them to sail this way.

Whether your ancestors came steerage in the Ellis Island Era, or by a leaking pesthole of a sailing ship during the Famine years, or by some even more wretched vessel during the colonial period of this country, thank God through their sufferings you were able to be a citizen of this country. You have won the global lottery by being able to live in the greatest nation on earth.

Even if your ancestors came aboard a ship in the 1500s or the 1600s like the *Pinta* or the *Mayflower,* they had it good compared to some of our nation's ancestors. Although their stories are outside the scope of this book, there are four other groups of Americans whose ancestors also came here across water, in conditions even tougher than steerage.

For those of you readers whose Polynesian or Inuit (Eskimo) or Native American Indian ancestors came here in open boats, there is no shame in your feeling sad or angry for the sufferings of your ancestors, who lost their American paradise to the greedy who took it from them. Only in recent years have the American people as a whole begun to realize what your ancestors contributed to this great nation. Your heritages are mighty heritages. America would not be what it is today without your peoples.

For those of you readers who are black, there is no shame in you feeling sad or angry for the sufferings of your ancestors who were forced to come here in slave ships by human vermin who bought and sold them like cattle. Even with its many flaws, the United States is the best nation on earth, in part, because of the gifts your ancestors brought here, and because of the sweat and blood they and their descendants invested in the building up of this land. Your heritage is a mighty heritage. America would not be what it is today without your people.

END NOTES

1. Statistics on slaves come from John Garraty's and Robert McCaughey's book The American Nation (page 373).

2. Information on press gangs comes from Nathan Miller's book The U. S. Navy: An Illustrated History (pages 77-78).

3. Statistics on shipping come from The American Nation (page 386).

4. Statistics on those who died aboard ships comes from Oscar Handlin's book The Uprooted (page 51).

5. Navy and merchant marine statistics come from J. Salwyn Schapiro's book Modern and Contemporary European History (1815 - 1940) (page 719), and from Ralph Tarr's and Frank McMurry's book New Geographies (page 410).

6. Info on America's pre-World War One manufacturing prowess and exports comes from New Geographies (pages 410-411).

7. The Abstract of the Report on Steerage Conditions was part of the "Reports of the Immigration Commission" (volume 37). It is available through the Internet and is available in the Historic Research Study, Statue of Liberty – Ellis Island National Monument, by Harlan D. Unrau, National Park Service, 1984 (pages 1132-1140).

8. Information on the cattle ships that plied the Baltic and North Seas with Jewish emigrés (and the quote) comes from Trains and Shelters and Ships, by Aubrey Newman, for the Jewish Genealogical Society of Great Britain, April 2000. This treatise is also the source for the posted notice about "couples making love too warmly."

WHAT WAS IMMIGRANT PROCESSING LIKE?

It is easy and irresponsible to criticize the majority of immigration agents at Ellis Island and elsewhere from the safety of today. The truth is no other country welcomed immigrants like the United States did, and as a nation the United States was barely 100 years old itself when Ellis Island opened for business. In that time, the United States grew from an Atlantic Seaboard country into a country roughly as large as Europe, and had withstood a terrible Civil War.

There was no federal immigrant inspection law until 1891. Until that time, state officials had admitted immigrants to the United States. Federal authorities had federalized immigrant processing in New York City's harbor in 1890, and they federalized immigrant processing in the rest of the country in 1891.

This chapter looks at how American officials screened immigrants coming through Ellis Island. We focus on Ellis Island for a very simple reason – volume. From when the U.S. government first started screening immigrants in New York in 1890 until the end of the great waves of immigration in 1924, federal agents on Ellis Island and elsewhere in the harbor facilities of New York City processed about 70% of all immigrants seeking to gain entry into the United States.

EVENTS THAT LED TO THE ELLIS ISLAND PROCESS

Since the opening of the Erie Canal in 1825, which tied the Great Lakes to the Atlantic Ocean via the Hudson River, New York City was the dominant seaport of the United States. Therefore most immigrants came in steerage through New York City's port. They simply got off the ships when they landed, and settled in New York or went elsewhere.

The first formal immigration station in New York City was at Castle Garden on Manhattan Island. New York state officials processed immigrants at Castle Garden starting in 1855 to protect immigrants from being ripped off by New York sharpies and other vermin in Gotham. However, the ongoing corruption of New York officials and other state officials in the immigrant processing business led the Feds to take over processing immigrants in the early 1890s. Federal officials started processing immigrants at the Barge Office on Manhattan Island in 1890 until Ellis Island opened for business in 1892. (After the fire destroyed the wooden structures on Ellis Island in 1897, federal agents processed immigrants at the Barge Office again until the new brick facilities on Ellis Island were ready in 1900.)

Ellis Island and the other federal immigration stations had a more thorough mission ... screening immigrants as well as protecting them. Processing of immigrants was supposed to screen out those deemed a detriment to the United States. The immigration officials proceeded on the reasonable standard that immigration should benefit the United States instead of benefiting only the immigrants.

As immigration officials learned their jobs and learned what to look for when inspecting would-be immigrants, they adjusted the inspection process to improve it.

The advance of science brought better medical techniques and public health practices. This allowed inspectors to screen out would-be immigrants with medical problems that forbade them from coming into the United States. This also allowed immigration officials to disinfect immigrants to prevent the spread of disease and allowed the immigration service's doctors and nurses to treat and cure many sick immigrants.

The advance of science brought better communication. The "wireless" radio telegraph joined the telegraph and the telephone as a means of rapid communication. This meant immigration officials could quickly get tips on unsavory individuals trying to enter the country, so they could detain them, arrest them, and deport them.

The advance of science also advanced industry. Industrial innovations included quantifiable standards, the discipline of quality control, and time and motion studies to improve products and production. Government officials – many who came from the private sector and after a few years went back, instead of too many of the careerists of today – applied these ideas to systematically organize the processing of immigrants.

There was at least one other factor which contributed to the treatment of immigrants at Ellis Island and other immigration stations – the growing participation of reformers in public life.

Labor unions were very controversial in the 1890s. That decade saw the bloody Homestead steel strike in Pennsylvania, several miners' strikes in the West that involved bloodshed, and the Pullman Car strike in Illinois, which escalated into a nationwide railroad workers' strike that soldiers broke with gunfire. It wouldn't be until Theodore Roosevelt that there was a president who was openly sympathetic with strikers when their strike was just. However, more and more people who were not manual laborers began to see the appalling conditions of many job sites and the

ELLIS ISLAND SCRAPBOOK

abysmally low wages for the jobs many workers performed were unjust.

Likewise, the blatantly crooked people who ran city, state, and federal governments inspired the outrage of many people. Since the people of the late 1800s were much more prone to react to corruption than we are now, there were politicians, publishers, and others who realized they could harness this anger to make reforms. Some politicians and writers decided to become reformers on principle; others did so to further their political careers or sell more newspapers.

Some of the best reformers in that era were women. Women as a rule could not work as white-collar employees in the corporations of the time, and they were by and large discouraged from being doctors or lawyers as well. As a class, about the only women executives in the United States were Catholic nuns who ran hospitals and school systems. As a class, about the only women who could shape public opinion were writers. Novelists Harriet Beecher Stowe (the author of Uncle Tom's Cabin), and Helen Hunt Jackson (the author of A Century of Dishonor and Ramona) changed many people's hearts and minds on the evils of slavery and the treatment of American Indians. Print media women Nellie Bly (who uncovered abuses at a mental institution by deliberately getting committed) and Ida Tarbell (the muckraker who wrote The History of the Standard Oil Company) had more impact than most male journalists of the late 1800s and early 1900s.

Women had the right to vote in some states, but did not win the right to vote nationwide until after World War One. However, women still had the right to act. Women like Jane Addams (the foundress of Hull House in Chicago) and Mother Cabrini (a Catholic nun – an immigrant from Italy herself -- foundress of many orphanages and schools) helped the poor and inspired others to do so.

More and more women became teachers, nurses, and social workers. Many of them worked with the working poor – the many families who needed Papa's wage, Mama's wage, and some of the children's pennies to eke out a living. Some of the women in these professions agitated for government officials to ensure the working poor got more decent treatment. The work of these women aided the work of some men of the day in trying to put government power to use to ensure fairer treatment for people.

The desire of many Americans for more humanitarian use of authority aided the people who processed immigrants at Ellis Island and elsewhere in doing their jobs more efficiently and humanely.

WHO WERE THE FEDS SUPPOSED TO KEEP OUT?

Commissioner of Immigration at Ellis Island William Williams, who ran Ellis Island from 1902-1905, and again from 1909-1913, in a 1912 report titled "Ellis Island: Its Organization and Some of Its Work" said the law required his agents to bar the following types of people from the United States:

"Idiots, imbeciles, feeble-minded persons, and epileptics.

Insane persons and those who have been insane within five years.

Persons who at any time have had two or more attacks of insanity.

Persons afflicted with tuberculosis or with a loathsome or dangerous contagious disease (including trachoma, an eye disease).

Persons suffering from any mental or physical defect which may affect their ability to earn a living.

Paupers, persons likely to become a public charge, and professional beggars.

Persons who have been convicted of or admit having committed crimes or misdemeanors involving moral turpitude.

Polygamists and anarchists.

Prostitutes, procurers, and "persons who are supported by or receive in whole or in part the proceeds of prostitution."

Persons coming to perform manual labor under contract.

Persons whose ticket or passage has been paid for by any association, municipality, or foreign government.

Children under 16 unaccompanied by either parent, except in the discretion of the Secretary of Commerce and Labor." (By 1913, lawmakers split this cabinet-level department into the Department of Commerce and the Department of Labor.) **(1)**

Yet, despite all these potential legal barriers to the immigrants, federal inspectors allowed 98 out of every 100 would-be immigrants into America during the Ellis Island era (1892-1924). Were the standards too lax? Or were the immigration agents at Ellis Island basically humane people? And were most immigrants in the Ellis Island era basically decent people able and willing to contribute to America?

We will take a quick look at how immigration agents processed immigrants in New York City's port facilities to show you how the process worked and how many people were able to get through it. Admittedly, immigration officials screened immigrants at many ports and border towns besides New York City since the start of federal control of immigration in the early 1890s, but still well over half the immigrants to the United States in the Ellis Island era (1892-1924) landed at Ellis Island.

All immigration stations had similar procedures. But since most immigrants were processed at Ellis Island, we will discuss the screening process at Ellis Island as the typical processing experience.

THE WORKERS OF ELLIS ISLAND

During the time commissioner William Williams ran Ellis Island, the day shift started at 7 a.m. and ended at 6 p.m. There was some staggering of inspectors' hours to ensure coverage during these hours. If there were many immigrants and many problems with these immigrants, the agents had to stay until about 8 p.m. inspecting immigrants. The night watch ran Ellis Island from 6 p.m. until 7 a.m. The workers of the night watch ensured immigrants staying overnight were fed, guarded, and otherwise attended to. Workers on the night watch also did a lot of cleaning and maintenance because of the hordes of immigrants passing through.

The flow of immigrants was constant. The immigration station on Ellis Island only closed Easter Sunday and four holidays in FY 1903, said Williams. Even on holidays, the place did not shut down like a typical government office building today. People being detained still had to be watched and fed, guarded, and treated. Ellis Island had dormitories for immigrants, holding areas for people being deported, a hospital to treat the sick, and a kitchen to feed everyone who had to be on the island. The power plant had to run constantly, and firemen had to be ready to put out fires and save lives. Plus, the place required constant cleaning to prevent outbreaks of diseases. So there were employees working at Ellis Island around the clock. Sometimes the Commissioner at Ellis Island lived on Ellis Island; there was a house there for his family.

The work went in shifts to provide around the clock coverage and overlap. Usually the agents didn't process immigrants at night, but hundreds of immigrants routinely had to stay overnight if there was a problem with letting them into the country. Hundreds and sometimes thousands of immigrants had to wait aboard their ships in the harbor overnight because their ships had arrived too late in the day for them to undergo processing.

Ellis Island had about 60 watchmen and gatemen to provide security during the day shifts and the night watch. Several thousand immigrants passed through Ellis Island each day during its busiest years, and it was not uncommon for the authorities to detain 2000 or so aliens overnight on Ellis Island. Most of the immigrants needed protection; some needed watching; a few needed incarceration.

Women who assisted in physical inspections, and in security and investigation work were called matrons. Some of these women boarded ships with the male inspectors; they assisted with inspecting first and second class female passengers. Others worked at Ellis Island, helping with the medical inspection of foreign women, helping with children, and investigating women detained on suspicion of "immoral character" (prostitutes, madams, and the like).

Doctors of Ellis Island's Medical Division performed the medical inspections (and as needed, the detailed mental evaluations) of the immigrants. Doctors, nurses, and other staffers of this group also operated the hospital on Ellis Island.

Agents in Ellis Island's Boarding Division boarded ships carrying immigrants when the ships entered New York harbor. The group had inspectors, matrons, and interpreters. Their job was to inspect all first and second class passengers aboard ship. Doctors also boarded ships to inspect non-steerage immigrants and to check for people with severe contagious diseases requiring quarantining. (The medical inspection and the primary inspection for first and second class passengers were the same as these inspections for steerage passengers, but they took place aboard ship instead of at Ellis Island.) The agents also had the job of escorting to Ellis Island the steerage passengers and any first and second class passengers they decided to detain for medical or legal problems.

The inspectors of Ellis Island's Registry Division performed the primary inspections (the legal inspections) of the immigrants. Most interpreters also belonged to this group. The interpreters also received assignments to help the other groups.

The men of Ellis Island's Special Inquiry Division formed the boards of special inquiry. Three or four three-member boards, composed of qualified inspectors, heard cases every day. They had stenographers and interpreters to help them. These boards made decisions on 50 to 100 immigrant cases a day, depending on the type of case, and the difficulty of communicating with the immigrants before them. This sounds like a huge caseload, but medical exclusions were open and shut cases, and pauperism cases were also fairly routine.

The people of Ellis Island's Discharging Division held immigrants temporarily detained due to problems such as lack of funds or inability to contact family or friends. They would try to reach immigrants' families or friends by telegram, mail, or other means. (In those days, most people did not have telephones.) They would release immigrants to people calling for them if the immigrants recognized them and agreed to go with them. Or they would release immigrants to railroad company agents once they received tickets or funds and were going to their final destination by train.

Sometimes these people would release immigrants to charitable organizations with the understanding they would help the immigrants find work and housing, and not harbor them as charity cases. Since there were many fraudulent boarding house operators posing as missionaries, immigration officials had to check on anyone representing his or her outfit as a charitable organization.

The men of Ellis Island's Deportation Division held aliens being deported, and escorted them to ships for deportation. There were two day watches and a longer night watch of deportation agents to guard and account for the detained immigrants to prevent them from escaping. At the change of each watch, the agents accounted for the detained aliens in their custody.

The men of this group also escorted detained aliens to the dining room for their three daily meals, and took them to the roof of the main building or elsewhere on the island for recreation at certain times. There was a group of men within this group who escorted the aliens being deported to the ship they were being deported on. If they had to put aliens on the ship the night before the ship was to leave New York, they would check on the ship just before it sailed to ensure no alien being deported escaped from the ship. Of course there were opportunities for aliens to bribe the immigration agents and the ship's officers to spring aliens, and some escaped or were "exchanged" and falsely accounted for.

There were men who ran and maintained the power plant on Ellis Island. They ensured the island had heat, light, water, and power. The workforce included engineers and skilled tradesmen, and about two dozen firemen.

There was a large force of janitors and charwomen who kept Ellis Island's buildings, dock, and grounds as clean as could be kept, considering the waves of people who passed through the immigration station. Besides cleaning showers, toilets, waiting rooms, work areas, and offices almost constantly, they disinfected bedding in the dormitories and other quarters where detained immigrants slept, they took blankets to be washed, and they spread disinfectants and pesticides everywhere. Many immigrants coming from Europe were dirty to begin with, and those who were clean usually became dirty in steerage because there were inadequate facilities for them to wash themselves in steerage.

The workers at Ellis Island rotated on and off night duty. They kept the place cleaned and guarded at night. Watchmen made the rounds through the dormitories and holding areas to check on the detained, and they patrolled on the outsides of the buildings as well. Matrons were available to help out. Men kept the power plant running and kept a fire watch. There were doctors, nurses, and other workers at the hospital around the clock.

The commissioner at Ellis Island had a staff and clerks, lawyers, investigators, phone operators, messengers, and runners. These people worked in the Executive Division.

The people of Ellis Island's Information Division gave family and friends of the immigrants information on the immigrants' whereabouts. These workers also kept records on the Boards of Special Inquiry and on the hospital, and kept records on people released to charitable organizations (such as religious groups or immigrant aid societies). They also dealt with inquiries by immigrants' families and friends, and gave telegrams and money orders to immigrants from relatives.

The commissioner had staffers who, besides paying the workers and handling expenses, made sure money and mail sent to immigrants on Ellis Island got to the immigrants. They also billed the steamship companies for hospital expenses run up by sick immigrants and billed the steamship companies for bringing inadmissable aliens to Ellis Island.

The people of Ellis Island's Statistical Division kept the records of all aliens arriving, verified ship landings, wrote most reports, and billed the steamship companies the "head tax" they had to pay for each of their passengers admitted into the United States. They also kept the ships' manifests as records and they kept the records of those detained at Ellis Island.

There was a tugboat for use in boarding ships, and another boat for the use of the immigration agents on Ellis Island.

Contractors operated the kitchen and dining hall for the immigrants detained on Ellis Island. There was also a laundry on Ellis Island that served the needs of the hospital, the dormitories, and the detention areas. Inside the Main Building were a telegraph office, an office for railroad and coastal ship companies, and a money changing office. The commissioners of Ellis Island also provided space for some private religious societies (who they called missionaries), and private immigrant aid societies. All this activity took place on Ellis Island, a built-up sandbar only a few football fields in size. Now let's go into the work of the immigration workers in detail. **(2)**

WHEN A SHIP CAME IN

Typically, a steamship loaded with immigrants coming into New York would anchor in Lower New York Bay, between Brooklyn and Staten Island and south of where the Verrazano Narrows Bridge is today. State health inspectors and federal inspectors would come out to the ship in a cutter, board the ship, and the federal inspectors would check the ship's manifest.

The manifest was a series of lists that American officials required the ship's officers to have prepared listing information about each alien intending to get off the boat ... the manifest would be organized by first class, second class, and steerage. If the one-page form used for those in first or second class had the entries for 30 people, for example, then it would take 10 of these forms to list the data on 300 aliens in first class and second class. The form for people in steerage was a two-page form because immigration officials screened them more tightly. If the two-page form had the entries for 30 people, for example, then it would take 40 of these forms to list the data on 1200 aliens in steerage. There would also be a manifest naming all American citizens on the ship, and it would also be organized by first class, second class, and steerage.

New York state doctors would quickly conduct a quarantine examination on all passengers aboard ship. During the quarantine examination, the state doctors would look for passengers with symptoms of serious contagious diseases such as cholera, smallpox, typhus, yellow fever, and bubonic plague. Likewise, a federal medical officer from Ellis Island would briefly check the passengers traveling in first class and more thoroughly check the passengers traveling in second class (because many immigrants who knew they might not pass muster at Ellis Island bought second class tickets to evade the medical inspection there) for these contagious diseases, and for diseases like trachoma, favus, tuberculosis, measles, chicken pox, scarlet fever, and diphtheria. The federal medical officer would also check the passengers in first class and especially in second class for other infirmities or other medical or mental disorders that would bar them from gaining entry to the United States.

If the inspectors found out people aboard the ship had cholera, smallpox, typhus, yellow fever, or bubonic plague, they would make the ship and passengers undergo quarantine. The ship had to anchor off of one of the islands used for quarantine and fly the yellow flag of quarantine. Those sick with the disease had to go to the New York Quarantine Hospital on Swinburne Island in Lower New York Bay. Those not sick but exposed to the disease had to undergo quarantine at the quarantine facility on nearby Hoffman Island. These people would have to bathe and undergo disinfection. Their clothing and baggage had to be disinfected or maybe burned. The ship would undergo fumigation and disinfection while empty. Only after the passengers passed quarantine – by waiting out the presumed incubation period of the disease and emerging without symptoms of the disease – would they be allowed to undergo processing. Those who died were buried or cremated and their belongings were burned or thrown into the ocean. Shipping companies had to pay for these costs because their agents were negligent in allowing diseased people aboard their ships.

If the inspectors found immigrants aboard a ship with milder contagious diseases like measles, chicken pox, scarlet fever, or diphtheria, these immigrants would have to go to a hospital in New York City until they were cured (or died). Later, Dr. Alvah Doty, who was the Health Officer of the Port of New York, had such unfortunates treated at the New York state hospital on Hoffman Island. When the federal government's Ellis Island communicable diseases hospital opened in 1911, immigrants suffering these less dangerous communicable diseases would receive treatment on Ellis Island. (The staffers of the Hoffman Island hospital treated some of the immigrants suffering these diseases even after the opening of the Ellis Island communicable diseases hospital. They would do so for a few more years.)

Dr. Doty personally tracked epidemics around the world. He kept in touch with American agents at port cities around the world, American Army and Navy military doctors stationed abroad, U.S. Marine Hospital Service officials, and foreign medical officials to find out what infectious diseases were cropping up in large numbers in these countries. He would then single out ships coming from ports in these countries, or ships carrying would-be immigrants from countries suffering epidemics, and order the passengers to be given the medical "third degree." His trademark, in the eyes of a reporter who wrote about him in 1908, was a globe studded with tacks representing outbreaks of cholera, bubonic plague, yellow fever, and other serious contagious diseases. **(3)**

Federal inspectors from Ellis Island would conduct a legal examination on each of the first class and second class passengers aboard ship. During the legal examination, they would question the passengers to corroborate the information about them on the manifest. Any of these passengers with medical problems or legal problems would have to undergo processing (and perhaps hospitalization) at Ellis Island ... and maybe deportation if they were not fit to enter the country.

The captain of the ship had to make sure there were on the ship's manifest answers from all the first class and second class alien passengers to questions such as the following:

- Passenger number on list
- Family name and given name
- Age (years and months)
- Sex
- Married or single
- Calling or occupation
- Able to read/Able to write
- "Nationality (country of which citizen or subject)"
- "Race or people (determined by the stock from which the alien sprang and the language they speak)"
- Last permanent residence (country, then city or town)
- "The name and complete address of nearest relative or friend in country whence alien came."
- Final destination (state, then city or town)

Immigrants who could afford to travel in first or second class didn't have to go through the processing at Ellis Island. They could be cleared aboard ship. Criminals and other undesirables often tried to sneak into the country by paying for a first or second class ticket in hopes of avoiding the screening at Ellis Island. Immigration officials who boarded the steamships would check for these lowlifes among the higher-income passengers. They looked for pimps, prostitute brokers, prostitutes, and madams – undesirables who were capable of paying to stay out of steerage. Armed with tips from American law enforcement officials, American officials overseas, foreign governments, and foreign individuals in America and overseas, the inspectors also looked for swindlers, common criminals, and other shady characters who were reported coming to America to escape prosecution or to create new trouble in America. The inspectors detained those they found for investigation.

The inspectors also checked second class passengers fairly thoroughly for another reason. Quite a few would-be immigrants with some money who had earlier come steerage to save money had a disease or a legal problem that caused the inspectors on Ellis Island to have them deported. Some of these people would then buy second class tickets and try again in a couple of weeks. Inspectors often caught these people and had them deported again. Other rejected immigrants with better sense would sail to Canada and sneak into the United States by rail or by horse or on foot.

After the on-board inspections were through, the ship would then usually dock at Manhattan Island. Immigrants got their first look at the Statue of Liberty on the way into port.

First and second class passengers who the inspectors cleared were free to leave the ship after it docked and go their way. (American citizens traveling in steerage who could prove their citizenship also got to leave the ship after it docked.) Only those first and second class passengers being isolated for a contagious disease that was not so serious, being medically inspected further, or being detained for other reasons would have to get on the ferry for Ellis Island instead of leaving freely when the ship docked.

Why was this?

In the 1800s and early 1900s, the only way to travel between Europe and America was by ship, so first and second class passengers who were not American citizens were usually tourists or businesspeople. They usually weren't trying to sneak into America.

The inspectors checked them aboard ship because usually there were not many of them. Also, since American officials presumed a person traveling in first class had enough money to live in good health, and the intelligence or the connections to have made a good living, they assumed such a person wouldn't pose a health problem to the public, be a burden to society, or risk becoming a criminal. American officials presumed a person traveling in second class – though poorer than a first class passenger – was also enough of a cut above the steerage passengers to warrant easier inspection than those in steerage. The inspectors assumed a second class passenger likewise was healthy, wealthy, and wise enough to contribute to the country instead of becoming a disease carrier, a lawbreaker, or a public charge.

So the inspectors didn't check these passengers quite as closely as they would check the immigrants in steerage. Certainly this was discrimination and profiling, but it was based on usually correct assumptions. Putting first and second class passengers through the poverty, medical, and mental capacity screening process the inspectors put steerage passengers through would usually be a waste of the Ellis Island inspectors' time ... and could put these usually healthy passengers at risk of catching a communicable disease from one of the many carriers who came in steerage.

The vast majority of our ancestors who came to America in that era came in steerage. This meant they would undergo processing at Ellis Island.

THE ELLIS ISLAND PROCESS

This section gives a "typical" picture of how Ellis Island immigration agents processed immigrants in the early 1900s. So the "typical" inspection process described here was a more stringent than it was in the late 1890s, and less stringent than it would be in the early 1920s. Of course, the processing changed a little from year to year, but we will present the overall picture instead of hanging you up on the minutiae.

Steerage passengers would get tags with their name and manifest number, they would collect their luggage, and they would get off the ship at the dock and board a ferry in groups corresponding to their places on the ship's manifest. The ferry would take them – groups at a time – across the Hudson River to Ellis Island.

Immigration agents inspected the steerage passengers on a ferryboat load by ferryboat load basis. They would try to keep these groups together (each group would consist of the people on each list of 30 people that was part of the manifest) as much as possible, except for those who the medical inspectors and legal inspectors detained for closer examination.

Sometimes the immigrants coming off of certain ships were so filthy that the immigration officials made everyone shower and have their baggage disinfected.

The inspection process, in a nutshell, went like this:

1. Brief physical and eye exam with your clothes on. If you pass, go to Step 5. If a doctor thinks you have a physical problem, go to Step 2. If a doctor thinks you have a mental problem, go to Step 3.

2. More thorough (strip to waist) medical examination, like a doctor's office physical exam. If you pass, go to Step 4. If you have a disease or handicap which excludes you, go to Step 6. If you have a less serious disease that you could recover from, you will be treated at the Ellis Island hospital (or at a nearby hospital), and if you recover and pass the medical exam, go to Step 4.

3. Up to three mental examinations. As soon as you pass a mental exam, go to Step 4. If you fail all three, go to Step 6.

4. If you pass the medical examination, go to Step 5. If you pass the mental examination, and you don't appear to have any physical or medical problems, go to Step 5. If you pass the medical exam, but a doctor thinks you have a mental problem, go to Step 3. If you pass the mental examination, but a doctor thinks you have a physical or a medical problem, go to Step 2.

5. You undergo the primary exam (the legal exam). If the inspectors decide you will be a burden on society (someone liable to be a public charge), are a contract worker who will depress American wages, or are an undesirable such as a pimp or a whore or an anarchist or someone else of anti-American beliefs or a common criminal, go to Step 6. If not, go to Step 7.

6. You go before officials of a Board of Special Inquiry for a hearing. If they decide you are inadmissable for medical, physical, mental, or legal reasons, and you don't appeal successfully, you will be deported. (If you need a hospital stay to get well enough to go home, you will get it.) If the board members decide to admit you, or you appeal their decision and win, go to Step 7.

7. You are free to enter the United States. You have the status of resident alien, and have the opportunity to become an American citizen in a few years if you support yourself, obey the laws, learn the language, and pass a citizenship test.

Recapping, the people sent to Ellis Island would undergo a brief physical exam. If they passed the physical exam, they would undergo a brief legal exam. If they passed the legal exam, they were free to enter the United States.

People who didn't pass the quickie physical exam had to undergo a more thorough medical exam. If they passed, they could continue screening. If they didn't pass, they were either sent home, or were given some medical treatment and sent home if they weren't fit, or were allowed to continue processing when they were healthy again. People who didn't pass the medical screening were deported, usually at the expense of the steamship company.

Likewise, during the screening process, inspectors looked over immigrants for signs of mental disorders. People judged to be very stupid, insane, feeble-minded, unbalanced, or senile could not gain entry. People pulled out of line for suspected mental defects had to undergo a simple mental evaluation. If they failed, they had to undergo a second evaluation. If they failed the second evaluation, they had to undergo a third evaluation. As soon as a person passed a mental evaluation, he or she was free to continue processing; he or she didn't have to undergo more mental evaluations. Aliens had to fail all three mental evaluations to be deported, and they were deported, usually at the expense of the steamship company.

The following sections will discuss the various screening processes in detail.

MEDICAL INSPECTIONS AND MENTAL EVALUATIONS

The immigrants didn't know it, but in a way, their medical inspections started as they carried their luggage from the ferry up the steps to the first floor of the Main Building where the Baggage Room was.

U.S. Public Health Service doctors watched immigrants as they climbed up the stairs. Was someone limping, or otherwise struggling to get up the stairway with his or her luggage? Was someone having trouble breathing, or was he or she coughing on the way up? Was someone rubbing his or her scalp or eyes? Did someone seem dimwitted or burdened with a mental problem? Doctors who watched the immigrants sometimes had them rushed up the stairs so they could see symptoms of heart and lung ailments and other handicaps more readily. They would mark people they saw having problems.

People would leave their luggage in the Baggage Room and get a claim ticket. They would claim their baggage upon completing inspection successfully or upon being sent for deportation back to where they came from.

Inspectors would inspect immigrants' luggage, then move them on, while luggage handlers took charge of the luggage. This verified no contraband was coming into America, but it also made it easier for thieves among the luggage handlers to steal. Occasionally crooked luggage handlers, by watching the inspections, would know what luggage had the best items; these crooks would break into the people's luggage and steal their things while they were undergoing processing.

The immigrants would next undergo medical inspection. Two doctors checked each immigrant as he or she got in line.

Dr. E. H. Mullan, a surgeon with the U.S. Public Health Service, summarized the diagnosis as follows:

"It is the function of this officer (the first doctor to check the immigrants in his line) to look for all defects, both mental and physical, in the passing immigrant. As the immigrant approaches the officer gives him a quick glance. Experience enables him, in that one glance, to take in six details, namely the scalp, face, neck, hands, gait, and general condition, both mental and physical. Should any of these details not come into view, the alien is halted and the officer satisfies himself that no suspicious sign of symptom exists regarding that particular detail. For instance, if the immigrant is wearing a high collar, the officer opens the collar or unbuttons the upper shirt button and sees whether a goiter, tumor, or other abnormality exists. A face showing harelip, partial or complete, is always stopped in order to see if a cleft palate, a certifiable condition, is present."

"It often happens that the alien's hand can not be distinctly seen: it may be covered by his hat, it may be hidden beneath his coat, or it may be deeply embedded in blankets, shawls, or other luggage. Of all the physical details in the medical inspection of immigrants it is perhaps most important to watch the hands. In many cases where the hands can not be plainly seen at a glance further searching has revealed a deformed forearm, mutilated or paralyzed hand, loss of fingers. or favus nails."

"Likewise, if the alien approaches the officer with hat on he must be halted, hat removed, and scalp observed in order to exclude the presence of favus, ringworm, or other skin diseases of this region of the body. Pompadours are always a suspicious sign. Beneath such long growth of hair are frequently seen areas of favus. The slightest bit of lameness will show itself in an unevenness of gait or a bobbing up-and-down motion. After constantly observing the passing of thousands of immigrants the experienced eye of an examiner will quickly detect the slightest irregularity in gait. Where the alien carries luggage on his shoulder or back, it may be necessary to make him drop his parcels and to walk 5 or 10 feet in order to exclude suspicious gait or spinal curvature. Immigrants at times carry large parcels in both arms and over their shoulders in order that the gait resulting from a shortened extremity or ankylosed joint may escape notice. In like manner they maneuver in attempting to conceal the gaits of Little's disease, spastic paralysis, and other nervous disorders. All children over 2 years of age are taken from their mothers' arms and are made to walk. As a matter of routine, hats and caps of all children are removed, their scalps are inspected, and in many cases palpated. If care is not exercised in this detail, ringworm and other scalp conditions are apt to escape the attention of the examiner."

"Immigrants that are thin and of uncertain physical make-up are stopped while the officer comes to a conclusion as to the advisability of detaining them for further physical examination. A correct judgment is often arrived at in these cases by the officer placing his hands against the back and chest of the alien, so as to obtain an idea of thoracic thickness, and also by feeling the alien's arm. Very often a thin and haggard face will show on palpation a thick thorax and a large, muscular arm."

"Many inattentive and stupid-looking aliens are questioned by the medical officer in the various languages as to their age, destination, and nationality. Often simple questions in addition and multiplication are propounded. Should the immigrant appear stupid and inattentive to such an extent that mental defect is suspected, an X is made with chalk on his coat at the anterior aspect of his right shoulder. Should definite

OPEN FOR BUSINESS

Top: Ellis Island in its heyday. **Right:** Immigrants land at Ellis Island. Immigrants (mostly the steerage folks) left the ships that brought them across the ocean and boarded ferryboats that were small enough to dock at Ellis Island. **Below:** "Ticket in Her Teeth." Imagine bringing what little you could pack to come to a new land, and keep alert so your children wouldn't stray. **Bottom right:** Italian immigrants ready to land at Ellis Island.

Credits: Bottom right picture by Lewis Hine, and other three pictures from New York Public Library.

Top: Immigrants undergo processing in the Registry Room aka the Great Hall. Credit: New York Public Library

Bottom: Immigrant children and adults on Ellis Island, 1908. Credit: Brown Brothers.

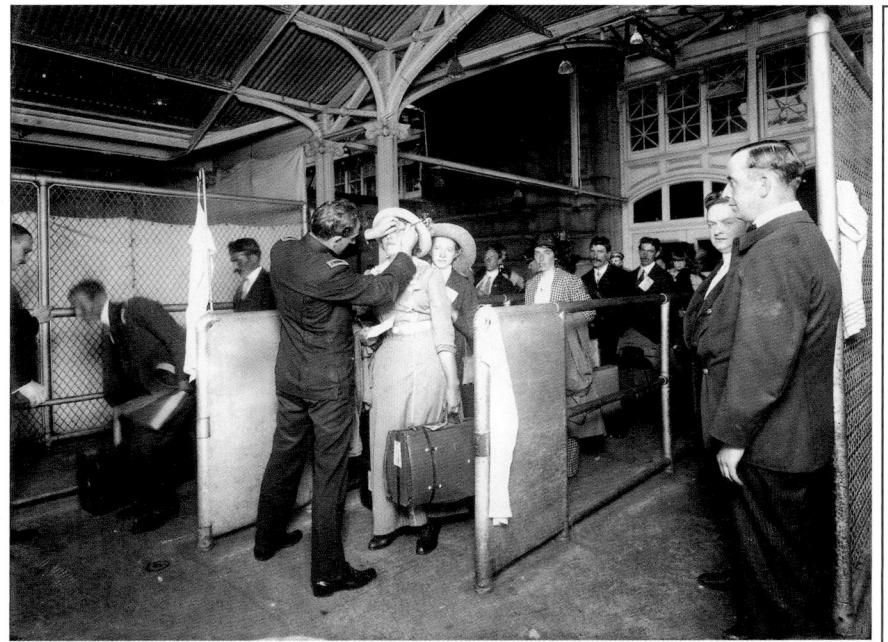

SCREENING IMMIGRANTS

Just showing up at Ellis Island didn't give you an automatic pass into America. You had to pass physical and mental evaluations.

Top: Medical inspector examines immigrant's eyes. They were looking for evidence of trachoma, a very infectious eye disease. Credit: Brown Brothers.

Center: Mental exam of woman. Corrupt European officials tried to dump people with mental problems on America. American doctors tested people suspected of having such problems. Credit: Brown Brothers.

Bottom right: Jewish teenage girl undergoes exam. Many European women were embarrassed by such exams and by semi-public showers and delousing. It was not common practice to be seminaked or naked in front of anyone but a spouse. Credit: Ellis Island Immigration Museum.

Bottom left: This nurse is checking an immigrant girl's hair for lice. Many immigrants practiced very poor hygiene. Credit: U.S. Public Health Service.

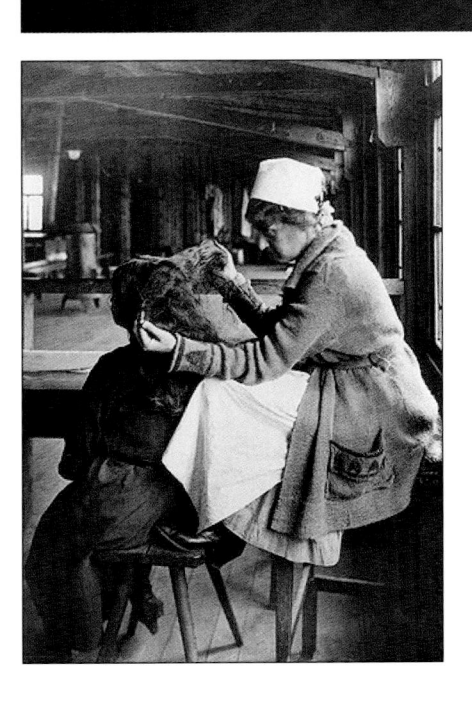

DETENTION AT ELLIS ISLAND

Officials detained hundreds of thousands of would-be immigrants at Ellis Island. About 400,000 had to return to Europe from America from 1892 through 1924; most gained admission.

Top: Stoic mother and her well-cared-for children look out at New York harbor from behind a chain link fence. Is Father a little late getting to Ellis Island to claim them? Is another child sick and recovering in the hospital on Ellis Island?

Bottom: A meal at Ellis Island. Americans fed the immigrants they detained three square meals a day. Most detained immigrants ate better at Ellis Island than they did in their homelands.

Right: Detained youngbloods find a good way to pass the time – meeting and dancing with detained ladies. An accordion player gives this couple some melodies of home.

Credits: New York Public Library.

PRIMARY INSPECTION
at Ellis Island.

Top: Inspectors checked immigrants to make sure they were legally able to become U.S. residents. They asked questions and profiled immigrants who were questionable.

Center right: Ellis Island commissioner Robert Watchorn (sitting, second from left) and Special Board of Inquiry members hear a case to decide if they will deport or admit a questionable alien. Watchorn was himself an immigrant from Britain.

Center left: William Williams, legendary Ellis Island commissioner.

Bottom: Inspector prepares German family for a railroad trip. He is tagging them so railroad employees will help them get to their destination safely.

Credits: Wiliams photo in public domain. Watchorn picture courtesy of Ellis Island Immigration Museum. Other pictures courtesy of New York Public Library.

HEALTH CARE AT ELLIS ISLAND

Many thousands of immigrants became sick on their voyage to America, no thanks to steerage conditions, or other less sanitary immigrants traveling with them. American doctors and nurses treated thousands upon thousands of sick aliens at the hospital on Ellis Island and in other hospitals and quarantine facilities.

Top: Nurses and doctors of the Ellis Island hospital. Credit: Ellis Island Immigration Museum.

Center: Nurse checks baby at Ellis Island. Many infants came through Ellis Island with their mothers. Doctors on Ellis Island also delivered 500 babies on Ellis Island. They were counted as aliens, not anchor babies. In the Ellis Island Era, a baby born in America to alien parents had the national status of his alien parents. Credit: U.S. Public Health Service.

Bottom: Ellis Island officials allowed detained women and children to get milk and crackers during the day besides getting their three meals. The Ellis Island "milkman" is taking care of these eager detainees. Bottom line? Ellis Island's staffers by and large treated immigrants kindly, even the ones they had to deport. Credit: New York Public Library.

QUARANTINE FACILITIES AND PUBLIC HEALTH FOR IMMIGRANTS

Top: The Lazaretto, Tinicum Township, Pennsylvania, was a quarantine facility for diseased immigrants. Philadelphia authorities built this facility on an island in the Delaware River a few miles south (downriver) of Philadelphia in 1799, after a devastating yellow fever epidemic traced to European immigrants from Caribbean islands. Ship captains had to offload sick immigrants here. Local health authorities operated the Lazaretto until 1895. They closed it because federal immigration officials opened a quarantine facility at nearby Marcus Hook. The locals named this place after the quarantine facilities of Europe which Catholic clergy and nuns ran to tend to the sick and protect the public. The word "quarantine" itself comes from the Italian word for 40 – the number of days that those sick with communicable diseases or exposed to them were traditionally isolated. Credit: Library of Congress.

Top middle: Hoffman Island. Staten Island residents, tired of losing loved ones who contracted yellow fever from immigrants being isolated at a quarantine hospital in their neighborhood, burned it down in 1858. As a result, New York authorities had Swinburne Island and Hoffman Island built from landfill nearby in Lower New York Bay to handle quarantine cases. Credit: Library of Congress.

Bottom middle: Teacher weighs detained children on Ellis Island. Teachers and nurses checked on children's health and taught them sanitation practices. Credit: Ellis Island Immigration Museum.

Bottom: Sunlight, sea air, and exercise are great tonics for health. Children exercise at Ellis Island. Credit: Ellis Island Immigration Museum.

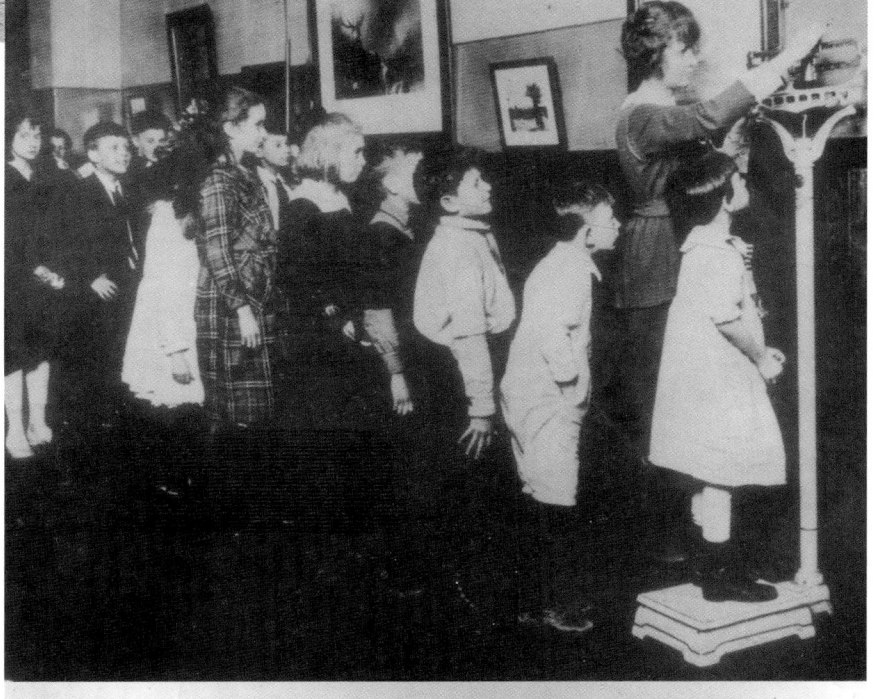

ANGEL ISLAND

in San Francisco Bay was where American agents processed 200,000 immigrants (mostly Asians) from 1910 through 1940. It is now a state park.

Top: Buildings for immigrants. These buildings at Angel Island were undergoing renovation when the author took this photo in 2006.

Bottom right: Angel Island commanded the Golden Gate. The Golden Gate Bridge was built during the Depression. Before then, artillery batteries pointed west to blast any unfriendly foreign naval vessel. The island was big enough to handle being an immigration station and a harbor defense fort. It would later host women soldiers and Army missile men. Photo by author.

Bottom left: Asian immigrants arrive at Angel Island to undergo processing. Photo courtesy of Angel Island State Park.

Center: Katherine Maurer, in black with pompomed hat, teaches detained Asian female immigrants English. Miss Maurer, a Protestant deaconess, ministered to the immigrants from 1912 through 1940. She was remembered for her kindness; she put the "Angel" in Angel Island. Photo courtesy of Angel Island State Park.

IMMIGRATION SCRAPBOOK

Top: Jewish immigrants from Russia. Roughly 2 million Jews came to America in the Ellis Island Era. Credit: New York Public Library.

Center: Immigrants from Galicia (either Polish or Ukrainian) land in Montreal. Many immigrants to America came to Canada, and then took the train to America. Many immigrants from Ukraine and Russia settled in the Prairie provinces of Canada. Credit: New York Public Library.

Bottom left: Mum and seven children, immigrants from England, at Ellis Island. Credit: Augustus Sherman, Ellis Island Immigration Museum.

Bottom right: Before the Clintons' and the Bushes' presidencies, most Arab immigrants to America were Catholics or Orthodox Christians from Lebanon and the Holy Land. These Christians were escaping Ottoman Moslem oppression. This contrasts with the Moslems and the large numbers of sleepers and overt jihadists in their midst who come to America today with the assistance of the State Department. This attractive young Lebanese woman is Arab and Christian also. Credit: Alamy. Many Catholic, Coptic, and Orthodox Christian women like her face kidnaping, rape, forced conversion, and forced marriage in too many Moslem lands today. Christians in these lands today also face similar indications of Moslem intolerance, like robbery and murder. Ironically, the safest overwhelmingly Moslem country for Christians today is probably Turkey.

WOMEN AT ELLIS ISLAND

Top left: Ruthenian woman. **Top right:** Albanian woman from Italy. The Turks ruled Albania until 1912; most Albanians were and are Moslems. Many Catholic and Orthodox Christian Albanians lived in safety in nearby Italy. **Bottom left:** Lapp woman from Norway. Did her headgear inspire pilots' helmets? **Bottom right:** Greek woman. She was no stranger to the needle, judging from the embroidery on her clothes. Credits: Augustus Sherman, Ellis Island Immigration Museum and New York Public Library.

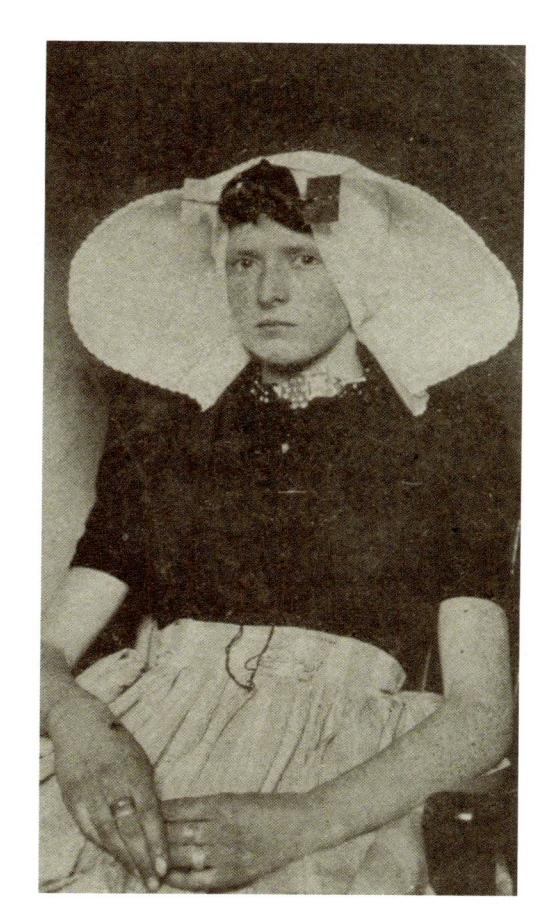

PAGEANT OF ELLIS ISLAND
Many Europeans displayed the picturesque clothes of their homelands when they came through Ellis Island for processing. **Top left**: Cossacks from Russia or Ukraine. They look somewhat prepared to fight street crime in New York. **Top right**: Dutch girl in native dress. She doesn't look too happy about being photographed by Augustus Sherman, long-time Ellis Island civil servant and shutterbug. **Bottom left:** French girl. She was probably from Alsace, because she is wearing the huge black ribbon headdress of that region. **Bottom right:** German man from Bavaria. Was he slyly eyeing the frauleins at Ellis Island? Credits: Augustus Sherman, Ellis Island Immigration Museum and New York Public Library.

MOTHERS AND CHILDREN AT ELLIS ISLAND

Top left: Italian mama and bambina. This well-loved photo got the nickname "Madonna of Ellis Island." **Top right:** Hungarian mother takes her baby for an airing in front of the Main Building of Ellis Island. **Bottom left:** Little Swedish girl wins hearts at Ellis Island. **Bottom right:** Scottish boys. They undoubtedly didn't show up for school in America like this, or if they did, they would have had to be good with their fists. Credits: Augustus Sherman, Ellis Island Immigration Museum and New York Public Library.

NEW WORLD FASHION vs. OLD WORLD FASHION AT ELLIS ISLAND

Top: This trio of pretty women from Guadeloupe in the West Indies make a fashion statement at Ellis Island. Their dresses were not much different than what American women were wearing at the time. The tallest lady of the three will soon be adding a child to America to help build it.

Bottom left: This girl, the sister of Danish painter Vilhelm Hammershoi, displays garb typical of many young Western European women of the middle class in the late 1800s – dark and simple, yet thoroughly feminine. She didn't come to America, but many who dressed like her did.

Bottom right: These Slovak sweeties are wearing peasant dresses and boots long before this look was "in." Boots were a must as women's footwear in snowy and muddy Eastern Europe, as were skirts that were relatively short for that era, compared with Western and Southern Europe. Who needed to spend time washing a long skirt that got muddied so easily?

ASSIMILATION BEGAN AT ELLIS ISLAND

Left: School at Ellis Island. Many families were detained for awhile at Ellis Island. The commissioners brought in teachers to teach the children the American language, American ways, and basic hygiene. Credit: Brown Brothers.

Right: Christmas at Ellis Island. Ellis Island officials tried to help the detained make the best of their situation. They had festivities for the immigrants. They arranged for Catholic Mass, Orthodox Divine Liturgy, and Protestant worship service for the detained. (They also arranged for rabbis to minister to Jewish detainees on their holy days.) Christians and Jews alike got presents from the aid societies. Pro-American schooling and celebrating Our Lord's birth were natural to officials who had patriotism and Christian charity. In today's poisoned world of political correctness, celebrating American culture and Our Lord's birth would cost some official his or her career. Credit: Ellis Island Immigration Museum.

ETHNIC NEIGHBORHOODS like these blocks in Little Italy, above, and the Jewish neighborhood of the Lower East Side, below, in New York City and many other cities of the East and Midwest formed before World War One as immigrants settled close to their countrymen. Credits: Granger, above, and the New York Public Library, below.

SCHOOL AND STREET helped immigrant children become real Americans. Back in the day teachers taught patriotism along with readin', 'ritin', and 'rithmetic.

Top: Gary, Indiana school children. Top row standing; left to right, American black, Romanian, Lithuanian, Italian, Polish, Croatian, Hungarian. Middle row; Greek (white dress), American white (with book), Austrian, German, Bulgarian. Front row, all seated, Scotch, Russian, Irish, Assyrian, "Slavic," Jewish and Spanish. Gary was a steel mill town with a very high immigrant population. Credit: New York Public Library.

Bottom: Kids play ball in a tenement neighborhood in New York City. Being with American kids helped alien kids learn the language and some of the customs of their new homeland. Credit: Lewis Hine.

signs of mental disease be observed, circle X would be used instead of the plain X. In like manner a chalk mark is placed on the anterior aspect of the right shoulder in all cases where physical deformity or disease is suspected."

The doctors would mark in chalk on the outer clothing of anyone they spotted who had problems. If an immigrant's coat had an L on it, they saw him limping and figured he was lame. A B on his coat meant the doctors noticed a back problem. An H marked on an immigrant's coat, shirt, or dress meant they suspected he or she had heart trouble.

An SC on a person's garments meant the doctors saw a scalp problem. A P meant the doctors suspected a lung problem or some other "physical" problem. A G meant the doctors saw the person had a goiter. Likewise, F for face, FT for feet, and N for neck was doctor shorthand for problems with these body parts. Often, the doctors wrote out the words "hand," "measles," "nails," "skin," "temperature," "vision," or "voice" on an immigrant's outerwear if he detected any of these problems.

A K meant the doctors thought the marked man had a hernia. A Pg on a woman's clothing meant she was pregnant, although in many cases, this was self-evident without the chalk mark.

A C, CT, or E on someone's coat, shirt, or dress wasn't a good sight. This meant the doctors thought the marked man or woman had conjunctivitis (pinkeye), trachoma, or some other eye problem. Having trachoma was grounds for being barred from entering the United States.

A person marked with an X or a circled X on his or her garment was truly branded. The X meant the doctors suspected the person had a mental problem. If the X was circled, this meant the doctors decided they observed actual signs of mental illness. Also, doctors marking S on immigrants' garments were telling the inspectors they suspected these people were senile. People marked with an X, a circled X, or S would have to be checked further; mental problems were grounds for being denied entry to the United States.

Mullan continued:

"The alien after passing the scrutiny of the first medical officer passes on to the end of the line, where he is quickly inspected again by the second examiner. The examiner is known in service parlance as the "eye man." He stands at the end of the line with his back to the window and faces the approaching alien. This position affords good light, which is so essential for eye examinations. The approaching alien is scrutinized by the eye man immediately in front of whom the alien comes to a standstill. The officer will frequently ask a question or two so as to ascertain the condition of the immigrant's mentality. He may pick up a symptom, mental or physical, that has been overlooked by the first examiner."

"He looks carefully at the eyeball in order to detect signs of defect and disease of that organ and then quickly everts the upper lids in search of conjunctivitis and trachoma. Corneal opacities, nystagmus (involuntary rapid eye movement), squint, bulging eyes, the wearing of eyeglasses, clumsiness, and other signs on the part of the alien, will be sufficient cause for him to be chalk-marked with "Vision." He will then be taken out of the line and his vision will be carefully examined. If the alien passes out of this line without receiving a chalk mark, he has successfully completed the medical inspection and off he goes to the upper hall, there to undergo another examination by officers of the Immigration Services, who take every means to see that he is not an anarchist, bigamist, pauper, criminal, or otherwise unfit." **(4)**

Matrons would then eye the female immigrants, especially the teenage girls and young women without husbands or other adult male relatives accompanying them. They were there to check for prostitutes. Prostitutes were not allowed to immigrate to America.

All immigrants processed at Ellis Island underwent the legal inspection (called the primary inspection) after being cleared medically. Most immigrants (80 percent and more) passed the medical inspection without being marked and diverted to the medical examination or mental examination line, so after the eye doctor cleared them and they passed the matron looking for prostitutes, they went immediately to the legal inspection. (Doctors marked about 15 to 20 percent of immigrants, according to Mullan.)

There were up to 15 doctors checking as many as 5000 immigrants a day for 250 to 300 days a year at Ellis Island. They gave exams to almost a million people a year in the busiest years. This works out to each doctor checking as many as 60,000 immigrants a year or 200 to 240 immigrants each a day ... or one every two minutes in an eight-hour shift. **(5)**

Those who were marked were sent into another line for further medical and/or mental examination. For a few pages, we'll talk about these people being diverted for suspected medical or mental problems. Then we'll come back to describing the legal inspection, which all immigrants processed at Ellis Island underwent after being cleared medically and mentally.

What happened to those marked for a medical defect?

A person who the doctors determined had a minor curable disease had to go to the hospital on Island 2 which was part of the Ellis Island complex. (Because of the Ellis Island fire of 1897 that burned down the hospital along with other buildings, immigration authorities had to have immigrants with medical problems sent to the Hospital of the Health Department of New York City until the new hospital was ready on Ellis Island in 1902.)

A person who the doctors diagnosed with a contagious disease had to go to a hospital. Those sick with a serious contagious disease like cholera, smallpox, typhoid fever, yellow fever, leprosy, or bubonic plague had to go to the New York Quarantine Station on Swinburne Island at the entrance to New York's harbor.

Before 1911, authorities sent aliens of all classes having milder communicable diseases such as measles, chicken pox, scarlet fever, or diphtheria to the Port of New York quarantine hospital on Hoffman Island, or to one of several New York City area hospitals for quarantining until they were cured. However, immigrants – especially those coming in steerage — frequently escaped from these hospitals still carrying the disease and still unscreened as to whether they were fit to enter America. Commissioner Williams pushed for having another hospital built on Ellis Island to isolate immigrants being quarantined for these lesser communicable diseases. Authorities had Ellis Island physically expanded with fill; this became Island 3. They then had a quarantine hospital built on the fill; it opened in 1911. This hospital was for immigrants with less serious diseases requiring isolation. The hospital's doctors and nurses treated immigrants who had pneumonia, whooping cough, measles, scarlet fever, diphtheria, mumps, chicken pox, tuberculosis, trachoma, favus, or venereal diseases.

When doctors certified a person had recovered, officials would let him or her finish screening and hopefully enter the United States.

People deemed incurable or suffering from certain severer diseases or defects could not gain entry into the country. U.S. officials had the steamship companies take these unfortunates back to the ports they sailed from in Europe, usually at the expense of the steamship company for doing negligent or dishonest screening of the would-be immigrants they chose to transport.

Likewise, people who had trachoma or favus or contagious tuberculosis or leprosy or venereal disease or another ailment or handicap that would make them unable to earn a living would have to be deported.

Trachoma is a disease of the cornea and the conjunctiva (the eyelid membrane) caused by the *Chlamydia trachomatis* bacteria. In fact, a related disease, inclusive conjunctivitis, is a venereal disease that attacks the eyes as well as the genitalia. The *Chlamydia trachomatis* bacteria causes growths on the conjunctiva and damage to the cornea that can lead to blindness. Trachoma is a contagious disease that spreads through close contact of people (coughing, exhaling, touching, sexual contact, etc.) who are not used to washing their hands or bathing; flies also carry the disease. Trachoma was widespread in southern Europe, Russia, the Middle East, and North Africa in the late 1800s and early 1900s. (It is still common in North Africa and is widespread in much of Asia. It is also present in rural areas of the American Southwest, where dry climate and a lack of water encourage its spread.)

During the Ellis Island era, Italians, Greeks and other people from the Balkans, Turks, Jews and others from Russia, and people from the Middle East were most likely to have trachoma. Sadly, many people who boarded a ship with undiseased eyes contracted trachoma from someone else in steerage.

Doctors inspected immigrants' eyes for trachoma by turning their eyelids up with their fingers or with leather loops used to button women's high-button shoes. Assistant Surgeon General H.D. Geddings, who checked the medical inspectors and the hospital facilities at Ellis Island in 1906, said the doctors inspecting immigrants' eyes disinfected their hands before inspecting each immigrant's eyes. He did not say if the doctors washed any of the loops; he said they used them only when their fingers got tired from checking so many immigrants' eyes. It is likely, and sadly ironic that some immigrants got trachoma from medical inspectors who didn't sanitize properly before touching their eyes.

Favus is a severe skin infection, usually in the scalp; it is a type of ringworm. Fungus, not worms, causes the disease. Favus is related to athlete's foot and jock itch but is more serious; favus is also highly contagious.

Doctors ordered marked immigrants to strip to the waist. (Female doctors and nurses would check women and girls who had to strip. There were different exam rooms for female patients.) The doctors would examine the immigrants for the problem the line doctors marked on their clothes. The doctors would check the immigrants for tuberculosis and for a number of contagious diseases. The doctors would perform ear, nose, and throat exams on them. As circumstances warranted, they would check the women's breasts and would check pregnant women.

Occasionally some of the immigrants would have to strip a little more.

William Williams in 1903 ordered inspection of some unmarried male adults being processed at Ellis Island for venereal diseases. He did this to see if VD was a large health problem among arriving immigrants and if there were enough cases of VD to warrant making such inspections part of the general inspection process. The chosen few had to strip and have their genitals inspected. The doctors as normal males did not like to check other men's privates ... and among the 3400 or so foreigners they spot-checked they found only five immigrants who were visibly infected, so Ellis Island's chief medical officer put a halt to the short-arm inspections.

If a doctor found an immigrant who had a medical problem that would keep him or her from entering the United States, two other doctors would have to check the immigrant and certify the first doctor's diagnosis. The immigrant would have to appear before the Board of Special Inquiry on Ellis Island if two other doctors agreed with the first doctor. The board members would rule on whether to deport the immigrant. **(6)**

An observer, commenting on immigrant inspection in 1913, noted, "The surgeons mark about half of the immigrants with chalk marks as they file by (a high proportion compared to the norm of about 15 to 20 percent; maybe the ship was from a questionable port in Europe), and those so marked go to another pen for further examination. Families are torn asunder, and no one has the time or opportunity to explain why. Mothers are wild, thinking their children are lost to them forever; children are frantic, thinking they will see their parents no more. Husbands and wives are separated and for hours they know not why or how." **(7)**

Children who were inadmissable posed other problems. If a pre-teenage child had to be deported, the child's mother or father had to accompany the child back to where they came from. A teenager who was inadmissable could be deported by himself or herself, or a parent could accompany him or her back home. (In the early 1900s, teenagers had more responsibilities than they do now. Most were already out of school, and were working. Many were married.) Sometimes all family members went home; often they split up so the husband could find work and lodging for the other children while the mother took the rejected child home and waited until the child was well enough to pass the medical exam or tried to get relatives to take care of the child if there was no chance of getting the child into America. Since wages were much higher in America than in Europe, immigrants could send home money for a child's care.

Having a child deported was undoubtedly a cruel blow to a family, but from a coldly practical point of view, their plight wasn't America's problem. American officials understood immigration was supposed to benefit America, not burden Americans with cripples from other countries whose own people should have been helping them. Crooked officials in the homeland countries and crooked steamship company officials should have told these people they could not all gain entry to the United States, but selfishness and greed motivated them instead of decency, so they encouraged these people to go to America anyway.

Now that we've discussed how an alien could get rejected for medical reasons, let's note the vast majority of aliens marked for further medical inspection passed. According to federal statistics from 1892 through 1924, doctors determined 129 people had tuberculosis, 42,319 had "loathsome" or dangerous contagious diseases, 25,439 had other medical problems serious enough to prevent their becoming residents of America, and 87 were chronic alcoholics. Compared to the 20,390,289 aliens who American immigration agents inspected from 1892 through 1924, and the 20,003,041 aliens who American immigration agents allowed into America from 1892 through 1924, these 67,974 immigrants rejected for medical reasons equaled a rejection rate of about 33 out of every 10,000, or 0.33% of the immigrants screened. These numbers show doctors as a rule weren't trying to exclude aliens just because they could. **(8)**

What happened to those suspected of mental illness or senility?

According to Dr. E. H. Mullan, this was the gist of the screening of immigrants suspected to have a mental disorder:

"From 50 to 100 percent of the immigrants who enter the inspection plant (the Main Building) are questioned by the medical examiner in order to elicit signs of mental disease or mental defect. The exact number that are stopped and questioned will depend upon the race, sex, and general appearance of the passengers undergoing inspection as well as upon the total number of immigrants to be inspected."

Mullan said the medical examiner would observe immigrants for abnormal behavior and ask immigrants simple questions, like, "How many are 15 and 16?" He said the medical examiners would ask children how old they were and what their names were.

Mullan said experienced line inspectors knew idiosyncrasies of various ethnic groups and did not judge immigrants by American standards of normal behavior, speech, and mannerisms.

What kinds of symptoms got a doctor's attention? Some behavior is considered eccentric in all cultures and times. Persons exhibiting compulsive drooling, abnormal staring or fidgeting, spastic and repetitive motions, disorientation, strange actions, excessive filthiness, talking to oneself, or biting or otherwise mutilating oneself, Mullan said, would get marked. Likewise, a person who exhibited a number of other behaviors, from extreme talkativeness to refusal to co-operate with the exams to extreme withdrawal, he noted, would be a person the doctors might consider to be exhibiting signs of insanity.

Mullan said persons who engaged in inappropriate laughter, crying, yelling, or other noisemaking, meddling with other people, compulsive lying, peculiar affected manner, or excessive antisocial behavior would also find themselves marked and in line for further mental evaluation. (Using these standards, many many politicians, media people, lawyers, and entertainers would be rightly certifiable on some or all of the above behaviors.)

Doctors were supposed to screen out, besides the insane, those they judged to be "feeble minded" (mentally retarded), "imbeciles" (moderately or severely mentally retarded), "idiots" (profoundly mentally retarded), or senile. Questioning of immigrants led doctors to mark others who they thought might be retarded or senile. Although epilepsy is a brain malady that is not a mental illness, doctors were supposed to screen out epileptics also.

If a medical examiner thought the immigrant was insane or had a mental illness, or was senile, he would mark the person's outer garment with an X, a circled X, or an S. The X meant the doctor suspected the person had a mental problem. If the X was circled, this meant the doctor decided he observed actual signs of mental illness. The S meant the doctor suspected the person was senile.

Those marked for mental screening went through what the inspectors called the "Weeding-Out Process." They would go to the Mental Room and one of the doctors would question them.

The doctor would ask the alien to walk up to his desk, sit down, count, do some simple addition, maybe make a simple drawing, and figure out a simple puzzle. He would also ask the alien some simple questions. If the doctor observed what he considered obvious signs of a mental disorder, he would fill out a list of symptoms he observed and have the alien sent to the mental ward of the Ellis Island hospital for observation. If the doctor observed the alien could not perform the test, but didn't display any other signs of a mental disorder, the doctor would have the alien detained overnight in a detention room for a more thorough mental examination the next day.

Most of the immigrants would pass the "Weeding-Out Process." The doctor would release them to undergo the legal inspection.

Doctors evaluated aliens sent to the mental ward of the hospital for observation. If three doctors who observed the alien in the mental ward determined he or she was insane or suffering from another mental illness that would not allow him or her to gain entry, they would certify the alien was insane or suffering from a mental illness. People who the doctors considered insane or idiots or imbeciles or senile or feeble-minded or mentally ill would be deportable. People having none of these problems, in the doctors' judgment, could be cleared for further processing or might still have to undergo mental examination.

An alien who failed the "Weeding-Out Process" but was not in bad enough shape to be easily certifiable as having a mental disorder had to undergo a second mental examination. He or she would undergo this exam with a different doctor than the one who ordered him or her detained. The doctor would spend 20 to 60 minutes with the alien and ask him or her questions about home life customs, his or her occupation, and his or her intentions if he or she could gain entry to America. The doctor would give the alien a brief psychological test. The doctor would sometimes give the alien a vision test and a neurological exam. The alien would often also have to count, do some simple addition, make a simple drawing, and figure out a simple puzzle. Many detained aliens were able to collect themselves and satisfy the second doctor they were at least dull normal. The doctor would then release such aliens to undergo the legal inspection.

If the second doctor observed what he considered obvious signs of a mental disorder, he would fill out a list of symptoms he observed and have the alien sent to the mental ward of the hospital for observation. (And if three doctors at the mental ward who observed the alien decided he or she had a mental disorder, they would certify it and the alien would be deportable.) If the second doctor deemed the alien was merely substandard or questionable, he or she would undergo yet another mental exam from a third doctor on another day.

If the third doctor decided the alien was off-center but not abnormal, or was slow but not stupid enough to warrant deportation, he would then release the alien to undergo the legal inspection. If the third doctor decided the person was "feeble-minded" or worse, then the alien would be deportable. Why? As in medical screening, it took the opinion of three different doctors to deem the would-be immigrant mentally defective in some way.

If three doctors at the Ellis Island hospital's mental ward certified an alien was mentally defective, or if three doctors doing "weeding out" exams in the main building certified an alien was feeble-minded or worse, the alien would appear before a Board of Special Inquiry on Ellis Island. The board members would rule on whether to deport the alien.

Mullan said the line doctors marked about 9 out of 100 immigrants undergoing processing for suspected mental problems. Most of these, he said, passed the mental evaluation the doctors gave them in the Mental

Room, and they could return to the line for legal examination. He said 1 or 2 of the 9 sent for mental evaluation typically showed symptoms serious enough to warrant a thorough mental exam. **(9)**

The medical inspectors tried hard to keep mental defectives out of the country. One of the doctors at Ellis Island said the doctors who inspected people and certified 59 people as being mental defectives (which meant these unfortunates had to be sent back) in 1905 saved taxpayers more in not having to care for immigrants with mental problems than the entire cost of the medical inspectors in that year. This was probably the case for most of the years from the early 1900s to 1924. **(10)**

Most of those detained for mental evaluation did pass inspection. According to federal statistics from 1892 through 1924, doctors determined 384 people were "idiots", 518 were "imbeciles", 3215 were "feeble minded", 2473 were "insane", and 550 had other mental problems serious enough to prevent them from becoming residents of America. They also kept 416 epileptics out of the country. Compared to the 20,390,289 aliens who American immigration agents inspected from 1892 through 1924, and the 20,003,041 aliens who American immigration agents allowed into America from 1892 through 1924, these 7556 immigrants rejected for mental reasons equaled a rejection rate of 4 out of every 10,000, or 0.04% of the immigrants screened. These numbers show the doctors didn't find very many mental defectives among the immigrants.

How busy was the hospital on Ellis Island?

The hospital on Ellis Island was busier than many hospitals in the United States at that time. Here's a sample of what the doctors and nurses did there:

From July 1905 through June 1906, roughly 7500 immigrants (about 1% of the more than 800,000 immigrants passing through the port of New York in those 12 months) required hospital treatment at the hospital on Ellis Island, or at the New York Quarantine Station on Swinburne Island or at one of the New York City hospitals which did contract work for Ellis Island. The average patient stayed in the hospital for 12 days. This is an average of about 250 admitted patients per day for the 12-month period. Most of these immigrants were treated at Ellis Island.

They were busier in the next 12 months. From July 1906 through June 1907, the medical people detained about 9300 immigrants for hospital treatment. This was again about 1% of the roughly 950,000 immigrants passing through the port of New York in those 12 months.

Commissioner Robert Watchorn (who was Commissioner of Immigration at Ellis Island from 1905 through 1909, between the two terms of William Williams) blamed the steamship companies for much of the hospital staffers' workloads. He noted in 1907 his people found 1506 immigrant children were suffering from measles, diphtheria, and scarlet fever, "all of which diseases are due, more or less, to overcrowding and insanitary conditions." Of these sick children, he said, 205 died. The next year, Watchorn noted, 267 immigrants who his people treated or who they had sent to hospitals in New York City died. Of these, he said, 229 were children suffering from communicable diseases like measles and scarlet fever.

Watchorn billed the steamship companies $104,000 for medical treatment rendered to immigrant children in fiscal year 1907 (July 1906 through June 1907), much of which took place at New York City hospitals. He said it cost another $30,000 to detain a parent or a teenage brother or sister of these children so these children would have relatives to protect them when they could be released. (These dollar figures seem small by today's standards, but in the early 1900s, a family could live in America on $800 a year without being below the poverty line.)

The hospital on Ellis Island also had a mental ward for observation and treatment of would-be immigrants who had or were suspected of having mental disorders. In 1907, medical officers opened the psychopathic ward a.k.a. the "insane pavilion" for isolation and treatment of aliens with mental disorders until they could be deported. Commissioner Watchorn pushed for such a facility in 1906 following the suicide of a man who strangled himself with a light fixture cord while being in a detention cell for behaving hatefully, and the suicide of a woman being detained for mental evaluation who killed herself by crawling out a window and jumping to her death. **(11)**

In fiscal year 1911 (July 1910 through June 1911), doctors and nurses treated more than 6000 aliens at the Ellis Island hospital – about 1% of the roughly 700,000 immigrants passing through the port of New York) They also referred 720 people suffering contagious diseases to the New York Quarantine Hospital on Swinburne Island.

In 1911, the contagious disease hospital complex opened on Ellis Island's Island 3. The hospital's 11 buildings had a capacity of 450 beds, and its medical people treated anywhere from 30 to 130 patients per month in 1911. Doctors and nurses at the contagious disease hospital on Ellis Island treated patients with pneumonia, whooping cough, measles, scarlet fever, diphtheria, mumps, chicken pox, tuberculosis, trachoma, favus, and venereal disease.

Doctors continued to treat those suffering the more serious contagious diseases like cholera, smallpox, typhus, yellow fever, leprosy, or bubonic plague at the New York Quarantine Hospital on Swinburne Island. They continued to isolate those exposed to these terrible diseases but not visibly sick from them at the facility on Hoffman Island. They also treated some of the immigrants suffering less serious contagious diseases at the hospital on Hoffman Island for a time.

In fiscal year 1928 (July 1927 through June 1928), after the quotas took effect in 1924 and only about 150,000 people processed through Ellis Island that year, the Ellis Island hospital's doctors and nurses usually were treating on average 325 patients a day. Many of these unfortunates were merchant seamen. **(12)**

LEGAL INSPECTION OR PRIMARY INSPECTION

If an immigrant passed the in-line medical exam and no doctor decided he or she was diseased, crippled, or mentally defective, and no matron decided she was a prostitute, they would route him or her to the Registry Room, a huge auditorium-sized room that occupied the center of the second floor of the Main Building of Ellis Island.

In the Registry Room, she or he would undergo the legal inspection. (People pulled out of line for closer medical or mental evaluations who passed these evaluations would also then undergo the legal inspection in the Registry Room.) Ellis Island agents also called this inspection the "primary inspection."

During this inspection, the inspectors questioned the immigrants to account for them and to verify the information about them on the ship's manifest. They also were looking for potential "problem children" that they would have to bar from entering the United States.

The ship's captain had to turn in the manifest to American immigration officers at the port of arrival. He had to list American citizens in steerage aboard his ship and his crew members also. (Many Americans and immigrants who weren't citizens yet made more than one trip across the ocean for business or family reasons.) The ship's manifest for steerage passengers contained many more questions than did the manifest for first class and second class passengers. The captain of the ship had to make sure there were answers for all of these questions from the steerage passengers.

Each inspector had a copy of the ship's manifest, so he could double-check the immigrants' verbal answers with the entries about them on the ship's manifest. This is another reason the inspectors tried to keep the immigrants who were listed on the same manifest page grouped together as much as possible.

Inspectors asked the immigrants the "29 Questions" (or whatever questions the law said steerage aliens had to answer at the time) on the two-page form, such as:

- Passenger number on list
- Family name and given name
- Age (years and months)
- Sex
- Married or single
- Calling or occupation
- Able to read/Able to write
- "Nationality (country of which citizen or subject)"
- "Race or people (determined by the stock from which the alien sprang and the language they speak)"
- Last permanent residence (country, then city or town)
- "The name and complete address of nearest relative or friend in country whence alien came."
- Final destination (state, then city or town)
- Passenger number on list (repeated because this was the first line on the second page of the form)
- "Whether having a ticket to such final destination"
- "By whom was passage paid? (Whether alien paid his own passage, whether paid for by any other person, or by any corporation, society, municipality, or government)"
- "Whether in possession of $50, and if less, how much?"
- "Whether before in the United States; and if so, when and where?"
- "Whether going to join a relative or friend; and if so, what relative or friend, and his name and complete address"
- "Ever in Prison, almshouse, or institution for care and treatment of the insane, or supported by charity? If so, which?"
- "Whether a Polygamist"
- "Whether an Anarchist"
- "Whether coming by reason of any offer, solicitation, promise or agreement, expressed or implied, to labor in the United States"
- "Condition of Health, Mental and Physical"
- "Deformed or Crippled, Nature, length of time, and cause"
- Height
- Complexion
- Color of hair/Color of eyes
- Marks of Identification
- Place of Birth (country, then city or town) **(13)**

Inspectors would ask these questions of the men, women, and teenage boys and girls.

Starting in 1917, the inspectors would ask would-be immigrants 17 and older to read a selection in their own language, because now the law required immigrants to be literate in their native language. (They made exceptions for illiterate immigrants whose literate husbands or children or grandchildren were legally admitted immigrants or American citizens who sent for them. Immigration officials would still allow these people entry even if they could not read. Officials also made an exception for the unmarried or widowed daughters of legally admitted immigrants or American citizens who were 17 or older and illiterate.) **(14)**

Interpreters fluent in almost every language in Europe and the Middle East stood by to help the immigrants understand the inspectors' questions and the inspectors understand the immigrants' answers. (At Angel's Island in San Francisco Bay and in other ports along the West Coast, interpreters fluent in Oriental languages were available to help the immigrants and the inspectors.)

Registry inspectors (the inspectors who performed legal or primary inspections) asked immigrants how they expected to support themselves, and other simple questions aimed at determining why the immigrants were coming to the United States. They were supposed to screen out contract laborers whose presence threatened the livelihoods of American workers. They were also supposed to screen out burdens on society like paupers and the unemployable. (Medical inspectors had presumably already screened out the physically and mentally defective.) And they were supposed to screen out the chancres of human society, such as common criminals and sociopaths, anarchists and other troublemakers, and perverts such as pimps, prostitutes, and polygamists.

An observer, commenting on the primary inspection in 1913, noted, "The line moves on past the female inspector looking for prostitutes, and then past the inspectors who ask the (then) twenty-two questions required by law. Here is where the lies are told. Most of the immigrants have been coached as to what answers to give. Here is an old woman who says she has three sons in America, when she has but one. The more she talks the worse she entangles herself. Here is a Russian Jewish girl who has run away to escape persecution. She claims a relative in New York at an address found not to exist; she is straightaway in trouble." **(15)**

Many immigrants, subject to human failings like all of us, would lie if they thought it would help them gain entrance to the United States. It was the job of the inspectors to sniff out those who could be a detriment to American society, and hold them up so the authorities could decide whether to deport them.

In the following paragraphs, we will discuss some of the main reasons agents rejected would-be immigrants.

CONTRACT LABOR

Some of the first federal immigration laws – the Act of March 3, 1875, the Chinese Exclusion Act of 1882, and the Alien Contract Labor Law of 1885 – aimed to keep robber barons from importing unskilled foreign laborers to break the wage scale of American workers. In fact, the first of these laws went into effect only six years after the completion of the Transcontinental Railroad. Robber baron Charlie Crocker had imported many coolies from China at dirt-cheap wages to build the railroad line from the Sacramento area through the Sierra Nevada Mountains, across Nevada, and into Utah. Most immigrants came to seek better conditions in America, but the goal of American immigration policy was not to let the robber barons import so many people willing to work for next to nothing that the standard of living of the average American would decline to European or even down to Asian standards.

This is in stark contrast to today, where immigration from Latin America and Asia – even illegal immigration – has official encouragement because government leaders and the corporate types who bankroll their campaigns evidently have no problem with breaking the wage scales in America's basic industries.

Immigrants had to convince the inspectors they had trade skills or at least the willingness to work, so they would not get classified as losers who would be deported because they were "liable to become a public charge." However, if they told inspectors they had jobs lined up, the inspectors would pull them out of line as suspected contract laborers, and the officials would likely deport them. The best thing for an immigrant to do was to tell the truth, and not lie or exaggerate in hopes of impressing an inspector who had heard it all before.

Fiorello La Guardia, an interpreter at Ellis Island from 1907 through 1910, had this to say about the dilemma of many people on the contract labor and pauper questions:

"It is a puzzling fact that one provision of the Immigration Law excludes any immigrant who has no job and classifies him as likely to become a public charge, while another provision excludes an immigrant if he has a job! Common sense suggested that any immigrant who came into the United States in those days to settle here permanently surely came here to work. However, under the law, he could not have any more than a vague hope of a job. In answering the inspectors' questions, immigrants had to be very careful, because if their expectations were too enthusiastic, they might be held as coming in violation of the contract labor provision. Yet if they were too indefinite, if they knew nobody, had no idea where they were going to get jobs, they might be excluded as likely to become public charges. Most of the inspectors were conscientious and fair. Sometimes, I felt, large batches of those held and deported as violating the contract labor provision were, perhaps, only borderline cases and had no more than the assurance from relatives or former townsmen of jobs on their arrival."

However, La Guardia said, "The history of immigrant labor in this country fully justified such a law (contract laborer exclusion). He said before the contract laborer exclusion law went on the books in the 1880s, "Our country went through a period of exploitation of labor which is one of the most sordid and blackest pictures in our entire history. The railroads and our young industries were built by exploited immigrant labor brought here under contract."

"Shipload after shipload of immigrants were brought into this country by contractors, or padrones, who had already made contracts with the railroads and other large corporations for their services. The wages, at best, were disgracefully low. In the eighteen nineties these wages averaged $1.25 to $1.50 a day. The padrone was paid by the corporation. In addition to the low wages he paid the laborers, he took a rake-off from their meager daily earnings. In addition to that, he boarded and fed the immigrants, for which he often made exorbitant charges, deducted, too, from their small pay. Often he had a company store as well, in which he sold them supplies at excessive prices. How they ever managed to save enough to send for their families is a wonder. The twelve-hour day was not unusual, and the seven-day week was common." **(16)**

"LIABLE TO BE A PUBLIC CHARGE"

The inspectors were also looking to keep out of the country those foreigners who would be a burden to society. Besides asking them about what their trades were or what their plans were, inspectors would ask immigrants how much money they had on them. Being virtually penniless at first was no bar to getting into the country. In the 1890s and through most of the first decade of the 1900s, inspectors let even the indigents in. After all, many people made it in America after arriving with little more than the clothes on their backs, including Robert Watchorn, the Commissioner of Immigration at Ellis Island from 1905 through 1909. Watchorn had come from England in 1880.

Williams in his second term as commissioner at Ellis Island stirred up controversy by enforcing the "pauper" and "public charge" portion of the immigration law more strictly. Williams tried to have barred some of those immigrants who came to America with less than $25 per adult. His argument was immigrants would need that much money as a minimum to pay their expenses until they could get jobs. People who showed up with almost no money, he argued, were likely going to have to receive charity in America.

In a memo he wrote for his agents, he acknowledged there was no legal minimum in cash an immigrant needed to enter America. However, he said, "In most cases it will be unsafe for immigrants to arrive with less than twenty-five ($25) besides railroad tickets to destination, while in many cases they should have more." He wanted inspectors to take this into consideration when deciding whether to admit immigrants.

There would be no formal requirement for an immigrant to show he or she had at least a certain amount of cash to avoid being sent back as a pauper during Williams' second watch. But Williams instructed his inspectors to use the $25 amount as a guideline to determine if an immigrant could be excluded as being likely to become a public charge. He noted, "This notice is not, as many have claimed it to be, a rule under which inspectors must exclude immigrants with less than $25, and thus an attempt to create a property test not found in the statutes. It is merely a humane notice to intending immigrants that upon landing they will require at least some small amount of money with which to meet their wants while looking about for employment." **(17)**

Williams said common sense dictated setting a minimum amount of cash needed and letting would-be immigrants and shipping companies know what America expected of them. He blamed shipping companies for bringing large numbers of practically penniless people to America, where they would require charity to survive until they could eke out meager livings. As an example, Williams noted 189 of the 251 passengers a steamship offloaded for processing at Ellis Island on the 4th of July 1909 had $10 or less.

Williams aimed his policy not so much at the poorest immigrants themselves, but at the steamship line operators who didn't care who they hauled in steerage, as long as they made money. Williams figured setting such a money requirement, even informally, would make steamship company officials stop carrying so many paupers to America. This is because every immigrant rejected by the inspectors when the steamship company's people should have known he or she couldn't be allowed into America meant a $100 fine to the steamship company. This also meant the steamship company would have to bring the immigrant back to the port at which he or she got on the ship at the steamship company's expense.

Williams' policy caused an uproar. Many people accused him of discriminating against the poor from Italy and Eastern Europe. However, his policy was a guideline rather than an absolute rule. Many immigrants who were in their 20s in this period would say later the inspectors let them in despite not having $25 because they looked like vigorous young men and women capable of finding work and making good.

Inspectors allowed another common-sense exception to the indigence guideline. Most of the time, women coming with their children and very little money were able to gain entrance to America after they telegramed their husbands or relatives and their husbands or relatives sent back word they had money and would support their wives and children or family members.

Officials of the steamship companies found a dodge that still enabled them to transport large numbers of indigents to America and make money doing so. Percy Baker, a superintendent at Ellis Island, said, "The steamship companies often advanced ten or fifteen dollars to aliens without money. And I have an idea they got most of it back." **(18)**

An observer, commenting on the primary inspection in 1913, noted, "Sometimes men (would-be immigrants) are turned back for trivial cases. Four Greeks were going to Canada, via New York. The Canadian law requires each immigrant to have twenty-five dollars. They have $24.37 each. When they found their funds short, they wanted to come into the United States, but could not. A child is taken down with a contagious disease and is carried to the hospital. The mother must wait and cannot even see her child. A man and his son have had their money stolen from them in the steerage; they lack twenty dollars and must go back. And so the sad tale goes on every day."

He noted if there were no standards, "Then sixteen thousand debarred aliens a year would lay siege to their (the inspectors') sympathies and each would regard his own as a special case, and innumerable difficulties would result. All authorities agree that the system in vogue is just about as humane and as free from hardships as any system that might be devised, and that would maintain the interests of the nation as paramount to the interests of the individual immigrant." **(19)**

The $25 "guideline" no doubt kept many would-be immigrants at home. One of these was apparently a young mechanic from the former Yugoslavia named Josip Broz. When author Louis Adamic, an American citizen and native of Slovenia, visited Yugoslavia in 1949, Broz told him the combined expenses of a train ride to Hamburg, a steerage ticket on a ship crossing the Atlantic and the $25 he thought he would need to gain entrance to America kept him from coming here in 1910. Instead, he stayed home. He eventually became famous, infamous, or notorious, depending on your point of view. For this Josip Broz would become the dictator commonly known as Tito. **(20)**

CRIMINAL SCREENING

Inspectors asked aliens if they had been convicted of and imprisoned for any crimes. Some people told the truth. Others lied about their criminal records, thinking they could get away with it.

Many people who had committed political offenses were likely to admit to what they had done, knowing that Americans admired people who fought authoritarian rule. (We need more of that in this country today!) After all, America became free by revolution against Britain. American authorities did not hold political arrests, except those for anarchism-related offenses, against would-be immigrants. The United States welcomed large numbers of Irish rebels and German dissidents throughout the 1800s.

Others told the truth because they were honest by nature. Public disorder arrests, like for drunkenness or fighting, were not uncommon among people in the 1800s and early 1900s. (Nor are they uncommon today.) Likewise, many people, especially peasants, were arrested for acts of petty misbehavior that would not be illegal in the United States. Inspectors didn't automatically flag aliens who admitted to such problems.

Note that the inspectors asked aliens if they had ever been <u>convicted</u> or <u>imprisoned</u>, not <u>arrested</u>. This reflected the American notion that a person accused of a crime was innocent until proven guilty. Being arrested for a crime didn't make a person guilty, unlike in Europe or Asia. An alien who was wise to the American way could conceal his arrest record if he hadn't actually received a prison sentence.

On the flip side of the coin, European officials did try to send some of their losers to America. And many other immigrants tried to hide their brushes with the law because they were common criminals instead of patriots, union people, poor peasants, or guys who got into scrapes after a little too much booze or after some lowlife said something uncalled-for to his wife. (Bear in mind many Americans are the descendants of English thieves and whores who were essentially dumped here by British authorities before the American Revolution.)

Most criminals probably did escape detection, but some did not. Here's why:

The Ellis Island era (1892 through 1924) did not have international police computer networking, the computer database or the Internet. Likewise, in those days there was no DNA sampling. Forensic science, first widely popularized in Arthur Conan Doyle's Sherlock Holmes books of the 1880s and 1890s, was just becoming a formal discipline. Fingerprinting, trace evidence analysis, document examination, ballistics, and blood typing and grouping would all become acceptable forensic procedures during the Ellis Island era.

Immigration officials in that era did have the telephone and the telegraph. The Atlantic Cable connected Europe to America for telegraph messages, so American diplomats and European officials could contact American immigration authorities about wanted or suspicious people who might be sailing to America.

Because of the development of the long-range radiotelegraph ("wireless") around the turn of the century, ships at sea could receive and send telegraph messages also. In fact, such a ship-to-shore message led to the 1910 capture and hanging of Dr. Hawley Crippen, an American who fled England for Canada aboard a steamship with his young lover after he reportedly killed and dismembered his unfaithful and domineering wife in their London house. Likewise, authorities in Europe or American officials stationed in Europe could use the radiotelegraph to relay messages about criminals trying to escape to America so immigration officials would be ready for them. **(21)**

American immigration officials would use these methods of quick communication to get tips on incoming bad guys. One of the most famous cases, according to Edward Corsi, the commissioner who ran Ellis Island in the early 1930s, a generation after he underwent processing at Ellis Island himself, was that of his former fellow countryman Benito Mussolini. Corsi said Mussolini, before he became dictator of Italy, was in hot water with Italian authorities. He was reportedly contemplating fleeing to America, according to a confidential source. Word of Mussolini's potential escape to America somehow reached the State Department in Washington, Corsi said, and that agency's officials immediately gave immigration officials at Ellis Island and other inspection stations the heads-up. "If he (Mussolini) had attempted to land in the United States," Corsi said, "he would have been detained and examined by a board of special inquiry."

Mussolini might not have needed an interpreter for such a hearing. Corsi, when he was a reporter, had interviewed Mussolini in the 1920s, after he took over Italy. Evidently Il Duce was confident enough in his foreign language skills that he didn't use a single word of Italian in answering fellow Italian Corsi's questions!

Corsi's own father had been a prominent Italian politician. People in Italy elected the elder Corsi to the Italian parliament while he was in exile in Switzerland. On his return to Italy in triumph, Filippo Corsi dropped dead as he was giving his victory speech. Corsi's mother eventually married an army officer, and they decided to try life in America. She became ill after three years in the tenements of New York City and returned to Italy to die. The stepfather raised young Corsi and his brother and sisters in America. **(22)**

Even though technology in that era was not as advanced as it its now, immigration agents were not necessarily dumber than the airline screeners of today who fail to catch weapons being smuggled aboard aircraft despite having metal detectors and X-ray machines.

There were some agents – like good policemen in all eras – who were naturals at finding people who were criminals or other undesirables. Profiling, noticing behavior untypical for a situation, and figuring out when someone is lying by listening for contradictions or improbable statements are skills not dependent upon technology. American officials had the ability to interrogate suspicious aliens or those who knew them. And they did not have anywhere near the interference from professional obstructionist groups and money-sniffing attorneys as immigration officials do today. American officials also had at their disposal the oldest of criminal investigation tools – the informants. European officials and American officials overseas and in America received many tips from informants for reasons ranging from a desire to help to a desire for revenge to a desire for money.

William Williams said, "Criminals and other bad characters, usually bearing no earmarks, seek to enter the country by taking passage in the cabin (second class), and yet the intelligent work of the boarding inspectors often results in their apprehension." Williams noted the tips his agents got were usually valid, "yet some of them are lodged here through spite." He added, "The power of the immigration officials is so summary that foreign authorities desiring to have an alien apprehended often seek to accomplish through the Immigration Service what should be accomplished through extradition proceedings. This office always declines to allow itself to be used in this manner." **(23)**

Europe was authoritarian, America was democratic. Even in alleged democracies like France and England, the government had the legal power to punish dissidents that the American government did not have. (Woodrow Wilson, FDR, LBJ, Nixon, and Clinton and their minions had to break the law to punish dissidents.) British officials routinely jailed Irish patriots who spoke their minds. French officials sentenced Emile Zola to prison on a libel charge for writing "J'accuse," a tract concerning the Dreyfus case, even though what Zola wrote was true. (Zola fled to Britain to avoid prison.) American officials, aware that America became free because Americans rebelled against British rule, would never bar immigrants just because they had committed political offenses in other countries. (Anarchists, Nazis, and Communists would be about the only exceptions to this policy.) Political offenses were not crimes of murder, rape, assault, arson, robbery, theft, dishonesty, or sexual depravity. It would be un-American to turn over immigrants to the officials of another country just because the immigrants had broken some political law that wouldn't stand in The Land of the Free. Williams, by refusing to be the toady of European and Asian governments, was simply affirming America's tolerance for most malcontents.

Williams had no similar qualms about getting information on common criminals so he could have them detained and deported. He thought America's leaders weren't doing enough to ensure the steamship companies checked immigrants and weeded out common criminals instead of making money dumping them in America. He wrote, "As matters stand to-day our Government makes no effort to obtain the valuable information undoubtedly contained in foreign criminal records as to many immigrants who come here. The transportation companies should be required to satisfy the immigration authorities as to each immigrant above a certain age that the criminal records of the locality from which he comes have been searched, and they should also be required to furnish a statement as to what, if anything, has been found therein, and a civil penalty should be imposed for furnishing false information." **(24)**

Williams' idea was a good one on paper, but it would not have worked that well in the Ellis Island era.

There was not the level of co-operation between European officials and American officials that there is today. European leaders still underestimated American power (America did not take part in World War One until 1917, and Woodrow Wilson was no Theodore Roosevelt), and viewed America as a dumping ground for their riffraff. European officials were authoritarian and much more corrupt than American officials, and American officials had a natural distrust of the slimy European officials.

It is true that most immigrants had no criminal record anyway. It was also true that many European government officials <u>wanted</u> *some of their people to leave, especially if they were ethnic minorities or poor people who didn't seem to be able to help their national economies. They would have been only too willing to help these people emigrate, and furnish clean criminal records on these people, even if they had to doctor their records.*

European officials also figured it would be cheaper for them to allow some of their petty criminals to come to America than to jail them, if only they could be assured these criminals would come to America and not somehow hide in Europe or come back. So they might falsely give these losers clean criminal record reports to deceive American authorities.

On the other hand, European officials punished many opponents of their regimes as criminals. Likewise, they oppressed ethnic minorities within their borders. Since many immigrants were refugees from corrupt or oppressive regimes, it would have been impossible for these people to have gotten a favorable report from police authorities in their countries. And this wasn't just countries like Russia or Germany. Officials in Britain and France jailed dissidents also, and sought to extradite those who escaped their clutches.

One last practical difficulty with Williams' idea was that the methods of record keeping and identifications weren't as good then. Criminals themselves could get false documents to hide their true identities. They still do it today, even with supposedly better technology and supposedly better trained agents opposing them.

If an inspector determined an immigrant was a worker coming to the United States on a labor contract that put him in direct competition with American workers, the inspector could pull him or her out of line and refer his or her case to a Board of Special Inquiry on Ellis Island. Likewise, any immigrant the inspector believed was likely to become a public charge (on grounds of anything from having no money, to having subnormal intelligence, to having no definite goals, to having no normal job skills to engaging in begging on a regular basis) could wind up in front of a Board of Special Inquiry.

Any alien who was found out to be a common criminal overseas (as opposed to being a political criminal, who Americans tended to welcome) was definitely going before a Board of Special Inquiry. Any alien involved in an immoral means of making money (such as being a prostitute or a pimp or a madam) or in other immoral behavior (such as being a polygamist – profiling aimed at Moslems and Mormons) could find himself or herself in the line for a Board of Special Inquiry. Someone who was honest enough and dumb enough to admit he or she was an anarchist, a Communist, or any other crackpot who advocated the overthrow of the American form of government would get to know a Board of Special Inquiry better as a detainee trying to argue why they should not have him or her deported from the United States. And finally, people who were caught lying to the inspectors were liable for detention and a hearing in front of a Board of Special Inquiry. The board members would rule on whether to deport the immigrant based on his or her legal fitness, ability to earn a living, and character attributes.

The largest number of aliens who the immigration officials refused entrance to from 1892 through 1924 were people they figured would be drains upon society ("likely to become a public charge," they called it). They barred 196,208 aliens on these grounds. The second largest number of aliens denied entry from 1892 through 1924 were the 72,640 aliens barred from entering the United States because immigration officials determined they were physical or mental defectives. The third largest group of people the immigration officials kept out of America from 1892 through 1924 were the 38,630 aliens deemed to be contract laborers, people who the American working public figured the robber barons were importing to break the wage structure. **(25)**

Officials at Ellis Island "temporarily detained" a large number of aliens. They were presumed qualified to enter the United States, but they needed relatives or friends to contact the officials at Ellis Island and vouch for them, and make arrangements to pick them up, or send them money for train fare. When the relatives or friends did what they needed to do, then the immigrant was free to go. If there was no contact from the immigrant's professed relatives or friends for five days after the immigrant landed, he or she would have to go before the Board of Special Inquiry. Robert Watchorn said his people detained 121,737 immigrants "to be called for by relatives" from July 1906 through June 1907, roughly one out of every eight immigrants who landed in the port of New York. **(26)**

Officials at Ellis Island "medically detained" a fair percentage of immigrants because they had an ailment needing hospitalization. (This was typically about 1% of the number of immigrants processed at Ellis Island any given year.) The immigrant would have to undergo treatment in the hospital on Ellis Island, and had to stay there until a doctor discharged the immigrant from the hospital and cleared him or her medically. When the immigrant recovered, he or she was free to go.

Now that we've covered all the potential ways the agents could detain and send back would-be immigrants, let's give the big picture. Despite the immigrants' fears, and the critiques of self-appointed do-gooders and immigrant societies, the inspectors let in the vast majority of immigrants they questioned.

Philip Cowen, an American-born son of Prussian Jewish immigrants who worked at Ellis Island as an inspector, said in 1907 (the busiest year at Ellis Island, at which a million would-be immigrants landed), there were many days when the Registry Division inspectors checked 5000 or more immigrants, and since there were at most 21 inspectors available for the two shifts during the day, this meant an inspector could count on checking about 250 immigrants on his shift on such a day. **(27)**

A 1909 labor force report by special immigrant inspector Roger O'Donnell noted there were 17 inspectors in the Registry Division, where the primary inspections took place. (This does not count the 14 inspectors serving as members of Special Inquiry Boards, or the 12 inspectors who were part of the Boarding Division, or the 21 other inspectors sprinkled throughout the other divisions on Ellis Island.) Since 580,000 immigrants came through the port of New York in 1908, and the vast majority of these landed at Ellis Island, the average primary inspector in the Registry Division inspected more than 30,000 immigrants that year, an average of more than 100 per day (assuming a six-day workweek and no help from the inspectors in the other divisions). O'Donnell noted the authorities on Ellis Island only asked for four more inspectors. **(28)**

When the inspectors were satisfied immigrants passed all the requirements for gaining entry to the country, they would hand "landing cards" to the immigrants. The inspectors sent them down to the first floor of the Main Building so they could get their belongings and make arrangements to go to their destinations.

We'll pick up this aspect of the immigrants' progress after we talk about the Boards of Special Inquiry.

BOARDS OF SPECIAL INQUIRY

Slightly more than 20 million immigrants came to the United States during the busiest years of the Ellis Island era (1892 through 1924). Of these, more than 14 million immigrants gained entry through the Port of New York; the vast majority of these gained entry through Ellis Island.

Most immigrants who came through Ellis Island and other immigration stations were able to gain entrance into America. But about two percent did not. While this is a small percentage, it means the officials at Ellis Island and other American immigration facilities turned away about 400,000 people in that era.

The members of the Boards of Special Inquiry heard the cases of those who the medical and mental inspectors and/or the registry inspectors (the legal inspectors) believed should be denied entry to the United States. An inspector could pull someone out of line, but he did not have the authority to exclude him. The board members could.

The members of the Boards of Special Inquiry reviewed each inspector's reason for sending each immigrant to them, reviewed the documents pertaining to each immigrant, questioned each immigrant themselves (usually through interpreters, but often enough someone on the board could speak the immigrant's language), and made a quick decision on whether to admit or deport each immigrant detained for possible deportation.

Each immigrant had the right to appeal a board of special inquiry decision to deport him to the commissioner at the immigration station. It was also possible for an immigrant to appeal a board of inquiry decision to the Department of Commerce and Labor (and after the split of the department into two departments, the immigrant could appeal to the Department of Labor). It was also possible for an immigrant to appeal to the Secretary of the Department himself. In reality, appeals to the Department rarely happened, because most immigrants lacked the skill to argue a technical case themselves and the money to hire a lawyer to do it for them.

It was possible for an immigrant to appeal a board of inquiry decision at Ellis Island if he could provide proper evidence that the board members had overlooked when hearing his case, or if evidence turned up later that he didn't have when he landed at Ellis Island. Such evidence, for instance, could include a witness who could come to Ellis Island and vouch for an immigrant, or a telegram from a relative proving the immigrant had a place to go, or proof of other disputed issues. Williams said on his second watch as commissioner there could be from 15 to 70 appeals a day.

Williams said hearing appeals enabled him to see how good a job each of his board members were doing, and also gave him another tool to spot-check the work of his line inspectors. He said he wanted to make sure the board members put the proper questions to immigrants to get the relevant facts of the case so they could make just decisions based on the record and the law. Williams said even if he overturned a board's decision and allowed an immigrant entry to the country, this often meant he had more discretion in hearing an appeal than the board members did in reaching a decision, and not necessarily that his board members had done wrong in denying the immigrant entry in the first place.

"Good board members are not easily found," Williams said. "They must, amongst other things, be intelligent, able to exercise sound judgment and to elicit relevant facts from immigrants and witnesses who are often stupid or deceitful." **(29)**

Each of these boards at Ellis Island made decisions on 50 to 100 immigrant cases a day, Williams said in 1903, depending on the type of case, and the difficulty of communicating with the immigrants before them. (Medical exclusions were open and shut cases; public charge cases were also fairly routine most of the time.) Williams said in 1903 three boards were at work every day, and on days when a larger number of immigrants landed at Ellis Island than usual, a fourth board would work on cases. Williams in 1912 noted that there could be as many as eight boards hearing cases on Ellis Island on given days.

The men on the Boards of Special Inquiry worked at traffic court speed on cases where much more was at stake for the accused than points on a license. Were the board members of the Boards of Special Inquiry "hanging judges?"

In fiscal 1907 (July 1906 through June 30, 1907), Robert Watchorn said his people at Ellis Island processed more than 1,100,000 aliens from 3818 ships, detained 64,510 aliens for a Board of Special Inquiry, and the board members ordered 7408 aliens (including 288 first class or second class passengers) deported. In other words, about 6 percent of the aliens who came through Ellis Island in the previous 12 months had to go before a Board of Special Inquiry, and almost 90 percent of these aliens received permission to enter the United States. **(30)**

In 1911 and again in 1912, more than 600,000 people immigrated to the port of New York, and the vast majority of them underwent processing at Ellis Island. William Williams, in his 1913 annual report, noted the Boards Of Special Inquiry heard more than 60,000 cases a year at Ellis Island. This means about one in ten would-be immigrants had to appear before a Board of Special Inquiry in those years. Dividing 60,000 cases by 300 work days per year meant the Boards of Special Inquiry heard about 200 cases a day.

In 1911, Williams' workers at Ellis Island barred close to 13,000 would-be immigrants. In 1912, they barred about 8000. This means in the two years before Williams' 1913 report, the Boards of Special Inquiry at Ellis Island apparently ruled in favor of the aliens often enough (and aliens' appeals were successful often enough) that more than 80% of the more than 120,000 aliens who appeared before a Board of Special Inquiry in those two years received permission to enter the United States. **(31)**

These numbers imply the men of the Boards of Special Inquiry were fair-minded enough in spite of any prejudices they might have held.

DETENTION AT ELLIS ISLAND

Even though most aliens inspected at Ellis Island received permission to live in America, quite a few of them had to stay at Ellis Island one or more days until immigration officials allowed them to leave.

Quite a few immigrants had to stay in the hospital while they recuperated from their illnesses. Hospitalized immigrants, especially those who were children, often had a relative stay on the island to be near them. About 1% of those who landed at Ellis Island were hospitalized, and perhaps another 1% to 2% of those who landed at Ellis Island had to stay on Ellis Island to wait for their loved ones to get well.

There were many immigrants who had to wait for friends or relatives to pick them up, or for the arrival of money for train tickets, or for instructions from friends or relatives or proof that they had some place to go and friends or relatives to help them. Immigration agents had them telegraph their relatives or friends, or send postcards if they lived in or not too far from New York City. Agents at Ellis Island also tracked down detained immigrants to deliver them telegrams concerning travel arrangements from spouses, relatives, or friends. (Depending on the year, at least 10% of those who landed at Ellis Island were detained for such reasons.)

Then there were those who were being held for cases before the Boards of Special Inquiry, and those who were awaiting evidence that might overturn a Board of Special Inquiry ruling against them. (Depending on the year, anywhere from 5% to 10% of those who landed at Ellis Island were detained for hearings before the Boards of Special Inquiry.)

There were the unfortunates being held for mental evaluation.

And there were those being deported. Some were in the hospital awaiting the end of their treatment. Others were in confinement as criminals or other undesirables. The majority were in less stringent detention; they were being sent back because they were contract workers or people who the authorities deemed would be objects of charity. (About 2% of those who came to Ellis Island and at other immigration stations were detained for deportation.)

The immigration agents on Ellis Island provided food, shelter, security, and surveillance to all of these people.

Temporarily detained immigrants awaiting friends or money or instructions stayed nights under the charge of the Discharging Division (or later, under the charge of the Information Division).

Aliens being held for a board of special inquiry were under the charge of the Deportation Division (later known as the Deporting Division).

"Deferred" aliens (those who had appeared before a board of special inquiry but whose cases were delayed while awaiting further evidence) were under the charge of the Deportation Division.

Excluded adult male aliens (those the boards of inquiry ruled ineligible to enter the United States and were therefore deportable) stayed overnight in the "excluded" room. Excluded and deferred adult female aliens and children stayed overnight in another room. These were under the charge of the Deportation Division.

Other detained aliens without medical problems stayed in the dormitories or barracks on Ellis Island.

Agents segregated aliens being deported by sex and condition (pauperism, physical problems, contract workers). They held criminals being deported separate from the aliens who were unfortunate in their physical or mental or financial condition. The quarantine stations, local hospitals, and the quarantine hospital on Ellis Island (when it opened in 1911) held aliens being deported for contagious diseases.

In Ellis Island's busiest years, it was common to detain as many as 1800 aliens at night on the island. Sometimes the agents had to detain as many as 2100 aliens a night if an especially large number of immigrants had come to Ellis Island. These people needed to be fed, sheltered, and protected. Robert Watchorn said in his 1907 annual report that his staffers <u>averaged</u> detaining 1400 people overnight each night for the entire year. **(32)**

This meant the cooks and kitchen attendants could have served immigrants about 500,000 dinners and another 500,000 or so breakfasts that year. (They also served lunch to immigrants being detained for some reason during the day.) Fines collected from the steamship companies, not taxpayers' dollars, were the main source of money to pay for the food, the equipment, the furniture, the dishes, the utensils, and the salaries of the workers who fed the immigrants being detained.

Most aliens being detained behaved themselves, but there were some being deported who were upset about it and liable to cause trouble. Some would try to escape; others would attack immigration agents. Occasionally despondent aliens would attempt suicide. Also, there were some criminals being detained, and the violent offenders were by nature dangerous to others. Others detained as thieves, beggars, or prostitutes might try to ply their criminal trades while awaiting deportation unless they were kept away from the other immigrants. Thieves in particular required watching and disciplining. Other immigrants being detained on Ellis Island usually didn't have much disposable income to give the beggars. And usually there was not enough privacy for prostitutes to consummate the transactions of their trade with other immigrants. However, they might try to bribe or blackmail immigration officers with sex.

Occasionally there were riots that needed quelling. Riots by Italians, Gypsies, and Moslems on Ellis Island were not uncommon.

There were some immigrants who were coming to America as a group to make trouble or perpetrate evil. The underworld imported a number of immigrants from Sicily and Southern Italy for criminal activities. There were prostitute brokers in Jewish communities in Russia and Eastern Europe who sold Jewish teenage girls and young women – *their own people and sometimes their own kin* – into sexual slavery in the United States. Their prey were only a couple of days from finding out about entry the hard way. Many of the Gypsies were organized thieves and con artists. And organized beggars from the Middle East were a nuisance to many cities and towns in America in the early 1900s.

There were some immigrants were used to committing acts of violence and other unsociable acts in their own countries. Some immigrants were thieves or bullies who hadn't been caught. Some of them had criminal records but were able to escape detection as criminals because employees of the steamship lines that brought them to America had not made them prove they had clean records when they bought tickets.

And immigrants had the same kinds of flaws as people in America or anywhere else, thanks to the fallen nature of humanity that none of us is exempt from. Many immigrants had trouble behaving themselves in their homelands, and local officials all across Europe convinced many of them that getting a fresh start in America was a viable alternative to a life of crime and jail at home.

Guards would have to keep these scumbag would-be immigrants under control. Many women and children were frightened and needed protection. Despite the segregation of immigrants by sex (and younger boys with mothers also), if there weren't guards and matrons present, some aliens would undoubtedly try to sexually assault women, teenage girls, or young girls or boys.

AFTER INSPECTION

After the immigrants passed inspection, most of them were free to leave Ellis Island. Families gathered, and groups of people traveling together gathered after everyone in their family or group got through inspection. Usually this would be on the first floor of the main building, where the baggage office, the railroad office and lobby, the waiting room, and the "New York Room" were.

If a family member had to wait because he or she was sick and was being medically detained, the family would make arrangements to pick up the sick family member later, or send money for the person's train fare to rejoin them.

After passing inspection, the immigrants could exchange their European money for American money at the day's official exchange rates for a small charge at the money exchange office. Those immigrants needing to send a telegram could do so at one of the telegraph offices. Telegrams coming to immigrants from relatives and friends with instructions came through one of these telegraph offices.

Those immigrants needing railroad tickets to other cities could buy them at the railroad ticket office. Some immigrants needed ship tickets if they were sailing to another port on America's eastern seaboard. They could buy these tickets at Ellis Island also. Roughly two-thirds of the immigrants bought tickets from one of the railroad lines or one of the Atlantic Coast steamship lines.

The immigrants would get their luggage from the Baggage Room, or make arrangements to have their luggage put on the proper trains or ships.

Immigrants going directly to New York City didn't have to worry about train tickets. Once they were free to go, they would gather in the "New York Room," and then board a ferry to Manhattan.

It was a little different for the train passengers. Each railroad company had a holding area for its immigrant passengers in the railroad ticket office lobby or a nearby waiting room. The railroad company agents would ferry their westbound and southbound customers to a railroad terminal at Jersey City or Hoboken, New Jersey. Immigrants would board the proper trains here.

Immigrants going by ship to other East Coast cities would wait for their rides elsewhere. They would take a small boat to the ship that would take them to the East Coast port they wanted to reach.

Roughly one-third of the immigrants went through the door out of the New York Room marked "PUSH TO NEW YORK", and took the Ellis Island ferryboat to

Lower Manhattan. Many of these people would settle in New York City. Immigrants with train tickets to towns in New England or upstate New York would also go to the "New York Room," take the ferryboat to Manhattan and get on the proper trains in Manhattan.

Friends and relatives could meet incoming immigrants at Ellis Island and escort them out. Agents on Ellis Island would question these people closely to make sure they were the people they said they were, and that they could prove their ties of blood or friendship to the people they came for. The immigrants themselves had to verify the callers were their friends or relatives before the immigration agents would let them go in their company.

Unaccompanied men could leave Ellis Island on their own, without having to have anyone come for them or without having to have any telegram confirm they had a place to go to.

Likewise, families with men, and groups of people traveling together with men in the groups could leave Ellis Island on their own. Ellis Island agents figured they ought to be able to protect themselves.

It was different for women and children who had no men accompanying them. Immigration officials temporarily detained these women and children and insisted they contact spouses, relatives, or friends by mail or telegraph. They insisted on the spouses, relatives, or friends verifying they were coming for their women and children, or that they were sending train tickets and money, or instructions on how to get to the places they needed to get to if the women and children had enough money.

Immigration agents tagged children younger than 15 who were unaccompanied by adults with linen tags spelling out the name and address of the relative they were going to. They also telegraphed the relatives so they would be at the train station to meet the children. Only then would they release these children to the railroad company agents.

Immigration agents also temporarily detained unaccompanied women and children going to New York City or someplace nearby. They would have to wait for husband or fiancé or relative or friend to call for them at Ellis Island. **(33)**

Sometimes charitable organizations agreed to sponsor single women immigrants. Catholic nuns, Protestant ministers, Jewish groups, and others agreed to sponsor these women and ensure they found housing and work that was not illegal or immoral. (Sometimes these organizations even put up cash bonds certifying that these women would not become public charges.) These groups daily had to account for these girls and women to the authorities at Ellis Island. **(34)**

If a man coming to pick up a woman at Ellis Island said he was her husband, she had to identify him and they had to have proof of marriage. If they didn't have such proof, then the officials would have the man and woman undergo a civil marriage ceremony at Ellis Island. If a man coming to pick up a woman at Ellis Island said he was her fiancé, then the officials would have the man and woman undergo a civil marriage ceremony at Ellis Island as well. Of course, the woman would have to consent to undergo this ritual with this man!

The authors of these policies did not intend to demean women or demean religious marriages. Immigration officials feared for the safety of women, because there were many predators in organized crime able and willing to steer them into prostitution or other degrading situations against their wills. There were also many unorganized swine who would sexually abuse unaccompanied foreign women and girls if they thought they could get away with it.

A woman could refuse to go with a purported fiancé or relative and the immigration agents would be there to protect her. Many times women needed such protection.

And as for the religious issue? Fiancés and fiancées who were religious could still refrain from consummating their marriage (having sex with each other) until they married according to the laws of their religion, in front of a priest, rabbi, or minister. Immigration officers by and large were members of religions themselves. They just wanted to make sure alleged fiances were who they said they were.

Frank Martocci, an Italian immigrant who was an interpreter and an inspector at Ellis Island from the 1890s until the 1930s, said, "We could not let a woman with her children out on the streets looking for her husband. This also applied to all alien females, minors, and others who did not have money, but were otherwise eligible and merely waiting for friends or relatives." **(35)**

The immigration officials could care less about the alleged equality of the sexes. (Remember, American women didn't have the right to vote in all states until 1920.) Their job was to protect immigrants as well as screen them. They knew it was easier for the unscrupulous to victimize immigrant women than immigrant men, so they put appropriate safeguards in place to protect them.

There was an area where immigration agents questioned callers coming for immigrants to verify they were legitimate. Immigrants, usually women and children, waited in a large waiting room nearby. When the immigration officials were sure the callers were telling the truth, they would bring out the immigrants they called for. The caller, most often an immigrant husband who had come to America alone some time earlier and had worked to bring his family over, would meet his wife and children at this post when the agents brought them out of the waiting room. Engaged couples would also reunite there. As you can imagine, the overflow of joy at these reunitings brought laughter, tears, and emotional hugs and kisses. The area naturally got the nickname "Kissing Post" or "Kissing Gate."

Now you have an idea of how it was to be an immigrant going through Ellis Island. If any of these people were ancestors of yours, thank God for their willingness to come to this great land!

Now you also have an idea of how American leaders and their subordinates did their jobs in an era when American leaders were not ashamed to put America first ... in an era when the public demanded such loyalty to our nation and people. Pray to God for the return of this type of public spirit, and do what you can to further it in your circles!

END NOTES

1. Statistics on immigration come from the immigration tables of the Historic Research Study, Statue of Liberty – Ellis Island National Monument, by Harlan D. Unrau. Page 490 of Unrau's study contains Williams' quoted statements.

2. Information on the workers of Ellis Island comes from William Williams' 1903 report "Organization of the U.S. Immigration Station at Ellis Island, New York," and his 1912 report "Ellis Island: Its Organization and Some of Its Work." The Unrau study reprinted the former (pages 312-383) from the General Immigration Files RG 85, and the latter (pages 489-543) from his papers (New York Public Library). Specific pages referenced included pages 21-28 and 31-33 of the 1903 report and pages 5-12, 14-21, 28-31, 37-43, and 45-53 of the 1912 report. Other sources include "Summary of Labor Force Report by Special Immigrant Inspector Roger O'Donnell" dated 4/15/1909 (pages 397-399 in the Unrau study), and Barry Moreno's book Encyclopedia of Ellis Island (pages 40-41, and 56-57).

3. Staten Island residents, tired of losing loved ones who contracted yellow fever from immigrants being isolated at a quarantine hospital in their neighborhood, burned it down in 1858. As a result, New York authorities had Swinburne Island and Hoffman Island built from landfill nearby in Lower New York Bay to handle quarantine cases. After the heyday of the Ellis Island Era, the U.S. Public Health Service took over the islands in 1924. The U.S. Maritime Service took over the islands in 1938 and used them for bases to train merchant marine sailors and to put up artillery, submarine nets and other items to bolster the Port of New York's harbor defenses during World War Two.

After the U.S. Maritime Service stopped using the islands, New York scavenger thieves broke out all the building windows and stripped out all the usable fixtures by the early 1950s. The U.S. National Park Service now controls the islands as part of Gateway National Recreation Area. Ironically, these two man-made islands are now bird refuges off-limits to the public.

Some information on Hoffman and Swinburne islands come from 5/7/198 and 8/25/1951 New Yorker articles, a May/June 1997 Ancestry Magazine article by Rafael Guber, and an article in the March 1944 Mast Magazine, courtesy of the U.S. Merchant Marine.

Other information about the facilities of Swinburne Island and Hoffman Island include a 11/27/1910 New York Times article titled "A Little Island Near New York Peopled With Babies,"

a 9/6/1879 Harper's Weekly article called "Quarantine at New York," a 3/19/1905 Washington Post article, the General Laws of New York State 1900, Article VI, Sections 80-91, and a 5/27/1934 New York Times obituary of Dr. Doty. Reprints of these articles came from Cathy Horn's website "The Forgotten of Ellis Island." It is a nostalgic and tearjerker site well worth your time to check. (Especially read her article "My Search for Apollonia Speigel," about how she located the grave of a child from Hungary who died in quarantine on Hoffman Island in 1910. Little Apollonia would have been Cathy Horn's aunt had she survived.) Cathy Horn also reprinted an article about Dr. Doty's work from the New York Times issue of 10/4/1908 titled "How Plagues are Watched the World Around."

Further details of medical inspection of immigrants aboard ships comes from the Unrau study (pages 590-593).

4. Dr. Mullan's comments are in the Unrau study (pages 853-855).

5. Statistics on medical exams come from the Unrau study (page 916).

6. Information on how immigration officials treated those with medical problems comes from the Unrau study (pages 324, 584-587, 591-593, 598, 608, 612-613, 634-635, 656, 668, and 671-672).

7. The observer's quote comes from the Unrau study (page 549).

8. Statistics on those rejected for medical reasons come from the Unrau study.

9. Dr. Mullan's comments on mental health screenings come from the Unrau study (pages 854-865).

10. Statistics on those barred for mental health reasons and the cost benefits to the United States of these examinations comes from the Unrau study (page 594).

11. Information on the suicides and Watchorn's response comes from the Unrau study (page 597).

12. Statistics on the workload of medical people comes from the Unrau study (pages 186, 239, 601, 602, 608-609, 612-613, 669, and 921). Information on the wards in the contagious disease facility comes from Encyclopedia of Ellis Island (pages 40-41)

13. The "29 Questions" come from the form "List or Manifest of Alien Passengers for the United States Immigration Officer at Port of Arrival."

14. The law in question is the Act of February 5, 1917 (39 Statutes at Large 874-898).

15. The observer's comments are in the Unrau study (pages 548-549).

16. La Guardia's comments come from his book The Making of an Insurgent (pages 66-67).

17. The sources for William Williams' quotes on his unofficial $25 per immigrant yardstick are his Annual Report dated 8/16/1909 in his papers (New York City Public Library) and the Unrau study (pages 251-252).

18. The source of Baker's comment is Edward Corsi's book In the Shadow of Liberty (pages 123-124).

19. The source of the observer's comments is Frederick Haskin's 1913 book The Immigrant: An Asset and a Liability (pages 75-81). The excerpt appeared in the Unrau study (page 551).

20. The source of Tito's claim he almost emigrated to America is Louis Adamic's book The Eagle and the Roots (pages 109-110).

21. Information on the wireless assisted arrest of Dr. Crippen comes from Crimes of the 20th Century (page 53). People in Crippen's family tree in America and some independent forensic scientists recently cast doubt on his guilt. They blamed sloppy British police work and prosecutor work for his conviction and hanging. This book doesn't speculate on his guilt or innocence, but points out the communication technology was available to have him nabbed. And the wireless was also available to authorities to check on travelers to America or receive warnings about them.

22. Corsi's accounts of Mussolini come from his book In the Shadow of Liberty (pages 28 and 229).

23. Williams' remarks about tracking European criminals and declining to short-cut the extradition process come from page 19 of his 1912 report "Ellis Island: Its Organization and Some of Its Work." The excerpt appeared in the Unrau study (page 507).

24. Williams' comments about crime come from his 1912 Annual Report. The excerpt appeared in the Unrau study (page 57).

British officials today still demand the extradition of Irish patriots who are using the same methods in Ulster as the American patriots did to fight British rule. After the jihadist London bombings of 2005, British officials reached out to Moslems in their country, including the sizeable Moslem criminal and terrorist element. British officials never made that sort of gesture to the Irish under their control.

25. Statistics on excluded aliens comes from the Unrau study. I did some math to come up with the totals.

26. Watchorn's detention statistics come from the Unrau study (page 239).

27. Cowen's comments on inspector workload are in the Unrau study (pages 247-248).

28. "Summary of Labor Force Report by Special Immigrant Inspector Roger O'Donnell" dated 4/15/1909 is the source for O'Donnell's remarks. This report is in the Unrau study (pages 397-399).

29. Williams' comments about boards of special inquiry come from pages 32, 35, and 36 of his 1912 report "Ellis Island: Its Organization and Some of Its Work." The pages appeared in the Unrau study (pages 520, 523, and 524).

30. Watchorn's statistics come from the Unrau study (page 239).

31. Other information on boards of special inquiry comes from the Unrau study (pages 270, 334, 522). Page 334 is a reprint of Page 23 of Williams' 1903 report "Organization of the U.S. Immigration Station at Ellis Island, New York."

32. Watchorn's statistics on detentions and other statistics come from the Unrau study (pages 239 and 533). Page 533 is a reprint of Page 45 of Williams' 1912 report "Ellis Island: Its Organization and Some of Its Work."

33. Information about agents detaining unaccompanied women and children for their own safety comes from Williams' 1903 report "Organization of the U.S. Immigration Station at Ellis Island, New York" (page 21). The page appeared in the Unrau study (page 332).

34. Information about the charitable organization's aid of single female immigrants comes from Williams' 1903 report "Organization of the U.S. Immigration Station at Ellis Island, New York" (page 30). The page appeared in the Unrau study (page 341). Charity works better when it is private and personal than when it is governmental and impersonal.

35. Martocci's quote comes from In the Shadow of Liberty (page 77).

THE DEMISE OF ELLIS ISLAND

Immigration from Europe peaked before World War One, fell off during the war, then started to peak again. Americans were less friendly to the tide of Europeans in the 1920s because of the war and the fallout on American society related to the war. They moved to restrict immigration. The resulting lower flow of Europeans to America from the mid 1920s to the mid 1950s would lead to the shutdown of Ellis Island as an immigration station.

Immigration to the United States was high until the World War One years. Immigration dropped dramatically, from 1.22 million in 1914 to 327,000 in 1915, to 299,000 in 1916, and to 296,000 in 1917, the year America entered the war. Immigration bottomed at 111,000 in 1918, the final year of the war.

The British navy bottled up the German passenger ship fleet. The German navy sunk British and French and Russian and Italian passenger ships. It was too dangerous to cross in a passenger ship. The war trapped millions of people in place in Europe. Many of the most likely immigrants wound up drafted and dead. Millions of civilians died from starvation and disease. Many were killed when they got in the way of armies.

In 1919, there were 141,000 immigrants to the United States, (and only 25,000 from Europe) largely because American ships were busy transporting American soldiers home from Europe and many British and French ships were taking colonial troops home, because many British and French and Italian merchant ships were sunk in World War One, because the German merchant fleet was due to be delivered to the Allies, because the former subject peoples of Austria-Hungary were now independent, and because Soviet authorities forbade emigration.

But immigration started to return to prewar levels in 1920. In 1920, there were 430,000 immigrants to the United States. About 250,000 of these came directly from Europe, 90,000 came from or through Canada (many of whom were European nationals), and about 50,000 came from Mexico.

In 1921, more than 800,000 immigrants flooded into the United States. About 650,000 of these came directly from Europe, and of these, more than 220,000 came from Italy. Poland was in second place with 95,000 immigrants, and Britain, Czechoslovakia, Spain, Greece, Ireland, and Yugoslavia followed with between 20,000 and 30,000 immigrants each. The British had high unemployment, and all of the other countries were experiencing warfare or internal unrest in addition to unemployment problems. More than 70,000 came from or through Canada (many of whom were European nationals), and about 30,000 came from Mexico. **(1)**

World War One brought a mess of problems to the people of America. Four million men had to enter the Armed Services during the war. More than 110,000 of them died in combat or of disease or of their wounds. Roughly 240,000 others were wounded; many were blinded or crippled or mentally damaged for life.

American businessmen entangled the nation financially with Britain and France. President Woodrow Wilson and his top people were Anglophiles. American food, fuel, ordnance, and credit kept Britain, France, and Italy in the war. When the German high command moved to choke off the British from theses items by resorting to unrestricted submarine warfare, Congress declared war in April 1917.

Once America was in the war, Woodrow Wilson and his underlings incited ethnic hatred against Americans of German ancestry, and to a lesser extent to Americans of Irish ancestry. The first group was not happy American businessmen and politicians were aiding the Allies who were fighting the Germans; the second group was not happy American businessmen and politicians were aiding the British who oppressed the Irish. Wilson got laws enacted to restrict freedom of speech and protest. He and his people soon branded certain union officials and many other critics of his regime as traitors and subversives. His attorney general started a Red Scare that was largely unjust to aid his own quest for celebrity and power. The Wilson regime and many state and local prosecutors and judges sent many innocent people (and a few actual miscreants) to prison for political offenses.

Wilson was a Progressive. The Progressives were all too often elitists who thought they knew better what was good for other people. They claimed to stand for justice and efficiency, but they really stood for increased government interference in people's lives. They had a lot of disdain for the working people of America, especially the non-WASP working people of America.

Wilson as a tolerant Progressive didn't really like blacks either. He extended segregation to the entire federal government. The suffragettes won the right to vote during Wilson's second term; they also used anti-black bigotry to get members of Congress and the state legislatures to give them the vote. White suffragettes claimed white women were smarter, purer, and more numerous than black men (who had the right to vote) and black women (who didn't) put together. They rebuffed black suffragettes who tried to work with them.

Progressives, suffragettes, and prohibitionists also managed to enact Prohibition during Wilson's second term. They used the need for food for troops and refugees during World War One as an excuse to cut down on, then ban, the making of beer, wine, and booze. This criminally negligent push for Prohibition strengthened organized criminals, because they moved to fill Americans' need for alcohol and made hundreds of millions of dollars in the process. The rotgut they peddled poisoned thousands of people. The money they made trafficking alcohol allowed them to buy judges and politicians to thwart law enforcement against booze-running and their other enterprises, like prostitution and female trafficking, freight hijacking, protection, loan sharking, numbers, money laundering, and murder for hire. Among the American people, the silly Prohibition laws led to diminished respect fo the law and for those who made and enforced the laws.

During the years after the war, Americans saw some terrible race riots, large numbers of strikes, large numbers of organized crime killings, and some horrible cases of foreign anarchist violence. They also started to learn the truth about World War One ... that it was a war to make the world safe for British and French imperialism.

Americans became disgusted with the ingratitude, lying, and thievery of their British and French and Italian allies. Americans lost more than 100,000 of their bravest men, they were stuck with a bill of billions of dollars for the American war effort, and they inherited a debt of another $10 billion because their European allies welshed on $10 billion worth of war debt to the United States government. Meanwhile the British and French and Italians scrambled for more colonies and extorted hundreds of millions of dollars out of the peoples of Eastern Europe.

Americans found out the hard way European leaders were far more crooked than even their own venal politicos. Americans didn't want to be responsible for Europe's problems.

One of the reminders of Europe's problems was the constant stream of immigrants. A high proportion of them seemed to be unpatriotic and prone to labor violence or political violence or organized crime. Regulating immigration was one thing Americans could do something about fairly easily. Most Americans in the 1920s favored fewer immigrants and more reinforcement of the American way of life. The politicians saw which way the wind was blowing and took steps to drastically reduce immigration.

Their first attempt was the Quota Act of 1921. After Warren Harding won the 1920 election, members of the House of Representatives and the Senate, in the "lame duck" session before Inauguration Day, passed a one-year quota bill that would limit maximum immigration of each nationality to 3% of foreign-born members of that nationality who were living in the United States in 1910.

In practice, this bill, if signed into law, meant Americans would allow about 200,000 to come from western and northern Europe, and about 155,000 to come from southern and eastern Europe. This was aimed at lowering the percentages of Italians, Poles, and Jews coming into the country. The overall limit of 355,000 immigrants per year from Europe was lower than the number of legal immigrants who entered the country from Europe in every year between 1900 and 1914.

Members of Congress presented the bill to Woodrow Wilson on February 26, 1921. (Wilson had to leave the White House for good on March 4, 1921. Before 1937, Inauguration Day was March 4.) Wilson, who suffered a breakdown and then a stroke in 1919 while trying to peddle to Americans the fatally flawed World War One peace treaties and the League of Nations (the impotent predecessor of the anti-American United Nations), was now incapacitated in everything but his own selfish ego. He was bitter because of the public's repudiation of his dream of the League of Nations, and he was angry because the Democrats would not renominate him for a shot at a third term in 1920. He vetoed the bill with a pocket veto.

But the congressmen were not overly perturbed. They passed the bill again and president Warren Harding signed it into law anyway three months later, on May 19, 1921. It went into effect June 3, 1921 as an addition to existing American immigration laws. This bill would become known as the Quota Act of 1921 (aka 42 Statutes at Large 5-7).

The Quota Act of 1921 had several problems, and immigrants kept coming in larger-than-expected numbers. So members of Congress devised another law to reduce immigration.

The new immigration law they drafted was known formally as the Immigration Act of May 26, 1924, and was more commonly known as the Immigration Act of 1924. This law, which Congress passed and president Calvin Coolidge signed into law, proposed to limit maximum immigration of each nationality to 2% of foreign-born members of that nationality who were living in the United States in 1890. (Harding died in office in 1923, so Coolidge became president.)

This would be at first much more discriminatory toward the Italians, Jews, Poles, and others from Eastern Europe and Southern Europe than the Quota Act of 1921 had been. It limited total immigration from around the world (except for the independent countries of the Western Hemisphere) to about 165,000 per year.

This proportion was to last for three years, and then starting in July 1927, the total number of quota immigrants could only be 150,000. However, starting in July 1927, maximum immigration of each nationality would be 2% of foreign-born members of that nationality who were living in the United States in 1920.

This would be much more fair to Italians, Jews, Poles, and other would-be immigrants from southern Europe and eastern Europe.

They exempted most people from the Middle East and Iran as not being Asians from the "barred zone" spelled out in the Immigration Act of 1917. (The 1882 Chinese Exclusion Act and the 1907 "Gentlemen's Agreement" with Japan put a lid on immigration from China, Taiwan, Korea, and Japan.) However, the quotas limited the number of Turkish immigrants to under 200 a year, the number of "Syrians" (essentially Lebanese and some Syrians – the French ran both lands as a colony under one government) to fewer than 600 a year, the number of people from "Palestine" (essentially Israel and Jordan, run by the British as colonies) to 100 a year, and the number of people from "Hedjaz" (the Arabian Peninsula), "Mesopotamia" (Iraq) and "Persia" (Iran) to 100 a year.

The 1917 law had added exclusions against unskilled laborers from most of Asia (besides unskilled Chinese laborers, who were already banned). The law established a "barred zone," which was "west of the 110th meridian of longitude east from Greenwich and east of the 50th meridian of longitude east from Greenwich and south of the 50th parallel of latitude north ....," from which they would allow no immigrant laborers. In essence, they barred non-white-collar immigration from India (which at that time also included present-day Pakistan and Bangladesh), Ceylon (Sri Lanka), the small Himalayan countries, the interior of China, Mongolia, Burma, Thailand (then known as Siam), Indochina (Laos, Cambodia, and Vietnam), the Malay States (Malaysia and Singapore), Afghanistan, the eastern part of the Arabian Peninsula, and what we have known as "Soviet Central Asia" – Kazakhstan, Uzbekistan, and the other khanistans collectively called "Turkestan" in geography books and atlases.

Ironically, the congressmen did not forbid immigration from the lands the Turks controlled – present-day Iraq and Kuwait, much of the Arabian peninsula, present-day Israel, Jordan, Lebanon, Syria, Turkey, and some of Armenia. Most of these areas were full of Moslems, but there was not much immigration from these lands, except for the Greeks and Armenians and Christians from Lebanon and Syria and Assyria (today's northern Iraq), who the Turks were running out.

By cutting a rectangle into the globe bounded by the 50th and 64th meridians in the west and east, and the 24th and 38th parallels in the south and north and exempting the people of this area from the Asian Barred Zone, the congressmen allowed immigration from present-day Iran – almost totally a Moslem land -- to continue. (Immigration from the land, then known as Persia, was also a trickle in those days.)

The 1917 law also forbade non-white-collar immigration from the many East Indian Islands (present-day Indonesia, New Guinea, and Timor) and Pacific islands west of the 160th meridian and between the 20th parallel above the Equator and the 10th parallel below the Equator not under United States control. The law allowed immigration from Australia and New Zealand, two countries south of this area whose people were predominantly of British or Irish blood.

Laborers from the British-controlled Indian subcontinent had been coming to Canada, which at the time was under much more British control than it would be after World War One. British leaders were upset Australian, New Zealand, and South African politicians in the British Empire banned immigration from the Indian subcontinent. They wanted to prevent nationalists in the Indian subcontinent from having another reason to act against British colonial rule. So they leaned on the Canadian government to allow immigration from the Indian subcontinent. The "Hindoos" (and Sikhs and Moslems) from the Indian subcontinent undercut Canadian workers. Finally the Canadian government restricted their immigration to Canada in the early 1900s. Some from the Indian subcontinent then started filtering across the Canadian border into America. The American people didn't want these people from the Indian subcontinent undercutting Americans either.

America operated the Philippines and some other islands in the western Pacific Ocean like Guam, so this law didn't apply to Filipinos or the natives of the other American-run islands. Filipinos and other such native islanders were able to emigrate to the United States. Most of the people of the Philippines and Guam were Catholics; Spanish missionaries had evangelized the people of these islands.

Commissioner General of Immigration W.W. Husband noted he understood the 1924 law (aka 43 Statutes at Large 153-169) allowed his people at Ellis Island and elsewhere to admit only whites and blacks. In his annual report for 1924 he noted, "Included in the category of persons ineligible to citizenship are the Chinese, Japanese, East Indians, and other peoples indigenous to Asiatic countries and adjacent islands."

The 1924 immigration law also aimed at diminishing Canada's business of laundering Europeans for export to America. The law closed the loophole allowing a European to evade the quota on his or her homeland by living in the Western Hemisphere for five years. People born in Europe would count against the quotas for their homelands regardless of where they were living when they decided to come to America.

In 1922, 310,000 immigrants had gained entry to America; 210,000 of them had done so through the port of New York and 100,000 had done so at other stations. Of the immigrants, 47,000 listed Canada as their place of last permanent residence. In 1923,

523,000 immigrants had gained entry to America; 295,000 of them had done so through the port of New York and 228,000 had done so at other immigration stations. Of the immigrants, 117,000 listed Canada as their place of last permanent residence. In 1924, 707,000 immigrants had gained entry to America; 316,000 of them had done so through the port of New York and 391,000 had done so at other immigration stations. Of the immigrants, 201,000 listed Canada as their place of last permanent residence.

Was the drop in immigrants coming to Ellis Island as a percentage of the national total a coincidence? Was the rise in immigrants at other immigration stations and the rise in declared Canadian residents due to less-thorough screening of those who claimed Canadian residency at other immigration stations?

In 1925, the first full year the Immigration Act of 1924 would be in place, 294,000 immigrants would gain entry to America; 137,000 of them would do so through the port of New York and 157,000 would do so at other immigration stations. Of the immigrants, 103,000 would list Canada as their place of last permanent residence. The Canada trend reversed. **(2)**

Congress did not discriminate against immigration from Canada, Mexico, Latin America, or natives of free countries of the West Indies. Congressmen realized men and women from Quebec or Ontario or Mexico or Cuba or Brazil or Argentina were more desirable immigrants because of similarities in religion and culture. There was no quota on people from these places (other than the total number of immigrants American officials were going to allow into the country in any given year), and they only had to show they were admissible when processed.

One very reasonable provision of this law was a proviso that would place the burden of proving admissibility on immigrants. Before this time, the U.S. government had the burden of proving a would-be immigrant was inadmissible.

Another very good provision of this law made each would-be immigrant get an American consular official in their country of origin grant him or her an entry visa. This meant immigrants would receive proper legal vetting and proper medical inspection to verify they were eligible to enter the United States – pending immigration station inspection – when they arrived. This also meant very few immigrants would be sent home because they failed some legal or medical test for admission to the United States.

The law also had a provision enabling the limiting of the number of visas American officials could hand out to would-be immigrants. This was a nod to the thinking of people like then-Ellis Island commissioner Henry Curran, who argued Congress should allow U.S. consuls around the globe to hand out only enough immigrant visas to meet the quotas for the countries they were stationed in.

The lawmakers put a fine of up to $10,000 and a prison term of up to five years into the law as punishment for those who forged immigration visas or permits. They ordered the same penalties for aliens using other aliens' visas to get into the United States, aliens who sold or gave their visas to others to allow them to sneak into America, and aliens who lied to American officials to gain entry into America.

In the law, the congressmen and senators prescribed a $1000 fine per alien for ship companies whose ships brought in aliens without unexpired visas or with falsified nonquota visas. A nonquota visa usually applied to Latin American, Caribbean island, and Canadian natives. (Some nonquota immigrants were wives or minor unmarried children of immigrants of citizens. Others were clergy members, college professors, and college students.) It was usually fairly easy for shipping company officers to determine if someone carrying a nonquota visa deserved to have one.

The lawmakers also put into the law a provision fining shipping companies $1000 for each excludible alien seaman an officer of one of their ships allowed to go ashore or failed to detain aboard ship or failed to prevent from escaping due to lax ship security. (This didn't count if the sailor in question required medical treatment unavailable aboard ship.)

The Congressmen raised the penalty on shipping companies to $1000 per seriously diseased or disabled person found in inspection in America for bringing such persons to America if a competent doctor in Europe or elsewhere outside of America could have detected the disease or disability. They also applied this fine to shipping companies for negligence or indifference in screening out the mentally defective from the would-be immigrants. The lawmakers added a $250 fine per mentally or physically defective person as an extra fine to the $1000 already being assessed. The law also called for jumping the fines on shippers who negligently or indifferently brought in aliens from the Asian Barred Zone or inadmissible illiterates from anywhere to $1000 per inadmissible Asian or illiterate. The lawmakers ordered the custom collectors at American ports to take enough money from the shippers to pay for the return of the inadmissible aliens in the same class to the same port as they came from.

Among quota immigrants, the Immigration Act of 1924 gave preference to immigrants "skilled in agriculture" and their families. Although this law did supersede the Quota Act of 1921, the authors of the law intended it to add to rather than replace the Immigration Act of 1917 (the law that put the Asian Barred Zone into place) and other immigration laws still on the books. **(3)**

Some controversy surrounded the law. The bill's authors aimed at dropping the numbers of all immigrants. Since the law favored immigration from the WASP nations of Europe, people of Italian, Jewish, Polish, Greek and other ethnic ancestries from southern and eastern Europe felt demeaned. Many immigrant societies and some ethnic groups complained about the numbers of immigrants to be allowed entry to the United States.

On the inherent fitness of WASP immigrants compared to other European immigrants, the immigrant pressure groups had a point. Based on the behavior of the leading people of their homelands, it was naive to think British and German and Scandinavian and Low Country immigrants would be the most prone to be democratic. Britain's leaders were ruthless colonialists and liars, and naval militarists besides. The practice of piracy was ingrained in too many Britons. Too many Germans believed in authoritarian rule because they were natural followers, and they took back seat to nobody in terms of militarism. The Scandinavians and Low Country people submitted to rule by kings and queens also. Conversely, most Italian, Slavic, and Jewish immigrants were Christians (though not Protestants) or Jews. They were not at odds with the Judeo-Christian ethical underpinning of American society.

The quota system's unracist proponents argued America had a certain ethnic mix, and should keep it. They argued quite rationally that people from Asia and the Moslem countries did not agree with most Americans on religion or customs, and would be very hard to assimilate. They did not make this same argument against people from Canada, Latin America or the West Indies because most people from these areas adhered to one of the Christian religions, and most had some exposure to American ideas. Other backers of the law believed Americans had taken in a huge amount of foreigners over the previous three decades, and Americans would need time to assimilate these newcomers into the American way of life.

Millions of honest men and women felt threatened by the rise of organized crime in the 1920s. Mafiosi from Italy, Jewish gangsters in New York whose roots were in Russia or eastern Europe, and Chinese tong wars did nothing to allay their fears. The lawlessness of these individuals gave their countrymen a black eye in the mind of the American public and made many an unbigoted person support severe limits on immigration.

Of course there were those who supported immigration limits and quotas for reasons of racism. The Ku Klux Klan, endorsed by president Woodrow Wilson, peaked at roughly four to six million members in the 1920s, including many suffragettes.

The Klansmen were white Anglo-Saxon Protestants. Since the nation in the early 1920s had about 110 million people, this meant possibly as many as one household in six across the country had a bedsheet-wearing Kluxer in it. (Assuming some wives of Kluxers were in the Women's Ku Klux Klan, the actual percentage was still probably above one household in seven nationwide.) The Klan was almost as strong in certain parts of the Midwest as it was in the South. The Klan was powerful in other states like Oregon, where they tried to destroy the Catholic school system in that state by pushing into the books a law that required children to attend only public schools. (The Supreme Court threw out the unconstitutional law in 1925 with their ruling on the Pierce vs. Society of Sisters of the Holy Names of Jesus and Mary case.)

The Klan had friends in places even higher than the state governments of the South and other states like Indiana and Oregon. Woodrow Wilson watched the pro-Ku Klux Klan film "Birth of A Nation" at a private screening in the White House in 1915. He said of the hate flick, "It is like writing history with lightning, and my only regret is that it is all so terribly true." **(4)**

The service of many blacks in World War One and the factory jobs that were opening up in the Northeast and the Midwest caused many blacks to leave the South. This led to anti-black race riots in a number of cities up North, and to a rise in Klan membership north of the Ohio River and the Mason-Dixon line. The Klan's leaders expanded their anti-black message of hatred to Catholics and Jews also. This gave many Midwestern and Western bigots who couldn't hate blacks in person some targets to attack in their towns. Immigrants were mostly Catholic or Jewish, so they were instant targets to Klan members.

There were millions of more racists who didn't become Klan members simply because they were not joiners.

Beyond these garden-variety knuckleheads were those who were truly evil sociopaths – the eugenicists. Eugenicism was a social disease too many American elitists caught from interfacing with their infected British and German counterparts. Of course, racism was institutionalized in America's laws against blacks and American Indians, and in practice against Hispanics. But eugenicism – the belief in breeding of human beings from "the fittest" parents and the sterilization of the "least fit" – was an even worse doctrine that came from the imperialistic circles of the British Empire, and in the cities of defeated imperial Germany, because it justified the "birth control" and enslavement of perceived weaker people and in many cases the extermination of these people once they were deemed incapable of being useful to the elites. This pathological viewpoint would lead to continued British oppression of black and yellow people around the globe, and to Hitler's wars upon Slavs and Jews and the handicapped.

Margaret Sanger, the common-law mother of Planned Parenthood, was the most effective of the eugenicists. In her 1920 book Woman and the New Race, the genteel bigot Sanger noted, "Among our more than 100,000,000 population are Negroes, (American) Indians, Chinese, and other colored people to the number of 11,000,000. There are also 14,500,000 persons of foreign birth. Besides these there are 14,000,000 children of foreign-born parents and 6,500,000 persons whose fathers or mothers were born on foreign soil, making a total of 46,000,000 people of foreign stock. Fifty percent of our population is of the native white strain. ... So it is more than likely that when the next census is taken, it will be found that following 1910 there was an even greater flow from Spain, Italy, Hungary, Austria, Russia, Finland, and other countries where the iron hand of economic and political tyrannies have crushed great populations into ignorance and want. The census of 1920 in all probability tell a story of a greater and more serious problem than did the last."

Margaret, who passed herself off as a nurse even though she was a quack without a nurse's license, considered blacks and American Indians to be "foreign stock." By her own twisted definition, she had to consider Hispanics with black or American Indian blood (virtually all Puerto Ricans, Cubans, and Mexicans, and most Latin Americans) "foreign stock" also. She didn't have much love for the non-WASP immigrants of Europe either. Maybe it was because nearly all of them were Catholics or Jews.

In 1939, the year after she publicly acknowledged her *liaison* with Klanswomen in the 1920s, Ms. Sanger set up a birth control project aimed at American blacks which she called "The Negro Project." She duped a few prominent blacks into supporting her. In a letter to her accomplice Clarence Gamble, she wrote, "We do not want word to go out that we want to exterminate the Negro population and the (black) minister is the man who can straighten out that idea if it ever occurs to any of their more rebellious members." Gamble claimed in the proposal he wrote that won funding for the project, "The mass of Negroes, particularly in the South, still breed carelessly and disastrously, with the result that the increase among Negroes, even more than among whites, is from that portion of the population least intelligent and fit, and least able to rear children properly." He continued, "Public health statistics merely hint at the primitive state of civilization in which most Negroes in the South live."

Margaret Sanger clearly meant blacks no good. In her 1938 autobiography, she was petty and low enough to quote each black she quoted talking like Mammy or Stepin Fetchit. She used a "feeble-minded" black woman who had 16 children who got into various scrapes with the law as her poster child for the "need" to control the breeding of the "defective."

In her 1922 manifesto Pivot of Civilization, Ms. Sanger falsely claimed 75 percent of America's schoolchildren were physically or mentally defective, 10% of the American public were mental defectives or morons who were encouraged to reproduce, and 2/3 of men of military age in America were "physically too unfit to shoulder a rifle." Margaret was in Mein Kampf territory.

Although she publicly bemoaned the lives of the poor, and claimed she was pushing population reduction on them for their own good, Margaret Sanger did little or nothing to help them gain better wages and working conditions once she started pushing birth control. In fact, she said charity was useless for the poor because they kept overbreeding, which negated the good done for them. She made fun of the Chicago Vice Commission, whose members had done much to rescue girls and young women from sex trafficking, something she never attempted. She criticized the Communists and the Socialists for blaming capitalism for the woes of the working class; she said overbreeding of the working class was to blame for their problems.

Ms. Sanger condemned American government programs for assisting poor mothers with prenatal and postnatal care, because, she said, "Instead of decreasing and aiming to eliminate the stocks that are most detrimental to the future of the race and the world, it tends to render them to a menacing degree dominant." Margaret Sanger was AWOL when Al Smith was pushing labor reforms through the New York legislature in the 1910s. She worked against Smith when he ran for president in 1928 because she despised practicing Catholics.

During the time of the debate over immigration quotas, Ms. Sanger argued, "The most urgent problem to-day is how to limit and discourage the over-fertility of the mentally and physically defective. Possibly drastic and Spartan methods may be forced upon American society if it continues complacently to encourage the chance and chaotic breeding that has resulted from our stupid, cruel sentimentalism."

What sort of Spartan methods, Margaret? She noted, "Every feeble-minded girl or woman of the hereditary type, especially of the moron class, should be segregated (from men) during the reproductive period. Otherwise, she is almost certain to bear imbecile children, who in turn are just as certain to breed other defectives ...We prefer the policy of immediate sterilization, of making sure that parenthood is absolutely prohibited to the feeble-minded."

Bear in mind Ms. Sanger claimed most military age men were physically defective, most American children were mentally or physically defective, and at least 10% of the American populace was mentally defective. If she had gotten her way, her sterilization gulags for Americans would have been Nazi or Soviet in size.

Money from robber barons and crooked financiers like the Rockefellers, Carnegie, Paul Warburg, and Henry Morgenthau, and money from millionaire lawyers and socialites supported Ms. Sanger's programs, so many of the elites put their money where their hard hearts were on their desire to cut down on the numbers of the masses who were not useful to them.

Ms. Sanger supported ethnic quotas on immigration. In a speech she gave in Oakland, California in 1929, she remarked, "Up to 1914 Uncle Sam was rather negligent about the kind of folk who emigrated [sic] here; he was like the parents who, although they scarcely know what they will do if their family is increased, yet do nothing to prevent it ... Not until 1924 was it necessary to recognize that there was a population problem and that SOMETHING must be done for the future of the country. So bars were put up at the entrance of the United States ... If it is necessary to keep such types out of the country, why is it not just as important to stop their breeding?" (5)

Harry Laughlin, one of Margaret Sanger's many associates who shared her eugenicist views and her bigotry, designed a model compulsive sterilization law that 18 states' lawmakers passed. The Nazis would later use Laughlin's model sterilization law for their own war against those they deemed inferior. In 1936, Nazi Germany's Heidelberg University would award Laughlin with an honorary doctorate for "services on behalf of racial hygiene."

Tragically, Laughlin, a high school teacher, had another claim to infamy – that of a quack statistician pushing ethnic restrictions based on the false science of eugenics. (This was like Margaret Sanger's false claim she was a real nurse.) Money that robber barons Andrew Carnegie and E. H. Harriman stole from their workers and the public funded the Eugenics Record Office, which Laughlin directed. Laughlin used this post to worm his way into the fight for the Immigration Act of 1924. Using false and flawed statistics, Laughlin testified extensively to congressmen on the "need" to restrict immigration of non-WASP countries. Sadly, this lying crackpot had an impact on the law the lawmakers enacted. (6)

Because of the input of twisted people like Laughlin, and the support of twisted people like Margaret Sanger and the elites of industry and finance, and because of the agitation of the Ku Klux Klan, the Immigration Act of 1924 would be a flawed product.

The specific bias the Immigration Act of 1924 had against Latin Europe and Eastern Europe made it a flawed law. However, it had many good provisions. Just because many racists and deviates supported the Immigration Act of 1924 because of their own demons doesn't mean the law was totally worthless.

The intent of many nonracists who backed the passage of the Immigration Act of 1924 was to lower the total number of immigrants per year to assist Americans in assimilating immigrants without being overwhelmed by them. According to the censuses of 1890, 1900, 1910, and 1920, the percent of foreign-born in America was 15% in 1890, 14% in 1900, 15% in 1910, and 13% in 1920. In 1930, the percentage of foreign-born would drop to 12%. By 1940, the percentage of foreign-born would drop to 9%; this would lead to better assimilation and national cultural cohesion. Americans could keep their ethnic identities and still be loyal Americans, as the military service of the many with roots only a generation old in America would prove during World War Two. (7)

Henry Curran, the commissioner of Ellis Island in 1924, said, "The foreign groups fought it (the bill) tooth and nail. They behaved more like foreign colonies than American citizens, and they were powerful."

"My own estimate of the situation, in a nutshell, was that our country needed a rest from the task of assimilating so many millions of foreigners piling in here from every part of the world to become voting Americans in five years from the day they came ashore at Ellis Island," Curran said. "The art of self-government is not acquired so easily. It is a long, hard road. There must be a habit of it, a strong element of matured experience in it, if the composite sum of our American population is to succeed at it. We have done pretty well so far, but we are still an experiment, with only a hundred and fifty years of national life behind us – a tick of the clock, against the ages! And most of the immigrants were coming in from countries where for centuries they had lived under the heel of dictators, knowing nothing of the obligations of self-government that must go hand in hand with its blessings – if self-government is to survive."

Curran was also prophetic about the need for jobs for Americans. In 1941, while Americans were still digging out of the Great Depression, he said, "Incidentally, it would be good to have enough jobs to go around among ourselves – if we ever get near that millennium again – without letting in more impecunious millions to compete with us for relief and for such jobs as we have." (8)

The Immigration Act of 1924 was a needed fix because the steamship companies and shifty Europeans were still using the loophole of unregulated immigration from Canada and elsewhere in the Western Hemisphere to evade the intent of the 1921 law. In 1922, there were 310,000 immigrants to America. The number jumped to 523,000 in 1923, and to 707,000 in 1924. Roughly 200,000 of the total came in through Canada, and another 90,000 came in through Mexico. In 1924, another 75,000 came directly from Germany, 56,000 came directly from Italy, 36,000 Poles and Jews came directly from Poland, 33,000 came directly from

Scotland, 26,000 came directly from England and Wales, 18,000 came directly from Sweden, and 17,000 came directly from Ireland. In all, more than 360,000 immigrants came directly from Europe and at least another 100,000 Europeans came in by way of Canada.

The 1924 law caused a large drop in immigration. In 1925, there were 294,000 immigrants admitted to America. In 1926, 1927, 1928, 1929, and 1930, the numbers were 304,000, then 335,000, then 307,000, then 280,000, then 242,000, respectively. **(9)**

Harry Hull, the Commissioner-General of Immigration, noted the following about Ellis Island in 1928:

"Ellis Island was the great outpost of the new and vigorous Republic. Ellis Island stood guard over the wide-flung portal. Ellis Island resounded for years to the tramp of an endless invading army. Its million or more immigrants a year taxed its resources to the utmost. It was the target of the demagogue, the sob-story writer, the notoriety seeker, and the occasional fault-finding busybody puffed up with conceit, who meekly submitted to every form of official surveillance in his own country, accepting the same as a matter of course, but felt it unbefitting his dignity on entering free America to conform without protest and criticism to reasonable and necessary immigration regulations. Ellis Island is freed of this inundating horde and largely freed of carping critics, but Ellis Island has lost its proud place in the grand immigration scheme. Its million or more immigrants yearly have shrunk to several hundred thousand." **(10)**

During the 1920s, Congress and the presidents and the courts addressed several other immigration and citizenship issues. Their most overdue action was in enacting the Indian Citizenship Act of 1924. Many American Indians had received American citizenship, through individual treaties their tribes signed with the American government, through marriage with whites, through military service, or through the 14th Amendment in 1868 if they lived in states or territories under effective American government control. But many tribes not under effective U.S. government control in 1868 had *not* received citizenship under the 14th Amendment. American politicians did not give citizenship to American Indians after the soldiers, settlers, and speculators forced them into reservations. The Dawes Act of 1887 promised American Indians *might* become citizens only if they left tribal life and adopted white man's ways. The Dawes Act allowed the theft of most of the reservation lands. The nation's leaders put the Indian Citizenship Act of 1924 on the books only after the valiant service of many American Indians in World War One. This long-overdue law granted all American Indians American citizenship automatically. **(11)**

Congress and President Coolidge put two more significant immigration laws into effect during the "lame duck" session in early 1929. The first law, approved on March 2, 1929, updated a number of existing immigration and naturalization laws. This law also allowed any alien without a record of admission for permanent residence who had been in the country before the Quota Act of 1921 became law to register as a permanent resident. The alien had to have resided in America since before the enactment of the Quota Act of 1921, show "good moral character," and not be subject to deportation according to current immigration laws. Some might claim this was possibly the first bill that had an "amnesty" provision. Others would claim otherwise. If the alien could not have gotten into the country legally in the first place because he or she was liable to be a public charge, sick with a "loathsome" disease, an illegal contract worker, an illegal entrant, one of the immoral classes, a person convicted of a crime of moral turpitude, or an anarchist, Communist, proponent of violent overthrow, or someone else with views inimical to the United States, he or she would have been deportable when he or she first came to America, and would not be eligible for registering as a permanent resident.

The second law, approved on March 4, 1929, made it a felony for an alien to try to enter America illegally after being deported. Instead of merely deporting these individuals again so they could try again, federal officials would have to imprison illegals for up to two years. The law permanently banned any illegal alien who the feds had deported earlier. **(12)**

The two 1929 laws in a way tied together American fairness with the American desire that people do things the right way. Congress and the president gave immigrants a chance to clear up their status to avoid being rounded up and deported for not having proper proof of legal resident status. They also banned illegals who tried to enter after already being caught and deported after a fair hearing.

In the years 1931 through 1939, there were 457,000 immigrants total admitted to the United States. Many thousands of immigrants left America for their homelands during this decade, hoping they could do better. In 1940, immigration picked up some, as 71,000 immigrants came to the United States; 50,000 of these came from Europe, and of these, 22,000 came from Germany. This was the year of the Nazi blitzkrieg over Denmark, Norway, the Low Countries, and France, and the air battle over Britain.

From 1931 through 1940, American officials would deport 117,000 aliens. Roughly 50,000 of these they caught trying to enter the country illegally without inspection, or illegally with forged, false, or faulty documents. Another 15,000 had to leave because they violated laws pertaining to their permission to be in the country, and 10,000 or so joined them on a boat ride back to Europe or a train ride back to Canada or Mexico for being caught after previously being barred or deported. The feds sent home another 17,000 convicts, 5000 members of "immoral classes" (mostly pimps and prostitutes), 1000 drugrunners, and 253 subversives. They also expelled 8000 illiterate adults, 6000 physical or mental defectives, and 2000 public charges. They deported about 3000 for miscellaneous causes. American officials "required to depart" another 93,000 aliens for various reasons. These people had to get back to their homelands on their own.

From 1941 through 1945, 171,000 immigrants came to the United States. Of these, only 53,000 came from Europe. This was because of World War Two. **(13)**

Hitler was the main cause helping president Franklin Delano Roosevelt limit immigration. Hitler's secret police were very effective at limiting the escape of people from the countries of Europe his forces controlled. And his submariners sunk many more ships. The Netherlands, Denmark, and Norway, which had great merchant fleets and were neutral nations during World War One, were under German occupation during World War Two. Sweden, another World War One neutral with a decent merchant fleet, was surrounded by German-occupied Norway and Denmark, and by German ally Finland. (The Finns were fighting a revenge war against the Soviets, who had attacked them and stolen some of their land in the winter war of 1939-1940.) The Germans also occupied Greece, another country with a good merchant fleet.

There was some movement of refugees, but not many of them came to America. The Turks were neutral during the war, so Pope Pius XII's envoys operating out of Constantinople (Istanbul) smuggled many thousands of Jews out of Eastern Europe with fake baptismal certificates. The Pope's men helped many Jews relocate to neutral Portugal and neutral Ireland, and even helped many hide out in Italy, which was an Axis country but whose people were not enthusiastic in helping Hitler murder the Jews. Even the Spanish took in some Jews and helped others make it to Portugal despite Franco's "official" attitude against receiving refugees. Some Jews sneaked into the Holy Land, braving Arab attacks and the British blockade. Pope Pius XII paid ransoms to free Jews. He also hid 3000 Italian Jews in his own summer palace near Rome from the Germans who essentially were occupying Italy after the overthrow of Mussolini. Pope Pius XII also had hundreds of other Jews hidden from the Nazis in the Vatican itself. **(14)**

Spanish and Portuguese authorities allowed refugees from elsewhere in Europe to escape to America and other places.

As Hitler rose to power, rearmed Germany, and started persecuting the Jews, many Jews in Germany sought to emigrate to America. Many Jewish leaders in the United States pleaded with FDR to allow more Jews fleeing Hitler to come to America. FDR was worried about how Southerners and union members would react to the importation of roughly a million Jews from Germany, Austria, and the Czech lands (which Hitler's army controlled before the outbreak of World War Two). They would compete for jobs and would not be Christians. Since Southerners and union members formed a large percentage of FDR's voting base, he did nothing.

In one notorious case, FDR in 1939 turned away the *St. Louis*, a German ship carrying 930 Jews who were fleeing Hitler. American officials tried to cajole Cuban officials and other Latin American officials into taking them in, but failed. The captain had to return the ship to Europe. Many of these Jews perished during the Holocaust when German armies overran western Europe. The plight of these Jews was memorialized in a book and later a movie called "Voyage of the Damned."

It is easy to criticize FDR now for not helping Jewish refugees. But in FDR's defense, his job was to be president of the United States, not runner of a refugee camp for Europe. In America, many patriot groups and labor unions opposed more immigration during the Great Depression because of the competition immigrants would offer for scarce jobs. In FDR's first eight years in charge – 1933, 1934, 1935, 1936, 1937, 1938, 1939, and 1940, unemployment stood at 25%, 22%, 20%, 17%, 14%, 19%, 17%, and 15%, respectively. (In Hoover's four years of 1929, 1930, 1931, and 1932, unemployment percentages were 3%, 9%, 16%, and 24%, respectively.) The unemployment figure for 1940 would have been higher if FDR and Congress hadn't started a peacetime military draft. The unemployment figures for 1939 and 1940 would have been higher if FDR hadn't allowed businesses to sell implements of war and related supplies to the British and French. They would also have been higher in the 1930s if Hoover's men hadn't deported or forced to leave on their own hundreds of thousands of illegals from Mexico to lessen competition for jobs in America. **(15)**

The Jews weren't the only victims of genocidal oppression, as the Chinese and the Slavs could point out. The patriot groups and labor unions noted if America had to take in Jewish refugees because no other country would, then they would be obligated by a sense of equality to take in millions of other non-Jewish victims of Nazi, Soviet, and Japanese genocidal aggression. And they understandably viewed these mass murders and oppressions as evils the people of Europe and Asia should deal with, not the people of America. Americans were still paying for World War One, a quarrel between rival groups of European imperialists. They didn't want to have to shoulder the burden for a second such war. However, FDR was essentially a political schemer, so his decision to do nothing essentially looks like a calculated move on his part to protect his political power.

The United States' population during the war rose from about 135 million to about 140 million. About 16.3 million able-bodied people were in uniform. Roughly 11.2 million served in the U.S. Army and Army Air Force, 4.2 million served in the U.S. Navy, 700,000 served in the Marines, and 200,000 served in the Coast Guard. Others served in the merchant marine during the war; due to submarine attacks, this was essentially a combat branch also. The vast majority of these were young men, including all the men of my family who were of service age. During the war, my Dad, my uncles Chuck and Rusty (Uncle Don was too young for the war; he fought in the Korean War), and my wife's father all served in the Navy or the Army. So did virtually every man who was a friend of my father's that was roughly his age. So did virtually every father of every friend of mine. My aunt Wilma served as an Army nurse. (That's how she met Uncle Chuck.) Roughly 200,000 other women who were not Armed Services nurses also served in uniform during World War Two. My Dad's Uncle Joe, who was too young for World War One, tried to enlist in World War Two, but Uncle Sam kept him at his job as a foreman in a shipyard. Grandpa Charlie, who had served in the U.S. Navy in World War One, did training films for the Armed Services in World War Two. Grandpa Leo, who served in combat in the U.S. Army in World War One, was an armed guard at a defense plant during World War Two. Both my grandpas had been Chicago police officers crippled in the line of duty.

Also, many women worked in industrial jobs the men had to leave behind to join the Armed Forces. And since there was a greater demand for manufactured items such as ships, tanks, planes, artillery pieces, explosives, rifles, trucks, and uniforms, many men and women worked at these jobs, which paid better than farm work or semiskilled manual labor.

This meant the largest group of aliens in the United States legally during World War Two would be braceros (manual laborers) from Mexico. These people replaced refugees from Oklahoma and other Dust Bowl states as the people who picked crops in California. (Most of the young men who were "Okies" were serving in uniform in World War Two.) The braceros soon started doing farm labor across the country. They also did railroad maintenance work and other work requiring raw muscle throughout the war. Roughly 220,000 Mexicans signed bracero contracts and worked in America during the war. The Bracero Program would last until 1964. There were roughly 4.5 million bracero contracts signed by Mexican nationals during this two-decade period. But since the average bracero signed many contracts while working in the United States after World War Two, the actual number of braceros was much lower – about 400,000 braceros. **(16)**

In the final four years of the 1940s, the Cold War replaced the war against Germany and Japan as the main concern of American foreign policy. American taxpayers spent billions of dollars to rebuild an ultimately ungrateful Europe, Japan, and China. During these years, at least 610,000 people immigrated legally to the United States. Of these, roughly 370,000 people came directly from Europe; most came from Britain (105,000), defeated enemy Germany (91,000), and defeated reluctant enemy Italy (44,000).

Formal immigration from Eastern Europe was much lower because the Red Army occupied most of these countries and Stalin essentially forbade emigration. However, the great majority of the roughly 215,000 refugees and asylees American officials admitted from 1946 through 1950 came from Eastern Europe. Of these, almost 80,000 came from Poland, more than 20,000 came from Latvia, almost 20,000 came from Lithuania, roughly 10,000 came from Yugoslavia, more than 8000 came from Czechoslovakia, 7000 came from Estonia, 6000 came from Hungary, 4000 came from Romania, and 14,000 or so (most probably from Ukraine or Belarusia) came from the Soviet Union. We also admitted more than 35,000 refugees and asylees from Germany and about 5000 from Austria.

Throughout the decade, far more legal immigrants came to America via Canada than via Mexico. However, some of the braceros did not return to Mexico when they stopped doing farm labor under the terms of their contracts. Instead, they stayed illegally in the United States.

From 1941 through 1950, American officials would deport 111,000 aliens. Roughly 65,000 of these they caught trying to enter the country illegally without inspection, or illegally with forged, false, or faulty documents. Another 14,000 had to leave because they violated laws pertaining to their permission to be in the country, and 18,000 or so joined them on a boat ride back to Europe or a train ride back to Canada or Mexico for being caught after previously being barred or deported. The feds sent home another 9000 convicts, 759 members of "immoral classes" (mostly pimps and prostitutes), 822 drugrunners, and 17 subversives. They also expelled roughly 2000 illiterate adults, 1600 physical or mental defectives, and 143 on public assistance. They deported 812 for miscellaneous causes. American officials "required to depart" another 1,471,000 aliens for various reasons. These people had to get back to their homelands on their own. Most of these people were illegal immigrants from Mexico. **(17)**

Dwight Eisenhower and his underlings would close down Ellis Island as an immigration station in November 1954, after moving the last of the detainees off the island. Meanwhile, rival government agencies scavenged the facilities at Ellis Island for goods like grave robbers.

Eisenhower tried to sell Ellis Island to private businessmen from 1956 through 1960. The prices they offered were so shamefully low the feds had to pull Ellis Island off the real estate market. **(18)**

Ellis Island lay barely guarded or largely unguarded through the 1960s and 1970s. The buildings deteriorated because of bad weather, salt fog, and lack of preventive maintenance. Vandals broke windows; thieves stole electrical wire, plumbing fixtures, and anything else of any conceivable resale value. Millions of pigeons and sea birds lived in the derelict buildings, and defecated heavily inside all of them. The degradation and violation of Ellis Island mirrored a similar breakdown in American government and society in those years.

John Kennedy's underlings offered Ellis Island to the United Nations, but the racketeers of the world organization turned it down. Lyndon Johnson pulled the guards off of Ellis Island in 1965, only to be chagrined when professional criminals not in government service looted the island for scrap metal and other items. The old ferry boat that offloaded so many immigrants from passenger ships to the island was allowed to deteriorate and sink in 1968.

This devastation of a place many Americans viewed as hallowed ground because of the sacrifices their ancestors made to leave Europe behind was to be expected from a string of self-serving politicians and bureaucrats without an appreciation for history or the practical worth of a facility designed and maintained with such care as the facility on Ellis Island. It wouldn't be until Ronald Reagan's presidency, and several years of work in the 1980s after Reagan pushed for the renovation of Ellis Island, that dedicated people would finish renovating Ellis Island and reopen it as a living monument of Americana – an immigration museum.

END NOTES

1. Immigration statistics come from the Historic Research Study, Statue of Liberty – Ellis Island National Monument, by Harlan D. Unrau, National Park Service, 1984.

2. Immigration statistics come from the Unrau study. I did some math to come up with totals.

3. Info on the Immigration Act of May 26, 1924, and Husband's interpretation of it as a guide for who from Asia to bar comes from the act itself and from the Unrau study (pages 124-125).

4. Info on suffragettes in the Ku Klux Klan comes from Kathleen Blee's book Women of the Klan: Racism and Gender in the 1920s and an interview she did with Dinitia Smith for the 1/26/2002 issue of the New York Times. Info on Wilson's approval of "Birth of a Nation" comes from a PBS website on the film, and from Thomas Fleming's book Illusion of Victory (page 189).

5. The main Information sources on Margaret Sanger (including her quotes) are her own books. Margaret Sanger: An Autobiography, (pages 40-41, 57, 68-87, 94-96, 104-105, 119-162, 176-190, 192-250, 268-291, 312-313, 315, 355, 366-367, 370-371, 388-391, 395, 409-410, 433-459, 490), her book Pivot of Civilization (Chapters I, II, IV, V, VI, VII, VIII), and her book Woman and the New Race (Chapter III) are the sources for most of the info on Margaret Sanger.

Only a thorough racist who viewed people like breeding stock like Ms. Sanger did could offhandledly drop a ridiculous observation like the following in her much more cautious autobiography (page 490): "Not only the features of the cultured types of the Island, but even those of the coolies, the longshoremen, struck me as growing less Oriental and more Anglo-Saxon, the foreheads fuller, the eyes less slanting."

The Speaking of Margaret Sanger in the Birth Control Movement from 1916 to 1937, by William Morehouse (pages 184-185) is the reference for her 1929 Oakland speech.

New York University maintains the Margaret Sanger Papers Project. The school has copies of many of her writings (speeches, letters, pamphlets, etc.) and researchers dedicated to preserving her twisted legacy. Info sources include their articles "Biographical Sketch," "Birth Control or Race Control? Sanger and the Negro Project," "American Birth Control League," "Birth Control Clinical Research Bureau," and "Birth Control Federation of America."

Harry Laughlin's ties to Margaret Sanger are noted in the papers he donated to Truman State College in Missouri. Info on Ms. Sanger's "Negro Project" comes from the book Woman's Body, Woman's Right by Linda Gordon (pages 332-334).

6. Virginia state officials used their Laughlin law and Laughlin's shysterish testimony to forcibly sterilize Carrie Buck. Laughlin didn't even meet Miss Buck, much less examine her clinically (because he didn't have the skill set or the formal training to do so). He claimed Carrie and her kin were part of the "shiftless, ignorant, and worthless class of anti-social whites of the South."

Carrie Buck, placed with a foster family after her mother was committed to an institution, dropped out of school after sixth grade to help her foster parents. The foster parents' nephew raped Carrie when she was 17, and she became pregnant as a result. The white-trash foster parents covered up the rape, falsely claimed Carrie was stupid, incorrigible, and promiscuous, and put her in a state facility for the feeble-minded.

When state officials tried to sterilize Carrie, her court-appointed appealed. Carrie's lawyer was in cahoots with the state's lawyer; the shyster was in on the fix to make Carrie's case a test case to support the Virginia sterilization law. The state's lawyer falsely claimed Carrie's infant daughter was mentally defective also, and Carrie's lawyer didn't challenge this. (Nor did he attribute the child's supposed backwardness to the genetic defectiveness of the white-trash vermin who raped Carrie.) The case (Buck vs. Bell) went to the Supreme Court in 1927. Justice Oliver Wendell Holmes, in ruling with most of the other justices it was okay to sterilize

Carrie against her will, made the idiotic statement, "Three generations of imbeciles are enough." Medical hacks sterilized Carrie and her sister Doris. Doris didn't even know about it; they sterilized her without her consent when she was having her appendix taken out. Carrie's child by the rapist nephew had average grades, but died before she could enter third grade; the white trash foster parents had taken her from Carrie and let her die of an intestinal disease. Carrie eventually was released; she married and always regretted she could have no more children. News reporters and scholars visited Carrie over the years and determined she was of normal intelligence, something a slew of pinhead judges, including Holmes, who was no Sherlock, failed to do. Carrie's forced sterilization was a crime against her on several levels. And hers was the first of 60,000 or so sterilizations that doctors in Virginia government pay would commit in the Old Dominion.

Information on Harry Laughlin and Carrie Buck comes from the University of Virginia's series of articles "Eugenics" on the school's Claude Moore Health Sciences Library website, and from Stephen Jay Gould's article in the July/August 2002 issue of Natural History. Both acknowledged Paul Lombardo, a lawyer and ethicist who befriended Carrie Buck, and became her advocate.

7. Census statistics for foreign-born residents of America come from the U.S. Commerce Dept. book Historical Statistics of the United States: Colonial Times to 1970 (Bicentennial Edition). I did some math to come up with percentages.

8. Henry Curran's observations come from his book Pillar to Post (pages 304-305).

9. Immigration statistics come from the Unrau study.

10. Hull's quote was in the Unrau study (page 127).

11. The Dawes Act of 1887 aimed at destroying the tribal system. On paper, the bill allowed Indians who left tribal life to get portions of the reservation land and the possibility of becoming citizens. However, dividing all the acres of reservation by the number of acres each Indian could own under the Dawes Act left plenty of land. White speculators got their hands on this land. They also bought up land cheaply from American Indians who left their tribes and sold land that was due to them under the Dawes Act. Under the Burke Act of 1906, which amended the Dawes Act, the federal government could seize land from American Indians who they deemed incompetent.

By 1934, American Indians would lose 86 million acres out of the 138 million acres in the reservation system in 1887. To this day, federal bureaucrats mismanage land that belongs to the American Indians, and steal money that rightfully belongs to the various tribes and individuals in these tribes. At the rate our government expands and arrogates authority and steals from the public, some argue we are all becoming American Indians.

Information on the Indian Citizenship Act comes from the act itself (43 U.S. Statutes at Large 253), Nebraska State Historical Society articles on the Dawes Act and on the Indian Citizenship Act, the Dawes Act itself (24 Statutes at Large 388-391), the Burke Act itself (34 Statutes at Large 182-183), and an article by Gary Mitchell about the theft of the land of American Indians in Kansas in the 5/18/1995 Topeka Capital Journal,

Evon Peter, an Alaskan Native American, in a 10/3/2008 article, noted Congress in 1971 put the Alaska Native Claims Settlement Act onto the books. This law, he said, invalidated all Alaska Native American land claims and took away hunting and fishing rights, much like the Dawes Act did more than 80 years earlier. There is nothing new under the sun.

12. Information on the Acts of March 2, 1929 and March 4, 1929 were the acts themselves (aka 45 Statutes at large 1512-1516, and 45 Statutes at Large 1551-1552).

13. Immigration statistics come from the Unrau study, and from the U.S. Commerce Dept. book Historical Statistics of the United States: Colonial Times to 1970 (Bicentennial Edition).

14. Father Pierre Blet, in Pius XII and the Second World War (pages 229 and 230), noted the Churchill government refused to lift the blockade of Greece for a number of months so the Vatican could send food to starving Greeks. The British rationale was the food would help the German war effort. The British had hampered Herbert Hoover from getting food to the Belgians during World War One on the same grounds. Churchill, who ran the British Navy until he was canned in the wake of the Gallipoli fiasco, was consistent in both wars. Churchill reportedly called Hoover a "son of a bitch" for trying to feed the Belgians instead of letting the effects of the British blockade starve many of them to death. The source for this unoriginal Churchill utterance was Thomas Fleming's book The Illusion of Victory (page 323).

15. Unemployment statistics come from the U.S. Commerce Dept. book Historical Statistics of the United States: Colonial Times to 1970 (Bicentennial Edition).

16. Statistics on the braceros comes from a 1/14/2004 Associated Press article by Juliana Barbassa, a Smithsonian Institute website article titled "Opportunity or Exploitation: The Bracero Program," a University of San Diego website article titled "Bracero Program," and an Associated Press article that appeared in the 1/8/2007 Madera, California Tribune. Madera is in the heart of California's San Joaquin Valley, as great an agricultural area as our great nation is privileged to have.

17. Immigration and refugee/asylee statistics come from the Unrau study, from the U.S. Commerce Dept. book Historical Statistics of the United States: Colonial Times to 1970 (Bicentennial Edition), and from the 1999 Statistical Yearbook of the Immigration and Naturalization Service.

18. Something similar happened in 1995. Bill Clinton and his administration closed the San Francisco Presidio military base. Congress made it a national park but also allowed commercial development of the picturesque military base on the north coast of the city. The feds allowed "Star Wars" movie tycoon George Lucas to put a megamillion dollar commercial development inside the Presidio in 1999. Other big-money deals followed. Because of the shortsightedness of the feds, the Presidio is now basically unavailable in case of another major earthquake in the San Francisco area (like those in 1906 or in 1989) as a place to muster emergency workers or to shelter large numbers of victims.

MEMORIES ARE MADE OF THESE

One December Sunday many years ago, when I was home on leave from the Army, Mom, God rest her soul, was cooking a wonderful dinner for us all. When dinner was just about ready to serve, she called us all to the table. Dad in the meantime, had put the Advent wreath on the table, and had lit some candles on the wreath. Before dinner, Dad recited some Advent prayers to God, and finished with this impromptu prayer while we were all gathered around:

"Remember those who have gone before us,
those who founded our people,
who gave our people the gift of faith in God,
who gave us the gift of strong character."

This is one of my favorite memories of Dad, God rest his soul. He was a big, blunt World War Two veteran who was a real man in every sense of the word. "Remember those who have gone before us."

We have seen pictures of our parents and grandparents when they were young people. We have heard the family stories our old ones have told.

I was fortunate enough to have a great-great aunt old enough to remember Teddy Roosevelt as a young president when she was a young bride, and with a good enough mind to remember the stories her father had told her about his time as a soldier under the command of General Sherman in the Civil War, and she would share these with us. I also had the good fortune of having a grandfather who remembered and spoke often of his childhood days in Ireland and his rowdier days as a teenager on the streets of Chicago. Our family cherishes these memories and the pictures and other mementoes Aunt Albie, Grandpa Charlie, and our other ancestors have left us.

This chapter serves the same purpose for this book. It is not a collection of statistics or dry facts, but of stories. History is a STORY ... or more correctly, MANY STORIES that make up an overall truth. This chapter contains stories, some funny, some happy, some sad, and some instructive, about immigration during the Ellis Island era. Featured in this chapter are newspaper articles about Ellis Island while it was in business, and the observations of a few of the people who worked at Ellis Island who wrote down their experiences. This chapter lays out like a series of short newspaper articles with headlines.

Featured in this chapter are the reminiscences of Henry Curran, a Commissioner of Immigration at Ellis Island from 1923 to 1926, and those of one of his successors, Edward Corsi. Corsi, who ran Ellis Island from 1931 to 1934, was himself the son of an Italian politician; his mother remarried after his father died, and the family came to New York in 1907. Corsi interviewed Frank Martocci, another Italian immigrant and an interpreter at Ellis Island. Martocci quite likely questioned Corsi's mother and stepfather when they were being processed. Fiorello La Guardia, a one-time interpreter at Ellis Island, and William Williams, also a Commissioner of Immigration at Ellis Island and the one-time boss of both La Guardia and Martocci, are also quoted in this chapter.

The women of Ellis Island are also well-represented in this chapter. Maud Mosher, a civil service matron from Illinois assigned to Ellis Island in the first decade of the 1900s, left us her reminiscences and some of her field notes. Miss Mosher had worked with the American Indians in Kansas. Maud had been a schoolmarm and a traveling saleswoman as well. Ludmilla Kucharova, a Czech girl who emigrated to America through Ellis Island in 1894 with her family, later married an English immigrant named John Foxlee. She was known to the immigrants she served as Ludmilla Foxlee. Ludmilla served as a social worker for the YMCA and the National Institute of Immigrant Welfare in the 1920s and the 1930s. She left a compelling record of the immigrants she served. The donations of many good Americans funded Ludmilla's work at Ellis Island.

We close the chapter with the childhood reminiscences of two very famous American sports figures. One was an immigrant from Norway, who would become the legendary coach of an ethnic team known as the Notre Dame Fighting Irish. And the other man, who was a fair major league ballplayer but an excellent manager, was the son of a French Canadian immigrant woman from Quebec.

Laugh, cry, reflect, and enjoy. Upon such people our generations of today rest.

ELLIS ISLAND'S FIRST IMMIGRANT

(New York Times, 1/2/1892)

The new buildings on Ellis Island constructed for the use of the Immigration Bureau were yesterday formally occupied by the officials of that department. The employees reported at an early hour, and each was shown to his place by the Superintendent or his chief clerk. Col. Weber was on the island at 8 o'clock, and went on a tour of inspection to see that everything was in readiness for the reception of the first boatload if immigrants.

There were three big steamships in the harbor waiting to land their passengers, and there was much anxiety among the new-comers to be the first landed at the new station. The honor was reserved for a little rosy-cheeked Irish girl. She was Annie Moore, fifteen years of age, lately a resident of County Cork, and yesterday one of the 148 steerage passengers landed from the Guion steamship *Nevada*. Her name is now distinguished by being the first registered in the book of the new landing bureau.

The steamship that brought Annie Moore arrived late Thursday night. Early yesterday morning the passengers of that vessel were placed on board the immigrant transfer boat *John E. Moore*. The craft was gayly decorated with bunting and ranged alongside the wharf on Ellis Island amid a clang of bells and din of shrieking whistles.

As soon as the gangplank was run ashore, Annie tripped across it and was hurried into the big building that almost covers the entire island. By a prearranged plan she was escorted to a registry desk which was temporarily occupied by Mr. Charles M. Hendley, the former private secretary of Secretary Windom. He asked as a special favor the privilege of registering the first immigrant, and Col. Weber granted the request.

When the little voyager had been registered, Col. Weber presented her with a ten-dollar gold piece and made a short address of congratulation and welcome. It was the first United States coin she had ever seen and the largest sum of money she had ever possessed. She says she will never part with it, but will always keep it as a pleasant memento of the occasion. She was accompanied by her two younger brothers.

Besides those of the *Nevada*, the passengers of the *City of Paris* and of the steamship *Victoria* were also landed at the new station. They numbered 700 in all, and the many (features) of the mammoth structure for facilitating the work of landing were made manifest by the rapidity with which this number was registered and sent on to their various destinations. It was quite a populous little island about noon, when the steerage passengers from the three big steamships were being disembarked but within a very short time they had all been disposed of. Those destined for local points were placed on board the ferryboat Brinckerhoff and landed at the Barge Office. Those going to other places were taken to the various railroad stations by the immigrant transports.

The first ticket sold by the railroad agents in the new building was purchased by Ellen King, on her way from Waterford, Ireland, to a small town in Minnesota.

Col. John J. Toffey and Major Edward J. Anderson, who has succeeded to the contract for the supply of subsistence, signalized the day by entertaining Col. Weber, the Superintendent of Immigration; Major Hibbard, the Superintendent of Construction; Surgeon Toner and staff, and all the employees of the station at a New Year's Day spread. Capt. Charles W. Laws, their chief, had prepared the board for 300 guests, and the throng had a merry time at the tables.

Col. Toffey and Major Anderson had planned to have a pretentious opening and their friends were to have been invited, but the authorities at Washington directed that the opening be made without any ceremony.

All connected with the Immigration Bureau expressed themselves as exceedingly well pleased with the change from the cramped quarters at the Barge Office to the commodious building on its island site. The railroad people were the only ones who were heard to express any dissatisfaction. Their grievance is that the building is so large as to involve much running about on their part in getting their various passengers together. Others said that when the tremendous number of immigrants who had to be handled in this building was considered finding fault with its size was like complaining of a circle for being round.

"We can easily handle 7,000 immigrants in one day here," said Col. Weber. "We could not handle half that number at the Barge Office. At the old place the greatest delay was in the baggage department. All that is now done away with, as the baggage department has the entire first floor and the arrangement is perfect."

The building was erected by the Federal Government at a cost of $500,000. The wharves are so arranged that immigrants from two vessels can be landed at the same time. As soon as disembarked the passengers are shown up a broad stairway on the southern side of the building. Turning to the left they pass through ten aisles, where are stationed as many registry clerks. After being registered, those of the immigrants who have to be detained are placed in a wire-screened inclosure. The more fortunate ones pass on to a similar compartment, where those going to the West are separated from those bound for New England or local points.

There is an information bureau in the building for the benefit of those seeking friends or relatives among the immigrants. There are also telegraph and railroad ticket offices and a money changer's office. Except the surgeon, none of the officials will reside on the island. The surgeon occupies the quarters formerly used by the gunner when Ellis Island was a naval magazine.

THE ORDEALS OF STEERAGE

FOUR HUNDRED MAY GO BACK
(New York Times 7/15/1893)

The 800 immigrants brought by the tramp steamship *Red Sea* were not landed on Ellis Island yesterday, and it now looks as if at least half of them would have to return.

The majority of the passengers are Russian Jews. It appears that they have been made the victims of gross misrepresentations on the part of the agents of the vessel.

Health Officer Jenkins gave the vessel clearance papers early yesterday morning. She left Quarantine at 8 o'clock and made fast to a pier at the Woodruff Stores, Brooklyn, where she was visited at noon by a board appointed by Immigration Commissioner Senner, which was instructed to make an investigation into the status of the Immigrants and their eligibility to land.

The board comprised Supervising Inspector Quinlan of the Contract Labor Bureau, Register Clerks Arbeely and Wetzler, Dr. Prochazka and Mr. McDowell of the Ellis Island medical staff, Matron Stucklin, and Boarding Officers Wank and Bruno. The party was in charge of Assistant Commissioner McSweeny. It was accompanied by five Custom House Inspectors, who were detailed by the Collector for this service.

Assistant Commissioner McSweeny had instructions to make a thorough examination of the ship, ascertain the number of passengers that was entitled to land, and the number the vessel was permitted to carry under United States laws.

Col. Thomas F. Lee, the Quarantine Inspector of the Immigration Department, who boarded the vessel at Quarantine, made his report to Commissioner Senner before the board visited the ship. He stated that there were 794 passengers on board, exclusive of the six stowaways who were not discovered until the vessel had sailed from Bremen.

Of this number 684 were Russians, mostly Hebrews; 84 Austrians, 1 German, and 1 Armenian. Col. Lee said that 427 were entered on the manifest as having no money whatever, 258 had between $1 and $5, and 11 had $50 and over.

Col. Lee In his report also said that the ship was in a fair sanitary condition, no worse and no better than the usual class of Italian vessels which bring immigrants to this port. According to his report her passenger accommodations and sanitary conditions are not so good as those on the regular liners.

After receiving the report of his subordinate, Dr. Senner said that he was very much surprised that Dr. Starkloff, the United States Consul at Bremen, should have permitted the 427 penniless persons to embark on the *Red Sea* for America.

The Commissioner said: "The majority of the *Red Sea* passengers I have been informed, if not actually refused passage by the regular liners, are not of the class that would be accepted by them. I demanded a bond of $10,000 to cover expenses of deporting such of the number as may prove to be undesirable and their maintenance during the period of detention."

"I did not regard the bond as exorbitant; on the contrary, I thought it very moderate. I received no response from Barber & Co., who I had been informed would furnish the bond, and a few days ago again asked them what they intended to do. A member of the firm informed me that three days ago a cable had been sent to the Bremen consignors, Schoed & Moeler, asking them to guarantee indemnity in the case of all immigrants who were refused admission. I was yesterday informed that no answer had been received and that the firm had declined to assume responsibility for the *Red Sea's* passengers, so I decided to make the ship a security."

Note: *In other words, Senner ordered the ship seized until its owners came up with bond money. Back in the day, American officials were not shy at backing America's interests over those of foreign corporate pirates.*

"Subsequently a representative of C.B. Richards & Co., 61 Broadway, called upon me and said that his firm would be responsible for the ten thousand-dollar bond which I had required."

Dr. Senner received the report of his assistants at a late hour yesterday afternoon. After hearing it he ordered that the immigrants be transferred to the Island at an early hour today, and that each of them be accorded a separate and rigid examination.

It is expected that at least 400 of the passengers will be debarred as paupers. All who are excluded will be sent back in some other ship at the expense of the owners of the *Red Sea*. This, it is estimated, will cost the company fully $8,000 for transportation alone. The maintenance of the immigrants during detention will doubtless bring the total to $10,000, the full extent or the bond required.

To prevent any of the immigrants escaping during the night the vessel was ordered to haul out from her pier and drop anchor in the stream (the channel of the Hudson River on its way out to the Atlantic Ocean). This was done about sunset.

Assistant Commissioner McSweeny, when seen last night, said that he had heard numerous complaints about an insufficient food supply from the immigrants of the *Red Sea*. He thought they were true, because when he visited the vessel several women fainted within his sight from lack of food. After hearing the complaints, he ordered a quantity of food, which was placed on board the vessel last night.

The officers of the ship deny that there is or has been any lack of provisions. They say that the complaint of insufficient food was made by the Jewish passengers who refused to eat meat. The Inspectors, however, affirm that they saw many passengers fighting like wild animals for loaves of bread.

Mr. McSweeny was told in the course of his investigation that passage money ranging from $21.50 to $60 had been exacted from each of the passengers. Several of the passengers have made affidavits to the effect that they were told when purchasing tickets that the vessel would sail the next day. Day after day for twenty days they were told the same thing, and as they had to pay their own expenses during period, what little money they had was exhausted before the vessel finally sailed.

Commissioner Senner says he understands that the fitting out of the *Red Sea* as a passenger vessel and the sending of her here with a load of immigrants is an experiment that will be followed by other such shipments should it prove successful. He has been informed that another vessel has been chartered for a similar purpose, and that the owners are now awaiting the result of the *Red Sea* experiment before dispatching her to this country.

The follow-up story follows.

RED SEA'S HAPLESS VOYAGERS
(New York Times, 7/16/1893)

The tramp steamship *Red Sea*, which came into port to find herself famous, spent all of yesterday anchored in the stream off Ellis Inland. In the afternoon her crew went to work on her decks with holystones and sand.

They will have hard work to got the vessel clean, but it is nothing compared to the task to her agents will have to explain satisfactorily some charges that have been made against them.

It now appears that these same immigrants have been more sinned against than sinning. According to their statements, they have not only been defrauded by the agents of the *Red Sea* but maltreated during the voyage. They were transferred from the *Red Sea* to the landing bureau on Ellis Island early yesterday.

The examination, which was at once begun, resulted in the barring of nine Slovaks, who were found to be contract laborers. and the detention of 430 as paupers. These will be held until friends guarantee that they will not become public charges.

Nearly half of the penniless crowd was released in the afternoon, friends and relatives having furnished the requisite guarantee.

In addition to those who were found to be paupers, forty-five others were detained on the recommendation of the examining surgeon. Eight of these were afflicted with favus, a contagious disease of the scalp. The thirty-seven others were healthy, but were relatives of those having favus.

The sorriest-looking lot of all were the six young Russian stowaways. They were discovered when the vessel was one day out from port.

They were put to work in the fire room, and. were worked so hard that each lost nearly thirty pounds during the sixteen days' voyage. They will be held until the prescribed fine of $10 for each is paid by the agents of the vessel.

The immigrants say it was represented to them that the vessel would have good accommodations, and all applying for passage were told she would sail within a few days. It was represented to them that they would be second-cabin passengers, and thus escape the strict examination of steerage passengers.

They paid $40 to $60 apiece, which was to include railroad fares from the various towns they emigrated from. Instead of sailing immediately from Bremen, it was twenty days before the *Red Sea* started. The immigrants were huddled into berths, seven deep. The food, they say, consisted mainly of corned beef, barley broth, and bread, only the bread being fit to eat.

One Jewish immigrant, who was provided with $750 when he left Bremen, claims to have spent $60 for food for himself and family on the voyage. Two others made affidavits that they were compelled to pawn their watches for food.

One, whose exchequer had been exhausted by the long detention in Bremen, applied for bread, but got only severe bruises and a discolored eye.

Capt. Bustin's account is different from that of the passengers. In a written statement to Commissioner Senner he says he had thirty days' supply of food on board when he started. He heard of only one complaint about the food. It was made by an immigrant who said he had been compelled to buy food of the steward or go without. Capt. Bustin says in his report that the stewards were threatened with prosecution if other complaints were made.

To the reporters who boarded the Red Sea last night Capt. Bustin admitted that there was a small-sized bread riot on the fourth day out. It was brought about, he said, by the passengers recovering from their seasickness and demanding more to eat than the daily allowance called for.

When the bread was refused they made a charge upon the galley. Capt. Bustin seized the two ringleaders, handcuffed them and stood them upon the bridge as an example for the others.

C.B. Richard, who filed the $10,000 required by Commissioner Senner to cover expenses that may be incurred in the detention or return of the Red Sea's passengers, said yesterday that he had assumed the responsibility purely as an act of humanity to prevent their indefinite detention.

THEY MUST GO BACK TO EUROPE
(New York Times, 5/8/1895)

WASHINGTON, May 7. -- Commissioner General Stump to-day issued a letter of instructions to Commissioner Senner at New York, in which he says:

The bureau is in receipt of your letter of the 5th inst., inclosing a communication from Messrs. Wing, Putnam & Burlingham of New York City, attorneys for Henderson Brothers, agents for the Anchor Steamship Line, requesting that the said Henderson Brothers be permitted to furnish bond, under Section 7 of the act of March 3, 1893, for the 87 alien immigrants who arrived at your port per steamship Victoria from Naples April 28, 1895, and who were debarred a landing by the Board of Special Inquiry as likely to become public charges.

From the records in this office it appears that this vessel brought 470 steerage passengers; that 280 of them were landed after inspection by the immigration authorities at Ellis Island, and 190 were detained for special inquiry. The board, after duly considering each case, finally ordered 87 of these detained passengers deported. The unusually large number ordered deported clearly indicates that the Anchor Line Steamship Company, to which this vessel belongs, does not carefully inspect its steerage passengers at the port of embarkation prior to sailing, thus ignoring the plain requirements of the act of March 3, 1893, which was intended to save the immigrant a fruitless voyage, the steamship companies the expense of returning rejected immigrants, and the United States from an undesirable class of people.

The decision of the board of special inquiry in each case is final, unless appealed from, and the permission to receive a bond is a special privilege, only granted where the circumstances justify the interposition of the Commissioner General and the Secretary of the Treasury.

I am informed that certain steamships touching at Havre, and some sailing from Mediterranean ports, are bringing to New York steerage passengers, most of whom appear to the Inspectors who board the vessels at Quarantine as undesirable. In such cases you may, in your discretion, examine such passengers on board the vessel, thereby avoiding the overcrowding of immigrants on the island at this busy season of the year, and placing the responsibility for the neglect to observe the reasonable requirements of our immigration laws upon those who may violate their provisions.

An application to give bond in each of the cases to these immigrants would be considered and granted, if the circumstances presented any sufficient reason for interposition on the part of the department; but this, it must be said, is not apparent.

The application of Messrs. Henderson Brothers to give bond for all these eighty-seven immigrants will therefore have to be refused.

The Immigration Bureau heretofore has in many cases taken the bonds of steamship companies that immigrants debarred for cause should not become public charges, and has permitted them to land until their cases should be passed upon. But under this system there are now awaiting examination at the one immigrant station of Ellis Island more than 300 immigrants, and they test to the utmost capacity the accommodations of the Island.

Commissioner Stump's letter, which was sent this afternoon to Commissioner Senner at New York, supplements a telegram sent earlier in the day, directing that eighty-seven immigrants be returned to Europe tomorrow, and fully explains what the policy of the department will be in the future.

SWARMING WITH INSECTS

Ellis Island Commissioner of Immigration William Williams pretty much attacked everyone who he believed was taking advantage of immigrants, no matter how powerful they were. Here is a letter he sent to officials of the French Line on December 9, 1910 concerning their sanitation practices.

Sirs:

By "La Gascogne" there arrived a girl named Michelina Trapanese covered with vermin. Her head in particular was and, notwithstanding the hair has been cut, still is literally swarming with insects. I have caused your landing agent to look at the condition this girl is in, even after attempt was made to clean her head. Do you think it is right to allow immigrants to board your vessels in such a condition?

Respectfully,

*WM. WILLIAMS,
Commissioner.*

ALMOST 40 NOBLES IN STEERAGE
(New York Times, 10/3/1923)

The National Greek liner *Constantinople* docked at Pier 22, Brooklyn, yesterday morning with 1,536 passengers from ports in the Near East and was escorted from Quarantine by a fleet of motor launches filled with Greeks eager to greet the folks arriving from their native land. Among the young women on the *Constantinople* were 135 so-called picture brides, who had been selected by their husbands-elect on this side through photographs.

Included in the steerage list were a number of Russian refugees from Constantinople, among whom were said to be eleven former Princes, twelve former Princesses, six Barons, eight Baronets and two Counts belonging to the old regime. Count Ivan Peterhof, a former Captain in the Imperial Guards, explained to the reporters that he and his countrymen on board no longer had titles, but were immigrants coming here to live and become citizens of the United States.

Note: *The Communists had recently seized power in Russia and in other lands associated with the old Russian Empire. They were trying to hammer these countries into the Soviet Union. These nobles were escaping death sentences.*

The yearly quota allotments of Spain, Palestine, Egypt and other African and Asiatic countries being exhausted, no more non-exempt immigrants from these nations may be admitted before the new fiscal year, July, 1924, according to a statement last night by Henry H. Curran, Commissioner of Immigration.

Additional aliens examined at Ellis Island yesterday totaled 1,755, of whom 883 were brought here by the United States liner *George Washington*, 865 by the French liner *Paris* and 7 by *Columbia* of the Pacific Mail Steamship Company.

MANY IMMIGRANTS BEAT DEPORTATION

TEDDY ROOSEVELT AT ELLIS ISLAND
(New York Times, 3/14/1897)

Police Commissioner Roosevelt visited Ellis Island yesterday and observed the work of receiving, examining, and landing immigrants. He was invited to a seat beside Chairman Ellis of the Board of Special Inquiry, and was permitted to examine some of the immigrants himself.

The first immigrants to come before the board were a man and woman who turned out to be elopers. The woman said her husband was a "card sharp" in Germany. She had left him because he had beaten her. The man said he was going to marry the woman as soon as her husband got an absolute divorce.

Another couple then appeared for examination. One was a young man, who gave his name as Henry Smith, 23 years old, son of a wealthy Scotchman. His companion was a German girl, only 20 years old, who had been a servant in his father's family, but had been sent away some time previously. Her name was Alice Laybonn. Henry's father had sent him away also to travel, but he was true to the girl. At the suggestion of the Board of Special Inquiry, all hands adjourned to Deputy Commissioner Mc Sweeney's room, and the Rev. Dr. Dalton made Henry and Alice man and wife. Commissioner Roosevelt witnessed a typical day on the Island, and seemed much interested.

Note: *Theodore Roosevelt was police commissioner of New York City in the mid 1890s. This was the start of his rise to national prominence. He would later serve as Assistant Secretary of the U.S. Navy, as a colonel in the Rough Riders, and as governor of New York before he received the vice-presidential nomination in 1900.*

WOMAN IN MALE GARB ADMITTED
(New York Times, 10/6/1908)

Mary Johnson, who has lived fifteen years of her life as Frank Woodhull, and whose sex was discovered when she was held up on Ellis Island, was discharged yesterday by the immigration authorities after landing from the American liner *New York* and allowed to go out in the world and earn her living in trousers. The Board of Special Inquiry came to the conclusion that Miss Johnson was a desirable immigrant and should be allowed to win her livelihood as she saw fit.

The woman, whom nature has endowed with a mustache of proper proportions, left the station on Ellis Island Yesterday afternoon very much elated. She did not land in New York, but went direct to Newark. There she took a train for New Orleans, where she will make her home. She left the building wearing her neat black sack suit and with her overcoat hung over her arm.

"Women have a hard time in this world," she said. "They are the walking advertisements for the milliner, the dry goods stores, the jewelers, and other shops. They live in the main only for their clothes, and when now and then a woman comes to the front who does not care for dress she is looked upon as a freak and a crank. With me how different. "See this hat?" and she leaned over and picked up the black slouch hat. "I have worn that hat for three years, and it cost me $3. What woman could have worn a hat so long? Bah! They are the slaves to whim and fashion."

"What could I do when fifteen years ago I faced the crisis in my life? There was only housework to which I could turn, and I had been subject to rheumatism. Men can work at many unskilled callings, but to a woman only a few are open, and they are the grinding, death-dealing kinds of work. Well, for me, I prefer to live a life of independence and freedom."

Before she went out again to face the world as Frank Woodhull, Miss Johnson was asked whether she feared detection of her sex. She replied that she feared nothing from grown-up persons, but strangely enough her experience had told her to beware of children. They have been the only ones who have seen through her disguise or had an inkling of the truth concerning her, she said.

Comment: *This story shows immigration officials would have allowed K. D. Laing's spiritual ancestresses into the country if they didn't suspect lesbianism. A century ago, people were understandably leery of sexual deviate behavior, but they were less prone to assume someone who was merely eccentric was also a deviate.*

WRITER WON'T BE DEPORTED BECAUSE OF OLD CRIME IN HUNGARY
(Special to The New York Times, 7/7/1909)

WASHINGTON, July 6 -- Gyula Rudnyansky, a Hungarian poet and journalist of note, who has been detained at Ellis Island since last November, will be released tomorrow, on orders from the Department of Commerce and Labor, when he will be free to return to his home, in Cleveland, Ohio.

The case of Rudnyansky attracted the attention of Hungarians all over the United States, and the department has been visited by scores of delegations seeking his release and has been inundated by petitions seeking the same end. The prisoner was held on charges that he had been guilty of a crime in his native country and that, according to the law, he could be deported.

Rudnyansky is the editor of an influential Hungarian paper in Cleveland, and has been a power in Hungarian circles in the United Stats since he came here, three years ago last January. Last November charges were filed against him with the Department of Commerce and Labor.

Assistant Secretary McHarg declined to divulge the names of Rudnyandky's accusers, but it is intimated that they were the publishers and proprietors of a rival Hungarian newspaper. The charge was that more than a quarter of a century ago Rudnyansky was convicted of distorting some declaration of a civil debt, and on conviction was sentenced to serve six months in jail in Hungary.

A complete investigation of the editor's subsequent career satisfied this Government that he had lived this down and was fully qualified for citizenship.

Here's the follow-up story (7/8/1909):

Acting under orders from the Department of Commerce and Labor, Commissioner of Immigration Williams yesterday released from custody Gyula Rudnyansky, the Hungarian poet and journalist. He had been detained on Ellis Island since Saturday. His release came through the influence of friends in the Middle West. The order for his release reached the Commissioner early in the morning, and immediately Rudnyansky was notified that he was free.

Some months ago, after a quarrel with another newspaper man of his own nationality, Rudnyansky, who manages a Hungarian newspaper at Cleveland, Ohio, was arrested by the Federal authorities on the charge that he had been convicted of a crime in Hungary twenty-five years ago, and was therefore not a desirable citizen. He was taken to Ellis Island at that time, but investigation showed that the conviction was in a civil case and he was released.

Last week a similar charge was made against the editor, and he was rearrested and sent to Ellis Island. Influential Hungarians appealed to Congressman Cassidy of Cleveland. The result was that the Washington authorities agreed to release him. He left at once for Cleveland.

BEAU DIDDLING OVER HARVESTING RIPE RUSSIAN FARM GIRL
(Arthur Train, Saturday Evening Post, 3/5/1910)

A handsome, clear-eyed Russian girl of about 20 years, the daughter of a farmer, comes in and sits down before us. She is clean and intelligent looking. She nervously clasps and unclasps her hands and the tears are welling in her eyes.

"That girl over there," says the commissioner, "is an interesting and puzzling case. Her father is a farmer in moderate circumstances. A young man with whom she grew up, the son of a neighbor, came here two years ago, and last year wrote to her father that if the girl would come over, he would marry her. So she came alone. But the prospective bridegroom didn't show up. I wrote him -- he lives somewhere in New Jersey — and last week he appeared and looked her over. Finally he said he wasn't sure whether he wanted to marry her or not. Naturally her pride was somewhat wounded, and she decided that she had doubts herself."

"So everything is at a standstill. The girl says she doesn't want to go back, to be laughed at; and I can't let her land. You don't know any lady who wants a servant, do you? She could work! Look at her arms. A nice girl, too. No? Well, I don't know what to do."

(The commissioner asks the girl:) "Are you willing to marry Peter if he comes again?" The girl nods, the tears brimming over.

"Well, I'll write to that fellow again and tell him he's a fool. He'll never have such a chance again."

Note: The commissioner in the story was William Williams. He could overrule his boards of special inquiry and admit certain aliens under the law. The Russian girl appeared able to work, but without a place to stay until she found work, she might wind up a public charge or prey to those who meant her no good. A middle-aged California man sent Williams a letter offering to marry the girl (or at least hire her) because he read about her plight in the Saturday Evening Post and clipped out the story to accompany the letter.

STOWAWAY PRINCESS STAYS
(New York Times, (9/26/1922)

WASHINGTON, Sept. 25 -- Princess Ivan(a) Pschernitscheno(va) of Russia, who came to this country as a stowaway after trudging across Russia and Germany afoot, today established to the satisfaction of immigration officials that she is an American citizen.

Arrested upon her arrival in this country last July, the Princess declared she was the daughter of Frederick Schlich, who was a naturalized American and who at the time she was born was living at Louisville, Ky.

Immigration officials at the time were unable to verify the woman's story and she was ordered deported, but Secretary Davis later permitted her to remain in the United States pending a further investigation. Records produced by the woman and her friends recently and verified by Government officers, it was officially announced today, disclosed her story to be correct.

The Princess is said to be living in New York City at present.

ITALIAN BRIDES BEAT QUOTA LAW
(New York Times, 12/4/1922)

Five prospective brides just got under the barrier at Ellis Island late on Saturday afternoon after they had come very near to being excluded under the quota law. Yesterday they were honeymooning their ways to different parts of the United States.

It was just before the gates slammed against Italy, her yearly quota exhausted, that these girls were counted "safe" and passed to the accompaniment of "Bravas!" from waiting on-lookers as they flung themselves into the arms of the anxious bridegrooms. The girls were Teresa Benedetti, Rosa Desimone, Oneglia Soccaglia, Maria Gianetti and Angela Simonassi.

The arrival of three ships, racing from Italian ports to land passengers brought 3,436 Italians, with a balance of only 3,100 to be admitted. Clearly 336 must be left out. In enforcing the quota law preference is given to the "wives, parents, brothers, sisters, children under 18 years of age and fiancees of citizens, aliens who have applied for citizenship ... persons eligible to citizenship who served in the World War and were honorably discharged." So it was that the bridegrooms were able to claim the brides ahead of some others less fortunate.

SCOTS GO TO HALIFAX, SPEED TO AMERICA TO BEAT OUT OTHER BRITS
(New York Times, 5/20/1923)

HALIFAX, N.S., May 19 – Winners in a race with other British groups now on the high seas to reach the United States before the immigration quota of the United Kingdom was exhausted, 399 Scottish immigrants who were landed here today from the steamship *Cameronia* tonight left the city by special train for New York.

Cutting off two days on the ocean voyage by landing at this port, the canny Scots were examined at Halifax under a special permit from the United States immigration authorities at Washington and quickly resumed their trip.

A special train of thirteen sleeping cars bore the immigrants on the last lap of their race, leaving here soon after 6 o'clock tonight. The train was routed over the Canadian National Railways to St. John, N. B., and thence to New York, via Worcester, Mass.

Hearing that large numbers of British immigrants were on their way to America, the Scots on the Cameronia persuaded the captain to land them here in order to reach American soil before their fellow-countrymen.

Commissioner General Husband said tonight that the immigration authorities at Halifax had telegraphed him asking whether the 347 Scottish immigrants landed there from the Cameronia exhausted the quota for the United Kingdom, and that he had replied that they did not, and, therefore, would be allowed to enter the United States. Halifax, he said, was a port of entry the same as New York.

Robert E. Tod, Commissioner of Immigration, said last night that the 347 emigrants from Scotland who had landed at Halifax might possibly come in when the new quotas went into effect in July.

"If their passports are visaed to the United States they can remain in Canada a few weeks and then come in," he said. "If, however, their passports are to Canada, according to the law they will have to remain there a full year before they can be admitted into this country for residence."

Commissioner Tod said that he had not heard from Commissioner General Husband on the cases of the emigrants at Halifax. Two inspectors have gone from the Ellis Island Station to Halifax to examine those who desire to come here.

THEY KNOW THE BABY IS A POLE
(New York Times, 7/23/1923)

If our immigration laws have any purpose except that of putting every possible obstacle in the way of foreigners desiring to come here – if those laws have even incidentally the purpose, while restricting immigration, to do it in a reasonable, common-sense way – there is at least one change in them that should be made as soon as Congress can get around to the job.

The present method of letting birthplace determine nationality and race sometimes is obviously absurd. That is, not infrequently, it leads to absurdity.

Our law makes a mistake like the one common among ethnologists of another day, who deduced race from language, forgetting the frequency with which languages not their own have been imposed on subject peoples or voluntarily adapted by inferior ones.

Last week there arrived at this port a baby that had been born on the way over from Europe. Its parent were Poles, but the ship was British. Under the law our immigration officials had to reason thus: A British ship is British territory: therefore this baby cannot enter on Poland's unfilled quota, but must be excluded because the British quota is exhausted for this month.

So a difference of nationality between a new-born baby and its parents was gravely announced! That this ruling will be reversed may be expected with some confidence, but no self-respecting official should have been require to render himself ridiculous by making it.

Henry Curran, then the Commissioner of Immigration at Ellis Island, explained the situation this way in his book Pillar to Post (pages 300-302):

The Polish wife of a Pennsylvania coal miner – both good Poles, admitted a year before – had gone back suddenly to Poland to visit her old father and mother, who had taken sick and might soon die. The visit over, she returned quickly to America. She would be admitted at once, for little visits do not count against quotas. The coal miner was at the island, waiting for her. We told him everything would be all right, but he was unaccountably nervous. Then the ship came in, the Lapland of the Red Star Line, from Antwerp, and we found out why the husband was so nervous. On the day before the ship made port, a baby Pole had been born to the returning mother. The expected had happened, "mother and child both doing well," in the Ellis Island hospital, everybody delighted, until – the inspector admitted the mother but excluded the baby Pole.

"Why?" asked the father, trembling.

"Polish quota exhausted," pronounced the helpless inspector.

Then they brought the case to me. Deport that baby? I couldn't. And somebody had to be quick, for the mother was not doing well under the idea her baby would soon be taken from her and "transported far beyond the northern sea."

"The baby was not born in Poland," I ruled, "but on a British ship. She is chargeable to the British quota. The deck of a British ship is British soil, anywhere in the world."

"British quota exhausted yesterday," replied the inspector. That was a blow. But I had another shot in my locker.

"Come to think of it, the Lapland hails from Antwerp," I remarked. "That's in Belgium. Any ship out of Belgium is merely a peripatetic extension of Belgian soil. The baby is a Belgian. Use the Belgian quota."

"Belgian quota ran out a week ago." Thus the inspector. I was stumped.

"I've got it! How could I have forgotten my law so soon? You see, with children, it's the way it is with wills. We follow the intention. Now it is clear enough the mother was hurrying back so the baby would be born here and be a native-born American citizen, no immigrant business at all. And the baby has the same intention, only the ship was a day late and that upset everything. But – under the law, mind you, under the law – the baby, by intention was born in America. It is an American baby – no baby Pole at all – no British, no Belgian – just good American. That's the way I rule – run up the flag!"

It took the inspector some time to recover. "What is the exact legal reference that I enter into the papers?" he asked finally, looking out to sea hard.

"Yes – ah, yes, the legal reference, of course." I needed more time. Then it came to me. Necessity is the mother of invention. "It is the 'High Law of Innocence,'" I replied solemnly. "Yes, yes – I had nearly forgotten – the High Law of Innocence – unwritten but supreme – supersedes all other laws. Put it down to that. I don't think the judges know about it yet, but – maybe the case will never get to them!"

"Baby admitted," said the inspector, grinning.

WEEPING MUSIC TEACHER PLAYS HER WAY INTO AMERICA
(New York Times, 12/28/1923)

Her rendition of Schumann's "Traumerei" on her violin before a special Board of Inquiry at Ellis Island convinced the authorities that Regina Kohn was entitled to classification as an artist, and won her admission to the United States. She had been threatened with deportation because the Rumanian quota was exhausted when she arrived Monday on the Celtic. Miss Kohn is a Hungarian, but the part of Hungary in which she always lived is now occupied by Rumania and its inhabitants are classified as Rumanians under the immigration regulations.

Her case came up before the board Wednesday and Miss Kohn was informed by the Chairman that if she could play the "Traumerei" well enough she would be admitted as an artist, if not she would be deported. Feeling as if she had "one foot in America, the other in Europe," as she expressed it yesterday, she played the composition so artistically on a violin she had with her that she was told she could enter at once. So feelingly did she play that she broke down and wept in the midst of the piece, but controlled herself well enough to finish.

Miss Kohn, who is 38 years old, has taught hundreds of children in her native land, but seldom has played in public and then only in her own city of Nagy Warad. She intends to open a studio here and possibly give concerts or go on the stage. She will live with her brother, Ignatz Kohn, at 1475 Second Avenue.

Henry Curran, in his book Pillar to Post (pages 298-299) recalled Miss Kohn's ordeal as follows:

In the quota law there was an exemption for artists. Strolling through the island, I found a pale-looking girl from Hungary pleading with the inspectors to be admitted. She was alone, and the tears were coming. The inspectors were sorry but helpless, for the quota was exhausted.

"Is that a violin?" I asked her suddenly, pointing to her luggage in the corner.

"Yes, it is mine," she answered fearfully.

"Will you play for us?" I grinned at her in reassurance.

"Yes, sir, but – but why?"

"Just play – please!" I persisted, still grinning.

"What should I play for you?" she asked as she took up the violin. Her fingers were trembling, the bow shaking in her hand, her whole little frame quivering.

"Oh, let's say – Schumann's 'Traumerei.' "

"Ah, yes."

She played it, her confidence growing. She played it so beautifully we were all spellbound. When she had finished and lowered the violin uncertainly, still lost in the happier land of her music, I turned to the inspectors.

"Artist, don't you think?" I asked vaguely, winking one eye. "Exemption – perhaps?"

"Yes, yes, yes," answered the three inspectors together, vigorously and in unison.

A letter writer whose missive made the New Year's Day 1924 edition of the New York Times, summed up the case as follows:

"Mark Twain once remarked that God first made idiots for practice, and then made Boards of Education. It is a pleasure to commend the Board of Inquiry at Ellis Island. In listening to Miss Kohn so sympathetically and understandingly this board deserves to be placed on record as being guilty, at least, of harmonious intelligence."

DEPORTATIONS OF IMMIGRANTS

DEMENTED GERMAN GIRL DEPORTED
(Maud Mosher)

On Feb. 17, 1904 I was sent to the Elizabeth St. Police Station to escort a demented girl to the Barge Office.

Just as I arrived at the Police Station the Inspector, Mr. Palmer, who had brought her from Minneapolis as one had become a public charge, was standing cap in hand before the judge saying: "I came into the city late last night on the train and this morning have telephoned to the Barge Office for a matron to come here to escort the girl to the Island."

The rules of the Immigration division are such that if it be necessary for an officer to take a woman or girl anywhere off the Island he must have a matron with him.

Just as the Inspector said this I came in the door and not realizing that I was in the presence of the court stepped up to Mr. Palmer and said: "And here I am, Mr. Palmer -- how-do-you-do?"

At that the judge, policeman and all the others laughed.

Mr. Palmer then said: "So you are going to help me are you? I hope you are not afraid. She has 'done up' two trained nurses and broken two pairs of glasses -- she seems to have an antipathy for people wearing glasses." I took off my spectacles and handing them to Mr. Palmer, asked him to put them in his pocket as I could go without them a while and had no place to put them.

He took them and said, in answer to my question: "Is she violent?" "Well, yes, she gets violent spells. The woman who came with me from Minnesota was deathly afraid of her and had several fights but then the girl knew she was afraid. I guess you will get along all right."

When I said: "Oh, yes. I guess I shall," the judge said, "Aren't you afraid?" in quite an astonished way.

"Oh, no," I replied, "If she acts very badly I'll just fall on her." At that, of course there was another laugh.

Just then the police matron brought the poor demented creature in. She was a small, slender, dark haired German girl of seventeen but her face was drawn and old -- she looked nearer thirty than seventeen. On her head was an old hat which kept falling off as of course they did not dare let her have hatpins. She wore a dark red dress but the skirt she had put on wrong side out. The police matron said she had tried to get her to change it and also to eat something but she would not.

I took her by the arm and Mr. Palmer walked on the other side; in this manner we escorted her to the elevated railroad. We got inside the car; she seemed quite interested in watching the flying buildings, etc.

In the seat facing us were a young lady and a boy. She regarded us quite curiously for a while and then all at once it dawned on her that the reason that queer looking girl opposite had her dress on wrong side out was because she was crazy. It didn't take them very long to leave the car and then Mr. Palmer came and sat opposite us.

When we got to the Barge Office I took Anna (her name was Anna Mallinger) to the Matrons' Office and there persuaded her to eat something and drink some coffee.

By-and-bye I pointed to her skirt and turned up the bottom showing the right side. She just glanced at it. Pretty soon she looked at it again then impatiently looked away again. But she was not just satisfied for soon she gave it a closer examination and began to laugh. Then she got up and started laughing, hastily took it off, turned it and put it on again right.

By this time Mr. Willits, the deporting officer had come to take her to the ship. I accompanied him and we took her to the *Troonland* and put her in charge of the ship's officer.

By this time she had taken a great fancy to me and clung to me -- she seemed to fear I was going to leave her and when I finally did go I had to attract (her) attention to something else and then slip away.

Anna had come to this country (evidently on her own) ... and became insane sometime afterward. Her mania was that she was intensely afraid of men -- afraid they would do her harm or take advantage of her. She was deported because she had become a public charge in less than a year from the time she landed.

Note: Perhaps the poor girl had been raped or had been forced into acts of prostitution or had thwarted an attempt of slavers to catch her ... and she had a reason to be afraid of men.

NORWEGIAN WOMAN THROWS BIG MONEY INTO NEW YORK HARBOR
(New York Times, 10/30/1915 and 10/31/1915)

About an hour after the Norwegian-American liner *Kristianiafjord* arrived at her pier at the foot of Forty-fifth Street, South Brooklyn, yesterday morning from Bergen, an excited-looking woman, who was being detained by the Immigration Inspector for further examination, rushed on deck and threw a packet of papers into the water.

Walter Lillie, the ship's baggage master who saw the act, said that a few minutes before he had been watching a motor boat with a green painted hull and a gray top that had been hanging round the stern of the liner for some time in a suspicious manner. It was close by when the woman threw the package overboard, and before he could take any action in the matter, Lillie said, one of the men from the motor boat picked it up. And then the little craft started toward the Manhattan shore.

Lillie reported the matter to the Captain of the *Kristianiafjord*, who notified Brooklyn Police Headquarters, and two detectives from the Sixth Brooklyn Detective Bureau are trying to identify the owner of the motor boat. All the woman would say about the package was that it contained 5,000 kronen in Norwegian paper money, which is worth about $1,300 in United States money.

Note: *That amount of money would keep a family alive for almost a year in 1915.*

Here is the followup:

The name of the woman passenger who threw a package of Norwegian money worth $1,456 into the water on Friday morning from the steamer *Kristianiafjord* at the foot of Forty-fifth Street, South Brooklyn, on which she arrived from Bergen, according to the immigration authorities, is Mrs. Marie Andersen, 50 years old. She is now in the observation ward of the medical division in the hospital on Ellis Island, suffering from mental trouble. Mrs. Andersen told the immigration officials that she had thrown the money overboard because she was going back to Norway and did not need it.

Detectives William Lohman and Thomas Hylands of the Sixth Branch Detective Bureau, who were assigned to the case, reported yesterday that the owner of the green motor boat who was seen to fish the package out of the water was Richard Gallagher, a junk dealer of 756 Third Avenue, Brooklyn. In restoring it to the detectives, Gallagher said that he had intended to carry it to Police Headquarters in Brooklyn that morning if it had not been called for by the officers. They believe him, as Gallagher has the reputation (of being honest).

POLE ATTACKS GUARDS, TORCHES BAGGAGE; GYPSIES AND BLACK-HANDERS SCUFFLE
(New York Times, 7/18/1909)

It became known last night that serious trouble occurred at the Ellis Island Immigration Station on Friday evening, when 227 aliens were shipped on the transfer steamboat *Millard* to be taken aboard the various liners on which they were to be deported.

Fifteen of the number were Russian gypsies, who appeared to be very unruly. They fought with some "Black Handers," who had been arrested on warrants in various cities. The deportation staff had to be increased by a number of clerks, and officials from other branches of the Immigration Bureau to quell the trouble.

Note: *"Black Hander" was a moniker applied to Sicilians and Corsicans and Italians from south of Rome, and Serbs and others from the Balkans suspected of being in organized crime or in terrorist or anarchist activities.*

The turbulence began when Jan Gyvan, a Pole of powerful build, who is six feet three inches tall, objected to going on board the *Millard*.

The Pole could not speak English enough to make his protests against being deported understood, so he drew a long keen-bladed knife from his boot and went for the nearest deportation officer. It took six husky men to hold Gyvan till he was disarmed and carried, kicking and struggling, on board the vessel.

The immigration officials were not armed, and had a hard job to get the enraged alien's knife away. To prevent him causing more trouble he was lashed to a stanchion on the main deck of the steamboat forward, while the officers went aft to get the fifteen gypsies on board.

Shortly after the *Millard* left Ellis Island for the North River piers Capt. Burns, who was in the pilot house, saw a cloud of smoke rising from the fore part of the main deck. He sang out, and the mate and crew rushed forward to find that Gyvan had freed his hands and set fire to the bundles of bedding and baggage around him. The flames were subdued before much damage was done. The thing happened so quickly that the 226 aliens in the after part of the *Millard* did not have time to start a panic before the danger was over.

When being taken aboard the *Cincinnati* the big Pole tried desperately to jump overboard, but was restrained by the deportation officers and crew of the *Millard*. Gyvan will be carefully watched on the voyage back.

It was 1 o'clock yesterday morning when the deportation officers got through with the last steamship on the list, the *Prinzess Irene*, and the officers of that ship complained bitterly at having to rouse up at that hour to receive aliens who should have been brought on board in the afternoon.

The officers from Ellis Island had been working for eighteen hours at a stretch without extra pay and were tired out. They complained, too, that, as they are unarmed, they are in danger of their lives in handling such desperate aliens as are now being deported in batches.

Otto Grumach, who came over on the *Amerika* as a second cabin passenger and who was formerly Assistant Secretary of the German Legation in Belgrade, Servia, has been detained by the immigration authorities for examination. Grumach said he had come to this country to look over American industries. He had $7 in cash and tickets to the West.

He also carried a letter of credit from his father allowing him to draw $12.50 a week for twelve weeks.

POLICE CAPTURE LAUNCH WITH PRETTY GIRL IN MENSWEAR
(New York Times, 2/3/1922)

Detective Sergeants Donohue and Corcoran and Sergeant Whalen of the harbor police were patrolling the waters of the bay in the vicinity of Ellis Island in a police launch shortly before last midnight, when they discovered another launch speeding in the direction of Brooklyn with its lights out.

A chase ensued which ended at the ferry slip at the foot of Thirty-ninth Street, where two men jumped from the mysterious launch to the landing and escaped. The two detectives then boarded the abandoned launch and were surprised to find what appeared to be another man crouching in the bottom of the boat.

When they dragged the "man" to his feet, however, they discovered that their prisoner was a pretty Italian girl about 18 years old dressed in male attire. The girl was unable to speak English and the detectives carried her to the Barge Office at the Battery, where though an interpreter, she said she was Dele Donato. She refused to say anything more about herself, however.

Superintendent Cromer at the Barge Office telephoned over to the Immigration Station on Ellis Island and later announced he would detain the girl until an investigation could be made this morning to learn whether the men had attempted to smuggle her into the country to evade the recent amendment to the law restricting the number of immigrants to be admitted to the country.

The detectives said that examination of the boat revealed the name "Luba No. 3" on the bow and a license which had been issued by the Government to J. A. Armgren of 230 95th Street, Brooklyn. They said they would question Armgren with a view to identifying the two men who made their escape.

ALIEN SAYS HE'S AN ACTOR, BUT JUDGE GIVES HIM THE HOOK
(New York Times, 7/14/1922)

Federal Judge Knox was asked yesterday to permit Benedetto Messina, now held at Ellis Island, to land in this country despite the fact that the Italian quota is exhausted. His counsel contended that Messina was an actor, and, as such, privileged to land without regard to the quota. The immigration authorities doubted Messina's calling because his hands were rough from manual work, and because, when asked to display his histrionic talents, he had failed lamentably.

His counsel insisted that the Court accept a certificate by the steamship company that brought Messina over that he is an actor, and showed a contract with a Bowery theatrical company at $3.50 a day. Judge Knox replied that if any one could be admitted upon such evidences all a man would have to do would be to say he was an actor and then get a job in a barber shop. Benedetto will be sent back to Italy.

FINNISH GIRL WHO ELOPED WITH SAILOR DEPORTED
(New York Times, 5/22/1923)

BOSTON, May 21 -- Loser in a three months' battle for the right to remain in the United States, Bertha Laine, a 19 year-old Finnish girl, left for New York tonight to sail for Copenhagen tomorrow on the steamship *Frederick VIII*.

While the American steamer *Bellingham* was frozen in at Raumo, Finland, last Winter, Bertha met and fell in love with Arturo Alvarez, a Porto Rican, a member of the vessel's crew. The night before the *Bellingham* was to sail Alvarez persuaded the girl to elope with him. They walked out over the ice to the steamer and Bertha was smuggled into the firemen's quarters in the forecastle, where she remained hidden for sixty days.

The day before the *Bellingham* was to reach Boston the skipper was informed of the girl's presence on board. An immigration Board of Inquiry ordered her deportation, despite Alvarez's plea that they were to have been married. An appeal to Washington failed to upset the board's ruling and habeas corpus proceedings in the United States District Court also failed of result.

IRISH STOWAWAY BREAKS HANDCUFFS IN ESCAPE ATTEMPT
(New York Times, 8/6/1923)

Because he did not wish to be sent to Ellis Island today, Patrick Walsh, 17 years, a stowaway on the Royal Mail liner *Ohio*, which docked at Pier 42, North River, yesterday from Southampton and Cherbourg, made a desperate effort to escape by breaking his handcuffs and diving down into the water thirty-five feet below him. He swam to Pier 45, where he was assisted to the stringers by one of the ship's detectives. He was taken back to the *Ohio* and locked up with a new set handcuffs and will go to the island today.

The *Ohio* brought eight stowaways, six ex-firemen, including Walsh, who stowed away in the coal bunkers at Southampton, where two Germans had been concealed since the ship left Hamburg. At Quarantine yesterday morning they were all locked up in some cabins with a steward on guard in the alleyway.

Walsh, who was described as an active lad, had been advised to drop overboard as the ship was passing Liberty Island and land at the Battery with excursionists as if he had fallen off a tugboat. He did not succeed in breaking the handcuffs until the ship had been made fast for an hour at the pier.

Walsh wriggled out of the port in the cabin and went down head first into the water. The loud splash attracted the attention of Ed Cleary, the company's detective, on duty on the deck. The stowaway still had a handcuff on his left wrist, but it soon slipped off in the water as he struck out for Pier 41.

In spite of the heat, Detective Cleary did a sprint on shore and managed to get to the next pier just in time to assist the nearly exhausted Walsh to climb the stringers.

When he recovered his breath, instead of being grateful to his rescuer, Walsh said: "If I had know you were here I would have gone on further." He was a bit dazed from the shock he received on hitting the water, but soon recovered.

ITALIAN IMMIGRANTS ESCAPE
(New York Times, 11/2/1923)

News of the escape of twenty-three Italian immigrants from the liner *Dante Alighieri* on Oct. 10 became known yesterday. A check of records by immigration officials showed that of 132 immigrants returned to the ship to await examination, because of crowded conditions at Ellis Island, only 109 were sent back to Ellis Island.

A fine of $300 for each immigrant who escaped will be levied on the steamship company, Commissioner of Immigration Curran announced yesterday. Dominic A. Truda, local agent of the Transatlantica Italiana, vigorously denied reports that immigrants had escaped with the aid of passes which had permitted them to get by the guards at the gate.

BRITISH PREACHER GETS DEPORTED, DEFROCKED ON MORALS CHARGES
(Edward Corsi, In the Shadow of Liberty, Page 265)

Ellis Island once deported a preacher, serving a warrant of arrest on him in his rectory in Brooklyn and bringing him up before the Board of Inquiry which proved that he had served two prison terms in England for a crime involving moral turpitude. Under the laws of this country any person who has been less than eighteen months in the United States must be deported if it is proved that he was convicted abroad for something which comes under the moral turpitude clause.

Note: "Moral turpitude" means crimes of dishonesty, such as perjury, burglary, fraud, theft, embezzlement, and fencing stolen goods, or sexual crimes such as rape, sodomy, sexual assault, and child molesting, or acts of malicious violence such as murder, felony assault, and robbery, and acts against public decency such as adultery, incest, bigamy, homosexuality, and child abandonment.

The Rev. Alfred Hart had taken over his pastorate about six weeks before, and had remained a mystery man to his congregation. At the time of his arrest none of them knew anything about him.

The immigration officials had information that Hart was born in a Whitechapel slum, and had been found and educated by a wealthy woman who sent him to Oxford to prepare for the ministry.

The Church of England, with which he claimed affiliation, repudiated him after his arrest.

CONVICT GETS RUSSIAN TRIP
(Special to The New York Times, 4/15/1923)

OSSINING, April 14 – Sing Sing Prison is accustomed to pay the fare of departing convicts when they are formally released, but Jacob Harris, alias Meyer Herson, who was paroled today, will get a longer free ride than any other inmate who has left the prison in years.

Harris, who is a Bolshevik, was taken in custody by a United States Immigration Department attendant and started for Ellis Island on the first lap of a 5,000 miles journey to Russia. He is being deported as an undesirable alien.

The defendant reached Sing Sing twenty months ago on a sentence for attempted burglary. He always spoke in praiseworthy terms about the Red rule in Russia until he learned today that he was headed for there, and then he protested vigorously and vainly pleaded for a chance to remain in this country.

DEPORTATIONS FROM ELLIS ISLAND – AN ESSAY
(New York Times, 8/12/1906)

You can run the entire scale of human emotion in the deportation division in the big Federal building on Ellis Island. But for the asking you will hear stories of hardship and disappointment that have the power to seek out an unpetrified corner of a heart of flint and to cause that strange lump to rise in the throat.

The Government ferryboat *Ellis Island* leaves the Barge Office on the hour and soon glides into its slip in front of the big red building across from the Battery. A sea of eager, expectant faces peer down at you from the roof garden of the building. Friends and relatives are expected, and a great cry goes up from the roof as the passengers begin to walk ashore. Families are to be united and made happy after a separation of many years; sweethearts are to be joined who before had the great Atlantic between them.

Yet in this great sea of faces above are many who will never set foot on American soil, save to come and go from the little island controlled by Uncle Sam.

Those aliens who do not qualify physically and mentally – and often morally – are not permitted to remain in this country. They must go back to the land from which their long journey began. The Immigration Department presents a strict examination for the aliens, and they must pass letter-perfect in every subject if they would come under the protection of this Government. Those who do not satisfactorily pass the examination are detained as "undesirables," and after a sojourn of a few days in the deportation division, are returned to Europe, at the expense of the steamship company responsible for their crossing the Atlantic.

A complete record is kept of this undesirable alien element, and it is stated that an average of 1,000 aliens are monthly refused admission to this country and are compelled to journey back to the land from which they came.

Many of them had for years saved a few pennies each day, denying themselves even the bare necessities of life, in order to realize the price of a steerage ticket to this mystical land of wealth. The cost of the ticket meant many a supperless night. Then with light hearts and an abundance of ambition they traveled across the ocean, to find another cup of bitter disappointment awaiting them, filled to the brim by watchful immigration officials.

A little Russian boy, ill-shapen and pale from long suffering, was found packed in among a number of his fellow-countrymen in a large room on the upper floor of the immigration building. The bent piece of humanity could not have been more than 16 years old, and yet his pain-pinched features made him appear much older. He was eager to talk of his shattered hopes and to tell his story of bitter disappointment.

Less than two months ago this boy left the town of Kishinef in Russia. He could not make a living at home because he was a cripple and too weak to go into the fields. No one wanted to look on him, for his bent and twisted figure was unsightly to the superstitious peasants. Other children would cry after him and taunt him with his deformity. A deep sadness came into the life of the little fellow and he had given up all hope of ever wringing one moment of happiness out of life.

Note: *Kishinev, now a city in Moldova named Chişinău, was the scene of a lethal anti-Jewish pogrom in 1903 and another one in 1905.*

Then a letter written by an uncle arrived from America. This letter told of the great opportunities awaiting those who should hasten across the ocean. The hunchbacked boy read the letter over and over again, every word sinking deep into his memory. Through years of toil his parents had saved a sum sufficient to send the little fellow to America. They willingly gave up their all in the hope that their crippled son should find a place with his uncle. The uncle's address was written at the end of the letter, and with this the hunchbacked boy started on the long voyage.

When the big liner steamed slowly past the Statue of Liberty the boy stood on the forward deck, his eyes feasting on the beautiful scene. In a provincial dialect, hardly intelligible to one speaking Russian, the little fellow described his emotions on sighting the shores of America:

"I stood at the front of the ship with several of my fellow-countrymen, who, like me, were bound for America. As we came closer to the shore my joy knew no bounds. I was soon to be in a land where my race is not persecuted. I heard of this gold that could be had for the asking, and I longed to gather some of it and return to my old parents in Russia. Now they tell me I must return home, for they cannot find my uncle, and, furthermore, cripples like me are not wanted here."

Tears came into the cripple's eyes as he looked up appealingly to the knot of visitors who had gathered around him. An Inspector shambled up and after a casual glance at the little fellow turned to the crowd and vouchsafed the information that "Hunchy is clean loco."

But "Hunchy" isn't "loco," though the pain and sorrow that have been thrust upon this poor bent weakling have been enough to drive the strongest man along the straight road to the insane asylum.

Insanity among immigrants is daily increasing. The matron in charge of the women's quarters on Ellis Island explains that homesickness and lack of knowledge of the English language are the chief causes of mind derangement among female aliens. This is more so the case with servant girls who are permitted to land, but who later become insane and must be returned to their native lands. For three years after landing aliens are under the watchful eyes of the Government, and if during this period of probation they in any way step aside from the strict laws governing their conduct they are liable to be returned without notice. Matrons are kept busy traveling throughout the country and collecting female aliens who are found undesirable even after having been permitted to land.

Note: *Many of the "undesirable" females were servant girls or low-paid workers in stores or elsewhere who stooped to try prostitution, or were lured or forced into the sex trade. Others were females who lost their heads and fell in love with heels who used them for sex, then ditched them by turning them in as moral turpitude cases so they could chase other cuties.*

A short time ago a mother and son arrived from Poland. Both expected to gain lucrative employment as factory hands. But during the voyage the son developed a severe type of trachoma – that dreaded disease of the eyes, which closes the gates on so many aliens. The mother gained the consent of the immigration authorities to land, but the son was ordered to immediately return to the port of departure. When the mother and son found they were to be separated, a scene was enacted which brought tears to the eyes of every one standing about. The mother threw her arms about the lad, weeping all the while as if her heart would break. The son endeavored to hide his feelings of emotion and bitter disappointment, but like a mighty flood of water breaking through a dam his pent-up feelings passed beyond his strength and broke forth in a wail that sounded more like the cry of some hunted animal than of a man. He would have fallen to the floor had not his mother placed her loving arms around his neck. The boy continued to cry out at the top of his voice, while the mother's deep sobs sounded the accompaniment. It was a hard scene to look upon, and the visitors walked away.

When it is understood that an average of 5,000 aliens daily seek admission at the Port of New York, many incidents similar to the foregoing are bound to occur.

Up on the roof garden of the big building on Ellis Island the "undesirables" look out through a wire netting. Across the river they gaze longingly at the line of skyscrapers bordering the opposite shore. The strange sight of appalling greatness seems to taunt them and to take voice and whisper in their ears: "Look on me, so near and yet so far." Soon they shall take ship and travel back empty-handed to their homes. There they must again take up their old lives of wearisome toil, under slave-driving masters, in a land where corruption and oppression often run rampant. They return from the new world with only a view at that formidable wall of skyscrapers that seemed to bar their way.

Love plays strange pranks on Ellis Island and often causes the officials no end of worry and trouble. Young girls from Europe arrive (coming after) lovers who had gone before to prepare the nest. These girls from Europe are simple in their ways and modestly look forward to a simple life in a little home, and wish for nothing more than to be looked on as good housekeepers and mothers. The swain knows this and appreciates the girl's worth until he meets in this country girls of his own nationality who have been here for some time and have acquired somewhat the atmosphere of individuality that surrounds the real American girl. This is a novelty to the rustic fresh from the fields in Hungary or Russia, and with but little difficulty he soon forgets his promises made to the fair maid across the water. When the sweetheart arrives from Europe she often finds that her intended does not claim her at the island, so in tears and vowing vengeance on the fickle swain, she returns home at the expense of the steamship company by which she traveled to this country. Cases of this character are very common on the island.

A pen full of cattle crowding each other about before the entrance to a slaughter house is the comparison one makes while visiting the deportation division. And in truth Ellis Island is a slaughter house, for daily hundreds are sacrificed, their ambitions and hopes slain, to guard the interests of higher bred animals who fear contamination.

A feeling of depression comes over you while seeing these unfortunates and hearing their stories, and even after you have left the island, and Uncle Sam's ferryboat is gliding through the water, that depression is still with you. All the way over you say to yourself: "If I had my way I'd throw down the barriers to every one of these poor unfortunates with his hard-luck story." But this is your sentimental side asserting itself. Wait until you have taken the elevated; then look down through the crowded streets near the Battery; observe the congested state of the street traffic, and where thousands are battling for daily bread. This sight knocks out sentiment with one blow, and your better judgment says: "It is much better so."

CRIMES AND RIOTS AND ELLIS ISLAND

GYPSIES RIOT AT ELLIS ISLAND
(Frank Martocci, as interviewed by Edward Corsi, In the Shadow of Liberty, pages 85-86)

Whether they were Italian or Russian, Swedish or Spanish, German or Greek, many of the immigrants came in their native peasant costumes – a strange and colorful procession of fashions in dress from all parts of the world. One would think we were holding a fancy dress party, judging by the variety and oddness of the styles. And the gypsies – I mustn't forget the gypsies!

The Cunard liner, *Carpathia*, brought them in September of 1904, two hundred and eighty of them, in all the picturesque gorgeousness of their various tribal costumes. But what wasn't so picturesque was the fact that forty-eight gypsy children had measles and had to be sent by the immigration doctors to the Kingston Avenue Hospital in Brooklyn.

Note: *The Carpathia was the ship whose captain and crew rescued the survivors of the Titanic in 1912.*

This taking of the children was what started things; and what fanned the fire was the fact that several members of distinctive families were taken from the detention room and placed before the Board of Special Inquiry.

More and more gypsy forces arrived – gypsies from Long Island, New Jersey, and other adjacent points flocked into the Island to meet those detained. Then some gypsy spread the rumor that all the children taken by the doctors had been drowned, and you can imagine what happened!

At eleven o'clock that night a doctor, who tried to feel a gypsy child's pulse, was attacked by the gypsies as a murderer. This started a riot which could not be checked or stilled, and which raged all night. Every time the gypsies saw anyone wearing an immigration uniform or cap they opened fire, using as weapons anything on which they could lay their hands.

But at last a way of explaining things was worked out. The next gypsy child who developed measles was sent to the hospital like the others, but the parents were allowed to go along and see how the other gypsy children were being cared for. They brought the news back to the other gypsies, and this was successful in appeasing them. But as long as I live I shall never forget the picture of those gypsy women pulling off their heavy-soled slippers, and sailing into us inspectors and the doctors with fire in their eyes!

THE MIDDLE EASTERN CON MEN
(Edward Corsi, In the Shadow of Liberty, pages 265-266)

About 1880 our country was deluged with numbers of fakers. These people spoke Arabic and came here from Lebanon, in Syria.

Note: *Corsi called these people Maronites. These beggars posed as Christians instead of as Moslems.*

They began coming in small groups in the garb of mendicants. They wore red fezzes, short open jackets, short baggy blue trousers to the calves of the legs, and ill-fitting shoes. As soon as they had passed the immigration authorities they would at once go out into the street to ply their trade. At the end of his first day in America the whining (beggar) would have added five dollars to his board, while the Irish or German immigrant would be bustling around trying to find work to enable him to earn a dollar.

The first comers returned richly laden with spoils, whereupon their admiring friends began selling their land and possessions in order to come also to America. They arrived in droves until about eight thousand were living in New York City alone.

Soon they were a nuisance, and the policemen were ordered to arrest all those caught begging in the streets. The story goes that a policeman arrested one of them for this offense, but before reaching the police station the expert mendicant not only had persuaded the officer to let him go but had actually got a quarter out of him. Upon returning to his friends he boasted about having got the better of that "goat" of a policeman.

An entire family of (Lebanese), landing at Castle Garden, remained there a week pretending to have no money. Sufficient funds were raised to send them to a southern state. Then it developed that they had twenty-four thousand dollars invested in sheep and railroad bonds.

After they were arrested for begging the fakers would produce little trinkets to sell whenever a policeman was watching them.

Gradually the padrone system was organized, and professional Syrian tramps were hired and shipped to this country, the principals taking mortgages on their property and paying their passage. They printed a directory of American cities and towns, giving the population, together with the names of priests and clergymen, who could be easily deceived. The country was divided into districts and a definite gang went to each district. An alphabet of signals and signs was invented. Inscriptions in Arabic chalked on fences often informed members of the gang, "We have begged this village thoroughly," or "Don't waste time here." Two always travelled together, the padrones depending upon one tramp watching the other.

When the inspectors learned of the racket and tried to keep the beggars out, they came dressed as Greeks or Italians.

RARE SMUGGLER TAKES RAP FOR CUSTOMERS IN SNOWY CHASE
(Edward Corsi, In the Shadow of Liberty, pages 162-163)

Uncle Sam's immigration inspectors frequently encountered stern opposition and dangerous resistance from the smugglers. Their escapades would furnish suitable material for a modern detective story. One report from Inspector Thomas D'Arcy which was submitted from his post at Plattsburg on February 5, 1905, is of especial interest.

Although the inspector failed to capture a gang of smugglers and their human contraband, the chase he describes was a hair-raising one from start to finish, and he succeeded in blocking the plans of the "villains." His narrative related the attempt of a notorious smuggler, Frank Castine, to bring a sleigh load of Chinamen over the border.

Word reached Inspector D'Arcy from Douglass Corners of Quebec, on the night of January 30, that Castine and his Celestials had left there for La Prairie. Hurriedly summoning and arming Inspectors Weeks, Maher, Ketchum and Mac Gregor, D'Arcy proceeded to Dewey's Corners, where the inspectors had decided to intercept the smugglers and the smuggled. They waited until after two o'clock in the morning before their dogs gave the alarm. The thermometer stood at twenty degrees below zero, and it was necessary to keep the horses moving constantly to prevent their freezing to death.

Finally a huge sled filled with Chinamen came into sight. It was followed by a small cutter carrying one man. The inspectors barred the road and ordered the strangers to halt. Instead of obeying, the two sleds were quickly wheeled around and started back in the direction of Canada. The inspectors set forth in hot pursuit. They raced mile after mile over the snow-covered road, in the words of D'Arcy: "In the teeth of the wind, which nearly blew the breath from our bodies, and the hail of ice thrown back by the heels of the horses, which pelted us like a Gatling-gun bombardment."

Gradually the inspectors gained on the smugglers, and when within calling distance shouted for the fugitives to surrender. But the pursued only replied with curses and whipped their horses the harder. Finally D'Arcy fired his revolver after the speeding sleighs, but the shots went wild. When it was apparent that the fugitives could be overtaken in the next two or three hundred yards, the man in the small cutter, who later proved to be Castine, seeing the danger, resorted to a desperate ruse. Rising to his feet he deliberately overturned the cutter in the middle of the road. A minute later D'Arcy and his men were sprawling atop of Castine and his wreck. Castine was captured but the Chinamen escaped.

IMMIGRANT ESCAPES ELLIS ISLAND ONLY TO BE MURDERED
(Edward Corsi, In the Shadow of Liberty, pages 157-158)

There were instances when the finger of crime moved all too fast for the protecting hand of the law. Such a case was the remarkable disappearance of Isadore Termini from immigration custody in May, 1900.

Although mystery will always surround this extraordinary case certain facts are known. Isadore Termini, an old Italian immigrant, reached New York about May 25. He went to the United States Immigration Station at the Barge Office, and his dead body was picked up in the harbor three days later.

Meantime his son, Calegro Termini, lived in Buffalo, and when, after three days, the father failed to arrive, he consulted Immigration Inspector de Barry at Buffalo about the matter. De Barry found that the old man had been under detention at New York, classed as liable to be a public charge. This seemed strange under the circumstances, for he found also that the Italian had landed with a money order for thirty-four dollars, a ticket on the Erie Railroad to Buffalo, and about sixty dollars in cash.

After several days the old man still had not come, so Inspector de Barry wrote several letters to Immigration Commissioner Fitchie at New York. The Commissioner reported that the immigrant had apparently escaped illegally from the Barge Office, and he intimated that the son's inquiries were a pretext to keep the old man from being found.

Young Termini hired a lawyer who soon found that his father had not returned to his relatives in Italy. Inspector de Barry reported the case to the Treasury Department in Washington. During the investigation it developed that the body of an Italian, evidently Isadore Termini, had washed up on the shore of New Jersey near the coal docks of the Jersey Central Railroad. The description of the missing man, as he was last seen, fitted the body exactly. Two boys fishing off the docks saw the corpse floating. They shouted to a (man) who was passing and the body was taken to the morgue.

OPPRESSION LED MILLIONS TO COME TO AMERICA

Top left: "Execution of the Jewess" by Alfred Dehodencq. Morrocan officials had Jewish teen Solica Hatchouel beheaded in 1834 for refusing to convert to Islam and marry a Moslem nobleman who coveted her. Public domain.

Top right: Atrocities at Batak. In 1876, Turkish soldiers and police killed the young men defending this Bulgarian town, then entered the town, captured and raped the young women and teenage girls for days, killed most of the people at the village's Orthodox Christian church, then beheaded the unfortunate females they had been raping. Irish-American war correspondent Januarius MacGahan and American diplomat Eugene Schuyler saw the dead and the severed heads of the females, and exposed the atrocities the Turks and their allies the Disraeli government of Britain wanted covered up. Picture courtesy of the Bulgarian government.

Center: Pogrom victims. Russian officials from time to time incited peasants and laborers to attack Jews. The rioters killed several thousand Jews in the pogroms of 1905. Russian officials wanted Jews to convert or leave Russia. They limited where Jews could live and work. Public domain.

Bottom: Turks hang Armenians during World War One. Armin Wegner, a German officer, took this and other pictures to prove Turkish atrocities. Armenian National Institute.

Turkish officials had hundreds of thousands of Armenians, Bulgarians, Serbs, Greeks, Lebanese, and other Christian peoples in the Middle East murdered in the late 1800s. During World War One, the Turks genocidally murdered more than a million Armenians.

POVERTY AS WELL AS OPPRESSION SENT MILLIONS TO AMERICA

British officials, police, and soldiers helped kill more than a million Irish in the late 1840s by starvation; they confiscated food the Irish grew for export, and often tried to make the Irish give up Catholicism to get a small amount of food. **Bottom left**: A newspaper artist sketched famine victim Bridget O'Donnell and her girls. They are gaunt from starving. Public domain. **Top left:** British police and soldiers evicted Irish peasants by battering their cottages to destroy them. This 1870s picture is from the National Archives of Ireland.

Poles and Lithuanians suffered poverty and oppression, thanks to the Prussians and Russians. **Top right:** Polish artist Artur Grottger's picture "Warning" shows a Lithuanian couple alerted in the dead of night. **Center:** Many Poles and Lithuanians came to America, like these Polish girls in the 1890s. Credit: Indiana Historical Society.

Bottom right: These Serbs, like many in Europe, suffered poverty. Credit: New York Public Library. Some poverty was the result of natural disaster, but most poverty was due to the greed of those who ruled the countries of Europe. The rich and the politicians and the nobility caused wars of aggression, and stole from their own people through excessive taxation and refusal to allow them to make a wage that was just for the work they did. More people came to America for economic reasons than for any other reason.

OVER A MILLION IRISH came to America in the wake of the Potato Famine in the 1840s. British authorities turned the natural disaster into genocide by seizing Irish crops for shipment to England, hamstringing relief efforts, and withholding relief unless the Irish gave up land and Catholic faith. More than a million Irish died because of the Famine and the British.

Center left: Woman and children search desperately for unspoiled potatoes. **Top:** Irish steerage passengers. Note the terrible conditions aboard the ship they were on. Many British landlords sent their Irish tenants away in leaking hulks. Many Irish died of disease or drowning at sea. **Center right:** "Defenders of the Faith," by Kevin O'Malley, for the Ancient Order of Hibernians. The Irish ran into anti-Catholic fanatics in America. They had to guard their churches from Protestant mobs who wanted to burn them down. **Bottom:** Hundreds of thousands of Irish immigrants and Irish-Americans served in the Civil War, most for the Union. After the war, Irish vets from both sides invaded Canada to force British officials to free Ireland. Some American officials wanted to take Canada because the Brits sold the South warships, so they made the Irish return to America. Photo by author.

BEFORE ELLIS ISLAND

New York officials processed immigrants at Castle Garden and state and federal officials processed immigrants at the Barge Office. Both were in the Battery district at the bottom of Manhattan Island.

Top: Castle Garden. Photo by author.
Center right: The Barge Office. This building was the first building the feds used to process immigrants. It was demolished in the early 1900s. Credit: Library of Congress.
Center left: Photo from a Manhattan building looking southwest shows Castle Garden, the Statue of Liberty, and Ellis Island, where the boats are clustered. Credit: New York Public Library.
Bottom left: Statue of Liberty (left) and Ellis Island (right), 2008. The author took this photo from Manhattan Island, on a pier a couple hundred feet south of Castle Garden.
Bottom right: Immigrants know they are in the right place when they see Lady Liberty in New York harbor. Credit: New York Public Library.

STEERAGE PASSENGERS by the millions came to America in ships in the late 1800s and early 1900s.

Top: Passengers come on deck to breathe fresh air and pass the time. A sailing ship could take weeks to cross the Atlantic. Credit: New York Public Library.

Center left: Immigrants land at Castle Garden in New York City. Before the feds took over immigration, such landings were often disorganized messes. Criminals lined the waterfront, looking to scam immigrants and lure pretty unattached females into "white slavery." Credit: New York Public Library.

Bottom right: Steerage immigrants on a newer ship, early 1900s. These ships were not as filthy, but still crowded. Credit: Ellis Island Immigration Museum.

Bottom left: A couple find a pleasant way to while away the time aboard the S.S. *Patricia*. Credit: Museum of New York City.

Center right: Good-looking German fraulein debuts at Ellis Island, 1920s. Steerage by now was a much cleaner place to be, and her well-scrubbed look shows it. Credit: Lewis Hine, Ellis Island Immigration Museum.

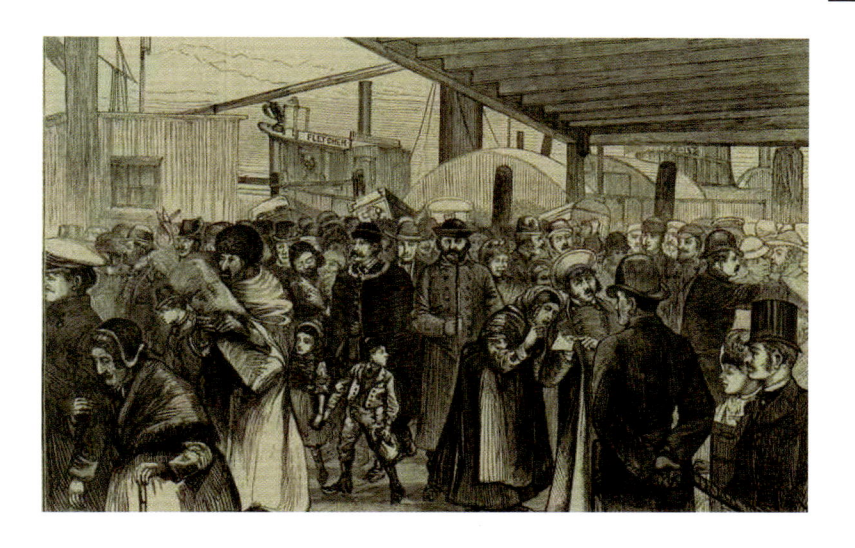

ELLIS ISLAND SCRAPBOOK

Top left: Ludmilla Foxlee in her native Czech finery. She was a cheerful and kindly social worker at Ellis Island. Credit: Ellis Island Immigration Museum. **Top right:** Mother Cabrini. This immigrant from Italy founded many schools and orphanages in America. She tirelessly served the immigrants and also worked to help them assimilate. Credit: Mother Cabrini Shrine. **Bottom left:** One of the nearly 1000 Irish colleens and other European bachelorettes who came to America on the *Baltic*. A little girl and her dolly get in on the photo op. Credit: Ellis Island Immigration Museum. **Right:** "The Letter" by Slovenian artist Jozef Petkovsek. Many a wife and sweetheart waited in Europe for their menfolk to earn enough money to resettle them in America. Letters were cherished and saved. Public domain.

ELLIS ISLAND – AMERICA'S FRONT DOOR

Top left: Statue of Annie Moore, the 15-year-old Irish girl who was the first person processed at Ellis Island when it opened for business New Year's Day 1892. She was responsible enough to get herself and her young brothers to America. The author and thousands of other Ancient Order of Hibernians members paid for the statue. **Top right:** Clothing items from Eastern Europe donated to the Ellis Island Immigration Museum. The thigh boots on the right belonged to a Czech teenage girl with very slender legs. **Bottom left:** Alsatian immigrant couple Edouard Loesch and Eugenie Herter (Loesch), 1920s. They both had German last names and French first names, which summed up the mix of the region. Jeanne Loesch donated their photo to the Ellis Island Immigration Museum. **Bottom right:** "The Kissing Post" by Eileen Sherlock. Often, the husband came first to America, and then saved enough to bring his wife and children to America. Husbands would call for their loved ones at this part of the Main Building on Ellis Island. The tears and embraces and kisses as husband and wife reunited earned this post the nickname "The Kissing Post."

PRESIDENTS AT ELLIS ISLAND

Top: This blurry picture of Theodore Roosevelt and his men, taken in September 1903, reflected the fact that they came in the midst of a hurricane with a driving rainstorm. The weather delayed Teddy (second from right, outstretched hand), but would have spelled mission scrub for virtually any other president. Ellis Island agents bet he'd show up that day, and he did. Public domain.

Center: William Howard Taft plays chief of Special Inquiry Board for a day at Ellis Island in 1910.

Bottom right: Ronald Reagan makes a speech at Ellis Island in 1987. Reagan was the driving force behind the restoration of Ellis Island, dramatically unlike his predecessors Eisenhower, JFK, LBJ, Nixon, Ford, and Carter, who allowed it to be looted and vandalized. Reagan assisted the people of captive nations of Eastern Europe in their quest for freedom, also dramatically unlike these other presidents, and unlike the Bushes, the Clintons, and Obama, who followed him. Behind Reagan's right side are the Twin Towers, which are now gone, thanks to hostile jihadist immigrants and incompetent screening of these murderers by politically correct agents on orders from our top officials. Credit: Ronald Reagan Presidential Library.

Bottom left: Loreta Asanavičiūtė, victim of Soviet Communist Gorbachev's "glastnost." Red tankers crushed her to death beneath their treads in 1991, because she and other Lithuanians dared to demonstrate for religious freedom and civil liberties like we in America take for granted. Hundreds of thousands of her countrymen and women came here in the Ellis Island era; the ancestors of Johnny Unitas, Dick Butkus, and Kimberly Bergalis were among these people.

AMERICANS FLEX THEIR MUSCLES

In the Spanish-American War, American sailors, soldiers, and marines showed their stuff. **Above:** Admiral Dewey's fleet KO's the Spanish fleet in the Philippines. Another American fleet does likewise in Cuba. **Left:** Col. Teddy Roosevelt (on horse) rallies the Rough Riders in combat against the tenacious Spanish infantry in Cuba. Teddy Roosevelt would become president three years later. He would start the building of the U.S. Navy into the world's best. Pictures courtesy of the U.S. Navy and U.S. Army.

"Speak softly and carry a big stick" was Teddy Roosevelt's motto. He sent the Great White Fleet on a round-the-world voyage to remind other countries' politicians of America's growing might. **Right:** American and Japanese officers pose aboard the USS *Missouri* in Japan. The battleship's guns were covered to keep water out. Credit: U.S. Navy. **Below:** The Great White Fleet's 16 battleships anchor in San Diego harbor ... a breathtaking sight! Credit: San Diego Historical Society.

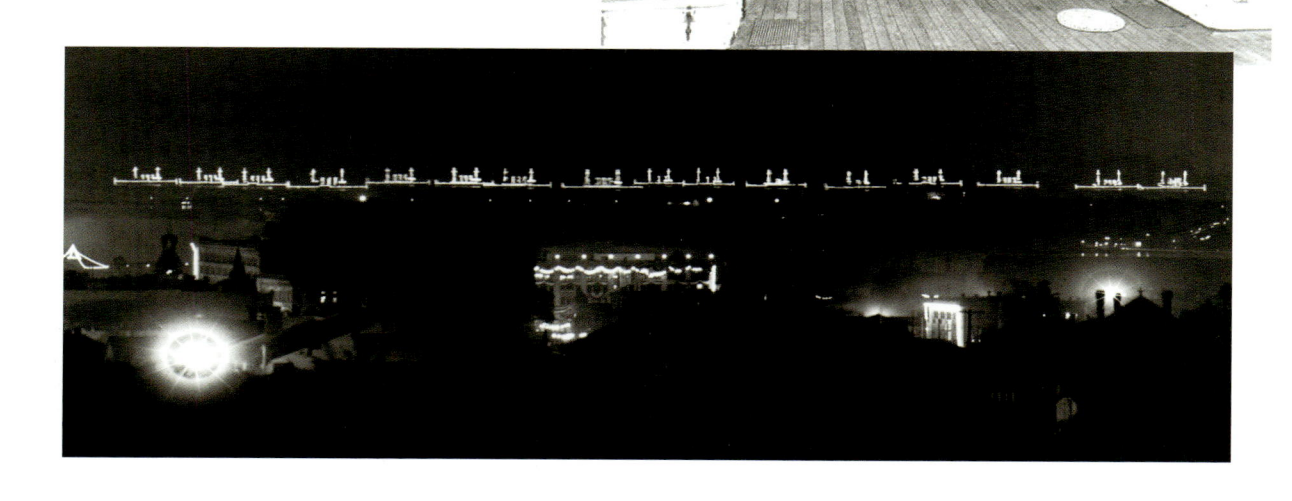

THE PANAMA CANAL

became a reality thanks to Teddy Roosevelt and many other worthy Americans. American doctors beat yellow fever and malaria, and American engineers and men beat the jungle and the mountains to build the canal. It would be ready for ship traffic in 1914.

Top and center: "Gatun Dam" and "Installing a Lock Gate", both by W. B. Van Ingen. American men and machinery went to work in incredible heat and humidity to dig the canal and channel the rivers and bolster unstable land that the canal went through. Jamaicans and other men from the Caribbean Basin joined the Americans in building the canal. Courtesy of the Panama Canal Society.

Bottom right: "The Conquerors" by Jonas Lie, 1913. The Panama Canal was not an easy sea level canal over desert terrain like Suez, but one that had to crack a barrier of mountains and jungle. The mountains dwarf the steam shovels and locomotives used to cut earth and rock out of the area and haul it away. Credit: U.S. Army.

Bottom left: The USS *Minnesota* passes through the Panama Canal. The canal was a geopolitical triumph of the first magnitude. It enabled American naval officials to shift warships between the Atlantic and the Pacific. It also saved merchant sailors the expense and the danger of going around Cape Horn at the bottom of South America.

By 1976 (when the author was undergoing military training in the Canal Zone), incompetents like Gerald Ford, Jimmy Carter, and Henry Kissinger were planning to give it away. The author visited his congressman and tried to talk him out of supporting this idiocy. The Bushes and the Clintons completed this sell-out of American policy. The Chinese now have working control of the ports at both ends of the American-built canal.

TEDDY ROOSEVELT was a man of action, courage, justice, and vision. He pushed to protect the public from corporate abuses. He built the U.S. Navy and the Panama Canal. **Top left:** TR is being TR ... animated and forceful. **Top right:** TR checks out a steam shovel on the Panama Canal project. **Left:** TR's pretty and spirited daughter Alice – America's best known bachelorette of that era – captured the hearts of the American public. Her sister Ethel did not come of age until TR was back in private life. Ethel served with honor as a nurse in World War One. **Bottom:** Left to right, TR's sons Archie, Theodore Jr., Kermit, and Quentin all were wounded in World War One; Quentin died when a German pilot shot down his biplane. Their cousin FDR held a cushy government job during the war. Credits: Alice is courtesy of the Library of Congress. The other photos are courtesy of the National Park Service.

TR Jr. was the only general who landed in the first wave at D-Day in World War Two. He got his tankers and infantry men inland. He died weeks later of a heart attack. Archie would see combat against the Japs in that war, and get wounded again. Kermit raided the Nazis in Norway and had coastal defense duty in Alaska. Kermit saved TR's life in the Amazon but would take his own during the war due to depression. Alice said it was unfair that her gallant brothers always were measured against their father.

LABOR CONDITIONS

in America would improve thanks to men like Al Smith (bottom right) and Teddy Roosevelt.

Top: Farm children did farm work in usually reasonable conditions with their parents and neighbors, like the boy helping the men run a team of horses to grade this North Dakota road. Credit: Fred Hultstrand, Library of Congress, and North Dakota State University

Many cannery owners paid children and their mothers pennies an hour to harvest and process crops. **Center:** Children harvest onions in Illinois. Credit: Chicago Daily News, Chicago Historical Society. **Bottom left:** Children shuck oysters in South Carolina. Credit: Lewis Hine, New York Public Library.

Conditions were bad in many industries, especially the coal industry. The needle trades were not as dangerous, but girls working as seamstresses received serf wages and often received unwanted advances from the men who worked them. Many immigrants worked in these trades.

Top left: Boy mine workers at a Pennsylvania mine. Credit: Library of Congress. **Top right:** Slavic coal miner. Credit: Lewis Hine, New York Public Library. **Center:** Slavic woman washes clothes in a coal camp. Credit: Lewis Hine, New York Public Library. **Bottom right:** These girls worked for a clothing manufacturer. They seem startled; perhaps because the business was being inspected. Credit: Chicago Daily News, Chicago Historical Society. **Bottom left:** Nellie Bly and other muckrakers exposed evil conditions, and pushed for reform.

AMERICANS FIGHT TO VICTORY IN WORLD WAR ONE

The "can do" sprit of American soldiers and their physical prowess and courage helped them beat the Germans and help the British and French do likewise. American entry in the war saved France from defeat and Britain from cross-channel retreat.

Top: American infantrymen advance behind a smoke screen. One way to avoid the withering fire of soldiers in good defensive positions was to put up a smoke barrage to conceal your own men in the assault. They couldn't see the enemy either, but artillery shells would find the enemy as ground troops advanced to be close enough to see them, surprise them, and shoot them or bayonet them.

Center: Americans march into Germany to help occupy Germany west of the Rhine after the Germans quit the war on November 11, 1918. American soldiers were much easier on German civilians than the British and French soldiers who they bailed out.

Bottom left: .American men drink German beer out of captured German beer steins.

Bottom right: Crippled black soldier comes home. He still manages a smile as he visits with a lady among the home folks who have come out to welcome his unit home.

All pictures public domain, some courtesy of U.S. Army Signal Corps.

AMERICAN SAILORS, MARINES, AND NURSES HELPED WIN THE WAR

Top left and right: Many American women served as Red Cross nurses during the war, or entered the Army or the Navy, as this nurse did, shown with two of her Marine patients. Teddy Roosevelt's resolute daughter Ethel served as a nurse in France. She was also active in the Red Cross for at least 60 years.

Center: U.S. Navy men lay antisubmarine mines in the North Sea. This crippled German submarine operations against British shipping and against ships bringing Americans to the war. **Bottom**: U.S. Navy warships enter a British port. Churchill and other British officials schemed to get America into the war. They needed American naval strength as well as ground troops to avoid disaster.

American warships protected convoys of supplies and soldiers from submarine attack. After the war, the Brits downplayed the U.S. Navy effort. British officials also tried to pressure America's leaders into not expanding the U.S. Navy. We did surpass their navy, and we would bail the Brits out of a second world war they helped cause.

All pictures public domain, most courtesy of the U.S. Navy.

THE THIRTIES saw worldwide depression and the rise totalitarian states. **Top:** Ticked-off Ukrainian city girls are forced to harvest crops. Stalin had 5 to 7 million Ukrainian peasants starved to death or executed in 1932-1933; the resulting labor shortage in the Soviet Union's most productive farmland area led to the dragooning of these girls and many others. **Center left and center:** Criminals of Munich Hitler and Chamberlain, Nazi-Soviet Pact criminals Stalin and Ribbentrop. Cowardly sell-out of Czechs by British and French leaders, and Stalin's backstabbing the Poles led to the carve-up of Czechs and Poles, World War Two, the Nazis' murder of six million Jews and 20 million Slavs (the holocaust you never hear about), and Red domination of Eastern Europe. Nazi German archives. **Lower mid left:** Japanese soldiers use live Chinese for bayonet practice. Japs murdered 20 million Chinese, a million Filipinos, and several million other victims in Asia. Japanese photo, public domain.

Bottom left: Hitler murdered Jews in Germany. He later ordered Jews in captive lands dragged to his gas chambers. These Jews from Salonika in Greece were among his victims. Nazi German archives. **Bottom right:** It took American might to destroy the power of the Nazis and the Japs. Might in the service of right is justifiable homicide. US Army photo. **Center right:** Nazi bitch Inge Viermitz pleads not guilty to war crimes. She was a RuSHA agent; these vermin sterilized Slav women and girls and forced abortions on them. She escaped justice. Photo from US Holocaust Memorial Museum.

But when the body was officially identified at the New Jersey morgue, a complete change of clothing had taken place. The shirt and coat had been exchanged for a sweater. Obviously this and the other changes had been made to prevent identification. It was said in explanation that the clothes first found on the body had been given to the (man) to pay him for his trouble.

Old Isadore Termini was buried in the garments the crooks had put on him. It was found that the old man's ticket over the Erie Railroad had never been used and his money order had not been cashed. The case remains one which was never solved, and yet it serves to show the lengths to which criminals will go in order to get the immigrants' money.

ISLAND TAKES A BITE OUT OF CRIME
(Frank Martocci, as interviewed by Edward Corsi, In the Shadow of Liberty, pages 89-90)

We had criminals of all types and descriptions and from all parts of the world. (Martocci was speaking of 1907, when over a million immigrants came to New York City and Ellis Island.) My most interesting case was that of Alfano, who was wanted by the Italian police and who was a menace to my fellow Italians in the city. I mention this case because my friend Petrosino, one of the greatest detectives New York has ever seen, had come into it.

This man Alfano, commonly called Erricone here, had escaped from Italy under a false name and had come to this country through France. He had gotten through at the time, for we knew nothing about his Italian background.

Now Petrosino, one of the finest men I ever met, had been put in charge of the Italian squad at Police Headquarters in New York. His name was anathema to the Italian criminal here, who feared and hated him. It was my good fortune to have known Petrosino even before his detective days, and yet, though we had been friends for many years, he was so tight-lipped he never let out a word to me about his police activities.

But the time came when he had to. One day he looked me up and announced briefly: "Say, Martocci, I've got a fellow down at Mulberry Street who's wanted by the Italian police – I happened to jump into a reception his pals were giving for him. His name's Alfano. He says it isn't, but I know it is."

Petrosino brought his man over to Ellis Island, where he was locked up pending action by the immigration authorities. But they couldn't deport him — they couldn't do anything — till they had established his identity.

The prisoner gave us no co-operation whatsoever, for he would not admit his true name. Together with the immigration lawyer, Mr. Govin, I went to consult Alfano in his cell a number of times, but he would not confess who he was. Even before the Board of Special Inquiry, where we had him testify, and at which I happened to be the interpreter, he still refused.

We had just about given up the affair in desperation when one day, I don't know just why – perhaps out of sheer disgust at the constant hounding of him – he admitted: "Yes, yes, all right. I'm the Alfano you want. Do whatever you want with me."

This admission he later made in a sworn statement, and he was deported to Italy where, with one hundred or more, he was prosecuted in the famous Abbatemaggio case. It was the conspiracy of this Camorra for which Alfano, by the way, is now serving a life sentence. And it was Alfano's group which, in 1909 in Italy, killed my friend Petrosino while he was tracking them down. They say sometimes that criminals are colorful or interesting, but Petrosino had more color and picturesqueness than any criminal we ever harbored at the Island.

A SAINT'S OBSERVATIONS ON IMMIGRANTS AND AMERICA
(Courtesy of the Mother Cabrini Shrine)

Francesca Saverio Cabrini, a Catholic nun from the Lombardy region of Italy, emigrated to America in 1889 on the orders of Pope Leo XIII to help the Catholic immigrants to America. Some anti-Catholic fanatics would call her an agent of the Vatican; many grateful immigrants would call her a saint. For Mother Cabrini would establish an orphanage in New York, and other institutions in Philadelphia, Chicago, New Orleans, Los Angeles, Washington State, and Colorado. (Mother Cabrini's middle name was "Saverio" – Italian for "Xavier." Saint Francis Xavier was one of the greatest of the Jesuit missionaries, so Francesca Cabrini would have an apt middle name.)

Mother Cabrini and William Williams, the great commissioner of Ellis Island, shared the view that more immigrants should move out West, and to rural areas where they were needed and where they might feel more at home. Here is a letter she wrote from her facility in Colorado on that theme, and on the themes of immigrants being cheated and the terrible working conditions of many immigrants who labored in construction and mining in the early 1900s. At the end of this letter, she voices her awe at the awesome craftsmanship of God in His creating the United States.

Letter to the Students of the Magistero, boarders of the Missionary Sisters of the Sacred Heart of Jesus in Rome
A.M.G.SS.C.J.
February, 1906

My Dear Daughters,

I think I wrote to you of my work in Denver for the enlargement of the Orphanage we have in that city for the daughters of our emigrants. It will be enough for you to know that, with the help of the Sacred Heart, always ready to favour us, I have been able to acquire a beautiful property at the foot of the Rocky Mountains, standing upon a pleasant hill which descends with a gentle slope to the banks of the Rocky Mountains Lake. The house, to which a wing is being added, because space is already limited on the account of the thirty orphans which are gathered there this first year, is surrounded by trees laden with fruits and enhanced by the proximity of the clear waters of the lake. To the west extends the imposing Rocky Chain with its summits covered with snow; to the east is the beautiful city of Denver. To the south and north are great plains, three-fourths of which include the territory of Colorado.

Meanwhile, seated in a comfortable carriage of the Santa Fe railway, which was taking me to Los Angeles, my glance swept across those immense plains which, around Denver, are dotted with the cottages of our Italian agriculturists, and which, further on, are uninhabited, there being immense tracts still of virgin soil. My thoughts flew to our emigrants, who, in such great numbers, land every year on the Atlantic shores, overcrowding still more the already populous city of the east, where they meet with great difficulties and little gain. In the west there is still room for millions and millions, and its most fertile soil would offer occupation more congenial to the Italian emigrants, as well as a field in which to develop their activities and their agrarian knowledge, and to crown their efforts and labors with copious results....

Poor emigrants are so often cheated by those who pretend to be their protectors. This deception is all the more cruel, because these so-called protectors know well how to colour their private interests under the cloak of charity and patriotism.

During my journey I saw these dear fellows of ours engaged on the construction of railways in the most intricate mountain gorges, miles and miles away from any inhabited region. Hence they are separated for years from their families, far from the Church, deprived of the holy joys which in our own country the poor peasant has on Sundays at least. In Italy the peasant is able to put his hoe aside, and, in his best clothes, after having consecrated the morning to Divine Service and heard the words of the priest, who reminds him of the nobility of his origin and of his destiny, and of the value of work consecrated to God, has one day in the week to devote to his family and to honest amusements, and is thus able to resume his work the next morning with his mind invigorated.

Here the hardest labor is reserved for the Italian worker. There are few who regard him with a sympathetic eye, who care for him or remember that he has a heart and soul: they merely look upon him as an ingenious machine for work. It is true that here the Italian wins esteem because he is sober, honest, faithful and industrious, but how much real joy does he not give up in leaving his native country for foreign lands, without anyone to guide him on the road of true happiness, which does not consist in hoarding heaps of money, which, more often than not, cannot be enjoyed when misfortune comes. How much better his little field in his native country would be for him. What a great social and philanthropic work could be achieved by anyone who knew how to turn these hands, which waste their activity to the advantage of foreign countries, to the benefit of our own lovely land! I do not mean to deny that there are advantages in these immense fertile virgin lands. They certainly offer the emigrants work and a comfortable life, but I trust that some really generous minds may arise who will take to heart the interests of the poor, and direct them well and conscientiously when they land on these shores.

I can assure you, now, that in my journey through our Missions, the evidence of the good that is being done by our Institutions for the emigrants is of the greatest comfort to me. That which, being women, we are not allowed to do on a large scale, such as helping to solve important social problems, is being done in our little sphere in every State and in every city where our Houses have been opened. In them, the orphans, the sick and the poor are sheltered, but the good done by coming into contact with a great number of people, which such institutions of charity make it easy for the Sisters of the colony to get into touch with, is immense.

The relations between the Sisters and the people are very cordial. The latter call the former Mothers and Sisters, and they feel these words are not without meaning, for they know that with such titles hearts truly maternal correspond. They know that the hearts of the Sisters palpitate in unison with theirs, and that, having put aside all thoughts of themselves, the Sisters make their troubles their interests and their jobs their own. All this, however, is not merit, but the fruit of the love of Christ and of the prodigious fertility of our Holy Religion, the true friend of the people, the light which guides them in the darkness, the house of refuge, tower of strength and post of safety.

While I am conversing with you, we have reached the Colorado Springs, the aristocratic city of Colorado, which rises out of the shadow of Pike's Peak, one of the highest summits of these mountains. The weak and consumptive are attracted here by the mildness of the climate, the salubrity of the surrounding mountains and the many and various mineral waters, which on every side spring up fresh, foaming and gaseous. The Indians, astonished at such a wealth of mineral waters, thought their god Manitou, an Indian word which means Great Spirit, lived in these mountains, and especially in the one called the "Garden of the Gods." On my return I will show you a view of this natural park, several hundred acres in extent, in which brightly-coloured rocks are scattered in thousands and sculptured by Nature in the most strange forms, now imposing, now grotesque, sometimes austere, sometimes frivolous, as it were, presenting the strangest appearances. Here, a little farther on, General Palmer, one of our good benefactors, possesses a private "Garden of the Gods," a real jewel of art, both as regards the palace has built and the natural beauty of the rocks, which here form very high peaks, reflecting the most varied colours. Among the rocks can still be seen the nest of an eagle, which for years lived here as queen of the mountains. But a short time ago the young eagle was killed, and since that day the noble bird has deserted the nest, to the great regret of the General, as may be imagined, as he had become very proud of it.

Leaving the Colorado Springs, we reach Trinidad in a few hours. This is an important field of various mines, especially coal, in which direction many Italians are employed. Our Sisters visit them regularly, and to these poor people such a visit is like a ray of sun in the darkness of the bowels of the earth. They speak to them of their daughters whom they have under their charge, and of their families whom they have visited. They remind them of their religious duties, comfort them in the sadness of their miserable conditions, and always leave them happier, or at least more resigned to their poverty. The fatigue of the Sisters in climbing up the steepest mountains is rewarded by the smiles which light up the faces of these poor people on hearing the maternal tongue resounding in these dark vaults. Poor miners! Do you want to know what their life is? Those who work on a day shift enter the mines at six o'clock and remain buried there till mid-day. They come out at twelve o'clock for a short meal, and go in again at half-past twelve to leave at five. Half-an-hour is spent in washing themselves and preparing for supper. When they have finished this meal, feeling worn out, they throw themselves on their little beds, to rise again the following morning at the sound of the whistle which calls them to work. On Sundays they smoke and sleep. This is the life they lead far from their families and separated from the company of men. They continue uninterruptedly year in and year out, until old age and incapacity creep over them, or at least until some day a landslide or explosion or an accident of some kind ends the life of the poor worker, who does not even need a grave, being buried in the one in which he has lived all his life.

Oh, if the voice of religion at least could reach all these poor people and teach them to make holy and noble such fatiguing work, and to render it fruitful for Eternity, what a boon it would be for them!.....

Having left the large manufacturing city of Trinidad, the train enters the heart of the mountain district. As the locomotive ascends slowly, we are able to admire the beauty of the landscape. Every minute the view changes. We behold austere mountains whose summits are whitened with shining snow, hills quite green with pine trees and reddened by the colours of the rock and soil, sharp peaks which seem to touch the sky and on which the eagle alone rests, plateaus where the hardy goat back from his mountain excursions comes to browse upon the sweet grass in which they are so rich, and where the slow ox and the proud buffalo pasture together quite unconscious that in the neighbouring glen the howl of the white bear resounds. Here and there silver streams descend among the rocks and soon become threatening torrents which, in rapids and waterfalls, follow their beds of many-coloured rocks. The name Colorado was never better applied than to this enchanting country, to these most beautiful natural parks, where the hand of man could never add greater beauty than that with which Nature has enriched it.

In truth, here one exclaims spontaneously: How wonderful is God in His works!....

Yours most affectionately in Christ Jesus,
Mother Frances Saverio Cabrini

Mother Cabrini became an American citizen in 1909. She crisscrossed the country and crossed the Atlantic Ocean many times for her life's work. She was in Chicago at Christmastime 1917; she was busy wrapping presents for children when she died suddenly. She was 67. Mother Cabrini was the first American citizen to be named a saint by the Catholic Church. In her era, she was a member of about the only class of women who were executives – Catholic nuns. In an era when most American women didn't have the right to vote, Mother Cabrini and others like her founded and ran schools and hospitals and orphanages across the United States.

PROTECTION OF THE IMMIGRANTS AT ELLIS ISLAND

INTRODUCTION
(Edward Corsi, In the Shadow of Liberty, pages 156- 157)

In the old days, when the immigrant got off the Ferry at the Barge Office he was in America; and when he got through the Barge Office, he ran into very serious danger of exploitation. The police did all they could to protect the aliens, but still some got into the clutches of the cheats. Most of the runners for boarding houses were of foreign extraction, and those who were crooks would get the confidence of the aliens by speaking to them in their own language, afterwards luring them to places where they would be held or robbed, or, in the case of women, detained in questionable houses where the police had sometimes to be sent to rescue them.

PATERNALISM PROTECTS WOMEN
(Frank Martocci, as interviewed by Edward Corsi, In the Shadow of Liberty, page 75)

A woman, if she came alone, was asked a number of special questions: how much money she had; if she were going outside of New York; whether her passage had been paid by herself or by some charitable institution. If she had come to join her husband in New York or Brooklyn, we could not let her loose on the streets of a strange city looking for her husband. Actually he might have been waiting outside the Barge Office for a week, but the inspector would detain the woman, and her children if she had any, until the husband came for her, for there were too many unscrupulous people preying on the ignorance of the immigrant in those days.

The woman had to remain in the detention room, where employees looked out for her while she was detained. If her husband were on the Island when her name was called, he would accompany her to the inspector whose duty it was to discharge such persons to their relatives or friends. With the wife safely and happily in her husband's care, the case was closed so far as the immigration inspection went.

If no callers came for the woman, the person in charge of those being detained had to wire the immediate relative who was expected to call for her. This telegram or other communication also stated that it would serve as a pass to Ellis Island.

When the person claiming the immigrant called, he or she was first directed to the information division, and then into the presence of the woman, but only after due inquiries by the inspector handling the case, to make sure he or she was the right person. If the inspector saw any discrepancies, or if the names or previous history did not agree, he referred the case to a Board of Special Inquiry, which would hear the case and then make its decision.

CRANKS SEEK MONEY, LABOR, SEX, AND MAYBE LOVE AT ELLIS ISLAND

William Williams, formidable commissioner of Ellis Island, was not known for his sense of humor. But he did keep a number of letters that he said tickled his funnybone. A number of them were on the same topic: old fart wants younger wife to work like a dog for him and bring money. A typical one follows:

I am looking for a good woman (Age from 35 to 40) to be Wife & Housekeeper for me on my Place of 63 Acres. Must be Protestant Faith Speaking Good English and not given to liquor, also of healthy body. Looks don't cut any great figure with me, and if she should have a child I wouldn't mind (but not a whole crowd) Good Disposition and accustomed to Farm Life. Another very important thing, she must have 500 or 600 Dols (dollars) and be willing to use it to outfit us. This means I have the only the Place and nearly Empty House as I had to sell off Stock, Tools, & Furniture to satisfy the Heirs when I lost my wife 15 months ago. I am not what is called a young man, being 60 years old, but I have dark brown hair and am as strong active and healthy as almost any of those 20 years younger. I hope I may hear something soon as Spring is very near.

S. Brigham

Comment: *Either "Brigham in Young" was lying about selling off gear and livestock or he married the now-dead wife for her property when she had children by a previous marriage and she didn't give her property up to him when she married him. Spring is also a very busy time in a farmer's year; hence the sense of urgency in the greedy old coot's letter.*

DETAINED ALIENS PROTECTED DURING WORLD WAR ONE
(Frank Martocci, as interviewed by Edward Corsi, In the Shadow of Liberty, pages 91-92)

(During World War One) we had practically no immigration from the northern countries of Europe. The only immigration during War days was from the Mediterranean, and a good many vessels from the area were torpedoed. One Italian ship, the *Ancona*, was sunk, but fortunately her passengers were saved.

Note: The Italians joined the war in 1915 on the side of the British and French.

Finally we had to resort at that time to the inspection and detention of aliens on board ship, because all our accommodations on the Island were taken up by the interned enemy aliens and individual hospital cases brought back from the War. We had, in fact, about two thousand aliens on the Island.

For persons being detained, these enemy aliens were treated royally. There were concerts on Sundays in the large detention room upstairs. Friends of the enemy aliens came in such numbers that three or four trips had to be made by the Island ferryboat.

The police department was kind enough, when we held the concerts, to furnish police women in uniform to guard the entrance and exit of the reception room where the concerts were held. It was exceedingly difficult to explain to visitors how they could see the aliens and under what conditions, and arguments were endless. To cap it all, one day one of the police women tried to push me out of the room where I was going to see my chief. How could she know I was not a visitor?

MISSIONARIES TO THE IMMIGRANTS

One of the most well-known missions in New York City was the Mission of Our Lady of the Rosary. It also had the name "Mission of the Immaculate Virgin for the Safekeeping of Irish Girls." Irish Catholic priests ran this mission in Lower Manhattan for more than 50 years, from 1881 through the 1930s. At least 120,000 girls and young single women from Ireland received help from the missionaries.

The Hebrew Immigrant Aid Society served Jewish immigrants from the 1890s until President Eisenhower closed Ellis Island as an immigration station in 1954. They provided legal help to Jews facing possible deportation. The society even ran a kosher kitchen at Ellis Island.

These were two of the many mission and immigrant aid societies which had representatives at Ellis Island. Since the men who ran Ellis Island were usually men of great judgment, they welcomed the help of legitimate religious workers. However, like William Williams, the commissioners sensed there were wolves in sheep's clothing among these professed men and women of God, so they tried to check on these people to ensure they weren't fleecing the faithful. Williams kicked some immigrant aid societies off of Ellis Island for exploiting immigrants. He would also burn at least one preacher for the same sins.

In time, virtually every ethnic community in America sponsored one or more immigrant aid societies. They were most active at Ellis Island and in the New York area. They were also active in other port cities and in towns where large numbers of immigrants were living.

Clergy members of the various faiths would maintain a steady presence on Ellis Island as well. Most looked after their co-religionists from Europe, some came to proselytize, and eventually they came to work together for the good of the people coming to America.

More people of the Catholic faith came to America from its independence until the practical end of the Ellis Island Era (FDR's administration) than those of any other faith. The Italians and Irish who held a faith were almost entirely Catholic. So were the vast majority of the immigrants from Austria-Hungary (Czechs, Slovaks, Ruthenians, Slovenes, Croatians, as well as Austrians and Hungarians) who were churchgoers. So were most churchgoing immigrants from Poland (which through most of the Ellis Island Era was divided between Germany, Russia, and Austria-Hungary). About 30% to 40% of Germans, Swiss, and Dutch who practiced a faith were Catholics. Lesser numbers of immigrants came from France, Belgium, Spain, and Portugal; almost all people professing a religion from any of these countries were Catholics. So were most of immigrants from Lithuania, a large minority of those from Ukraine, and many from Lebanon.

This does not count the people coming from Mexico and the rest of Latin America, or a sizeable number of people coming from Quebec and elsewhere in Canada who were also Catholics. Therefore, it stood to reason there were many prominent Catholic missions and immigrant aid societies.

Most Jewish immigrants fled from the Russian Empire, which also included Ukraine, half of Poland, Lithuania, and Moldova. Most of the remainder of the Jewish immigrants came from Austria-Hungary, Germany, and Romania. It stood to reason the Jewish communities of New York would rally to assist their co-religionists, most of who came fleeing oppression in the Russian Empire.

Most Orthodox Christians came from Russia, Ukraine, and Greece. Lesser numbers of Orthodox immigrants came from Romania, Bulgaria, Serbia, Macedonia, Montenegro, Moldova, Georgia, Armenia, and Syria; almost all of these who practiced a religion were Orthodox faithful. Many Lebanese immigrants were Orthodox Christians. They formed a small percentage of the total number of immigrants, but their churches provided priests and religious workers to aid them.

Almost all immigrants from England, Wales, Scotland, Norway, Denmark, Sweden, and Finland who attended church were Protestants. So were a majority of the German, Dutch, and Swiss immigrants. A sizeable minority of Hungarians and Austrians were also

Protestants. And so were most of the churchgoing people from Estonia and Latvia. This doesn't count a large number of people coming from Canada who were also Protestants. Immigrant aid societies were there for these immigrants also. There were more Protestant immigrants than Jewish or Orthodox Christian immigrants during the Ellis Island era. There were more Catholic immigrants than Protestant immigrants.

The main reason there have been more Protestants than any other religion in America is that the British virtually excluded non-Protestant immigration to the parts of America they colonized from the early 1600s through the Revolutionary War. And until the Famine in Ireland in the late 1840s, there were no large-scale movements of European Catholics to the United States.

This means there was about a ten-generation period from the beginning of English settlement in America to the start of the Civil War in which the population of the lands that would become the United States went from a few hundred English settlers along the Eastern Seaboard to more than 30 million people. And more than 90% of the people who came to America or were born in America up until 1861 were Protestants. This demographic advantage would be enough of a head start to ensure Protestant supremacy in America even when most of the 20 million or so immigrants to America from 1890 to 1930 were not Protestants.

Of course, there were Spanish and French settlers, trappers, and miners in Florida, Louisiana, along the Great Lakes and Mississippi Valley, and out in Texas, New Mexico, and California, but their numbers were much smaller than those of the British. More than a million Irish poured into America in the 15 years before the start of the Civil War. Likewise, in the late 1840s, Americans admitted Texas into the Union and beat the Mexicans in the Mexican War; this means the United States took in perhaps 100,000 Mexicans and Spaniards in Texas, California, and other parts of the Southwest and quite a bit more than 100,000 Native American Indians. Almost all of the Spaniards and Mexicans and some of the Indians were Catholics.

One phenomenon of America not known to Europeans since the days of the wars of religion and the centuries of British persecutions of the Irish for their faith was the hectoring Protestant minister urging other Christians to convert to his brand of Christianity. Since America had no established church after 1776 (colonies had them), ministers of rival sects have competed for adherents like rival insurance salesmen ever since the Calvinist Pilgrims landed on Plymouth Rock in Massachusetts and the rival Anglican adventurers built Jamestown in Virginia – and both groups started to eliminate the American Indians they ran across.

A very large segment of the American populace was anti-Catholic during the Ellis Island era. The Ku Klux Klan had millions of members. Al Smith would lose an election to Herbert Hoover during the Ellis Island era essentially because he was a Catholic even though he was a much better political leader than Hoover.

In that social climate, it would stand to reason that some misguided militant ministers would see it as their job to try to convert incoming immigrants to their brand of Christianity. They believed one had to be Protestant to be a real American. And they hated the Catholic Church, which was a larger and much older Christian denomination, and also was one whose leaders enforced a consistent and well-defined belief system and formal ordination of their clergymen instead of individual interpretation of Scripture and in many cases, self-chosen appointments to the preaching ministry. After all, it is the nature of many people, especially Americans, to want to be their own religious authority. It is much easier to do so as a Protestant than as a Catholic or an Orthodox Christian.

The hectoring of some of these Protestant missionaries no doubt confused some of the immigrants. In most countries of Europe one church or another had a favored position relative to the others. In Scandinavia, some Lutheran ministers told immigrants leaving for America it would be all right if they converted from the official Lutheranism of their lands to Anglicanism (Episcopalianism) to get along because they mistakenly believed America had an established religion and Anglicanism was it. The aggressiveness of some of the preachers caused some of the immigrants – especially those of the Catholic and Orthodox faiths -- to think they had to become Protestants to be considered fully American. And some of them did convert for this superficial reason.

Fortunately, most Protestant ministers who came to Ellis Island were not anti-Catholic fanatics. Many ministers, honest and understanding, would target the unchurched but leave those alone who were settled in their Catholic or Jewish or Orthodox faiths. After awhile, the missionaries of the various religions would work together to help the immigrants. No doubt the harmony and honest spirit of charity shown by these people on Ellis Island made Our Lord smile.

WILLIAMS BANS CROOKED CLERIC

Commissioner William Williams revoked visiting privileges on Ellis Island for a Protestant pastor because he was trafficking immigrant girls, swindling them, and threatening them with deportation. He notified the crooked cleric of his condemnation in this October 10, 1902 letter:

Pastor Berkemeier,
12 State Street, New York City.

Sir:

You have for some time past represented at Ellis Island the Lutheran Immigrant Home of 12 State Street, New York City, and you were allowed the freedom of this Island under the supposition that your only object was to assist immigrants. I have recently had occasion to suspect the sincerity of your motives and now I have conclusive proof that instead of assisting immigrants you are in the habit of actually preventing recently arrived girls from meeting their friends and compelling them to accept employment against their will with people who have previously directed you to look up servants for them at Ellis Island. Your action is the more reprehensible because you have prefixed to your name the word "Pastor".

On October 1, Marie V. Rhein, a German immigrant girl of about twenty, reached Ellis Island by steamship "Kaiser Wilhelm". She desired to go to East Orange, New Jersey, with Mrs. Ambrose Vernon, a cabin passenger on this steamer, and the wife of a clergyman, who had come to Ellis Island to meet her. Through the privileges accorded you at Ellis Island, you were enabled to secure the release to you of this girl for alleged missionary purposes. Your real object was in fact wholly different. This girl told you both at Ellis Island and later at your "Home" that she wished to go to Mrs. Vernon, who again called for her on Thursday morning while she was still under your immediate care. On this occasion you treated both Mrs. Vernon and her husband with the utmost discourtesy, said that the girl had left you, declined to say where she had gone, and falsely stated that she had expressed a desire to have nothing further to do with Mrs. Vernon. What really happened was this: you told the girl that she could not go to Mrs. Vernon, asked her whether she had an arrangement with the latter for work (to which she said no), talked to her about the contract labor law, and frightened her by saying that she would have to return to Germany unless she took for one year a certain position which you had found for her. Having made these misrepresentations you turned her over at noon on October second, to a man who has a place of business in New York City, and he took her to his home in Flatbush where she went to work. Both you and this man declined to tell Mr. or Mrs. Vernon where this girl could be found, and it required the services of an expert Treasury agent to ascertain her whereabouts.

On Monday, October 6, learning these facts, I summoned you to my office where you repeatedly contradicted yourself and misstated the facts. In ignorance of the fact that both Mrs. Vernon and the girl were at Ellis Island you stated (1) that the girl said she did not wish to go to Mrs. Vernon, which statement was promptly shown to be untrue, (2) that when at the "Home" on Thursday Mrs. Vernon had not asked to see the girl, whereas you later admitted that she had made such request, (3) that you accidentally received the girl, whereas Mr. Burlingame, an attorney of this city, stated that the man to whom you discharged her told him that he had made application to you sometime ago for a servant girl and that this girl was turned over in compliance with such application and (4) that the wife of the man to whose house she went was an invalid and that you were requested to tell that girl not to "speak of any transaction that transpired when she passed through Ellis Island so that his wife might not grow suspicious and nervous" all of which I do not believe to be true. Upon presenting herself in my office, shortly after my interview with you, the girl told all of the circumstances of this case, and particularly how she had insisted that she wished to go to Mrs. Vernon, until you had threatened her with return to Europe unless she took the place you had selected for her. I personally witnessed the delight with which she greeted Mrs. Vernon in my office, and later in the afternoon she voluntarily went with her to East Orange, as she would have done in the first instance but for your interference.

The foregoing will cause surprise only to those who are not familiar with your method of dealing with immigrants. Upon investigation I find that the case of Anna Krajicek, who arrived at New York on S.S. "Neckar" in May, 1901, was another instance where you attempted to subject an ignorant foreign girl to similar treatment. In an affidavit verified January 1, 1902, this girl swears that you took her against her will to your "Home", there placed her at work which was "very hard", refused to let her see or communicate with her relations to whom she was going, treated her harshly until her aunt procured possession of her through legal proceedings, and that when you were finally compelled to let her go, you endeavored to swindle her by paying her far less than the small amount you had agreed to give her. Most of these facts were brought out in the New York Evening Sun of December 31, 1901. Other cases have come to my attention in which your care of immigrants has inured to their distinct disadvantage.

Your actions above referred to are in marked contrast with your words; for you have recently stated to me that your object was: To provide the immigrants on their arrival with a Christian home, and to assist them with necessary counsel and protection, in connection with which there is a chapel and the service of a chaplain, to be helpful to them in the discharge of their highest religious duties.

Your boarding-house rates range from 75 cents to $1.25 a day per person. This is business, not charity. The time has come when I propose to draw a sharp line between the true missionaries (of whom there are a number at Ellis Island) and the boarding-house runners who, parading under false colors, are for that reason the most dangerous people to whom an immigrant may be turned over.

I now inform you that neither you nor any one representing you will be further allowed to come to Ellis Island or the Barge Office. Orders to this effect have been issued.

Respectfully,

WM. WILLIAMS
Commissioner.

WILLIAMS GETS ARCHBISHOP'S HELP

Commissioner William Williams took aim at some of the self-styled immigrant aid groups and clergy from Ellis Island when he determined they were corrupt. He banned representatives of the Swedish Immigrant Home, St. Joseph's Home for the Protection of Polish Immigrants, and the Austrian Society of New York from coming to Ellis Island to waylay immigrants. Many special interests and immigrant groups attacked him. One mighty representative of many immigrants, on the other hand, saw Williams was doing right and pledged his assistance. Here is New York Catholic Archbishop Farley's offer for aid.

ARCHBISHOP'S HOUSE
452 Madison Ave.,
New York

April 15, 1903.

Commissioner William Williams,
U.S. Immigration Service,
Office of the Commissioner, New York.

Dear Sir:

I am very grateful for your courteous and exhaustive communication on the subject of the relations of the Polish Immigration Home with Polish immigrants at Ellis Island. I have just placed your letter in the hands of a Polish clergyman, in whose good judgment I have the utmost confidence, and instructed him to make a thorough inquiry into the management of the Home and trust that the result will be, that if changes are found to be necessary, they will be made without regard to anything but the interests of the immigrants.

I shall let you hear of the outcome of the investigation and am confident that the former friendly relations between the Home and the U.S. Immigration Service authorities will be restored.

Meantime I am, with much regard,
Very truly yours,

JNO M. FARLEY,
Abp, N. Y.

DUTIFUL MATRON HELPS IMMIGRANTS

Maud Mosher, an Ellis Island matron, followed up on a large number of women. Some she suspected were coming to work in America as prostitutes; she watched to make sure others would not fall into the hands of white slavers. Some of her field notes follow:

Dec. 18, 1904

Miss Louise Dubois (French) said she had $100.00, was to go to Hotel Martin on Broadway and there wait the arrival of her sister from Butte, Mont. Case appeared <u>very</u> suspicious to me as well as girl's appearance and I told Mr. Jackson I considered it a good S. I. (Board of Special Inquiry) case.

Mr. Miller told me Miss D. was not made S.I. but was sent to N.Y. Div. and was there made S.I. on appearance. He said a Mrs. Butcher came next morning to St. Paul for her and Insp. J. failed to get Mrs. B's. address.

Miss Margaret Harold told me she was going to a friend, Major Armstrong -- said her name should be Mrs. not Miss on Passenger list. I found Maj. Armstrong on pier and took him on board. He told me he had lived with Miss H. 5 years as his wife, had never married her but intended to do so -- that he had paid her -- that for family reasons could not marry her -- reported above to Inspector. In my presence he gave her what looked to be a large amount of money. She was made S. I. She was one of the most beautiful girls I ever saw -- about 25. He was rather nice looking and very prepossessing in manner and speech.

Note: *"Prepossessing is a now archaic word; it means "creating a favorable impression." I had to look it up, too.*

Miss Dutoit (French) said she was an orphan -- coming here to get a position. She was a nice appearing girl. She had no place to go and I took her to the French Evan. Home, 341 W. 39th St. N.Y. where Mme. Bolliet received her.

Dec. 24, 1904

Ordered on cutter. Boarded "Campania." Found friends for detained passengers as follows: son of Mrs. Archdale (& Mrs. and Miss Ashton), uncle of Misses Bannister & Hesketh, brother of Miss Hepburn, son of Mrs. Lewis, Husband of Mrs. Linscott. Miss Butcher a French girl was detained -- I could not get to see her as she was allowed to leave the cabin & "could not be found." When I went on the deck she was there & as I came back in just a minute on ship from pier met this girl in company with a woman (tall, large, coarse-looking) who had come for her and had been taken on ship by someone else beside myself.

It seems to me that suspicious cases on Cunard ships always get off in just a similar way.

I believe this girl comes within Sec. 3 but as I could not see her before she was discharged. Said nothing to Mr. Keep - Inspector in charge.

Mrs. Butcher is said to be name of woman who came for Miss Dubois (St. Paul) next morning -- wonder if this isn't same one.

Jan. 1, 1905

Boarded "La Champagne" from cutter. Mr. O'Conner told I could go on cutter if I wished. Messrs Bock and Pearsall, Inspectors, and Mr. Markus Braun and Interpreter Tedesko and Capt. Neucome were on ship. Mr. Braun asked my opinion of two women, Mrs. (X) & Miss Beigirrger. I regarded them as suspicious cases. Mr. B. had same opinion and they were made S.I. on his order by Mr. Bock. Miss Dessegns told me she was going to Skonazi Bros. as companion to a sister of theirs. Got position thru an uncle in Paris -- she knew nothing of them except thru her uncle. She came from Constantinople -- was a teacher. She told me this in a way which impressed me as a story learned and recited. When I saw her card marked "cousin." I started to tell Mr. Bock but he very impatiently said: "I don't see what difference it makes whether she is going to a cousin or not." I replied: "I can't understand why when I tell you something you ought to know, you should get angry." According to instructions I went to Inspector Chg. Pearsall and told him what I tried to tell Mr. Bock. At Mr. Bock's request went to Dr. Parkes and asked him why Mrs. Ferrando and Mrs. Maretich were to be held -- Dr. P. said "trachoma".

Note: *Back in the day, most civil servants really worked, even on holidays.*

Jan. 3, 1905

Boarded "Statendam" at pier. Almost perished with cold going from ferry to pier -- such cutting wind & stinging snow.

Found friends for detained passengers as follows: husband of Mrs. Bos (& child), husband of Mrs. Ceitlen and child, husband of Mrs. Jarahebracha, son-in-law of Mrs. Pollak, Miss P., husband of Mrs. Wolnausky, Miss W., bro-in-law of Miss Weintraub, son of Mr. Vos, uncle of Mr. Gottlieb, uncle of Mr. Schaap, husband of Mrs. Ratner & 2 children. Signed off at 6 P.M. Such a dreadful dreadful snow & wind storm -- never saw anything like it except the blizzards in Kansas.

Jan. 5, 1905

Boarded "Graf Waldersee" at pier. Found husband of Mrs. Danziger & 2 children, found Herr Folokewicz for cousin who had come to meet him on pier. Did some pier work.

Mr. Pearsall did not give me all the names of detained passengers -- 2 women were detained who names I did not get. Heard after returning to office that a woman came over 2nd cabin as Miss ___ who had come over previously as Mrs. ___. This must be Miss S. Perrox as I know who all the other unmarried women were. Also heard there were a number of men who frequented her stateroom. Was told it (she) was the first passenger discharged (let go) by Mr. O'Conner.

Jan. 7, 1905

Did not go down bay as Capt. Neucome told Mrs. Waters, "Weather is too bad for men let alone women." One of the Customs Boarding Officers told me the sea was not rough -- & added, "Never is much sea in a fog you know." Heavy fog till about 10 A.M.

Boarded "Lucania" at pier. No detained passengers. Mr. James Wallace of Marquette, Mich. 1st cabin pass. U. S. Cit. was arrested on pier so I heard for a theft of $30,000.00 of securities from his employees.

Told Mr. Pearsall what I had heard & he went out on pier to "see about it." At time I spoke to him did not know name nor all of story & he knew nothing about it.

Jan. 9, 1905

Boarded "Zeeland" at pier. Found following friends for detained passengers: brother of Mr. G. Strauss, brother of Miss Sandler. Leo Haus, representative for Mr. U. Zuckermayer. When I first saw Miss Helene Danziger as I went in cabin I thought from her appearance she was pgt after I had observed more went to Mr. Keep & asked to have an opportunity to talk more with her. Got a stewardess to interpret, asked her if she were not pgt. She denied it. Was not entirely convinced. Reported to Mr. Keep but as no one came for her he decided to make her S.I. & <u>requested</u> me to write on card - "Appearance - pgt. M. Mosher." Did so. Also wrote a little note to Mrs. Stucklen telling her I had talked with girl, etc. Miss D. said she was going to a brother in Elizabeth, N.J.

Miss Sophie Stowik going to Minneapolis, $5.00 & no ticket was also made S.I. I wouldn't be surprised if she went insane before long from her rather queer way. Polish visitors were called for by the Leo Haus man. First time I was ever officially recognized on a ship & allowed to go on cutter!

Notes: *"Pgt." is short for "pregnant. "Queer" was most people's way of saying "odd," not "lesbian."*

ELLIS ISLAND SCRAPBOOK

Jan. 11, 1905

Went to pier for "Krownprinz Wm." as I did not know whether Mrs. Mooney would be allowed to board her or not from cutter. Mr. Brown told me to let "Mexico" pass & go to "K. Wm." but when I got to pier found Mrs. Mooney had started work so let her finish altho it was my ship.

As I sat in 2nd cabin a man whom Mrs. Mooney had brought on board showed me a letter of instruction which he had concerning two young girls from the bro. of one of the girls saying they were to be sent on "Penna R. R." and making careful arrangements to meet them in Chicago & take them to Oswego, Ill. Miss _ had already bought ticket to Oswego over B. & O. R. R. as he was only agt. on board. I called Mr. Keep's attention to case & he called Mr. Jackson's attention but as Mr. J. said "he was not going to get into any R.R. tangle" nothing was done & the other girl was virtually compelled to buy her ticket of B. & O. man so they could travel together. I also heard the B. & O. agt. tell a steward to tell a woman (poor looking - several little children) "She's got to give me $4.00 dif. in a first class ticket." The way he said this last & the way he acted about other two tickets did not look to me like straight business. Reported to Mr. Flannery, Officer in Chg. of ship.

Jan. 20, 1905

Boarded "Alene" at pier 28 shipwrecked sailors from "Valencia." No work of course.

Boarded "Astoria" at pier. Found brother-in-law of Miss Scott, intended husband of Miss Nelson. A passenger on ship after he got on pier sent money to Miss Kate Murray who was going to Terre Haute, Ind. so she would have sufficient to take her on.

Spoke to Insp. Jackson who sent for the man and had a conference with him after which he held Miss Murray of which I was very glad. Miss Murray was a very pretty young girl & I feared the man wanted to get possession of her for no good purpose. Mr. Nickols came & asked me to take friends on the ship as the Customs men refused to allow anyone to go on the ship unless I took them on.

Comments: *Maud Mosher was a sharp-eyed and dutiful woman. Her notes indicate she was looking out to protect Kate Murray from possible sexual slavery, that she detected a possible railroad scam being pulled on immigrants, and that she found an unmarried girl (Miss Danziger) who looked pregnant (and, if so, very likely had to leave her home in Europe in shame), and might be deportable as a public charge.*

Her notes also indicated she suspected a woman (Mrs. or Miss Butcher) of being a procuress, that she suspected another female (Miss Perrox) of being a prostitute, that British shipping officials of the Cunard Line were engaged in unethical conduct regarding immigrants, and that an immigrant (Miss Dessegns) was rehearsing her story to enter the country on false pretenses. She uncovered the sad story of a young British woman (Margaret Harold) hoping for marriage to her swain (who had been keeping her on the side for years with no intention of marrying her), and watched as he gave her money and then let her be put before the Board of Special Inquiry for probable deportation on moral turpitude or public charge grounds. And she helped a poor French girl (Miss Dutoit) get to an immigrant aid society.

Maud mundanely noted the immigrants she found for people who were waiting for them. (I left out a number of notes of hers listing these people.) And by way of noting the events of her days, she commented on foulups a couple of her co-workers made, noted the miserable weather conditions of her outdoor work, and indicated she worked on a holiday to help others hoping to come to America. And Maud's note of the shipwreck indicated traveling across the ocean was not a certain thing.

LOVE, LUST, AND MARRIAGE AT ELLIS ISLAND

HUNDREDS OF IRISH GIRLS WARM ELLIS ISLAND
(Unnamed New York newspaper, April 30, 1897 (as retold by Edward Corsi, In the Shadow of Liberty, page 53))

The record of recent years for the number of Irish immigrants landed at Ellis Island in any day was broken yesterday. Seven hundred of them, mostly red-cheeked, laughing girls, were brought there from the steamers *Majestic* and *Servia*, which arrived yesterday from Queenstown (the port is now called Cobh, Ireland). Of these sixty-five percent had had their passage prepaid by friends in this country.

Three-fourths of the immigrants started at once out of town, most of them going into New England states. The remainder will stay in the metropolitan district. Only some half dozen of the arrivals were debarred from landing.

Note: Corsi implied these young Irish females were mostly coming to be brides.

A THOUSAND EUROPEAN WOMEN FOLLOW ON BACHELORETTE SHIP

The New York Times and the New York World reported on a ship bearing an even larger cargo of pretty unmarried females from Europe a decade after the landing of the Irish girls in 1897, and made no disclaimer about the intentions of some of the flirty femmes. Here are the rival papers' stories.

SHIPLOAD OF GIRLS SEEK HUSBANDS HERE
(New York Times, 9/28/1907)

When the White Star liner *Baltic* tied up at the foot of West Eleventh Street yesterday morning 1,002 young women tripped down the gangplank and looked about them for husbands. Some of the young women found those for whom they looked awaiting them on the pier, but there were many left over, and be it said to the shame of Manhattan bachelors that these announced it as their intention to look far inland for their affinities.

Little Gena Jensen, from Christiania (Norway), pretty and golden haired, said she hoped none of the men on the pier would try to take possession of her. "Because," she announced, "there is some one waiting for me in a place called Connecticut."

The arrival of the young women had been heralded from abroad when the *Baltic* sailed. The girls were booked from every country in the north of Europe, the majority of them coming from England, Ireland, Wales, and Scotland.

The State Board of Immigration of Michigan, which has been for some time trying to increase the population around Kalamazoo, immediately wired to the towns in that district, advising that delegates be appointed at once to meet the *Baltic*. The result was the appointment of a general committee of the young farmers of Northern Michigan. They arrived in the city early yesterday, prepared to do their best to persuade the maids that Michigan was the best place in the country to live. The result of the young Michiganders' endeavors will not be known until to-day, for only a few of the girls were taken off Ellis Island yesterday after their trip there from the liner's pier.

Comment: Leave it to the New York Times to screw up basic American geography. Kalamazoo is in southern Michigan, about 40 miles north of Indiana.

Most of those who did land were Irish girls, who went back this year to attend the Dublin Exposition, and did not have to go through all the red tape that their fellow-passengers in the steerage will experience. Some interesting and embarrassing incidents attended the arrival of these returning voyagers at the Battery. They were awaited by a large delegation in Battery Park. When the ardent ones greeted them with Sunday-go-to-meeting smiles, a chorus of "Go 'long wid yez" filled the air. The immigration officers finally had to explain to the prospective bridegrooms that there were many young women on the boat who were not looking for husbands and whose wishes in the matter would have to be respected.

Purser H. B. Palmer of the *Baltic* when asked about his cargo said: "They're here all right. We took on a bunch of them at Liverpool and gathered in over 700 more when we reached Queenstown (Cobh, Ireland). You ought to have seen them come up the side of the ship. They did it just as if they expected to find husbands awaiting them on the steerage deck."

The deckhands of the *Baltic* said that they had the greatest difficulty all the way across in keeping the passageways from the first and second cabins to the decks overlooking the steerage cleared. It was plain that the value and beauty of the cargo were appreciated to the full by those who traveled on the decks above.

Comment: Most of the females were Irish. This explains why they were so desirable.

The White Star officials could give no explanation of the sudden influx of maids on the *Baltic*. It is believed, however, that it is due to the fact that the report has been circulated in Europe that wives are scarce here and that those that are to be had demand too much of their would-be mates. It is also undoubtedly true that a certain percentage of the passengers of the Baltic have come with no higher ambitions than to work as servants.

Not so with Clara McGee from Roscommon (Ireland). She admitted that she had never been inside a theatre, but, nevertheless, said that she had decided to be a great actress. Others want to be the wives of railroad engineers, and some decided, after they arrived in the lower bay, that the only men that could win their hands, were the ones who built the skyscrapers, One little blue-eyed girl from Liverpool showed that she was strictly up to date by declaring that "it's a Pittsburgh millionaire for me."

OLD WORLD BEAUTIES GREETED BY AMERICAN BACHELORS
(New York World, 9/28/1907, noted in This Fabulous Century (1900-1910), Time-Life Books)

No marriage mart of the Orient where brides were merchandise ever presented so bewitching a picture as the decks of the "Baltic" yesterday when 1,002 beauties, colleens from Ireland, lasses from Scotland, maidens from Wales, girls from England and blondes from Scandinavia, rosy, dimpled and roguish eyed, marriageable every one, stood there, fascinated by their first glimpse of the New World.

"I like tall men and blondes," said Susan Thompson frankly, and then her companions all screamed and Susan laughed until she could hardly speak. "I have read much about Americans making good husbands."

Miss Agnes McGirr's home is in Edinburgh (Scotland). "I want a man with dark hair," she chirped. "A city man? No, a farmer. A man who is making $1000 a year will do. That isn't too much to ask in this country is it? How old? Thirty. He has some sense, then."

"They tell me," remarked Nellie O'Brien from Loch Crae, Tipperary (Ireland), "that there are no men in Pittsburgh but millionaires. I'm going there, and it's soon I'll be riding in my own carriage, I suppose."

As for the accomplishments of these girls, no list would be long enough to enumerate them, and no rash man so ungallant as to abridge them. They can cook, sing and play the piano, scrub, take care of a house and mind children, milk cows, raise chickens, weed garden beds, go to market, sew, patch and knit, make cheese and butter, pickle cucumbers and drive cattle.

Comment: *These are all talents that most American women lack today. Most men of today couldn't milk cows or drive cattle, either.*

No wonder when he heard they were coming, a farmer out in Kansas wrote: "John Lee, Vice-President of the Merchantile Marine Steamship Company: Dear Sir: I am a widower with a couple of married daughters, but I want a new wife, who is to come out here to Kansas the minute the Baltic gets in. There is only one other house near mine. She can tell my house by the green shutters. Tell her not to make a mistake."

The Kansas guy didn't luck out. You have to pounce on good fortune, it doesn't come to you. A large crowd of bachelors, and the farmers' delegation from Michigan descended on the docks when they got word the ship bearing the Irish girls and other Euro-babes was about to land.

A band also showed up to welcome the ladies to America and add to the carnival atmosphere of that magical fall day by playing hits of the era like "Cupid's Garden" and "I Want You, Honey, Yes I Do." Photographers took pictures of many of the young women, who were only too happy to pose and display their most winning smiles.

In your mind's eye, can't you see the beer wagons rolling in, being pulled by teams of horses, and the pushcart vendors hawking "veeners und zouzages?" And all the young women in their most festive dresses, and the guys with straw hats or derbies and handlebar mustaches cheering and whistling and offering their arms to them? Who said our ancestors were prudes?

YOU SAY I SHOULD REMARRY MY WIFE? WHAT A COUNTRY!
(Frank Martocci, as interviewed by Edward Corsi, In the Shadow of Liberty, page 86)

One of the most disgusted men we ever had on the Island was a young Hungarian who, in 1905, had, as he complained, to marry his own wife!

They were two young Hungarians, and I remember them well, though it was back in 1905 that they got to Ellis Island. They had come from London separately, on tickets bearing different names and at that time they had said they were cousins.

Once they arrived at the Island, however, they explained that they were really man and wife, adding that they had bought return tickets for other people, and so had been forced to represent themselves as the people whose names were on the tickets.

The immigration authorities brought the case to the attention of the superintendent of the Home for Jewish Immigrant Girls, requesting her to become responsible for the girl. She agreed and took the girl to the Home. Later the man appeared with several of his countrymen and demanded his wife. A conference followed, in which they were asked for evidence of their married status. Their explanations, given convincingly, were that they had been too poor to get a wedding ring and that the wedding certificate had been in a trunk which was lost.

Finally the superintendent said: "Well, if you're married already, it won't do you any harm to be married all over again. If you will marry here and now, you can go away as you like, but if not, I will have to keep the girl, for in spite of what you say, you have no real proof that you are her husband."

The man looked dazed. "What kind of country is this," he asked hoarsely, "that makes me remarry my own wife?"

He agreed, however, to the proposition, and after a rabbi had been called in they were married again, to the bewilderment of the bridegroom and the amusement of his naturalized friends. The couple went away happy, however, with clear sailing ahead.

TWO-TIMING SOONER POLITICIAN PLOTTED BIGAMY OR ADULTERY
Special to The New York Times (10/28/1922)

OKLAHOMA CITY, Okla., Oct. 27 – Frieda Giovetta is due in New York tonight and expects to sail for Italy Saturday. Signorina Giovetta, who arrived in this country in the latter part of July, was held up at Ellis Island until George Hoke of Stillwater, Okla., met her and induced the immigration officials to admit her.

Oklahoma was startled when press dispatches carried the story that she had come to this country to marry Mr. Hoke, who is a member of one of the most prominent families in the State and already married. He returned to Oklahoma accompanied by Signorina Giovetta, who in an interview declared that she had come to America to marry him. She professed her astonishment to find Mr. Hoke married, and said that she could not return to her home and face her family, as she had come against their wishes.

Mr. Hoke had just been nominated by the Democrats for a Judgeship at Stillwater, having no Republican opponent, but the publicity attendant upon the case caused him to withdraw his candidacy.

Signorina Giovetta stayed at Stillwater for a few days and met members of the Hoke family, and then went to McAlester and appealed to the Italian consul for advice. When she left McAlester she said: "I came to America to make a home, not to break one up."

Mr. Hoke met Signorina Giovetta in Italy in wartime while he was in the army. He knew her for only about two days. She does not speak English, nor he Italian.

"We talked with the eyes," she said.

Signorina Giovetta is said to be a member of a wealthy and aristocratic family. She is a woman of about 40. Mr. Hoke is possibly ten years younger.

THE ITALIAN WITH TWO WIVES
(Maud Mosher)

One day an Inspector came to me in the New York room and said, "Come here quick and see this discharging case."

I went to the discharging cage and there saw an Italian who had been compelled to come there for his wife and child by the Italian Society.

The man it seemed had been in this country two or three years and had married again. The expression on his face was a study as he stood there -- the Italian Immigration Society man telling him that if he abused his wife and child, they would prosecute him for bigamy. The Italian priest was telling the woman that if her husband did not treat her right to let him know and he would see that her husband was punished.

It was a sad time for both. The woman was broken-hearted for of course, she did not know her husband had married again until she arrived here and telegraphed him to come for her, and his brother came and in simple, unconcerned language told the Inspector her husband "don't want her, he has another wife now."

And the husband when he was compelled to come for her evidently was thinking of the scene when the two wives met.

THE MAN AND THE "OTHER WOMAN"
(Maud Mosher, May 10, 1904 and May 11, 1904)

One of the matrons, Mrs. Waters, heard on the pier that a woman had arrived on the *Kaiser Wilhelm 2nd* and had gone to a hotel nearby who suspected that her husband had come here with another woman.

Mrs. Waters took an interpreter and went to the hotel and talked with the woman who was a bright, nice appearing Hungarian woman with a frank, good face.

The woman told Mrs. Waters that her husband had sailed on the *Frederick der Grosse* and on his arrival here was to get the home ready and she was to follow in two weeks with the two little children.

After her husband had sailed she for some reason thought that her husband had come with another woman and so she had taken passage on the *Kaiser Wilhelm 2nd* and sailed immediately. The *Kaiser*

Wilhelm 2nd being a faster ship arrived in fact before the *Frederick der Grosse*.

She said she did not know for a certainty that her husband had come with this woman as they might have just happened to sail on the ship and she did not wish him to know she suspected anything unless it really was so.

The matron said she would find out and let her know if anything seemed wrong. She would come to the pier when the *Frederick der Grosse* came in.

When the steamer arrived the husband was on board with the other woman registered as his wife. He was seated facing the door with the woman by his side. When the wife came into the cabin, four of the ship officers preceded her, hiding her from sight so that the husband had not the faintest idea she was anywhere within several thousand miles until the officers stepped aside and just before him stood his wife.

The wife when she saw her husband broke down and cried and the other woman came to her and tried to comfort her.

The husband begged to be allowed to go to his wife and would have gladly deserted the other woman for her but both were detained and sent to the Island for Special Inquiry.

The woman upon being questioned said that she took that way of getting to the U.S. At the Inquiry the man was admitted to his wife who received him with open arms. So her husband was home -- but the other woman was deported.

SLATTERNLY SCHATZI SENT HOME
(Ludmilla Foxlee, How They Came: The Drama of Ellis Island, pages 95-96)

Elizabeth W., 23, German, from Rumania, recognized no difference between right and wrong. She was brought to Ellis Island for entering the United States unlawfully. A relative by marriage, Mr. B, who lived in the Bronx, New York City, obtained her release on a $1000 bond but my plea to reduce it to $500 succeeded and Elizabeth was free for a few weeks. She then often visited an Englishman who was detained on a warrant of arrest, and she also cultivated a Polish cook in the Ellis Island kitchen. She obtained the address of any man she met on Ellis Island and elsewhere.

Shortly after she was released on bond she led her relative, Mr. B., on a merry chase. The search for her seemed to lead to nowhere. When he time for deportation arrived, Mr. B. thought she might have gone to Buffalo, New York, where her sweetheart – yet another man – had a sister or brother; but Mr. B. did not find Elizabeth. The Buffalo Immigration Office took over the chase and soon found her and sent her to Ellis Island.

Mr. B. then discovered that Elizabeth had indeed lived dangerously. She was widowed once, divorced once, and she managed to cross the International Bridge at Niagara Falls by creeping across it in the underside, clinging to rafters. Her English sweetheart complained to a high official that we were making obstructions to his plans to marry Elizabeth. This official wanted to know what right we had to counsel persons old enough to make their decisions. We replied that such an alliance would create complications since the woman would be sent to Rumania and the man to England. Even so, what we thought had no influence on the affairs of these two persons; the official could have sent them to New York City to marry if he approved of their romance. But the Englishman was deported soon after and Elizabeth was free to look for new alliances. We were glad to see her deported on the S.S. *Mauretania*. Even while she was waiting in the Deportation Office she was making new contacts to enliven the coming voyage.

THE CASE OF THE FLEEING FIANCÉE
(Superintendent Percy Baker, as interviewed by Edward Corsi, In the Shadow of Liberty, pages 121-122)

Once, I remember, a young Italian girl arrived on a French ship. She announced that she was on the way to her intended husband at Streator, Illinois. Of course we detained her until we could hear from her future husband, since Washington was very strict in those days.

We requested the man in Streator to send affidavits as to his intentions and ability to provide for her. We permitted her to telegraph him under government supervision.

A day or so after her detention a man appeared, saying he had come for her, and that he was her brother. The case was cited for Special Inquiry in order that a record might be made. It was apparent to me that the man who alleged he was her brother was an impostor, so she was further detained, pending receipt of the affidavits.

The affidavits were received, and at the hearing she again expressed her desire to join her intended husband at Streator. Everything being in order and according to law, we admitted her. Two weeks passed and nothing had been heard, when a communication was received from the man in Streator claiming that his fiancée had not reached him.

Since a railroad ticket to Streator had been furnished her, it was easy for one of our officers to trace her journey. He reported a few days later that she had detrained at Buffalo. It was also soon discovered that her ticket had not been used beyond that point. The officer next set out to locate the alleged brother. The man was found in Brooklyn, but he had married the girl the day before. The man in Streator had paid the freight for the other fellow.

We finally learned that she had met the alleged brother at a steamship boarding house in Havre. He had taken a fast boat after they had fallen in love, so that he might comply with the technicalities of entrance into the country and be on hand to claim her after her own voyage on a slower boat. So far as I know the man in Streator is still waiting for a refund.

GALLANTRY AT ELLIS ISLAND
(Maud Mosher, April 14, 1904)

A fine looking old gentleman of about 60 years asked one of the Customs men to help him find a lady who was a passenger on the "Zeeland" saying that he would not know her. He gave the Custom's man a card and when he spoke to an old lady and asked her if she recognized that name. She at once said "yes," and was taken to the old gentleman.

He (the old man) talked with her a few minutes then took some photographs out of his pocket and showed them to her. They were pictures of herself from childhood up. She looked at them and then threw her arms around the old man's neck. They embraced and kissed and cried.

He then took out a jewel case and gave it to her -- she opened it and I caught sight of what looked to be a beautiful pin.

Of course the Customs man and myself thought we had discovered a very charming romance. Had they been lovers in youth and changed so much they did not recognize each other? Was it an arranged marriage or what?

With much interest we watched the pretty and amusing scene.

A while afterwards we learned that they were brother and sister and had not seen each other since the old lady was twelve years old.

Speaking to a ship's officer about it an hour or so afterward, he told me that the lady was the Baroness Munchhausen and that she claimed that her husband, the Baron was a lineal descendent of the renowned Baron Munchhausen of anecdotal fame.

Note: Baron von Munchhausen had the reputation for telling hilariously exaggerated tales about his life. He was the Al Gore of his era.

SHIP'S OFFICER CAUGHT AT ROMANCE
(Maud Mosher, April 19, 1904)

One of the officers on the "Zeeland" and myself were quite good friends. (It was he who told me that the woman whose old brother met her was the Baroness Munchhausen.) I teased him a little after we had talked of the above about seeing him kiss a lady passenger as he said goodbye. This lady with several other friends was at one end of the pier and I at the other when the officer, Mr. X went up to them to bid adieu. Of course when I mentioned it he protested that he only "whispered a word in her ear," and finally that they were old, old friends, really, etc.

Maud then made a poem of the incident, which followed in her diary:

Out on the pier she walked.
Wandering up and down.
So out on the pier he walked.
Wandering round and round.

Old friends from long ago.
Friends of a by-gone year.
Dear are the old friends to us.
Dearer and yet ever dear.

Her hair rippled low on her brow.
So tempting but why should he fear?
He bent low and touched her fair cheek.
While he "whispered one word in her ear."

Twas just for the days that are gone.
Days that may come back no more.
Twas just for the memories sweet.
Dear dreams of the days of yore.

"Only in remembrance?"
Tell us something true,
Say that why you did it.
Was because you wanted to.

"Only in remembrance"
Cheeks are fair to kiss;
"Only in remembrance!"
Think I believe all this?

Find a civil servant with that sense of rhyme and gentle humor on the federal payroll today, if you can.

ELLIS ISLAND SCRAPBOOK

MARRIAGE AT CITY HALL
(Maud Mosher, June 11, 1904, ship *Campania*)

When I was talking with passengers on the steamer I learned that Miss ___ was coming here to meet her lover, Mr. Miller, and to be married to him.

I told her that I would find him on the pier and bring him on board ship to her, and also asked her when she expected to be married. She replied that she had expected to be married on the ship as she had understood people often were married there and although she could trust her lover she preferred being married before going out in the city.

I found Mr. Miller and in answer to my question, "What relation are you to the young lady?" he answered in a very embarrassed manner. "A friend."

"Aren't you the gentleman Miss ___ expects to marry?" I asked.

He was much relieved and said, "Yes." And on the way up the pier told me he had a home already for her and that he had expected to go right to the City Hall and be married. He also told me he was a bricklayer and was making 65¢ an hour and could take good care of his wife.

I talked with Miss_ again and told her that unless she wished to be married she did not need to be as she could land in some other way -- that it was not a necessity, etc.

The Inspector discharged Miss ___ with the understanding that the couple were to go to the City Hall and that I should accompany them as a witness for the young lady and for the government.

We all went then to the City Hall and got there just in time as the (alderman) was just about to leave the Marriage Room.

The ceremony was performed and the young husband and wife went away happy.

Mr. Miller was determined to pay me for my trouble but of course I would not take anything and told him, "Just be good to the little girl!"

FUTURE NEW YORK MAYOR WITNESSED IMMIGRANT MARRIAGES
(Fiorello La Guardia, The Making of an Insurgent, pages 68-69)

There were some rare cases of husbands who had sent for their wives after two or three years of hard working and saving from their small wages, only to learn for the first time that a child had been born in the meantime. We also witnessed scenes of great generosity, understanding, and forgiveness.

Often we interpreters at Ellis Island had to accompany couples to the city to be married. These were cases of young men who had sent for their fiancées. The men would arrive at Ellis Island all prepared to marry before admission had been granted to the young ladies. We would take them to the City Hall in New York, where marriages were performed in those days by aldermen. The aldermen took turns performing the ceremonies and getting the fees. Some of the aldermen were not averse to getting a little extra, above the two dollars prescribed by the law. I know that most of the Immigration Service personnel protected the immigrants and were not parties to these overcharges.

I was assigned to only a few of these cases, but a few were plenty. I would escort the bridegroom and his bride and their witnesses to the City Hall to see they were properly married and then give the bride clearance for admission to the country. In the few instances I attended the aldermen were drunk. Some of the aldermen would insert into their reading of the marriage ceremony remarks they considered funny and sometimes used lewd language, much to the amusement of the red-faced, cheap "tinhorn" politicians who hung around them to watch the so-called fun. I was happy when years later the law granting aldermen authority to perform marriages was repealed.

Who was behind the repeal? La Guardia's future fellow Republican and occasional opponent Henry Curran was. (Yes, he is the same Henry Curran whose recollections are in this chapter.) As an alderman, Curran objected to the aldermen pocketing fees from $2 to $5 for each short ceremony. He convinced the state legislators to make the fee a flat $2 fee, that the city clerk perform the ceremony, and that the money go to the city treasury instead of to aldermen. (Henry Curran, Pillar to Post, pages 178 - 182)

THE OVERSEXED SAX PLAYER
(Edward Corsi, In the Shadow of Liberty, page 106)

In my own time at Ellis Island the detention case which afforded the most amusement and certainly the greatest degree of satisfaction to certain Americans was that of a noted saxophone player.

It seems that the crime for which this saxophone player was deported (other than saxophone playing) was that of bigamy. And strange to say, when he was first indicted, there appeared in the courtroom to confront him, not just his first legal wife who had brought the suit, but other women, all insisting that they too had entered into the relationship of marriage with the defendant. As was to be expected, he was convicted. On the night before he was deported from Ellis Island, he entertained the others who were in detention quarters at the same time, by walking up and down the floor and playing Victor Herbert's celebrated musical composition: "Ah, Sweet Mystery of Life."

THE FREEWHEELING FRAULEIN
(Ludmilla Foxlee, "A Social Worker's Ellis Island," page 7)

Hedwig Bodenbach, German, 25, blonde and pretty, might have avoided her Ellis Island experience, had not her impetuous young friend form Michigan claimed her at the pier in New York. Were they engaged to be married? No. They explained that they could not be because they were not acquainted personally. Yes, he had paid her steamship fare, but that did not place her under obligation to him, the young man declared.

He was a baker, comfortably situated, ripe for marriage, but unable to find the right girl in the United States. His sister in his home town in Germany was instrumental in bringing Hedwig to the attention of the young man, and after they had corresponded a year, they wanted to meet. Being unable to go to Germany, the young man invited Hedwig to come to the United States. If they found each other desirable, they would marry; if not, Hedwig would return home.

In the eyes of the Ellis Island Board of Special Inquiry this case was entirely irregular. A young woman should not be discharged to a young man if he did not intend to marry her immediately. So Hedwig had to be excluded, but her appeal to the Secretary of Labor against exclusion was sustained and she was admitted on a departure bond of $500, furnished by the young man. We took a firm stand against immediate marriage, advocated by another interested person, because we believed these young people needed to see each other against a normal, workaday background, free from excitement and tenseness, before they married.

Apparently they found each other desirable. Some three months after Hedwig's departure from Ellis Island we received an invitation to their wedding, and next Christmas a card came from a small Ohio town, where, Hedwig said, they lived contentedly.

THE KISSING POST
(Frank Martocci, as interviewed by Edward Corsi, In the Shadow of Liberty, page 87)

It seems to me now as I look back that in those days there were crying and laughing and singing all the time at Ellis Island. Very often brides came over to marry here, and of course we had to act as witnesses. I have no count, but I'm sure I must have helped at hundreds and hundreds of weddings of all nationalities and all types. The weddings were numberless, until they dropped the policy of marrying them at the Island and brought them to City Hall in New York.

Incidentally, as you may have heard, there is a post at Ellis Island which through long usage has come to earn the name of "The Kissing Post." It is probably the spot of greatest interest on the Island, and if the immigrants recall it afterward it is always, I am sure, with fondness. For myself, I found it a real joy to watch some of the tender scenes that took place there.

There was a line of desks where the inspectors stood with their backs towards the windows and facing the wall. Further back, behind a partition, the witnesses waited outside for the detained aliens. As the aliens were brought out, the witnesses were brought in to be examined as to their rights of claim. If the inspector found no hitch, they were allowed to join each other. This, because of the arrangement of the partitions, usually took place at "The Kissing Post," where friends, sweethearts, husbands and wives, parents and children would embrace and kiss and shed tears for pure joy.

KISSING POST GREETINGS
(Arthur Train, Saturday Evening Post, 3/5/1910)

Now and then one of them (women detained near the "Kissing Post") will wave excitedly to a man at the rail. Occasionally the men outside indicate to one another someone in the crowd of women – but it is very quiet, very restrained. They are so afraid something may go wrong and that they (their wives or sweethearts) will not be let out of the cage. Presently the inspector turns around and shouts: "All right – Becky Lipsky!"

There is a flutter in the cage and a little birdlike woman, leading a four-year-old boy by the hand, rushes to the opening at the side. A curly-haired young man with a serious, determined face walks unemotionally from the rail, and paying no attention to my presence greets the woman with a mere nod and takes her bundle. Then, without speaking, they pass into the covered gallery leading to the dock.

"Humph!" I remark. "Didn't even kiss her!"

"Take a peek through the door," answers the gateman. "Sure, they don't do it here. They wait!"

I walk to the door just in time to see Becky Lipsky throw herself sobbing into her husband's arms, while he rains kisses upon her cheeks and that of the child.

MISFORTUNE AND TRAGEDY AND ELLIS ISLAND

THE DEAD BABY
(Maud Mosher)

Mrs. (Regina) Stucklen, Chief Matron, told me that one day she was examining immigrants on the line when a woman carrying a small baby came through. The baby was wrapped up closely and ordinarily Mrs. Stucklen would not have touched it, as it was such a little thing, for fear of waking it but the mother's face looked so white and wild that she felt that something might be wrong so she insisted on uncovering the little face although the mother protested bitterly.

Mrs. Stucklen drew back the covering only to see that the baby was dead. Upon inquiring of the now weeping mother she learned that it had died three days before and that the mother had carried it in her arms ever since knowing that if it were discovered it would be taken from her and, as she feared, buried at sea.

Notes: *Roughly 3500 immigrants died at Ellis Island; 1400 or so of them were children. About 500 mothers in detention at Ellis Island gave birth to children. Barry Moreno's excellent* Encyclopedia of Ellis Island *is the source of this information.*

Also, babies born at Ellis Island were not automatically American citizens. American officials ruled each such baby had the citizenship of his or her father. In the Ellis Island era, there was no such thing as an anchor baby automatically getting a load of aliens, legal or illegal, residency and citizenship they didn't deserve.

THE DESERTED WIFE
(Maud Mosher)

One day in May, 1904, I was showing a party of friends over the Island and went to the "Deferred Room." At once I saw what seemed to be a familiar face. I went up to the woman and she at once took my hand and kissed it and began to pour out a story in Polish.

I remembered then that she had come to the Island with her two pretty fair little girls along in November. We had a great time locating her husband but finally found him and he came and took her away.

When I saw her again in the "Deferred Room" of course I was greatly astonished and asked her what was the reason she had come back. She held in her hand a photograph of her husband -- a rough working man and said with tears in her eyes rough translation, "He has gone away and I know not where he is working."

She, poor thing, had become a public charge and was to be deported.

DEPORTED YOUNG MOTHER DIES WITH BABY AT SEA
(New York Times, 12/4/1923)

The story of the death at sea of Mary Brennon, an eighteen-year-old girl who (was) to (be returned to) County Sligo, Ireland, and her newly born baby girl, was told yesterday when the White Star liner *Celtic* arrived from Liverpool and Queenstown (now Cobh, Ireland).

Mary Brennon arrived in New York on Nov. 1 on the White Star liner *Celtic* and went to Ellis Island. On Nov. 3 she was ordered excluded. The deportation order was marked "L. P. C.," which is used when the immigrant is liable to become a public charge, and also when the exclusion is ordered on moral grounds. She was not married and was about to become a mother. She had not told her parents of her condition, according to the letter left by her for her mother, and she was coming to an aunt in well-to-do circumstances here, to remain with her until her baby was born.

While detained at Ellis Island from Nov. 3 until Nov. 9, when she was taken to the White Star liner *Baltic*, the girl had caught a severe cold, which developed into pneumonia two days after the vessel left New York. The baby was born, and died on Nov. 15, and the mother died the next day.

SMUGGLERS KILL CHINESE
(Edward Corsi, In the Shadow of Liberty, page 166)

In the days when Canada admitted them in wholesale quantities upon payment of the Canadian head tax, it was not uncommon for sailing vessels to pick up entire boat loads of Chinese at a Canadian port and attempt to land them at some harbor or point upon the American coast. At times the smugglers were frightened by the approach of strange vessels or learned that they were about to be detected. Overboard went the Chinamen. More tragic still are instances where the smugglers made no effort to land them, merely taking them a few miles out to sea from the port of embarkation and dumping them mercilessly into the ocean. These practices finally led to payment only after safe delivery inside the country.

On one occasion a boat load of Chinese was being brought into New York harbor. Suddenly with success in full view, an immigration cutter was seen approaching. The smugglers, in a frantic effort to do away with the evidence, began to throw the Chinese into the harbor. But strange to say, the pacific Chinese turned the tables on the smugglers, and threw every one of them into the water instead. They were picked up eventually in small boats, and the vessel manned by the untutored Chinese sailors was finally boarded and taken in command.

YOUNG LITHUANIAN WOMAN PUNISHED FOR HER CHARITY
(Edward Corsi, In the Shadow of Liberty, pages 264-265)

A nineteen-year-old Lithuanian girl, Miss Hamel Weshner, was ordered deported in 1906 because her medical examination showed that she had trachoma. She was a first-class passenger who was coming to live with three naturalized brothers, one a priest, in Pittsburgh. The brothers had had her educated abroad; when her school-days were over one had gone across to bring her to this country.

Before sailing the brother obtained a certificate from a physician stating that she had no disease. It was believed she had contracted the illness through attending to several of her countrywomen who were sick in the steerage. Federal authorities could find no way to help her, as she had the disease in a malignant form. Her brothers in Pittsburgh were broken-hearted when told that she would have to return.

SERB WAR ORPHANS WIN HEARTS OF CONSUL AND OTHER AMERICANS
(Edward Corsi, In the Shadow of Liberty, page 156)

I doubt if any more appealing group ever arrived at Ellis Island than five little Serbian orphan girls whose ages ranged from two and a half years to twelve.

They arrived under the charge of a Serbian nurse. They were all unusually beautiful and dressed in their picturesque native costumes. They attracted the attention and sympathy of everyone. The American Vice-Consul at Athens was said to have given instructions that one of the five little orphans be sent to his wife in Alabama. The Department of Labor investigated. Assuming that one of the little girls thus found a home, what of the other four?

That was in June of 1916. The Great War had had its part, one assumed, in sending these five children to us. Those who saw them say that they were quiet, gentle, and trusting, obviously accustomed to love and tender care. They constituted another example of the complex responsibilities imposed on our immigration authorities and the Department of Labor, another example of problems far outside th ordinary routine.

As in so many other cases, when the press announced the plight of the Serbian children, scores of volunteers rushed to adopt them, and the immigration laws were finally complied with in the case of all five.

Note: Serbia and Montenegro were under German, Austro-Hungarian, and Bulgarian occupation in 1916. One-fourth of all Serbs and Montenegrins would die during that horrible war.

LITTLE JEWISH MOTHER DEPORTED
(Edward Corsi, In the Shadow of Liberty, page 104)

Perhaps fully as tragic as death have been some of the separations caused by deportation. Old-timers at the Island recall the case of Clara Schmitzky and her two children. Mrs. Schmitzky and her children arrived August 13, 1904. The 13th proved to be her unlucky day.

Frail and weak, practically a dwarf, Mrs. Schmitzky was unable to pass the medical examination.

While she was in detention, her husband Maurice haunted the Island, prowling distractedly about the buildings. The case was appealed to Washington and every effort was made by the Hebrew Immigration Aid Society to prevent a separation of the family. For Maurice Schmitzky had been here nearly two years and had established a home for his wife on Rivington Street in New York.

When Mrs. Schmitzky was ordered excluded and the order had been affirmed she sat in the "excluded room" nervous but with a brave attempt at dignity. "I look very poorly now," she told one of the newspaper reporters, "because I have had such a long journey, and such a long stay here. But I am really in perfect health." She pushed her two toddlers forward. "You see," she said, "I am perfectly able to bear children."

POLISH RAPE VICTIM'S DAUGHTER BORN ON ELLIS ISLAND
(Ludmilla Foxlee, How They Came: The Drama of Ellis Island, page 141)

Pradseda M, 28, Polish, arrived on S.S. *Berengaria* August 3, 1928, with her child Stefania, four, to go to her husband in North Dakota. Mrs. M was in the last stage of pregnancy, and on August 10th a child was born, whom she named Julia. This child was illegitimate and was begotten one night by her brother-in-law who had come to the village to help with the harvest.

The Board of Special Inquiry would not believe her, but she said she was helpless in the hands of this man and that she could not avoid her trouble. When she was discharged from the hospital August 24th, she took her baby as a matter of course and took good care of it.

The first child, little Stefania, did not appear bright, but she loved the doll I gave her as well as a curious paper cap. Her mother enjoyed seeing her dressed in pretty

American clothes and she took good care of her and the baby.

We were astonished when Washington admitted newborn Julia as an American citizen. In all the earlier years children born on Ellis Island had not been acknowledged to be American-born.

Mrs. M appeared to be willing to learn new ways of doing things and she was amiable. We found her some thin summer clothes to replace to two heavy linen petticoats and the heavy linen shirt and the tight-fitting woolen dress, all of which were uncomfortable in the August heat. Her husband seemed much concerned over what she had suffered and was glad to take her in, even with the new baby.

Comments: *The husband was a good man. All too many rape victims have seen their husbands leave them.*

Immigration officials had rightly denied automatic American citizenship to babies born in America of un-naturalized foreign parents. If Ludmilla was correct, then officials in the Labor Department twisted the law to admit Julia. A better solution would have been assigning babies born in America the status of the mother or the father, instead of just the father, especially if the mother had custody. Assuming Pradseda was telling the truth, the immigration officials could have still admitted Julia because she was the child of an admitted legal alien. The problem with twisting any law out of context, even for a charitable purpose, is that doing so allows dishonest lawyers to argue such an action makes a precedent. A bad decision should not make precedent.

UKRAINIAN ESCAPES AFTER BEING DUPED BY COMMUNIST CON ARTISTS
(Ludmilla Foxlee, How They Came: The Drama of Ellis Island, page 188)

Joseph K., 36, Russian (Ukrainian), was misguided by Amtorg (a Soviet trading company), which offered him work in Stalingrad when employment in the Detroit Ford factory came to an end. He said that he fared well in the beginning, but when he refused to become a member of the Communist Party and expressed a wish to return to the United States, he ran into difficulties. He had departed without a re-entry permit and thus he found himself trapped in Russia.

"At this time," he said, "the people were dying like flies of want. I tried to go to Ukraine to visit my sister, but half-way to my destination I decided to return to Moscow, because the sights that I encountered filled me with horror. There were so many dead persons that decent burials couldn't be thought of. The dead bodies were piled up in carts and taken to burial places where huge holes were made in the ground; into these the bodies were deposited. Many persons died because they ate the meat of loathsome carcasses of diseased animals; they could find no other food."

When desperation seized Joseph he made his way to Riga (in then-independent Latvia), where the American Consul gave him a non-quota visa. He was detained on Ellis Island because he lacked money for transportation, but a friend living in New York lent it to him and he was permitted to proceed to his destination.

"Because I saw all these horrors with my own eyes, I shall never take any newspaper propaganda seriously," he said before leaving. "The agricultural collectivism is the sharp rock on which the whole communistic set-up will break apart, for it is evident that the people cannot be driven to satisfactory production of food or scientific animal husbandry. Young persons will not stay on the farms, and the old ones, accustomed to individual ownership of farms, cannot understand why they should work hard when what they produce is taken by the State."

Note: *About 10,000 people went from America to the Soviet Union during the Depression to work. Most would die of overwork, starvation, or execution; Stalin couldn't risk letting them leave and tell the truth about his regime. FDR's ambassador Joseph Davies ignored the plight of these people. Big leftists like Planned Parenthood's Margaret Sanger and traitor tycoon Armand Hammer covered for Stalin. Henry Ford built a huge auto plant in Russia and did millions of dollars of business with Stalin. Tim Tzouliadis' book* The Forsaken *covers this evil saga.*

OLD OR FORGOTTEN
(Frank Martocci, as interviewed by Edward Corsi, In the Shadow of Liberty, page 80)

In the case of aged people it was particularly pitiful. You see, in nine cases out of ten, an old person was detained until called for by some relative or friend. At the Island, these poor unfortunates would wander about, bewilderment and incomprehension in their eyes, not even knowing where they were, or why they were being kept. It was touching to see how, whenever they saw anyone who spoke their language, they would ask hopefully: 'Have you seen my son? Have you seen my daughter? Do you know him, my Giuseppe? When is he coming for me?'"

There were times, of course, when all our efforts to locate the immediate relative failed. Sometimes a married woman had come to join her husband, or a young woman to marry her fiancé, and the man could not be located. Perhaps he had died, or moved, or the correspondence hadn't reached him – who knows? In any event, the results were tragic indeed, as I well know from personal experience. There was no way of soothing these heartbroken women, who had traveled thousands and thousands of miles, endured suffering and humiliation, and who had uprooted their lives only to find their hopes shattered at the end of the long voyage. These, I think, are the saddest of all immigration cases.

PROBLEMS AND CHALLENGES OF ELLIS ISLAND AGENTS

PEEPING TOM AGENT BEATEN UP BY CO-WORKERS
(New York Times, 11/8/1896)

The Portuguese Consul General has begun to interest himself in the young Portuguese girl whose case led to an investigation some weeks ago by the Ellis Island authorities.

Report had it that she had been the victim of an outrage, but an investigation showed that the accused man had been guilty only of peering into the section of the detention pen set apart for women. He was a night watchman, and he received a drubbing at the hands of other employes who were attracted to the scene by the cries of the young woman.

Note: "Outrage" was a euphemism for "rape."

Recriminations among the employes of the Island led to further investigation, and recently several of the employes were discharged. Some of them have since been trying to stir up a scandal regarding the conduct of affairs at the island, and it is supposed that their stories may have induced the Consul General to revive the matter.

The girl in the case was deported some time ago, as ineligible to land. The Consul General called on Immigration Commissioner Senner on Friday. After the evidence brought out in the case was shown to him, he expressed himself as satisfied that his young countrywoman had not been the victim of outrage, and went away. Some surprise was felt at the Island when the following advertisement appeared yesterday morning:

CONSULATE GENERAL OF PORTUGAL AT NEW-YORK.

Reference having been made by some daily papers of this city to a case in Ellis Island of a comely Portuguese girl having been assaulted by minor employes of the Board of Immigration there, without her name or actual whereabouts being set forth, the undersigned, with a view to cause through the American authorities the punishment of the accused, would like to hear (at his chancellery, Produce Exchange, Annex B, 18) from any person, American or foreigner, who might know something of the alleged fact and its circumstances.

LOUIS AUGUSTO DE MOURA PINTO DE AZEVEDO TALVEIRA, Consul General of Portugal.

The Consul General would say nothing when seen. He is seeking news, not giving it. He became greatly excited when questioned. He persisted in misunderstanding the mission of a reporter who called. He speaks English indifferently, and when the reporter's query for information was put to him through an interpreter, he arose and with some vehemence dramatically exclaimed, "What I know is locked in the bosom of my heart!"

INSANE GREEK KILLS AGENT
(New York Times, 12/18/1913)

When a party of thirty Greeks on their way to Europe from Chicago arrived last night at Communipaw, they were met at the train by several Ellis Island employees, including Robert Walsh, 60 years old, who lived at 310 East Fifty-fifth Street, Manhattan. The Ellis Island employees had been sent to get an insane man among the Greeks who was to be deported by the Government. This man was seized and was handcuffed to Walsh.

It was arranged for a revenue cutter to take the insane Greek to Ellis Island from the Battery. Walsh and his prisoner were standing on the pier near the place where the revenue cutter was tied when the Greek suddenly pushed Walsh.

Both men fell to the deck of the boat, fifteen feet below. Several Government employees ran to the place where they were lying and found the Greek unhurt. Walsh was lying very still. A Government surgeon said that he was dead of a broken neck.

NIMBLE-FINGERED ITALIAN EXPOSES MONEY CHEATER
(Frank Martocci, as interviewed by Edward Corsi, In the Shadow of Liberty, pages 90-91)

Another source of trouble in those hectic days was the money exchange. Perhaps there was no other financial institution or procedure like it anywhere in the world, and it would have provided a real thrill for those who make antique and foreign money collections.

Before going out of Ellis Island to the mainland, the foreigner changed his money into American dollars and cents. There were so many aliens in those days that even for this we had to line them up after inspection had been made. A hundred lire, for example, came to $19.30, and the alien was given a receipt to show that he had received the right amount in American money for his one hundred lire.

The money-changers usually paid in gold. From time to time a number of immigrants complained of being cheated in the exchange. I don't mean to say that the person in charge was dishonest, but perhaps an occasional helper was found to be untrustworthy. We could not place the guilt on any money-changer, and we found the aliens' receipts correct; but the fact remained that sometime the alien did not have his $19.30.

One day an alien can to me, complaining that he was short five dollars. Incidentally it wasn't often that an alien knew enough about the money to know when he was cheated. Another inspector and I returned with the alien to the money-changer and asked him for an explanation. The alien, mind you, had just had his money exchanged by this man, who insisted he had given him the right amount. The alien insisted just as loudly-more so, in fact – that he had been short-changed five dollars. Although I suspected the money-changer, I had no proof and was about to try to close the matter, when the alien, who happened to be an Italian, after fumbling through all his pockets again, reached over and pulled the missing five dollar bill out of the money-changer's pocket. It was done so cleverly that to me it seemed a sleight-of-hand trick.

WILLIAMS BUSTS STAFF THIEF

Commissioner William Williams made the following release on July 16, 1903:

NOTICE.

Yesterday the Commissioner received an affidavit from Vaclav Vacek, an immigrant now at Omaha, stating that he had received from a telegraph boy at Ellis Island, in partial exchange for a twenty-dollar gold piece, two pieces of metal which he supposed to be respectively $10 and $5, gold. An immediate investigation was instituted from which it appeared that the boy in question was John Kuklis, Jr. He was summoned this morning to the Commissioner's office where he at first denied the charge, but was eventually compelled to admit its correctness. Someone on his behalf restored the $15, and young Kuklis was sent in charge of Supervising Inspector Weldon before U.S. Commissioner Shields, who remanded him to the Ludlow Street Jail, where he will remain until trial, unless bail in the amount of $1,000 is furnished.

Swindling immigrants is contemptible business, and whoever does this, under whatever form, should be despised. It is the duty of all Government officials to go out of their way to protect immigrants against every kind of imposition. Let everyone at Ellis Island clearly understand that all impositions, whenever detected, will be punished as severely as the law permits.

WM. WILLIAMS,
Commissioner.

I WAS ACCUSED OF STEALING MONEY
(Maud Mosher)

One day at the Island I was examining cards of steerage passengers detained for various reasons and came across two Italian (women) whom I thought might be discharged.

They each had a prepaid ticket to Philadelphia and one of them had over $4.00 in money. They were cousins going to the same address.

I examined their papers, tickets, cards, address, etc. and handed them back and then turning to the older woman, said, "Quanto Denaro?" (How much money have you?) She pulled out something white from her bosom as I thought and taking her money from it handed it to me to count. After doing so I turned to the other woman and asked her the same question. She replied that she had none.

I then went to an Inspector (Mr. Leonard) and stated the facts in the case to him. He came back with me to discharge the woman and taking their cards began asking the usual questions. When he asked, "How much money have you?" they both began to talk excitedly in Italian. He did not understand and upon seeing that they talked and gesticulated more than ever.

All at once it dawned on me that they were saying I had taken their money so turning to Mr. Leonard I said, "They say I have their money -- but I haven't -- I looked at it but I handed it back."

I then turned to the women and told them to look for it and motioned to the woman I thought had it to look in her bosom, placing my hand on her. She jerked away and they both began to cry and gesticulate more than ever and talk, talk, talk.

The Inspector said, "I will go out of the room and -- I guess -- they will find it all right."

In a little while (they) came back and then began to cry again and beg me to give the money back. I then began to think it might prove to be a serious matter so (I) went to the Chief of the Division and said: "Mr. Hise, two Italian women here claim I have taken money belonging to them and won't give it back."

He looked at me and smiled in his grave fashion and said: "I guess we'll have to have (them) searched."

"That is just what I was going to request." I replied.

Calling an Italian interpreter, we all three went into the "New York Room" and to the women together.

The women went through the story again both talking, crying and gesticulating at the same time. (They told the interpreter the same story), that the "Donna" (myself) had taken all their papers and money and had returned the papers and kept the money and would not give it back.

The chief, turning to me, said: "How much money had they?"

"Only one had money and I think it was this one," I answered, pointing to the older woman. She had four silver dollars, one fifty cent piece, a quarter and some small change."

"Where did she have it?"

"I think she had it in a white handkerchief in her dress," I again replied.

By this time I was beginning to feel somewhat worried. I knew I hadn't stolen their money but at the same time they kept saying so emphatically that I had done so that I found myself hunting unconsciously in my apron pocket for it.

The chief now turned to the Interpreter and said: "Ask the women if they are willing to the searched."

"Oh, yes, yes, yes" -- with more gestures and tears.

"Ask them," he again said, "if they are willing to go into a room and have a woman take all their clothes and hunt for the money."

At that the younger woman without a word put her hand in her bosom and pulled out a white bag containing the money.

I would never dream that other one had it and so gave it to (the older woman), that they made up the story together thinking I would give them some money to keep still as hush money "blackmail."

After that .... they begged forgiveness for their (racket) and begged me to shake hands. ... They (told) the Italian Agent their case, (to ask) to me to forgive them. But I would not do so.

They were discharged and sent on their way, probably to work the same game more successfully on (someone) else.

I told Mrs. Denny about my experience with the Italian women who accused me of stealing their money.

Mrs. Denny had been at the Island many years, first as chairwoman and afterwards as matron. She was a shrewd, kindly old Irish woman, very capable and full of fun.

She spoke with a broad Irish brogue and according to her usual manner many ejaculations.

"Yes," she said, "and didn't I have almost the same experience meself! One day, we hadn't had our checks for a long time and everyone was hard up, and bliss the Lord I didn't know what to do for I had to pay my rent that day, and not a cent did I have to bliss myself with. And I was talkin' to one of the officers about it and he loaned me tin dollars."

"Well, I was feeling pretty gay and I went along wavin' the bill in my hand and callin' to the boys -- "Do you wish you had your check too?" whin, Bless the Virgin! didn't it slip out of my hand and fall on the floor just inside the door where a lot of Italians were waitin.' "

Note: *In that era, "gay" meant "happy," not "homosexual."*

"I reached down to get it and an Italian woman was reaching for it to but I got it first and if she didn't begin to raise a howl and say, I had taken her tin dollar bill. Bless the Lord but she did!"

"I knew it was me own money I dropped and picked up again but, praise the Lord! I thought I would be mobbed by them Italians because I wouldn't give it up."

"The woman kept on crying and callin' on all the saints to make me give the tin dollar bill back to her, until I began to think to meself "and maybe it is her money I've got" and yet I knew it was me own that I had picked up.

"Bliss the Lord! I had an awful time before she quieted down. But she finally did, praise the Lord for that."

WILLIAMS CANS INTERPRETER FOR TRYING TO STEER FEMALES

Commissioner William Williams gave this notice to an interpreter of his named Emile Schamcham on January 15, 1903:

Sir:

I have recommended your dismissal from the service for the reasons which appeared in two interviews which took place this morning. Amongst other facts it was there made to appear that you gave yesterday to an immigrant woman, while she was awaiting release to a friend who had called for her, in the Discharging Bureau, a paper marked M.L. Shawy, 89 Washington Street, New York City. When asked to explain why you did this you stated that it was "for fun", and on the ground that she had asked you for your address. You further stated to me that the address was fictitious. The woman in question and her friend both denied that any such request was made of you, and allege that you handed them this paper of your own motion. Furthermore I caused an investigation yesterday to be made as to whether or not anyone named Shawy resided at 89 Washington Street, and found the affirmative to be the fact. You later admitted that you were in the habit of going there occasionally for your meals. You now insist that this man's name is George, and not M.L. Shawy. This is a mere quibble. Since there is a man named Shawy at the 89 Washington Street the address is not fictitious, and it did not occur to you to make this quibble until after I had shown you that I know of the existence of one Shawy at this place. I do not find it necessary to investigate whether or not this man's initials are M.L. or G. He is a Syrian, and you are a Syrian interpreter at this station. I am further satisfied that the reasons alleged by you for giving this paper to such immigrant woman are false. You are hereby suspended from duty.

Respectfully,

*WM. WILLIAMS,
Commissioner.*

MIDGETS vs. MIGHTY MOUSE
(Henry Curran, Pillar to Post, pages 295-296)

The mice ... did not earn their way. They increased and they laughed at me. It was a losing fight. I was about to call back the cats (Curran had to get rid of cats which overbred after eating the rats and food scraps at Ellis Island) when a troupe of Austrian midgets came incredibly to my rescue. The midgets had come over the ocean to join an itinerant American circus and they had to be detained at the island until bonds could be put up against their becoming public charges. If the circus should go broke – and circuses do – the midgets would be left stranded and helpless. Midgets cannot get regular jobs. They would be "on the country" – hence the bonds.

It was not until the second day of the midgets' visit to my Ellis Island hotel that I saw what was going on. At each mouse hole that evening I found a midget waiting, crouched and tense. Shortly a mouse ventured from one of the holes. As he emerged, the midget's arm made a horizontal motion like a sickle, silently and so swiftly it could not be seen. The midget's hand grasped the mouse. In a moment the mouse was no more. The midget stayed as he was, waiting for the next mouse. Mice are fast, but midgets are faster. I did not hurry about the bonds. When the midgets finally departed they had cleaned out the mice. They did it for me every year, at circus time.

RAILROAD MEN ROUTE IMMIGRANTS
(Edward Corsi, In the Shadow of Liberty, pages 123-125)

(In the early days of Ellis Island) all the leading railroads sold tickets at Ellis Island, but later this privilege was narrowed down to an Immigrant Clearing House of the Trunk Line Association.

The Trunk Line Association included the New York Central, West Shore, New York, Ontario and Western, Pennsylvania, Lehigh Valley, Erie, Delaware, Lackawanna and Western, B. and O. and the Central of New Jersey. Both the money-changing concession and the Trunk Line Association still operate in the big railroad room at Ellis Island.

In the flood-tide years the railroads got about fifty per cent of their business in cash and the other half in orders from the steamship companies. It was not uncommon for the ticket sellers to take in forty thousand dollars gross per day, which meant that, including the orders from the steamship companies, their day's business had amounted to eighty thousand dollars from tiny Ellis Island. The present joint agent, Benjamin Sprung, who came to the Island as an office boy, has held that job 27 years.

Strangely enough, many of the aliens destined to points beyond New York, never saw the city. They were ferried to Jersey piers and there embarked for their destinations.

What a scene the old railroad room must have presented with aliens waiting all day for their tickets and hours of departure! What jabbering! Twelve men sold tickets at the windows, while linguists worked the floors separating the aliens into groups. The Germans were usually en route to Wisconsin, Illinois, North and South Dakota, there to work on the great northwestern farms.

The Hollanders and Germans always had the biggest families. Superintendent Baker recalls one Dutch family who paid nine full fares, eight half fares, and had three or four children too young to require any fares.

"The steamship companies," he recalled to me, "often advanced ten or fifteen dollars to aliens without money. And I have an idea they got most of it back."

On occasion it happened that women waiting for tickets would have babies born in the waiting room. Hurry calls would go forth to the hospital, and attendants with litters would come and carry them off. Others died in the waiting room ... It cost nine dollars to bury a dead alien.

Only the Jews, of all the races in the world, have a perfect record for burying and administering the last rites to their own dead from Ellis Island.

The railroad ticket business frequently caused repercussions in Superintendent Baker's office. Primarily, it was a concession, and as such was beyond his control except for his responsibility for supervising it along with other concessions in order to prevent or eliminate graft. The office now sells two hundred and fifty tickets a month, but there used to be that number in ten minutes. Each ticket seller had to have a number of languages at his command in order to ask the alien where he or she was going. Agent Sprung, then a ticket seller, could ask an alien where he was going in any language in the world except Chinese or Japanese, two which he could never master.

But the repercussions which fell upon Superintendent Baker were often the result of mistakes made by Sprung's men. Once fifteen Italians bound for Amsterdam Avenue in New York City wound up in Amsterdam, New York. The chief of police of that city wired: "Get wise at Ellis Island. Fifteen Italians sent here want to go to Amsterdam Avenue, New York."

Sometimes the states were confused, as in the case of a party of Austrian laborers who got to Johnstown, Pennsylvania, when in reality they wanted to go to Johnstown, New York.

Once the leader of a group of Italians walked up to the window to buy a block ticket for himself and companions.

"Where are you going?" the ticket seller demanded in Italian.

"P-p-p-p-p-p-p-p-" stuttered the Italian in consternation and distress. Then he tried it again.

"P-p-p-p-p-poo-poo poo-poo-"

But that was as far as he could get. Finally he reached into an inner pocket of his coat and produced a typed slip. The name of the town was Punxsutawney, Pennsylvania.

Note: *This is where many people, some with beverages that don't freeze easily, wait for the groundhog to emerge and look for his shadow each February 2.*

One immigrant in endeavoring to ask for a ticket to Detroit, Michigan, said something which was a variation of Detroit-a-Mich. Charley McCullock, the agent at the window, thought the alien had called him a dirty mick, and resented it.

In those days it cost thirteen dollars for a day coach ticket to Chicago. One morning about ten o'clock an elderly Jew with a flowing black beard and a skull cap arrived in the railroad waiting room with his family. The wife, who appeared to be about his own age, had her hair bound in a handkerchief in typically foreign fashion. There were ten children, and each carried a basket.

Approaching the old man, the interpreter questioned him: "Yiddish? Russian? Deutsch? Italiano? English?" The was no answer. Merely an imperturbable countenance and a shake of the head. At four o'clock in the afternoon the family still occupied the same bench. Finally someone thought of asking the old man if he spoke Gaelic. With a big smile he replied that he did, and the interpreter learned that he wanted to go to Chicago.

CHINESE DRUGRUNNER RATTED OUT
(Edward Corsi, In the Shadow Of Liberty, pages 167-169)

In my own time at Ellis Island we had duplications not only of the old practices but many novel efforts of the Chinese to circumvent Uncle Sam's rigid restrictions. The case of Chen Chee is one that I can never forget.

Inspectors of the service in the New York area had for a long while been watching certain sections of Brooklyn, in the belief that Chinese aliens were more likely to frequent the resorts of their fellow countrymen there than the more public resorts of Mott and Pell Streets, which are the main arteries of New York's Chinatown.

One March afternoon in 1933 a Brooklyn apartment house, where, it had been previously determined, large numbers of Chinese were used to gathering and playing cards, was raided. True to expectations, the detectives found the card game going on in a small apartment on one of the upper floors of the building. Arrests were made at once, but in the confusion, one of the Chinese escaped. Two hours later, standing in the snow, attired only in his pajamas and with bare feet, he was discovered on the roof.

"Me slitizen!" he asserted vigorously to the man who had found him. "Me born San Flisco!"

"Then what are you doing up here in your pajamas when it is freezing?" the inspector asked, undoubtedly amused by the Chinaman's answer.

"I come takee sun bath," said the Chinaman.

"What?" demanded the inspector. "A sun bath when the roof is covered with snow?"

"It is my custom," retorted the alien blandly and with utter composure.

The inquiry which followed failed to shake the Chinaman's story. He offered to provide the usual witnesses in corroboration and immediately announced his desire to appeal to the courts. It was learned a few days later that he had engaged counsel. Meanwhile the following letter came to Ellis Island:

Flatbush Avenue, Brooklyn
March 8, 1933.

To Mr. Carsi,
Immigration Commisher,
Ellist Island
Dear sirs:

I writing this line to let you know the truth of the poin, you remenger your men arrested the china man Henry Mar Sow on 5th inst. last Saturday in apt no Flatbush Ave. Brooklyn you success for this right man, I know very weel bacause I live near him the same day morning about 7 a.m. I standing out door Saw your men go in he house he home be too much room he hearing your men ask for Henry Mar Sow he run out roof after your men arrested him at roof, your men carry him out I saw it right man, no matter what name he say I know this right man your success Sirs.

Henry Mar Sow himself came from Trinidad, B.W.I. by smuggle since Aug. 1930. He doing contractor for bringing Chinese from Trinidid B.W.I. try to send he back to China to fight with Jap.

All above to be very truth by god believe me Sirs.

Yours truthly,

Joam.

Notes: *The letter is printed here as it was shown by Corsi, with misspellings and grammar problems intact. Bear in mind the average public high school kid today doesn't do much better in composition. Also, B.W.I. meant "British West Indies." The British held Jamaica, Trinidad, and a number of other islands in the Caribbean Sea when Corsi was commissioner.*

At a subsequent hearing Chen Chee testified under oath that he was a laborer of the Chinese race, but that he was not in possession of documentary evidence showing him to be lawfully in the United States. He claimed birth in San Francisco, but did not know exactly where in San Francisco he was born. He said that he did not know his mother's name, as he was told that she had died when he was very young. He could not remember who told him this. He testified that he did not remember the full name of the man who brought him East at the age of about five years, and that he did not know whether any one living could swear that he was born in the United States. He also testified that he had never heard of Trinidad, that he had been living on the bounty of friends, and also depended upon them for a place to sleep. He said that he had no money, and that he had once worked as a relief waiter, in various restaurants.

But when questioned by his attorney on July 21, in the court of the United States Commissioner Epstein, the defendant seemed to have in some way acquired information as to his birthplace, the name of the street, number of the house, etc. He had also learned the name of his mother, and had changed his mind as to occupation and places of work. He produced witnesses, none of whom were members of his Clan, the Mar, and these corroborated his story.

In rebuttal the government submitted the following from the Consul at Trinidad, B.W.I.:

Chen Chee is the correct name of a Chinese who, under the name of Edward Marso or Edward Chong Marsow, which he used in Trinidad, was convicted in Trinidad on February 4, 1930, of being in possession of raw opium, and fined 150 pounds Sterling, which he paid, and that record of the said conviction, (a record of which was submitted with the aforementioned evidence), is in Criminal Register No. 94, page 203, Trinidad, B.W.I. This evidence also shows that when the said Chen Chee, under the name of Marsow, applied for a Section 6 Merchant's Certificate, which was denied by the U.S. Consul at Trinidad, on April 8, 1929, he, the defendant, testified that he was born in Hong Kong, China, on September 10, 1900.

But for the tip-off letter which enabled the government to get the finger-prints, photographs and evidence against Chen Chee, his case would have been air-tight. Needless to say, his counsel and witnesses were rather confused when confronted with the proof.

These tip-off letters, frequently attributed to clan or tong enmity, have proved invaluable in the apprehension of Orientals illegally in the United States.

MONEYCHANGER COUNTS PROBLEMS
(Edward Corsi, In the Shadow of Liberty, pages 125 - 126)

George O'Donnoghue, formerly of the Cashier's Office at the Island, which handled financial matters and maintained a depository for alien funds, always had difficulty with orthodox Jews who would not sign for the receipt of their money on holy days. They would wait until after sundown before accepting their money from our office.

"Some aliens were reluctant to admit that they had money for fear of being robbed," he said. "It turned out that one Greek, who claimed he had no money, was carrying over five thousand dollars on his person."

"Some would squander the money which relatives had sent to them in our care, while going to their destinations. On arrival they would contend that we had short-changed them, and soon we would receive threatening letters from attorneys," O'Donnoghue recounted. "The cash business of our office was as high as five hundred thousand dollars monthly and for a time reached eight million dollars per year."

THE KISSING GATE
(Maud Mosher, Ellis Island as the Matron Sees It, page 20)

There are so many joyful meetings at this place that the officers call it the Kissing Gate. The manner in which the people of different nationalities greet each other after a separation of years is one of the interesting studies at the Island. The Italian kisses his little children but scarcely speaks to his wife, never embraces or kisses her in public. The Hungarian and Slavish (Slavic) people put their arms around one another and weep. The Jew of all countries kisses his wife and children as though he owned all the kisses in the world, and intended to use them all up quick.

FIGHTING HER OWN BIASES
(Maud Mosher, excerpts from her letter to the Epworth League, 1/20/1905)

I really believe that no one who is not situated so as to see the immigrants coming in as we do day by day, month by month can have any idea of what it means to our country to have these great hordes of people continually pouring in to it.

Why people right here in New York City, who have lived here for years have no idea of the numbers of foreigners who are coming, coming, coming.

There have been many weeks in the 15 months I have been here that enough people have been landed here sufficient to make a city the size of Wichita – and that, just steerage passengers. Poor ignorant, degraded, filthy people a large proportion of them.

Just now and for months back thousands of Russian Jews have been coming and oh they are a dirty, degraded lot of human beings.

A week or so ago I was on a ship coming into port and the steerage deck was crowded just as thick as they could stand with men and boys – nearly all Russian Jews – and actually they didn't seem to have one ray of intelligence on their faces, crowding, pushing, any way to get off the ship to the coveted America – the "land of gold."

Of course I feel sorry for them but it does seem too awful bad that a class of people should be admitted to our shores in such great numbers as to be a menace to our government within a very short time.

Comment: *Maud Mosher had to fight her prejudices against these and other immigrants to do right by them. It is a tribute to her character that she didn't let her biases interfere with her performance of her duties.*

FRENCH MADAM TRIES TO BUY MAN TO AVOID DEPORTATION

A high-roller Euro-procuress used to selling women tried to loophole her way out deportation from America by offering to buy an American man for marriage. This caused William Williams and his staff at Ellis Island major headaches.

The 4/15/1911 New York Times covered the saga as follows:

Interest was aroused yesterday at Ellis Island by the appearance in the deportation pen of a tall, attractive looking French woman, who wore a smart tailor made blue serge costume and a large black picture hat trimmed with white velvet and covered with ostrich plumes which she said cost $150.

The woman was Annie Gold, who was arrested in Portland, Ore., after being ten years in the country, and ordered deported at the expense of the Government as an undesirable alien for keeping a disorderly resort in that city.

Note: *A "disorderly resort" was a euphemism for a "whorehouse."*

Annie Gold told the detectives who arrested her that she had $55,000 in cash and about $50,000 in jewels, and that she would pay $10,000 down in cash to any citizen of the United States who would marry her so that she would not have to return to Europe.

In view of the excitement created at Ellis Island by her offer she will be guarded by a matron as well as two deportation officers until she sails to-day, on the Hamburg-American liner Pretoria.

In all there are 219 undesirable aliens to be deported to-day on the ten steamships sailing for European ports.

Williams had to take the precautions because gigolos, grifters, gomers, and other gravy-trainers across the country besieged his office with offers to honor Annie's offer to offer her honor.

A typical letter from one of the cheapskate losers who surfaced at the smell of easy money, which Williams made available to the public, was this:

Dear Sir: Authorities

I saw an "Ad" in the Post-Express paper about a woman. She want to get married, and she offer 10,000 dollar and her name is Annie Gold. I want to know if she is sane or insane. I want to know if she got all that money. Is it any humbug. And if she got all that money, then be ready and come to Monroe County, New York. I am waiting.

ELLIS ISLAND SCRAPBOOK

Respectfully truly yours
Jacob E -------
Webster, New York

She have to pae her own fare and come to Rochester, New York.

THE HOOKERS' ONE-NIGHT STAND AT ELLIS ISLAND
(Henry Curran, Pillar to Post, pages 292-293)

Occasionally there was a hunger strike, but I had a technique for that. The shortest of the hunger strikes was put on by seven alien prostitutes, convicted over and over again in American courts and awaiting deportation. They objected to the presence of a matron to curb their hell-raising proclivities in the dining room. I took away the matron and had their meals served to them in their own separate sleeping quarters. They threw the first meal, which was luncheon, out of the window, and sent me a letter saying they were ladies and would not eat separately, would not suffer such an insult, would not eat at all. So I sent in to them in the evening a special dinner so tempting that no one on earth could long resist it. The waiter withdrew and the dinner remained. In the morning the matron told me what happened. The rebels held out till midnight, when one of them, supposing the rest were asleep, reached quietly from her bed and captured a generous corner of the dinner. Instantly the rest, who were all silently and hungrily awake, made each a lusty dive toward what was left. It vanished, even as snow in April sunshine. The war was over. The other hunger strikes responded to the same treatment.

PRESIDENTS AT ELLIS ISLAND
(Edward Corsi, In the Shadow of Liberty, page 126)

Presidents Theodore Roosevelt, William Howard Taft and Woodrow Wilson all made personal visits to the Island in their times. Roosevelt arrived on a day so stormy that he had to be taken from the *Mayflower* and brought ashore in the launch, *Samoset*, at that time provided by the government for the personal use of Commissioner William Williams. It is said that President Roosevelt came in his usual breezy fashion with a swinging stride and smile for all. He had lunch, took a hurried excursion through the buildings, and went away.

The visit of President Taft was a bit more leisurely. He came, as did Roosevelt, accompanied by the usual bodyguard of Secret Service men, visited the buildings, peeped in at the immigrants and deportees in detention, and left again.

But Woodrow Wilson actually attended a hearing. It was on a day when a case of national interest was being decided. The press had worked up great sympathy for the immigrant. Accompanied by Mrs. Wilson, the then President-elect with some friends and Secret Service men filed into the hearing room. It is remembered that Wilson listened attentively to the testimony, but showed no evidence of sympathy and made no comment as he was leaving.

Here are some details Corsi left out:

A hurricane blew up the day Theodore Roosevelt came to Ellis Island. The storm sunk dozens of boats in New York Harbor and nearly swamped his yacht. Some worried if the president would chance coming to the island in a hurricane. One official said, "Oh, he'll be here. If it was anyone else, this function would be postponed on account of weather."

The "bull moose" didn't disappoint. Soggy but cheerful, Teddy landed with his posse and inspected the island. He talked through an interpreter with a German woman coming with her boy to join her husband, who worked as a baker in New York City, and he praised her.

President Roosevelt objected to the unsanitary way the doctors were conducting eye exams. Before examining each immigrant, the doctor was supposed to wash his hands and wipe with a disinfectant-soaked towel the buttonhook he used to turn up eyelids so he could inspect each eyelid's now-exposed inner side for trachoma. Roosevelt noted the doctors hurried and didn't always sanitize their tools or wash their hands between immigrants.

Theodore Roosevelt praised William Williams, but used the visit to announce the appointment of a committee to check on the operation of Ellis Island. A reporter who covered Roosevelt's visit mentioned he did this at Williams' request to clear him of the many false charges lodged against him. (Sources: "Trachoma Through History," by Katherine Schlosser, and an article in William Williams' papers.)

Commissioner Williams offered Taft his "judgment seat" to hear the appeal of a Welshman named Thornton marked for deportation because of his physical defects. Taft ordered him admitted because he answered a few simple questions, including who the President of the United States was. To Taft's embarrassment, it came out that the Welshman had fled debts in his homeland, was unable to find work, and his relatives in America were unable to support him and his family. At Thornton's request, immigration agents deported him. (Source: Encyclopedia of Ellis Island, by Barry Moreno, page 232).

Note: *President, Ronald Reagan pushed for the restoration of Ellis Island after Eisenhower, Kennedy, Johnson, Nixon, Ford, and Carter let the historic immigration station rot and decay and suffer theft and vandalism. Reagan would visit Ellis Island to inspect the restoration, the first president since Woodrow Wilson to step foot on Ellis Island.*

FOOD AT ELLIS ISLAND

PASS THE PRUNES
(Frank Martocci, as interviewed by Edward Corsi, In the Shadow of Liberty, pages 78-79)

The feeding of immigrants! It was a sight, back in those days, and I hate to think of it. One employee brought out a big pail filled with prunes, and another some huge loaves of sliced rye bread. A helper would take a dipper full of prunes and slop it down on a big slice of bread, saying, "Here! Now go and eat!"

Now this would make a novel sandwich for once, but when you have it all the time, morning and evening, evening and morning, it becomes revolting. Even though they were peasants and many of them poverty-stricken, they had never been reduced to such monotony in their food in their own homes.

It was a case of profiteering. The man in charge of the food was making money out of those poor devils by giving them the cheapest food he possibly could, for, you see, he was allowed so much per capita. That was the sort of thing they had to eat from about 1898 on, but Mr. Williams, the Immigration Commissioner, changed all that and saw to it that better food was provided, though it still was not so good as it is today.

WILLIAMS THREATENS TO THROW FOOD DEALER OFF THE GRAVY TRAIN

Commissioner William Williams sent the following letter on May 28, 1909 to Fritz Brodt, whose firm held the feeding contract at Ellis Island, over the latter's price gouging on box lunches for train-bound immigrants:

Sir:

Pending the adoption of more definite regulations, you will forthwith cease selling to an immigrant travelling alone any package of food for which he is charged more than fifty cents, excepting that an immigrant travelling to a point as distant as Chicago may purchase a dollar bag of food, provided he ask leave to do this of his own motion. You will report to me daily how many bags of each class you have sold.

The slightest coercion on the part of any of your employees in compelling an immigrant to buy even a fifty cent bag of food will be punished with dismissal from the island.

For your information I will state that I was dissatisfied at the manner in which food was being sold at the only one of your stands which I have thus far had time to inspect, and a radical change must occur in these matters.

Respectfully,

*Wm. Williams,
Commissioner.*

DINNERS FOR THE DETAINED
(Edward Corsi, In the Shadow of Liberty, page 121)

At times there have been 25 or 30 races in detention at one time. The Italian cares nothing for the dried fish preferred by the Scandinavian, and the Scandinavian has no use for spaghetti. The Greek wants his food sweetened, and no one can make tea for an Englishman. The basis of all Asiatic and Malay food is rice, which they will mix with almost anything. The Chinese take to other foods but want rice in place of bread. The Mohammedans will eat no food across which the shadow of an infidel has fallen. And in big years it has been Superintendent Baker's problem to serve thousand(s of) meals per day, trying to please all.

Bread was bought at the rate of seven tons a day, both for these meals and for the box lunches formerly sold to immigrants departing for inland points. Those who did not buy box lunches usually found themselves at the mercy of grafters.

EGGING ON THE DERVISHES
(Frank Martocci, as interviewed by Edward Corsi, In the Shadow of Liberty, pages 79-80)

Speaking of food reminds me of the thirty howling Dervishes we once had on the Island. It was the *Trinacria* of the Anchor Line, from Mediterranean ports, which one bright day brought in the Dervishes: Mohammedan priests who had come from the East to give exhibitions in the United States.

They were a colorful, bizarre sight in their red fezzes, loose, flowing trousers, soft sandals, and coats of bright blue. They were in the charge of Sheik Maluck, of Damascus, said to be a personal friend of Emin Pasha, whoever he was. An Americanized Arabian, Josef Maluck, managed them while they were in the United States.

As I remember it, one of the papers announced: "It is expected that an exhibition will be given in this city." And it certainly was – right on the Island, for it turned out that they would eat no food over which the shadow of an infidel had passed. This was absolutely forbidden by their religion. Now of course the cook, the employees, waiters, helpers, and in fact everybody connected with the Island were infidels to them. So the serious question arose: What were we going to feed those howling Dervish dancers?

Fortunately, before they starved themselves, someone had a brilliant idea. Why not give them eggs? We tried eggs, and to these they had no objection.

These same Dervishes, incidentally, had given another unexpected exhibition on the ship coming over. A queer sort of light showed in the sky one day over the *Trinacria*, and suddenly, without any warning and to the amazement of the other passengers, the whole troop of thirty Dervishes began spinning around on one toe and howling in a way that brought everybody up on deck. I suppose they could howl for food or anything else, when they felt like it.

HAVE IT OUR WAY

Henry Curran, the Commissioner of Immigration at Ellis Island from 1923 through 1926, said he tried to have the immigrants served some ethnic foods, but immigrants whose native dishes were not on the menu would complain. He said with a twinkle in his eye, "If I added spaghetti, the detained Italians sent me an engrossed testimonial and everyone else objected. If I put pierogi and Mazovian noodles on the table, the Poles were happy and the rest were disconsolate. Irish stew was no good for the English, and English marmalade was gunpowder to the Irish. The Scotch mistrusted both. The Welsh took what they could get. There was no pleasing anybody. I tried everything, then went back to United States fodder for all. They might as well get used now to the baked beans, assorted pies, and anonymous hash that would overwhelm them later on."

If the immigrants weren't getting food their way, a 1908 food contract request for bid and four immigrant dining room menus from 1917 indicate they sure weren't getting starvation fare.

The 1908 food service bid requests from the U.S. Immigration Service (made when Robert Watchorn was the chief at Ellis Island) specified the winning food service vendor would have to provide immigrants hot cereal and milk, hash or pork and beans, and bread and butter for breakfast. For "dinner" (the midday meal), the vendor would have to provide immigrants meat or fish, potatoes, vegetables, bread and butter, and soup. For "supper" (the evening meal), the vendor would have to provide stew, pork and beans, or hash, a fruit dessert or pie or pudding, and bread and butter. Coffee and tea, and milk and sugar were to be available. Kosher substitutes for pork were to be made available.

This was a step up from the fare Williams was allowed to offer immigrants in 1902. On Williams' recommendation, fines against steamship companies for violations increased, and this undoubtedly led to better food for detained immigrants.

The 1917 dining room menus (made when Frederic Howe was the chief at Ellis Island) showed for breakfast, immigrants got hot cereal, milk, bread and butter, and fruit. For "dinner," immigrants got meat, vegetables, potatoes, bread and butter, and soup. For "supper," immigrants got a one-pot entree such as stew or hash or meat and beans, bread and butter, and fruit. Coffee and tea, and milk and sugar were to be available. Food service people served milk and crackers to children between meals.

After William Williams took over, no one starved at Ellis Island. In fact, most steerage immigrants ate better at Ellis Island than they did in their homelands.

HOW SWEET IT IS!
(Edward Corsi, In the Shadow of Liberty, pages 175-176)

One of my last recollections of Ellis Island is of a shipload of coolies, who had been working for the British Government in one of Great Britain's insular possessions and were detained overnight, just before Christmas in 1933, preparatory to their departure by rail for San Francisco.

While waiting for supper they became inquisitive about the bowls standing on the table. This particular group had never before tasted or seen sugar. The head man asked an attendant what it was and received an explanation. He tried some in his tea, some more on his bread. A moment later his face was rippling with smiles. He screeched the good news down the long table to his companions who all joined him in sampling the sugar. In two minutes the bowls were emptied and the coolies were asking for more. The bowls were refilled and as quickly emptied again. In three more meals at the Island, the coolies "killed" three sacks of sugar and left for San Francisco with an unexcelled appreciation of the hospitality of Uncle Sam.

DUMPING ON AMERICA
(Edward Corsi, In the Shadow of Liberty, pages 145-148)

I have often wondered why these sick and infirm people wished to make the long and hard trip to the New World. It would appear that life to them would seem the same anywhere, and that the dangers and troubles of getting in here ought to deter them from such a hazardous attempt. One of the immigration officials told me that many wanted to reach a place where a poorhouse system existed which would enable them to be cared for and to obtain free medical attendance. They paid huge sums of money to be smuggled in, and I wondered where this money came from. The only plausible explanation, I was told, is that those who have had to care for these people on the other side will pay any amount to get the responsibility of their care transferred to someone else.

Before ever going to Ellis Island I remember reading in the papers the story of a Syrian girl who committed suicide by jumping out of the window of the train that was bearing her to New York to await deportation. The story of the girl in the press of the United States attracted a great deal of sympathy for her, and placed much undeserved odium on the officers who were carrying out the law.

Upon applying at Montreal for a certificate to enter the United States, the girl was examined and found to be suffering from an incurable disease which, of course, prevented her admission to the country. A man who claimed to be her fiancé came from Iowa and told a romantic story of his love for the girl. He had worked hard, he said, to earn enough money to bring her to this country. The immigration officers at Montreal explained simply that if he married her in that city she would then have a legal right to enter the country as his wife. He demurred, protesting that he had prepared a wedding feast at Cedar Rapids and did not want to deprive his friends of the pleasure of assisting at his wedding. The officers suggested that he have a second ceremony after their arrival at home.

So the two stole away one night and were caught trying to cross the river at Detroit. The man was held for a time, and after his release went back home, giving up all attempts to help the girl. She was ordered deported. After her suicide it was found that the fond lover had a wife in Dubuque, Iowa, and was merely earning a bit of extra cash by bringing her across the border. It was also discovered that the girl had previously been deported from New York, and had been sent back by the Canadian route to the United States.

Probably the worst case on record of the way in which immigration agents (of foreign governments) send undesirable and inadmissible people to this continent to get rid of them, was brought to the attention of the authorities a few years ago. A man named Conrad von Walloghren landed in Quebec and was "steered" into the United States illegally. He tried to obtain admission to a Detroit workhouse, and was turned over to immigration officials who sent him back to Canada. He was a hopeless idiot, who had occasional lucid moments when he remembered incidents of his past life. He had been confined for years in an institution for imbeciles in Belgium. He had been released and shipped from Liverpool to Quebec, with the United States as his ultimate destination.

The smuggling in of cripples, paupers, the sick and the unfit began on a professional scale as soon as the local governments in Europe realized the value of the "dumping" process. As early as 1891 a whole colony of Russian paupers were slipped past the inspectors by some ruse and landed at Pennsboro, West Virginia, where they said they had been told they could find work. The dispatch from Parkersburg stated:

"This is the fourth lot of paupers sent direct to Pennsboro in a few weeks. Other lots of about twenty have been sent to other small places in this state and there seems to be no doubt that a systematic arrangement has been made to ship hundreds of paupers into the country by false promises and by evasion of federal laws."

About 1900 paupers began slipping across the Mexican border. In 1906 a large group of Syrian peddlers suffering from trachoma were sneaked into the country from Mexico, the smugglers receiving twelve dollars a head for their work.

The records of the Island show that in 1901 an investigation was made of all employees, to determine which were in collusion with the stewards of Atlantic liners to admit diseased and other undesirable foreigners into this country. It seems that at the period of the great flow of immigration, many inspectors, and those who boarded the ships, were tempted by bribes to betray their official standing. In 1903 a Russian immigrant, who came as a stowaway and was given a job in the immigrant hospital, confessed that he had long been working in conjunction with allies to get diseased foreigners into the United States. Often the agents at the embarkation points in European countries designated a certain city as a clearing house for the undesirable immigrants of their race, and the aliens were then brought from Canada on sailing vessels or by some other means to the assigned city. Early in the century Portuguese undesirables were found to be cleared at New Bedford, Massachusetts.

The worst wave of this smuggling process was probably over before I went as Commissioner to Ellis Island; but it can never be eradicated. So long as we have a reputation for space and wealth and poorhouses, so long will the crowded and poor and decrepit of Europe and Asia, South America and even Africa long to enjoy the fruits of our advantages. With our gates strongly barred and our borders closely patrolled, most of these cannot get through. Yet they will still make the long trip and suffer the hardships, many of them again and again, on the faint hope that a mere chance will get them through and they will be free to begin a new life here.

CANADIAN GOVERNMENT TRAFFICKED CHINESE
(Edward Corsi, In the Shadow of Liberty, pages 161-162)

Canada was permitting the entry of alien Chinese upon payment of a one-hundred-dollar head tax. Canada got the one hundred dollars, and Uncle Sam got the Chinaman.

Note: *Canadian authorities also let in people from the Indian subcontinent, then another part of the British Empire. They would encourage these people to head south to America. The crookedness of the Canadian government and of British Empire pooh-bahs was one of the reasons Congress drastically restricted immigration from China, the Indian subcontinent, and Southeast Asia with the Asiatic Barred Zone legislation.*

According to the 1930 census there are 74,954 Chinese living in the United States. But the number here illegally can never be determined, although they are gradually being apprehended and deported, and a veritable international dragnet guards the circumference of the country against their surreptitious entry.

But as far back as 1882 it became apparent to Uncle Sam's agents that the law was being flouted by every conceivable means. And the Orientals were becoming so adroit that a special Chinese Division of the Immigration Service was eventually established so that the government might better match wits with the canny John Chinaman.

In the New York Tribune of October 3, 1901, there was published the following comment upon the cleverness of Chinese disguises:

The average citizen can form little idea of the character of cunning which immigrants, especially Oriental, will resort to in order to deceive the authorities. One of the most novel disguises, which had been adopted extensively for Chinese aliens, is the garb of a priest or clergyman. A party of Chinese immigrants with their pigtails under cover, their slanting eyes disguised by some means, and gowned in robes like those of Montreal monks, is likely to be picked up by Government officers any time in the next few days. Authorities here say that prominent men in various sections of the country are interested in the work of smuggling Chinese into America and allow their agents generous amounts for purchasing disguises. These immigrants are willing to spend from $100 to $500 each to get into the United States.

In Baxter Street, New York, it is said, gowns of priests and clergymen's garments in general are available at $2 or $3 each for this purpose. In other places there are shops that make a specialty of selling Quaker garments. The Quaker disguise was worked successfully last year, until a sharp inspector caught a party of twenty.

For miles along the border east of Vancouver, the smugglers disguise the Chinamen as (American) Indians. When this scheme is followed, the Chinaman is schooled to drop his natural walk and articulate like an Indian. When disguised as priests the Celestials are taught to act the part. Smugglers have been known to drive twenty or thirty Chinamen from 75 to 150 miles away from an immigration station. This is to obviate the necessity of presenting credentials.

A few months after the foregoing exposé, it was definitely determined that soldiers of the 11th United States Infantry, stationed at Fort Niagara, were engaging in the lucrative Chinese smuggling racket on the Canadian border. On December 27, Private John Brown was arrested and turned over to civil authorities.

IMMIGRATION BEFORE THE QUOTA – AN ESSAY
(New York Times, 5/18/1924)

Waiting for the cry of "All ashore!" The sea-worn steerage passengers of the coppered and copper-fastened brig *Europa*, twenty-one days out from Liverpool, hung over the rail while the little merchant packet was being warped into her berth at the foot of Wall Street, interfering with the preparations of the sailors for knotting her, stem and stern, to the pier. In the long hours after they had seen the lighthouse on Cape Cod few of them had slept and not many of them had prepared a meal, routine having been interrupted by the glorious hope of a landing.

The steerage itself had been like a bedlam, women packing trunks and chests, men tying up uncouth bundles, children crying because they were neglected except for a push out of the way or a slap administered to give them something to cry for. Then this task was interrupted by a word, and on deck swarmed the emigrants again to cluster round the bows and watch the sail drawing (near) that brought the pilot. Once on board and the ship's guidance in his hand, by short tacks she passed through the Narrows so close to shore at times that the delighted passengers could almost snatch a leaf from an overhanging tree, while as they passed Staten Island and held their breath in fear lest a Quarantine officer should come out to detain the ship, they mechanically counted the whitewashed buildings on the hillside and the scores of vessels lying here at anchor.

Sailing up the bay but too slow for their impatience, they saw New York at last, outpost of the promised land! Houses and steeples took the place of waves and whitecaps! Governors Island, Castle Garden, the East River! Would the sailors never drop anchor?

Paying little attention to the boats that clustered round the ship or to the shouting, waving people crowding the pier, the single concern of the steerage passengers was their baggage. Unlisted, uninspected, with or without means of support so far as anybody knew or cared to know, they were free to swarm on shore. With a rush and a shout the tumultuous crowd fled from their fetid quarters and bounded on shore, becoming almost at once and by that simple act citizens of the Great Republic!

Note: *Actually the immigration laws as early as 1795 required an alien to reside in America for five years, renounce their allegiance to any foreign government, swear an oath of allegiance to America and the U.S. Constitution, and display "good moral character."*

Yes, it was as easy as that – yesterday. For these were the days of what is called the "old immigration," before the topic soon to become and to continue to be a national worry was agitated – whether the hordes of foreign poor should be permitted to land on our American shores. "These people have a right to come," cried a writer of 1837, "because the whole world is the patrimony of the whole world and, although they bring all the miseries of Europe with them, let them come if they can get here!"

To get here was the trick, that is, to be able to survive the horrors of a passage in an emigrant ship, occupying, if she were a greyhound of that day, from eighteen to twenty-one days, but frequently lengthening her voyage to thirty, forty and more. The privation they might have to endure in the new country, the misery they had left at home, both were insignificant beside the incidents of that awful voyage.

Today it is different. Immigrants brought over by the great passenger fleet fare better than the cabin passenger of the rude 1840s. They are no longer herded like cattle; they are not compelled to furnish their own food nor to prepare it; they have their own staterooms and their own deck; in a word, the drawbacks of a steerage passage nowadays are what the steerage passengers themselves supply. All they need dread is the quota.

So used have we become to discussions about the benefits and the disadvantages of the quota and the other immigration laws that preceded it on the State and Federal statute books that we have forgotten that it was only between the years 1837 and 1849 that the subject began to interest Congress and laws were passed restricting ships to a limited number of emigrants, according to a certain rate. About the same time laws were made in England to compel the provision of a fixed supply of food for every emigrant embarking from a British port. For several years thereafter these laws of either country remained ornamental, they were not enforced, nor did it seem likely that any legislation would reach and improve the hard lot of the emigrant.

Legislation tinkered with the problem through many years (legislation is tinkering with it still) and one may judge how urgent it was when it is recalled that the immigration flood had swollen before 1914 to more than a million annually. Long before the law of quota restriction was passed (in 1921) other means had been discussed and some measures tried, compelling immigrants to pass all sorts of tests or be deported. When the sailing vessel as a means of transport gave way to steamships a place of reception had to be provided while the immigrants' claim to a right to enter was being considered.

How slowly we moved, how dilatory were our methods, may be realized when we remark the date of the setting apart of Ellis Island as a reception centre for immigrants. The United States Government took it over in 1890 and opened it two years later. Before that recent time and for the same purposes, Castle Garden had been used and incidentally the Barge Office.

Around 1870 the Government first began really to tackle the problem, learning its early and elementary lessons of inspection at Castle Garden. Strange sounds and stranger sights began to be seen and heard in that quaint building around which still faintly lingers an aroma of society and Jenny Lind.

Are there ancient employees of the Immigration Bureau still living and working who recall the old days of Castle Garden, Barge Office and the early occupation of Ellis Island? Three or four of these worthies have been connected with the department for fifty years and more and they, happily, are full and running over with anecdotes of the old days. A particularly vivid memory of Bookkeeper Murphy at Ellis Island is that he began business life at Castle Garden for a wage of $1.50 per week. He wasn't a bookkeeper then, being employed to help "hustle the baggage." Also he used to see more of the immigrants in those days than he does now, for his ordinary view of the possible new citizens of the present is when, all preliminaries settled, they pass out of the building on their way to the city.

"Friendly souls I used to find many of the newcomers in them days, for mostly the grist was from Ireland and it was from little old Ireland I come myself. Plenty of young lads were among them and I could take them around the Battery and up as far north as Fourteenth Street, for there were no prisoners in Castle Garden in my time."

"Here and there one of the young fellows would be after wanting to stay in New York and these were the boys I showed the town after my work was done. But mainly then, and it is pretty near so today, the Irish came over in families. There would be the old grandfather and the man and his wife and their children: over thy come all altogether and after the "free land." Mostly, too, they went West to find it."

"That ignorant they were of what was before them but nothing daunted! The oldest of 'em wasn't frightened at my talk of Indians and all the bogys I scared up, for I liked to have my jokes. They just shut their faces and nodded. There couldn't anything be worse than what they had been through, for they knew the big famine. And ignorant as they was they didn't talk much to show it."

"I mind a little fellow who found a potato in the grass outside the garden and come runnin' to his mother, crying: 'Mother, you need not be hungry any more, they has potaties here!' "

"Was we crowded at Castle Garden? Well, mostly not. It was comfortable enough to what I have seen here. An handful as we'd say now, mostly Irish, Welsh and Cornish, coming over on the Black Ball Line and the Top Scott Line. A jolly crowd, taking things as they come and singing in the top of the morning as well as at night. Hardship beyond belief they had on some of the packets, but they made light of 'em and bore nobody a grudge. They made up songs about the ships and well do I remember how they would laugh as they sang about the yellow meal which was about all the food some ships provided and tired they got of the color of it before they struck New York. Some one would start it and they would all burst out:

> Bad luck to Captain Top Scott,
> And his dirty old yellow meal!"

"Had they money to take them to their journey's end? Yes, mainly they had when they came as families, but the boys that came over alone didn't many of 'em have a bawbee. It was the custom then to let the young men do some work around the Garden and anyway I never knew of anybody going hungry. The immigrants with money to buy food were wiling to share it with those who were strapped. And the hearty way they did it saved a man from feeling like a pauper."

"As I tell you, I was but a lad those days and just beginning life, and I"ve forgotten many things or remember them only when I hear somebody discoursing about old times, but this I get right, all my time over in Castle Garden was more of a picnic than it was work. The people coming over was a class I understood; we thought about the same things and when I got a chance to rest I didn't run off home, but could sit down in comfort and listen to one of them immigrants tell about Ireland. It ain't the same about here now, nor it couldn't be. This has grown to be a big business and nobody has any time to waste in talk."

Another old employee at Ellis Island is Miss Prokupek of the Information Department. She began her long career in Castle Garden and has witnessed all the changes and heard (and refuted) all the criticisms which have been aimed at the bureau since Washington took it over from Albany. She has not missed a day in her long service of fifty years except during the war, when a very small part of the force was needed to answer the questions of the few immigrants landed at Ellis Island during a little less than two years. This period of enforced inactivity is not pleasant for her to dwell upon.

Inspector Sven Smith, a Scandiavian born, is Miss Prokupek's contemporary. Like her, he felt lost when the Island was full of soldiers and sailors and his occupation was temporarily gone. He is at his inspection desk every day and can do a longer day's work there without weariness than most of his younger assistants. Said Sven Smith:

"I began at Castle Garden when the head tax of 50 cents was first levied on the immigrants. Colonel Weber, late Congressman had come over from Washington to take charge. He was a fine man, a big-hearted man. If an immigrant proved that he was penniless, the Colonel used to lend him enough to pay his railway fare to where he wanted to go and he took the money for this out of the head tax fund. I recollect well there was a row about it and an investigating committee."

"I never blamed the Colonel, for whoever got the help was deserving of it. It was a fine, upstanding crowd we would to get in those days at the old Castle, mostly strong young men with their young wives, bound to be a credit to any country. No sniveling and all hoping for the best. You could see these boys would all get work and that they did. It's different now with the Italians, Slovaks and Poles. But I don't want to judge them, and I guess they do the best they can."

"The accommodations at Castle Garden were pretty good: oh, yes, pretty good, considering. When we had a crowd and the barges kept on urging more people, we were pretty hard put to it finding places for them all to sleep. I've seen hundreds of men stretched out on the floor of the old Castle, and there wasn't any more room betwixt them than there is between sardines in a box. But we got along all right and never knew how lucky we were until the Government said we couldn't stay at Castle Garden any longer and moved us over to the Barge Office. There we were up against it, had to make beds frequently in the filling rooms and use the papers for mattresses."

"In those days when anybody was detained for any reason, including observation for a disease, we sent them over to Ward's Island. A part of that island was given up for our use."

The old Inspector stroked his head to find a reply to the question of the biggest number of immigrants that had to be housed in Castle Garden in his day. At last he said:

"Well, I guess it was in '88, the blizzard year. A regular fleet of ships had to lie off on account of the storm and then they all came up together. We had 9,000 to take care of and it was pretty crowded."

"The best times I've seen around here – on Ellis Island – were in the first years when we had the wooden buildings. Everybody was clean and comfortable and happy. I don't know what there was about it, but the old wooden buildings seemed more homelike."

"Our job was harder then than now; we didn't have manifests and we had to find out everybody's name and write it down. When you come to write down some of the outlandish names these people bring over you find that it takes a lot of time. I'm referring to the date now when everything was different, to the time when people mostly came from my country or from Great Britain. As soon as South Europe got wind of this country about 75 per cent of the immigration began coming from there – yes, easy – 70 anyway."

Comment: *From Sven's perspective as a Scandinavian, everyone in Europe except the Scandinavians was from "South Europe."*

After the destruction by fire of the buildings on Ellis Island the Bureau was taken back to the Barge Office to await the construction of new buildings and considerable enlargement. Then, said Sven Smith, his work in the Inspection Department was abridged as to hours, for it did not take so long to convey the immigrants to that centre.

"Expedition in the work here does not always depend on our force in the building," said he, "and it varies with steamboat companies. Some lines never will learn how to handle immigrants quickly, the Italian lines do it fastest. When we know that an Italian ship is in with, say, 1,000 steerage passengers, we get ready to look 'em over, for we are sure they will be here within three or four hours. And there are other lines which take all of a day to get 400 immigrants over to the island."

If ever the case of the Immigrants vs. Ellis Island comes up for judgment in a court not presided over by Idle Gossip staunch witnesses for the good conduct of the bureau are to be found in the ancient servants who have spoken here. It may be true that it is the glamour of youth which makes Castle Garden and the first state of Ellis Island look rosier than they actually were, but these veteran persons see no wrong in the present state of things. They have heard immigrants describe in many tongues what may be translated as the detention pens of European ports and none of the evils they enumerated is to be found in America.

The bookkeeper put it: "Sure, and it's a palace they think they come into when once they pass the big door!"

Said Sven Smith: "When there was no quota the immigrants of the old days couldn't fairly complain of Castle Garden: now with the new quota they will not be able fairly to complain of Ellis Island."

ALL IN A DAY'S WORK

TO THE HOTEL IN NEW YORK
(Maud Mosher)

One day while I was on duty in the New York room at the Island a young Irish girl came in who detention card was marked. "To aunt."

After some inquiry I learned that her aunt had come over on the same ship with her but 2nd Cabin - so had not come to the Island. The girl was only about sixteen years old and was very much excited because she was not allowed to go as she insisted that she was to meet her aunt.

I told her that her aunt would have to come for her and asked her (thinking to get a telegraphic address) where she was to meet her aunt. She replied, "At the hotel in New York!" in rich Irish brogue.

I asked, "What hotel?"

Looking at me in the most disquieted fashion as much as to say, "Didn't I tell you once?" she replied, "The hotel in New York."

Another Irish girl wished to send a telegram and was asked by the operator, "Where is the address?"

To his astonishment she replied, "In my mouth" meaning she could say it.

IRISH COLLEEN PROTECTED BY ELLIS ISLAND PEOPLE
(Edward Corsi, In the Shadow of Liberty, pages 155-156)

Now and again in those old days came striking, even touching, evidences of the immigrant's faith in us – the faith, for instance, of Bridget Coughrey, a charming young Irish girl from Clifden, County Galway, who landed at the Barge Office in June, 1900, with a shilling in her pocket and not one word of any language except her native Gaelic.

So far as making herself understood, she might have been born without the power of speech. The only interpreter at the Barge Office who understood Gaelic was absent. Young, comely, touchingly earnest, she tried in pantomime to explain, to make the immigration authorities understand what was such an open fact to her.

Then finally an interpreter was found who "had the Gaelic", and Bridget's story came out. She was one of a large family of children and was used to farm work. Her uncle, Patrick Coughrey, living in Pittsburgh, would advance the money for her transportation there, if he knew she had landed, and Bridget trusted the immigration officials to tell him. He was promptly informed, and the pretty young Bridget was kept under safe auspices until her uncle came, proved himself, and took her away.

"A GENTLEMAN, SON"
(Maud Mosher, May 14, 1904, ship *Campania*)

An old Irishman was questioned by the Inspector as follows:

"What is your name?"
"Pat Maloney."

"Your age?"
"68 years, son."

"How much money have you?"
"Four thousand dollars, son, a little more or less."

"On your person?"
"Yes, son."

"What is your occupation?"
"A gentleman, son."

"Have you always been a gentleman?"
"No, son -- sure and I worked hard in the South Africa mines to git me four thousand dollars and now I'm going out west and rest on me laurels, son."

SICILIAN GIRL CRIES VENDETTA TO ESCAPE SUITOR
(Edward Corsi, In the Shadow of Liberty, pages 151-153)

Those who remember Marie Casacello say she was beautiful. They say of her what was said of another Italian girl, that "Hers was the beauty to make an old man young and a young man mad." Marie Casacello was nineteen when she and her father and brother left Messina and came to this country.

The family took a house in Brooklyn, and Marie was almost instantly the center of a group of admirers. They vied with each other for her favor, and the most ardent among them was Francesco, a stone-cutter who also owned a macaroni store or factory.

All seemed to be going as merrily as a marriage bell. But the fact was that Marie had left behind her in sunny Sicily a determined lover named Terlazzo, to whom Marie, her father now remembered, was engaged to be married. What had reminded her father of this fact was her growing attachment for Francesco – Marie's father preferred the absent Terlazzo and warned her that she must remain true to him.

In addition to an amazing pair of eyes, Marie had a mind of her own and she told her father that she preferred Francesco. After all, her father was only her father; to Marie it was a matter simply between her and Francesco.

Marie unquestionably had inherited her obstinacy from her father, for at this point he announced that he would go back to Italy and get Terlazzo, who would know what Sicilian justice demanded under the circumstances. The old man sailed for Italy. That was the end of the first act of this Italian drama.

The second act opened in April, 1895, with the North German Lloyd steamer *Werra* arriving and landing at Ellis Island Giuseppe and Vincenzo Terlazzo, the two younger brothers of Marie's absent lover. Marie herself went to the Island that day, not to welcome the brothers, but because she remembered her father's oath. She was determined to prevent the brothers from being admitted to this country if she could.

In this mood she was taken before the Commissioner and told her story. The Terlazzo brothers protested that they had come to this country as immigrants and not as agents of their brother, Antonio; they said over and over that their intentions were simple and honest rather than bloodthirsty, and they explained further that they were going to launch out here in the chestnut and fruit-cart business and referred to a compatriot, Frank Chioari, of 116 Thompson Street.

Marie was not convinced and she begged that the two brothers should be sent back to the vineyards and lemon groves of their native Sicily. In the face of her fears, one would have thought that this was Corsica and that a vendetta was brewing.

The Commissioner decided to sleep over the matter. At that point Marie's brother came to the Island and said that Marie was over-wrought and that the two brothers Terlazzo wouldn't make any trouble. And Marie had to accept this view of it, for the Commissioner allowed the two young men from Sicily to land.

SOMETIMES I SWEAR?
(Maud Mosher, June 19, 1904, ship *Etruria*)

An old white haired Englishman was before the Inspector McGregor. He was quite deaf and so had not heard other passengers examined.

The inspector asked: "What is your name?"
"John Smith"

"Are you a citizen?"
"Yes, sir."

"Do you swear to that?"
"I will, sir."

"Yes, you will swear, but do you swear?" (the inspector asked) impatiently.

"Well, yes, sometimes when I get mad I swear some -- I say "damn" or something like that."

The old man went off with (a perplexed) look on his face. Probably he couldn't understand why swearing was necessary in order to get into (America or) why the Inspector laughed.

WELCOME IMPORTS
(Ludmilla Foxlee, How They Came: The Drama of Ellis Island, page 132-133)

Sometimes simple peasants show a fine family spirit, as did Despot B., 40, Yugoslav (Serb), who arrived with twin sisters Zorka and Milica, 26, on the *S.S. Aquitania* January 5, 1928. When I saw them in the Railroad Room, they were ready to depart for Cleveland, Ohio. Despot had lived in the United States for 15 years prior to 1920, when he returned to Yugoslavia to see how things were there. He was unable to return to the United States then, and he earned his living by repairing "threshing machines and any old thing." While he lived in Yugoslavia, a man one day said that he, Despot, was an alien and not an American. This disturbed him, for he did not consider himself to be an alien. He had lived in the United States, he had been drafted into the United States Army.

Note: Yugoslavia came into existence because of World War One. Serbia (which also included Kosovo and much of Macedonia) and Montenegro were independent before the war, but Croatia, Slovenia, Bosnia, Hercegovina, and Vojvodina were under Austria-Hungary's rule. Despot (great name, by the way) was drafted for World War One by American authorities when he was 30 or 31.

He closed himself into a room for three days and composed a wonderful letter on four pages of foolscap paper to the Commissioner of Immigration in Washington. One statement that he made was: "Please answer this soon. I need it."

Comment: A request for speed from today's bureaucrats would likely meet with indifference or ridicule or a glacial response.

This letter moved the hearts of Washington officials so much that they gave him and his sisters immigration visas. He bought the girls dresses made American style and taught them neat English phrases before they started for the United States. Returning residents of the United States were startled by the clarity of their English expressions when the girls spoke their pieces. Some listeners even thought the sisters knew more English than they did. Mr. B was also an excellent carpenter; he made a fine wardrobe trunk with a combination lock, which he showed to me proudly.

WELCOME ABOARD
(Edward Corsi, In the Shadow of Liberty, pages 261-263)

Among the welter of those undesirables who had to be turned back to their native countries, there came thousands of sturdy and intelligent families who have put their strength and intelligence into every county of every state in our union. I have already paid tribute in a general way to this steady stream of fine citizenship which has so impregnated our country.

It would have been better if, during the growth of this nation, more publicity had been given to some of the desirables who chose us for their fellow citizens. I am sure there must have been many a family like the de Jongs, for instance, who came here in 1920.

This Dutch family was termed the model immigrant family of that year at Ellis Island. It was headed by Jacob C. de Jong, a sturdy ship chandler from Holland. He was accompanied by Mrs. de Jong and eight healthy, rosy-cheeked children, Marrigue twenty, Gerrigue eighteen, Johannes seventeen, Johanna sixteen, Neeltje fourteen, Cornelia twelve, Mengo ten and Pilter eight.

When asked for some cash guarantee that his family would not come to want if admitted, de Jong produced five thousand dollars in American money and a great deal more than five thousand dollars in British currency and foreign checks. With a broad smile he explained that he had come to buy a farm and wanted to see his children grow up with the country.

"We believe this is a great country," he said, "and as I have been successful at home, I purpose now to invest my money in America and live here. We are all anxious to buy a farm and knuckle down to hard work."

The de Jongs were not the only family to bring money into the country.

An amusing story is told about Mrs. Margaret Moraitis, an English woman, who came here to live with her daughter in 1922. She was bringing over three thousand dollars in cash and seventy thousand dollars' worth of titles to real estate. On the boat she met a gentleman who said he was an "English detective," and who cautioned her against speaking about her wealth at Ellis Island.

"Don't, whatever you do, tell them about your German real estate," he said. "There is a very deep hatred for anything German among the Americans."

A week after landing she left the Island, laughing at herself for her credulity in taking the "detective" seriously. She had declared herself practically penniless, and had been obliged to wait a week until her daughter in San Francisco could wire affidavits of support. She was a gay little old lady, with dimples and curly grey hair, and after finally confessing her wealth to the Island officials, she went away convinced that the joke was on herself.

We received a band of Russians, once, who boasted of untold wealth, but would not let Ellis Island inspectors see it. They were gypsies, about fifty in all including the women and children, and they intended to found a colony in Louisiana or Kentucky. They brought a huge chest, tightly locked and bound and guarded, which they said held over one hundred thousand dollars in treasure and money. Some of the gypsies sat on the chest night and day, and doctors and inspectors had to examine them there. I believe this was about 1897.

The leader of the party was a big, fine looking fellow who acted as spokesman for the whole group. He had been in America some ten years before, and spoke fairly good English. His wife wore a necklace of United States twenty dollar gold pieces and large pearls. The whole party held themselves aloof from the other passengers on their ship, and seemed to shun publicity.

The various races who have come here have been proud of their contribution to our country, as indeed they may be. I am told that an Italian priest, glowing with pride, once headed a group of eleven men, mostly laborers from Pennsylvania, who were waiting for the arrival of a ship from Italy. When the boat had docked and her passengers had been examined and passed, this group met with rough dignity another group of eleven shy women who had come over to be the wives of the laborers. The priest ushered his charges importantly down to the Marriage License Bureau, and afterwards to the chapel of St. Raphael's, where he married them. These weddings were culminations of war romances.

CHINESE EXTORTIONIST BUSTED
(Edward Corsi, In the Shadow of Liberty, pages 174-175)

Last year an extortion case was reported to Ellis Island by Louis Sing, a legal resident of the country and a respectable laundryman on Amsterdam Avenue in New York. As I recall the facts, Sing related that one morning he was visited by a white man and a Chinaman. The Chinaman introduced the white man as an inspector of the Immigration Service, who was calling to examine Sing's citizenship papers. The papers were produced, and found by the white man to be out of order due to various technicalities. Sing was informed that for the payment of two hundred dollars he could have the papers validated. When Sing protested that he did not have that amount of money on the premises, Harry Lee, the Chinaman, announced to Sing that he would be arrested then and there.

The fear of arrest threw Sing into such a panic that he immediately dug up the last penny in the laundry treasury, a sum approximating sixty dollars. He paid over the money on condition that he would not be arrested, and agreed to have the remainder ready the following morning. His visitors departed.

The next day Sing, true to his agreement, had the rest of the money, but only the Chinaman, Harry Lee, returned. This naturally aroused Sing's suspicion and he refused to make the payment. Harry Lee left the laundry and did not return.

Several days later, Sing, through his connections with the Chinese Chamber of Commerce, made inquiries and learned that he had been made the "goat" by an extortionist. In recollecting the appearance of Harry Lee, Sing recalled that he had a peculiar, livid scar upon his forehead. Upon further inquiry, he verified the identification. The extortion was reported to Ellis Island.

Working through the police of New York, Inspector Zukor, in charge of the Chinese Division, learned from Albert Huang, an extortionist, who had been arrested previously and was being held for civil trial, that Harry Lee was his room mate. Early the following morning Detective Curry of the New York Police, and Inspector Zukor went to the Bronx flat where Huang had lived with Lee prior to his arrest.

Inspector Zukor knocked on the door.

"Who is it?" came a voice from within.

"Compie!" replied Inspector Zukor, which when translated means "detective," or literally, "hidden shield."

The door was opened and there stood a Chinaman with a livid scar on his forehead. A white girl was vainly endeavoring to conceal herself under a ragged bed covering. Lee was arrested and taken to a waiting taxicab, which conveyed the Inspector, Detective Curry and their captive to Sing's laundry on Amsterdam Avenue.

It was about eight o'clock in the morning. New York's rush hour was in full swing.

The cab pulled up in front of the laundry, and Inspector Zukor with the aid of Detective Curry, forced Lee to accompany them. The entrance of the trio produced a scene of mad commotion. Sing, seeing the Chinaman who had filched the sum of sixty dollars, commenced to scream and gesticulate. The crowds hurrying by the window paused, then hurried on. Someone reported to the policeman on the corner that the laundry was being held up. Detectives and patrolmen arrived a moment later, their guns trained upon Inspector Zukor and Detective Curry. It took some time for Inspector Zukor and the detective to explain and to confirm their identities.

SMASHED SWISS STAGGERED SIDEWAYS AT ELLIS ISLAND
(Edward Corsi, In the Shadow of Liberty, page 155)

If Uncle Sam ever decided to deport the alcoholics from the United States, the chances are there would be world-wide repercussions. But that is exactly what Switzerland did to the United States in the late nineties.

Among the extraordinary affidavits recorded at Ellis Island are those of Emil Kunni, 27 years old and a farmer, and Gustave Kammerer, 20. Both of these men came from Blauer, Switzerland, and swore that because of their intemperate habits the authorities there gave them thirty dollars in cash and steamship tickets to New York. Their story might have seemed fantastic except for the fact that their appearance fully verified their description. They gave ample evidence of being alcoholics.

Of course they were deported; and the Treasury Department was set investigating the action of the Swiss authorities in shipping their drunkards to this country.

TEASING THE GIRLS
(Maud Mosher, Ellis Island as the Matron Sees It, page 21)

The Irish girls were so shy and bashful and green – no other word expresses it but just green – but they were always good-natured and it was difficult for the men officers to keep from teasing them just a little. The girls would giggle and scurry away like half frightened rabbits. One joke was to ask the girls if they could play on the piano and when they answered "No," the officer would shake his head as though that were a very grave defect that a girl could not play the piano. This was not done by the grave and dignified officer on the examining line, but by the other officers along the way to the Discharging Division. As the "praste" (Irish priest) was always near and smiling too the girls were sure they were all right.

One day an officer gravely asked a German girl the same question. She answered "no," frowning. He asked her if she sang; again she answered no. Shaking his head in deep thought, he asked her if she could dance. At that question, she also answered no. Big boy that he was, to tease her a little more, he asked, "Well, what can you do?" In a dignified manner she answered, "I can work." He did not tease any more immigrant girls that day nor for a long time afterward.

AN APPLE (ANN EPPEL)
(Maud Mosher, ship Umbria)

Inspector McGregor had finished examining all the passengers on his sheet except one -- Ann Eppel who for some reason had not appeared.

Calling a steward he said, "Steward, I want Ann Eppel." The steward went away and returned in a few minutes with a plate of nice apples.

Mr. McGregor thanked him but did not notice that the steward had misunderstood the order and said quite impatiently: "Steward, bring Ann Eppel here! I must have Ann Eppel."

The steward somewhat dismayed ran on his errand and returned bringing a plate of a different variety of apples.

Mr. McGregor by this time was wild -- he pounded the table as he more impatiently again ordered Ann Eppel to be brought. The poor steward now was in despair -- he had done the best he could and that did not seem to be what was wanted but a bright thought struck him -- he went out of the cabin and returned with a fine large red apple on a plate with a fruit knife and placed it in front of the Inspector.

WICKED STEPMOTHER, KINDLY AUNT
(Ludmilla Foxlee, "A Social Worker's Ellis Island," page 6)

Zorka Vlastinich had some hard moments in her life, although she was only eight years old when she came to Ellis Island with her grandfather to wait for an affidavit of support for her uncle, her mother's brother, living in a large Western city. Her grandfather, a tall, dignified man aged 72, had cared for Zorka since her mother died five years ago. Her father and his new wife had refused to rear the child, and now her uncle intended to adopt her.

I did not like the high rubber boots that she was wearing when we met. When I promptly proceeded to make a change to new stockings and second-hand shoes from our clothing supply, an idea that she accepted without comment, the old stockings would not come off, because they had adhered to many sores on both legs. Three weeks of continual wearing of rubber boots had caused impetigo.

Three hours later I visited Zorka in the hospital. She stood at the door of the ward, the very personification of grief and loneliness. Astonishment quickly appeared in her face when I thrust into her arms a baby doll clothed in proper infant garb. As she shyly looked up at me, her eyes asked was this doll really to be her own? She had never possessed one.

Two days later she joined her grandfather, who had received the required affidavit, and they were off for the West. A letter of gratitude soon came from the kindly aunt, who was delighted with the beautiful, quiet child.

ELLIS ISLAND DOCS CURE CROATIAN GIRL'S TRACHOMA
(Ludmilla Foxlee, How They Came: The Drama of Ellis Island, pages 144-145)

Danica M, 17, Yugoslav (Croatian), arrived on S. S. Ile de France July 19, 1928, to go to her parents in a small town in Nevada. She was placed in the hospital for observation and on July 30th she was excluded because she was afflicted with trachoma. She had prepared to go on ship to be deported when we obtained the necessary $165 to make possible a petition for her treatment. Because her father was an American citizen, the petition was approved In Washington and treatment started at once, to last almost 11 months.

Her father had lived in the United States for 17 years. Four years before he had sent for his wife and daughter, but when they reached the port, Danica was sent back to Yugoslavia because she had trachoma. The hospital in Zagreb (Croatia) believed they had effected a cure after 18 months' treatment, but when she reached Ellis Island the terrible disease still clung to her eyelids.

Her father, a miner, sought to shorten the treatment because the girl's mother grieved over Danica's situation. The father thought he might be successful if he appeared on Ellis Island. The doctors in the hospital had become accessible at the time; after consulting together over Danica's condition, they decided that she could be discharged.

The stay in the hospital improved Danica to such good measure that I could hardly believe that the girl who came to my desk with her father was the same person who had appeared to be a cringing, expressionless peasant whom I had seen awaiting deportation. Her body was well filled out, her hair neatly dressed, she wore a brilliant brown satin dress, neat shoes, and she flashed a fine set of teeth as her broad kindly face broke into a smile. She had learned English and seemed able to answer almost any question we asked her. Her father had taken on American ways in a manner seldom seen in immigrants from the East. ***He had to live in American communities where English only had been spoken and had adopted the ways of his neighbors.*** (Emphasis the author's.)

"LITTLE EGYPT" DANCES FOR THE FOLKS AT ELLIS ISLAND
(Edward Corsi, In the Shadow of Liberty, pages 153-154)

We must go back to the year 1893 to find one of Ellis Island's greatest treats. It occurred when the steamer *Guildhal* arrived from Alexandria (Egypt), and Mohamet Nur, the mightiest soothsayer of the Soudan, found that he had lost his book of necromancy.

Against a colorful back drop of bearded, brown and black Egyptians, Turks, Arabs and Nubians (Sudanese blacks), who had come to assist in representing a Cairo Street at the World's Fair, Mohamet Nur uttered his grievance through an interpreter: "The unlucky son of Mohamet el Kabir mourns in darkness of perplexity without a lamp unto his feet. Give but a piece of American money to him that his good fortune may return."

Then, as a Bedouin came up, Mohamet said to him in swift English: "Great joke, that! I made joke, you understand? Show me American cent, I grab him. See? Great joke! I say, good-by."

Mohamet Nur was not the only Oriental [sic] ready and willing to accept American coins; some two hundred other children of the desert gathered round him at the Island that day, all of them offering everything from heirlooms to trinkets made on the ship, for coin, and all complaining of their sad straits; but unquestionably Mohamet Nur, son of Mohamet el Kabir, was the deepest mourner of them all.

Then there came in a missionary. He listened to their laments and, good man that he was, his heart was touched; he went out and got an armful of Bibles and started giving them out to these brothers and sisters of the desert places, to make them glad. He started with Mohamet Nur, giving him a Bible as a substitute for the lost book of necromancy.

The soothsayer of the Soudan thrust the Bible into his hairy bosom. The rest of them saw that the son of Mohamet el Kabir had received a present and they closed in on the missionary from every side. They grabbed every one of his Bibles and then cried out for more. The soothsayer of the Soudan, with a readiness which would have done credit to a visitor at the Ford Exhibition when offered coupons as a chance for a car, went to the end of the line and came through again, to get another Bible.

When the last Bible had been given out, these denizens of the desert wanted to show their gratitude, and Fatima Osmar said that she would dance. This modest, unassuming girl was one of the most famous dancers in all Egypt. She had rings on her fingers and camel bells on her slender ankles. Silk like gossamer was rolled about her. Her perfect body moved under strings of jewels and she was most divinely tall; and as she danced she became a thing of joy and life and speaking, sinuous curves.

How they had ever let her leave Egypt no one could imagine. She had said that she would dance. Ellis Island had never seen anything like that dance before, and I seriously doubt that it ever will again. For that dance must have made the senses take wings. Not differently had Salome danced! Anything that fair Fatima might have asked then she would have been granted!

The appreciation of all was expressed to Fatima through an interpreter. I believe that she and her dance came as close to astonishing Ellis Island as anything in the world could have done.

THE COLORFUL SIDE OF ELLIS ISLAND
(Remsen Crawford, Outlook, 7/7/1926)

No, the color has not all gone from Ellis Island. Though its dwindling pilgrimage, decimated by the Quota Law and the new plan of inspection abroad, may have brought a tinge of rust to the hinges of our national gate, once stormed by a million a year, there is yet what the artists call atmosphere there.

Endearingly quaint and picturesque are the immigrants at times. The dainty little bodice from Bohemia is still in evidence; boys and girls form bonny Scotland occasionally come over sporting their kilts and tartan plaids; the Spanish and Italian men are still wearing corduroy velveteen; the mantilla has not been discarded by the adorable senoritas from Spain; the dark-eyed girls from Italy continue to put on white satin they day they land in America, no matter how cold the weather may be; and the sober-minded Amazons from the hinterlands of northern Europe mock solemnly at modern modes of scanty skirts by wearing sixteen of them at a time, with cowhide boots away up to their knees, defying all laws of comfort and symmetry.

POLISH SISTER'S AMERICAN POLISH
(Maud Mosher, Ellis Island as the Matron Sees It, page 19)

One day a Polish girl came to the Island to meet a sister who had just come over. Upon being questioned the girl said that she had been in this country a little over a year, and she has a married sister in the city who would give the new sister a home until she could get "a place."

The immigrant sister was dressed up in the peasant costume, heavy knee-high boots, kerchief over her head, about 12 short skirts (petticoats), one on top of another such as the Polish women wear. The one-year-in-the-United States sister wore a cheap but pretty blue silk dress, a white hat with blue forget-me-nots on it, and white cotton gloves. She had blue eyes, thick golden hair, rosy cheeks, and altogether was very sweet and fresh looking. It was a picturesque sight to see the two girls typical of the Old World and the New embracing each other and so overjoyed at the meeting.

GREENHORNS DITCH THEIR CLOTHES
(Edward Corsi, In the Shadow of Liberty, page 267)

An amusing sight that it is now no longer possible to see, since the immigration tide has turned backwards, was the scene at the Battery when the Ellis Island ferry-boat landed with its human freight. Many people have told me that half an hour after the boat came in, the dressing rooms in the adjacent ferry-houses, the bushes at the lower end of Battery Park, and even the gutters along the sidewalks presented the appearance of a junk shop. Queer headgear of women lay about, the familiar black-visored caps of the men and boys, waists and skirts or coats and trousers that undoubtedly went well in the outlying districts of Moscow but would not go far in Manhattan without causing comment and ridicule.

American friends and relatives hurriedly dressed the newly arrived immigrants to disguise the fact that they had come in the steerage. Modern American clothing and luggage were handed to the arrivals as soon as they stepped off the ferry-boat, and they were forced to put it on in the nearest convenient place, before meeting anyone in America. Typical immigrant valises and bags were discarded in the street, thrown overboard from the ferry-boat, or abandoned in public dressing rooms. Such are the ways of vanity!

JUNOESQUE SLOVAK BEAUTY KNOWN AS MISSUS BIG BOOTS
(Ludmilla Foxlee, How They Came: The Drama of Ellis Island, page 116)

To see a lovely woman among the many who passed my desk gave me pleasure. Jan P., 25, Slovak, and Suzanna, 20, his wife, arrived on the S.S. Majestic December 21, 1927, and were detained temporarily because they lacked transportation money. The man had an innocent young face that made him appear about 18, instead of 25. His wife was as tall as he; she was clothed in a light tan cotton dress with a very wide skirt and she wore a kerchief on her head.

She had a long narrow face with an aquiline nose, a strong, large mouth with large heavy teeth beautifully shaped. Her abundant blonde hair was tightly done into braids that were attached in a stiff formation to her head. Her large eyes were hazel and her complexion lovely.

We found a complete wardrobe of modern clothes for her but we were horrified when we discovered that her feet, then enclosed in huge, heavy felt boots with leather soles, were about size 12 and our storeroom had no shoes of that size. The change that the American clothes wrought in her appearance astonished us. Her features took on a new dignity when her head was freed of the shawl. Given a pair of pendant earrings, and clothed in a finely draped dress of soft material, she made a splendid modern Juno.

She was delighted with her American clothing, but decided to go about in her old dress until she could buy a pair of shoes to go with her new outfit. She and her husband went to Ohio to a friend to work on a farm.

OTHER SISTERS AT ELLIS ISLAND
(Maud Mosher, Aug. 13, 1904, ship La Touraine)

I was quite surprised to hear a very sweet, modest looking lady dressed quietly in ordinary garb say to the examiner, "I am a nun," in answer to his question, "What is your occupation?"

One always expects a nun to be dressed in costume of the order. This sister belonged to the order of "St. Paul." but on this same ship were seven other sisters, some young, some old, all dressed in "everyday clothes."

One of the sisters was an American by birth and she told me she belonged to a "congregation in Belgium" but had been sent here with the six others to take care of them on the journey to go with them to their new convent home in Bristol, Maine and teach them the English language and how to get along in America.

"Oh," she said, as she put her hands up over her ears. "I feel so queer without my sisters' dress -- it seems as though I hadn't any clothes on -- my face and ears so bare and I had worn the costume of our order 27 years."

"No," she said. "We have nothing to pay duty on, we are so poor now. They took everything, everything from us. But I do not believe that will ever happen to us in America because in America religious freedom is guaranteed."

"Our priest thought best for us to dress like other people as he feared we might not be allowed to land -- so many of us coming -- they might think it was a Catholic invasion."

The 'Sister of St. Paul' gave me a little toy room made with infinite pains. It was a Sister's cell with its pictures, crucifix, tiny bed, predieu (kneeler for prayers) and two sisters; the whole thing only about 4 inches high.

I showed it to a steward and in awestruck tones he said: "It will bring you good luck, great good luck."

I hope it will! Sweet little Sister of St. Paul!

GERMAN GIRL GETS IN ON CHARM
(Arthur Train, Saturday Evening Post, 3/5/1910)

A good-natured looking chap in uniform stands, pencil in hand, at the head of one of the waiting rows. A flaxen-haired German girl of about eighteen, with big, lustrous eyes and winning smile, waits helplessly at the desk, while the inspector asks her in her own language some twenty questions, the main object of which is to make sure that her answers tally with the information contained in the manifest furnished by the steamship company. Her statement having proved satisfactory, the inspector asks her how much money she has brought with her.

The girl answers: "Fifteen marks!"

The inspector shrugs his shoulders and glances at the doctor.

"Goin' to work for her aunt who runs a Dutch boarding-house in Newark. Bought her own ticket. Brother Hans works in the brewery and is coming for her. I guess she's all right. She's got three dollars."

"Sure," assents the doctor. "Send her along."

The girl, seeing she is the object of our discussion, blushes and gazes at us appealingly. We nod sympathetically. "Gut!" remarks the doctor.

The inspector motions her toward the stairs leading to the outside world. The girl picks up a wooden trunk painted pink, with leather hinges and brass nails, curtsies, and murmurs: "Danke Schön!"

"She'll be married to the fellow that owns the brewery inside of a year!" grunts the inspector.

Note: The German girl didn't have the $25 that inspectors used as a guideline when William Williams was running Ellis Island. But the inspector figured she had a job, a place to stay, and family. Plus he couldn't help but like the cutie.

PUT THE STARS OUT
(Maud Mosher, May 1, 1904)

Last night a little three year old in the apartment house opposite put his head out the window and seeing no stars as the night was cloudy, called in a sweet baby voice: "God, oh God, put the stars out. God there aren't any stars in the sky. Please God, put the stars out."

"I WILL REMEMBER YOU IN HEAVEN"
(Maud Mosher, June 8, 1904, ship *Potsdam*)

I had helped a man -- a jolly German -- to get his wife and child who were temporarily detained and he was very grateful indeed and said, "Oh, I thank you. I will remember you in Heaven."

ASSIMILATION BEGAN AT ELLIS ISLAND
(Harriette Ashbrook, 4/27/1924)

Children from every corner of the globe, speaking twenty different languages and carrying with the traditions of twenty different countries, a heterogeneous mob of small, eager foreigners united by a common desire to gain admission to that marvelous place called America – this is the picture presented by the Ellis Island kindergarten.

Certainly no other schoolroom in the country assembles such a wide variety of tongues, types and temperaments. Blue-eyes Norwegians mingle with dark-eyed Armenians; ruddy little Germans sit side by side with dusky-skinned Greeks, while big, clumsy Russian lads play with their smaller and more agile brethren from Italy. Slav and Teuton, Jew and Gentile, and even an occasional slant-eyed Chinee race and romp and sing and squabble together in a spirit of spontaneous, childish friendship, as they wait for the day when they shall cross that misty stretch of water which separates them from the land of their dreams.

The realization of these dreams rests with the department of immigration, for these are the children whose families are detained at the island for investigation. Some stay a week, some six weeks, some six months. Some leave with a glad expectant light in their young eyes when the magic word "Admitted" is written across the family passport, while others less fortunate are turned back to the old country, heartsick and disappointed.

But while they wait for departmental red tape to be untangled they make good use of their time preparing for the days when they may be real Americans.

At first glance the schoolroom presents much the same aspect as the average kindergarten. On the walls are illustrations from well-known fairy tales, animal pictures and blackboards, while the sides of the room are lined with small chairs, work tables and boxes of toys.

The children themselves are in appearance not unlike so many average young Americans in the average public school – gingham dresses, patched pants, holy pants, dirty faces, clean faces, children losing their teeth and children who have just acquired new teeth several sizes too large for their small mouths. The cosmopolitan influence of the war has (deprived) Ellis Island of its picturesque pleasant costumes.

When you listen to the (children, it is then) that you realize that this is no ordinary school. Yiddish, Polish, Lettish, Finnish, Italian, German, Lithuanian, Armenian, Russian, Esthonian – all mingle in an unintelligible babble. But above all there is a high, firm voice in English, the only language spoken by those in charge.

"Teacher" is almost the first English word the children learn. Then comes "Name" and "Where from?" and "How old?" and "Where mother and father?" By the end of the second or third week the older children have a fairly good command of pidgin English, and if you are sufficiently graphic with your explanatory gestures, there is no limit to the lively conversation which you can maintain with these young foreigners.

As you enter the room the morning exercises are in progress, with fifty small children in a circle in the foreground and "Teacher" in the middle.

"Now, children, what do we do in the morning?" she asks. The response is instantaneous and vociferous.

"Good morning, Teacher," comes from fifty young throats. The music starts, the children begin marching and for a moment it almost seems as if you were back in the little red schoolhouse as there follows that time honored classic of schooldays, every word clear and distinct despite the diverse lingual tendencies of the young singers:

> "Good morning to you,
> Good morning to you,
> Good morning, dear Teacher,
> We're glad to see you."

"And now, what do all the boys and girls in America do each morning after they get up?"

It is quite plain, you reason in the interim which elapses between the question and response, that the idea which the instructor no doubt means to suggest is that young Americans who are property trained indulge in such matutinal (done in the morning) ablutions as will render them acceptable members of society for the remainder of the day. But how is she going to put it over with no five of the children speaking the same language?

You're stumped because you've forgotten to include in your calculations the one universal language – the language of music, rhythmical music, which lends itself to a delightful {lesson) with a wealth of pantomimic gesture ...

"Teacher" at the piano strikes up the tune. It is so familiar that you almost instinctively join in as fifty lusty voices launch forth upon the old, old chant.

> "This is the way we wash our face,
> wash our face, wash our face.
> This is the way we wash our face
> to go to school in the morning."

And then follows the long this-is-the-way-comb-our-hair, brush-our-clothes, tie-our-shoes rigmarole, accompanied all the while by the most energetic and descriptive gestures.

At this opportune moment the children are presented with wash rags, soap and toothbrushes and given vigorous object lessons in their use. The wash rag is familiar enough, but the soap they regard with mingled delight and skepticism, and persist in looking upon it as a fascinating souvenir rather than a household necessity to be applied lavishly and with great frequency.

The toothbrush also is to most of them a curiosity. Small Ivan in particular just can't understand why he is not permitted to share with his father in the detention room downstairs the pleasures of this strange new toy. Coming as he does from Russia, a country which of late has been leaning toward the all-for-one doctrine, he finds it difficult to grasp what he instinctively regards as a somewhat selfish viewpoint.

Three times a week the children are permitted to use these new possessions in the performance of that altogether amusing rite – the American bath. Permitted is used advisedly, for, unlike the proverbial American youngsters, these little immigrants regard a bath as a wholly delightful diversion. For its sanitary aspects they care not the slightest, but as a form of indoor sport they find it vastly entertaining.

Two of them are permitted to bathe together. The very tub itself, white and shining, is a curious, interesting affair. At first they wonder where the water is coming from, for they see no buckets at hand with which to fill the tub. Then "Teacher" turns the faucet and the water gushes out. They are entranced. They can hardly wait to get off their clothes and plunge in and experiment for themselves with the faucets and drain.

"Well," says young Abraham who hails from Galicia, "they tell me lots of things about America, but they never tell me you can have the ocean in the house when you just turn a thing."

While some taste the delights of indoor bathing, others are playing in the kindergarten room ... A great, hulking Russian of 10 or 11 is crawling along on his stomach, while another young person from Sweden stealthily creeps up from behind on hands and knees. The two are the center of a peering circle of eyes, eyes from Poland and China and Italy and Scotland and Armenia, all intent on the dark business at hand.

Suddenly young Sweden utters a blood-curdling yell and falls upon young Russian. Reinforcements flock in from all sides. They shout. They writhe upon the floor. They wave their arms and legs. Bedlam! Pandemonium! Inferno! And in twelve different languages and twenty different dialects to boot!

You clap your hands to your ears and tremble for the future of America if it is to be swamped with such blood-lusty vandals as these. What is it all about?

Just a nice friendly game of Jesse James, that's all. Perhaps the young participants don't recognize it under that title, but that's what it is, nevertheless. You can tell from the murderous glitter in their eyes as they lunge at each other's throats and the hair-raising war whoops they emit that the spirit of Jesse James, Dick Deadeye and Captain Kidd, that beloved triumvirate of boyhood, still lives and flourishes despite mere barriers of race and language.

In another part of the room the older girls are sewing dresses for themselves, while the older boys study reading and writing at the blackboards.

The star pupil is Max, a young Russian Jew of 12, who has been on the island for seven months while lawyers employed by relatives in New York are fighting to bring him and his mother into the country. Her illiteracy is one of the chief bars. During his short stay Max has learned to read and write English, and who in turn is passing this knowledge on to his mother. Attendants in the detention room say that for long hours each day while the other children are playing he sits beside her and patiently directs her faltering fingers in the formation of letters which he himself has learned so recently.

At one of the small tables building block houses is a wee, dark girl of about 6. At first she looks like a Negro, but closer observation shows the straight black hair and fine features of a Hindu. Her little teeth, so white against their dark background, flash a gay smile as you approach and ask, "Name?"

"My name is Rachael Margaret Brooks."

From "Teacher" you learn that Rachel Margaret – she insists on both names – was a Hindu orphan whom an American missionary found destitute in one of the remote parts of India and brought to the mission school at the seacoast. Each day she looks forward to the time when she shall be united once more with her "father."

"I'm going to American school," she announces, "and be doctor."

At another table bent intently over a drawing board is Kahon, thirteen-year-old Armenian lad who has been on the island four months. As he copies a lurid lithograph of a bunch of jaundiced flowers he confides to you in his queer mixture of Armenian and English that he is going to be an artist. And then, with no more heroics than one ordinarily expends upon the multiplication tables, he calmly tells you his story – the massacre of his parents, the abduction of his sisters, the disappearance of his brothers and his own wanderings without food or clothing until picked up by a kindly foreigner. Kahon is destined for a faraway Canadian town where he is to be legally adopted by a farmer.

Near by are two handsome young Russian girls of about 10, both wearing the picturesque high boots of their native land. In appearance they are almost like twins, but the eyes of one are bright and sparkling, while the other's hold a faraway, vacant look. Feeble-minded. The whole family of seven will probably be deported because of it.

In the playground adjoining the schoolroom games are in progress – American games. The children insist on them. In fact, they can't be induced to play their native games. They much prefer puss-in-the-corner, Ruth and Jacob, prisoner's base and drop the handkerchief.

Occasionally some of them pause in their play and press their small faces against the steel netting which separates them from the water and look towards the mainland in the distance.

A stocky little Polack catches hold of your hand and points toward the city. "There America" he tells you eagerly.

"But you're in America now," you assure him.

"No," he protests, and his small face grimaces. "This not America." And once more the eager light comes into his eyes as he points across the water and gazes longingly ...

CHRISTMASES AT ELLIS ISLAND

Christmas at Ellis Island was often a sad day for the immigrants and would-be immigrants, because those on Ellis Island were often there against their will. And of course, these people missed their extended families and friends in the home country.

Some were being treated in the Island's hospital. Many were being detained for a legal matter or were awaiting being discharged or being claimed by family or spouse, or awaiting the recovery of a loved one in the hospital. And some poor souls were awaiting deportation.

The authorities at Ellis Island did try to make Christmas as festive as they could for the immigrants. They also used the Christmas festival as a gentle way to aid in assimilation of immigrants to American customs.

Barry Moreno, a National Park Service historian at the Ellis Island Immigration Museum, shared the following information about Christmases at Ellis Island in his excellent book Encyclopedia of Ellis Island and his monograph Christmases at Ellis Island:

Many priests and ministers from the various ethnic communities of the New York City area came to perform religious services for the Catholic, Orthodox, and Protestant immigrants in their native languages. The priests and ministers also did their best to console those facing deportation.

The Registry Room (also known as the Great Hall), a huge auditorium-sized room that occupied the center of the second floor of the Main Building of Ellis Island, was the site of most of the Christmas festivities. A huge Christmas tree and a huge American flag and many smaller decorations adorned the massive hall, which was almost a half-acre in size. Sometimes there could be as many as 2000 aliens present for the Christmas service at Ellis Island. The deportees were welcome to these celebrations, along with those other detainees not in the hospital.

Robert Watchorn, one of Theodore Roosevelt's Commissioners of Immigration at Ellis Island, and an immigrant from England himself, presided over one such service in 1905 and ensured "My Country 'Tis of Thee" was sung. In 1914, Anthony Caminetti, the Labor Department's overall immigration chief, came up from the nation's capital for Christmas, and the staffers provided a concert and a silent movie show.

The Christmas festival always included speeches, singing of carols in various languages, and gift-giving to the immigrants. For those who were too ill to attend, the hospital staffers threw them a Christmas party in the hospital's Service Room. "Father Christmas" personally came to visit the sick boys and girls, bearing them presents.

Ludmilla Foxlee, in her work How They Came: The Drama of Ellis Island (pages 7-8), remembered the following about Christmases on Ellis Island:

Christmas was regularly observed on the island. Missionary societies sent toys and fruit for the children. The General Committee of Immigrant Aid decided to buy small, useful articles for adults, so that everyone could have a Christmas gift. An appeal was made for bags about 18 by 18 inches with a draw string at the top, made of bright cotton prints. Girls' bags contained a doll, a towel, washcloth, and soap, a game, a toy set of dishes, three handkerchiefs, a writing tablet, a pencil box, and a pair of stockings. Women received a sewing bag, needles and thread, pins and safety pins, scissors and buttons, a bead necklace, an apron, a bath towel and washcloth, toothbrush and toothpaste, soap, a writing tablet and pencil, stockings, and three handkerchiefs.

For men the bags contained a comfort bag (with needles, thread, some buttons, et cetera) a safety razor, toothbrush, toothpaste, pins, safety pins, washcloth and soap, a towel, a writing tablet and pencil, a pair of socks, and three handkerchiefs. For boys, the bags were similar to those for the girls, with a game substituted for the doll.

A Christmas tree with lights and a silver star brightened the hall. Benches in long rows with an aisle in the middle accommodated the detained. Chairs at the side of the hall were for the General Committee of Immigrant Aid and their friends. A musical program occupied the major part of the afternoon, and the talent was donated. For two successive Christmases, a group of the Social Service workers appeared in national costumes and sang English, Italian, German, Polish, Spanish, and Czechoslovak Christmas carols.

However, the Commissioner decided later that professional talent must be provided. He persuaded a broadcasting company to present a musical program, and that one was heard coast to coast.

The radio company provided a full orchestra and a Metropolitan Opera soprano to sing a Puccini aria. The grandeur had no visible effect on the audience. Probably they were thinking of home and loved ones. After the program, the immigrants were given their bags and an orange.

Jews and other non-Christians on Ellis Island of course could not in good conscience celebrate Christmas as a religious holiday. Jewish immigrant societies tended to Jewish detainees' religious needs on Hanukkahs. However, the non-Christian aliens on Ellis Island got gifts at Christmas and were welcome to the Christmas festivals just like the Christian aliens were.

CHRISTMAS WITH THE YOUNG POLKA KING
(Frank Yankovic)

I remember years ago when I was just a little boy laying awake in my room waiting for Christmas. I didn't think about toys very much 'cause I knew Mom and Dad didn't have very much money.

Mom rented rooms to boarders from the old country (Slovenia). And as the holiday grew near they would all become kind of sad thinking about their wives and sweethearts they left far behind in their homeland. Then before you knew it, they'd start singing and drinking some of our homemade wine and listening to the old button accordion.

Christmas Eve was special because Mom and Dad would let us (kids) stay up late so we could all go to Midnight Mass. The best memories of all were waking up on Christmas morning to the smell of the great holiday dishes that only Mom could make.

Even though I'm fortunate enough to buy all that I can for my children and grandchildren, thinking back, I know that I remember the true meaning of my Christmases long long ago.

Comments: *Frank Yankovic's parents were immigrants from Slovenia. He grew up in the Cleveland area, started his band "The Yanks" and ran a successful bar, all before World War Two. Frank joined the U.S. Army and earned a Purple Heart while fighting in the Battle of the Bulge. He pressed his own records and sold them at gigs. When Frank became well-known, Columbia Records execs offered him a recording contract. Frank kept them from dictating to him what to record; he recorded songs he believed in and made himself, his band, and them a lot of money.*

The story Frank told about Christmas he made into a recitation in the middle of the song "Silent Night." Singers sang the first verse of the carol, then Frank told his anecdote, then the singers resumed. It is on his 1984 album "Christmas Memories." Frank's widow Ida is due special thanks for talking with me about Frank, and providing me with a recording of his Christmas story.

THE ROCK AND THE ISLAND
(Knute Rockne, excerpts of "From Norway to Notre Dame" in Collier's Magazine, October 1930)

How a youngster from Voss, a hamlet in Norway that lies between Bergen and Oslo, could find himself in his mid-twenties captain of a typical, mid-Western American football team may require explaining. Perhaps it's sufficient explanation to say that this evolution is a typical American story – in business, athletics and politics. It has occurred so often that it's ordinary. The breaks came my way when I had sense enough to take them; and while that's an unromantic way of explaining a career, it has the advantage of being the truth.

Her celebrated majesty Queen Margaret of Norway had something to do with it. At least, there's the word of a student Norse genealogist to that effect. It's on an elaborately inscribed piece of parchment that looks like a map-outline of all the football plays ever invented. This, on close perusal, informs me that I'm descended – among others – from one Enidride Erlandson of Losna, Norway. He and his tribe were landowners of some consequence. When Queen Margaret merged the three kingdoms of Norway, Sweden, and Denmark, she did not retain the best features of each. At least, my pride of ancestry won't permit me to believe that she did. For the Erlandsons of Losna refused to have anything to do with the merger, retiring, in a collective huff, to the town of Voss and there establishing themselves in the hills. Generations elapsed, the hills remained the same, but it became harder and harder to make a good living.

The traditional venturesomeness of the Norsemen, aided by infiltration of Irish blood obtained when the earlier and hardier Vikings invaded Ireland looking for trouble and returned to Norway with colleens for wives, breaks out at intervals. With my father it broke out when I was about five (in 1893). The World's Fair (the Columbian Exhibition) was to be held in Chicago. Dad, by profession a stationary engineer and by avocation a carriage builder, wanted to show his wares at the World's Fair. He went to America. Later, he sent for his family. My mother took her three daughters and her only son to New York and we were duly admitted through Castle Garden

Notes: *Actually, Castle Garden – where fellow Scandinavian Jenny Lind once sang in concert – closed as an immigration station in 1890. The Barge Office, nearby on the lower west side of Manhattan Island, served as the first federally controlled immigration station, and Ellis Island replaced the Barge Office from 1892 through 1897, and again from 1900 through 1954. (The Barge Office reopened as an immigration station from 1897 to 1900 because of the fire which destroyed the wooden buildings on Ellis Island, and the time it took to rebuild Ellis Island buildings in brick, concrete and stone.) But in its day as New York's state immigration station from 1855 through 1890, Castle Garden was the point of entry for roughly eight million immigrants. Many of the first immigrants through Ellis Island like Knute Rockne simply called it Castle Garden because the old place was so well-known in Europe.*

ELLIS ISLAND SCRAPBOOK

My only equipment for life in the new country was a Norwegian vocabulary, a fervent memory of home cooking combined with pleasant recollections of skiing and skating among the Voss Mountains.

How my mother ever managed that tedious voyage, which I still recall with qualms; how she guided us through the intricacies of entry, knowing nothing of English, and took us into the heart of a new, strange, and bewildering country without mishap – how, in brief, she achieved the first step in our Americanization unaided by anybody, is one of the millions of minor miracles that are of the stuff and fabric of America.

Perhaps it was a trick of Fate that the first natives of the new country to register favorably with me were not only natives, but aborigines – Indians. In the Elysium of the World's Fair, with its glittering palaces, and amazing crowds, a tow-headed young Norwegian youngster was lost for one day. Elated by an award of a medal for his exhibit of a carriage, Dad had failed to check my natural curiosity. So I wandered all over the paradise of sights and sounds and smells; having a glorious time on popcorn, pink lemonade and the new and delightful rite of the hot-dog. At length – and it must have been a long time – I wound up before a reduced facsimile of an Indian reservation.

The contrast between me, a white-haired Nordic fresh from the original source of supply, and the jet-haired Indian papooses must have struck some minor Indian chief. When the fairgrounds police, in their mighty hunt for youngsters lost, stolen, or strayed, came to item 181-B, specifying a Norwegian boy who knew no English but might respond to the name Knute Kenneth Rockne if pronounced with pressure on the Ks, they gave it up. Until morning. Then a weary copper, passing the Indian reservation, beheld a blond head surmounted by feathers, bobbing through a scampering mob of Indian kids, wielding a wooden tomahawk and yelling for scalps.

They promptly collected me, stripped me of my Indian finery, and restored me to my puzzled parents. Ever since then I've held Indians in affection and esteem, unmodified even by collision on the football field with the greatest Indian athlete of them all. For when, as a professional player for Massillon, Ohio, I undertook the job of tackling Jim Thorpe and learned, when prostrate, following sudden and severe contact, that Mr. Thorpe was no respecter of even All-American persons – the Indian sign became more than an empty phrase.

Before I was to see and meet Indians again, a Chicago childhood and youth had to be gone through. It was not unpleasant going. The new, spacious city, with its endless corner lots and tolerant police, was a great place for a boy to grow up in, in the era B.C. – Before Capone. Our baseball and football games were undisturbed by rifle fire and the popping of pineapples (grenades), At that, there was excitement enough for everybody.

Rockne coached at Notre Dame for 13 years, and fielded five undefeated teams, including his last two squads (1929 and 1930), before he died in a plane crash in early 1931. The 1929 team played all their games at opponents' stadiums because Notre Dame Stadium was under construction that year. They are the only college team to win a national title with zero home games.

Frank Leahy, one of Knute Rockne's players and successors, was the most dominant coach in college football of his era. In 11 years at Notre Dame, he coached six undefeated teams, which included his first Irish team, the 1941 squad, the 1946, 1947, 1948, and 1949 squads, and the 1953 squad, which was also the last team he coached. (The 1943 squad lost a close game to a team of football all-stars at the end of the 1943 season, but they beat all the regular college teams they played. Their quarterback Angelo Bertelli, whose parents were immigrants from Italy, was so dominant he won the Heisman Trophy despite only playing six games before reporting to the U.S. Marines. Bertelli served as an officer in the Pacific Theater against the Japs.)

Leahy, who served as a U.S. Navy officer in World War Two in 1944 and 1945, had this to say about the immigrants and sons of immigrants who played football for him:

"Many people have poked fun at Notre Dame because of some to the unpronounceable names that have appeared in her lineups down through the years. (For every Gipper at Notre Dame, there was a Gmitter, a Gladieaux, a Savoldi, and a Czarobski.) However, we are extremely proud of all of these boys, and we feel that they are to be highly congratulated for the sacrifices they have made to receive their degrees. Several of these lads came from homes where English is not even spoken, and when they arrived in college they found it was necessary for them to work much harder than other boys in order to grasp the subjects. Yet down through the years we have had very few boys of foreign descent fail out of school. Many boys get up early and spend all their spare time with the books in order that they may become well-educated American citizens by the time they leave school. These lads are to be admired, and we shall always be happy to have boys with the long names on our football team, because in many cases the long name is synonymous with long hours of hard work and sacrifice, and for this, there is <u>no substitute</u>. (Source: <u>Notre Dame Football, the T Formation,</u> by Frank Leahy, page 234)

THE DRUMMER BOY

See if you can guess who this famous American sports figure was before the end of this story.

I was born on the kitchen table on the top floor of a three-decker wooden house on Merrick Street in West Springfield, Massachusetts. Two days later, my mother was back at her work. That's the way it was done in that kind of neighborhood, at that time.

I was the youngest of four sons, spaced two years apart. My brothers, in order of their age, were Clarence, Raymond and Armand. Not very long after I was born my father, who had been an engineer for the Boston and Albany railroad, suffered a heart attack. Not serious enough to completely disable him but enough to wipe out whatever small saving he might have had and to limit his activities.

And so my earliest memory is quite probably of my mother leaving the house to work as a maid in a downtown Springfield hotel.

We were so poor, I sometimes say, that we didn't live on the wrong side of the track, we lived in the middle of the track. A joke which has a certain bite to it, in our case because my father had gone back to work for the railroad. His job was to go from locomotive to locomotive and make sure the fires were properly banked.

We never had a Christmas tree; I remember that particularly. Christmas was always held on the linoleum floor in the kitchen in front of the old iron stove. When I was five or six, I wanted a drum. Oh, Lord, how I wanted that drum. More than anything I have ever wanted before or since. When I went to bed on Christmas Eve, I remember my mother and dad saying, "Well, you've been a pretty good boy; not the best but pretty good. Santa Claus may stop by."

When I woke the next morning there was a drum right there alongside me on the bed. Well, let me tell you, no rich kid ever got a Mercedes-Benz that meant so much to him as that drum meant to me. That's something poor people have on rich people. Anything my parents gave me I knew they were giving me out of sacrifice and sweat and love.

Not, as you may have guessed, that I didn't give them immediate cause to regret it. I started banging on that drum as soon as I woke up, and I never stopped. For three days, I went marching around the neighborhood with the drum hanging from around my neck, whacking away at it. At night I went marching around the house. The three-decker houses that were so common in those days had two apartments to each floor, six families in all. After a couple of days, five families in our house and twelve families in the adjoining houses were screaming to shut that kid up.

The shouts were in French, because it was a neighborhood of French Catholics. My mother, whose maiden name was Clara Provost, was born in a little town just outside Montreal. My father, George, came from the little French community of Cohoes, in upper New York. He was a small man, possible five feet four inches. My mother was barely over five feet. Nothing except French was spoken in our home, or, except for the Latin liturgy, in church. I didn't know one work of English when I started public school.

When I began to mix more with the other kids in town, socially and in athletics, their nickname for me was Swamper. After a while it was, anyway. It developed something like this: Frog ... Bullfrog ... Swamp ... Swamper. Jeez, do you know the last time I heard that name? I was sent to Atlanta in the Southern Association in my second year of organized baseball, and we were playing the inmates at the Atlanta prison. I hit a ground ball and was running to first when I heard some guy in the stands holler out, "Hey, Swamper." One of my classmates had got out of Springfield the hard way.

Until I began to play professional baseball, my name was always pronounced the French way; not De-*roach*-er but Doo-roe-*shay*.

(Leo Durocher, Nice Guys Finish Last, pages 27-29)

ELLIS ISLAND SCRAPBOOK

PRESSED BETWEEN THE PAGES OF OUR MINDS

The Ellis Island Immigration Museum has a huge number of immigrants' stories recorded and typed. For every one in this book, I could find hundreds as good there. But since time and costs limit all book projects, I regret I was only able to give you the stories this book contains.

Many of you enjoyed reading about the ships of Irish girls and other Euro-babes coming to America looking for husbands. Several hundred women on each vessel – full of hopes and high spirits, young and in the full bloom of life, coming to America looking for romance .... do you wonder how their lives unfolded?

Did the image of Irish teenager Annie Moore, who traveled with two little brothers in tow grab your attention? And when Colonel Weber gave her the $10 gold piece, and she said it was the most money she ever held in her life, did that not tug at your heart? (Annie turned 15 the day she landed at Ellis Island.) And did you notice Annie had enough maturity to cross the ocean with two younger children in her care?

The rest of the story is this: Annie's mother and father picked them up at Ellis Island. Annie married Joseph Schayer, a son of German immigrants, in 1895, three years later. She and her husband and family lived in Al Smith's old stomping grounds on the Lower East Side of Manhattan. In fact, they were married at Al's parish, St. James Catholic Church, and like Al, Joseph worked at the Fulton Fish Market. Annie bore 11 children; five of them made it to adulthood. Annie died of heart failure in 1924; she was 47. Annie's body lies at rest in Calvary Cemetery in Queens with six of her children.

Agents at Ellis Island had the duty of protecting girls and young women from predatory males – and sometimes from their own looseness. The well-fixed French procuress looking to buy a man to stay in America, the "fleeing fiancee" who used her guy's money to hook up with another stud, the hunger strike of the hookers, and the deported skank who was "making new contacts to enliven the coming voyage" back to Europe caused extra work for the people of Ellis Island.

Sadder were the tales of rejection and abandonment of wives. These tales prove unfaithfulness has been with us almost since the dawn of time. Infidelity has never ceased to hurt the innocent with a sorrow that is beyond words to express.

The plight of the people aboard the *Red Sea* was a fairly revolting tale. So was the story of the girl covered with insects. The tale of the stowaway princess and the Finnish girl who eloped with a sailor by stowing away on his ship indicates the trouble many people would risk just to get here.

If any of the very sad stories – the Jewish mother being deported, the Irish girl and her baby dying at sea, and the Lithuanian girl being deported because she caught trachoma while ministering to the poor souls in steerage – didn't affect your emotions, then your heart came from a quarry.

The story of the Communists duping thousands to come to Russia was sad and anger-inducing at the same time. It shows what happens when fundamentally evil politicians get their hands on power. Being a politician means never having to say you're sorry, so you lie and have your minions lie for you. If that doesn't get the job done, you imprison and murder those who speak the truth about you. This is why no politician, even one as public-spirited as Abraham Lincoln, should get too much authority.

The letters of William Williams and the stories about him confirm he was a man of ire and iron-bound integrity. But he had a bit of a sense of humor, as his collection of letters of greedy goobers looking for love demonstrates. And he was not without pity for the immigrants as the dilemma of the well-built Russian farm girl whose guy stood her up shows.

Henry Curran was an author as well as a politician. The stories "Weeping Music Teacher Plays Her Way into America" and "They Know the Baby is a Pole" showed his decency as well as his sense of humor and his flair for the dramatic. Newspaper articles backed up his recollections.

However, Mother Cabrini, in my opinion, was the better dramatist. Even though English was a second language to her, she mastered it and made her points well in it. She contrasted the lives of misery of the Italian laborers to the homes and loved ones they left behind, and she contrasted the meanness and tightness of too many bosses in America to the power and generosity of God Himself in creating the great land of America.

Maud Mosher talked about the workaday problems of inspectors and immigrants. She revealed her prejudices, her fears, and her hopes, as she went about her business of protecting America from bad immigrants and protecting immigrants from the bad in America and in their own circles. She showed real character in mastering her prejudices and doing right by the immigrants. By comparison, too many of our immigration agents (and other bureaucrats) <u>say</u> all the right things but do not always <u>perform</u> their jobs with competence, diligence, honesty, or charity.

Maud's little poem about the mariner who stole a kiss provided entertainment value in its own right. So did Ludmilla Foxlee's story about the Slovak giantess in the big big boots. Ludmilla's story about helping the Slav girl escape the clutches of her evil stepmother and Maud's admonition to a German husband to take care of his new bride provided a picture of their practical concern.

The account of the Peeping Tom employee whose co-workers beat him up for peering in on the Portuguese girl showed there were many honorable people working at Ellis Island. The problem some employees had with immigrants lying to try to take money from them indicates not all immigrants were innocent people. The riots of the Gypsies and some of the assaults detained immigrants committed showed the agents at Ellis Island had to be ready for trouble at any time. The agent who died of a broken neck when some idiot foreigner decided to push him down, the nurses and matron who the demented girl attacked, and the officers who had to subdue the loser who tried to knife them and who later started a baggage fire all suffered injuries so the American people would be protected.

Edward Corsi's accounts of the illegal immigrants (usually the Chinese in his day) shows illegal immigration has been a problem as long as there has been a need to regulate immigration. As a famous detective once noted, any list of crimes essentially contains the violations of the Ten Commandments. What has changed through the years is the technology criminals use to commit crimes.

Was it paternalistic to make men marry women who they said were their fiancees at Ellis Island itself or at City Hall in New York City? Yes. This way, female immigrants had status and rights under American law. Was it paternalistic to require a family member or someone else known to a woman or a child to show up at Ellis Island personally or provide proper instructions and wire money for the woman or child? Yes. These policies prevented many women and children from being victims of abandonment, abuse, kidnaping, and sex trafficking. Do you have a problem with that?

The agents' lives were not all tedium, overwork, and danger. "Little Egypt's" dance at Ellis Island was a much more welcome diversion than escorting volatile foreigners to deportation. Like guys anywhere, some of the agents enjoyed themselves teasing the immigrant girls in a harmless way. And they enjoyed seeing the separated husbands and wives melt with emotion when they reunited at the Kissing Post.

The accounts of the missionaries and volunteers who did right by the immigrants showed the basic charity of many in this country toward the newcomers. People not burdened by an intrusive government staffed with power grabbers and money grabbers were capable of great things. (Nowadays some buttinsky "separation of church and state" bedwetter would sue the "Mission of the Immaculate Virgin for the Safekeeping of Irish Girls" for their mission of protection and their overtly religious and ethnically exclusive name.) Once again, for sheer reach, the account of Mother Cabrini dramatized the work religious people freely did to make people's lives better.

The article on the school at Ellis Island, and the recollections of Christmases at Ellis Island indicate those who worked at Ellis Island tried to help the detained adjust to American ways and tried to show them friendship and Christian charity. (Jewish groups did likewise for immigrants of their faith.)

These stories collectively showed the humor, the sadness, the drama, and the decency of the lives of those who came here in the Ellis Island Era and of those whose job it was to screen and process them.

At one time the old were young. At one time the dead were alive and happy and productive. We rest on the labors of the many generations of these people who discovered, settled, and built this land. History books mention the names of the most prominent. But it took millions of people, known only to their loved ones and friends and others whose paths they crossed, to do the work that was needed but unrecorded to aid in the process. May we live our lives like the best of them. Future generations may not know our names, but they will depend upon the good or suffer from the bad that we do in our lives.

Top left: Slovak relatives of author's wife, late 1800s. He was in the Austro-Hungarian army. **Top right**: Czech-American great-great uncle of author. He served in Spanish-American War. **Bottom left:** German-American couple, wedding day, 1921. Wife is a relative of author. **Bottom right**: Leo Hurley, son if Irish immigrants, World War One vet, Chicago police officer, grandfather of author. Author's Grandpa Sherlock, who came through Ellis Island from Ireland, also served in World War One and with the Chicago Police Department. *May God rest their souls, and the souls of your loved ones!!*

THE TRUTH ABOUT ELLIS ISLAND

Over the years, many people have made many comments and complaints about immigration to America during the Ellis Island era. Since there are public histories and public records on the facts, we'll discuss how many of these were true and how many were lies that got good PR.

TRUTH, LIE, OR URBAN LEGEND?

"We came to America packed in like sardines, in filthy quarters, with little food and with many sick people."

That all too often was true until into the 1900s.

Steerage passengers were almost pure profit for steamship companies. Officers and employees of these companies sold cheap tickets to people, and fed them very little and provided them with very little in the way of sanitary facilities. They advertised all over Europe to lure poor people to buy tickets, and they were greedy enough to transport people who were sick, handicapped, or otherwise unfit to gain entry to America. They figured enough of these unfit people would somehow get by the inspectors and get into America.

American officials put laws with teeth in them into effect, and this pressure forced the steamship companies to do better. American officials started fining steamship companies for bringing in undesirables. They made steamship companies pay to feed, shelter, and provide medical treatment for aliens detained at Ellis Island or elsewhere in America, and they made steamship companies take rejected people back to Europe for free. They also quarantined ships in harbors and made steamship companies pay for related medical, feeding, lodging, and sanitation costs.

The more astute steamship company officials got the point. In the ports of Britain and Germany, the two greatest European maritime powers, there were fairly well-organized facilities for immigrants to clean themselves and undergo some medical screening. In some of the other countries, officials likewise upgraded their standards when they figured out America meant business.

American immigration officials wanted to save American taxpayers from having to bear the burden of caring for and sending back people they didn't want to admit to America. They also wanted to save would-be immigrants the expense and shattering experience of being turned back from America. So they made the standards known and prompted the steamship companies to follow them or lose money.

"Immigration officials and agents were corrupt."

Before Ellis Island opened in 1892, this was very true. In fact, the reason Congress federalized the immigration process was to cut down on the rampant corruption of state and local officials who had been processing immigrants.

Some corrupt employees continued in office. But when the incorruptible and cantankerous William Williams and his successors found them out, they became former employees and often became inmates of prisons.

Williams ordered railroad ticket agents to stop selling unsuspecting immigrants railroad tickets that would take them way out of their way to their destinations or face punishment. His successor Robert Watchorn had employees check on the levels of service railroad companies were giving immigrants. Based on what they found, Watchorn concluded the railroad company officials were cheating immigrants. Watchorn, himself an immigrant from Britain, filed a complaint against the railroad companies with the Interstate Commerce Commission to make them give immigrants better services or reduce their ticket prices. **(1)**

Unscrupulous vendors and agents could take advantage of immigrants who paid for services such as telegrams or train tickets or food for travel or baggage handling, and immigrants who exchanged their foreign money for American money. Williams and his successors tried to stomp down hard on this sort of corruption.

In one such case, Williams had a telegraph office employee jailed for short-changing a Czech immigrant by five dollars. In another case, Williams noted a money-changing contractor was turned out of Ellis Island because of his crookedness. Williams cancelled a vendor's baggage handling contract in 1911 when his people discovered the vendor was cheating immigrants. Williams canned a food contractor who was not feeding immigrants properly. Williams punished or assisted in jailing many others who broke immigration laws for financial gain. Williams' toughness and integrity set the standard for the men who followed him at Ellis Island. **(2)**

"They fed us swill at Ellis Island."

This was probably true before William Williams took over.

Frank Martocci, the interpreter at Ellis Island, was probably the agent who admitted immigration commissioner-to-be Edward Corsi and his mother, stepfather, brother, and sisters when his family passed through Ellis Island to New York from Italy in 1907.

Close to a quarter-century later, when Italian immigrant Corsi became the head man at Ellis Island in 1931, Martocci was still on the job. Corsi asked the old interpreter to reminisce about the early days of his service.

One of the things Martocci said he remembered was food service workers slopping ladles of stewed prunes onto rye bread to dole out to the immigrants for several meals in a row. He said the quality and quantity of food served changed for the better when Williams became commissioner. **(3)**

Williams cancelled the contract of the food vendor in 1902, his first year at Ellis Island. He cancelled the contract of another food vendor not long after he returned to Ellis Island in 1909, the first year of his second term as commissioner. He determined the vendor was not feeding immigrants properly. **(4)**

The 1902 food service bid requests from the U.S. Immigration Service was the first dealing done for food by Williams. Williams noted the previous food service vendor collected $65,000 from the steamship companies for a year at 10 cents a meal for breakfast and "supper" (the evening meal), and 15 cents for "dinner" (the midday meal, which typically was the big meal for rural people). This meant the vendor served at least 433,000 meals to as many as 650,000 meals to detained immigrants during the previous year.

Since it was often the fault of shipping companies that many would-be immigrants were detained at Ellis Island for sickness and unfitness, American officials decided it was only right to fine the shipping companies and use the money they collected from these outfits to pay for the food and shelter they gave to aliens they detained. Shipping companies did not directly have to pay for meals served for those being detained until family, fiancé, or friends could come for them or send them money for transportation to their new homes.

Williams specified the winning food service vendor would have to provide immigrants bread for breakfast, beef or fish, soup, and potatoes for "dinner," and bread and stewed prunes for "supper." (The prune ladles still found use, even after Williams took over.) Coffee and tea, and milk and sugar were to be available.

Williams also allowed the food service vendor to sell bread, ham, cheese, bologna, smoked fish, bread, pies, donuts, fruit, milk, soft drinks, and beer to people leaving Ellis Island so they would have something to eat while they were taking train rides to their final destinations. (Later, puritanical feds would ban alcohol sales at immigration stations.) Williams allowed the vendor a 20 percent profit margin on food to go.

Henry Curran, the Commissioner of Immigration at Ellis Island from 1923 through 1926, said he tried to have the immigrants served some ethnic foods, but immigrants whose native dishes were not on the menu would complain. He said with a twinkle in his eye, "If I added spaghetti, the detained Italians sent me an engrossed testimonial and everyone else objected. If I put pierogi and Mazovian noodles on the table, the Poles were happy and the rest were disconsolate. Irish stew was no good for the English, and English marmalade was gunpowder to the Irish. The Scotch mistrusted both. The Welsh took what they could get. There was no pleasing anybody. I tried everything, then went back to United States fodder for all. They might as well get used now to the baked beans, assorted pies, and anonymous hash that would overwhelm them later on." **(5)**

If the immigrants weren't getting food their way, a 1908 food contract request for bid and four immigrant dining room menus from 1917 indicate they sure weren't getting starvation fare.

The 1908 food service bid requests from the U.S. Immigration Service (made when Robert Watchorn was the chief at Ellis Island) specified the winning food service vendor would have to provide immigrants hot cereal and milk, hash or pork and beans, and bread and butter for breakfast. For "dinner" (the midday meal), the vendor would have to provide immigrants meat or fish, potatoes, vegetables, bread and butter, and soup. For "supper" (the evening meal), the vendor would have to provide stew, pork and beans, or hash, a fruit dessert or pie or pudding, and bread and butter. Coffee and tea, and milk and sugar were to be available. Kosher substitutes for pork were to be made available. This was a step up from the fare Williams was allowed to offer immigrants in 1902. On Williams' recommendation, fines against steamship companies for violations increased, and this undoubtedly led to better food for detained immigrants.

The 1917 dining room menus (made when Frederic Howe was the chief at Ellis Island) showed for breakfast, immigrants got hot cereal, milk, bread and butter, and fruit. For "dinner," immigrants got meat, vegetables, potatoes, bread and butter, and soup. For "supper," immigrants got a one-pot entree such as stew or hash or meat and beans, bread and butter, and fruit. Coffee and tea, and milk and sugar were to be available. Food service people served milk and crackers to children between meals. Okay, so maybe the onset of World War One led to the cutoff of the breakfast ration of pork and beans. (Or was it complaints of gas?)

So what's not to like? Do you and your children eat as heartily today? **(6)**

"Ellis Island was a filthy zoo where sadistic officials mistreated immigrants."

After Theodore Roosevelt became president, this was basically untrue.

Imagine having to undergo processing with 5000 other people on a very hot or very cold day. Underpaid and overworked immigration officials and employees – many working 6 or 7 days a week -- would be sorely tempted to lose their tempers, especially if crying children puked on them, or if greasy immigrants coming out of a two-week stretch in steerage tugged on their coats trying to get their attention, or if lice and other vermin hopped off of dirty foreigners and onto them.

Children's shrieks, women's crying, men's arguing, and the constant pushing and pulling and ordering going on would make an unpleasant mark on anyone's memory. So would being detained while waiting for loved ones to pick you up. *Ellis Island was not a hotel, but a gateway*.

By the early 1900s, immigrant groups in the cities made reasonably powerful blocs of voters. If they complained, there would be some vote-chasing politicians with no more morals than an ambulance-chasing lawyer looking to attack the workers at Ellis Island to endear themselves to these ethnic communities.

Journalists of a German-language paper in New York City started criticizing William Williams and his people for allegedly mistreating immigrants and deporting and excluding people cruelly. Theodore Roosevelt in 1903 appointed a commission to investigate the charges the Germanic newspeople made. The commissioners cleared Williams and his people and praised Williams for the job he did. **(7)**

Among immigrants, the British were the biggest complainers. A typical British bitcher was a minister named Sydney Bass who whined that he had to wait with other immigrants. This alleged disciple of Christ bitched because American immigration officials made him and other Englishmen and Englishwomen stay in the same area with unwashed immigrants from presumably less genteel lands.

Bear in mind the British were colonial masters of the Indian subcontinent, much of Africa, portions of Southeast Asia, many places in the West Indies, and Ireland when Bass tried to come to America. The British also were among the leading commercial plunderers of China at this time. They also had a lot to say about the running of Australia, Canada, and New Zealand. In short, their tentacles stretched around the globe, which gave many of them a dangerous sense of ethnic and racial superiority, every bit as objectionable as the "love myself, hate my neighbor" attitude many of the Germans had.

"I objected to being placed there in such close proximity with the filthiest people of all nations, covered with dirt and vermin," he complained in 1911. Besides showing a high amount of bigotry and persnicketyness for someone who was allegedly a follower of Jesus, Bass demonstrated a flair for dramatic exaggeration as well. He moaned, "I was peremptorily ordered back into the common room. There were 600 people in that little room, crowded together. It seemed to me the most like the black hole of Calcutta of anything that I have seen."

The short but large-mouthed Bass complained about taller Italians in the room. "They were eating garlic, and you can imagine how offensive it was," he whined. "It was very unpleasant. It made it difficult for me to breathe." Were his delicate sensitivities to blame, or was it anti-Catholic bias – against the people in whose land the Pope lived and usually was a native of – on the part of this alleged man of God?

Maybe Bass was miffed at being labeled an undesirable. Bass had to stay overnight on Ellis Island, and a board of special inquiry declared he should be deported as being liable to be a public charge. Bass admitted complaining about the filthy foreigners he as an Englishman was cooped up with when he appeared before the board members. The immigration officials might have considered his attitude unworthy of a real minister of the Lord. Maybe they considered him a charlatan akin to many of today's televangelists.

Evidently someone higher up than the agents at Ellis Island gave Bass a break, because six months later he was preaching in Pennsylvania. Maybe it was a catch and release situation for Bass.

Corrupt New York congressman William Sulzer fished Bass out of Pennsylvania and put the crabber in front of Congress in 1911 to make the above charges. Bass also complained the British gave him a clean bill of health before he emigrated. Because of his stay at Ellis Island, Bass carped, he couldn't get such a clearance anytime soon. Bass produced a note from a local doctor saying he (Bass) couldn't perform many of his functions as a minister for some time after he came to Pennsylvania because "I found him in a state of collapse." (In other words, the Ellis Island people evidently got it right about Bass' problems.) Bass also made the spurious charge that some young women being detained at Ellis Island were being denied religious services. This was a ridiculous lie, because priests, ministers, and rabbis routinely held religious services for the detained.

Williams wrote his boss a letter that refuted Bass' fish story. He said Bass was a liar on all his charges and cited facts to support his charge. He said a Protestant minister on Ellis Island had checked on Bass at Ellis Island and Bass said he had received good treatment. He said Bass thanked his deputy Byron Uhl for his treatment. Williams also noted his agents detained Bass for physical deformities affecting his ability to earn an honest living. So, Williams concluded, Bass turned to earning money dishonestly by making up stories about Ellis Island so he could hit the lecture circuit. (Before radio and TV, traveling lecturers made good money as entertainers.) He noted Bass claimed he was not only a minister, but also a journalist, lecturer, and salesman. (All four occupations unfortunately hide many charlatans.) Williams closed his blast with, "I do not know what part of the Scriptures he read; but he failed to read, or reading it failed to heed, the commandment – "Thou shalt not bear false witness against thy neighbor." **(8)**

Sulzer, a Democrat, was likely angling for the ethnic vote in his 1912 campaign to become governor of New York when he made charges against Williams in 1911. Members of the U.S. House of Representatives investigated Williams, a Republican, for "atrocities, cruelties, and inhumanities" that were allegedly taking place on Ellis Island under his watch. Certain immigrant protection group officials, foreign-language newspaper publishers, and those who resented Williams for his bulldog attitude in upholding immigration laws as he interpreted them witnessed against Williams. One of the fishy witnesses Sulzer produced was Brother Bass.

Williams, in writing, and in his verbal testimony before the congressmen, said Sulzer and the witnesses were lying about their key charges, and offered proof to back his counterattack. He noted he was not going to argue every detail with his detractors because they were caught lying on the gist of their most important accusations.

Sulzer in essence took back his complaints, and instead asked for more money for Ellis Island's administration. Williams had proven to the congressmen's satisfaction the charges Sulzer and others had lodged against him were false.

Sulzer would win the governor election later that year because the Republicans split into pro-William Howard Taft and pro-Theodore Roosevelt factions, each of whom ran candidates, splitting the anti-Sulzer vote. (His election as governor occurred in the same way as the election of Woodrow Wilson to the presidency that same year.) New York state assembly speaker Al Smith and other Democrats in Sulzer's own party – with the help of Republican legislators – would impeach Sulzer in 1913 for violating the state's Corrupt Practices Act. Sulzer had broken this law by diverting money donated to his campaign into his own pockets. A court made up of state senators and state judges tried Sulzer for the charge and removed him from office later in the year. **(9)**

There were many complaints from British immigrants about Ellis Island that were publicized. Every one of the complaints I reviewed revealed the Britishers' bigotry and classism at having to share the facility with other nationalities. I used Sydney Bass' complaint as an example of the tone of condescension typical of the British who complained.

Frederic Howe, the Commissioner of Immigration at Ellis Island during the World War One era, said, "The British gave the most trouble. When a British subject was detained, he rushed to the telephone to communicate with the consul-general in New York or the ambassador in Washington, protesting against the outrage. When ordered deported, he sizzled in his wrath over the indignities he was subjected to. All this was in effect a resentment that any nation should have the arrogance to interfere with a British subject in his movements. All Englishmen seemed to assume that they had the right to go anywhere they liked, and that any interference with this right was an affront to the whole British Empire."

In 1922, politicians in Britain criticized the treatment of British immigrants at Ellis Island, and sniped at the sanitation and the food service as well. They were shocked – *shocked!* – that migrating Britons didn't have separate eating, bathroom, and sleeping facilities and actually had to mingle with other foreigners while awaiting processing, admission, or deportation in America. **(10)**

The British had no right to talk. Dr. Alvah Doty, for many years the epidemic-tracking Health Officer of the Port of New York, blamed the British (and Moslems and peoples of the Indian subcontinent) for the spread of many epidemics. Doty said the British didn't regulate sanitation in their colonial ports well enough, and didn't do enough for public health in the Indian subcontinent (which they ruled as a colony). Moslems coming from British colonies in Asia and Africa (and from elsewhere) on pilgrimages to Arabia didn't use proper sanitation. Many of them passed through the British-run Suez Canal or came to and from British colonial ports aboard filthy ships. These wandering Moslems, Doty said, carried the germs of epidemics far and wide. **(11)**

These British blowhards overlooked the fact their own countrymen and countrywomen had chosen to leave their country for ours.

Ohio congressman John Cable expressed the thoughts of many when he shot back, "I cannot understand how these particular people (British aliens) can travel from seven to 14 days in steerage accommodations on the steamships (British ships, by the way) and do so willingly, and then suddenly develop the most acute culture and sensibilities as soon as the Statue of Liberty comes into view."

Congressman Cable said British officials should investigate the immigrant quarters at their own ports before critiquing American immigration stations. He added the admission of immigrants to America should be "for the benefit of America and not for Europe." In the 1920s, it was not politically incorrect for American politicians to be proud of America and put America's interests ahead of those of other nations.

James Davis, President Warren Harding's Labor Secretary, was the Cabinet member responsible for immigration stations during this flap. Davis was himself an immigrant from Wales. He seemed much too worried about what politicians in his homeland thought. He leaned toward segregating British immigrants from other immigrants.

Ironically, William Williams had favored a kind of segregation of immigrants at Ellis Island ... a segregation of immigrants by class. He noted the relatively few second class passengers detained for reasons other than disease might be held apart from the mass of steerage passengers so they might avoid exposure to the germs and vermin the poorer passengers were carrying. Even though Williams was a WASP of the bluest type, he would never have allowed the British such privileges as native Britisher Davis was contemplating granting them.

Davis invited British ambassador Auckland Geddes to inspect Ellis Island. Geddes did so late in 1922. Geddes saw that isolation of British immigrants from others could not happen at the small Ellis Island facility. So he said Americans should spread out the work of Ellis Island at several facilities. Geddes made this kibitz (which if carried out would cost Americans millions of dollars but the deadbeat British nothing) in a report made public in August 1923. **(12)**

Henry Curran, who Harding had just appointed as the Commissioner of Immigration at Ellis Island before he died in office in August 1923, blasted the British and those American officials who sucked up to them. Curran, during his three years as boss of Ellis Island, scuttled other attempts to show favoritism toward British immigrants and make it easier for aliens to avoid proper screening. Thanks to Curran's vociferous efforts, segregation of nationalities on Ellis Island for the satisfaction of the British would not take place. **(13)**

Curran, a reform politician in New York City, an Army officer in World War One, and a man of letters, was more known for his puckish sense of humor than for bombast. When a noblewoman emigré from Russia made fantastic and well-publicized charges against Ellis Island in 1923, Curran used this gentler touch to debunk her complaints publicly.

Baroness Mara de Lillier Steinheil said she was imprisoned by the Communists during the Russian Civil War, and the Reds murdered her husband and brothers. But instead of being grateful for the chance of coming to America, she claimed conditions at the immigration station were in many ways worse than a Bolshevik prison.

Even though she said she had titled relatives all over Europe, Madame Mara chose to come to democratic America. (Maybe her blueblood kin didn't like her act either.) Agents at Ellis Island detained her for three days and made her go before a board of special inquiry. The board members allowed her entry to America. Then she complained to the press.

Curran deflated the balloon of the boorish baroness by producing a letter from a Russian Orthodox priest who edited a Russian ethnic paper in Newark thanking him for helping the Russian refugees who underwent processing at Ellis Island. Curran added, with the tongue-in-cheek humor that was his style, "It is to be regretted that we can't provide a kaiser's suite for each immigrant." **(14)**

Curran said the immigrants who complained the most while he was commissioner were the English. "They talked a good deal about their rights as British subjects. To many of them Americans were still "colonials" while the other nationalities were always "foreigners." The English refused to sleep in the same room with "foreigners." They sent delegations to me about it. One batch of detained English immigrants even objected to living in the same room with another batch of English, who had come in on a later ship. 'They are English but they are newcomers,' said the leader of the delegation. 'We are the same as old inhabitants. We have been here for a whole week. Why do we have to associate with them?' " **(15)**

Curran did improve the sleeping arrangements for detained immigrants. He said, "In several small rooms for the detention of special cases there were beds, but in the large rooms that served as dormitories there were no beds at all. There were bedbugs, but no beds. It took me two months to exterminate the bedbugs. It took me two years to exterminate the wire cages that served as beds and replace them with real beds. To do that I had to have an appropriation by Congress, and the argument and red tape that had to be gone through with in Washington were such that it seemed to me sometimes as though Washington were the one place in the world that was completely motionless. Finally I got a couple of congressmen to come up to Ellis Island and stretch out in the cages for a few minutes. Those congressmen were flaming missionaries for beds instead of cages." **(16)**

What Curran referred to as cages were essentially wire grids held together with steel frames and steel rails and steel posts, stacked three high. Since the mechanics on Ellis Island tied these together head to foot, the end result looked like a series of giant rabbit hutches (minus the sides) instead of a series of three-bunk bunkbeds. Sleeping on a wire grid with only a blanket instead of a mattress would be uncomfortable, like sleeping directly on the lateral springs and wires of a military bed frame.

Several well-heeled immigrants singled out black workers at Ellis Island as being too forward. In this they shared the prejudice of most American whites of the time. Most Europeans had never seen a black person, and those who did had seen them in colonial servitude. (The prostitutes of France were exceptions. They cheerfully serviced black American servicemen during World War One.) They were surprised to see blacks in government service in the United States. They were surprised the black workers they ran into at Ellis Island could be as blunt and as unapologetic as white workers.

Without question, some employees at Ellis Island and other immigration stations were jerks or crooks or both. That's true with all organizations. Individuals will remember injustices done to them. However, the archives of Ellis Island bristle with personnel paperwork proving Williams, Watchorn, and other commissioners in the 1900s suspended, fined, fired, and/or had jailed employees who were abusive, dishonest, or criminal. This means they cared about how their people were doing their jobs and treating immigrants.

Will researchers a hundred years from now checking on the discipline of civil servants today find as many disciplinary cases proportionately on the many government employees who loaf, lie, cheat, steal, commit negligent acts, are inefficient on their jobs, seize property wrongfully, commit sexual abuse, or shoot or burn people alive without cause or due process? Given the strength of government employee unions today and the poor quality of government officials in general today, I doubt it.

<u>Ellis Island was not a hotel</u>. It was a station designed for the protection of America as much as it was designed for the temporary quartering of immigrants until they could leave or be deported.

The conditions I described at Ellis Island were Spartan by our standards of today, but not by the standards of the late 1800s or early 1900s. People were harder back then. Almost all immigrants were peasants who lived in small cottages or city laborers who lived in slums. Most lived without electricity or indoor plumbing. Most raised their own food, and made their own wine or beer. Most slaughtered their own livestock.

Many European immigrants slept in fields, haystacks, and wagons on their way to the ports of departure. They then tolerated days to weeks in steerage, packed closely in the poorly-ventilated filthy holds of ships with less-than-outstanding food. Many immigrants were beaten and/or stolen from on their way to the immigrant ships, and many were mistreated by the ships' crews or other steerage passengers on the way to America.

By comparison, the immigrants were fed and housed for free at Ellis Island, and they were guarded for their protection. They had access to shower and toilet facilities that were being cleaned constantly. Accommodations at Ellis Island were better than what a poorer person would have to endure while traveling in Europe, or traveling in steerage.

The immigrants would not dare to complain about their treatment at home. But since they were free in America, and moved on to a higher standard of living and political freedom than they knew at home, they could vent about Ellis Island without fear of jail.

"They changed my name at Ellis Island."

This was an "urban legend" long before there was such a term. I have heard people make that excuse to me for their ancestors many times, and I have read this charge many other times. On the whole it is not true.

Some immigrants did walk out of Ellis Island with different legal names than they had when they left their villages in Europe because of clerks' errors, clerks' rudeness, clerks' laziness, and clerks' obtuseness ... not only Ellis Island clerks, but clerks for the steamship companies and clerks at the ports where immigrants boarded ships for America.

However, these immigrants were not the norm. Starting with Theodore Roosevelt's administration, there were enough interpreters at Ellis Island to get immigrants' names straight. Many interpreters were themselves immigrants or children of immigrants. These agents would be naturally sympathetic to the immigrants and would be conscientious enough to record their names correctly.

Some immigrants undoubtedly got "name changes" because of ignorance ... their own and the ignorance of local officials in their homelands. Before World War One, there was no literacy requirement for adult immigrants. Many people came here not knowing how to spell their own names. Civil servants in Europe were not as a whole known for their honesty or efficiency. So any papers from home an immigrant carried (except, perhaps, a baptism certificate or a marriage record from his or her parish) might have his or her name misspelled. So how were the agents at Ellis Island going to make sure every immigrant's name was spelled correctly? They likely copied the immigrants' names off the ships' manifests and the tags they were wearing when they got off their ships. In other words, they were relying on papers the shipping companies' clerks prepared and maybe they relied on papers some people carried with them.

But these two reasons only account for some of the immigrants. The sad truth about most immigrants whose "names were changed at Ellis Island" is that they did it themselves.

Some immigrants changed their names when they left their villages to avoid problems on their trips to the ports where they would board the ships. Europeans and Turks were much more brazen in their mistreatment of minorities in their own countries and nationals from other countries passing through their countries than they are now.

Some immigrants changed their names for other rational, if less honorable, forms of deceit. These were criminals and other undesirables leaving their homelands. They needed to change their names to avoid detection.

Then there were the cowardly young men running from young women they impregnated. And there were the shamed young women who had to leave their villages because they conceived without the benefit of husbands. No doubt many of them felt they needed new names in their new country.

But most of the immigrants who left Ellis Island with names different than names they had at home simply wanted to fit in and avoid discrimination. They had heard enough about America and knew enough about human nature to figure out they would fit in better with Anglo-Saxon sounding names than with names ending in "ello" or "iani" or "vich" or "wicz" or ""witz" or "ski" or "sky" or "stein" or "berg" or "olsen" or "enko" or "poulos" or "anian."

In the Ellis Island era, it was a common sight for heaps of peasant clothing from Europe to lie discarded at or near the immigration stations. Why? Many people who were already established in America met their relatives at the immigration station bearing changes of clothes so the newcomers could throw away their Old World garments on the spot. They didn't want their loved ones being marked as foreign bumpkins because of their clothes. And they didn't want the embarrassment of being seen in public with their "greenhorn" relatives.

It was also not too unusual for some immigrants to change religion to fit in. For example, many Scandinavians, going from countries where Lutheranism was the state-established religion, heard from their pastors the advice that they should become Episcopalians in America because the pastors thought that was the dominant or established religion in America, even though America as an independent nation has never had an established religion. Lutheranism in Europe was a religion whose leaders and adherents tended to submit to civil authorities. **(17)**

That sort of thing still happens today. In the wake of the American hostage crisis in Iran during the Carter administration – and the resulting anger toward Iranians by the American public – many natives of Iran who were living in the U.S. in the late 1970s and early 1980s petitioned the courts to Americanize their names. And even today, Hollywood is full of actors and actresses who Gentilicized their Jewish names for business purposes. So the mindset of wanting to sound "mainstream" to the American public on the part of these immigrants was understandable, if regrettable.

Years later, many of these people, ashamed of denying their heritage in order to get off to a good start in America, did what many people do. They blamed others for their own weakness. It's easier to claim you were a victim of the authorities than to admit to being cowardly enough to want to fit in or avaricious enough to want to make it big that you willingly turned your back on your heritage.

If there was a scheme by Ellis Island officials to neuter immigrants of their ethnic names, there would be far fewer ethnic names in America today.

If these allegedly renamed foreigners didn't like their new moniker, then why didn't they file in court to have their names officially restored, properly used, and properly spelled? Under American law, they had that right! Ethnic societies could have helped them do so if they really wanted the help to right such an injustice, if it actually took place.

Bottom line? The people who processed immigrants at Ellis Island did much finer jobs than they were ever given credit for. Millions of people and their descendants owe these people gratitude for their basic decency and devotion to duty.

INSPECTION'S BOTTOM LINE

How tough on immigrants were the inspectors at Ellis Island and other American immigration stations?

U.S. immigration officials admitted 3,127,245 immigrants into the United States from 1892 through 1900, and excluded 22,515 aliens from entering the country. Of these, they kept out 15,070 on grounds they were "likely to become public charges," 5792 manual laborers claiming they had contracts, 1309 mental or physical defectives, 89 "immoral classes" (prostitutes, pimps, and the like), 65 criminals, and 190 people for other reasons. They allowed 99.3% of all would-be immigrants into the country.

U.S. immigration officials admitted 8,795,386 immigrants into the United States from 1901 through 1910, and excluded 108,211 aliens from entering the country. Of these, they kept out 63,311 on grounds they were "likely to become public charges," 12,991 manual laborers claiming they had contracts, 24,425 mental or physical defectives, 1277 "immoral classes" (prostitutes, pimps, and the like), 1681 criminals, 10 "anarchists or subversives," and 4516 people for other reasons. They allowed 98.8% of all would-be immigrants into the country.

U.S. immigration officials admitted 5,735,811 immigrants into the United States from 1911 through 1920, and excluded 178,109 aliens from entering the country. Of these, they kept out 90,045 on grounds they were "likely to become public charges," 15,417 manual laborers claiming they had contracts, 42,129 mental or physical defectives, 4824 "immoral classes" (prostitutes, pimps, and the like), 4353 criminals, 27 "anarchists or subversives," 1904 stowaways, 5083 people 17 or older who were illiterate, and 14,327 people for other reasons. They allowed 97.0% of all would-be immigrants into the country.

From 1921 through 1924, the year of the big quota law, U.S. immigration officials admitted 2,344,599 immigrants and turned away 78,413 would-be immigrants. In other words, they allowed 96.8% of all would-be immigrants in those four years into the country.

Overall, immigration inspectors at Ellis Island and elsewhere barred 387,248 would-be immigrants for medical, mental, or legal reasons from 1892 through 1924. When compared to the 20,390,289 aliens the inspectors inspected, and the 20,003,041 immigrants the inspectors allowed to enter in these years, this means the inspectors kept only 1.9% of all would-be immigrants out of America. *In other words, 98% of all would-be immigrants to America in that era got in.*

These numbers show doctors and inspectors as a rule weren't out to exclude people maliciously or obtusely. A majority of Americans would have been happier if they had rejected more people for medical, mental, or legal reasons. It appears the doctors and inspectors erred more on the side of leniency than on the side of firmness in deciding whether to allow immigrants into the country.

Paradoxically, Ellis Island inspectors were known for their firmness but barred a slightly lower percentage of immigrants than inspectors at other stations. Probably a lot of the questionable immigrants tried to avoid Ellis Island and sneak past inspectors elsewhere. But they were caught anyway.

Who did they keep out?

According to federal statistics from 1892 through 1924, inspectors at Ellis Island and elsewhere barred 196,208 would-be immigrants as paupers or people likely to become public charges. They refused entry to 38,630 people on grounds they were contract laborers. They barred 6 people as "coming in consequence of advertisement."

They refused entry to 3690 people who were "assisted" in coming to America with money from foreign governments or private organizations. They did so to combat European governments who were dumping their misfits and unwanted on America. They sent back 10,043 people who "assisted" themselves in getting to America as stowaways.

They barred 6037 children younger than 16 coming in without a parent if no parent would call for them at Ellis Island or send them money for train tickets from New York to join them. (Before 1908, there was no restriction against taking in unaccompanied teenagers.)

They refused entry to 11,585 people 17 and older who could not read in their native language. (Before 1917, people who were illiterate could gain entry.) The literacy requirement took effect in 1917; but there were several exceptions. The biggest loophole allowed admission of illiterates if they were females immigrating with a husband or immediate family member who could read.

They barred 384 "idiots," 518 "imbeciles," 3215 "feeble-minded," 2473 "insane persons," 292 people diagnosed as "constitutional psychopathic inferiority," and 258 people branded with a surgeon's certificate there was something else wrong with them mentally that could keep them from earning a living. They also barred 416 epileptics. In all, they excluded 7556 aliens with a mental problem severe enough to make them threats to others or make them unable to earn livings.

They refused entry to 129 people with tuberculosis, 42,319 people with a "loathsome" or dangerous contagious disease, and 25,439 people marked with a surgeon's certificate there was something else wrong with them physically that could keep them from earning a living. They also turned away 87 people for "chronic alcoholism." In all, they excluded 67,974 aliens with a severe disease or a medical problem severe enough to make them threats to others or make them unable to earn livings.

They barred 44 anarchists. From 1917 through 1921, they barred 101 aliens from enemy nations. (America entered World War One in 1917, and Germany signed the armistice ending the war on November 11, 1918, but America was technically at a state of war against the Central Powers (Germany, Austria, Hungary, Bulgaria, and Turkey) until 1921. The U.S. Senate refused to ratify the peace treaties Woodrow Wilson signed because they favored Britain and France over America, and they would allow globalist Woodrow Wilson to subject America's sovereignty to the League of Nations, a pipe-dream multinational group he wanted to form that the rulers of the British Empire and France intended to dominate. The senators declared the end of the state of war with the Central Powers in 1921, after Wilson had to leave office.)

They barred 7363 criminals. They barred 4350 aliens (almost all females) coming to America to be prostitutes or for "immoral purposes," 2771 procurers and pimps of females for "immoral purposes", and 70 people "supported by the proceeds of prostitution."

They excluded 1210 people for passport violations. They excluded another 2562 people from 1921 through 1924 for not having proper passports.

They excluded 6139 Chinese under the Chinese Exclusion Act. They excluded 140 people coming from other Asian countries America didn't allow immigration from in the "Asiatic Barred Zone." They barred 399 polygamists.

They barred 298 people as professional beggars, and barred 10 as vagrants. They barred 220 aliens trying to come back into America because they had been already deported within a year or less earlier.

They sent back, from 1921 through 1924, 14,457 people who "exceeded quota." In other words, American officials decided there were enough people from these countries coming in as it was, and their "crime" was getting to America after officials had let in all of their countrymen and countrywomen they were going to let in for that month.

They barred 4992 people for "accompanying aliens." These were usually aliens who were the guardians or protectors of rejected aliens, like infirm children. They had to go back with the rejected aliens because the rejected aliens needed their help. Also, such aliens and their charges had to go back even if the dependents were admissible but the guardian aliens were not.

They barred 689 people on "last proviso" of Section 23 of the 1917 immigration law or Section 17 of the 1924 immigration law. These were aliens who claimed residence in Canada or Mexico but hadn't lived in one of those countries for at least two years before applying for admission to America. After the passage of the Immigration Act of 1924, such aliens would be subject to quotas applying to the land of their birth anyway. **(18)**

* * * * * * *

An incredible fact about the Ellis Island process is that most people passed the medical and legal inspections and cleared the island in three to five hours.

Clerks at motor vehicle license bureaus, smog check stations, unemployment offices and other government agencies seem to need almost that much time to issue you a license, check your car, or do whatever else they have to do for your case!

On average, about 80% of the immigrants got through the screening process on Ellis Island in three to five hours. Officials detained perhaps as many as 20% of the immigrants for medical or legal reasons. Of this 20 percent, nine-tenths of them (or 18% of the overall total of immigrants coming through) were eventually able to enter the U.S. after their sicknesses cleared up or after immigration officials decided they wouldn't pose any threat or be any burden to the citizens of the United States. Officials only had 2% of the sea of humanity flooding through Ellis Island and other U.S. immigration stations sent back to Europe or the Near East or elsewhere as undesirables.

Two percent was still close to 400,000 mostly decent people (well, not the criminals, subversives, pimps, or other sociopaths), heartbroken and abandoned, who had to go back to a way of life they were hoping to escape. Their personal hardships were no doubt overwhelming.

However, the vast majority of would-be immigrants got in. The agents at Ellis Island and other American immigration stations by and large tried to treat immigrants fairly, but tried to serve the interests of the American public first. In other words, they tried to keep out criminals, people liable to be objects of charity, those who carried dread diseases, and those whose contract-labor presence would undercut the wage structure of the American worker.

Despite their prejudices against immigrants of other ethnic groups and religions (or maybe because there were so many former immigrants working at Ellis

Island and other immigration stations), the immigration agents still let in almost all of those seeking to come to America.

Most commissioners at Ellis Island were kindly men, and most of them were honorable men. Some of them were immigrants themselves. Many took huge cuts in salary to be Commissioner at Ellis Island. Many were disillusioned by their higher-ups. Most of these men were worthy commissioners because they were asked to do the job ... most of them didn't seek it. There was nowhere near the careerist mindset among major government officials then that there is now. Back then, many worthy men served as government leaders for a time then went back to the private sector.

In summary, the large majority of immigration agents and officials tried to protect the American public. And while they were at it, they tempered justice with mercy. And they did it on unexorbitant salaries. The aliens they processed by and large got a square deal like Teddy Roosevelt and other leaders of good will expected. Can the same be said of the attitude and the dedication and the competence of all too many government employees today?

END NOTES

1. Information on Watchorn's actions against railroad companies comes from the Historic Research Study, Statue of Liberty – Ellis Island National Monument, by Harlan D. Unrau, National Park Service, 1984 (pages 245-246).

2. Information on Williams having crooked employees punished and cancelling contracts comes from the Unrau study (pages 224, 257, 535).

3. Martocci's comment about the prunes comes from Edward Corsi's book In the Shadow of Liberty (pages 78-79).

4. Information on Williams firing the food vendors comes from the Unrau study (pages 257, 535).

5. Curran's comedic comments on chow came from his book Pillar to Post (pages 291-292).

6. Information on the food service at Ellis Island comes from the Unrau study (pages 386, 866-869).

7. Information on the 1903 charges against Williams comes form the Unrau study (pages 229-230).

8. The complaints of Sydney Bass, the peewee preacher, come from pages 130-135 of the Hearings on House Resolution No. 166 Authorizing the Committee on Immigration and Naturalization to Investigate the Office of Immigration Commissioner at the Port of New York and Other Places. (This was the Congressional investigation of William Williams.) The investigation record started May 29, 1911. William's comments were in a letter he wrote to Commissioner-General of Immigration Daniel Keefe dated 3/9/1911. This letter, like his other letters and many reports he wrote, are part of the collection of papers he donated to the New York Public Library.

9. Information on Williams' fight against Sulzer comes from his Annual Report dated 10/10/1911 in his papers (New York City Public Library) and the Unrau study (pages 262-264). Information on Sulzer's rise and fall comes from the Unrau study (pages 417-419), Al Smith's book Up to Now (pages 123, 130-132) and Richard O'Connor's book – a biography of Smith -- The First Hurrah (page 76).

10. Frederic Howe's quote comes from his book The Confessions of a Reformer (pages 257-258).

11. Information on the blowhard British politicians comes from the 12/7/1922 and 12/8/1922 issues of the New York Times. The source of Dr. Doty's comments on the disease-carrying Moslems and the British who negligently allowed them to spread diseases around the globe comes from the New York Times issue of 10/4/1908 titled "How Plagues are Watched the World Around." A reprint of this article came from Cathy Horn's website "The Forgotten of Ellis Island."

12. Cable's quotes come from the 12/9/1922 New York Times. Information on the Geddes report and the flap between the British and Americans over Ellis Island in the 1920s comes from the Unrau study (pages 284-285, 563-570) and the 8/16/1923 New York Times. Davis' comments come from the 12/17/1922 New York Times.

13. Sources of information on Curran's attacks on the British when they complained about Ellis Island include New York Times articles of 7/31/1923, 8/18/1923, and 8/12/1925, an 8/18/1923 London Times article (reprinted on Sue Swiggum's and Marj Kohli's TheShipsList.com website), 8/27/1923 and 8/24/1925 Time Magazine articles, and Pillar to Post (pages 309-310).

14. Information on Curran's handling of the Russian noblewoman comes from the 7/9/1923 and 7/10/1923 issues of the New York Times.

15. Curran's comments on the English come from his book Pillar to Post (page 309).

16. Curran's account of the "cages" comes from his book Pillar to Post (page 293).

17. Information on Scandinavian Lutherans whose pastors told them to convert to Episcopalianism in America comes from Oscar Handlin's book The Uprooted (page 139).

18. Statistics on immigration come from the immigration tables of the Unrau study. I did some math to come up with totals.

THE CLOSING OF THE SCRAPBOOK

I farm part-time. It's a hard way to make a living.

The vast majority of your ancestors earned their livings farming. They didn't have many options, until the Industrial Revolution provided factory jobs and farming machinery and greedy landlords ran many workers off the land. Our ancestors really did have to toil and sweat daily to make ends meet.

That was still true In the Ellis Island Era; most people even in the United States still earned their living by sweating. More people were farmers in the early 1900s than any other profession. The miners, loggers, and construction workers were also many in number and percentage of the work force. The steel mills and slaughterhouses employed many under conditions appalling by today's standards.

Women's trades were not easy either. Just ask the seamstresses who worked long hours and regularly got cheated out of their money and risked burning to death in firetrap buildings. Or ask the servant girls how long they worked and how little they made and how often they had to defend themselves from sexual assault. Or ask the female farmworkers of that era if they would prefer an office job of today to their farm labors in terms of pay, hours, and wear and tear on the body.

Because they were tough and independent-minded, our people in the Ellis Island Era demanded better performance from their politicians and bureaucrats than we demand today. Likewise, the immigrants themselves were used to hardships and were independent-minded enough to leave home and adopt our land as their own <u>and assimilate</u>. Half of my ancestors from Ireland and my wife's grandmother passed through Ellis Island along with millions of other people from the early 1890s through the end of the 1920s. My other ancestors who came to America (and hers) passed through Castle Garden.

The chapter on the growth of America is a sketch of how we as different types of people formed a Union and rose to greatness. Yes, there was a lot of wrongdoing in the process. Yet we are still head and shoulders above any other country that ever existed. Those who hate our way of life have nothing better to move to.

The chapters on immigration regulation and immigrant processing show the development of our laws and techniques for assuring decent people came to America to help it grow instead of allowing undesirables to come and leech off of America and work against America.

No laws are perfect, but the goals of any politician who actually wants to serve America should be to limit immigration to the nation's actual needs, and to preserve the existing culture of America. We have the right to value our traditions and cultural practices, and we have the right to insist all of those who would live here do so as well. We don't <u>have</u> to take in any immigrants who won't add to this nation. No other nation has dealt as charitably with systematic waves of immigration as our nation has done.

If you were a normal person with a reasonable sense of decency and humor, the chapter of stories in this book would have made you laugh, broken your heart, and given you some food for thought.

You got the point that immigrants in the Ellis Island era were a decent class of people. You also got it that the agents whose job it was to enforce immigration laws in the Ellis Island era were by and large reasonable and dedicated. Most agents covered in this book thought about people, America, and God, instead of careerism.

They cared about the safety of immigrants, about their ability to make their way in this country, and about their spiritual needs. They did not on the whole exclude aliens from America arbitrarily. And if their methods were paternalistic, Christian, and America-centric, so be it. That was who they were and what they did. And it worked fabulously.

They also cared about serving the people of America. They tried to keep out those who would pose a burden, an unfair competition, or a safety threat to Americans. They tried to include people as often as they could, as the 98 percent admission rate shows. They were not mean people, but conscientious and decent people.

Numbers don't lie. The chapter titled "The Truth About Ellis Island" shows how few people the agents turned away and how hard they tried to make a necessary process like immigrant screening decent as well as efficient and thorough.

There is a reason there is nothing like Ellis Island today. Those who come here legally get inspected and approved overseas. There is no real "quality control" or screening like there used to be at Ellis Island and other immigration stations in America, when the political leaders of this country were more responsive to the American people. State Department and Homeland Security people allow many spies, saboteurs, wage scale breakers, and other undesirables into America legally. That doesn't count the millions who come in illegally across the Mexican and Canadian borders, or the millions who fly here on visas, then overstay their visas, like some of the 9/11 murderers. Other 9/11 murderers got in "legally" when Middle Eastern bureaucrats falsely vouched for them or our bureaucrats wrongly let them in.

Due to the moral failings and psychological disorders of those in charge (yes, compulsive lying and power grabbing, self-aggrandizement and narcissism are objectively disordered behaviors), we could never have immigration stations like Ellis Island today.

If there was an Ellis Island today, having a government-sponsored Christmas festival would never happen. It would be in violation of the sacrosanct concept of separation of church and state according to the gospel of the ACLU and militant atheists. Likewise, there would be no tolerance for the missionaries at an Ellis Island of today.

And how could a government today allow the culturally hegemonistic kindergarten on Ellis Island, whose insensitive teachers taught our "diversity detainees" in English and frankly intended to assimilate the young children of the immigrants? How <u>dared</u> they?

And the paternalism the commissioners at Ellis Island ordered in protecting women and girls would be grounds for dismissal today. After all, the attitude underlying the actions of men like William Williams and Henry Curran would be undeniably sexism and chauvinistic piggery, according to radical feminists and executives of the sex trade in this country today.

Oh, the humanity!

William Williams would never see civil service today. Most of us who call ourselves adults are too immature to hear someone like Williams bluntly telling us our shortcomings from a position of moral authority as well as organizational authority. Government employee unions would target a man like Williams, who dared to demand people do their jobs and not cheat or exploit people or get fired.

Humorous Henry Curran would be in hot water also. Prune-faced politicians, paper-pushers, and pundits with no sense of humor or humanity would gripe that he "doesn't take governance seriously" and "lacks gravitas" or some other similar catchphrase of jargon that means the person who said it is a functionary without originality or a sense of independent thought.

Ludmilla Foxlee, as a private social worker in today's politically correct society, would be out of the picture also. She wouldn't be very welcome on a government facility as a non-government worker. And besides, who did she think she was to protect girls and young women from predator males, or express disgust at the sexual behavior of some of the more liberated females who came through Ellis Island on her watch?

In today's atmosphere of tolerance, Edward Corsi, Maud Mosher, and Sven Smith would be unemployable as civil servants. Certainly Maud Mosher's remarks about the Jews in steerage were biased. Inspector Sven Smith's remark about Italians, Slovaks and Poles was not kind, either. (As a man of Slavic descent, I have a personal reason for not wanting to hear such prejudice coming out of a civil servant.) And no public servant today could say the things about the Chinese that Commissioner Edward Corsi said so matter-of-factly in the 1930s. Bear in mind Sven and Corsi were themselves immigrants, and yet they held these sentiments like many natives of America did.

Believe it or not, when your ancestors elected leaders, they expected them to hire people like Williams, Curran, and the others. They wanted America's interests protected, and they wanted decency shown to the immigrants.

In the Ellis Island era, our agents got little co-operation from foreign governments. Foreign politicians who wanted to get rid of people falsified their records or falsely certified them. They lied about the backgrounds of spies they sent here. Immigration agents at Ellis Island and other American immigration stations worked hard to determine the truth about would-be immigrants. They had to – the American people demanded it.

A test of a person's character is whether he or she does the right thing despite his or her prejudices or financial or personal interests. Abraham Lincoln was prejudiced against blacks, but he eventually decided he would do the right thing and end slavery. It would cost Honest Abe his life. Likewise, men like Williams and Sven Smith and Corsi suppressed their prejudices and did their duty. They passed this character test.

Maud Mosher, despite her prejudices, performed actions and expressed thoughts that showed she had a basically kind heart, and also a sense of duty. She wanted good people to come to America. She trembled for the future of America if enough low-quality immigrants were to bring the country down. Yet her heart still went out to people in need. And she did not exclude people for trivial matters. This shows a nobility of purpose in her that enabled her to do the right thing.

She, Ludmilla Foxlee, and the others whose stories are in this book tried to do what is right. They tried to serve the American public and help immigrants. They weren't officious department chiefs or time-serving loafers.

Politicians today do not necessarily run immigration for the benefit of the people of this country. They run immigration for the benefit of their business donors who want cheap labor, and for their own perceived benefit of getting votes. Instead of men like William Williams and Henry Curran running things, there is a steady stream of careerist bureaucrats who help the politicians thwart the will of the people.

The fear of running into trouble on the job no doubt prevents many an immigration agent from making an arrest he should make. The fear of running into trouble on the job prevents many an immigration employee from ensuring all checks are properly done on visa applicants when a supervisor screams she's not working fast enough.

The 9/11 Commission report "Entry of the 9/11 Hijackers into the United States" noted business, government, and college educator pressures led immigration officials to soften the immigration entry inspection process, the overstay tracking process, and the student tracking process.

The results? The 9/11 hijackers got in when Middle Eastern bureaucrats falsely vouched for them and our bureaucrats and agents wrongly let them in. They also were able to stay because immigration agents didn't screen them properly in America and American law enforcement agents did not track them down after they violated immigration laws. This laxity was in large part the result of top-down pressure from government officials, college officials, and corporate interests. Thanks to these meddlers, the hijackers were able to murder 3000 Americans on 9/11.

Not counting the 9/11 murders, aliens murder roughly 4400 Americans a year, kill another 4700 or so Americans a year due to acts of negligent homicide, and rape tens of thousands of American girls and young women yearly. In the Ellis Island Era, those statistics would have provoked wholesale vigilante activity by the American public.

Most of the Asian and Middle Eastern aliens who have committed crimes in this country came here legally. By comparison, most Latin American-born criminals are illegals. This points to a flaw in our immigration screening processes. It also points to flaws in the Asian and Middle Eastern governments whose agents falsely certify these people. And it points to flaws in our politicians' desires to secure our borders.

What would immigration today look like if immigrants had to meet Ellis Island standards? If the Ellis Island yardstick was used on immigrants today, many of them would not measure up.

Any immigrant unwilling or unable to earn a living would be barred or deported. Immigrants would not be able to daisy-chain in elderly relatives and ask the American taxpayers to give them benefits.

Illegal entry would earn millions of illegals a trip home.

Criminal conduct would force deportation of hundreds of thousands of other immigrants. Not only street crime, but white collar crime, industrial espionage and other espionage would send criminals home.

The ban on most immigrants with labor contracts would drastically drop the number of immigrants looking to displace Americans in the technical fields at lower wages and lower skills.

The ban on polygamy would ban Moslems and others who practice this relic of barbarism.

Enforcing "inimical (hostile or harmful) attitude" laws would ban a very large number of people from the Middle East and a large proportion of other Asians. It would also ban other aliens who disagree with American institutions and are unwilling to adjust to them.

Ellis Island Era officials made sponsors and others put up bonds of up to thousands of dollars apiece for questionable immigrants whose causes they advocated. Applying that law to today and adjusting for inflation to as much as $40,000 per bond could stop many immigration advocacy groups and businesses from bringing in so many questionable immigrants.

Millions of European immigrants had to play by these rules I just outlined. The American public in the Ellis Island Era demanded they do so. They are still fair and reasonable standards for today.

Likewise, the example of men like William Williams and Henry Curran and of women like Maud Mosher and Ludmilla Foxlee would make most of today's government employees look like mental and moral midgets.

Maud Mosher recalled an incident in which she found an immigrant teenage girl weeping on a street in the Battery area of Manhattan, obviously lost, while she was off-duty. She contacted an immigration aid society of the girl's ethnicity, took her there, and waited with her until her people could be located. They were frantic, because they were aware of the dangers the white slavers posed in New York City.

Technically, Maud was not supposed to intervene with immigrants while off-duty, but she did so out of basic charity. She wrote about this episode the following:

"That was the first time I thought of myself as an American citizen since I had taken the oath of office ... (what I had done) seemed to be a terrible crime against Red Tape ... People employed in the government service forget after a while that they are American citizens. Perhaps they do not so much forget as they get out of the habit of thinking themselves as real loyal American citizens with rights of thought, the right to do good, the right to speak at the right time, the right to tell the truth, rights of conscience and loyalty and citizenship. (Some officials and employees) bow to the master Red Tape so completely that they forget that to serve this master (the government) is not always to serve their country nor to serve their God."

I believe most of us would like more civil servants like Maud and fewer of those whose salaries we pay today.

Notre Dame coach and World War Two veteran Frank Leahy said after World War Two, "All of the things that go together to make this country great must be continually defended from any attack." He listed faith in God, hard work, democracy, competitiveness, and the American Spirit (the can-do attitude we as a people used to have), as the things that made America the finest nation on earth.

We need to heed Frank Leahy's advice. We also need to heed the example of our ancestors, who came across the ocean in an open boat or a wooden sailing ship, or a barbaric slave ship, or in a beat-up steamer in steerage class, and built up this country. Likewise, we need to heed the example of our ancestors who descended from those who threw their lot in with this country (or were forced to) and who worked to provide us with the wonderful nation we enjoy today.

We should be grateful for the advances in safety and pay and liberty these people won for us, and we should not look down on them because their book learning wasn't what ours is. We should seek to defend and improve what these people provided us. And we should live our lives in a way that would make them proud of us, and our descendants grateful to us.

Grandpa Charlie Sherlock, Granny Theresa Sherlock, and Uncle Chuck Sherlock home on leave from the U.S. Army during World War Two. God rest your souls!

Granny Ruth fixes the hair of a not-too-happy author. He can't write yet, but he can complain and fidget. God rest your soul, Granny Ruth!

CHILDREN FROM THE FAMILY TREE IN THE ELLIS ISLAND ERA

Top left: Grandpa Leo, standing, right, and his brother and sister, late 1890s, Illinois. His parents came from Ireland. Many parents in that era dressed babies like Popeye's adopted son Swee' Pea.

Top right: Granny Ruth, early 1900s. Is she sad because her Teddy looks dead? Teddy bears became popular toys because Teddy Roosevelt saved a bear cub. The day before her birthday, Ruth's grandfather, Bohumil Legro, the "love child" mentioned earlier in this book who came from Bohemia with his family, was murdered in his Chicago saloon by the Car Barn Bandits. A posse of armed farmers caught the punks, and Illinois lawmen hanged them within a couple of months of their trial. The U.S. has four times as many people as it did a century ago, and almost 80 times as many murders. Back then, most murderers were executed by the law, or by vigilantes if the government failed the people.

Left: Author's wife's "Aunt Silky" and friends prepare for First Holy Communion at their parish in Alabama. (She's the second girl from right.) Menfolk in Aunt Silky's family (including her brother, the author's wife's grandfather), like many Slovaks, came to America and worked in the mines. But the immigrants didn't leave faith in God behind, as this picture shows.

ELLIS ISLAND SCRAPBOOK

CHARLIE SHERLOCK came from Ireland through Ellis Island with his family in the first decade of the 1900s. They settled in Chicago. **Top left**: British troops burned the roof off of the tiny Catholic church in Islandeady Parish, County Mayo, Charlie's home parish, during their centuries-long oppression of the Irish. Religious and political persecution caused many Irish to come to America. **Top right:** Headline is wrong. Dad and older brother Uncle Chuck asked God to save their father Charlie's life. He was severely wounded while serving as a detective with the Chicago Police Department. Most people have no idea about the cost in blood many emergency workers pay to serve. **Below left:** Dapper detective Charlie Sherlock was well known to Chicago criminals and reporters. He was one of the first cops to arrest Jack McGurn, Al Capone's enforcer. He worked on the Leopold and Loeb murder case. Back in the day, policemen even in the big cities were known as people to the public. People cared more, and so did the media of that era. **Below right:** The fighting Irish. Grandpa Charlie holds up Dad's hand in victory after a back yard sparring match against another boy. The cameraman didn't get the other competitor in the picture. Granny Theresa and a family friend did make the photo op.

244   THE CLOSING OF THE SCRAPBOOK

WORLD WAR ONE – SUICIDE OF EUROPE

Top left: Relative of wife of author and fellow squad members. Many American units had men who were born in Europe or had parents born in Europe. Wife's relative was of Irish heritage. Author's great-uncle Emil was the son of German immigrants, but that didn't stop him from fighting against the Germans. **Bottom left:** An ancestor of wife of author and friend in Austria-Hungary's army. Although America was formally at war with Austria-Hungary, contact was basically limited to Fiorello La Guardia and other American pilots vs. Austria-Hungary's pilots on Italian front, and some Austria-Hungary artillerymen vs. U.S. Army units on the Western (French) front. Austria-Hungary's beefs were with Serbia and Italy and Russia. Austria-Hungary's emperor and empress sought an honorable end to the bloodshed but could not get the other countries' leaders to agree to stop the suicide of Europe. **Top right:** "Her Boy Too," by Cyrus Baldridge, sums up the gratitude many French wives and mothers and sisters and soldiers' fiancees showed to American soldiers who came to France's aid. Note the portrait of the kepi-wearing French soldier on the wall; the poor wooden-shoed woman's son was fighting for his country. French politicians and generals were ungrateful, but the average Jeannes who loved their France and whose loved ones were risking their lives for France appreciated the Americans. **Bottom right**: "Madonna of Sorrow," National Geographic, June 1917. A French woman and little girl mourn the death of a husband and father. Behind is a bombed-out church. The masses of people of a nation pay in blood and sorrow for the selfish adventures of their politicians, or (like in France and Poland's case) those of an invading country's ruling classes. Author's Grandpa Leo and great-uncle Emil fought in France; both suffered gassing that greatly harmed their health. Uncle Emil died as a relatively young man; Grandpa Leo would eventually lose most of his sight. Author's other grandfather, Grandpa Charlie, was in the U.S. Navy but never left the Great Lakes.

ELLIS ISLAND SCRAPBOOK

WORLD WAR TWO featured many of the sons and grandsons of the Ellis Island Era rescuing what was left of the Old World. So many of the bravest of Europe died in the World War One era that many of the fathers of the coming generation were at best lesser men. Europe hasn't been the same since. **Top:** Dad Sherlock (center) and fellow deck apes aboard the U.S.S. *Sargent Bay*, an escort carrier. They fought against the Japs in the Pacific Theater. **Right:** Parents of author's wife. Her father was a tanker who took part in the Battle of the Bulge. **Bottom left:** Liberation American Style. Pretty Czech woman is obviously happy to see General Patton and many thousands of his manly and handsome American subordinates as they liberate her part of Bohemia. "Old Blood and Guts" and his men could have saved more people; Eisenhower stopped them from going farther east. Ike's and FDR's blunders helped lead to the Soviet enslavement of Eastern Europe. **Bottom right:** Liberation or Home Invasion? Red Army men and/or Czech/Slovak Red "comrades" show collective concern for scared Slovak civilian. The first wave of Russian Army soldiers were usually well-disciplined, but those following them cheerfully looted Slavic towns and raped Slavic women. They later angrily looted German towns and raped German females in revenge. Civilian was an uncle of wife of author. Author and wife visited him in Slovakia a few years before his death. He had to ransom a relative forced to enlist in the Russian Army. He lost possessions when comradely Soviets "generously shared" Communism with Czechs and Slovaks.

Immigrants and their descendants helped crush Nazism and contain Communism. Are the immigrants of today doing their bit for the freedom of the Republic?

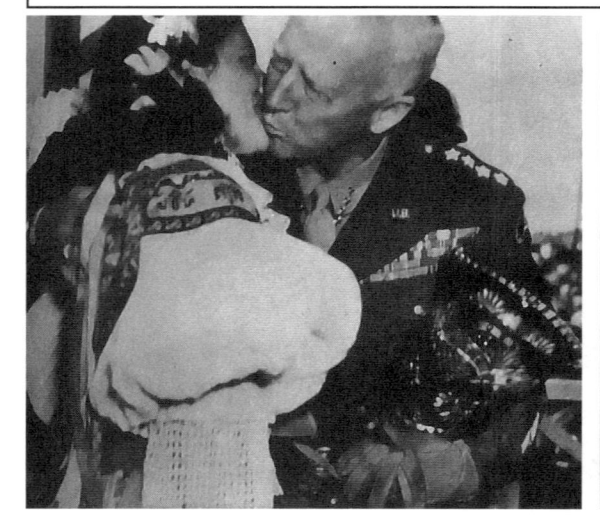

THE CLOSING OF THE SCRAPBOOK

INDEX

14th Amendment 84, 108, 154
9/11 . . . . 57, 239, 241

A Century of Dishonor 122
abortion 26, 28, 36, 39-41, 81
Acadia 43, 45, 46, 58
ACLU 38, 240
Alien Contract Labor Law 87-89, 135
Act of March 3, 1875 . . . . 86, 135
Act of March 3, 1891 . . . . 89, 109
Act of March 3, 1903 . . . . 95-97, 99, 100 110
Act of 1921 . . . . 148, 150, 154
Act of May 26, 1924 . . . . 148, 157
Adams, John 76
Adams, John Quincy 46
Addams, Jane 122
Alabama 34, 46, 195
Alaska 2, 29, 30, 33, 48, 52, 53, 68, 81, 111, 158
Albania 3, 13, 62, 67, 71
Alexander II (Russia) 12, 96
Alexander III (Russia) 12
Alexander VI (pope) 23
Alexandra (Tsaritsa of Russia) 27, 39
Alfano (criminal) 177
al-Qaeda 57
American Indians 2, 44, 50-52, 81, 119, 152
amnesty 154
anarchists 94-97, 127, 129, 134, 139, 148, 154, 170
Angel Island 109
Anglican 43, 182
anti-Catholic 22, 41, 46, 47, 55, 79, 83-85, 108, 178, 182, 231
Apache tribe 5
Arabs 107, 108, 155
Arabia 31, 63, 67, 232
Arapaho tribe 51
Argentina 13, 33, 34, 40, 52, 64, 65, 150
Arizona 37, 47, 50, 52, 54, 56, 58, 65, 86
Arkansas 24, 46, 54, 56
Armenia, Armenians 3, 23, 36, 62, 67, 71, 72,
107, 149, 161, 181, 220, 221
Ashbrook, Harriette 219
Asia 2, 29, 30, 61-63, 65, 71, 82, 109,
130, 135, 137, 149, 151, 155, 208, 231, 232
Asiatic Barred Zone 109, 149, 150, 208, 237
Assyrians 72
asylee 158
atheist 23, 38, 79
Augustus the Strong (Saxony) 25
Auschwitz 40
Australia, Australians . . 8, 14, 16, 29, 33, 38, 60-63, 109, 149, 231
Austria . . 3, 4, 11-14, 25, 26, 28, 30-32, 36, 39, 50, 60-64, 67,
69-71, 78, 82-83, 91, 93, 94, 96, 98-100, 104-106,
110, 147, 152, 155-156, 181, 184, 200-201, 213, 237
Austrian Society of New York 104, 105, 184
Aztecs 52

Baggage Room 128, 143
Balkan Wars 13, 70, 71
Balkans 2, 5, 9, 13, 23, 30, 35,
36, 61, 62, 70-71, 109, 113, 130, 170
Baltic lands and people 3, 4, 31-32, 35, 62, 63, 68, 120
Baltic (ship) 187, 188, 194
Baltimore (city) 79, 109
Baltimore, Lord 43
Barge Office 89, 92, 109, 121, 160, 169, 171,
173, 176, 180, 183, 210-212, 223
Bass, Sydney 231, 238
bastardy 28, 39
Bathory, Elizabeth (Blood Countess) 26, 39
Battery 83, 89, 92, 171-174, 187, 197, 210, 218, 241
Bavaria 2, 11, 25

Beaver Island 55, 81
Belarus, Belarusia 3, 4, 12, 23, 36, 67, 68, 156
Belgium, land and people . . 3, 4, 8, 12, 28, 31, 36, 53, 60-63,
66, 68, 78, 167-168, 181, 207, 218
Bell, Alexander Graham 34, 77
Bennett, John 55
Berkemeier, Pastor 183
Berlin Conference 31
Bessarabia 3, 71, 72
Bessemer, Henry 76
Big Foot (chief) 52
Billy Budd 111
Bismarck 13, 31
Blacks, aka African-Americans 31, 34, 35, 44, 45,47, 49,
52, 54, 55, 63, 84-86, 94, 102, 108,
111, 118, 147, 149, 151, 152, 217, 234, 240
blood atonement 57, 81
Bly, Nellie 122
board of special inquiry 90, 96, 99, 107, 123-124, 127,
131, 132, 138-142, 146, 163-166,
175, 177, 180, 184, 186, 193, 195, 231, 233
Boarding Division 123, 140
Bohemia 2, 12, 14, 70, 82, 217
Boleyn, Anne 25
Bolivia 52, 91
Borgia, Lucrezia 23
Bosnia, land and people 3, 4, 13, 67, 69-70, 213
Boxers (Chinese) 100
braceros 156, 158
Brandt, Karl 40
Brazil 33, 43, 52, 64, 65, 150
brides, murder of 23
Britain, British 1, 3, 4, 8-10, 12, 14, 16, 18-19, 21-27,
29-31, 33-39, 44-50, 52-53, 56, 58, 60-66, 73, 76, 79,
82-83, 87-89, 93, 96-99, 107, 111-113, 119-120, 137-139,
146-149, 151, 154-156, 158, 166-168, 172, 181-182, 186,
202, 206, 208-209, 211, 214, 229, 231-233, 237-238
British Empire 4, 29, 30, 82, 149, 151, 208, 232, 237
British navy 112, 147, 158
Brittany 24, 38
Brown, John (private) 208
Brown (Scottish equerry) 27
Brownsville "raid" 94, 110
Bryan, William Jennings 85
bubonic plague 125, 130, 134
Buck, Carrie 157, 158
Bukovina 3, 12, 36, 70-72
Bulgaria, Bulgarians . . 3, 13, 61-63, 67, 70-72, 181, 195, 237
Bunau-Varilla, Philippe 79, 80
Bushes (George) 85, 103

Cable, John 233
Cabrini, Mother 122, 178, 179, 226, 227
Cajuns 45
California 25, 33, 46-51, 56, 58, 62, 65, 66, 76,
80, 81, 83, 84, 86, 102, 153, 156, 158, 166, 182
Calvin, Calvinists 21-22, 37-38, 84, 148, 182
Caminetti, Anthony 222
Canada, Canadians . . 8, 13, 14, 29, 30, 33, 34, 43-47, 50-53,
58, 60-63, 65, 81-83, 87-91, 97-98, 102, 109,
111, 112, 126, 137, 138, 147, 149-151, 153-156, 159,
167, 176, 181, 182, 194, 207, 208,221, 231, 237, 239
Capone, Al 224
Caprivi, Count von 13, 14, 37
Captain Jack (chief) 51
Caribbean region 29-31, 43, 48, 79, 150, 202
Carnegie, Andrew 153
Carpathia (ship) 175
Carson, Kit 51
Carter, Jimmy 48, 80, 204, 235

ELLIS ISLAND SCRAPBOOK

Castle Garden 83, 88, 89, 92, 109,
　　　　　　121, 175, 209-211, 223, 239
Catholicism, Catholics 9-12, 16, 20-24, 28, 34, 36, 37-38,
　　　　　39-41, 44-47, 55, 57, 58, 63, 70, 77-79, 81-85, 100, 107, 108,
　　　　　122, 144, 151, 178, 179, 181, 182, 184, 218, 222, 226, 231
Carroll, Charles 79
Charles I (England) 25
Charles II (England) 22
Charles V (Holy Roman Emperor) 22, 26
Charles XII (Sweden) 25
Chen Chee 201, 202
Cherokee tribe 47
Cheyenne tribe 51
Chicago 1, 29, 30, 76, 109, 122,
　　　　　　152, 156, 159, 178, 179, 186, 197, 201, 205, 223, 224
Chicago Vice Commission 152
Chief Joseph 51
Chile 52, 65
China, Chinese 31, 34, 39, 50, 53, 58, 60-63, 80, 82,
　　　　　　83, 86, 87, 94, 100-102, 107, 109-112,
　　　　　　194-195, 135, 149, 151-152, 155-156, 176,194-195,
　　　　　　201-202, 205 208, 214, 215, 221, 227, 231, 237, 240
Chinese Exclusion Act 82, 87, 101, 109, 135, 149, 237
Chivington, J.M. 51
Choctaw tribe 47
cholera 90, 125, 130, 133
Churchill, Winston 158
Civil War, American 25, 29, 33-35, 41, 48-51, 56-58, 60,
　　　　　　65, 76, 84-86, 89, 108, 112-113, 121, 159, 182
Civil War, Russian 63, 68, 69, 233
Civil War, Spanish 37
Cleveland (city) 1, 213, 223
Cleveland, Grover 53, 85, 91
Castle Clinton 83
Clinton, Bill and/or Hillary . . 24-25, 80, 94, 96, 103, 138, 158
Cobh, Ireland 187
Cochise 52
Cold War 29, 156
Colombia 52, 79, 80
Colorado 36, 46, 47, 50, 51, 56, 58, 65, 178, 179
Columbus, Christopher 2, 22, 25
Communists 4, 27, 32, 62, 68, 108, 139, 154, 196
Compromise of 1850 48
Confederate Navy 112
Connecticut 187
Constantinople (Istanbul) . . 23, 30, 62, 63, 71, 155, 164, 185
contagious disease . 88, 90, 93, 96, 117, 122, 123, 125, 126,
　　　　　　130, 131, 133, 134, 137, 142, 145, 162, 237
contract labor 87-89, 108, 135, 136, 139, 161, 183
Coolidge, Calvin 148, 154
coolies 86, 101
Corsi, Edward 109, 138, 159, 172,
　　　　　　175-177,180, 187, 188, 190, 192-197,
　　　　　　200-202, 204-208, 212, 214, 215, 217, 218, 230, 240
Corsica 17, 213
Cortes, Hernando 52
COSCO 80
Costa Rica 80
Cotton, John 79
Cowen, Philip 99, 140
Crazy Horse 51
Creek tribe 46, 47
criminals, and screening of . . . 33, 41, 89, 97, 126, 127, 129,
　　　　　　137-139, 142, 143, 146, 177, 202, 234, 241
criminals, organized 57, 148
Crippen, Dr. 138, 146
Croatia, Croatians 3, 12, 26, 34, 36, 70, 73, 93, 213, 216
Crocker, Charles 50, 135
Cromwell, Oliver 10, 21, 44, 65
Cromwell, William 79
Crook, George 52
Cuba, Cubans 31, 48, 65, 85, 150, 155
Curran, Henry 96, 150, 153, 159, 164, 167, 168, 172,
　　　　　　192, 200, 204, 206, 226, 230, 233, 234, 240, 241
Custer, George 51

Cyprus 3, 29
Cyrano de Bergerac 27
Czechs, Czech lands 3, 9, 14, 29, 36, 37, 39,
　　　　　　69, 91, 155, 159, 229
Czolgosz, Leon 94, 95

Dalmatia 12, 70, 82
Damien, Father (Joseph De Veuster) 53, 54, 66, 81
D'Arcy (agent) 176
Davies, Joseph 196
Davis, James 233
Davis, Jefferson 51
Dawes Act 108, 154, 158
Decatur, Stephen 3
Delaware 30, 43, 47, 58, 200
Denmark, Danes 3, 4, 10, 11, 14, 28, 31, 36, 48,
　　　　　　60-63, 66, 73, 154, 155, 181, 223
deportation 47, 57-58, 73, 89-91, 93, 97, 99, 100, 106,
　　　　　　107, 121, 123-124, 126-128, 130-133, 135-136,
　　　　　　139-142, 154-156, 161, 163-174, 177, 181-182,
　　　　　　186, 190, 192, 194-195, 197, 203-204, 207-209,
　　　　　　215- 216, 221-222, 226-227, 231-232, 234, 237, 241
Deportation Division 124, 142, 173, 174
Deporting Division 142
detention 91, 92, 125, 132, 133, 139,
　　　　　　142, 146, 161-163, 175, 176, 180, 181, 190,
　　　　　　192-195, 197, 204, 205, 211, 212, 220, 221, 233
Detroit 1, 81, 109, 196, 201, 207
Dillingham Commission 106, 108, 110, 113
diphtheria 125, 130, 133
Discharging Division 124, 142, 215
Dole, Sanford 53
Don Juan of Austria 26
Doty, Alvah 125, 145, 232
Douglass, Frederick 94, 176
Drake, Edwin 77
Durocher, Leo 225
Dutch 4, 28, 31, 43-45, 66, 79, 85,
　　　　　　111, 113, 119, 181, 200, 214, 219

Earhart, Amelia 109
Eastern Europe 5, 9, 23, 27, 60, 61, 67, 68, 91,
　　　　　　107, 136, 143, 148, 149, 151, 153, 155, 156
Ecuador 52
Edison, Thomas 77
Edmunds Act 57
Edward VII (England) 26
Egypt 29, 164, 217
Eisenhower, Dwight 156, 157, 181, 204
El Paso 109
Ernst, Sigi 27
Ness, Eliot 66
Elisabeth (Empress "Sissi", Austria-Hungary) 26, 96
Elizabeth I (England) 10, 25, 44
Ellis Island 1, 2, 19-22, 33, 35-36, 43, 60-61, 65, 67,
　　　　　　72-73, 78, 81, 83, 88-89, 91-96, 98-100, 103-106,
　　　　　　108-110, 113, 119-127, 129-147, 150, 153-154,
　　　　　　156-157, 159-168, 170-178, 180-184, 187-198,
　　　　　　200, 201, 203-220, 222-223, 226-227, 229-241
England, English . 3, 10, 22, 24-25, 27-28, 30, 31, 34,36-38, 43-46,
　　　　　　52, 61, 64-65, 76, 79, 83, 98, 111, 112, 116, 136, 137,
　　　　　　138, 144, 154, 159, 161, 170-172, 174, 180-182, 187-189,
　　　　　　190, 197, 201, 206, 209, 220-222, 224-226, 230, 233, 238, 240
Erie Canal 83, 111, 121
Eskimos (Inuit) 52, 53, 119
Essex (Elizabeth I's courtier) 26
Estonia 3, 4, 12, 63, 66-69, 156, 182
Ethiopia 30, 31
Evans, Oliver 76
exclusion 55, 82, 87, 96, 99, 101, 102, 104,106-109,
　　　　　　128, 131, 135-136, 140, 149, 193, 194, 236-237, 239, 240

Fancher, Burr 81
farmers 8, 10, 12-14, 33, 166, 188, 215, 221
Fatima Osmar 217

favus	97, 125, 128, 130, 133, 162
feeble-minded	99, 122, 127, 132, 152, 157, 221, 236
Fenian Raid	50
Fernando of Aragon (King of Spain)	22, 23, 25
Field, Cyrus	34, 77
Filipinos	85, 86
Fillmore, Millard	48, 84, 85
Finland, Finnish	3, 4, 11, 36, 63, 66-69, 73, 152, 155, 171, 181, 220, 226
Fitchie, Thomas	92, 93, 95, 110, 176
Florida	1, 43, 45-47, 52, 65, 182
Ford, Henry	196
Foxlee, Ludmilla	159, 190, 193, 195, 196, 213, 216, 218, 222, 240, 241
France, French	1, 3-5, 8, 12, 14, 16, 18, 20, 22-25, 27-31, 34-40, 43-46, 50, 52, 58, 60-65, 71, 73, 78-81, 84, 96, 111-113, 138, 139, 147-149, 154-155, 159, 164, 177, 181-182, 184, 186, 190, 203, 216, 225, 226, 234, 237
Franz Ferdinand (Austria-Hungary)	31, 39
Franz Josef (Austria-Hungary)	26, 39, 50, 67, 78
Franklin, Benjamin	46, 79
Frederick the Great (Prussia)	25
French Canadians	44, 81, 159
French Revolution	3, 5, 23, 24, 30, 58
Fugitive Slave Act	48
Fulton, Robert	76
Gadsden Purchase	47, 58, 65
Galicia	2, 3, 12, 36, 66, 67, 69, 82, 220
Gamble, Clarence	152
Garfield, James	85
Garibaldi, Giuseppe; Garibaldi Guard	34, 41
gatemen	123
Geddes, Auckland	233, 238
Geneva, Switzerland	22, 38
Gentlemen's Agreement	102, 107, 109, 149
Georgia (state)	44, 46-47
Georgia (country)	3, 23, 36, 67, 181
Gerard, James	7, 19, 36
Germany, Germans	3-4, 7-8, 10-11, 13, 14, 19-22, 27-32, 34-37, 39-41, 45, 58, 60-64, 67-68, 70, 73, 77-78, 84, 91, 93, 98-99, 105, 108, 111-113, 119, 137, 139, 147, 151, 153-156, 158, 161, 164, 166, 169, 171, 175, 183, 190, 193, 195, 204, 213-215, 219, 220, 222, 226-227, 229, 231, 237
German Empire	70
Geronimo	52
Gibbons, James (cardinal)	39, 79
Gibbons, Jenny	37
Giraud, Marie Louise	40
Goeldi, Anna	22, 38
Gold, Annie	203
gold rushes	30, 33, 47, 49, 53, 58, 66, 84, 86
Goodyear, Charles	77
Grant, Ulysses	50, 56, 85, 86
Great Hunger (Irish Potato Famine)	37, 58, 64, 84, 99
Great Lakes	43, 46, 58, 83, 91, 111, 121, 182
Great White Fleet	102
Greece, Greeks	3, 13, 23, 24, 61-63, 67, 70, 71, 73, 104, 107, 110, 147, 151, 155, 158, 164, 175, 181, 197, 202, 205
Greenland	31, 43
Guam	149
guild	19
Gypsies	143, 170, 175, 214, 227
Haiti, Haitians	45, 58, 65
Hammer, Armand	196
Hanoverian dynasty	26
Hapsburg, Otto von	78
Hapsburg dynasty	4, 11, 12, 22, 26, 37, 39, 50, 69, 71, 78, 82
Harding, Warren	148, 233
Hart, Alfred	172
Harriman, E. H.	153
Harrison, Benjamin	85
Harrison, William Henry	3
Hawaii, Hawaiians	2, 29, 43, 48, 53, 66, 81, 85, 86, 102, 111
Hayes, Rutherford	85
Henry VIII (England)	10, 25, 26, 44
Hercegovina	3, 4, 13, 70, 213
Hermogen of Saratov	27
hijackers	241
Hildebrandt, Richard	40
Hindus	23, 36, 38, 221
Hispaniola	65
Hitler	28, 30, 39, 40, 78, 155
Hoffman Island	125, 130, 134, 145
Hohenzollern dynasty	26
Hoke, George	189
homestead	34, 49, 121
Homestead Act	49
Homestead Steel strike	121
Honduras	29
Hong Kong	29, 202
Hoover, Herbert	158, 182
Hopkins, Mark	50
Horseshoe Bend	46
Horn, Cathy	145
Howard, Catherine	26
Howe, Frederick	206, 230, 232
Hull, Harry	154
Hull House	122
Hull, Isaac	3
human sacrifice	23
Hundred Years War	30
Hungary, Hungarians	3, 7, 11-12, 14, 26, 28, 30-32, 34, 36, 39, 60-64, 67, 69-73, 78, 82, 93-94, 96, 98-100, 145, 147, 152, 156, 165, 168, 174, 181, 188-189, 195, 203, 237
Huntington, Collis	50
Husband, W.W.	167
Iceland	4, 31
Idaho	47, 50, 51, 56, 83
"idiot"	207, 227
illegal	7, 16, 18, 28, 33, 40, 63, 65, 85-88, 96-99, 108 111, 119, 135, 137, 144, 154, 156, 194, 227, 241
Illinois	46, 47, 55, 76, 121, 159, 190, 200
illiterate	18, 108, 135, 150, 155, 156, 236
"imbecile"	152
immigrant aid society	95, 181, 186
immigrant home	104, 183, 184
immigration act	106, 110, 148-150, 153, 157, 237
Immigration Act of 1917	149, 150
Immigration Act of 1924	110, 148, 150, 153, 237
immigration station	1, 83, 88, 89, 91-93, 97, 109, 121, 123, 124, 141, 145-147, 150, 156, 170, 171, 176, 181, 204, 208, 223, 233, 235
impressment	111
indentured servant	32, 86
India	2, 23, 29-31, 38, 57, 82, 149, 221
Indian Citizenship Act	84, 108, 154, 158
Indian subcontinent	23, 62, 107, 109, 149, 208, 231, 232
Indian Territory (Oklahoma)	45, 47, 52, 53
Indiana	46, 151, 187
Industrial Revolution	10, 19, 20, 33, 76, 239
Information Division	124, 142, 180
"inimical"	88, 154, 241
Inquisition	21, 22, 37, 38
"insane"	50, 96, 108, 122, 127, 132-134, 169, 174, 185, 197, 203, 236
"Insane Pavilion"	133
Inuit (Eskimo)	2, 52, 111, 119
Iowa	46, 47, 207
Iran	31, 149, 235
Iraq	3, 31, 63, 67, 107, 149
Ireland, the Irish	1, 3, 4, 8, 12, 14, 21-22, 23, 27-29, 31-32, 34-38, 44-45, 47, 50, 55, 58, 60-66, 72, 73, 83-85, 91-92, 94, 99, 108, 111-112, 137, 138, 146-147, 149, 154-155, 159-160, 172, 175, 181-182, 187-188, 194, 199, 206, 210, 212, 215, 223-224, 226-227, 230-231, 239
Isabella I of Castile (Queen of Spain)	22, 23, 25, 38, 44
Isabella II (Spain)	25, 26

ELLIS ISLAND SCRAPBOOK 249

Israel	3, 31, 55, 63, 107, 149
Italian Brides	166
Italy, Italians	3, 4, 11, 13, 20, 23, 26, 28, 31, 34-37, 60-64, 72-73, 78, 91, 93, 94, 96, 98, 100, 102, 107, 113, 122, 136, 138, 143-144, 147-148, 151-153, 155, 156, 159, 161, 166, 171-172, 175-178, 180, 189, 190, 197-199, 201, 203, 205, 211-214, 217, 219-222, 224, 226, 230
Jack the Ripper	28
Jackson, Andrew	3, 34, 35, 45-47, 58
Jackson, Helen Hunt	122
Jackson, Sheldon	53, 81
Jamaica	29, 65, 202
James I (England)	25, 44
Japan, the Japanese	30-31, 39, 48, 53, 61-63, 82, 85-86, 94, 99-102, 107, 109, 110, 112, 149, 155-156, 201
Jefferson, Thomas	46
Jesuits	44
Jews	2, 10, 12, 21-23, 31, 32, 34, 37-38, 40, 43, 57, 60-62, 66-69, 71-73, 77-78, 91, 94, 96, 99-100, 119-120, 130, 135, 140, 143-144, 148,-149, 151-153, 155, 161-163, 173, 181-182, 188, 195, 200, 202-203, 219, 221-222, 226-227, 235 240
jihadists	57, 146
"Jim Crow" (anti-black laws)	34, 95
Joan of Arc	22, 30
John Paul II (pope)	29
Jones, John Paul	25
John XXIII (pope)	23
Johnson, Andrew	48, 50, 56, 85
Johnson, Lyndon	80, 108, 138, 157, 204
Johnson, Mary	164, 165
Joseph II (Austrian Empire)	11, 12
Juárez, Benito	50
Kaiser Wilhelm II (ship)	183, 189, 190
Kansas	38, 46-50, 58, 65, 81, 158, 159, 185, 188
Kelly, William	76
Kennedy, John	157, 204
Kennedy, Teddy	108
Kentucky	46, 214
Kirkland, Lane	29
"Kissing Gate" or "Kissing Post"	145, 193, 203, 227
Kissinger, Henry	80
Know-Nothings (movement)	84
Koch, Robert	77
Kohn, Regina	168
Kosciuszko, Tadeusz	67
Kossuth, Lajos	11
Ku Klux Klan	34, 85, 151, 153, 157, 182
Kuklis, John	198
La Guardia, Fiorello	93, 110, 135, 136, 159, 192
labor union	101, 103
Lafayette, Marquis de	25
Lafitte, Jean	3
Latin America	3, 11, 16, 22, 30, 33, 34, 44, 45, 52, 61, 64, 65, 73, 82, 112, 135, 150, 151, 181
Latvia	3, 4, 12, 63, 67, 68, 156, 196
Laughlin, Harry	153, 157, 158
League of Nations	148, 237
Leahy, Frank	224, 242
Lebanon, Lebanese	3, 31, 61-63, 67, 71-72, 107, 149, 175, 181
Lee, Harry (Chinese)	215
Lee, John	56, 57
Lee, Robert E.	50
Lee, Thomas (inspector)	161
legal inspection	129, 132, 134
Leo XIII (pope)	20, 178
Lepanto (sea battle)	26
leprosy	54, 66, 130, 134
Liliuokulani (queen of Hawaii)	48, 53
Lincoln, Abraham	34, 48-51, 56, 85, 94, 226, 240
Lind, Jenny	83, 89, 210, 223
Lindbergh, Charles	66
Lister, Joseph	77
literacy	34, 90, 108, 234, 236
Lithuania, Lithuanians	3, 4, 12, 23, 25, 63, 67-68, 156, 181, 195, 220, 226
Little Big Horn	51
loathsome disease	96, 122, 131, 154, 196, 237
Lombardy	2, 3, 178
Los Angeles	1, 81, 109, 178
Louis XIV (France)	25, 30
Louis XVI (France)	23, 58
Louisiana	43, 45, 46, 54, 58, 65, 83, 182, 214
Ludwig I (Bavaria)	25
Lusitania (ship)	62, 113
Luther, Lutherans	20-22, 28, 37, 66, 182, 183
Luxembourg	22
Macedonia	3, 4, 13, 31, 62, 70, 71, 181, 213
Mackinac Island	55
Maine	46, 218
manifest, ship	125-127, 134, 146, 160, 161, 219
manifest destiny	22, 43, 53
Mann, Horace	41
Mann Act	108
Mannix, Daniel	27, 94
Marconi, Guglielmo	34, 77
Maria Theresa	25
Marie (Queen of Romania)	25
Marie Antoinette (France)	25
Marie-Astrid of Luxembourg	22
Marine Hospital	89, 92, 125
Martocci, Frank	144, 159, 175, 177, 180, 188, 193, 196, 197, 205, 230
Mary Queen of Scots	26
Maryland	30, 43, 79
Massachusetts	22, 41, 43, 79, 84, 98, 182, 207, 225
matrons	79, 105, 129, 134, 159, 161, 169, 174, 184, 190, 194, 199, 203, 204, 215, 217, 227
McCarran, Patrick	87
McCormick, Cyrus	76
McHaney, James	40
McKinley, William	48, 53, 85, 92-96, 101, 110
McSweeney, Edward	92, 93, 95, 110
measles	125, 129, 130, 133, 175
Mengele	40
"mental ward"	132, 133
mestizo	22
métis	44
Mexican Cession	65
Mexican War	47, 49, 55, 58, 65, 67, 76, 83, 84, 182
Mexico, Mexicans	1, 43-45, 47-50, 52, 54-55, 58, 60-63, 65-67, 76, 83-84, 86, 88-89, 91, 97, 102, 109, 147, 150, 153, 155-156, 181-182, 186, 207, 237, 239
Miami tribe	46, 47
Michigan	46, 55, 187, 188, 193, 201
Middle East	24, 31, 130, 135, 143, 149, 241
Miles, Nelson	52
miners	14, 15, 98, 103, 167, 216
Minnesota	29, 46-48, 50, 51, 76, 83, 160, 169
Mississippi	43, 45-47, 54, 58, 182
Missouri	38, 46, 49, 54, 55, 81, 157
Modoc tribe	51
Mohamet Nur	217
Moldova	3, 12, 36, 63, 67, 71, 72, 173, 181
Mongolia	149
Monroe Doctrine	30, 50
Montana	46, 47, 50, 51, 83
Montenegro	2-4, 13, 61, 62, 67, 70, 181, 195, 213
Montez, Lola	25, 89
Moore, Annie	91, 160, 226
moral turpitude	96, 99, 122, 154, 172, 174, 186
Moravia	12, 70, 91
Mormons	49, 55-57, 81
Morocco	3, 23, 30, 31
"moron"	152
Moreno, Barry	110, 204, 222
Morrill Act	49

Morse, Samuel 34, 77, 83
Mosher, Maud 159, 169, 184-186, 189, 191,
    192, 194, 198, 203, 212, 213, 215-219, 226, 240, 241
Moslems 3, 9, 21-23, 36, 57
    69, 72, 85, 86, 106-107, 146, 149, 151
Mountain Meadows Massacre 56, 57, 81
Mullan, Dr. 128-129, 131-132
Murray, Joseph 95, 98
Mussolini 23, 39, 138, 146, 155

Napoleon 3, 11, 12, 24, 25, 30, 37, 38, 46, 50, 58
Napoleon III 50
naturalization law 83
Nazis 4, 28, 32, 35, 38, 40, 41, 68, 78, 152-155
Nebraska 46, 50, 158
"Negro Project" 152, 157
net immigration 64, 72
Netherlands 4, 12, 31, 36, 60-63, 79, 155
Nevada 33, 47, 49, 50, 56, 58, 65, 66, 135, 160, 216
New England . 30, 43, 44, 46, 61, 65, 76, 79, 111, 144, 161, 187
New Jersey 28, 30, 44, 58, 76, 91, 98,
    103, 143, 166, 175-177, 183, 200
New Mexico 1, 43, 47, 48, 50, 54, 58, 65, 86, 182
New Orleans 1, 46, 50, 58, 109, 165, 178
New York 1, 25, 30, 34, 41, 43, 44, 55, 66, 76, 83,
    88, 89, 91-95, 98, 103-106, 109-111, 117-119,
    121, 123-125, 130, 133-135, 137, 138, 140-146,
    149-152, 157, 159-178, 180, 181, 183, 184,
    187-190, 192-201, 203, 204, 207-210, 212, 214,
    215, 221-223, 225, 227, 230-233, 236, 238, 241
New Zealand 29, 60-63, 109, 149, 231
Nez Percé tribe 51, 108
Nicaragua 79
Nixon, Richard 110, 138, 204
North Carolina 43
North Dakota 46, 47, 50, 94, 195
Norway, Norwegians 4, 6, 11, 28, 36, 58, 60-63,
    66, 73, 154, 155, 159, 169-170, 181, 187, 223-224
Notre Dame 159, 223, 224, 242
Nuremberg trials 40
nurses 152, 153, 156, 195

O'Donnell, Roger 140, 145, 146
O'Donnoghue, George 202
Oakley, Annie 51
Obama, Barack 103
Ohio . . 20-21, 43, 46, 58, 151, 165, 172, 193, 213, 218, 224, 232
Oklahoma, "Okies" 45-47, 52, 54, 58, 65, 156, 189
"Old World Beauties" 188
Omaha, Nebraska 50, 198
Ontario 46, 50, 150, 200
Oregon 37, 46-48, 51, 79, 83, 151
Orthodox Christians 2, 9-10, 13, 20, 23, 27, 53,
    57, 68, 70, 72, 107, 181-182, 222, 233
Ottoman Empire 23, 32, 63, 67, 71, 107, 109

Pacific Islands 109
Paiute tribe 51
Pakistan 23, 29, 38, 149
Panama, Panama Canal 48, 79-80, 102, 112, 118
Paraguay 52
Patricios 47
Pasteur, Louis 77
pauper 103, 104, 129, 135, 136, 210
Pennsylvania 30, 43, 76, 77, 92,
    98, 121, 167, 200, 201, 214, 231
Perry, Oliver 3
Peru 52, 65
Peter the Great 25
Petiot, Marcel 40
Petrosino (lawman) 177
Philippines 30, 31, 48, 85, 109, 149
Pius XII (pope) 23, 155, 158
Plessy v. Ferguson 57, 102
pneumonia 130, 133, 194

Pocahontas 44, 79
pogrom 21, 22, 173
Poland, Poles . . 2-4, 12, 14, 23, 26-27, 35-36, 45, 60-63, 66-69,
    73, 94, 99, 104, 105, 118, 147, 151, 153, 156, 167-168, 170,
    174, 181, 184-185, 190, 194-195, 217, 220-222, 226-227
Polish Immigration Home 184
Polk, James 47
polygamy 55-57, 96, 241
Polynesians 119
Portugal, Portuguese . . . 3, 11, 22, 31, 34-36, 37, 43, 60-63,
    65, 73, 78, 82, 155, 181, 197, 207
Potato Famine (Great Hunger) 58, 84
Powderly, Terence 92, 95, 110
pregnancy 24, 26, 29, 33, 36, 40, 55, 129, 130, 157, 185, 186
Presbyterians 22, 45
Presidio (San Francisco) 158
primary inspection 123, 129, 134, 135, 137
Prince Albert (England) 27
Prince Charles (England) 22, 26
Princess Diana (England) 22
Princess Stephanie (Austria-Hungary) 26
Progressives 4, 118, 147
Prohibition 147, 148
Prokupek, Miss (matron) 210
prostitutes, prostitution . 27, 31, 51-53, 86, 96, 100, 122, 126,
    134, 139, 143-144, 148, 169, 174, 186 237
Protestantism, Protestants . . . 9-10, 19-23, 26, 34, 37-38, 41,
    43-45, 53-58, 79, 83-84, 100, 107, 144, 180, 182, 222, 232
Prussia 3, 4, 10-12, 25, 26, 28
public charge 90, 96, 97, 99, 103, 104, 122, 126,
    127, 135, 136, 139, 141, 154, 166, 169, 176, 186, 194, 231
Puerto Rico 31, 48, 65, 85
Pullman car 121
Puritanism, Puritans 22, 40, 79

quarantine 93, 125, 130, 133, 134, 142,
    145, 161, 163, 164, 172, 209
Quarantine Hospital 125, 130, 133, 134, 142, 145
Quebec 43, 45, 46, 50, 79, 109, 150, 159, 176, 181, 207
Quebec Act 79
<u>Quo Vadis</u> 27
quota 62, 70, 91, 107, 148-151,
    154, 164, 166-168, 171, 196, 209, 211, 217, 236, 237
Quota Act 148, 150, 154

Race and Settlement Main Office 40
race riots 148, 151
<u>Ramona</u> 122
Rasputin 27
Reagan, Ronald 29, 157, 204
Red Scare 147
<u>Red Sea</u> (ship) 161-163, 226
refugees 78, 155, 158
Registry Division 123, 140
Reno, Janet 80
Revere, Paul 58
revolution 22, 1, 3-5, 10, 12, 19, 20, 23-25, 30, 33,
    35, 39, 45, 46, 49, 58, 63, 68, 76, 79, 83, 111, 137, 239
Revolutionary War 83, 111, 182
robber baron 103, 135
Robespierre 23, 38
Rockne, Knute 66, 223, 224
Rolfe, John 44
Romania, Romanians . 3, 13, 61-63, 67, 69, 71, 72, 156, 181
Roosevelt, Franklin 95, 102, 138, 155
Roosevelt, Theodore . . . 1, 30, 35, 48, 53, 61, 79, 80, 82, 85,
    94-96, 98-99, 101-103, 106-108, 110, 112,
    119, 121, 139, 159, 164, 204, 231-232, 238
Rudolf (Hapsburg crown prince) 26
Rudnyansky, Gyula 165
Ruef, Abe 101, 102
RuSHA 40

ELLIS ISLAND SCRAPBOOK

Russia, Russians 2-5, 7, 11-14, 20, 25-27, 29-32, 34-37, 39, 48-49, 53, 54, 60-64, 66-69, 71-72, 81, 94, 96, 98-99, 100, 102, 107, 113, 119, 130, 135, 139, 143, 147, 151, 152, 161-162, 164, 166, 170, 172-175, 181, 196, 201, 203, 207, 219-221, 226, 233, 238
Russian Empire 12, 34, 37, 60-62, 64, 66-69, 72, 96, 99, 100, 164, 181
Ruthenia, Ruthenians 3, 12, 36, 69, 71

Saint Louis (city) 1, 30, 84, 155
Salem, Massachusetts 22
Salonika, Greece 23, 31, 71
San Diego 1, 158
San Francisco 1, 66, 101, 102, 109, 110, 135, 158, 202, 206, 214
Sand Creek (massacre) 5
Sanger, Margaret 40, 152, 153, 157, 196
Sargent, Frank 9
Saxony 10, 25
Scandinavia 7, 13, 34, 35, 56, 60, 61, 73, 96, 182, 188
"Scarecrow of Romney Marsh" 111
scarlet fever 125, 130, 133
Schamcham, Emile 199
Schmitz, Eugene 101, 102
Scotland, Scots 3, 10, 26-28, 37, 45, 46, 58, 60-62, 64, 154, 167, 181, 187, 188, 217, 221
Scott, Dred 57
Scott, Winfield 3, 47
Seattle 50, 86, 109
segregation 95, 102, 110, 116, 118, 143, 147, 233
Senner, Joseph 91, 92, 110, 161-163, 197
Serbia, Serbs 3, 13, 31, 39, 61-63, 67, 70, 77, 181, 195, 213
Seward, William 48
sex trade 40, 100, 174, 240
Seymour, Jane 25
Shawnee tribe 46, 47
Shawnee Prophet 46
Sheridan, Philip 50, 56
Sherman, William T. 49, 51, 56, 159
Sicily, Sicilians 143, 212, 213
Sinatra, Dolly 39
Sioux tribe 51-53, 108
Sitting Bull 51
Skavronsky, Katrina 25
Slavs, Slavic people . 28, 40, 67, 70, 73, 151, 203, 219, 227, 240
slaves, slavery 1-2, 22-23, 32, 40, 44-45, 47-49, 51, 55-57, 63, 68-69, 77, 84, 86, 96, 103, 109, 111, 119, 122, 143, 174,186, 240, 242
Slovakia, Slovaks 3, 12, 26, 36, 39, 70, 72- 73, 218, 227
Slovenia, Slovenes 3, 12, 36, 70, 93, 137, 213, 223
smallpox 125, 130, 133
Smith, Al 152, 182, 232
Smith, Joseph 55, 81
Smith, Sven 210-211, 240
smugglers 80, 82, 104, 110, 176, 194, 207, 208
sneak 49, 51, 62, 96, 97, 102, 126, 150, 236
Solzhenitsyn, Aleksandr 38
Sooners 53
South Africa 16, 29, 33, 212
South Carolina 79
South Dakota 46, 47, 52, 200
Soviet Central Asia 149
Soviet Union 4, 26, 29, 36, 39, 48, 64, 68- 69, 72, 147, 149, 152, 155-156, 164, 196
Spain, Spanish 2-3, 11, 13-14, 21- 23, 25- 26, 28, 30-31, 33-34, 36-38, 43-49, 52-54, 61-63, 65, 76, 79, 82, 84, 85, 93-96, 111, 147, 149, 152, 155, 164, 175, 181-182, 217, 222
Spanish-American War 30, 31, 48, 53, 61, 79, 85, 93, 95
Special Inquiry Division 123
Speigel, Apollonia 145
Stalin 30, 39, 156, 196
Standard Oil 122
Stanford, Leland 50
Stevenson, Robert Louis 54
Statistical Division 124

Statue of Liberty 36, 81, 88, 108, 109, 120, 126, 145, 157, 173, 233, 238
steerage 22, 1, 2, 73, 83, 87, 88, 90, 93, 97, 100, 106, 110-121, 123-127, 130, 134, 136, 137, 160-164, 173, 187, 195, 198, 203, 206, 209, 211, 218, 226, 229, 231, 233, 234, 240, 242
Steinheil, Mara de Lillier 233
Steinmetz, Charles 77
Stowe, Harriet Beecher 122
Strang, Strangites 55, 81
Stucklen, Regina 185, 194
Stump, Herman 163
submarine 14, 32, 62, 113, 145, 147, 156
Sulzer, William 106, 110, 231, 232, 238
Sutter, John 66
Sweden, Swedes 3, 4, 6, 10, 11, 14, 25, 28, 36, 37, 58, 60-63, 66, 73, 83, 104, 154, 155, 175, 181, 184, 221, 223
Swedish Immigrant Home 104, 184
Swinburne Island 125, 130, 133, 134, 145
Switzerland, Swiss 3, 6, 12, 22, 34-36, 45, 58, 60-64, 73, 78, 138, 215
Syrians 72, 175, 200, 207

Taft, William 1, 103, 106, 108, 204, 232
Talveira, (consul of Portugal) 197
Tarbell, Ida 122
tariff 53
Taylor, Telford 40
Taylor, Zachary 47, 48
Tecumseh (chief) 46
tenement 17, 98
Tennessee 35, 46
Termini, Isadore 176, 177
Tesla, Nikula 77
Texas 33, 46, 47, 50, 58, 65, 69, 76, 94, 95, 110, 182
Thebes 24
Thatcher, Margaret 22
Titanic (ship) 2, 108, 113, 119, 175
Tito 137
Tod, Robert 167
Torquemada, Tomás de 38
trachoma 97, 122, 125, 129, 130, 133, 174, 185, 195, 204, 207, 216, 226
Trail of Tears 47
Train, Arthur 166, 193, 219
Transcontinental Railroad 60, 135
Transylvania 3, 12, 36, 63, 70-72
Treaty of Guadalupe Hidalgo 49
Triangle Fire 2, 108
Tschudi, Johannes 22
tuberculosis 53, 99, 122, 125, 130, 131, 133, 237
Turkestan 36, 149
Turkey, Turks 9, 13, 23, 26, 27, 31, 35, 61-63, 69, 71, 109, 149, 237
Tuscany 3, 82
typhoid fever 130
typhus 125, 134

U. S. Air Force 156
U.S. Army 51, 55, 56, 80, 81, 93, 156, 223
U.S. Dept. of Commerce 81, 95, 107, 122, 141, 165
U.S. Dept. of Commerce and Labor 95, 141, 165
U.S. Dept. of Homeland Security 239
U.S. Department of Labor 107, 122, 141, 195
U.S. Marines 3, 30, 53, 80, 85, 156, 224
U.S. Navy 80, 89, 94, 112, 156, 164, 224
U.S. State Department 45, 138, 239
Uhl, Byron 232
Ukraine, Ukrainians 2-4, 12, 23, 34-36, 63, 66-67, 69, 71-72, 156, 181, 196
Ulster 28, 146
Uncle Tom's Cabin 122
Union Navy 84, 112
United Kingdom 166, 167
Unrau, Harlan (and study) 36, 81, 82, 108-110, 120, 145, 146, 157, 158, 238

252   INDEX

Utah.	47, 50, 55-58, 65, 81, 135
Ute tribe.	56
Van Buren, Martin.	47, 66
Vendée.	24, 38
venereal disease.	26, 130, 133
Venezia.	3
Venezuela.	52
Vermont.	46, 106
Vetsera, Maria.	26
Victoria (Queen of England).	24, 26, 27
Victorian Age.	24, 29, 86
Vietnam.	30, 149
Vikings.	2, 43, 223
violent overthrow.	96, 154
Virgin Islands.	31, 48
Virginia City, Nevada.	49
visas.	36, 150, 213, 239
Vojvodina.	3, 12, 36, 70, 213
Wales, the Welsh.	3, 10, 14, 26, 28, 34, 44-46, 58, 60-64, 154, 181, 187, 188, 206, 210, 230, 233
Walesa, Lech.	29
Walsh, Robert.	197
War of 1812.	3, 43, 46, 58, 83, 111
Washington (city).	34, 35, 47, 80, 86, 91-92, 102-103, 138, 160
Washington (state).	51, 83, 178
Washington, Booker T.	94, 102
Washington, George.	1, 45, 58, 83, 164
watchmen.	123, 124
Watchorn, Robert.	98, 99, 103, 110, 133, 136, 140-142, 206, 222, 229, 230, 234
Watt, James.	76
Weber, John.	91, 160, 210, 226
Weeding-Out Process.	132
Weshner, Hamel.	195
West Indies.	44, 58, 60-63, 65, 86, 150, 151, 202, 231
West Virginia.	49, 207
white slavery.	2, 96
whooping cough.	130, 133
Wilhelm II (kaiser of Germany).	13, 14, 30, 112
William and Mary.	25
Whitney, Eli.	76
William of Orange.	25, 44
William the Conqueror.	30
Williams, William.	95, 97, 103, 110, 122, 123, 130, 133, 138, 141, 159, 164, 166, 178, 180-182, 184, 198, 199, 203-206, 219, 226, 229-231, 233, 238, 240, 241
Wilson, Woodrow.	95, 103, 108, 138, 139, 147, 148, 151, 204, 232, 237
Windom, William.	88, 89, 160
Wisconsin.	46, 55, 200
witches.	21, 22, 25, 37, 38
World War One.	1-4, 7, 14, 19, 20, 24, 28-32, 35, 39, 62-65, 67-73, 78, 84, 96, 100, 109, 112, 113, 120, 122, 139, 147-149, 151, 154-156, 158, 180, 213, 231-234, 237
World War Two.	1, 2, 4, 23, 28, 35, 39, 40, 48, 68, 69, 87, 109, 111, 145, 153, 155, 156, 159, 223, 224, 242
Wounded Knee massacre.	52, 53, 81
Wovoka (Ghost Dance).	51
Wright, Orville and Wilbur.	77
Wyoming.	46, 47, 50, 56, 58, 65, 83
yellow fever.	80, 125, 130, 134, 145
Yankovic, Frank.	223
Yorktown.	22
Young, Brigham.	55-57, 81
Yukon.	30, 33, 53
Zita (Empress of Austria-Hungary).	39, 78, 82
Zola, Emile.	138
Zukor (inspector).	215

Uncle Don Sherlock in Army basic training. He was awarded several Purple Hearts for enduring wounds in combat in the Korean War. Later, as an engineer, he designed aircraft that helped win the Cold War. Uncle Don, God rest your soul!

Eugene "Rusty" Karle and wife Lorraine with their adopted son Mark and her parents after his First Communion. Uncle Rusty was a gunner on a B-24 bomber during World War Two. He won the Distinguished Flying Cross for hanging in an open bomb bay and kicking bombs onto Jap positions when the bomb dropping gear malfunctioned. God rest your souls!

To Mom and Dad Sherlock — Thanks for Everything! God Rest Your Souls!